Sources of support	Curriculum	
Most privately supported; few public nursery schools today; Federal Emergency Relief Act of 1933 stimulated growth of public nursery schools	Informal curriculum planned to meet needs of children from ages two to four	
First were private and supported by gifts and student fees; public kindergartens supported by taxes; enabling legislation necessary in most states for kindergarten to become part of public education	Built around activity, self-development, social cooperation, and play	begin self-development education; Froebel's school admitted children between ages three and seven; today's kindergartens for children five years old
Students paid for instruction; some legal support in the Massachusetts Act of 1642	Reading and writing for boys; cooking and sewing for girls	To offer instruction in the rudiments
Student fees, fines, and sometimes taxes; town with population of 50 families required by Massachusetts Act of 1647 to have such a school	Reading and religion; some taught writing and arithmetic	To provide sufficient learning for children of any age to understand capital laws of colony and principal tenets of religion
Supported by taxes and hence entirely free; state constitutions adopted which established, or required legislatures to establish, systems of common schools	Originally three R's; curriculum enriched as need for broader elementary education arose; studies graded to meet maturity and ability of pupils; denominational teaching prescribed	To provide bases for a common citizenship for all the children of all of the people; citizenship replaced religion as the first purpose of elementary education
Tuition or rates; some public support—usually land grants; growth aided by Massachusetts Act of 1647; towns required to maintain schools for university preparation	Strictly classical; Latin and Greek grammar and literature; religion	To prepare boys and young men of upper social classes for college
Never a genuine public institution; often received land grants; many denominationally controlled and supported	College-preparatory curriculum of Latin grammar school; practical subjects such as surveying, navigation, and English	To prepare students for life; open to boys of the upper and middle classes who could read; some established for girls; elementary teachers sometimes prepared in academies
Supported as regular part of public education	Adapted to needs and interests of children in grades seven to nine; beginning of secondary education	To provide transition between elementary and high schools; to lessen time spent in elementary school; to improve educational opportunity
Legal foundation fixed in Kalamazoo decision of 1874; Massachusetts first state to pass law requiring high schools as part of public education, 1827 (James Carter High School Act); tax support	Intended to offer English classical course and practical subjects; curricula, in time, included mathematics and moral philosophy; modern high schools offer variety of curricula, sometimes hundreds of courses	Open to boys and girls who have completed elementary school; following objectives stated in *Report of the Committee of Ten*, 1893, high schools' main function now preparation for life
Public junior colleges supported by public funds, private by fees and gifts; enabling legislation necessary in many states; "Higher Education for American Democracy," 1947 report of President's commission, popularized community college movement	Terminal for students who are seeking vocational preparation; preparatory for students who expect to continue in higher education	Chief goal of junior college is general education; community college offers educational opportunity beyond high school to all people of a community
Early colleges, both private and state, supported by fees and gifts; Morrill Act of 1862 granted land to states for higher education and stimulated growth of state colleges	First colleges classical in content and religious in purpose; scientific, professional, and vocational curricula developed in nineteenth century	First colleges admitted only male students; co-education introduced at Oberlin College, 1833; liberal or general education college's chief objective
Private universities supported by gifts and tuition, controlled by boards of trustees; public universities supported by taxes, fees, and gifts, and controlled by public officers	Emphasis on graduate instruction and research in arts and sciences; professional schools of all types	To teach, discover, and preserve knowledge; open to all qualified students
Most normal schools and teachers colleges created by state law and publicly supported	Normal-school curriculum limited mostly to techniques of teaching; teachers colleges offer combined general and professional four-year program leading to bachelor's degree	Normal schools prepared teachers for elementary schools; teachers colleges for elementary and secondary schools; colleges for elementary and secondary schools; universities for college and university teaching

EDUCATION FOR
AMERICAN DEMOCRACY

Foundations of Education

Second Edition

McGRAW-HILL BOOK COMPANY
New York
St. Louis
San Francisco
Toronto
London
Sydney

EDUCATION FOR AMERICAN DEMOCRACY

Foundations of Education

EDWARD J. POWER
Professor of Education
School of Education
Boston College

EDUCATION FOR AMERICAN DEMOCRACY

50586

When Quintilian was importuned by friends and admirers to write a guide for the education of children, he agreed somewhat reluctantly. Earlier he had laid down the rhetorical principle that written discourse should be shielded from public view for ten years, and then after a full decade, if the oration still seemed meritorious to the author, it could be published. Being in a state of dormancy did not help the manuscript; there was no suggestion that it would ripen with age; but this great Roman teacher and writer did believe that an author critic would be in a better position to assess the quality of his writing after such an elapse of time.

We are not implying, of course, that this book has been put to such a severe test, but in bringing out a second edition, we have had an opportunity to update important, though not essential, points in the text and to incorporate into its context the outstanding recent occurrences in education that have an imperative quality about them. We have, moreover, with six years' experience with the first edition, learned a great deal about both the matter and form of textual presentation. This has led to some reorganization of first-edition chapters, to a suppression of parts of chapters because they no longer seem sufficiently pertinent to remain in a book where limitations on space, to say nothing of the student's time, cannot easily be ignored, and to the addition of new chapters that seem to make for greater integrity of treatment.

The general objective of the second edition is identical with that of the first: to describe education in the United States and to show the evolution of schools, educational systems, and educational thought in America in relation to the major traditions of education and the larger movements of American life.

No doubt this edition must share those dangers to which books used for basic courses in education are constantly subjected. If they do too much, if

v

their treatment attempts to achieve comprehensiveness, they are blamed for trying to usurp the proper boundaries of later courses in the education curriculum; if they concentrate on certain areas, issues, or problems thought to be appropriate, they are charged with narrowness and with having left out too much. The balance of satisfaction is not easy to strike. It is not easy to know when it has been achieved, but we have constantly aimed at it.

This book, while not exclusively a text for a first course in education, may be used for such courses and also for courses entitled American public education, school and society, school and American life, principles of education, or other courses which, though carrying different titles, have as their principal objective a thorough introduction to American public and private education.

A book used for a first course in education must, as we have already suggested, avoid involved considerations proper to later courses in educational theory and practice. Yet it should try to offer a base for the preparation of students to deal effectively with subsequent courses in educational history, philosophy, psychology, administration, and methods. This book is not a history of education, a philosophy of education, or a text in educational administration, but it does consider—it cannot help doing so— many of the basic questions in each of these areas. It should be added, while we are saying what the book is not, that it has not been written for our colleagues: this is a textbook for students and as such admits of no commission to push back the boundaries of knowledge. This is not the place to offer advanced, untested hypotheses, nor is it the place from which to disseminate personal or parochial ideas on education. I feel compelled to include what may appear to be a disclaimer, for no one should pretend more for the book than it claims for itself.

As an essential part of what may appear to be an introduction to education, the influences of court decisions, basic laws, and other important public and educational documents have been analyzed and discussed in their relation to the growth of American education and the determination of goals and opportunities for democratically oriented schools. The documents and decisions which seem to stand above all others in the contribution they made, and are making, to the essential structure of education in the United States—*Stuart v. School District No. 1; The Cardinal Principles of Secondary Education; Meyer v. Nebraska; Pierce v. Society of Sisters; Everson v. Board of Education; McCollum v. Board of Education; Doremus v. Board of Education; Zorach v. Clauson; Brown v. Board of Education; Engel v. Vitale; School District of Abington Township v. Schempp;* and Title IV, Civil Rights Act of 1964—are presented in the Appendix. The Appendix is integrated via the text, and the reader is referred to the appended material whenever the original language and sense of the documents or decisions will be useful in illuminating fundamental features of American education. Students are encouraged to give the appended material close attention while studying the text, for it seems clear that greater profit will come from studying original sources, along with the interpretations given of them in the text, than from merely reading about them.

A historical and philosophical emphasis may be found throughout the book. The justification for this emphasis is that with an understanding of education's most fundamental questions the student will be best equipped to cross the threshold of professional studies.

Although the author has tried to be objective and has in most cases tried to avoid taking sides on issues that have varying interpretations, this book is intended to represent both a Christian and a humanistic approach to education. Formal education is understood to be but a means to aid men in the achievement of their temporal and ultimate life goals. The temperate educational doctrine of Isocrates (in *Panathenaicus*, Loeb ed., pp. 32–33) offers a theme if not a guide:

> Whom, then, do I call educated, since I exclude the arts and sciences and specialties? First, those who manage well the circumstances which they encounter day by day, and who possess a judgement which is accurate in meeting occasions as they arise and rarely misses the expedient course of action; next, those who are decent and honorable in their intercourse with all with whom they associate, tolerating easily and good-naturedly what is unpleasant or offensive in others and being themselves as agreeable and reasonable to their associates as it is possible to be; furthermore, those who hold their pleasures always under control and are not unduly overcome by their misfortunes, bearing up under them bravely and in a manner worthy of our common nature; finally, and most important of all, those who are not spoiled by successes and do not desert their true selves and become arrogant, but hold their ground steadfastly as intelligent men, not rejoicing in the good things which have come to them through chance rather than in those which through their own nature and intelligence are theirs from birth.

Questions and exercises follow each chapter. Their purpose is not primarily to review the chapter; they are intended mainly to lead the student into other shades or avenues of educational thinking that could not be represented fully in the text. Pertinent selected readings appear at the end of each chapter. These reading selections are offered as tools supplemental to the text itself, which is only a tool. Explanatory and reference notes are found in a separate section at the back of the book.

Many people, both students and colleagues, have been of help to me in the preparation of this book. I owe a great deal to all of them and now to them I extend my sincere gratitude. Also, I wish to thank the publishers who generously granted permission to quote from copyrighted materials.

Edward J. Power

CONTENTS

Educational Ideals

chapter 1

Education in

Life and Society

EDUCATION AND SOCIETY

In every historical period education has had a social dimension, yet in the last half century education's social objectives have been given greater recognition than ever before. The sociology of education has emphasized a natural relationship between the school and the society it serves. Indeed, by now it is clear, schools are but arms or branches of society, performing assigned functions. As every other social institution, the school finds many of its goals in society.

If the school is an instrument of society, the prevailing social philosophy will certainly have a decisive effect on it. And this social philosophy may favor one or another of a variety of points of view. Conceivably, one social philosopher might argue for progress: in effect, he is deploring social immobility and encouraging formal education to assume a position of leadership in forging progress. Meanwhile, another social philosopher or sociologist may oppose the presuppositions of social dynamism and argue cogently for the preservation of the tried and tested values of the past. To put it another way, we may have, on the one hand, a revolutionary or evolutionary doctrine supporting change and, on the other, a theory of social conservatism. Who is right? Which position is more acceptable to a democratic society? Is the school better equipped to preserve the past or to build or rebuild institutions for the future?

Whether in a context of progressive or conservative thought, the school's relationship to the larger society needs clarification, and this relationship, it would seem, can be seen most clearly and understood most fully by employing valid data-gathering and research procedures.

Although relatively few persons doubt the benefits to be achieved by using scientific methods, many refuse to trust scientific vehicles alone as worthy guides for defining and maintaining social institutions. How much enthusiasm can be generated for scientific determinism, by which we mean, first, scientific determination of the goals of society; second, scientific determination of the objectives of education; third, scientific determination of the purposes of the school; and finally, scientific determination of the curricular means and the personal motives and goals of students? What we have just referred to are, in a sense, the promises of a school of thought expressing confidence in an exact socioeducational science with entirely dependable outcomes. In contemporary educational sociology the methods of science are in evidence, and results so gained and conclusions thus drawn are generally more acceptable than the evidences, observations, and conclusions of, say, the philosophical method, referred to by some as the "armchair" method. A more balanced view would hardly be exclusively scientific in its orientation, nor would it dogmatically assign infallibility to the products of science. Yet with all of their differences, social and educational philosophies enthusiastically adopt cooperation, interdependence, and teamwork as educational means and objectives.

Cooperation as a tool for progress has, perhaps, never been given a more exalted role than in the word picture of the ideal society envisioned in Francis Bacon's *The New Atlantis*. In this literary utopia we find Bacon constructing a perfect society, uncontaminated by greed or sloth, and basing all of its accomplishments on the technique of working together. Perhaps this technique of human cooperation was an application to the intellect of the physical principle of "strength in numbers." One man alone may apply all of his understanding and wisdom to a problem and be unable to solve it. But if he can illuminate his understanding by enlisting the aid of two additional men of at least equal intellect, he may—or, rather, they may—be able to arrive at a solution. Actually, Bacon was arguing for cooperation on a much more extensive scale. In fact, cooperation was to have been the central social principle. Despite the validity of the illustration, Bacon's imaginary world view was drawn hundreds of years ago, and as a point of departure, he undoubtedly depended on the realities of the world he knew. It is possible to find contemporary theorists trying to make the same points.

Interdependence and teamwork played a leading role in the social philosophy and the educational sociology of John Dewey. In his famous *Democracy and Education* Dewey said: "Social efficiency as an educational purpose should mean cultivation of power to join freely and fully in shared or common activities."[1] Ross Finney, well known for his strong attachments to educational sociology and for his book *A Sociological Philosophy of Education,* appropriated Dewey's assertion that education's large goal, to the extent that a goal could be assigned, was social efficiency.[2]

The Seven Cardinal Principles of education (health, command of the fundamental processes, citizenship, worthy use of leisure, vocational efficiency, worthy home membership, and ethical character) are set in a sociological context, as are many other lists of educational objectives and aims. The names of Edward Thorndike and Arnold Gesell, as well as those who in general represent the child developmentalists, might be called upon to support education as an ultimately social enterprise.

Whether or not an educator accepts the evolutionary or the conservative doctrine, he is likely to think of education as having multiple social dimensions. If he is conservative, he is marked as a social traditionalist; if he is evolutionary, he is called a social experimentalist.

So the question confronting us is not whether education is irrevocably attached to social purposes or whether its consequences are unequivocally social, but, rather, how are social goals achieved, and how is the social orientation protected? Education, it may be maintained, is first of all an adjustment enterprise, and the school's objectives are distilled in a broad and chaotic social environment. Or, it may be said, education is not concerned with adjustment but with guidance toward an objective to be refined and defined at the end of the process, never at the beginning. In general, then, the social dimension is either one of adjustment or guidance. Still, it is possible to be more specific and look more closely at ways in which distinctive social goals may be achieved through the instrumentality of the school.

In the first place, we have a definition of education's, or the school's, role as one of passing on or continuing accepted traditions. The inheritance of the race—or, better, the inheritance of mankind—contains goals, codes, and skills persons need to perpetuate social standards arising out of conventions invented in, and preserved by, preceding generations. There is, the argument proceeds, a common core to basic culture, and this cultural core must be given a position of academic privilege in the school. There is no new world, we hear, only an old world to be relived. So the school is put in the position of helping set the stage for each new generation. The school has no commitment to the novel; it does not create; to put it most simply, its commission is one of preserving the *status quo*. To see the school's objectives put in such blunt, apparently backward-looking company generates sympathy for students who must be confronted daily with motives of reaction. But the picture is hardly ever so black or so bleak as words paint it; the *status quo* may really mean nothing more than a devotion to the best ideals of the past, a dedication to the tested principles of the past without any necessary acknowledgment that the means of the past should be adopted as the only means of the present. To assume that any defense of the past, any acceptance of the doctrine of the *status quo,* any willingness to find a conservative context comfortable is a complete endorsement of a reactionary social philosophy is to miss the point of the really effective elements of such a social philosophy. Moreover, to misunderstand the doctrine of the *status quo* may well lead, as it appears to have led in the past.

to all kinds of protests in the literature of the progressives against what is called social and educational "perennialism," whereas the attacked doctrine may not be a veritable type but only a caricature of a social commitment that has never really been made.

Next, remaining within the context of the school as a social adjustment agency, we have a theory maintaining that educational institutions must anticipate the normal, gradual social changes of the coming years and prepare younger generations for them. The school is not a trail-blazing institution, according to this view. Instead, it tries to stay a safe distance behind the main currents of life, reacting favorably to them.

In the third place, there may be a highly structured social complex in which the school has a social blueprint of some future society and is instructed to realize this society by any means at its disposal, including indoctrination and instruction.

We have touched on sociological theories which persistently restrain schools from challenging the social order and have referred to educational theories wherein the school is indifferent to social change: either it reacts to larger social forces or it attempts to implement social anticipations or blueprints generated outside the school. Finally, we come to an educational-sociological theory committed not to adjustment but to guidance. Now the school becomes a flexible social unit daring to lead society, not with a preconceived or prearranged outline but by reacting to the pooled ideas and hopes of all the members of society. Seen in this light, the school becomes a leading social force; as much as, possibly more than, any other institution, it defines the realities of social philosophy. Within such a framework, the question asked in the title of George S. Counts's book *Dare the School Change the Social Order?* is easy to answer.[3] Either the school is an instrument for reform or it is failing miserably.

Thus, the implications of a sociology of education and perhaps, too, the variety of relationships possible between the school and the society it serves become apparent.

EDUCATION AND UTILITY

During the past three centuries, but especially in recent years, the utility of learning has been stressed, and this emphasis has at times come perilously close to swamping other justifications of the quest for knowledge. On the other hand, there is a cult of theory which, it may be said, advocates disinterested learning while belittling applied learning. Although the terms themselves may not be central to the issues involved, there is no error in saying that cultural ideals are accentuated when learning in its most liberal, nonpractical dimension is endorsed, whereas technique, skill, a science of application are the goal of the utilitarian. What benefits accrue from bodies of knowledge that cannot be used; what real value can be placed on esoteric culture? There would seem to be a total rejection here, one that goes beyond the merely cynical attitude that lack of utility is tantamount to lack of meaning. Although this cynical attitude may not be authentic pragmatism, it is an art of rejection which may have other applications. Rejection of another kind comes from another source: The cultural idealist may reject technique not because he misunderstands it, or is unable to see skill being used to make creatures more comfortable, but because he believes that technique leads to cultural deterioration and ultimately to destruction of the cultural idea. Besides deploring deterioration and destruction, the cultural idealist is vigorously opposed to any means endangering pure liberalism. Thus, there is little hope, so far as the two extremes are concerned, of following a principle which accepts both abilities of knowing and doing as the most legitimate objectives of learning.

Fortunately, many educational theorists and most practical schoolmasters have moved away from these extreme positions, despite the entirely respectable standing of their chief architects. For example, Plato was fairly certain that theoretical knowledge alone should provide curricular content to stimulate the best minds. He despised practical culture. Perhaps the point Plato missed, or chose not to notice, is that educational opportunity geared for the best minds may often be the most ineffective educational instrument for average students. Yet, irrespective of emphases, Plato seems to have eliminated from serious consideration any education that took practical knowledge seriously. Thus, young men who studied geometry with an eye on surveying, masonry, or irrigation or understood their study in its practical dimensions were, in Plato's view, wasting their talents in a shadowy, imprecise world. He would have them make a commitment to philosophy, which he understood as a theoretical means to wisdom.

The Platonic interpretation was not permitted to go uncontested; both in his day and in our own, critics have challenged its validity. Where Plato regarded philosophy as a principal means leading to wisdom, another theorist of enviable repute defined philosophy as an avenue to prudence. This was Isocrates. And this is what he said: Whatever men learn, if it is to be trusted, must be useful because it enables them to live complete lives as social beings. The ultimate business of education, and the only reason for philosophy, is to teach men what ought to be done in the real world in which they live. Knowledge, as well as systems of education, not meeting this criterion is severely criticized and then shelved.[4]

The animosities surrounding the theoretical and the practical, the liberal and the servile (although Isocrates was not really a spokesman for the servile) had their origin in the very early years of educational history, were given clear and vigorous codification and expression, and an element of authenticity, by the two giants of Greek educational theory, and were bequeathed to Western education, where they have been protected and preserved. In spite of the theoretical foundations these opposing positions boast, we must not remain too long on this level. What theorists think and say is not always what teachers and students accept and teach and learn. What is the case for the theoretical and the practical—liberal versus utility—in today's educational world? The lines that separate the two are not so tautly drawn as the verbalisms of theorists suggest, nor do teachers and learners always detect and defend the dichotomy of knowing and doing. Yet, preferences, if shown, are likely to be on the side of the practical. Few contemporary students show much patience with curricula promising nothing in the realm of action. Even liberal curricula today are preserved in environments assuming a short-lived interest in, and sojourn with, the liberal arts and then a more protracted journey into professional education. Learning, or the products of learning, are viewed as tools or instruments for manipulating the human world and adjusting to the physical world. "Knowledge," to use Francis Bacon's phrase, "is power," and without it, men are helpless before the inexorable forces of nature and hopeless in the densities of social pressures.[5] But Bacon did not mean, nor do educators today mean, that only those kinds of knowledge which are clearly manipulative may be embraced. It has always been hard to say in advance what kind of skill preparation will actually be the most practical. If this cannot be done, one may well criticize an overemphasis on what appears to be a job-analysis approach even in vocational education.

Although there are legitimate criticisms to be made of some vocational curricula, it would be hard, indeed, to insist that vocational education has no place in today's world. We know enough about interests and aptitudes to know that a broadly conceived educational program in and out of school must be organized. In this broad conception, we are bound to find vocational curricula.

What generalizations may be safely made on this topic of education and utility? We should think it unwise to accept the fallacy of the "nothing but" and to say nothing but liberal education is appropriate or nothing but utility-centered education may be justified. If we believe in educating men broadly and in exposing them to generative opportunity, this is what we are really saying: The whole man should be educated, although all educational opportunity need not be controlled or directed by the school. Wherever the responsibility may lie, educational opportunity, if it is to be adequate, must enable men to progress along broad fronts of learning and skill. Because men are human, this opportunity should be directed first at the most essential feature of humanity: thought. To do this, however, the necessary means or vehicles to thought must become part of the learner's intellectual equipment, and this is nothing more than acknowledging the tools of education—reading, writing, arithmetic—and inviting them cordially to a place in the school's syllabus. With these tools, both formal and informal education may proceed toward the goals of basic liberal education: to speak, to listen, to observe, to think. These goals are common to all human education, and opportunities of varying breadth and depth to pursue them must be made available to all. From this point on, though refining thought processes may still be the primary consideration in some curricula, the second distinctive human ability—expression—must make a clearer impression on formal education. Expression may lead one further into the liberal arts, the fine arts, or the practical or useful arts. Any one of these avenues is honorable and legitimate, and there is no reason to scoff at the student who chooses one rather than the other. The minimum requirement for all should be the basic (liberal) education to which we have referred, but there need not be, and in the interest of social and economic diversity there must not be, a total, exclusive, and irrevocable commitment to the liberal and fine arts. We should not act as if practical art does not exist, and we are not entitled to demean or chastise it. The man who is educated well is the man who knows some things well and is able to do some things well. The cold war between the practical and theoretical worlds should be settled by an honorable and intelligent treaty of peace.[6]

What has technology done for man? This question needs no detailed answer here. Perhaps the best way to phrase the answer is to admit forthrightly that because of technology, because of the application of science to the affairs of men, all men are better able to enjoy the fruits of the earth and some of the good things of life. And as far as education is concerned, it has prospered because men have, for the most part, used technology to create leisure for themselves and for their children, and this leisure has brought them to the threshold of a fuller intellectual life. The days of the sweatshop; the apprentice system, with all of its failures for the young; and child labor have passed from most of the Western world. They belong to a shadowy and unmourned past, largely because of the combined and dedicated efforts of educators and technologists. It is possible, of course, for technology to govern man, as it is possible for the monster to control, and perhaps destroy, his creator, but it is also possible for men to control technology. No one wants an irrational, ungovernable technology, and we need not have it: education is responsible for producing technology; education as an instrument of man is also the ultimate source of its control.

RELIGION AND EDUCATION

Long before educational implements were formalized, and also long before dichotomies arising among religious teachings were articulated, religion enjoyed a secure role in the education of the young. Mothers, fathers, relatives, and friends, by their actions and by their words, taught children basic values inseparable from their world view. What they believed about their relationship to God and their duty to Him was made clear in their daily lives. This was basic religious education; and from what is known of early societies, these methods of teaching were effective, and their impression on learning was stable.

Some commentators on religious history, however, purport seeing excessive rigidity in nascent religion along with a diminution of essential human values. The price paid for conformity, irrespective of the social benefits derived from it, may have been too high. And even today with the multiple and inevitable subtleties of knowledge and all of the sophistication with which men have surrounded themselves, the charge regularly appears: Religion is nothing more than superstition, good perhaps to order the life of the primitive or the medieval man, but too simple, too archaic, for the contemporary world. Perhaps we should not try to go further without trying to illuminate somewhat three fairly popular conceptions of religion.

If religion is codified superstition, its petition for recognition in the school's curriculum is indeed tenuous; its place in education would always be hard to justify. Opponents of religion often stress this. They dismiss a religious interpretation of the origin of the universe and a theological view of man's place in the world as having no factual basis. How, they argue, is it possible for modern man to know anything about the act of creation? How, they ask further, can these theological interpretations of creation be validated? Some go beyond this apparently agnostic attitude and state flatly that science and all the precise instruments supporting it disprove the theses of theology. None of the mysteries forming the foundation for a religious view of the world can be taken seriously by the tough-minded scientist. Natural laws of cause and effect are sufficient to explain the occurrences of nature, and what cannot be fitted into these explanations is disregarded as insignificant or is deferred for clarification until scientific methods and analytical techniques are more fully developed. Man is the master of his fate; the world is his to own, to know, and to understand; there is no transempirical reality; and even if there were, its relationship to the lives of men would be remote and, indeed, scientifically meaningless.

The person who sees religion in this light—as a carefully cultivated and articulated body of meaningless mysteries—can hardly welcome it in the school's curriculum and, what is more, must refuse to acknowledge its place in the broader educational arena wherein all men live and learn.

Moving on from a caricature of religion as superstition, we find a second interpretation in which religious experience is regarded as a compartment of total experience. That is, as other compartmentalized aspects of life, it should not intrude on, or interfere with, life in general. This is akin to maintaining that theories should not control or confuse practices, and it reminds us of the story told of the idealist philosopher who, when asked how he could continue to live a normal life while adhering to an idealist ontology, replied that his philosophy did not affect his life because he left his philosophy in his office!

There is a current tendency to set religion apart from life, to accept it if it does not cross parochial boundaries and to confine all related instruction to Sunday schools. These trends raise no question pertaining to the validity of religious experience; they neither doubt the importance of religion nor challenge the authenticity of religious traditions or the reasonableness of faith. Rather, they cultivate a dogmatic assumption relegating religion to a narrow role largely unrelated to man's life in society. When barriers are raised between religion and the vital tasks of life and when the relevance of religious faith is doubted, no one should express amazement at corollary inquiries as to the significance of religion for education or even to a lack of genuine cordiality toward religious ideals or institutions.

Finally, religion is understood to be a vital, even necessary, component in man's world view. Religious belief or lack of it permeates all of life and is basic to fundamental convictions and assumptions to be made relative to all man's relationships in the human world. A comprehensive religious orientation includes in the first place man's understanding of himself: his origin, nature, and destiny.

In this latter view, we see an unavoidable connection between religion and education. What is education (and it makes little difference whether it is formal or informal) really worth if it neglects the most essential questions men must face? How can the school experience be adequate if it is required to isolate students from the very foundations of life itself?

Even in this final conception, where religion is thoroughly understood and genuinely embraced, the route between religion and education is often obstacle-ridden. Religion or sectarian pluralism generates its own loyalties and its own special problems. At this point, the student of education is entitled to wonder how religious traditions—but, more especially, how sectarian doctrines—can be incorporated in instructional programs. The solution is easy, of course, when denominations maintain their own schools, but the acuteness of the issue cannot be minimized when public education is involved. Compromises, or even tolerable indifference to critical points, may be realistic expedients in the homogeneous Christian community—e.g., Bible reading in some states before 1963—but outrageous violations of the consciences of non-Christians, whose rights in the heterogeneous community and its schools must be respected and safeguarded. In other words, it is not enough, in a society whose religious pluralisms are so diverse, to think only of Christian religious teachings and observances.[7]

Educational history in the United States illustrates three ways of handling religious instruction in a nominally Christian society. A first solution with considerable support, offered by secularism, rests on premises endorsing religious neutrality, although privately an educational secularist may accept and follow the doctrines of a religious sect. Education may need religion; but in the domain of public education, which religious or sectarian beliefs can be permitted in the school? It is better, we are advised, to remain out of range of religious controversy, and not risk the disruption of other parts of the school's curriculum, than to open the curriculum to religious experience and eventually to denominationalism. If religious knowledge is wanted or needed, do whatever needs to be done in the home and the church; for the sake of educational tranquility, keep religion out of the school.

Secularism may lack appeal to many people who will, in turn, be impressed by a more humanistic approach to the religious question. Here an effort is made to interlace religion with education, though not on the level of faith or belief but as part of the broad range of historical and cultural experience. Religion has a long tradition; it has claimed the allegiances of men throughout a great part of modern history. It has been a principal motive force in the lives of great men and great empires. There are valid religious-cultural-political histories that can be viewed, studied, analyzed, and understood without any creedal commitment. The humanist wants to find a place for religion in the school's curriculum, but he thinks of religion as a human experience and would have it studied with the same approach—and possibly the same lack of involvement—as economic or political philosophy, or social revolution or evolution.

Finally, we come to an interpretation, and a practice, rejecting both secularism and humanism. The first is rejected because it is incompatible with basic realities and the needs of man; the second because it is inadequate—it pretends that human experience is a sufficient base for the formation of men and societies and places too much reliance on man. This final interpretation has a thorough theological orientation. Man is man because God made him, and he can understand himself and others only when he knows his God-given capacities, only when he understands his duties as a creature of God. This is an undertaking requiring more than mere exposure to humanistic traditions that, over the centuries, have attached themselves to religion, or a compartmentalization of religious belief and practice preventing its intrusion on really important things. It presumes a curriculum in which every learning activity is permeated by a theological orientation, and it assumes a friendly and objective attitude toward religion in every school subject. Moreover, it reserves a special place for theology, itself an independent discipline, and emphasizes the dependence other disciplines, none of them objectively constituted, have on it. In other words, there is no academic adequacy without theology. This is more than a theory of education; it is a theology of education with goals including the preparation of men for temporal pursuits and eternal destinies.

EDUCATION AND MORALS [8]

Every society observes certain conventions and hopes that oncoming generations will observe them too, for these conventions were honored in the first place because they were thought to contain practical values. At least, they were expected to guide the individual through a labyrinth of perplexing social issues: it is easy to understand men's trying to protect the things they value. In the course of history many conventions have been modified, and we have seen how the taboos of the past have been themselves rejected by succeeding generations. Perhaps everyone expects conventions to change; at least, few persons doubt the possibility of social metamorphosis or fearfully anticipate its coming.

What we have said about convention has some meaning for our general theme. Yet convention, though related to morals in a somewhat indirect way, is not in precisely the same category as morals. The source of convention is social intercourse; and as societies evolve, the agreements for social living are modified. The roots of convention, though having a certain stability, are far from permanent. Morals, on the other hand, find their bases either in natural or divine law. The law of nature permits certain freedoms and imposes certain restrictions on men; the laws arising out of divine mandate govern man's relationship to other men and to his Creator. In these laws, we find the foundation for morality, and we move from this foundation to build a moral structure for which we try to elicit zeal and devotion.

There is an explicit moral code, and there need be no mystery about its content. There has never been any real doubt about the possibility of teaching a moral code, although men have argued long and hard over proposals for doing more than this. Men can be taught what ought to be done—although disagreements over specific aspects of the content of the syllabus of morals must be admitted—but teaching them to accept the moral code and make it part of their personal value system is a second phase in moral education, a phase often questioned.

If, however, we admit learning is involved in all the dimensions of morals and morality, it is difficult to see how this learning must be reserved for agencies other than the school. Yet, the best moral education, we may be willing to agree, takes place in the home or in the church and not in the school. If moral education is possible, learning must be a necessary condition; and if this is true, there is no valid reason for proscribing schools' involvement.

Although moral education may not follow the same pedagogical prescriptions of intellectual education and the techniques employed may differ from those adopted for arithmetic or geography, this does not prevent schools from developing programs advancing moral learning that are different from literary, mathematical, or historical curricula. Yet, there is not always agreement on the necessity or meaning of moral teaching. Somewhat tangentially, this relates to questions of freedom and responsibility. Is man free? Is he responsible for his actions? Or does he merely follow blindly the forces, whatever they may be—social, physical, cosmic, or even, indeed, divine—dictating his actions? If men are not free, there is no need to spend time discussing morality or moral education. Men do what they are determined to do with total disregard for influences the school or any other agencies try to exert. Determinism, it must be understood, does not always appear in an ugly or evil context. If men are determined, they can as easily be determined toward good as evil. Rousseau's thesis assumed man's natural goodness, although it assumed also an inevitable human perversity arising out of institutional contamination. Traditional Calvinism contained little hope for depraved mankind; the elect, of course, were assured salvation, but most men were predestined for an unenviable life both here and in the hereafter.

Unhappily, man is not naturally good; he is deprived, not depraved, and must bear the burden of original sin. He must learn to be virtuous, a lesson not always easily managed, and must strive constantly to meet the standards of objective morality. Moral virtue, or adherence to the good, including character education and will training, is the objective of moral education. The first step toward moral education is shaping an environment, helping to build one, wherein goals may be identified and understood and where tools to reach these goals may be fashioned. We should expect the general social environment to contribute to what are particular functions of school, church, and home environments. Moral training supported by these institutions has fulfilled its commission when its good offices have helped form a morally autonomous person, by which we mean one with courage and strength of will to be fully moral irrespective of pressures to which he is exposed.

This is important work in which all social agencies must share. Despite the school's principal intellectual purpose, assigning responsibility for dealing essentially with what can be taught seems highly unrealistic if this principle is used to deny the school any significant role in moral education. For, as we have said, if man is not naturally good, he must learn to be virtuous; and what can be learned can be taught.[9]

One part of the syllabus of moral education which can be learned in the same way as any other school subject is ethics. The source of ethical knowledge is the law of nature, more exactly the law of man's nature. Another part which may be learned in the same way has its ultimate source in God, for God is the author of the divine moral law. To be complete, a system of morals must draw on both sources. If this is so, it is not easy to see how some educators can at once emphasize the importance of character (moral) education and ignore its relationship to religion and a basic religious morality. An abstracted system of morals is probably better than none, but, it should be obvious, such a system of moral knowledge is inadequate without religion.

EDUCATION AND POLITICS

The clearest sample to be found in the history of education or in the history of political philosophy of the intimate connection between politics and education is in Plato's *Republic*. He construed education as an instrument for statecraft; moreover, he hoped that in creating an ideal state, he would create a perfect educational society. Thus, Plato was using education as a means to an end, but only temporarily; for his ultimate purpose was to provide men with broad opportunities for transcending themselves and the brute world in which they lived. We need not try to probe the intricacies of Plato's political or educational views here, but we can say he would never have settled for totalitarianism, a political philosophy which subordinates the legitimate goals of mankind to the demagoguery and impersonalism of the state. It is easy but dangerous to misread Platonic intentions. He wanted men to become so intellectual and so moral that neither laws nor states would be necessary. This was an ideal, a utopian plan, never realized except on the pages of Plato's manuscript, but this should in no way invalidate the basic proposition: There are, or should be, open avenues of communication between educational theories and institutions, on the one hand, and government or states on the other.

It may be naïve to hope for a society in which education will be so good that government, with all of the machinery now indispensable to it, will not be needed; but is it excessively optimistic to believe in social and political progress as a direct result of superior education? The relationship between politics and education is cyclical: good educational opportunities strengthen political societies, and a good political order inevitably improves the quality of education. No society has ever been so fortunate as to have all of its citizens interested in, or prepared for, leadership. But every political system needs leaders whether or not they are prepared, and every state needs intelligent and loyal followers.

Both the Greeks and the Romans used the phrase "the public man." The public man was a leader, and in this ancient but valid way of thinking he did not become a leader by accident: he was educated for leadership. Theoretically, every citizen had the road to leadership open to him: he needed only to qualify as a public man. The citizen class was relatively small and closely knit; a majority of the population did not qualify for it.

In a later age, with political views modeled on those of more ancient times, efforts were made to give special educational opportunity to persons of royal blood to prepare them for leadership. We find in the literature many examples of tracts and treatises written to guide the education of a prince. These outlines left much to be desired, but they showed, despite the pretensions of royalty to superior status, that skill, understanding, and wisdom are needed for leadership and that these are not inherited but come from diligent study and broad exposure to formative experiences.

Aristocracies (the rule of the best), autocracies (the rule of one), oligarchies (the rule of the few), and plutocracies (the rule of the rich) were sensitive to the need for qualified leaders, and we in a democratic state should be especially ready to believe in education as the best preparation and safeguard for self-government.

Does this have any special relevance to education in the United States? What are the points of convergence between education and the state? A democracy, itself the best argument and justification for universal education, depends for its preservation on a high degree of developed intelligence among its citizens. Informed and interested citizens must be unrelenting in their efforts to improve their government. Yet, education is not merely a political tool; there are broader connotations: because of it, life in society is better, and opportunities for fuller, more human lives are made available. If education is a tool at all, it is one which enables individuals to seek and achieve abilities consistent with innate capacity.

Broadly educated men serve the state and strengthen it; enlightened states help education achieve quality. There may be sound administrative justification for local control—undoubtedly, responsiveness to local need is greater when schools are controlled on the local level—but the breadth of education is so great, and the need for opportunity so demanding, we are compelled to wonder how long education in the United States can afford to worship at the altar of localism. But whether archaic localism is to be rejected or retained, clearly government must convince education of its legitimate requirements and then support schools in creating an educational environment wherein broad and rich opportunities may be offered.

The state has the obligation to protect freedom and opportunity in teaching and learning and to hold high the ideal of excellence. This is all in the state's own self-interest. In addition, it must impose order when there is danger of academic anarchy, and it must support the educational enterprise in every legitimate way when it needs or requires support.

EDUCATION AND FREEDOM

The great German poet Goethe, who lived through a crisis of freedom, said to his generation: "What you have inherited from your fathers, earn over again for yourselves or it will not be yours." For members of a society who enjoy freedom, this may be hard advice, for confusion is possible, and it is easy to believe that freedom is the natural, relaxed, and happy state of ordinary humanity. If this were true, most men—possibly all men—would be free, whereas throughout a great part of human history, men have lived in some kind of servitude under some kind of tyranny. All too frequently, it may be said, tyranny becomes the normal pattern of government; freedom as an essential element in a system of government has prevailed only as the product of sacrifice, idealism, and intense dedication and thought. All the labor necessary to creating freedom is needed to sustain it in the modern world.

It is a mistake to regard freedom as a gift to us by our contemporary way of life. There are constant challenges to freedoms now enjoyed, as there are constant challenges to our way of life itself. We must not accept a purely defensive attitude, for the experience of recent years should have convinced us that such attitudes of self-defense still leave freedom on the defensive. Our community is perhaps the first one in the history of the world not lacking means to defend and advance freedom; if means are not lacking, it must be choice: not instruments but ends.

More exactly, what are these challenges to freedom? Internally, they are poverty, slums, disease, ignorance, discrimination, and despair; externally, they are materialism, collectivism, atheism, and communism. Our goals in the face of these challenges to freedom must be resolute and clear, and they must be defined in the context of reasonable ideology supported by faith, virtue, and intelligence.

In an age commonly characterized as one of conflict of ideology, technological explosion, and scientific quickening, it may not be easy to find the extra dimension of vision contributing to the formation of genuine, imperturbable, and selfless public spirit where disinterested reform will be achieved only by disinterested reformers. Ceremony, ritual, glamor, and veneers appended to ideals of the public good cannot take the place of patience, dedication, and personal responsibility in building a public morality advocating, and responding genuinely to, urgent and honorable human needs and interests. Our society did not slip into freedom, but a free society can slip out of freedom, or this freedom can be chipped away by an undisciplined, uneducated, irresponsible society of men and women.

The question now is: How can education strengthen freedom? How can it elicit the kind of dedication and devotion to freedom that guarantee its preservation? This is no simple question, and, unhappily, it is not one susceptible of a simple answer. Our purpose here is not to answer the question, for the answer would require a treatment going far beyond the purpose of this book. Yet, we should keep these questions in mind, for the processes of education and the goals, too, must be set in a total context where, with flexibility, resiliency, and imagination, we may examine the epitaphs of yesterday's educational doctrines. We must be wary of abstract generalizations used to govern education of the past, though we must be ready to reclaim dynamic ideas which once served education for freedom but were lost or submerged in the naked ambition or arrogance of modern political and educational philosophies.

We must not fall into the trap of believing an educational institution alone has responsibility for standing guard over our heritage of freedom. All of the social institutions must stand ready to assume their fair share in strengthening the structure in which free men may preserve and advance their precious way of life. But there are areas in which formal education must assume leadership and responsibility, and now we want to state the goals by which, if they are accepted, education may join in building faith in freedom and prescriptions for keeping it.

1.   The first objective rests on the proposition that men are political animals and must participate in political decisions. The ability of men to take an active and productive part in political dialogue depends on the sufficiency of their education, their political understanding, and the political information available to them. Free men in a free society cannot be expected to conduct a civilized dialogue if they refuse to examine or are prevented from examining all of the propositions of political philosophy or political doctrine. Proscribing a serious and objective study of communism, for example, has consequences as serious to a free society as proscribing the study of cancer in the medical school would have for our hopes of controlling or destroying this ugly and spreading malignancy. If men are to be free, they must be free to discover the dangers confronting them: they must be free to study and debate the strengths, the weaknesses, the plans, and the promises of their own and other political systems and philosophies.

2.   The second objective rests on the assumption that formal education must provide the leadership for eradicating indifference to education; it must become active in offering better opportunity for less money while the total cost of education mounts; it must disabuse what may be an indifferent public of the notion that good education can be had without sacrifice or that the very best learning is possible without some pain; and, finally, it must explain that our national life can no longer afford to relegate educational decision making to political subdivisions which have little relation to the economic, social, or political life of the nation as a whole. Unless this leadership is taken and made the most of, history will smile sardonically, as one astute commentator has said, at the spectacle of a great country's becoming interested, but only slightly and temporarily, in education because of the achievements of the U.S.S.R., and then being able to act only by assimilating education to the cold war and calling an education bill a defense act.

3.   Education can help us realize the hopes of democracy and back the cause of freedom by providing every citizen with opportunity up to the

level of his capacity. Training, amusing, exercising, adjusting may all have their place, but they should not replace the development of intellectual power.

4. The educational community must make greater efforts to broaden opportunities for adult education. This would seem to be the great possibility for the next generation. Life, in a very real sense, is learning, and its object should be a community living and learning together, to continue, expand, and improve the kind of dialogue that will make freedom a permanent reality.

5. Education must inspire media of mass communication to supply accurate and full information on which an alert and interested people can base their political judgments.

6. Finally, education must lead men toward a valid political sophistication rejecting as an archaic and invalid generalization the dogmatic assumption, long given the status of unassailable dogma, that governments are best which govern least. The object of political education should not be to weaken government, but to strengthen it as an agency assigned primary responsibility for the common good and for maintaining the structure in which freedom may live and flourish.

PROSPECTS FOR THE FUTURE

Education in this country has made steady improvement almost from the beginning, and in some periods, say 1890–1920, the progress bordered on the spectacular. It may be fair to expect the schools of the year 2000 to be more advanced than those of today. Can we look to the future and make some cautious predictions about schools and education at the end of the twentieth century?

Some classes in the schools of the first years of the twenty-first century will be smaller than those we are used to. For purposes of discussion, where students will learn to examine their own ideas and the ideas of others and where they will learn, too, to become better members of groups, some classes may be no larger than fifteen students, although other classes intended to fulfill other objectives may be conducted in auditoriums and admit one hundred or more students. The smaller-group sessions will offer, in addition to the values already noted, opportunities for teachers to assess the talents of their students and will open vast areas for experimentation with a variety of teaching techniques. They will also provide students with opportunities to know their teachers on a personal, individual basis, which should be a plus value of considerable significance in teacher-student relationships. Finally, through these means, students will be better able to see the relevance of the things they learn and their potential uses. There will be much less of passive classroom learning; a greater reliance on the principle of activity in learning will make classrooms and learning situations more vital.

The school of the future will be a more flexible educational unit than we have known in the past. Part of this flexibility will be seen in an encouragement of programs for independent study. In such programs it will be possible for students to study independently either in or out of school and to engage in reading, writing, handling automated learning devices, and experimenting in laboratories. Facilities needed to promote independent study will be evaluated by their contributions to initiative, problem-solving ability, ability to think, and individual responsibility for reaching individual goals. Teachers will become increasingly expert in teaching students the most efficient use of the school's learning tools.

We have said that some classes will be very small; others will be quite large. In the schools of the twenty-first century, more students will be exposed to skilled teaching in all subjects because the most capable and experienced teachers in specific fields will teach large classes. The large class will avoid the duplication of effort required when teachers must repeat a number of classes. And team teaching will be entirely common; it will capitalize on the strengths of individual teachers, freeing some to fulfill specialized professional responsibilities while others are engaged in large-group instruction. In order to carry on teaching and learning processes most expeditiously, classrooms and/or auditoriums will be equipped with electronic and technological devices.

Steps will be taken to assure the professionalization of teaching. Teachers will be the professional members of an educational team consisting of staff specialists, community consultants, general aides, clerks, and instructional assistants.

School buildings will reflect the public's interest in education rather than its prolonged attachment to the archaic notion that a simple room, reasonably warm and regularly dry, was sufficient for teaching and learning. Many multipurpose rooms, convertible in a number of ways by a simple flick of a switch, will be available.

Flexibility will be the mark of the school of the future. The school plant will be flexible with rooms and facilities being largely interchangeable; curricula will be adapted to student needs; teachers will have their individual differences recognized and capitalized on; regulations concerning the procurement of money and its disbursement will be relaxed, although waste or misappropriation will not be tolerated; the role of the principal as an educational leader will be more clearly defined, yet he will be able to act in his new leadership role with greater freedom; finally, the public will be closer to the school. On this last point, one may suggest that barriers to public understanding of the school will disappear because the lines of communication between the school and the community will be shortened.

The school will be recognized and accepted as a community enterprise of the greatest possible importance—not as a learning factory located in the area—and a clearer public understanding of the mission of education and the community's schools will be the result.

In addition to all of these, the school of the twenty-first century may be a year-round school.[10] By then, the public may have accepted the plan, proposed even today by some educators, for a coterminus school and calendar year, arguing that the cost and quality of education no longer allow for the luxury of a nine-month school year. Educational opportunity must span the entire year to reduce costs, and, furthermore, bodies of knowledge now accumulated are too extensive to fit dated educational traditions. These are the principal points, and they receive sympathetic support from the following:

1. Teaching is a full-time job and should be conducted on a twelve-month basis. There is no other way, it is said, to assure the teacher of full professional status.
2. The nine-month school year places a great burden on the school system, but it places an even greater burden on the recreational agencies of the community. In a brief two- or three-month period, the community must provide recreational facilities for the total school population of the community, and to a great extent these facilities lie unused for the other nine months. With the year-round school all of this could be done with less cost and more efficiency, with a fuller and finer recreational program.
3. No business establishment would attempt to conduct an economical operation and do what the school does: it permits its plant to stand idle almost three months of the year. The cost of school buildings is too great, proponents of the year-round school argue, to allow intolerable waste to add to the total cost of education. If the public wants a dollar's worth of education for its educational dollar, the critics of the present school year say, it must insist on instituting the year-round school as a first step toward this goal.

Whether or not the year-round school is to be a reality of the twenty-first century depends on how the American public reacts to the merits claimed for it. Whatever cogency the cost and knowledge arguments may have, they must be balanced against these counterarguments:

1. The year-round school will increase, not decrease, educational costs. The amortization of school building costs over a half-century life for buildings makes the annual cost rather modest, and the number of months' use to which the building is put neither adds nor detracts from its life expectancy. But increased use would increase maintenance and contract service costs. A year-round school operation promising teachers professional status would add the financial responsibility of paying teachers' salaries for an

additional quarter of a year. Would the year-round school be more economical?

2. More cultural and social structures, so firmly implanted in our society, make a year-round school disruptive and impractical. The academic year of experience is a nine-month year; and by adding to it, the point of diminishing returns is soon reached. Further, many seasonal activities have the strong support of seasonal motivation. Most of them would have to be sacrificed in the year-round school. Families would find away-from-home vacations difficult to plan with children in school throughout the year, and teachers would wonder where they were to find time to continue professional preparation and engage in independent study and travel. Finally, education is not limited to the school; some of the best education and some of the most important, too, goes on in society without the help or knowledge of the school. Could the school be a worthy substitute for these informal but highly worthwhile experiences?

SUMMARY

Whether or not the schools of the twenty-first century will be radically different or only slightly different from the schools with which we are presently familiar depends partly on the progress of education and partly on the imagination and generosity of the people. Whatever form educational institutions take and whatever structural and organizational changes are initiated will in no way alter the traditional affinity of education and life. Men will continue to be true to their past, and the societies they help form will honor their wishes. Education will continue to be the distinctive mark of a civilized society, and with all of its cultural dimensions it will still have a utilitarian aspect that is wholesome and worthwhile. It is easy to point to the need for skill in a complex society, and it is easy and natural to assign responsibility for the inculcation of these skills to the school.

Social skill, economic skill—who can gainsay their worth? The school of the present and the school of the future, however, may not ignore the relationships that exist between religion and education, education and morals, education and politics, and education and freedom. The schools' part is evident in all of these relationships, and in them dimensions are drawn that are not handled elsewhere. It is the business of education to help man toward a freer and a fuller life; it has no commission to stand in his way. With the enlightenment from the past and the hopes of the future, it shall not hinder man but help him.

QUESTIONS AND EXERCISES

1. How lasting are the traditions of education? Is there any danger that in honoring these traditions we shall become reactionary in our educational views? Do you see real value in tradition?

2. When does education begin? List, if you can, all of the evidences of informal education and formal education in the life of a child from five to ten years of age. Which is more important, formal or informal education?

3. What is the relationship between the school and society?

4. Do you believe that schools can build a new social order?

5. How valid is the distinction between education for utility and education for liberal purposes? Would the distinction, if made, be subject to change in a changing world?

6. Do you believe education needs religion, or do you prefer to claim that religion needs education?

7. Explore the possibilities of conducting a successful program of moral or character education having no connection whatever with religion or religious beliefs.

8. Do you believe that it is possible to teach what can be learned? Is it possible, then, to teach a man to be good?

9. What are the dangers of bringing political questions, political education, and ideologies into the schools?

10. Can education make men free? Isn't this talk about education and freedom really poetry, a kind of idealism without any grounding in reality?

ADDITIONAL READINGS

Brameld, Theodore: *Cultural Foundations of Education: An Interdisciplinary Exploration,* Harper & Row, Publishers, Incorporated, New York, 1957. See chapters 1 and 2.

Bredemeier, Harry C., and Jackson Toby: *Social Problems in America,* John Wiley & Sons, Inc., New York, 1963. A study of fundamental and persistent social problems. Consult index for those related to education.

Callahan, Raymond E.: *Education and the Cult of Efficiency,* The University of Chicago Press, Chicago, 1961. The author marshals evidence to show that the greatest force undermining intellectual standards in the schools is the cult of efficiency and the willingness of school administrators to follow "sound business practices" rather than educational goals based on the scholarly tradition.

Clancy, William: *Religion and American Society,* Center for the Study of Democratic Institutions, Santa Barbara, Calif., 1962. A broad study of the religious dimensions in American life and society.

Coon, Carleton S.: *The Story of Man,* Alfred A. Knopf, Inc., New York, 1955. May be read by the student who wants to gain some insight into anthropological and educational relationships.

Cox, Philip W. L., and Blaine E. Mercer: *Education in Democracy: Social Foundations of Education,* McGraw-Hill Book Company, New York, 1961. A survey of political and philosophical bases for education.

Cremin, Lawrence A.: *The Transformation of the School,* Alfred A. Knopf, Inc., New York, 1961. A moving account of the reshaping of the American school to fit the temper of democratic ideals.

Fletcher, C. Scott (ed.): *Education: The Challenge Ahead,* W. W. Norton & Company, Inc., New York, 1961. A thought-provoking book concerned with how we can best prepare ourselves for positions of economic, social, and political leadership in our own country and in the world at large.

Fuller, Edmund (ed.): *Schools and Scholarship: The Christian Idea of Education,* Yale University Press, New Haven, Conn., 1961, part 2. See Harbeson's chapter on the possibilities of liberal learning in a committed Christian context.

Haring, Douglas G. (ed.): *Personal Character and Cultural Milieu,* Syracuse University Press, Syracuse, N.Y., 1956. An interesting collection of readings on social and individual issues, all of which are meaningful for education.

Kluckhohn, Florence, and F. Strodtbeck: *Variation in Value Orientations,* Harper & Row, Publishers, Incorporated, New York, 1961. Read for the authors' conception of a value orientation and how it is constructed.

Ladd, Edward T., and William C. Sayres: *Social Aspects of Education,* Prentice-Hall, Inc., Englewood Cliffs, N.J., 1961. An examination of education's social objectives.

Machlup, Fritz: *The Production and Distribution of Knowledge in the United States,* Princeton University Press, Princeton, N.J., 1962. Pay particular attention to those sections dealing with the production of knowledge.

Nelson, Jack, and Gene Roberts: *The Censors and the Schools,* Little, Brown and Company, Boston, 1963. How free are the schools? This book offers interesting insights into both insidious and blatant means of censorship.

Riesman, David, Nathan Glazer, and Reuel Denney: *The Lonely Crowd: A Study of the Changing American Character,* Yale University Press, New Haven, Conn., 1953. A social-psychological study of search for identity in a complex society where identity is easily confiscated.

Russell, Bertrand: *Education of Character,* Philosophical Library, Inc., New York, 1961. The author does not hesitate to assert the primacy of character among a variety of educational goals.

Schultz, Theodore W.: *The Economic Value of Education,* Columbia University Press, New York, 1963. A study of the worth of learning. The conclusions, easily believed and generally accepted, were not previously documented.

Spindler, George D. (ed.): *Education and Culture,* Holt, Rinehart and Winston, Inc., New York, 1963. A multiauthored book; see especially part I.

Thomas, John L., *Religion and the American People,* The Newman Press, Westminster, Md., 1962. Read in connection with Butts's book *The American Tradition in Religion and Education,* and notice particularly the conflicting assumptions.

Wade, Francis C.: *Teaching and Morality,* Loyola University Press, Chicago, 1963. An excellent discussion of the possibilities of moral teaching.

Wakin, Edward: *The Catholic Campus,* The Macmillan Company, New York, 1963. Colleges have personalities that are as distinctive as those of persons. See especially for the varying qualities of the Catholic college campus.

Woodring, Paul, and John Scanlon: *American Education Today,* McGraw-Hill Book Company, New York, 1963.

chapter 2

The Distinctive Features

of Education

in the United States

The structure and ideals of education in the United States are considerably more complex than one might suppose from casual observation. Foreign visitors and students from abroad are often puzzled by the decentralization of our system, by the sharing of responsibility for educational programs among various units of government along with talk about the rights of states and local communities, and by the variety of teaching and learning programs available to serve the needs and interests of the people. They may, in addition, be amazed at the willingness of most people to agree to the practical necessity for educational opportunity while disagreeing as to the real or the fundamental meaning of education itself. We should not be surprised to know that our friends from other lands exhibit some difficulty in understanding education in the United States; nor should we be surprised to discover that many people who have lived their entire lives in the United States and have had direct contact with the schools do not fully understand or completely appreciate our educational ideals. This lack of understanding is in part inevitable and unavoidable and it can be deplored too much, for it would be hard to defend the view that in order to be a good citizen and a worthy member of our society, everyone should give special attention and study to education. But hundreds of thousands of teachers and millions of citizens directly concerned with basic school policies and programs have no warrant to be unaware of the distinctive democratic features of education in the United States which in many ways make it unique.

It would, of course, be inaccurate to claim indigenousness for every detail of education in the United States. In the country's first years a social tradition was borrowed from abroad, and this tradition included educational plans and practices. The American educational inheritance can be

25

traced to England and to the Continent and then all the way back to the ancient Greeks, who remain a lasting force in Western education; but the important point is not that we borrowed—every civilization and every culture has done so—but that the transplanted theories and practices were reshaped and cultivated in a sincere effort to meet the ever-changing needs and aspirations of a dynamic, demanding society and its people. As a result of this planned and guided (and at times even accidental) metamorphosis of older theories and practices, a total educational system without counterpart anywhere in the world evolved.

In Chapter 1 we touched on the importance of education and the significance of teaching in the world of the twentieth century. In this chapter we shall discuss the distinctive features or characteristics of education in the United States and attempt to describe both the evolution of these features and their practical significance for democratic education. The distinctive features of education in the United States are univeral education, equality of educational opportunity, public support, nonsectarianism, public-private dualism, and single-ladder organization.

UNIVERSAL EDUCATION

Interpreted strictly, the phrase "universal education" means everyone is educated; it is something like saying that learning is ubiquitous. If the interpretation is broadened slightly, it means that all adults or near-adult members of a society have had the advantages of formal schooling. Can either interpretation of the meaning of universal education be applied to education in the United States? If we said, for example, that

TABLE 2-1

Distinctive Features in United States Education

Universal education	Opportunity for some education is universal.
Equality of educational opportunity	Opportunity equal to student's capacity for achievement.
Public support	Universal taxation for support of public education.
Nonsectarianism	Sectarian doctrines may not be taught in public schools, and church-related schools may not share in public funds.
Public-private dualism	Democratic society being a pluralistic society, the right of individual responsible groups to provide education outside of the public school system is maintained.
Single-ladder organization	All the schools open to all the people.

everyone in this country has been exposed to formal schooling, we should be wrong. We should be wrong also in ascribing literacy to all our citizens. Possibly the figures on literacy, or percentages on illiteracy, are not as precise as we should like, for literacy tests are still being misused in some sections of the United States, and despite a citizen's ability to read he is judged to be illiterate and is thus deprived of one of the citizen's most important rights and duties—voting. The results of such tests may find their way into the national percentages and distort the picture. In general, literacy figures are based on the population over fourteen years of age, and even then almost $2\frac{3}{10}$ per cent (2.5 men, 1.8 women) of this group is illiterate.

We should not restrict our thinking by believing mere mastery of reading and writing is tantamount to education. Suggesting a difference between literacy and education must of necessity raise the question "What is education?" This is a good question, an entirely valid one, but it is too soon for us to try to answer it. This effort will be made in Chapter 11. Besides, it may not be necessary to settle on the meaning of education now in order to show that the goal of universal education has not been reached in the United States; the statistics on literacy are sufficient evidence of this. Although literacy and education may not be synonymous, they are unquestionably and intimately related: the former is obviously a prerequisite for the latter. Perhaps, then, what we in the United States are trying to achieve first, and are sometimes confusing with universal education, is universal literacy. The test for determining who is educated and who is not has yet to be constructed, and, of course, until we are surer of the meaning of education, we should not want to draw any definite conclusions. So far as political functions are concerned and for determining the qualifications of citizens to participate in these functions, demonstration of an ability to read and write is usually considered to be sufficient. Yet even the attainment of universal, or nearly universal, literacy needs the help of formal education. Another interpretation of the meaning of universal education must be made, an accurate interpretation to be applied to education in the United States. It is this: Education is available to all; opportunities for education are universal.

Taken in its strict meaning, universal education is an ideal, an objective, or a goal toward which we are aiming, but it is not yet within our grasp. Viewing this matter in the proper order of progression, we see that universal opportunity must precede universal education—the former is a necessary condition to the latter—and in the United States, schools with minimum facilities are now available for teaching and learning, enabling everyone, no matter how remote or seemingly isolated his home, to enjoy the advantages of some education. Here it is important to note and remember for future judgments that the commitment made in this context is only for *some* education.

Why have the people of the United States devoted their best energies to securing universal opportunity for education? What is the motivation that initiates and sustains efforts to attain this ideal? This devotion to education and the drive to establish more and better schools are nurtured by the democratic ideal relating truth and freedom: when freedom is protected, opportunities to achieve truth remain unfettered. This ideal was embraced by the founders of the Republic; it prompted them to lay theoretical and practical foundations for a government of the people, for the people, and by the people. Under such a political system, free men were commissioned to govern themselves and make public policy; since then, determination of public policy by public opinion has remained an essential feature of political democracy. On the level of practice, government by the people is achieved when citizens exercise their right to vote; but if government by the people is to be truly effective, the people must be prepared to discharge their rights and fulfill their responsibilities. In other words, government by the people depends upon a qualified electorate. How do the people become qualified? The best and perhaps the chief means so far devised is education.

The founding fathers knew, and other thoughtful men understood, that democracy's full potential depended upon a literate, sensitive, enlightened, and educated citizenry. Despite this, relatively little progress was made in creating conditions promoting the attainment of these essentials; real efforts to achieve universal opportunities for education were not undertaken until after the fourth decade of the nineteenth century when the United States was already more than a half century old. Even after the 1840s, although some impressive gains had been made, especially in the Northeast, most boys could not expect to attend school for more than a few years, and girls could hardly hope to attend at all. Nevertheless, as the democratic doctrine of universal suffrage was more clearly and generally recognized, the educational ideal of universal opportunity was given a more friendly hearing in most sections of the country.

In 1779, four years after the rupture in relations between the Colonies and Great Britain, the Virginia Legislature was presented with a bill purporting to lay a legal foundation for free, public education in the colony of Virginia. Thomas Jefferson, the author of the bill, proposed the establishment of a system of free schools giving every free child in the commonwealth three years of publicly supported elementary education; intellectually qualified but economically impoverished secondary school and university students were to be helped by public scholarships. The Bill for the More General Diffusion of Knowledge, despite the enviable reputation of its illustrious sponsor, did not receive sufficient support for passage in the Virginia assembly of lawmakers; yet it was not forgotten, even though it was defeated in the legislative hall, for Jefferson's plan was a model—it was accepted in theory as principal means by everyone who recognized citizenship as education's most important objective.[1]

Jefferson believed universal education was an essential instrument for building the civic virtue of citizenship, but besides citizenship other desirable outcomes were expected too. Universal education, it was argued, would increase national prosperity by raising the productivity of the people. Such a design for education, one might guess, would attract the sympathetic, if not the active, support of men of means, influence, and wealth. Despite the apparent validity of the claim, neither sympathy nor support came frequently or generously from these people. It is not difficult to understand why affluent early-nineteenth-century men were not entirely willing to lend their support to the cause of universal education and why, when this support did come, it came reluctantly. These men did appreciate the values to be derived from universal education, and they were willing to acknowledge education's vital and necessary role in the formation of a functioning democracy, but they maintained, nevertheless, that education on such a scale, embracing all the children of all the people, could succeed only at the cost of national bankruptcy. This, they thought, was too high a price, and at this point progress toward universal opportunity for education halted until a related feature—public support—was more generally understood and accepted. Effective economic arguments were mustered to support the cause of universal education. But in addition to the economic arguments pro and con, there were others: Universal education was supposed to prevent or greatly reduce crime. Schoolhouses could be built more cheaply than jails, and with the erection of a new schoolhouse, so the argument ran, one less jail would be needed. Another fairly effective argument found its basis in an expression of political philosophy: Elementary education is the natural right of every citizen.

Universal education, we have said, was a principle not always eagerly embraced, and we have referred to important and effective opposition to the extension of educational opportunity: cost. Other opposition was rooted in such ideas as these: Universal education would destroy traditional class structures of society; most hard-working citizens did not have time to bother with formal schooling; and, finally, book learning was important to neither men nor societies. Each of these positions made a contribution to a rather extreme generalization. It was this: Public responsibility does not reach down to the education of a private citizen. In other words, the principle of "educational opportunity depending on private or individual means" received enthusiastic support. Public means could not be used, it was agreed by those who shared this view, except to provide some education for paupers or others who were unable to care for themselves; beyond this, opportunity for education was to be secured out of individual initiative and resources. Public resources should be used only to educate and train indigent persons. One may estimate the strength of this conviction and the fervor with which it was held from a request by an Indiana legislator for the following epitaph: "Here lies an enemy of public education." Today it is hard for us to believe that political success could ever have been gained by endorsing a party policy opposing public education. And, it may be added, on matters of public education, Indiana was one of the more progressive states.

In the face of consistent and, at times, especially articulate opposition to universal opportunity for some education, the cause was a worthy one and made progress. Signs of this progress can be seen in the early constitutions of many states, where some responsibility for providing educational means was accepted. New Hampshire's constitutions of 1784 and 1792 indicate the people's awareness of relationships between education, public policy, and the common good. The section of New Hampshire's constitution for the year 1792 which alludes to the state's responsibility for education may be taken as fairly representative of many constitutions of the period.[2]

Knowledge and learning generally diffused through a community being essential to the preservation of a free government, spreading the opportunities and advantages of education through the various parts of the country being highly conducive to promote this end, it shall be the duty of the legislatures and magistrates, in all future periods of this government, to cherish the interest of literature and the sciences, and all seminaries and public schools; to encourage private and public institutions, rewards and immunities for the promotion of agriculture, arts, sciences, commerce, trade, manufactures, and natural history of the country; to countenance and inculcate the principles of humanity and general benevolence, public and private charity, industry and economy, honesty and punctuality, sincerity, sobriety, and all social affections and generous sentiments among the people.

By accepting the admonition contained in the Ordinance of 1787—"religion, morality, and knowledge [are] necessary to good government and the happiness of mankind"—by encouraging the establishment of schools and at times actually founding them, state governments took their first unsteady steps toward providing universal opportunity for education. But other and more certain steps were needed; broad acknowledgments and high-sounding phrases needed to be implemented in a number of ways. The founding and the support of schools were certainly high on the list of priorities. But what, or how much, could be gained by building schools and appointing teachers if the children of the communities did not attend them? Compulsory education with all of its refinements must be brought into the picture, and when this is done we begin to see compulsory education as a corollary of universal education.

With all of the present-day opportunities for education, there is something unreal, almost unbelievable, about our past where schools were hard to find, with many communities not having any, and where progress in popularizing education was slow and did not become steady until several important obstacles were removed. A mild, though general, interest in schools and education had to be transformed into actual districts, money appropriations, and schools where teaching and learning were realities. But this transformation was hardly ever effected apart from bitter and radical educational campaigns, which set the stage for the enactment of laws relative to the improvement, development, and expansion of educational opportunity. It is true, of course, education enjoyed a general though abstract reservoir of good feeling in most parts of the country; learning was commonly acknowledged as being important to the common good; but a practical implementation of either feeling or belief was realized slowly. The foundations for compulsory education, laid in the climate of the early colonial period, were supported by educational objectives keyed to religious rather than civic life.

Compulsory Education

Compulsory education is neither more nor less than a legal requirement that everyone be educated. Standing alone, without subscript, it needs little amplification for understanding. Yet in today's educational world, we are not likely to find compulsory education without refinements and amendments. These we shall consider later. Now we can best plumb the foundations of the distinctive features by seeing compulsory-education legislation in its earliest historical form. Clearly the best example in our history is the Massachusetts Act of 1642. This remarkable piece of legislation contributed considerably to the development of education in this country. It has even been called the original seed from which public education in the United States grew and flowered. Without pausing here to argue the strengths and weaknesses of such an assertion, the act, we can agree, did contain the first legal acknowledgment in the American Colonies of a state's right to exert some control over the education of its people. This Act of 1642 directed the selectmen of the towns to investigate the educational accomplishments of the towns' inhabitants and to require the skill of reading and an understanding of the principal tenets of religion and the capital laws of the colony. Other skills and knowledge clearly economic in their significance were also demanded, but, it should be noted, nowhere were provisions made in the act for schools or institutions to train or educate the people. The act, it is true, did require certain educational accomplishments of the people, but it neglected to say how they were to be achieved.

Compulsory-school Laws

Compulsory-school laws are intimately related to, and are a natural and inevitable development of, compulsory-education legislation. If the people must be educated, schools would seem to be essential; and the same authority requiring all persons to have the advantages of formal education must take necessary steps to provide the means. The first example of a compulsory school law in English America was the "Old Deluder Satan Act," or the Massachusetts Act of 1647. This act required towns with a population of 50 families or householders to establish a reading and writing school, or an elementary school, and towns with 100 families or householders to provide for grammar schools in addition to elementary schools. The act is quoted in full, with its spelling modernized: [3]

> It being one chief object of that old deluder, Satan, to keep men from the knowledge of the Scriptures, as in former times by keeping them in an unknown tongue, so in these latter times by persuading from the use of tongues, that so at least the true sense and meaning of the original might be clouded by false glosses of saint-seeming deceivers, that learning may not be buried in the grave of our fathers in the Church of the Commonwealth, the Lord assisting our endeavors,
>
> It is therefore ordered, That every township in this jurisdiction, after the Lord hath increased them to the number of fifty householders, shall then forthwith appoint one within their town to teach all such children as shall resort to him to write and read, whose wages shall be paid either by the parents or masters of such children, or by the inhabitants in general, by way of supply, as the major part of those that order the prudentials of the town shall appoint: *Provided,* Those that send their children be not oppressed by paying much more than they can have them taught for in other towns; and
>
> It is further ordered, That where any town shall increase to the number of one hundred families or householders, they shall set up a grammar school, the master thereof being able to instruct youth so far as they may be fitted for the university: *Provided,* That if any town neglect the performance hereof above one year, that every such town shall pay five pounds to the next school till they shall perform this order.

In this act, the responsibility of the town to open schools was clearly established, and many towns, if not all—we are led to believe—complied with the law. Still, it should be emphasized, at this point, regardless of the towns' response to the law, no one—child or adult—was required by the law to attend these schools.

Compulsory Attendance

On the popular level it is not common (it may not be important) to distinguish between compulsory attendance and compulsory education, but in this context—where, in addition to their historical evolution, the deeper meaning of these laws is being probed—a distinction would seem to be illuminating. We have already dealt with compulsory education, and its meaning need not be repeated here. So we can turn at once to the meaning of compulsory attendance. Perhaps it is too obvious to mention, surely it is too apparent to belabor: Compulsory attendance means one must attend school. In the United States, with each state having its own battery of educational laws, compulsory-attendance legislation has a variety of applications. For example, the age range for compulsory attendance is not uniform, although one would usually be correct in assigning age seven as a normal minimum and age sixteen as a common maximum. In general, the statutes covering compulsory attendance are construed to mean that all normal children whose age falls within the legal range for attendance must be enrolled in an authentic school. Once the legal maximum age is attained, withdrawal from school is permitted, or, as in some states, once a certain educational level is achieved, say eighth grade or high school graduation, compliance with the compulsory-attendance law is waived. We may liberalize these legal requirements further by reporting that some states accept instruction outside a regularly established school as fulfilling the compulsory-attendance statute. But where and when this is done, public-education officers are given the legal authority to assess the educational attainments of children of compulsory-attendance age who choose not to attend school. If these officers are satisfied with the child's work, he is left with his tutors; but if minimum standards are not met, attendance in a regular school becomes mandatory.

Both compulsory-education and compulsory-school statutes have been in force in this country for more than two centuries, whereas compulsory-attendance laws are of relatively recent origin. The first statute in the United States requiring attendance in school was passed in Massachusetts in 1852. Following the lead of Massachusetts, other states enacted similar laws, so by 1890, in addition to Massachusetts, the following states and territories had enacted compulsory-attendance legislation: District of Columbia, 1864; Vermont, 1867; New Hampshire, Michigan, Washington, 1871; Connecticut, New Mexico, 1872; Nevada, 1873; New York, Kansas, California, 1874; Maine, New Jersey, 1875; Wyoming, 1876; Ohio, 1877; Wisconsin, 1879; Rhode Island, Illinois, Dakota, Montana, 1883; Minnesota, 1885; Nebraska, Idaho, 1887; Colorado, Oregon, 1889; and Utah, 1890. By 1918, when Mississippi enacted this legislation, all of the first forty-eight states had compulsory-attendance statutes.[4]

It may be interesting at this point to sample some of the provisions of the first statute, so we shall quote briefly from the Massachusetts Law of 1852.[5]

. . . Every person who shall have any child under his control, between the ages of eight and fourteen years, shall send such child to some public school within the town or city in which he resides, during at least twelve weeks, if the public schools within such town or city shall be so long kept, in each and every year during which such child shall be under his control, six weeks of which shall be consecutive. . . .

By 1918, it was possible to close the books on the actual evolution of compulsory attendance. It had taken fifty-nine years for the forty-eight states to accept a necessary condition for universal education. In the face of some fairly effective and always persistent opposition, this may well have been a surprisingly short time in which to accomplish so much. There were two main sources to which the opposition to compulsory-attendance laws turned for their intellectual ammunition. In the first place, it was argued, such laws interfered with personal liberty and were a threat to free institutions. They were but the first step, it was often stated, toward tyranny. If the state could begin by requiring its citizens to attend schools, where could it be stopped? Many persons taking this stand seemed convinced of the lack of state authority to do anything but pay the educational bill, and others even withheld all financial responsibility for education from the state. Here we see a revival of the old philosophy of individualism, current—even dominant—for so many years in the colonial period. This view considered education as a private matter, or, if not exclusively private, it would never go beyond admitting the family and the church to the inner circle of responsibility. The other source for opposition so often instrumental in retarding educational progress on this as well as other fronts was grounded on economic predictions. Whatever good might have been counted for compulsory attendance, the unreconciled rightfully regarded it as a means to universal education. And whatever the short-range values of universal education might be, and there were probably many, the long-range outcome was inevitably fiscal catastrophe.

Neither of these broad and often well-stated arguments was ever successful in blocking educational progress completely in this area of required school attendance, but both unquestionably interfered with progress. In time, both positions lost their force: the claim that compulsory-attendance laws abridged personal liberty has been rejected by the courts, and all compulsory-attendance statutes whose constitutionality has been questioned have been upheld. The second objection, pertaining to financial ability to support education, always bordered on the thin edge of invalidity and in recent decades has been demonstrated to be without any substantial foundation.

EQUALITY OF EDUCATIONAL OPPORTUNITY

Of all of the ideological foundations supporting democratic education, none are more generally misunderstood and misinterpreted than equality of educational opportunity. And, it may be added, none are more important to the full realization of democratic education. Does equality applied to education mean the same thing as equality applied to politics? The Declaration of Independence, we know, sounded the call for political equality, and its high purposes have, over the years, been confirmed in scores of constitutions, statutes, promulgations, judicial decisions, and executive actions. There is really no reason to question the intimate relationship existing between politics and education; the correctness of Plato's doctrine has been ratified repeatedly in the political and educational history of the West. But can we be content with equality before the law, the fundamental meaning of political equality, or must we have a broader application of equality if the full promise of democracy is to be realized? We should think it incorrect to claim that political and educational equality are identical, but we should think it equally incorrect to insist on great differences between them. Educational equality is a natural and possibly an inevitable development of political equality. It may evolve more slowly than political equality, but it is necessary to the full realization of political equality. In other words, if equality of educational opportunity is not a reality, a political democracy is weakened and eventually may wither and die. So equality of educational opportunity is a vital tributary feeding democracy and keeping it viable.

What does equality of educational opportunity mean, and why has there been so much misunderstanding concerning its application? What stands in the way of equality of educational opportunity and impedes its general application? To put it another way, what obstacles must be overcome before equality of educational opportunity will be generally and fully realized?

Equality of educational opportunity is not achieved by exposing everyone to the same educational experiences. Individual interests or abilities are not served in a democratic way by instituting a single and uniform program of instruction. But equality of educational opportunity does imply giving every student the kind of educational experience best fitted to his interests and capacities. There is no good reason for believing, for example, that every high school graduate must be guaranteed a place in the state university. At the same time, some opportunity for education ought to be available to all who have need for it. But how is this need to be demonstrated? Is it enough for the person directly involved to indicate his desire to continue upward progress on the education ladder, or should there be tests of aptitude and achievement, screening applicants for various programs? There is a philosophy of educational opportunity built on the principle of the "right to try" or, one might say, the "privilege to fail." In this view, everyone who seeks admission to a school—especially to a public school— should be admitted. But admission does not mean retention. Students who succeed, remain—or may remain—in school; those who fall by the wayside have their places taken by others supposedly more worthy. This process of natural selection imposes immense burdens on the educational budget. Think of the facilities a state university must have if the law requires it to accept every high school graduate of the state. Such a plan would seem to be wasteful, and waste always detracts from equality of educational opportunity. Without going into the myriad difficulties facing the administration of an educational program committed to equality of opportunity, we can restate the principle: Every person should have educational opportunity commensurate with his talents. Anything short of this is inconsistent with the deeper principles of democracy.

Educational opportunity may be curtailed in any one of three ways: by discriminating among persons, i.e., by not giving similar persons similar opportunity; by treating everyone alike without regard for individual differences in capacities and interests; and by being unable to, or refusing to, provide the means for diversified educational programs to meet a variety of human needs. The first type of curtailment is the result of an unreasoned attachment to racist or sectarian doctrines. At different times in different places, otherwise well-qualified students have been denied admission to schools because of their race, their creed, or their color. The democratic doctrine of equality recognizes neither racial, religious, nor color differences among men. The United States Constitution is color-blind; it is also race- and sect-blind. The only important quality for democratic doctrine to recognize is capacity to achieve.

Despite the national mind's theoretical acceptance of the United States Constitution, there has been a long history of various types of educational discrimination in different parts of the country. The New England area did not welcome the Irish influx of the 1840s, and Irishmen were subjected to numerous discriminatory practices; the West felt uncomfortable with Chinese and Japanese immigrants; the Southwest often did its best to make Mexican-Americans feel uncomfortable; American Indians were badly treated in many sections of the country; and in the South, as well as some places in the North, Negro citizens have not been, and are not being, accorded full rights of citizenship. If the discrimination against the Negro in the South is not the only kind of discrimination in this country, it is at least the most deep-seated and the best known.

For several decades, and surely since 1896 when the United States Supreme Court in the celebrated decision of *Plessy v. Ferguson* endorsed the "separate but equal" doctrine, it was entirely legal to maintain a dual system of schools: One system was open only to white children, the other to Negro children. Although many perceptive citizens both in the South and the North doubted the possibility of providing separate but fundamentally equal opportunities for education, the practice persisted with regular but largely ineffective protests until 1954, when, in *Brown v. Board of Education,*[6] the United States Supreme Court overturned the "separate but equal" doctrine, ruling segregated schools should be integrated "with all deliberate speed." In its decision, the Court indulged in a detailed analysis of equal opportunity for education, concluding that an environment for education constrained in a strait jacket of dualism interfered with real equality. In effect, the Court argued, a school is more than buildings, however adequate they may be, and it is more than its teachers, too, although they may be well qualified. Students are educated by their environment both in and out of school, according to the opinion, and the artificial environment of the segregated school is detrimental to the students of both white and Negro schools.

A decade has passed since this memorable decision was rendered, and a great deal of progress has been made toward integrating schools: much more, in fact, than most arch segregationists approve; too little for the person who has chafed under the yoke of segregation for generations; but enough to satisfy the realistic expectations of sympathetic and reasonable observers. If progress in achieving the full rights of citizenship for those to whom those rights are denied is always too slow, then, it can at least be maintained that the social climate is far more conducive to accelerated rates of progress in the next ten years than in the past ten. Of course, a nation committed to equality of educational opportunity cannot rest until the ideal is achieved; as an ideal, equality of educational opportunity is a feature of education in the United States.

Equality of educational opportunity is blocked or interfered with when an effort is made to reach a dead level of uniformity in all educational programs. Then the problem is not so much one of too little as of too much. Think of a school system which tries to provide a rich educational program for all its students but at the same time is reluctant to permit any deviation from a single curriculum: a uniform curriculum for all. Inevitably, popular education caters to the average student, whatever "average" may really mean; and as numbers increase, the standard for an average intellectual or educational diet drops. There may be no special danger in this so long as deviations are possible and one student may take a course of studies quite different from other students because of special interest, need, or capacity. Because of either unique abilities or particular disabilities, a student may be given special attention, teaching, or freedom. His program may lead him off into what for the average student are unexplored and unchallenging regions. This approach we should think natural and commendable. But the doctrinaire uniformist would be quick to register his objections: Whatever is provided in a democratic system must be used by all. It is not only a question of opportunity; it is a question of actual use. Special courses taken only by the few are challenged as undemocratic, as undermining equality of educational opportunity, although in actual fact the opposite is true. To insist upon uniformity of educational experiences is the most certain way of destroying equality of educational opportunity. In addition to the harm it does to persons pushed ahead or held back, it places such a burden of cost on those paying for education that the general quality of educational opportunity declines. There is no reason to withdraw from a commitment made to the education of the common man, but this is only the beginning of the educational process. When the common man has been exposed to the advantages of the social inheritance, of the distilled wisdom of the ages, he will, it is hoped, have become an uncommon man. The purpose of democratic education is not to make men the same; it is to offer them a chance to strike a spark of individuality, to enable them to become more fully but individually human. Uniformity of opportunity is not the best way, if it is any way at all, to achieve this. Happily, the doctrine of the educational uniformist is less attractive today than it was from 1930 to 1950, although vestiges of this damaging point of view remain still.

Finally, we come to the economic factors and their bearing on equality of educational opportunity. Of the three major obstacles to equality of opportunity, the economic may be the most imposing and the most difficult to eliminate. There are many striking examples of economic inequality. Some states have resources adequate for supporting the educational enterprise; for other states the resources are more than adequate; in still others there are insufficient means to provide all of the opportunity needed. It may be put another way: A wealthy state may be able to spend four times as much on education as a poorer state and not really tax its ability in doing so. Why, it will often be argued, doesn't the state doing less resolve to do more and support educational budgets more generously? The answer is not to be found in effort but in wealth, and many states, as well as communities within a state, may not have the wealth upon which to draw.

Money, it has been asserted, will not guarantee equality, and educational inequality caused by unfavorable economic factors is greatly exaggerated. The merit of the claim that money alone is enough to assure high quality in education need not be tested, for no one really believes this. Adequate financial resources may, however, bring about the construction of a school plant large enough to house all the students in attendance in a single daily session, the procurement of those instructional facilities needed for the best learning, and the appointment and retention of fully prepared and highly qualified teachers. Flexible and diverse programs and curricula can be developed for the children of the school; educational experimentation and research can be carried out; special classes can be conducted for superior students or for students who may need remedial teaching. A full educational program designed to meet the needs of the students may be maintained. All of this and more can be done with adequate financing; none can be sponsored without it.

It is difficult to see how the economic obstacle can be overlooked or discounted. Perhaps as many as 12 per cent of the teachers in the United States are not fully qualified, as qualifications are defined in state certification codes. This is due largely to the financial inability of certain school districts to attract qualified persons or to motivate persons not fully qualified to seek the status, position, and income of the fully qualified teacher. The difference in ability of some communities to support education is so great that in some instances one school system is able to spend forty times as much per pupil as another. The economic impediment to equality of opportunity is very real, and despite an enlightened public opinion and the real achievements already stimulated, much remains to be done. All of the sources of inequality must be eliminated, and this is equally important to all parts of the country, to all states, to all communities, for the consequences of educational inequality know no state or local boundaries and actively undermine the stamina of a democratic society.

PUBLIC SUPPORT

Because they believed education was necessary to good government and the happiness of mankind, public men and public-spirited citizens stressed the natural relationship existing between universal education and self-government. A deep faith in the power of education and an unremitting pressure from an alerted people prompted the people's representatives to enact laws requiring the establishment of schools and their attendance by children. If it was not obvious from the outset, it became clear very quickly that school building, the implements of teaching and learning, all of the costs of instruction made heavy demands on the public purse, and a regular source of revenue had to be found. In New England during the colonial period, interest in education was relatively high, and, in spite of the private character assumed by schooling and instruction, attendance in school was definitely encouraged for those who could afford tuition charges. Later, during the first years of the national period, the inadequacy of private means for supporting universal education became apparent. And to bring the matter down to everyday realities, how could government demand attendance of children at schools unless they could afford to go? At this point, the public was asked to determine policy or choose between two different meanings of public support. In one meaning, public support was limited to a moral and verbal commitment to education; it hardly went beyond confirming the people's interest in education. The other interpretation was more realistic and held out greater hope for educational progress: it accepted the theoretical support of the people and commended them for their interest in education, but in addition, it promised, public money would be used for the support of schools.

By the 1840s, when the battle for public support was fought and won, most Americans believed that formal education was a good thing and that the influence of education on society was great. But a few prominent citizens, although they accepted the value of education, still regarded it as an individual responsibility. The use of tax money for the support of schools was held to be unjust. The spirit of economic individualism was so strong that collective efforts for education, it was feared, would discourage thrift and frugality and would encourage the poor to lean too heavily on the public treasury. It was held, moreover, that if education were used to extend suffrage, the poor, who had no property, would be empowered to use taxation to rob the few who did have property. A statement attributed to a Rhode Island farmer explains the reaction of many to the proposal that schools be supported by tax money. Henry Barnard, one of America's foremost education statesmen and the first United States Commissioner of Education, was traveling around the country, seeking support for the principle that schools should be supported by taxes and that they should be entirely free. Upon hearing that Barnard was in the vicinity, the farmer threatened to shoot him "if he ever caught him on his property advocating such heresy as the confiscation of one man's property for the education of another man's child."

Somewhat related to the argument that tax levies for the support of universal education were unjust and confiscatory was the proposition that public funds could be used to pay for the education only of those who could not afford to educate themselves. A poor man should not be ashamed of his condition, it was said, nor should he be required to pay for the education of his rich neighbors' children. The public purse should be opened only for paupers and charity cases.

Although neither of these arguments was sufficiently powerful to block progress toward public support, together they delayed the achievement of universal free education for some years. Even when public support was gained rather generally throughout the country, many parents refused to send their children to free schools because they thought of them as pauper schools, or they believed attendance at publicly supported schools was a sign of economic collectivism.

The *Philadelphia National Gazette,* July 12, 1830, carried an editorial which was typical of the opposition to public support for education:[7]

It is an old and sound remark, that government cannot provide for the necessities of the People; that it is they who maintain the government, and not the latter the People. Education may be among their necessities; but it is one of that description which the state or national councils cannot supply, except partially and in a limited degree. They may endow public schools for the indigent, and colleges for the most comprehensive and costly scheme of instruction. To create or sustain seminaries for the tuition of all classes—to digest and regulate systems, to adjust and manage details, to render a multitude of schools effective, is beyond their province and power. Education in general must be the work of the intelligence, need, and enterprise of individuals and associations. At present, in nearly all the most populous parts of the United States, it is attainable for nearly all the inhabitants; it is comparatively cheap, and if not the best possible, it is susceptible of improvement and likely to be advanced. Its progress and wider diffusion will depend, not upon government, but upon the public spirit, information, liberality, and training of the citizens themselves, who may appreciate duly the value of the object as a national good, and as a personal benefit for their children. Some of our writers about universal public instruction and discipline seem to forget the constitution of modern society, and declaim as if our communities could receive institutions or habits like those of Sparta.

In spite of spirited opposition, the battle for public support was won. At the present time the base for public support is rather general or broad. Many different kinds of taxes are used to raise money for schools—sales taxes, state income taxes, special excise taxes—but a levy on all real property is the most common means. A broad or general base for tax support, however, has not always been an accepted principle in American taxation. The early methods employed by communities to raise money for the support of schools did not include a levy on all the real property within the unit sponsoring the school. The first schools in this country, with the exception of certain schools founded under religious auspices in colonial Maryland, were not free schools but rate schools. The rate, a form of tuition, was charged for the instruction which each pupil received. It may be worth recalling that the Massachusetts Act of 1647, although it required the towns to establish schools, placed the major financial responsibility for supporting these schools on those who attended them. Subsequent legislation in Massachusetts tended to relieve the burden on those people with children to be educated by permitting the towns to collect special excise taxes for the partial support of schools, but many years passed before public support in the form of general taxation for the support of education became a fact.

During the second quarter of the nineteenth century, there was considerable agitation for a more generous support of public education. Eventually, public opinion became strong enough to demand the enactment of tax laws which required resident property owners to pay school taxes. In the early stages of the evolution of these tax laws there was a tendency to levy a school tax on property if the owner of the property had children in school but to exempt from school taxes those who did not have children, or those who did not have children in school. Absentee property owners, that is, property owners who lived outside the town or school district, were not usually taxed for the support of schools.

The taxing principle which called for a levy to be applied to all real property for the support of public education was accepted slowly and somewhat reluctantly. Several decades passed, and only shortly before the Civil War was this principle applied generally throughout the United States. Tax support had to battle its way through the strongholds of pauper schools and through those regions of the country where it was not considered wise or desirable to make the schools entirely free. Today, apparently having reached the end of this evolutionary process, public education is supported by every property owner.

Before concluding this brief consideration of public support, the two principal sources for the financial support of schools should be identified. Of course, the ultimate source is the people to whom the tax bills are presented for payment, but considered as local and nonlocal there are, as

Figure 2.1 Trends in Sources of Revenue for Education. (*School File,* September, 1962, p. 23.)

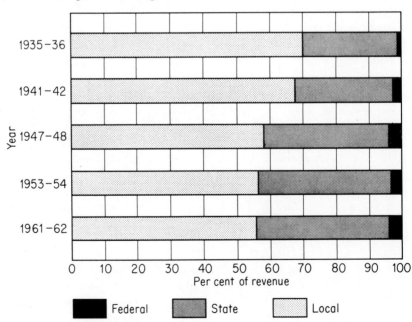

we have said, two principal sources. The major source from which schools derive their funds is the local community. On a national average about 56 per cent of the funds which are needed to finance education are furnished by the citizens of local communities. Nonlocal support may be distinguished as state or Federal. Recent figures computed for the United States as a whole indicate that approximately 40 per cent of support comes from the state, whereas about 4 per cent of support is in the form of special grants to education made by the Federal government. Trends in the sources for revenue for schools may be seen by comparing these percentages with those shown in Figure 2.1.

In 1961–1962, 17.5 billion dollars in revenue was collected in the United States for school support. The sources for these funds are shown in Figure 2.2a. The percentages given for the United States as a whole may vary considerably from state to state, as shown in Figures 2.2b and c.

Figure 2.2 Sources for School Revenue: (a) for the United States, 1961; (b) Michigan, 1961; and (c) Nevada, 1961. (Adapted from *Revenue Programs for the Public Schools of the United States,* U.S. Office of Education, Miscellaneous 38, 1961.)

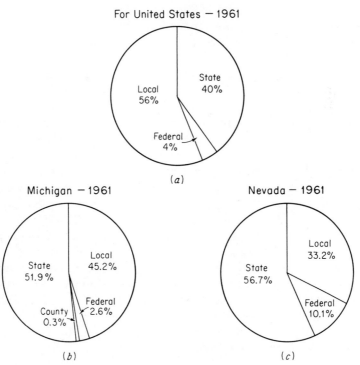

For United States — 1961

State 40%
Local 56%
Federal 4%

(a)

Michigan — 1961

State 51.9%
Local 45.2%
County 0.3%
Federal 2.6%

(b)

Nevada — 1961

Local 33.2%
State 56.7%
Federal 10.1%

(c)

NONSECTARIANISM OF PUBLIC EDUCATION

Most schools of the colonial and early national periods had some sectarian affiliation, and, naturally enough, the schools' goals and content were religiously oriented. With only a few exceptions, colonial churches had a privileged position in society and were supported by the colonial government. In this context, we find schools closely associated with churches, oftentimes considered to be their adjuncts rather than instrumentalities of the state. For many years after the beginning of the national period, these same conditions prevailed, and the religion which was considered to be official in the state or in the community enjoyed a privileged position in the schools. It was not unusual for church schools to receive land grants, money endowments, and other financial aid from the public treasury. Nor was it unusual when the first publicly supported schools were established for the doctrines of a religious denomination to be taught in these schools. Although such practices would meet with effective opposition today, they raised few special problems then because there was little diversity in religious affiliation within the communities. But increased immigration and continued mobility of the population tended to dilute religious homogeneity. And to these factors was joined the ideal of universally available and publicly supported democratic education. Under these conditions, the teaching of an official or approved sectarian doctrine in the common or public schools became unworkable, and sectarian teaching in these schools was prohibited by law.

Nonsectarianism as a public policy protecting the common schools from the invasion of sectarian beliefs passed through a process of gradual evolution. The Massachusetts Law of 1827, the first law dealing with nonsectarianism, did not go directly to the point of sectarian teaching; rather, it dealt with instructional materials used in the schools and said in part: "[school committees] shall never direct any school books to be purchased or used, in any of the schools under their superintendence, which are calculated to favor any particular religious sect or tenet." [8] Whatever precedents this law may have set in motion, it did not in itself assign to the school a position of neutrality with respect to religious teachings nor did it declare a policy of common-school hostility to religion. Bible reading, a long-standing practice in the schools of Massachusetts, was not tampered with by this law, and the employment of religion for the inculcation of morality was clearly encouraged. Neither by this law nor its immediate precedents were schools converted to irreligious or secular institutes, but they were defined as nonsectarian institutions. The act, moreover, did not touch on questions of school support, nor did it enjoin the use of public funds from religiously affiliated schools. It was only natural to expect, however, a gradual withdrawal of public support from all kinds of private schools as public education grew and as the costs of operating public schools mounted. This trend had no necessary connection with wanting religion in or out of the schools.

Nonsectarianism was first understood to mean that sectarian books or other tools or materials of instruction could not legally enter the classrooms of the public schools. Subsequently, this meaning was broadened to include all teaching in the school, and then it was applied to the use of public funds for church-related schools. In its final form, then, nonsectarianism has two dimensions: It prohibits sectarian teachings in the public schools, and it withholds public money from church-related schools. The precedent for the first was the Massachusetts Law of 1827, whereas the New York school controversy of the 1840s was probably responsible for generating a precedent for the second. At this time in New York City, the Public School Society, a nominally nondenominational group that was actually subject to Protestant control, received public money to conduct schools for thousands of children who did not attend, or could not attend, the church schools of the city. The schools of this society resembled in some respects the public schools of other cities; in any event the City of New York was not affected by state legislation which earlier had erected a district system in New York State. The Catholics of New York, following their principal spokesman Archbishop John Hughes, requested that their schools be permitted to share in funds coming to the Society from the state. They made this request, they said, not as Catholics but as citizens who felt entitled to some financial help for conducting their schools. Their appeal was refused. Renewed appeals brought no better results, so finally the matter was brought to the Legislature. Although the Legislature did not take action directly on the appeal made to it, its action in creating a school district for the City of New York did serve to quell the controversy. In addition, the legislators withheld the assignment of public funds to schools wherein sectarian doctrines were taught or where religious beliefs were inculcated.

The question of the use of public funds for church-related schools was not given any final answer by New York, for it was raised again many times in other states before the Civil War; and in the decade just before the war, many states adopted constitutional provisions or amendments, or enacted statutes, intended to withhold public support from religious schools.

State restrictions on the use of public funds for private schools have a fairly long history. Before 1870, twenty states had constitutional statements stipulating that public funds were to be preserved inviolate to the use of common schools. By 1912, all but three states had constitutional provisions which implicitly or explicitly forbade the use of public funds for sectarian purposes. There was, moreover, a tendency for the older states to revise existing prohibitory clauses to make them more explicit. Instead of broad and vague statements prohibiting the use of public money to sectarian purposes, the revised clauses contained detailed provisions to safeguard and direct the disbursement of public funds. In addition to constitutional provisions, a number of states enacted legislation intended to clarify the provisions and indicate the extent of their application. Despite this action taken by various states, the picture, as we entered the twentieth century, was not entirely clear. Some states prohibited the use of public money to all levels of private and sectarian education, but other states granted funds to higher schools and colleges regardless of their affiliation. The courts, moreover, did not always interpret the clauses or the statutes strictly, and some public money did find its way into the treasuries of private schools.

The policy of prohibiting public money to nonpublic schools evolved slowly. In the early years of American education, private and church-related school foundations were encouraged by grants of land and money. The door to the public treasury closed little by little, and legislative generosity in land grants, expecially for elementary and secondary schools, began to decline two decades before the Civil War. Still, private and church-related colleges continued to benefit from public magnanimity. Although the evolutionary process was dilatory, its progress was steady; and by the time Catholic schools became fairly common, the dim outlines of broad policy were apparent. When the Third Plenary Council of 1884 decreed the organization of a system of Catholic schools, it was a fixed policy. What policy might have been formed had the Catholic population during the first half of the nineteenth century been larger can only be speculated about. As it was, actual policies were developed without taking into account Catholics or their educational philosophy. The Catholics' special problem in relation to education became apparent only after the direction of public education was set and the policies with respect to the disbursement of public funds were securely established.

By 1870, many Catholics admitted that little could be done to change public schools to make them acceptable to Catholics for the complete education of their children. Catholic children could attend public schools and after the school day or on Saturdays or Sundays be instructed in the tenets of their faith. But this practice, while always having some shortcomings, had a special one during most of the nineteenth century. Public schools, though legally nonsectarian, went a step beyond and were often anti-Catholic. It would be unreasonable to expect Catholics to accept a practice where the child was, at worst, taught anti-Catholic doctrines and exposed to views prejudicial to the Church, or, at best, exposed to an anti-Catholic school atmosphere and then for a brief instructional period outside the school put in contact with positive Catholic teaching. The problem was real. Neither verbalism nor rhetoric could explain it away. What were Catholics to do?

Then, as now, it was contended that Catholics have a right to share in school-tax money because they pay taxes but cannot use public schools. This argument, coupled with the fact of compulsory attendance, had considerable force. In it we see a revival or a continuation of a "sharing" theory that Archbishop John Hughes had advocated during the New York City school debates. The rationale of the theory was this: Public benefits should be given to citizens recognizing the same principle requiring them to fulfill obligations of citizenship. Some spokesmen have found the "sharing" theory illogical. Money paid in taxes, they argue, is public money, and no individual or group has any claim on it. Even if some public money were distributed to parochial schools, they continue, their financial problems would not be solved.

PUBLIC–PRIVATE DUALISM

The first schools in America were private schools. That is, they were neither publicly supported nor publicly controlled. For many years, down almost to the middle of the nineteenth century, these private schools—although not always free from some public control and not always able to refuse some public support—provided the bulk of formal educational opportunity. This was strikingly true of higher education, for of 207 permanent colleges founded before the Civil War, only 27 were public.[9] But as the relationship between political democracy and education became clearer, public education became a reality: today about 84 per cent of all elementary school children (kindergarten through grade 8) in the United States attend public schools, 89 per cent of the secondary school population (grades 9 through 12) is in public schools, and over half of higher education's enrollment is in public colleges and universities.

Public-private dualism, or the partnership of public and private education, rests upon three propositions:

1. That, democratic society being a pluralistic society, the right of individual responsible groups to provide education outside the public school system must be maintained
2. That private schools accept and teach the fundamentals of the American democratic way of life and maintain standards equal to those of public institutions
3. That the choice of public or private education lies with the parent or the individual

The integrity of these propositions is protected by the Fourteenth Amendment to the Federal Constitution. In other words, the right of private schools to exist was guaranteed by this amendment in 1868, and before the enactment of the Fourteenth Amendment, there could not have been any Federal question, no matter what the states might have done in educational matters. These words are the legal foundation for private education in the United States:

> No State shall make or enforce any law which shall abridge the privileges or immunities of citizens of the United States; nor shall any State deprive any person of life, liberty, or property, without due process of law; nor deny to any person within its jurisdiction the equal protection of the laws.

In 1925 the United States Supreme Court made a definitive application of the Fourteenth Amendment to public and private education. This was in the famous Oregon decision. In 1922, under the system of initiative and referendum in use in Oregon, a compulsory-attendance law was enacted; it was to become effective in 1926. Prior to the effective date of the law, the Society of Sisters of the Holy Names of Jesus and Mary sued to restrain the public officials from enforcing this statute, which required, subject to some minor exceptions, every child between eight and sixteen years of age to attend a public school for the period of time that the public school was in session. The district court granted the decrees, and the public officers appealed. The United States Supreme Court upheld the lower court in a unanimous opinion. The legal precedents which protect the system of private education in this country originate in this decision.

What was protected? In the Oregon decision the property of the Society of Sisters was protected:[10]

> It [the Society of Sisters] has long devoted its property and effort to the secular and religious education and care of children, and has acquired the valuable good will of many parents and guardians.
> . . . All courses of study, both temporal and religious, contemplate continuity of training under appellees' charge; the primary schools are essential to the system and the most profitable. The business is remunerative—the annual income from primary schools exceeds thirty thousand dollars—and the successful conduct of this requires long time contracts with teachers and parents.

The opinion of the Court emphasized the threatened loss of property to the Society of Sisters if the statute were enforced. But this was not all. The Court held also that the act unreasonably interfered with the liberty of parents and guardians to care for the upbringing and education of their children. In this connection the Court held:

> The fundamental theory of liberty upon which all governments in this Union repose excludes any general power of the State to standardize its

children by forcing them to accept instructions from public teachers only. The child is not the mere creature of the State; those who nurture him and direct his destiny have the right, coupled with the high duty, to recognize and prepare him for additional obligations.

In this case, the right and liberty of parents are protected, but this protection is incidental to a specific right or interest of a private party actually in litigation with the state. In other words, parents are protected in their right to have their children educated in private schools because a corporation owning schools had a property interest which it attempted to protect from damage or destruction. Therefore, in its relation to the state the private school has the protection of the due-process clause in its property aspects. In its relationship to its students and to their parents, there is judicial recognition of the right of freedom of choice and control.

However, this protection given to private education in the due-process clause of the Federal Constitution is subject to some qualifications. The state does have considerable authority over the administration and management of schools within its borders. As Mr. Justice McReynolds wrote in *Pierce v. Society of Sisters* (the Oregon case):

> No question is raised concerning the power of the State reasonably to regulate all schools, to inspect, supervise and examine them, their teachers and pupils, to require that all children of proper age attend some school, that teachers be of good moral character and patriotic disposition, that certain studies plainly essential to good citizenship must be taught, and that nothing be taught which is plainly inimical to the public welfare.

The authority of the state to require attendance at some school is not questioned. And all the states have enacted such laws. What the decision in the Oregon case prohibits is enactment of laws compelling attendance in public rather than private schools. The educational program at private schools can be regulated by the state to ensure substantial equivalence to that of public schools. The state, moreover, may compel private schools to comply with standards of safety in the construction and maintenance of school buildings. It may prescribe the teaching of certain courses, and it may set standards of instruction. The sanction for this authority is the state's compulsory-attendance law: if substantial equivalence is not found between the educational programs in private and public schools, the pupils attending private schools will not be fulfilling the state's compulsory-attendance statute. Some states, to illustrate briefly the authority of the state over instructional programs, may require all elementary schools to provide instruction in eleven common branches: arithmetic, reading, spelling, writing, English, geography, United States history, civics, hygiene, physical training, and the state's history. In some instances, states demand that specific subjects be taught; sometimes this demand is applicable to public schools only, and sometimes it is applicable to both public and private schools. Typical of subjects required only in public schools are instructions relating to the flag, the study of certain holidays, and teaching on the subject of the effects of alcohol. Instruction in patriotism and citizenship, physical training, the nature and effects of narcotics and habit-forming drugs, highway safety and traffic regulation, and fire drills are usually required of all schools in a state.

Based on the substantial legal foundation of the Oregon decision, public and private schools are welded into a partnership to secure American democratic education. Often these schools exist side by side; and the public schools, although they educate about 90 per cent of the children, have no monopoly over education in the United States. Children who desire to do so may attend private schools.

More often than not, it is higher education that catches the public eye: at this level it is quite generally appreciated that private colleges make important contributions to higher education. One has little difficulty in indicating the vital role private colleges occupy in America, and they outnumber public colleges and universities more than 4 to 1.[11] But too frequently attention is not directed to the equally important position of private secondary and elementary schools. Private educational facilities, at all levels, supplement the work of public education by offering programs which public schools cannot offer. Private schools are usually sponsored by religious denominations who deplore the inability of public schools to offer a religious education and who establish their own schools in order to offer the members of their own denomination an education with religious perspectives.

Private schools often enjoy greater flexibility in their educational programs and are, therefore, able to experiment more readily in areas of curriculum and methodology and develop programs and techniques which otherwise would not be accepted so quickly. In some respects, private education has led the way in American education in making significant instructional innovations. Although this claim is sometimes contested, the record of history is clear on some of the more important contributions of private education. Private normal schools (the first schools for teachers in the United States) were forerunners of public normal schools and teachers colleges. Progressive education owes its origin to the private schools. The Northampton, Massachusetts, Round Hill School, opened in 1823 by George Bancroft and Joseph C. Cogswell, called attention to the importance of physical training in education. Bronson Alcott's Temple School in Boston (1834–1839) popularized the Pestalozzian principles of sense training and observation. John Dewey's Laboratory School at the University of Chicago (1896–1903) may claim to be the direct ancestor of today's progressive schools. The kindergarten was a contribution of private education; the education of girls was begun in private schools; schools for the deaf and the blind were products of private education in the United States. More recently, private schools have engaged in a variety of educational movements: the junior college, technical education, foreign-language instruction, the country day school, and remedial education.

All one should have to do to see the important effects of private schools is look around: their real contributions are obvious. Yet, despite their excellent record, the significance of private schools is not only not always recognized and appreciated, it is sometimes unequivocally denied. Some American educational spokesmen have always made the dogmatic assumption that democracy must have only one school system—the public—and that it alone can really contribute to the maintenance of a democratic society. They argue, moreover, that anything other than a monolithic educational program will actually rot away the foundations of democracy. In a word, private schools are called undemocratic schools. Such schools are thought to foster undemocratic sentiments and values by keeping the children of various races, national backgrounds, religious faiths, and, possibly, economic circumstances out of contact with one another. Because they do not have scholastic contacts, it is assumed they can have no contacts at all and, therefore, cannot possibly know or understand the differences between them or the similarities uniting them.

It should be understood, despite the school's influence on the values of children, there is another educational force whose influence is much greater and more constant, as well as more insidious than the school's. This force is society itself; in a sense, society is man's greatest teacher. If this is so, it would be hard to understand how attending nonpublic schools would effectively isolate students from democratic values and insulate them from the needs and aspirations of their fellow citizens.

Should the time ever come when the private school is a threat to democracy, when the very existence of the public school is challenged (and who could see such a challenge today when public education on all levels is becoming stronger, often at the expense of private education), it would be proper to raise voices in protest. But until the private school is demonstrated to be a dangerous undemocratic institution—until it is proved to be guilty as charged—it should be accepted for what it is: an institution wherein parents may exercise their democratic right of choosing and directing the education of their children. If the parent has this democratic right, it would be difficult to see how he could exercise it if private schools were eliminated and public schools were the only schools available.

It is interesting to speculate, but especially difficult to understand, how opposition to private education can be voiced along with an affirmation of principles of democracy, which include, it would seem, the right of citizens to differ in thoughts and actions, to be free to choose the church they attend or the school where their children enroll. Apparently, those who see a clear and present danger in the private school have an impaired understanding of democracy, or their application of its principles is somewhat myopic.

There is another threat to the stability of private education. Private schools have found it increasingly difficult to remain solvent, because of the great increase in educational operating costs over the past several years. This problem has been largely overcome for public education through larger legislative appropriations and higher school taxes, but private institutions, which rely on income from tuition and fixed resources such as endowments, have not received corresponding increases. Also, current tax practices tend to discourage the accumulation of great personal fortunes, which formerly provided a common source of funds for private education. Without dwelling on the financial aspects of education, it can be said that private education saves taxpayers hundreds of millions of dollars annually. If private schools were not in existence, the students now enrolled in them would be in public schools. And if this were the case, the cost of public education would be considerably greater than it is.

But more important than costs or savings, private education provides students with educational opportunities not available to them in public schools. In private education there need be no cleavage between a student's intellectual and spiritual life. Private schools may offer a complete religious education.[12] In this way, particularly, private education makes its greatest contribution.

Together, public and private schools can move with hope toward a conquest of the problems that threaten to engulf human living. In their partnership—within the dual system—these schools can perform their greatest service to individuals and to American society.

SINGLE-LADDER ORGANIZATION

We turn now to the last of the distinctive features of education in the United States: single-ladder organization. This is an organizational plan wherein elementary, secondary, and higher schools are closely articulated and one permitting students to move freely from one level of education to the next. Generally speaking, it is not necessary for students to attend a special elementary school in order to gain admission to a particular high school, or to attend a special high school to be admitted to a certain college. This is not to say, of course, that a given college may not set its standards at a point beyond the achievement of any student in a given high school. But this is not the point. The point is this: With a sufficient demonstration of achievement, candidates from such a high school can be admitted to the college in question. There are no artificial barriers excluding certain people from further progress on the educational ladder because they have not attended the right system of schools. Inability may stop or seriously interfere with forward movement on any educational level, but this is simply a fact of educational life which in no way invalidates the feature we are now discussing.

It is probably easier to see the strength of a single-ladder, or single-track, system by looking briefly at the weaknesses of another type of educational organization. During the last part of the eighteenth century and for the greater part of the nineteenth, European education was organized according to a two-track plan. There was, in other words, one system of schools for one class of the population and another system for the other class. Once a person was committed to the system of schools for the lower classes, to be educated not as a leader but as a follower, it was virtually impossible for him to extricate himself. And this system did not lead to higher education; although advanced trade schools, often called continuation schools, were available in the lower system, the door of the university was always closed tightly to anyone coming from it. The higher system was oriented to the preparation of leaders for church, state, and society, and even though it may be praised for the thoroughness of its work in taking children through elementary, secondary, and higher education, it effectively excluded many persons who, except for faulty social or economic position, were fully qualified to attend.

The system of education with which the colonists were familiar was really a dual system, perhaps not fully evolved, but one, nevertheless, which respected position more than individual capacity and dignity. To a large degree, this attitude was transplanted to colonial America, and schools were founded which tried to serve a class in society. Even in the national period, class schools were much in evidence despite the seemingly obvious undemocratic implications in them. The American commitment to democratic and universal education was coupled to an idealism deploring aristocracies of wealth and position; instead, it endorsed aristocracies of ability. But again, this idealism was real only, or largely, on the level of theory, and the schools themselves were still saddled with practices bespeaking social autocracy, if not actual tyranny.

The lines of evolution cannot be drawn here in great detail, for to do so would be to anticipate too much the development of the principal educational levels, but to give a fairly adequate though narrow picture now, we must say that elementary, secondary, and higher education in America grew up as independent enterprises. The elementary school was not thought to have any connection with the secondary school, and the high school, though this was not true of the earliest secondary schools, was not closely associated with higher education and did not try to gear its programs to college preparation. And the college, resting on top of the educational heap, felt entirely independent of the two lower levels.

Pressure was exerted from many sources to drive American education down the road to dualism. Persons misunderstood democracy or disapproved of it and were quite willing to restrict opportunity in education, which by this time was recognized as an important, necessary instrument to the broad objectives of democracy. But these pressures were unsuccessful: they did not drive American education further from the ideal. The best they could do was retard progress. In time, despite the differences in age and goal of the schools representing the three levels, these levels were welded together into one system, one we have called single-ladder.

Table 2-2A illustrates how each grade fits into the nineteen-step educational ladder. In addition, it indicates the effect the reorganization move-

TABLE 2-2A
Single-ladder Organization for American Education

Traditional plan	Age	Grade	Reorganized plan
University	24 23 22	19 18 17	Graduate and professional schools
College	21 20	16 15	Senior college
	19 18	14 13	Junior college
High school	17 16 15	12 11 10	Senior high school
	14	9	
	13 12	8 7	Junior high school
Elementary school	11 10 9 8 7 6	6 5 4 3 2 1	Elementary school
Kindergarten	5		Kindergarten
Nursery school	4 3		Nursery school

ment of the twentieth century had on single-ladder organization. Table 2-2B illustrates educational organization within the traditional European system. Even with the modifications of reorganization, the function of the single ladder is to start the student at the first educational level and carry him progressively through the various grades and school experience without leaving gaps in his education or creating too many adjustment problems for him. Without a single-ladder organization, many of the goals of democratic education could not be realized.

SUMMARY

The first schools in colonial America were institutions transplanted from Europe. Although these schools may have fulfilled the expectations and needs of their colonial patrons, they did not meet the needs or the emerging ideals of a democratic society. The American political system demanded an electorate that was educated, or at least literate, for its effective function-

TABLE 2-2B

Traditional Dual Organization for European Education

Secondary and higher education (for the elite)	Age	Grade	Elementary education (for the common people)
	24	19	
	23	18	
University	22	17	
Professional schools	21	16	
Teachers colleges	20	15	
	19	14	
	18	13	
	17	12	
	16	11	Peoples' high schools
	15	10	Adult education
Classical and scientific secondary education	14	9	Vocational schools
	13	8	Technical institutes
	12	7	Continuation schools
	11	6	
	10	5	
	9	4	
	8	3	
Foundation schools	7	2	Reading and writing schools
	6	1	
Kindergarten	5		Kindergarten

ing. This demand led from compulsory education to compulsory schools and finally to compulsory attendance. In its final form, compulsory attendance in school of all normal children means universal education. Along with the evolution of the ideal of universal education, policies for financing public education were developed. In order to support a rapidly expanding educational system, a variety of taxes was imposed, and eventually a principle of taxation was accepted: the support of public education is a responsibility of every citizen. With the recognition that the education of citizens was a public responsibility, it seemed necessary to remove distinctive denominational teaching from the publicly supported schools. However, the tradition that nonpublic schools at all levels were free to operate was not impaired by the principle of nonsectarianism, and this tradition was firmly reinforced and supported by the famous Oregon decision of 1925.

As these features of American education evolved, educational institutions were organized into a system which made all the schools available to all the people, and finally a feature that had always been implicit in American educational ideals was made explicit: Artificial barriers to educational opportunity have no place in democratic education.

QUESTIONS AND EXERCISES

1. What is your interpretation of equality of educational opportunity? What does the school system have to do with equality of opportunity?
2. Give examples showing how sections of the country differ in their ability to support education.
3. May society ask the school to prepare students in a special way? For example, is it proper for a democratic society to demand that schools prepare students for a democratic way of life? Is this some kind of indoctrination?
4. How was nonsectarianism in both its dimensions applied in your state?
5. What is your interpretation of education for citizenship? What is the school's part in making good citizens?
6. What social outcomes are proper to education? Do you believe that social values are at present being overemphasized?
7. Compare the American single-ladder system with that of another country. Do you think that a double-ladder system has any strengths? What are its chief weaknesses?
8. Prepare arguments for and against compulsory-attendance laws.
9. Give and evaluate the arguments against a dual system of public-private education. In what way is the Oregon decision a foundation for private education in the United States?
10. Can you think of any good reasons for changing the principle of nonsectarianism? If you had been a member of the Massachusetts General Assembly in 1827, how would you have voted on the bill requiring nonsectarianism in the common schools?

ADDITIONAL READINGS

Bailyn, B.: *Education in the Forming of American Society,* The University of North Carolina Press, Chapel Hill, 1960. A study of the role education has played in building the American social order.

Brown, Elmer E.: *The Making of Our Middle Schools,* Longmans, Green & Co., Inc., New York, 1903. An old but still valid analysis of the evolution of secondary education in the United States.

Brown, Samuel W.: *The Secularization of American Education,* Bureau of Publications, Teachers College, Columbia University, New York, 1912. Religion played a prominent role in early education in America. This volume shows some of the steps and how they were taken toward secularizing American education.

Conant, James B.: *Thomas Jefferson and the Development of American Public Education,* University of California Press, Berkeley, 1962. Conant regards Jefferson as an educational innovator and relates the fate of Jefferson's eighteenth-century proposals on nineteenth-century educational practices.

Cremin, Lawrence A.: *The American Common School,* Bureau of Publications, Teachers College, Columbia University, New York, 1951. A perceptive treatment of the rise of the common school: its ideals, purposes, and popularization.

Culver, Raymond B.: *Horace Mann and Religion in the Massachusetts Public Schools,* Yale University Press, New Haven, Conn., 1929. An especially competent treatment of the connection Horace Mann had with nonsectarianism. See especially the section dealing with Mann's role in and reaction to the Law of 1827.

Freeman, S. S.: *Yesterday's Schools,* Century House, Watkins Glen, N.Y., 1962. A treatment of colonial schools, including the early district and common schools and modern district schools and their equipment.

Good, H. G.: *A History of American Education,* The Macmillan Company, New York, 1962. A general history of American education which, in this edition, gives particular attention to educational metamorphoses since World War II.

Gross, Neal C.: *Who Runs Our Schools?* John Wiley & Sons, Inc., New York, 1958. Schools are pushed and pulled by superintendents, parents, boards of education, and general public pressures. This book tries to analyze the intensity of these pressures.

Hillway, Tyrus: *Education in American Society,* Houghton Mifflin Company, Boston, 1961. This book is intended to introduce the reader to school systems, levels of education, and the profession of teaching in contemporary America.

Jackson, Sidney L.: *America's Struggle for Free Schools,* American Council on Education, Washington, D.C., 1942. An imaginative and readable account of the movement away from individualism to collectivism on the point of support for public education.

Kimball, S. T., and James E. McClellan: *Education and the New America,* Random House, Inc., New York, 1963. A treatment which is preoccupied with the societal factors shaping education. Education is to be fully receptive to the changing society.

Mason, R. E.: *Educational Ideals in American Society,* Prentice-Hall, Inc., Englewood Cliffs, N.J., 1960. The author tries to isolate and describe the major traditions, scientific and democratic goals, and cultural and intellectual ideals as they helped form democratic doctrines of American education.

Rickover, Hyman G.: *Education and Freedom,* E. P. Dutton & Co., Inc., New York, 1959. American educational standards have been challenged before, generally by sympathetic but perceptive critics. This author indicts education for its failures and seems blind to its great successes.

Welter, Rush: *Popular Education and Democratic Thought in America,* Columbia University Press, New York, 1962. Educational precedents generated by Jacksonian democracy and liberalism are examined. The last half of the book treats of post-bellum consensus and twentieth-century innovations in education.

Whittmore, L. B.: *The Church and Secular Education,* Seabury Press, Greenwich, Conn., 1960. A study of the educational effects of separation of church and state. The author's general conclusion is that there were both debits and credits.

Woelfel, N.: *Educational Goals for America,* Public Affairs Press, Washington, D.C., 1962. Democratic goals for education are related to the essential elements of learning and needed reforms in teacher education. The role of teaching machines and learning aids is considered.

PART TWO

Organization and
Administration of Education
in the United States

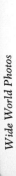

chapter 3

Local Communities

and Education

THE EVOLUTION OF
EDUCATIONAL ORGANIZATION

Education in colonial America began by living in the past. The people who came to North America in the seventeenth century were pioneers willing to brave the perils of the wilderness, but their spirit reflected a basic and imperturbable conservatism. Without question, many of them were searching for something, or they would not have ventured so far from a land they knew, but this search was never meant to extend to the point where it would lead to a confrontation with effective challenges to the fundamental values they held. This is not to say, of course, that there was a common motivation sustaining immigration: motives were quite dissimilar and ranged from the quest for wealth, to adventure, to religious freedom. Perhaps these principal motives were never required to stand alone (and alone they might not have been sufficient); in other words, there may have been a blending of motives and a mixture of reasons for leaving the world of the known for the world of the unknown. The possibility always existed for the man who sailed for America's shores with a determination to practice his religious beliefs unhampered by the local brand of intolerance to find ways to add to his treasures of worldly goods, and the man whose uppermost motive was economic gain might not have found the probability of adventure out of keeping with his hopes or expectations.

America's first colonists, despite the urgency of the motives bringing them to the eastern shores of this country, were not disinterested reformers committed to disinterested reform; they were leaving the old country behind, it is true, but this in no way implied a cultural rejection. They could shift their location without shifting their loyalties very much; and when they shifted their cultural inheritances, they retained much more than they discarded. So when we look at the cultural foundations of colonial America and the school policies emanating from them, what we see is not an original projection, but a reflection of the past, in which basic social and religious values are especially distinct. It may be too much to say that seventeenth-century colonial America was seventeenth-century Europe all over again; but if room were made for a few exceptions, such a generalization would carry a good deal of weight.

The colonial cultural attachment to religiously oriented education was undeniable and probably inflexible. There were changes in denominational patterns, of course, and the established churches of the old country did not always succeed in obtaining privileged positions in the new country. Yet, some denominational view was usually accepted as official, and formal education on all levels was expected (required would not be too strong a word) to serve both the doctrines and the development of this creed. Education became the servant of the established church, and the schools were under its direct control. With this general attitude toward education and religious control common in all parts of the new world, one might assume that educational patterns in colonial America were uniform. Though there were similarities among the colonies, there was hardly any educational uniformism. Yet, in three separate sections of the new country, a kind of educational homogeneity did develop.

Ecclesiasticism in New England

Systematically organized ecclesiastical authority imposed a social profile on the New England Colonies which, while not achieving all of the requirements of uniformity, did lead to the religious homogeneity referred to above. A common and reasonably accurate historical picture of colonial New England may be drawn by making religion the central figure on the canvas and by sketching in all other institutions as part of the background. In a social climate where the principal preoccupation was religion, it is reasonable to inquire about the basic religious convictions and theses, and to ask how they contributed to or directed life in society. The dominant theological doctrine was Calvinism—its special sectarian form was Congregationalism—but it and other creeds in evidence, mainly Separatism and Anglicanism, were imbued with a common spirit which at times seemed to subordinate doctrinal differences. This common spirit was Puritanism. Puritanism never became a clear-cut doctrinal belief to be exclusively absorbed by any one sect, so there was nothing extraordinary about its being the theme around which New England religiosity was built. This theme declaimed against enjoyment and comfort and seemed to endorse the view that the more miserable a man was, the more somber and severe his countenance, the more painful his exertions, the better off he was and maybe, too, the better he was. At best this was a hard doctrine, with austerity as its cardinal virtue.

Religion was public, more seen than felt, and compliance with codes of religion was prescribed irrespective of the inner feelings of men. Of course, the Separatists, who were poor and lacking in influence, and the Anglicans, who were few in numbers, did not always embrace the public attitude toward religion regularly taken by Calvinists, for their doctrines refused to acknowledge for the church that authority and power stated in Calvinistic dogma. Yet, on the level of practice, mainly because of their immersion in a Puritan milieu, the adherents to these creeds engaged in a religion of public display. It was not especially difficult for them, then, to acquiesce when religion was as apparent in the town meeting as it was in the Sabbath-day services. Both in theory and practice Calvinism was intent upon remaking the political world and subordinating the state to the church; in New England generally, but in Massachusetts especially, government rested with an oligarchy of ministers and magistrates. Political leaders and government officers were closely allied with the church, and the church-state relationship was so intimate it often became impossible to distinguish between the two. The church tried to avoid any intrusion on the state's law-enforcement machinery, but it was clearly and universally understood that, in return for this forbearance, the state would administer and enforce ecclesiastical canons whenever the clearly religious sanctions of the church proved ineffective.

It is sometimes believed the political dimension of Calvinism nurtured education in New England. While this may be a tenable view, it is important to remember educational ideals were first identified with the church and its functions and with religion rather than with politics. On the other hand, although the state may have followed the educational leadership of the church, precision on matters such as these is always difficult, but especially so when the church-state bond was as firm as in the case of colonial New England.

The educational system, if, indeed, it can be called a system, having its origin in doctrines of church-state relations, grew slowly, and with growth its influence spread. The most obvious signs of growth and sensitivity to educational causes were found in the enactment of educational laws supplemental to, or replacements for, older apprenticeship statutes, in the acceptance of some state responsibility for education throughout a colony, and in the private founding and public encouragement for Latin grammar schools and colleges.

The important educational legislation now forming the core from which further growth was possible was found principally in Massachusetts. The best examples are the Acts of 1642 and 1647. The Law of 1642 laid down the principle that everyone in the colony have some education; it designated the selectmen of the town to check on compliance or noncompliance; but while in these respects it gave ample evidence of its serious intent, it made no mention whatever of the establishment of local schools in which the educational achievements stipulated could be acquired. Yet, for all its worth as a law insisting upon the people of the towns being educated, the fundamental worth of the Act of 1642 must be sought in the recognition it gave to the state as a regulatory agency for education. Because the Act of 1642 was the first educational legislation in the English-American Colonies, and because it was enacted by the General Court (the legislative body for the Massachusetts Colony), it set in motion the precedent permitting states to exercise some control over education on the lower levels.

Further evidence of early growth in educational consciousness can be seen in the Massachusetts Law of 1647. Building on the solid foundation of the Law of 1642, the new law called for the founding of town schools in which the demands of the earlier law could be met. Towns were expected to provide educational opportunities, although there was no clear recognition of, or a commitment to, any doctrine of free schools; and even when schools were founded, no one in the colony was required to attend them. Despite what today may appear as weaknesses in the Law of 1647, and allowing, too, for its limited effectiveness, it was probably the most important step taken in American educational history toward the creation of a free public school. An undoubted outcome of the Law of 1647 was the town system of educational organization.

The Town System

A compelling conviction with many New Englanders of the seventeenth century was the importance of education. There was a convincing vividness to this firm and incontrovertible spiritual attitude toward moral and intellectual formation; and while there may not have been any real affection for learning, there was undoubtedly a realistic reaction to the promise it·contained. This was no brittle ivory-tower dream; it reached down to the level of action to be reflected in an effective public opinion, and it extended to the early, modest laws providing the initial framework for educational growth.

The Massachusetts Acts of 1642 and 1647 provided the foundation upon which the town system of educational organization was built. The New England town (not to be confused with a village) was the basic unit of local government, and in the town meeting decisions affecting life in the town were arrived at. The town was similar to the township of the Northwest Territory, but it did not have the township's uniformity in area or regularity of boundary. Some New England towns were extensive in area; others were small. The average area for a New England town was 40 square miles.

In addition to being the basic political unit, the New England town served also as the primary school unit. It was the town's responsibility to establish schools, provide for their maintenance, and decide the objectives for the schools.

The town's geographic profile, as well as the distribution of its population, sometimes generated problems for the schools. This was a time, of course, when transportation was slow and, compared to modern means, ineffective, and when unsettled or remote areas or wilderness paths were not safe places for the unescorted traveler or schoolboy. Yet, the town normally had only one school, for the early legislation had demanded no more, and not infrequently this school was inconveniently located for many of the inhabitants of the town who were also patrons of the school. The dilemma of school location was sometimes obviated by readapting the school to the locational and population needs of a town by creating such unique institutions as the *moving school,* the *kitchen school,* and the *divided school.* These institutions were responses to urgent needs, and they had an obviously impermanent character to them. Later, as community responses to education became more mature, other plans were advanced for organizing schools and putting them close to their clientele. From among the many plans and experiments tested, one stood out as being superior, and it came to have a relatively permanent value and status in American educational organization. This was the school district.[1]

The Parochial System of the Middle Colonies

Schools and education are nourished by the society which they are created to serve. In New England that element of society which counted was definitely homogeneous. Unity of outlook was preserved and in some instances strengthened by the unanimity in doctrinal beliefs. This attitude, it would seem, was indispensable to the achievements of the people of New England; without its consistent presence, educational precedents could not have flowed so freely from the Northeast, and early activities in education would not have been so uniform as they were.

Where the New England colonists were homogeneous in religion and nationality, the inhabitants of the Middle Colonies—New York, New Jersey, Delaware, and Pennsylvania—were heterogeneous in religion, nationality, economic status, and cultural background. The motives for immigration to this region were probably more diverse than in New England.

In New York the colonists were subjected to a despotic political regime which justified its extreme discipline in the accumulation of financial profits for the companies that had sponsored colonization. A feudalistic colonial society was evolved as an objective of wealthy landlords, who called themselves "patroons." In order to attain their objectives, the patroons coerced, maligned, and suppressed—to say nothing of exploited—the people of the colony. But even under these conditions, unfavorable as they were, the possibility for a kind of unanimity was there, for the first essential of this kind of unified society, an established religion, was found both in New York and in New Jersey. The fundamental tenets of this religion were the same as those of the established and official creed in New England. In New England this took the form of either Presbyterianism or Congregationalism; in New York and New Jersey it was Dutch Reform. However, in New York and New Jersey the state rather than the church was supreme, and the state found it possible to relegate the church to a position of little influence, although it officially acknowledged its devotion to the Dutch Reform Church. The church spoke with but little authority; it held no position of exclusiveness as in New England; and people of tender conscience might well have taken advantage of the religious toleration to be found in New York, New Jersey, and elsewhere in the Middle Colonies. At least a dozen different sects were permitted.

As was common during this period, in American Colonies and elsewhere, schools and education were the products of religious zeal instead of a real interests in intellectual formation of men. A religious denomination often established its own schools, where the articles of its faith could be taught. Such schools seldom enrolled the children of adherents to other creeds. Thus, from the refusal of the colonial governments in New York and New Jersey to take steps to provide for education, the parochial system gained its strength. When control in New York passed from the Dutch to the English in 1664, the pattern of political control and the educational structure, though not old, were so firmly established that the English decided to encourage existing practices rather than reform them.

In Pennsylvania, conditions were much the same as they were in New York. Of course, there was no established church in Penn's refuge, and no one religious outlook ever succeeded in absorbing the doctrinal diversity in the colony. Actually there was greater diversity in Pennsylvania than in New York, but, as in New York, the colonial government failed, except for a few abortive attempts by William Penn to organize education, to assume effective leadership in education, and the incentive for establishing schools passed to the several denominations.

Little can be said for the effectiveness of the parochial system, except that it made educational responsibility a local, and often a private, matter. Nevertheless, its persistence and durability were remarkable in the face of rather apparent and important disadvantages: lack of uniform standards, poor teachers, discrimination between sects, rigid and artificial social distinctions, and financial instability. Some of the educational traditions of the parochial system were so tenacious that they were not realistically reformed or completely removed until the last quarter of the nineteenth century.

Education in the South

We have examined some of the foundations of education in the Colonies of New England, where one religious denomination was dominant. We have seen that the Middle Colonies lacked uniformity in religious, social, and economic character and that this was reflected in their efforts to institutionalize education. Now we shall explore briefly the educational developments of the Colonies of the South, where certainly one religion was the official, and often the only, creed which could be accepted publicly. This was Anglicanism. But the official religion in the Southern Colonies did not influence education in the same way that religion in the New England Colonies did. The Colonies of the South offered nothing in the way of educational opportunities that could compete with the system taking shape in Massachusetts and elsewhere in New England. This claim has been made: If any section of the New World was to bear the name of New England, it should not have been the Colonies of the Northeast, but that area extending from Chesapeake Bay southward. Southern planters were not in revolt against anything. The established order had been good to them, and they had few, if any, religious problems. Their chief concern was to gain financial success and preserve their position in society. As a group, they seemed to consider it necessary to subjugate the members of society less fortunate than themselves in order to preserve their own rank. One method which they could understand, if they desired to keep the masses in their place, was to provide little or nothing at all in the way of educational opportunities. Sir William Berkeley, the Royal Governor of Virginia, spoke in defense of a way of life when he said: "I thank God, there are no free schools nor printing [in Virginia], and I hope we shall not have them these hundred years, for learning has brought disobedience, and heresy, and sects into the world, and printing has divulged them, and libels against the best government. God keep us from both." [2]

Out of this attitude—selfish, surely, but always consistent—grew the tradition that education was a private matter and that the means for its attainment were always problems for the individual to solve for himself: "every man according to his own ability instructing his children." This was an easy and acceptable conclusion or working hypothesis for the grandees and merchants who could afford the expenses of sending a son, and sometimes a daughter, to a private school or to Europe for an education. However, there was no way of making this lack of opportunity attractive to small farmers, artisans, indentured servants, and slaves. These groups combined to make up a majority of the population of the South, but in numbers there was little strength, and little was done to provide educational opportunities for the common man. Perhaps if geographic and economic factors had been different, the situation would have been altered quickly, but the population was dispersed, and there was little opportunity for the lower classes to cooperate or pool their main resource of numbers.

It should not be concluded, however, that nothing was done to provide some educational opportunity in the South. Orphans were cared for, and apprenticeship openings were secured for them. Apprenticeship laws were passed as early as 1642 in Virginia and 1695 in South Carolina. Children of paupers were trained for some useful occupation by the pauper schools. Here and there a school building could be seen, but whenever public funds were used for the construction of school buildings, the appropriations seldom exceeded $50. Public and private colleges were established in every colony of the South. However, if the colonial governments of the South gave evidence of conservatism in financial matters relating to education, they did encourage philanthropy in education. The schools of the South before 1800 were either endowed schools or charity schools; very few schools received any financial assistance from public sources.[3]

If the educational progress of the Middle Colonies was slow, and it was, the progress in the Southern Colonies was subject to even greater retardation. The early educational system of the South has often been referred to as one of *laissez faire,* which is really acknowledging the absence of any system. Although there were some laws enacted to provide for the training and education of the poor, early education in the South lagged far behind the educational accomplishments of the Middle Colonies and further behind the zealous, although somewhat limited, attempts to institutionalize education in New England.

Although there were clear indications of cultural, religious, economic, political, and educational diversity among the three colonial systems, the roots of later and more uniform organization for education were being cultivated and in time began to evolve. The principles of educational organization and administration that were evolving in New England, the Middle Colonies, and the Southern Colonies were primarily these:

1. The educational relationship between the individual and local government on the one hand and state or colonial government on the other was treated as a very one-sided affair. The state was taken holus-bolus, and either because of political backgrounds generating fear or political philosophy generating genuine opposition to central control, the limits of educational responsibility were coterminous with those of local government. Even this may have been a concession to a new spirit dominating public life, for, as a close inspection of colonial educational attitudes suggests, colonial men were happier when education was solely an individual responsibility. But if this could not be achieved in a political climate that was being altered somewhat by a collectivism considered by many to be a unique catastrophe, local government might play a role short of exerting a penetrating influence or having a negating effect on individual respon-

sibility for education. A succinct statement of the principle is this: *Education is either a local or an individual responsibility.*

2. While the colonists were harshly critical of any political principle leading to state responsibility for education, the ethics of individuals and the creed of the state had not drifted so far apart as to proscribe all state action in connection with education. The political philosophy embraced at the time implied a political structure charged with both the care of the soul and the building of a state. Paradoxically, the colonial mind could at once accept this implication and declare that in practice the two tasks—education and statecraft—should be kept unmixed. This mind regarded statecraft as realistic public policy and education as a part of private morality. In this context, there could not have been real harmony, but as with other questions touching on the relationship of individual and civic virtue, the state was permitted to employ its resources not to control education or to accept any direct responsibility for it, but, *in the interests of the general welfare, to regulate and encourage education at the local level.* Although existing conditions allowed for such a compromise, it was one which was bound to make the state either withdraw from education in silence or apply its own standards to education on the local level and demand compliance with them. This principle of partial state involvement was observed temporarily, but it led to conflict, as we shall see later.

TYPES OF LOCAL SCHOOL UNITS

Building on the tradition that schools belong to the people and inspired by the ideal of universal education and the promised benefits from it, the states began to create, or in some cases to recognize, local units for the administration of education. The most common local units are town, township, county, and school district. Figure 3.1 shows the various types of local organization and their distribution throughout the United States. The district system prevails in the West and Middle West, the county system is the typical organization in the South, and the town system is popular in the New England states.

The Town as a School Unit

When education in New England was ready for organization, i.e., when the time had come to fit local schools into an administrative pattern in order to conduct and control them, this organization, naturally enough, was provided in a governmental structure already present. This was the town. The New England town, then, has the distinction of being the oldest type of local school unit in the United States.

The town, of course, arose out of the peculiar circumstances and needs of the New England community and was not created for educational purposes. It was a compact type of settlement that was able to adapt itself to the needs of the people. The inhabitants of the town may have been farmers, fishermen, or businessmen. The town's area was not usually less than 20 square miles or more than 40, but in every case the size of a town depended upon the colony's legislative body. If a congregation or a group of people wanted to organize a town, they did so by petitioning the colonial government; and if the colonial government granted their petition, it marked out the boundaries of the town. The title to the land was assigned to proprietors, the affluent members of the community. The town, therefore, was a kind of corporate entity. With its legal creation, the town assumed an important place in colonial political life. Now it was able to send representatives to the colonial legislature, and it was given a good deal of freedom in the conduct of local affairs. There were broad areas for local action at this time; in some things—possibly education could be included—the local town unit was autonomous. But to return to town organization: When the town received its legal recognition from the colonial legislative unit, its officers began to assign plots of land in the village on which the proprietors and inhabitants could build their homes. Other plots were assigned for other purposes. A farmer would be allotted another plot of land on the outskirts of the village where he could till the soil; an artisan would be allotted a place in the village where he could build his shop. This land was assigned to the inhabitants of the town and was legally held by them. Yet not all the land of the town was assigned to private ownership. Pasture land and wooded areas, for instance, were reserved for common use, and there was no individual ownership of the commons. After all the inhabitants of the newly formed town had had their property designated, the town may still have had some undistributed land. Such land was simply held by the town for future assignment. A newcomer to the town could apply for a portion of the land that remained unclaimed, and if the town board voted its approval, a plot of land would be assigned to the newcomer.

It was in New England that the town meeting came into prominence. The town meeting was a forum in which the affairs of the community were conducted. In such a system, although there were many signs of democracy, there was no such thing as popular government even on the town level. Only qualified members of the town could participate in the discussions of the town meeting and vote the decisions, and usually the qualifications were stated in terms of an individual's status in the town: Was he a householder? What was his estate worth? Did he have a good reputation? All of these questions demanded a proper answer. In addition to these other requirements, an attained age of twenty-four was usually demanded.[4]

Education was a proper subject for the town meeting. In the meeting, decisions were made about schools: if the town would have them and how many. In addition, teachers were selected, their remuneration determined, questions of school support and the enactment of rates were settled, the height and breadth of the curriculum was stipulated, and every other question pertaining to education in the town was considered. In time, both because town affairs became more complex and because town meetings became large and unwieldy, the town meeting began to delegate some of its authority to special groups, boards, or committees. When this was done for education, we had the origin of the town school committee, which assumed effective control over education within the town, although it held itself accountable both to the town meeting and to qualified townsmen.

In the town organization for education, the town was the basic unit, and between it and colonial or state governments intermediate units with authority over education did not commonly intervene.

The Township as a School Unit

The township, like the town, is a unit of local government sometimes employed as a basic unit for school organization. The township is usually administered by a township board consisting of three or more members; when the township is also a school unit, the township board functions in much the same way as the local board of education for a school district. In some states there is an intermediate educational unit between the township and the state, usually the county, but in other states the township is the intermediate unit between the school district and the county or the state.

Townships came into existence as a result of the Northwest Ordinance of 1785. This ordinance required a rectangular land survey of the Northwest Territory. According to the design of the survey, the territory was laid out in areas 6 miles square, these areas being called "townships." Each township was divided into sections 1 mile square. The sections of each township were numbered from 1 to 36, and the sixteenth section of each township was reserved for the support of education.[5] When Ohio was admitted to the Union in 1802, Congress granted the new state the sixteenth section in each township for the maintenance of schools. Each new state admitted to the Union since, except Maine, Texas, and West Virginia, has received similar grants from the Federal government. Beginning with California in 1850, Congress increased the grant to two sections, and three Southwestern states, Utah, Arizona, and New Mexico, received four sections because of the low value of the land in that region.

The County as a School Unit

Twelve states employ the county as the basic unit for school administration (see Figure 3.1), although most states, with the exception of the New England states, delegate some authority to the county for the administration of educational affairs. Except in the twelve states where the county replaces such local school units as the town, township, and school district, the county functions as an intermediate school unit. An intermediate school unit does not duplicate the functions of basic units, nor does it conduct schools. Its role includes coordinating school affairs between local units and state departments, developing administrative procedures for supplementing the work of local units, and making available consultative facilities for the schools within its boundaries. Regional features of geography and population often influence the place the county will have in school organization and administration.

Whether the county functions as a basic unit or as an intermediate unit in educational organization and administration, the internal provisions for administering education are much the same. A county board, sometimes called the "board of county commissioners," with legislative and executive power, functions as the board of directors for the county. In many cases this board is charged with educational responsibilities, but in other places a separate county board of education is either appointed or elected. County boards or county boards of education will function in much the same way as the board of education for a school district.[6]

County boards of education may have some professional assistance in designing educational policies. Most states, without regard for the place

Figure 3.1   Types of Local School Organization in the United States. (Statistics of State School Systems, U.S. Office of Education, 1956.)

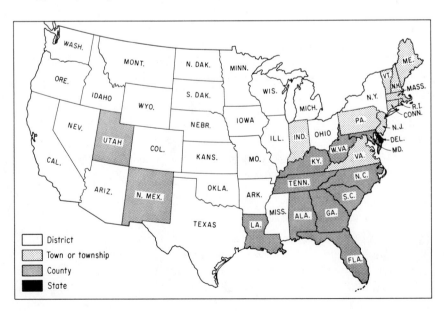

of the county in educational organization, have retained the office of county superintendent of schools. This officer is usually elected on a political ballot, although some county superintendents are appointed.

The county superintendent has an important role in the functioning of all the schools of the county, particularly in rural schools. His influence is sometimes underestimated by teachers and the general public. The county superintendent is usually responsible for distributing school funds to the county schools. Frequently he has the authority to certify teachers; without his approval no one in the county is legally qualified to teach. As a representative of the state he may interpret school law. His advice is sought by local boards of education. Sometimes he acts as an arbiter in disputes between teachers and boards of education. In many states the county superintendent occupies a central position in the movement to absorb or consolidate small districts with larger school administrative units. He is the chief educational supervisor in the county, and he is the direct representative of the state department of education in his county.

In addition to the county board and the county superintendent, the counties may maintain professional staffs to supervise and enrich education in the county schools.

The School District

Although towns, townships, and counties are important units for the administration of local schools, the school district is the most popular agency for school administration in the United States today. In 1962 there were 35,650 school districts (ten years before there were 71,100), of which 31,100 operated schools.[7] The school district was developed to fulfill special educational and community needs; in time this type of organization was recognized as one which could make a significant contribution to democracy in education.

The first schools in America were the products of local endeavor. In New England, for example, where the town organization prevailed, the towns established and conducted schools. In the Middle Colonies, schools grew out of private and denominational initiative. And in the South, public education was controlled and conducted by counties. Because each of these regions approached the question of public education in a somewhat different manner, in each the evolution of local school administration proceeded along different routes. New England was the birthplace of the district system. This system was developed in response to special needs, and its evolution reflected both the rising spirit of democracy and the localism in American education.

In early New England the people lived in and around the village, the center of town life and activity. As long as life in New England was village-centered, the town schools were adequate, but when the population grew and became dispersed throughout the town, the town school located in the village was no longer readily available to many of the inhabitants of the town. These settlements away from the original village were known as "quarters," "squadrons," "ends," "skirts," or "districts." When the disadvantages of the location of the town school were keenly felt, the people of these outlying settlements began to demand schools of their own. Obviously, they were somewhat unwilling to support a distant town school which their children could not attend, and they found such expedients as *divided schools* and *moving schools* out of keeping with their desire or need for education. In time, these various settlements asked that the funds for schools which were collected in their districts be left in the districts and that each district be empowered to establish its own school. These appeals had to be made to the town. An example of such an appeal is quoted in part:[8]

> We, the subscribers, living very remote from any district where we might be convenient to a school for our children, do humbly petition that the town would vote us off a district and grant that the money which we pay towards maintaining a school in this town may be laid out for schooling in the said district as near the center as may be convenient. . . .

The school-district system as it was first permitted was a local arrangement within the town. The towns that created school districts were not released from the educational responsibility which the colony placed on them, nor did they by this device relinquish any of their authority over education. The school district was the result of the peculiar circumstances of New England life, and it was created for educational purposes only. Consequently, the establishment of its boundaries took into account the citizens of the area to be served by the school. School districts originated in Massachusetts in the middle of the eighteenth century. They were given statutory recognition in 1800, and in 1817 were created as legal corporations by Massachusetts law. Historically, school districts owed their existence to the town; today, school districts are created by the state legislatures. In their present form, school districts are often coterminous in boundary with towns, townships, or counties, although this need not be so in the case of every school district.

Years ago, when transportation and communication were difficult and slow, the schools were located near their patrons. At that time the argument for small school districts was sound. Now, with our modern conveniences in communication and travel, the small district is probably a liability rather than an asset. There is, therefore, a tendency to suppress small school districts and to form large or consolidated districts with one school—the consolidated school—serving the entire district. Consolidation has the advantage of reduced building and overhead costs, and it provides greater educational opportunity for students as well as more attractive teaching situations for good teachers.

Local boards of education. Local school districts are created by the state and are delegated certain authority by the state to manage schools within the district. School districts as legal administrative units vary both in area and in population. Normally they are classified as Class I, II, III, IV, etc., according to population. Some of the more common types are designated as (1) rural school districts, (2) village school districts, (3) city school districts, and (4) suburban school districts.

Irrespective of a school district's geographic area or the number of people within its boundaries, its affairs are managed by a local board of education, whose members usually obtain office by election, although the board members of some districts are appointed. The terminology used from state to state or from locality to locality may vary somewhat: in a few states the phrase "school board," "board of trustees," or "school committee" is used to identify the group managing local schools, but the most common way of identifying the governing body for schools of a school district is to call it the "board of education." Whatever terminology is used to identify this board, it is everywhere the representative of the people of the district, and it organizes, administers, and supervises the schools for them. When the first school districts were organized, all of the people of the district assembled to consider the school's problems and formulate solutions to them. Eventually, however, this direct type of management became unwieldy, and permanent school committees were selected. This was the beginning, the first stages of district school activity, and from it the legally recognized board of education evolved, and the state delegated to these boards the function of seeing that the schools of the district were properly organized and conducted.

Although nearly 85 per cent of all local boards of education are elected by popular vote, the board of education derives its authority not from the local district whose schools it administers, but from the state. The only kind of legal authority local boards of education have is delegated to them. We shall not attempt to detail the authority of local boards of education or discuss all phases of the rules and regulations they may make governing the conduct of pupils and teachers, acquisition and use of school property, the employment, deployment, and dismissal of teachers, the issuance of bonds, and collection of taxes. We shall be content with the general legal principles governing the action of the board and determining the scope of its authority. School districts—with their boards of education—are quasi-corporations, created by the state with the express purpose of administering its educational policies. Being creatures of the state, they may be abolished at the state's pleasure, or their powers may be added to or altered as the state sees fit. They possess no inherent powers; the authority they may legally exercise is conferred upon them by statute. The courts have agreed that school districts (boards of education) may exercise the following authority:

1. That expressly granted by statute
2. That fairly and necessarily implied in the authority expressly granted
3. That essential to the purposes of the school district

The general view concerning the exercise of authority by boards of education has been codified in a decision of the Supreme Court of Arkansas:[9]

> School directors are authorized not only to exercise the powers that are expressly granted by statute but also such powers as may be fairly implied therefrom and from the duties which are expressly imposed upon them. School directors are public officers, and the rules respecting their powers are the same as those that are applicable to the powers of public officers generally. The rule respecting such powers is that, in addition to the powers expressly given by statute to an officer or board of officers, he or it has by implication such additional powers as are necessary for the due and efficient exercise of the powers expressly granted or which may be fairly implied from the statute granting the express powers.

Despite the legal limitations on its authority, the board's responsibility to education is considerable. In general, it is a twofold responsibility having to do with adopting local school policies and determining how effectively these policies are carried out. In other words, the general functions of local boards of education are *legislative* and *inspectorial*. More specifically, the board's responsibilities may be listed as:[10]

1. Interpreting the educational needs of the community and making provisions in the schools for satisfying these needs. This may mean, for example, that the board will have to decide whether certain schools under its jurisdiction will teach courses in agriculture or commerce, whether junior high schools will be organized in the school system, or how many months of the year the schools will remain in session.
2. Appointing a school executive or superintendent of schools whose chief responsibilities will be to carry out the policies of the board and to keep the board informed on all school matters.
3. Appraising the effectiveness of its policies and the extent to which they are carried out. This may be done by the board itself, employing such means as school visitations, teacher and principal conferences, and interviews with parents and pupils, or the board may delegate the actual information-gathering functions to others, either intramural or extramural agencies. Although very large school systems may have offices and

personnel doing nothing other than evaluation, it is probably more common for boards of education to call on outside agencies or persons to conduct evaluative surveys. Many different evaluative tools are used in surveys, including broad testing programs, to appraise the effectiveness of a school system. But surveys of this type may look to the future, too, and project school needs as far ahead as two or five decades; of course, both the present status and the possibilities of future adequacy of the system are of vital significance to the school board.

4. Furnishing the facilities for education and providing the local financial structure for schools is an important function of the board. The extent of the local financial obligation toward the support of local schools depends upon the size of the school budget, on the one hand, and on the amount of money the local community can expect from state or other sources on the other. The difference between these two sums must be raised by local taxation, and it is the board's responsibility to determine what the local tax levy for education is going to be.

5. Informing the people of the school district of the purposes, values, and needs of education in the district. Through the board of education the people of the community should come to know their schools.

Although special qualifications have not been determined for board membership, it is usually agreed, Mark Twain's famous remark notwithstanding —"First, God practiced on idiots, then he created school boards"—that candidates for board membership should be sensible, fair, tolerant, civic-minded, honest, and courageous. What citizens of the next generation will be, to some extent, will be determined by what the schools are today. It is the boards of education which chiefly determine what the schools will be like. Moreover, more money is spent in education, more people are employed, and more people are affected, directly or indirectly, by education than by any other public undertaking. This should be enough to indicate the importance of board membership.

Local superintendent of schools. The board of education determines educational policy and appoints an executive officer to carry it out. This executive officer is the superintendent of schools. Before 1836, the office of local superintendent of schools was unknown in the United States. Either the people themselves or the board of education tried to supervise all phases of internal school administration. In 1836 Providence, Rhode Island, and in 1837 Buffalo, New York, and Louisville, Kentucky, created the position of superintendent of schools. Other cities followed this example rather slowly. In 1870 only 29 of the 226 cities of the country with a population of 8,000 or more had school superintendents. After 1870, as education became more popular and as school organization became more complex, boards of education found that they did not have the qualifications to fulfill the responsibilities of day-to-day school supervision and management. The need for a professional educational executive became clear, and eventually most local school units created the office of superintendent.

While the office of local superintendent was in its formative stages, the superintendent was little more than a head teacher with supervisory duties. He was responsible for "housekeeping," having such duties as the purchase and distribution of supplies and the supervision and maintenance of buildings. The office has developed, however, and today the superintendent is expected to be an educational leader. He is selected because he knows how to manage a school system, but if, in addition, he is to be an educational leader in the full sense, other qualifications must be added: He must be a liberally educated man who is sensitive to the relationship between our intellectual inheritance and the pragmatic and current needs of men and societies; he must be a generalist in culture and in human relations and a specialist in the science and philosophy of education; finally, he must be personally dedicated to the vital meaning and means for human development and to the excellence of education.

A superintendent's strictly professional qualifications may be inferred from the multiple and complex problems directed to his office. He is expected to be expert in fiscal affairs relating to schools, including sources of educational revenues, theories and practices of taxation, budget building, and, of course, care and wisdom is expected of him in the disbursement of school funds. He is the principal interpreter of valid educational theories to the board, he is their main adviser when they select and reject educational goals for their schools, and he is the chief translator of these goals into curricula and teaching and learning policies. Because he is so fully informed about the school's policies—their source and their direction—he is the logical spokesman for the school, and he must represent it before the public. If he is not actually in charge of public relations, he is clearly responsible for them, and the board will recognize him as the key architect of the school's public image. The board may be committed to a policy of outstanding teaching in the schools, but personnel policies, both the induction and the deployment of academic personnel, are spelled out and implemented by the superintendent. The list of duties is long, and we may add to this list these additional functions: The superintendent must be conversant with law as it applies to education; he must assume leadership in curricular development; he must direct the supervision of teaching, for it devolves on him to provide the conditions favorable to teaching and learning; and he must communicate a sense of commitment and provide professional leadership for the educational staff. No listing of the functions of the superintendent could ever be judged entirely adequate, for the tasks of education are so broad and the number of superintendencies is so great that the possibilities of variety are almost infinite. For our purposes, we can be satisfied with something less than complete adequacy. It is apparent that the duties and functions enumerated above are fundamental, and we shall be satisfied with them.

Finally, the relationship between administration—what the superintendent and his assistants do—and the primary task of education must be made clear. It is easy to express the essential purpose of schools, but each school must have an internal organization, and it must be administered in such a way that the school's essential purpose will be fulfilled. The school's primary interest must be providing opportunity for learning, and a corollary of this is instruction or teaching. Because the teaching-learning relationship has become more complex with the expansion of formal education, internal administration of schools is necessary. What is the principal function of those who are charged with the administration of schools? It is to create and conduct a situation favorable for learning.

In creating this situation favorable to learning, administrators are expected to determine policies relative to teaching and learning. The board of education operates on the level of educational principle; it sets forth in broad strokes the outlines of an educational portrait for the community. Accepting these statements of principle, the administrator with his staff undertakes to formulate the day-to-day policies of the school system. These policies, if adequate, will touch every phase of the school system's operation. The next step after policy is practice, and here in American schools is where the faculty finds its role. There have been heated debates over the rights of faculty vis-à-vis administration and, it should be said, there are undoubted faculty rights, yet in American education the responsibility, as well as the authority, for academic policy has been vested with the administration. It would be too much to expect administrators to surrender policy-making functions to the faculty—traditions of educational administration and business models so religiously followed by schools should allay such fears or crush such hopes—but it should not be unrealistic to think of inviting faculties to share in the formulation of academic policies. Such a partnership or, if this word is too strong, such cooperation should better enable administration to fulfill its purpose, for unquestionably teachers have insights which administrators should want to share. On the most fundamental level and correctly understood, administration should be regarded as the servant of instruction. To be a servant of instruction does not demean, or require servility, of anyone or any office, for the concept of service—not servility —means administration exists to facilitate the operation of the educational enterprise, and its efficiency must be measured by the extent to which it contributes to teaching and learning. Administration makes its greatest contribution when highly qualified teachers are appointed and when they and their pupils are freed for teaching and learning in a stimulating educational environment.

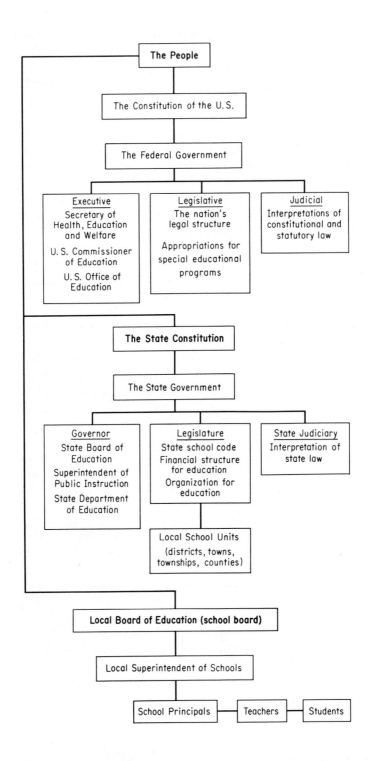

SUMMARY

Out of a diversity of sectional organizational patterns for education in the colonial and early national periods, principles of school organization evolved which emphasized local responsibility for education but established legal authority for education in the individual state. Thus the various types of local school units—county, town, township, or school district—are legal creations of the state legislature, although local school units establish, maintain, and conduct schools. Local schools are managed by local boards of education, which are empowered by state legislatures to act in school affairs. Members of local boards of education are elected by the people of the local school unit and function as a policy-making body for the local schools. The actual management of schools is usually delegated to a local superintendent of schools appointed by the local board of education.

QUESTIONS AND EXERCISES

1. What was the relationship between religion and education in colonial America, and how did this relationship affect early provisions for the organization of education?
2. Can you explain why educational control in the Colonies was generally vested in the local community? Why was this pattern of control modified with the passing of time?
3. Investigate and discuss the reasons for the types of local school organization shown in Figure 3.1.
4. Explain the functions of an intermediate school unit. Does educational organization in your state provide for intermediate school units?
5. Can you explain why the school district has become the most popular type of school organization in the United States?
6. If local communities do not have autonomy in educational control, what justification is there for the existence of local boards of education? What are their functions?
7. Investigate and report on the origin and evolution of the local school superintendency.
8. This statement is sometimes made: "The schools belong to the people." If this claim is true, what meaning does it have for local school organization and control?

ADDITIONAL READINGS

Edwards, Newton: *The Courts and the Public Schools,* rev. ed., The University of Chicago Press, Chicago, 1955. Education has been shaped by a number of forces; one important one is judicial interpretation. This book gives an excellent picture of the courts' role and is distinguished by the breadth of its treatment.

Figure 3.2 Educational Organization in the United States.

Fitzwater, Charles O.: *Organizing Districts for Better Schools,* U.S. Department of Health, Education, and Welfare, Office of Education, 1958. A summary of practices, policies, and procedures for school-district reorganization.

Garber, Lee O., and Newton Edwards: *The Law Relating to the Creation, Alteration, and Dissolution of School Districts,* The Interstate Printers and Publishers, Danville, Ill., 1962. Legal principles affecting education are stated and supported by illustrations from leading cases.

Griffiths, Daniel E., et al.: *Organizing Schools for Effective Education,* The Interstate Printers and Publishers, Danville, Ill., 1962. Discusses the advantages and disadvantages of formal and informal organization and offers case studies of administrative organization. The job of school administrators is described.

Hamilton, Robert, and Edmund E. Reutter: *Legal Aspects of School Board Operation,* Bureau of Publications, Teachers College, Columbia University, New York, 1958. The legal status of the school board is presented together with the authority of school boards over students, curricula, teachers, school property, and contracts.

Jackson, George L.: *The Development of School Support in Colonial Massachusetts,* Bureau of Publications, Teachers College, Columbia University, New York, 1909. An interesting portrait of the traditional foundations of educational support.

Knezevick, Stephen J.: *Administration of Public Education,* Harper & Row, Publishers, Incorporated, New York, 1962. This book works toward a definition of administration, an analysis of the structure of public education, and a discussion of major administrative levels.

McCoy, Raymond F.: *American School Administration: Public and Catholic,* McGraw-Hill Book Company, New York, 1961. An important introduction to basic administrative considerations, control of education, and responsibility for effective administration.

Mitchell, Herbert S.: *School Budget Policies for Financial Control,* The Interstate Printers and Publishers, Danville, Ill., 1962. A sound, practical, objective presentation of budgetary planning and preparation.

Moehlman, Arthur B.: *School Administration,* Houghton Mifflin Company, Boston, 1951. A general but basic book concerning the topic of school administration from the state through the local level. See especially the section on state organization.

Morphet, E. I., et al.: *Local Responsibility for Education in Small School Districts,* University of California Bureau of Public Administration, Berkeley, 1961. A book of particular interest to readers who come from or live in small school districts.

Noble, M. C. S., and H. A. Dawson: *A Handbook on Rural Education,* National Education Association, Washington, D.C., 1961. The problems of rural education are somewhat distinctive. This handbook is helpful in identifying them.

Osborne, E. G.: *Parent-Teacher Partnership,* Bureau of Publications, Teachers College, Columbia University, New York, 1959. On the surface, parent-teacher relations seem uncomplicated. The fact is, however, they are extremely complicated, ranging all the way from organization of the program to meeting shy parents at the door.

Pittinger, John C.: *The School Board Member,* McGraw-Hill Book Company, New York, 1951. An excellent treatment of the qualifications and role, as well as the importance, of the school board member.

School District Organization, American Association of School Administrators, Washington, D.C., 1958. A study of school district organization and its effects on teachers, school construction, school equipment, instructional programs, and school finance.

Suzzalo, Henry: *The Rise of Local School Supervision in Massachusetts,* Bureau of Publications, Teachers College, Columbia University, 1906. See especially section on establishment of state prerogatives in education, which laid the groundwork for local supervision.

Tuttle, Edward M.: *School Board Leadership in America,* The Interstate Printers and Publishers, Danville, Ill., 1958. The reader's attention is called to those sections treating of school-board services and school-board associations.

Updegraff, Harlan: *The Origin of the Moving School in Massachusetts,* Bureau of Publications, Teachers College, Columbia University, New York, 1908. This old but interesting book takes the reader back to the origin of the school district.

White, Alphius L.: *Characteristics of Local School Board Policy Manuals,* U.S. Department of Health, Education, and Welfare, Office of Education, 1959. This book gives us information on characteristics of a number of board manuals as an indication of what some boards believe to be important to the proper fulfillment of their functions.

Wilson, Robert E.: *The Modern School Superintendent,* Harper & Row, Publishers, Incorporated, New York, 1960. See the section dealing with the duties and qualifications of the modern school superintendent.

chapter 4

State School Systems

THE ROLE OF THE STATE IN EDUCATION

State Authority and Responsibility

Throughout much of our history as a nation, there have been disputes and debates over states' rights versus Federal authority. This is one side of the picture. On the other side, we see the unwillingness of local communities to subordinate what they think are vital local interests and surrender local rights in order to establish state unity. Proponents of local rights theories believe this endeavor to make the individual more fully and more permanently a servant of the state leads to social degeneracy; while state right theorists insist vis-à-vis local claims that a political and social life of matchless intensity and a realization of the highest form of human virtue and happiness are possible only if the legitimate appeals of the state for broader authority are granted. Perhaps the theory of state unity, or the one of state supremacy, goes so far as to be unpalatable to the delicate tastes in political philosophy fashioned by Americans in almost two centuries of political experience. But these tastes have not resulted in a rejection of the state's assumption of control over education, for in the United States legal authority and responsibility for public education are vested with the state. Little could be gained by disputing the legal bases and the traditions or the precedents of educational control making this conclusion so obvious. An evolution toward state authority in education began with colonial enactments which, although not asserting the state's educational authority explicitly, recognized the relationship between education and the general welfare and laid a foundation for the states to encourage, regulate, and supervise education. At the same time, these early laws were enacted with a clear implication of keeping schools close to the people, and they left many of the details of educational administration to local communities.

In the original draft, the Constitution of the United States did not mention education, and the possibilities of finding in it legitimate legal bases either for state or local control of schools seem remote indeed. Why education was not mentioned by the framers of our nation's most basic legal document may always remain a moot question. Of one point we may be sure: They did not neglect mentioning education because they thought it unimportant. Yet, in its totality, the Constitution does not remain entirely silent on questions such as the general source of educational control. The Tenth Amendment, ratified in 1791, is highly significant in this context; it provides: "The powers not delegated to the United States by the Constitution, nor prohibited by it to the States, are reserved to the States respectively, or to the people." Since there was no delegation of educational authority to the United States by the Constitution, educational control remained unassigned and was to be exercised either by the state or by the people; time determined which was superior in this area of action. In spite of the central position occupied by the Tenth Amendment in any discussion of state authority in education, it may not be accepted as a definition of state authority, although it is unquestionably the legal basis for state authority. Developing the doctrine of state authority was left to the states themselves and to the courts. Both shortly before and shortly after the ratification of the Tenth Amendment, many of the states inserted clauses in their constitutions, assuming responsibility for the establishment of some schools and for the general regulation of education. Pennsylvania, North Carolina, Georgia, Vermont, Massachusetts, New Hampshire, and Ohio accepted responsibility for education in their constitutions about this time, although such constitutional provisions did not go much beyond a general encouragement that schools be established. Indiana, however, in 1816, assumed broader authority and responsibility for education with these words:[1]

> It shall be the duty of the general assembly, as soon as circumstances will permit, to provide by law for a general system of education, ascending in a regular graduation from township schools to a State university, wherein tuition shall be gratis, and equally open to all.

By the middle of the nineteenth century, most of the states had accepted the responsibility for education which was left either to them or to the people by the United States Constitution, and they begin to establish, support, and control general systems of education within their borders. This action by the states resulted in some opposition and eventually, on certain issues, in litigation to determine whether or not the state had the legal right to maintain and regulate schools. Many judicial decisions have been rendered which recognized the state's right in education. For example, in *Louisville v. Commonwealth,* the relation of the public school to the state is given a clear definition by the Court of Appeals of Kentucky. The Legislature of Kentucky had enacted a statute fixing the minimum tax levy for school purposes in cities of the first class at 36 cents on the 100 dollars' valuation. The Board of Education of Louisville presented to the city council a budget fulfilling the requirements of the statute. The council, however, refused to apply the levy, arguing that the statute in question violated the following provision of the state constitution: "The General Assembly shall not impose taxes for the purpose of any county, city, town or other municipal corporation, but may by general laws confer upon the proper authorities thereof respectively power to assess and collect such taxes." In issuing a writ of mandamus which directed the council to levy the tax, the court wrote: [2]

> If the maintenance of a public school is a purely municipal purpose, then the section [of the state constitution] would seem to be conclusive of the matter. But education is not a subject pertaining alone, or pertaining essentially, to a municipal corporation. Whilst public education in this country is now deemed a public duty in every state, and since before the first federation was regarded as a proper public enterprise, it has never been looked upon as being at all a matter of local concern only. On the contrary, it is regarded as an essential to the preservation of liberty—as forming one of the first duties of a democratic government. The place assigned it in the deliberate judgment of the American people is scarcely second to any. If it is essentially a prerogative of sovereignty to raise troops in time of war, it is equally so to prepare each generation of youth to discharge the duties of citizenship in time of peace and war. Upon preparation of the younger generations for civic duties depends the perpetuity of this government. Power to levy taxes is an essential attribute of sovereignty. That is so because the necessity of conducting the government requires that money be raised for the purpose by some sort of taxation. So is the power to educate the youth of the state, to fit them so that the state may prosper; else the taxes raised could scarcely meet demands made upon a government in these times. Whilst the power named is older in point of adoption as a legal maxim, the other is modernly found to be of no less importance. It may be doubted if the state could strip itself of either quality of its sovereignty. Certainly it will not be deemed to have attempted it upon language open to debate.

In another case, *Leeper v. Tennessee,* the state supreme court was asked to decide the constitutionality of a state law which prescribed uniform textbooks for the schools of the state. In other words, the general legal question was this: "Does the state have authority to regulate education, and may the state legislature enact laws to this end?" The court said in part: [3]

It is immaterial whether we consider this act as deriving validity from the police power of the state or the public character of the schools. It is evident that the basic principle of it is the power of the legislature to subserve the general welfare by prohibiting certain contracts, and throwing around others restrictions tending to promote the general welfare, and protect the citizen from oppression, fraud, and wrong. That the state may establish a uniform series of books to be taught in the schools, which it provides and controls, seems to be a proposition as evident as that it may provide a uniform system of schools, which we take it is not now an open question. . . .

We are of the opinion that the legislature, under the constitutional provision, may as well establish a uniform system of schools and a uniform administration of them, as it may establish a uniform system of criminal laws and of courts to execute them. The object of the criminal law is, by punishment, to deter others from the commission of crimes, and thus preserve the peace, morals, good order, and well-being of society; and the object of the public-school system is to prevent crime, by educating the people, and thus, by providing and securing a higher state of intelligence and morals, conserve the peace, good order and well-being of society. The prevention of crime and preservation of good order and peace, is the highest exercise of the police power of the state, whether done by punishing offenders or educating the children.

Thus, in sustaining the constitutionality of the law, the court identified the maintenance and regulation of a system of public schools with the exercise of the police power of the state.

The state has not taken this interest in education from purely altruistic motives, but out of a consideration of the essentials of good government. It exercises control over education and directs the general educational purposes of local communities for the protection, safety and welfare of the citizens of the state. The relation of the school to the person, on the one hand, and to the social community, on the other, has been stated by the Supreme Court of New Hampshire:[4]

The primary purpose of the maintenance of the common school district is the promotion of the general intelligence of the people constituting the body politic and thereby to increase the usefulness and efficiency of the citizens, upon which the government of society depends. Free schooling furnished by the state is not so much a right granted to pupils as a duty imposed upon them for the public good. If they do not voluntarily attend the schools provided for them, they may be compelled to do so. While most people regard the public schools as the means of great personal advantage to the pupils, the fact is too often overlooked that they are governmental means of protecting the state from the consequences of an ignorant and incompetent citizenship.

These and other judicial interpretations have established the right and the duty of the state to support education and the right of the state to prescribe certain instructional materials. In addition, precedents have been set for state supervision and the definition of minimum standards, compulsory attendance, and the elimination of sectarianism from publicly supported schools. But the state may do even more. In 1897, the town of Watervliet, New York, closed its school. Various local factions were unable to agree upon school policies, but they were successful in suspending the school's activities. After a delay of about two months, the state commissioner of education ordered that the school be opened and he appointed teachers to conduct the school under the direction of an officer of the state department of education. Some of the citizens of Watervliet, regarding this action on the part of the commissioner of education as an illegal infringement of the educational rights of the local community, appealed to the courts to force the state commissioner of education to abandon his action to operate the school. The court, however, held the action of the commissioner to be legal and proper and recognized the superior jurisdiction of the state over the local community in educational affairs.

This principle was recognized by the Supreme Court of Indiana in an earlier decision (1890) in the case of *Indiana v. Haworth*. The legal issue involved was the constitutionality of a law which required township trustees to accept textbooks for the township schools which had been selected by the state board of education. The constitutionality of the statute was questioned on the ground that it was an unwarranted and illegal usurpation of local prerogatives in education. The court held that the right of local governments could not be exercised except in matters of purely local concern. The court went on:[5]

> Essentially and intrinsically the schools in which are educated and trained the children who are to become the rulers of the commonwealth are matters of State, and not of local jurisdiction. In such matters, the State is the unit, and the Legislature the source of power. The authority over schools and school affairs is not necessarily a distributive one to be exercised by local instrumentalities; but, on the contrary, it is a central power residing in the legislature of the State. It is for the law-making power to determine whether the authority shall be exercised by a State board of education, or distributed to county, township, or city organizations throughout the State. . . .
>
> As the power over schools is a legislative one, it is not exhausted by exercise. The Legislature having tried one plan is not precluded from trying another. It has a complete choice of methods, and may change its plans as often as it deems necessary or expedient. . . . It is clear, therefore, that even if it were true, that the Legislature had uniformly intrusted the management of school affairs to local organizations, it would not authorize the conclusion that it might not change the system.

In the United States, where education is regarded primarily as a state rather than a national function, the following fundamental legal principles may be noted:

1. State legislatures have the power to control public schools except as they are limited by constitutional provisions. (State constitutions generally turn over the actual control of education to the legislatures.)
2. The control of education is in no way inherent in the local self-government except as the legislatures have chosen to make it so.
3. Public education may be a separate field distinct from local government.
4. The legislature having tried one method of school administration and maintenance is not precluded from trying another.
5. Education is a state function even though the legislature provides no central state control or state agency for its administration.

The basic legal responsibility for education, we have said, rests not with the local community but with the state. Despite the validity of this statement, the power of the state over education is not absolute; there are both legal and theoretical limitations within which state educational systems in a democracy must be conducted.

Limitations on State Authority

In all matters of government, including education, the Federal and state constitutions are the fundamental law. However, except for the authority contained in the Fourteenth Amendment to the Federal Constitution, the Federal government or the Federal courts may not legally limit or regulate state activities in education. Education is one of the affairs of government reserved to the states by the Tenth Amendment, and the states, therefore, in their constitutions and by the action of their legislatures may exercise all powers of government except those expressly withheld. This does not mean that the power of the state is absolute, but it does mean that the states through their legislatures may pass any act pertaining to education not explicitly or implicitly forbidden by fundamental law. The fundamental law limiting a state's activity in education may be the state's own constitution, or it may be the Federal Constitution. If it is the state's constitution, such limitation may simply be considered to be a further expression of legitimate state authority over education; but if by the Federal Constitution, the activity of the state would be restrained by a law even more fundamental than that of the state's constitution. The limitations on the power of the state to control education may be illustrated in two concrete instances.

In 1919, a law was passed in Nebraska prohibiting the teaching of foreign languages to pupils in private, parochial, or public schools who had not finished the eighth grade. This exercise of the state's police power was challenged in the courts. The Supreme Court of Nebraska declared the law constitutional and called attention to the conditions which had been found to exist in the military service during the First World War. The court wrote that thousands of men from foreign-language-speaking homes and from foreign-language-speaking schools were "unable to read, write, or speak the language of their country, or understand words of command given in English." It was clear, too, the court believed, that anti-American and alien sentiments were being fostered by schools which did not use English as a medium of instruction. In its opinion the court declared that the Nebraska law was not an unreasonable interference with individual liberty:[6]

> Neither the constitution of the state nor the Fourteenth Amendment takes away the power of the state to enact a law that may fairly be said to protect the lives, liberty and property of its citizens, and to promote their health, morals, education and good order. "If the state may compel the solvent bank to help pay losses sustained by depositors in insolvent banks, if it may enact workmen's compensation laws, . . . it surely is not an arbitrary exercise of the functions of the state to insist" that the fundamental basis of the education of its citizens shall be a knowledge of the language, history and nature of the government of the United States, and to prohibit anything which may interefere with such education. Laws, the purpose of which are with respect to foreign language speaking children, to give them such training that they may know and understand their privileges, duties, powers, and responsibilities as American citizens, which seek to prevent a foreign language from being used as a medium of instruction in other branches, and as the basis of their education, are certainly conducive to the public welfare, and are not obnoxious to any provision of either the state or federal Constitution.

In 1921, the Supreme Court of Iowa upheld the constitutionality of an act similar to the Nebraska law. The state, the court wrote, had "a right to adopt a general policy of its own respecting the health, social welfare, and education of its citizens."[7] In its opinion the court saw no violation of constitutional privileges, for there was, it said, no inherent right to teach German to children, especially when the teaching of that language might prove to be inimical to the best interests of the state. In Ohio, in 1921, the Supreme Court reviewed the constitutionality of an Ohio law which prohibited the teaching of German to children who had not completed the eighth grade. In this case the court held that the constitutionality of the act depended upon whether the general welfare required such legislation. The court declared that the Legislature was the best judge of what the general welfare demanded.

According to the fundamental law of the states of Nebraska, Iowa, and Ohio and ten other states which had enacted such laws, the state had the right to proscribe the teaching of German. But the law of the states involved was not final; it was reviewed on the question of what constituted a proper exercise of police power. In other words, the constitutional protection of the Fourteenth Amendment may have been jeopardized by these laws, and the United States Supreme Court was called upon to determine whether the states were thus depriving any citizen of his constitutional rights and privileges. The fundamental legal issue in the case before the United States Supreme Court (*Meyer v. Nebraska*) was this: Did the act deprive any person of liberty or property without due process of law? The Court held that it did. The Nebraska law, the Court wrote, deprived a teacher of German of the liberty to pursue his lawful calling without due process of law. Incidental to this, parents were protected in their right to have their children instructed to German if they so desired. The Court wrote in part:[8]

> While this court has not attempted to define with exactness the liberty thus guaranteed, the term has received much consideration and some of the included things have been definitely stated. Without doubt it denotes not merely freedom from bodily restraint but also the right of the individual to contract, to engage in any of the common occupations of life, to acquire useful knowledge, to marry, establish a home and bring up children, to worship God according to the dictates of his own conscience, and generally to enjoy those privileges long recognized at common law as essential to the orderly pursuit of happiness by freemen. . . . The established doctrine is that this liberty may not be interfered with, under the guise of protecting the public interest, by legislative action which is arbitrary or without reasonable relation to some purpose within the competency of the state to effect. Determination by the legislature of what constitutes proper exercise of the police power is not final or conclusive but is subject to supervision by the courts.

Meyer v. Nebraska is one illustration of a limitation on the power of the state to control education; another is *Pierce v. Society of Sisters* and *Pierce v. Hill Military Academy* (the Oregon case).[9] The United States Supreme Court declared the Oregon law to be void because it violated the due-process-of-law clause of the Fourteenth Amendment and because it interfered with the liberty of parents to supervise the nurture and education of their children. The decision of the Court was, in part, as follows:[10]

> . . . The Oregon Compulsory Education Act which, with certain exemptions, requires every parent, guardian or other person having control over a child between the ages of eight and sixteen to send him to a public school in the district where he resides, for the period during which the school is held for the current year, is an unreasonable interference with the liberty of the parents and guardians to direct the upbringing of the children, and in that respect violates the Fourteenth Amendment. . . .
>
> The legislative power of a State in relation to education does not involve

the power to prohibit or suppress private schools and colleges. The familiar statement that education is a public function means no more than that it is a function that the State may undertake, because it vitally interests and concerns the State and that children shall be furnished the means of education and not left to grow up in ignorance. But the power of the State to provide public schools and colleges carries with it no power to prohibit and suppress private schools and colleges which are competent and qualified to afford what the State wants, namely, education. . . .

No question is raised concerning the power of the State reasonably to regulate all schools, to inspect, supervise and examine them, their teachers and pupils; to require that all children of proper age attend some school, that teachers be of good moral character and patriotic disposition, that certain studies plainly essential to good citizenship must be taught, and that nothing be taught which is manifestly inimical to the public welfare.

From these two important decisions rendered by the highest court in the United States, it seems clear that, although the state may establish educational policies and institute practices, the United States Constitution may limit the power of the state in education whenever that power threatens to interfere with either liberty or property of citizens. In addition to statutory and constitutional limitations on the authority of the state in education, there are limitations which may be imposed by natural law. According to the natural-law theory as it applies to education, every individual has the right to advance his own perfection; every individual has the right to the means necessary for the achievement of his natural end. But a child is unable, because of his immaturity, to exercise this right unaided. It is the responsibility of those who are charged with the child's care to provide the means for his education. By natural right, therefore, education is primarily and principally a function of the family, and consequently a parental function. The natural-law limitations on the right and authority of the state in education do not prevent the state from acting in educational matters. The state may act from that authority which families delegate to it because they are unable to perform fully the functions of education while they have to care for the multiple other necessities of providing for a family. Besides, the state representing civil society has a direct concern with education: the products of education are future citizens.

The natural-law theory giving parents the primary right in education has at times been extended to give parents the sole right in education. According to this interpretation, the state may contribute to the support of schools, but it may not have any other relationship to education. But this claim has never gained anything approaching general acceptance. Natural law places the parent first, but it does not ignore the special and proper rights of the state in education. The rights of the state as they are seen from the point of view of natural law may be expressed as follows:[11]

We say *special and proper* right, for there can be no question of a vague and general right: it were unreasonable to refuse to the state that which is granted to every legitimate association. Let us add that teaching, as far as the state is concerned therein, means establishing schools, appointing teachers, prescribing methods and programs of study: the state teaches in the same way as it governs and judges, viz., through delegates fitted for such functions. Finally, we are inquiring what is the right of the state considered in itself, omitting the consideration of the conditions and the circumstances under which it may prudently and legitimately use the right.

These considerations being premised to obviate all equivocation, we affirm unhesitatingly, and in accord, as we think, with the principles of sound theology and philosophy, and with the testimony of the tradition of the Church, that it must be admitted, as the larger number of theologians do admit, that the state has the right to educate. The following reasons, drawn from the very nature of things, and, in our judgment, thoroughly apodictical, will suffice. Civil authority has the right to use all legitimate, temporal means it judges necessary for the attainment of the temporal common welfare, which is the end of civil society. Now, among the most necessary means for the attainment of the temporal welfare of the commonwealth is the diffusion of human knowledge. Therefore civil authority has the right to use the means necessary for the diffusion of such knowledge, that is to say, to teach it, or rather to have it taught by capable agents.

There seems to be no question that the state has certain special rights in education, but it seems clear, too, that the activity of the state to regulate and control education is limited in the United States by fundamental constitutional law and by the claims of natural law. The family and the state have rights in education, and the right of the former tends to limit the authority of the latter. There is a third society which may limit the educational authority of the state. This society is the church. This right of the church is a supernatural right, and it is made effective through the exercise of the natural rights of parents, under the guidance of the church. The relative rights of the family, the state, and the church are treated in the encyclical *The Christian Education of Youth*:[12]

> There are three necessary societies distinct from one another and yet harmoniously combined by God, into which man is born: two, namely the family and civil society, belong to the natural order. The third society, into which man is born when through baptism he receives the divine life of grace, is the Church: a society of the supernatural order and of universal extent; a perfect society, because it has in itself all the means required for its own end, which is the eternal salvation of mankind; hence it is supreme in its own domain. Consequently, education which is concerned with man as a whole, individually and socially, in the order of nature and in the order of grace, necessarily belongs to all these three societies, in due proportion, corresponding, according to the disposition of Divine Providence, to the coördination of their respective ends.

A democratic view of society and the public good, based on a concept of natural law and natural rights, leads to definite conclusions about authority and responsibility in education. Freedom and creativity are among the individual and social goals to be achieved; the means to attain them must be proportioned to them. Because children are not creatures of the state but have their origin in the family, education is primarily a parental right. When parents cannot achieve the ends of education, they may form associations for the establishment of schools or entrust their children to the schools which they, the parents, cause the state to organize. Whether the schools which come into being are private schools or public schools, the state has the right to regulate them and, in the case of public schools, the obligation to support them. The state, moreover, may be said to have a duty to provide educational opportunities, that is, to create a system of public schools, and, as we have said, it may regulate education provided it does not deny parents the right to determine what is best for their children.

STATE ORGANIZATION AND ADMINISTRATION FOR EDUCATION

The power, importance, and prestige of the national government must not be allowed to obscure the fact that the states perform services without which the national government, on its present constitutional basis, could not be preserved. All state governments are organized on the same broad pattern and have functions and problems generally similar. The United States is a union of states; among the states there is legal and political equality. Rights and privileges belonging to one state belong to all the other states as well. Equality of states is basic to our constitutional system of government. Although, as we have seen, certain state activities may be somewhat circumscribed or limited by the national Constitution, the sphere of state activity is more extensive than that of the national government, and in its sphere each state is supreme. The powers of the state are not derived or delegated as are the powers of the national government.

The organization and administration of education is a function reserved to the states; this function may not be limited except as has been indicated in the preceding section. The general power of the state to provide for a system of public education is contained in the state's constitution.

The State Constitution and Education

The state constitution is the fundamental law of the state; neither state legislation nor local regulations may run counter to it. It takes its place as the source of executive, legislative, and judicial powers, and it exercises a general supervision over the action of these branches of government. The legislative mandate to organize a system of public education comes from the constitution and the constitution, speaking for the people, may, as we have seen, limit the actions and the authority of the legislature. Despite the surveillance exercised by, and the general authority vested in, the constitution, the legislature has a great deal of freedom, and, in general, may do anything the constitution does not proscribe. Thus, when questions of conflict arise—when a state statute's constitutionality is challenged—it is not enough to show an absence of constitutional acquiescence; it must be shown that the constitution prohibits such legislative action or the law will not be declared null and void. In this respect a state legislature enjoys a broader commission than does the Federal Congress.

Constitutional provisions related to education are *sui juris*, i.e., they have no connection with, and need not be integrated to, the constitutional statements of any other state. Such independence results in considerable variety among state systems of education. Some state constitutions do nothing more than direct the state legislature to enact laws creating a system of public education, whereas other state constitutions go to some length in stipulating kinds and imposing limits on legislative action. Constitutional statements relating to education are sometimes construed to be self-executing; i.e., no action by the legislature is needed. For example, the constitutional provision that public money may not be spent for private or church-related schools is usually considered to be sufficient, and statutory enactments are not necessary to its enforcement. However, the constitutional statement that public money may not be spent for purposes other than that for which it was collected may require some statutory clarification.

A review of educational provisions in state constitutions shows constitutions of the newer states and the more recently accepted constitutions of older states are content with a brief and general statement directing the legislature to take action in the field of education. Yet, whether or not the constitutional statements are long or short, general or detailed, they contain the fundamental legal authority over education within the state.

The State Legislature and Education

The state's basic educational policy is found, as we have said, in its constitution; the implementation of this policy is the responsibility of the legislature. It is pertinent to inquire of the direction legislative action may take. Without undertaking to present an exhaustive statement on the subject, we can give a few meaningful examples of legislative plenary power with respect to matters of educational policy and organization.

1. The legislature may determine the types of schools to be established throughout the state, and it can define the levels of education falling within the ambit of its constitutional commission. Of course, the legislature

cannot suppress schools created by the constitution, as is the case with some state universities, nor can it ignore a constitutional definition of the constituent parts of a "system of public education," but short of these two limitations, it can decide whether there are to be state colleges and universities and the curricular emphasis of each. Some schools of higher learning may be technical schools, others teachers colleges, and still others professional schools. The legislature is empowered to define the status of the junior college or the community college. We have seen how such colleges have flourished in the states where legislatures have enacted enabling laws for their founding, and we have seen also how the downward extension of higher education has been adversely affected in states where enabling legislation was either absent or tardy.[13] It is the function of the legislature to define the scope of elementary education and to decide, for example, whether kindergartens and nursery schools are to be part of the system of public education. On the secondary level, the legislature has broad powers to define the nature and scope of the high school course: technical high schools, commercial high schools, cosmopolitan high schools fall under its defining authority.

In addition to the control it may exercise over public institutions, the legislature may enact regulatory statutes applying them both to public and private schools, or only to one or the other. In higher education, by way of illustrating this point, the state legislature is vested with the prerogative of chartering colleges. Thus, the founding and the operation of colleges, either public or private, come within reach of legislative educational authority.

2. Another step toward implementing state educational policy is taken by the legislature when it develops plans for school support. It may, for example, provide for a system of free schools in which all the children of the state who elect to attend the public institutions may do so without cost to themselves. The public school system, it may again be emphasized, is a matter of state, not local, responsibility, and the establishment, maintenance, and control of public schools is a legislative function. To promote . the public schools within its boundaries, the state, acting through its legislature, may levy taxes directly, or, having, as it does, full control over its agencies—the counties, towns, townships, or school districts—may authorize them to levy a tax, or may by statute require them to levy a tax for the establishment and maintenance of public schools.

The courts have consistently ruled that the exercise of the taxing power to promote a system of public schools for all of the units of local government does not infringe upon the right of local self-government, because the public school system, like a highway system or a concern for public health, is not of purely local, but of state, significance. The state is a unit, and the legislature is the state's source of legislative power, from which flows the mandate of the state.

3. A third general commission of the legislature is to provide for the administration of schools. State authority over schools and school affairs is not necessarily distributive, to be exercised by local units of government. The state legislature may create a system in which there is a division of administrative labor between state, county, and district units, or it may reserve all administrative authority to itself. On the other hand, the state legislature may determine that the best way to administer schools is to entrust all, or most, of the management of school affairs to the local units. Whatever the legislative decision may be at any one time, it is not precluded from changing the system it has inaugurated.

The officers of educational administration are technically state officers, and they may be selected in any manner the state legislature determines. They may be elected by the people, appointed by the courts, or selected by any other officer or unit that educational policy may prescribe.

4. In carrying out its commission to organize, maintain, and control public education in the state, the legislature is empowered to exert generalized control over the curriculum, or it may delegate this function to a state educational office or agency. The state may prescribe a legal minimum for curricula; it may require English as the language of instruction in the schools; it may demand that all curricula include courses in health, safety, and citizenship. Some states not only exercise general administrative control over curricula but go to the point of preparing syllabuses for the courses and then administer state examinations assessing the attainment of minimum standards.

5. Finally, in summarizing legislative involvement in educational affairs, the legislature's control of teachers is listed. Every state requires its public school teachers to be certified or licensed: the legislature directly, or an agency created by it, sets standards for certification. In some states the legislature requires certification of all elementary and secondary school teachers in public and private schools alike. In addition to the certification of teachers, the state school code may provide for the licensing of other school officers: superintendents, principals, nurses, coaches, etc.

The State Board of Education

The evolution of state boards of education was accelerated by a determination on the part of the states to exercise closer control over the schools. As the states began to accept, or assume, more and more responsibility for education, they attempted to erect an administrative structure providing means of control and supervision. Despite this common purpose, the early history of state education authority shows considerable divergence. The first state board of education, the Board of Regents of the University of the State of New York, was established in 1784. Its duties at that time were restricted to the direction of higher education, including King's College (now Columbia University). In 1812, New York State created the first state office for superintendent of common schools, but abolished the office in 1821. Between 1821 and 1854, when the office was revived, the secretary of state acted as state superintendent of public instruction. The state board of regents became a quasi-legislative body for all education in the state, and in 1904 the superintendent of common schools became the executive officer of the board of regents. His title was altered to "President of the University of the State of New York and Commissioner of Education." If we accept 1784 as the date when the state began to assume some control over certain levels of education by creating a board, the evolutionary period which culminated in the state's supervising and generally directing all education in the state covered 160 years.

In Michigan, in 1817, the governor and judges of the Territory of Michigan created the University of Michigan, or the Catholepistemiad, modeled after the University of France. Despite its awesome title, this territorial unit was merely an administrative superstructure for educational control, and all schools in the territory were fitted into it. The first president, of what may be thought of as a state board of education, was Rev. John Monteith; Father Gabriel Richard, a missionary priest of the Society of St. Sulpice was vice-president. By 1821, the organization in Michigan was changed, as was the name of the board, although control over schools, academies, and colleges continued to be vested with a territorial board. In 1837, there were additional changes, and Michigan gradually developed a more diffused state authority for education, until in contemporary times the general supervision of elementary and secondary education is vested in an elected superintendent of public instruction; the control of higher education is divided among an elected board of regents, a board of agriculture, a state board of education, and appointed boards of regents. Thus, Michigan, which began the evolutionary period with centralized control similar to that currently existing in New York State, gradually developed considerable administrative diffusion.

The organization of a state board of education in Massachusetts in 1837 is illustrative of still another tendency in the evolution of state administrative authority. In that year, the legislature provided for a state board of education with ten members. It was to appoint its executive officer, who was the secretary to the board and commissioner of education for the state. The Massachusetts board was unique in this way: As constituted, it was a weak board; its executive officer (Horace Mann) wielded the real authority. The original Massachusetts plan for a single state authority with an appointed professional executive is now regarded as an especially sound one. But the original plan was not retained, and today the Massachusetts educational authority is considerably diffused.

From what has been said so far, it is obvious that the role of the state board differs considerably from state to state; it is almost impossible to classify state boards of education with any degree of precision. But admitting some lack of precision, it would appear that in the United States there are 348 state boards of control with some educational responsibility. To cloud the picture even more, there are nine states (Illinois, Iowa, Maine, Nebraska, North Dakota, Ohio, Rhode Island, South Dakota, and Wisconsin) without general state boards responsible for elementary and secondary education.

The 348 state boards may be divided by major types: There are state boards of education, boards of vocational education, boards of higher education, boards of trustees for state educational funds, library and art boards, and boards for textbooks and curricula.

State boards in forty states have some supervisory control for elementary and secondary education varying from extensive authority in Colorado to sharing authority with the state superintendent of public instruction in Michigan. Eighteen states give state boards control over state colleges of education. The state university comes under the board's jurisdiction only in three states. In many of the states, the board of education is almost as specialized in its functions as are boards of regents or trustees for colleges and universities.

The power to appoint all or a majority of members to state education boards has been given to the governor in twenty-four states. In other states, members are elected directly by the people, appointed by the legislature, elected by a convention of local boards of education (Utah), appointed by the state superintendent, or assume their position on the board ex officio. The usual size of state boards is seven members, with a range from three in two states to nine in one state. As a rule, state board members receive no salary and are compensated only for their actual expenses incurred in attending meetings.

Chief State Education Officer

Each of the fifty states has provided for a chief state education officer, most frequently called the state superintendent of public instruction (twenty-eight states), or state commissioner of education (fourteen states); the title "superintendent of education" is used in four states, "superintendent of schools" in two, "director of education" in one, and "superintendent of free schools" in one. Thirty-five states established the office by constitutional provision; fifteen states created it by statute.

The office is an old one; in some states it preceded the erection of other state educational agencies. New York created the office in 1812, Maryland in 1826, Vermont in 1827, Michigan in 1836, Massachusetts and Ohio in

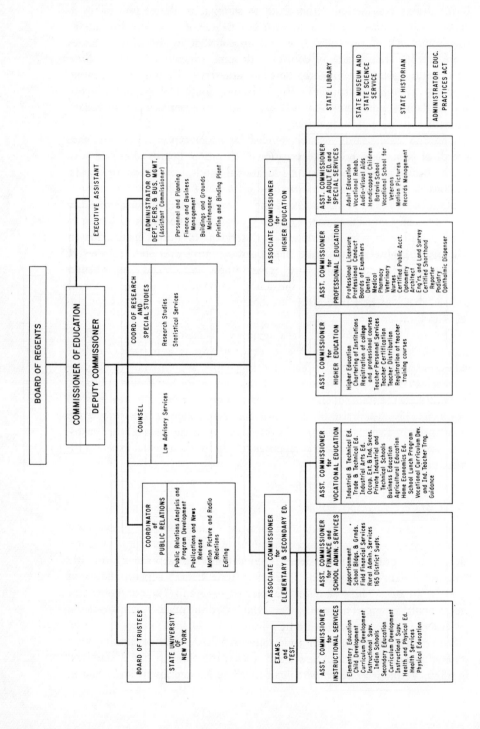

1837, Pennsylvania in 1857, and Tennessee in 1867. In the early years, the state superintendent occupied himself with administration of school lands, guarding permanent school funds, and keeping records and data. As education in the state became a great, complex human industry, the responsibilities assigned the superintendent were broadened.

A general statement concerning the duties of the chief state education officer is not easy to make. In states having general boards of education, the superintendent is frequently in the uncomfortable administrative position of having to share authority with the board. In some of these states, he is a member of this board; in others, he is not. In states without a general board, he is the supreme education officer and enjoys a wide authority and an enviable reputation. In the majority of states, it is fair to say, it is common to regard the state superintendent as the most powerful of state educational officials.

Chief state education officers are either elected by the people, appointed by the governor, or appointed by the state board of education. Over the past quarter century a noticeable trend has been detected favoring the appointment of a state superintendent by the board of education. But regardless of the direction of the trend, the people of twenty-nine states still insist on selecting their chief state education officer by popular vote.

The academic and experience qualifications a person must offer if he is to be considered for this office vary from none in some states to a college degree, experience, and state teachers' certification in others. The term of office is brief in most states, and the salaries are somewhat low (median, about $8,000) for attracting the most competent people.

State department of education. The chief state education officer has a staff which makes up the state department of education. In this department specialists in elementary, secondary, and higher education make themselves available to the school officers of the state and provide, in addition, a number of useful services. There are also divisions of school finance, architecture, vocational education, teacher certification, and adult education, among others, which are intended to give both direction and service to the local communities. It is the objective of the chief state school officer and the state department of education (the latter is charged with this especially) to promote efficiency in the management of state school affairs.

Although it is hazardous to present any so-called typical pattern of internal organization for the state department, its general activities may be summarized as follows:

Figure 4.1 Organization of the State Department of Education, New York.

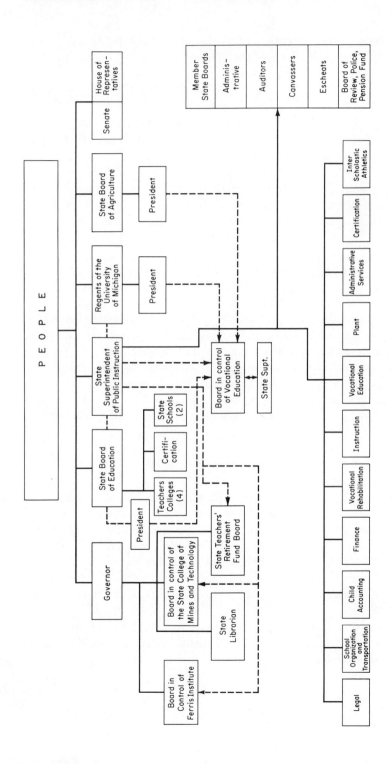

1. Gathering information on the status of education in the state and conducting or sponsoring research on various aspects of instruction, curricula, etc.
2. Regulating and supervising school practices and requiring conformity to educational law and standards
3. Providing educational leadership for the improvement of instruction by raising the quality of teaching, by carrying on or sponsoring research, and by offering broad consulting and field services to all school districts, or units, of the state

SUMMARY

Since authority over education was not delegated to the United States by the Constitution, education became a matter for each state, or for the people, to deal with. Law and custom have placed legal authority and responsibility for education with the state rather than with the local community. The power of the state over education, however, is not unlimited: legally, the action of the states in exercising their authority is subject to review by the courts to ensure that the constitutional rights and liberties of individuals are not impaired; philosophically, the state's authority is subject to the limitations placed on its action by the theory of natural law, which gives to parents the primary right in education.

Although the organization and administration of education may vary from state to state, the fundamental legal basis for education in every state is found in the state's constitution. Usually it is the responsibility of the state legislature to create a system of public education and to enact laws pertaining to the control or regulation of public and nonpublic schools in the state. Many states have state boards of education, and all states have a state department of education and a chief state school officer. These boards, departments, and officers have the function of seeing that the state's educational enterprises are operated efficiently and effectively.

QUESTIONS AND EXERCISES

1. What is the legal basis for state authority in education?
2. Investigate and discuss the evolution of state authority in education.
3. Review the significant court decisions which have defined the legal authority and responsibility of the state in education.
4. Discuss what you believe to be the most important and effective limitations on state educational authority.

Figure 4.2 Organization of the State Department of Education in Michigan.

5. In what way is the authority of the state limited by the Nebraska and the Oregon decisions?
6. Does your state have a state board of education? What are its powers and duties? Are its members elected or appointed?
7. What is the constitutional provision for education in your state?
8. Who is the state school officer in your state? How does he obtain his office; what are his duties; what is his salary?
9. Study and report on the organization of the state department of education in your state. What is the relationship between it and the local school in your community?

ADDITIONAL READINGS

Abbott, Frank C.: *Government Policy and High Education,* Cornell University Press, Ithaca, N. Y., 1958. This is of special value to the student interested in New York State's educational patterns. Abbott traces the history and outlines the work of the regents of the University of the State of New York.

Bailey, Stephen K.: *Schoolmen and Politics,* Syracuse University Press, Syracuse, N.Y., 1962. A study of state aid to education in the Northeast.

Beach, Fred C., and R. F. Will: *The State and Education: The Structure and Control of Public Education,* U.S. Office of Education, Miscellaneous Bulletin 23, 1955. See especially those sections dealing with the establishment and expression of state educational authority.

Blum, Virgil C.: *Freedom of Choice in Education,* The Macmillan Company, New York, 1958. This book contains definitions of freedom of choice in education and develops theories and practices of tax relief to guarantee this freedom.

Dubay, Thomas: *Philosophy of the State as Educator,* The Bruce Publishing Company, Milwaukee, 1959. A philosophy of the state and the state as an educational agent, a subsidiary, and a delegated subsidiary educational agent.

Gruber, Frederick C.: *Education and the State,* University of Pennsylvania Press, Philadelphia, 1960. This book of lectures is centered on a commitment to education for a free society and treats such important topics as mass education, delinquency, and citizen responsibility for public schools.

Hutchins, Clayton D.: *School Finance and School Business Management,* U.S. Department of Health, Education, and Welfare, Office of Education, 1958. See sections on responsibilities and authorizations among state educational agencies.

Keesecker, Ward W.: *State Boards of Education and Chief State School Officers,* U.S. Office of Education Bulletin 12, 1950. The section most relevant to this chapter is that on the chief state school officer. The variety in title and qualification from state to state is most interesting.

MacKinnon, Frank: *The Politics of Education,* University of Toronto Press, Toronto, Canada, 1960. The traditional affinity on the level of theory of politics for education is clear. This author involves us in politics vis-à-vis education but not on the practical level.

Martorana, S.: *State Boards Responsible for Higher Education,* U.S. Department of Health, Education, and Welfare, Office of Education, 1960. An overview, analysis, and evaluation of state boards and their relationship to public higher education in fifty states.

Remmlein, M. K.: *School Law,* The Interstate Printers and Publishers, Danville, Ill., 1962. See chapters on legal problems that touch the teacher in his life and activities as a schoolman.

Stone, J. C.: *California's Commitment to Public Education,* Thomas Y. Crowell Company, New York, 1961. Admittedly narrow, in that the concern is with California, but nevertheless interesting because of the cosmopolitan character of that state.

chapter 5

The Federal Government
and Education

We have seen that legal responsibility for education rests with the states and that the immediate supervision of schools is usually left to local communities. In the light of such a legal structure, what relationship does the Federal government have to education? Obviously, we have no national system of education; education is not controlled from the nation's capital. Nevertheless, the Federal government has long displayed an interest in preserving and extending the breadth and depth of educational opportunity. This interest has been made effective in two ways primarily: by making land and money grants to education, and by providing leadership to achieve the fullness of democratic education. And whenever the Federal government has guided or supported education, it has done so without disturbing the traditional constitutional principle that education is a state, not a Federal, responsibility.

Each of the branches of the Federal government has shown interest in education: the executive by creating agencies and commissions; the legislative by appropriating money for special programs; and the judicial by preserving liberty, freedom, and equality for the citizens of the United States. Although there have been many examples of Federal aid and interest in education, some of which will be reviewed below, the most striking recent example of Federal action contributing to leadership for education was provided by the decision of the United States Supreme Court of May 17, 1954. In this decision the Court declared that the doctrine of "separate but equal" facilities for education has no place under our Constitution. In coming to this decision, the Court held that only when public education is considered in the light of its full development and its contemporary position in American society can a judgment be made whether or not segregation in the public schools does in fact deprive citizens of the full protection of the laws. It regarded education as being possibly the most important function of state and local governments and noted how both great monetary expenditures and nationwide adherence to compulsory-attendance laws demonstrate the public's awareness of education's value to a democratic society. Education is a requirement for the performance of the most basic public responsibilities, even service in the Armed Forces; it is accepted as the very foundation of citizenship. The Court asked whether anyone could reasonably expect any citizen to succeed in life if he were denied opportunity for education. "Such opportunity, where the state has undertaken to provide it, is a right which must be made available on equal terms."

The Court proceeded, in part:[1]

> We come then to the question presented: Does segregation of children in public schools solely on the basis of race, even though the physical facilities and other "tangible" factors may be equal, deprive the children of the minority group of equal educational opportunities? We believe that it does. . . .
>
> We conclude that in the field of public education the doctrine of "separate but equal" has no place. Separate educational facilities are inherently unequal. Therefore, we hold that the plaintiffs and others similarly situated for whom the actions have been brought are, by reason of the segregation complained of, deprived of the equal protection of the laws guaranteed by the Fourteenth Amendment. . . .

This decision overturned the precedent established in an 1896 Supreme Court ruling in *Plessy v. Ferguson* (163 U.S. 537) and precipitated extreme statements, and sometimes radical and reckless actions, on the part of persons and groups dedicated to the principle that segregation serves the vital interests both of white and colored men. It would be impossible to present anything like a fair or typical sample of statements made by uncompromising segregationists, for they are all extreme and unworthy of a Christian and democratic position, irrespective of the moderate terminology in which they may be couched. On the level of action, however, it would be hard to overlook the illustrations of extremism presented to us by the eruptions in Little Rock, Arkansas, in 1958; Oxford, Mississippi, in 1962; and Birmingham, Alabama, in 1963. The Federal government had to intervene with Federal troops to restore order and ensure for certain classes of citizens the equal and full protection of the law. In Mississippi, the Governor cited the doctrine of "interposition" as a justification for action by the state. According to some constitutionalists, the state may place itself between the Federal authority on the one hand and local authority and citizens on the other. In other words, in interposing the authority of the state's segregation laws relative to education in public institutions, the state was trying to find a legal method to block any application of the Federal constitutional guarantees of equal opportunity before the law.

HISTORICAL BACKGROUND

It may be pointed out, regardless of the effect of the decision respecting segregation in public schools, that the United States Supreme Court was not engaging in educational activities primarily, but only incidentally. The Court's real purpose was to protect the rights of citizens under the Fourteenth Amendment. It is not difficult, however, to find in the record of history several clear examples of more direct Federal interest and aid to education.

The Northwest Ordinances

National interest in education antedates the adoption of the Federal Constitution. Under the Articles of Confederation the government decided to survey and organize the vast Northwest Territory—an area now embracing the eastern North Central states—in order to encourage settlement in that region. As a further inducement to the hardy men and women who were to push back the frontier, the Northwest Ordinance of 1785 reserved the sixteenth section of each township for the support of education.[2] Later, Congress extended this grant to the states which joined the Union after 1802. The Ordinance of 1785 was not enacted as a result of any clearly formed policy that the national government was responsible for supporting education, or even that the national government was to declare itself for universal opportunity for education. Nevertheless, few Federal grants to education have had more significant results. The land granted to the state according to the precedents of the ordinance—90,000,000 acres, or about 150,000 square miles—yielded revenue to the states which enabled them to establish permanent school funds, and the action of these states motivated the older states to do the same.

The importance of the Ordinance of 1785 as the motivating force for public support for education should not be minimized. It provided some of the means for state support of education, and the Ordinance of 1787, which may properly be thought of as a companion or complementary act, provided some of the inspiration for transplanting the culture, institutions, and values of the settled regions of the country to the Western frontier. The Ordinance of 1787 incorporated the Northwest Territory. In addition to this, however, one of its clauses was of special significance for eduction. It recognized the value of education both for the individual and for society; it became a cornerstone for democratic education in the states carved out of the North-West Territory. The clause was this: "Religion, morality, and knowledge being necessary to good government and the happiness of mankind, schools and the means of education shall be forever encouraged." [3]

Land-grant Colleges

During the colonial period, most of the institutions of higher learning were supported by grants of land or money from legislatures, by donations of money or in kind, and by miscellaneous means, such as lotteries. Although some public money was appropriated for higher education, colonial governments were by no means committed to a policy of supporting higher education; instead, they encouraged philanthropy. By 1800, twenty-six colleges had been founded in this country, but their facilities were inadequate, and their progress toward improvement was slow because they were usually close to insolvency. Throughout the first half of the nineteenth century, additional colleges were established and settled themselves into the traditional framework of American higher education.

However, the colleges could not remain immune to the changes taking place in American life; they began to feel the pressure of demands for a new kind of higher education. The classics, long the core of curricular experiences, began to lose their attraction for students; practical and scientific curricula were being demanded. The case for revised college curricula and modified college objectives was not difficult to make. The nation's boundaries had pushed all the way to the Pacific. New territories were opened for settlement. Frontier society brought the realization of democratic ideals: the dignity and worth of the individual. Class distinctions became less rigid. The rich agricultural lands of the West were drawn closer to markets through a network of railroads and waterways. As the ideals of democracy became more real, a demand for greater democratization of higher education was renewed with ever-greater conviction. A variety of powerful economic, social, political, and educational forces contributed to make the Federal government conscious of the need for a new kind of higher education and eventually to enact legislation which not only encouraged the establishment of certain kinds of colleges but contributed to their partial support.

During the 1850s, Congress debated the action to be taken in the area of higher education and finally passed the Morrill Act of 1859. President Buchanan vetoed it as a violation of traditional policy leaving control of education to the states. On July 2, 1862, the Morrill Act was passed by Congress and signed by President Lincoln.

The true intent of the Morrill Act has been pondered over the past century; in the act itself the purpose is stated in the following words:[4]

> . . . the endowment, support, and maintenance of at least one college where the leading object shall be, without excluding other scientific and classical studies, and including military tactics, to teach such branches of

learning as are related to agriculture and the mechanic arts, in such manner as the legislatures of the States may respectively prescribe, in order to promote the liberal and practical education of the industrial classes in the several pursuits and professions in life.

From the legislation itself and from Senator Justin W. Morrill's statements both before and after the law's enactment, it seems clear that at least three basic motives underlay the legislation: the privileged position of the classics in higher education was challenged; practical curricula for college were endorsed; and broader opportunities for higher education (especially professional preparation) for the common man were encouraged.

A system of colleges and universities, under the direct control of each state but conforming to certain broad policy stipulations of Federal law, has evolved from the legislation of 1862. The Federal support explicitly committed in the initial Morrill Act was to be the income from public lands (30,000 acres or equivalent in scrip for each representative and senator) made available to each state. The state, in turn, was expected to contribute to the maintenance of its land-grant institution and provide its physical plant. It may be added at this point, to underline the magnitude of this Federal grant to higher education, that a total of 11,367,842 acres of land was conveyed to the states. About two-tenths of the grant consisted of land in place (land still part of the national domain and at the disposal of the Federal Congress); the rest was in the form of scrip certificated equal to the value of land that would have been granted had it been available. The land was sold by the states, or the scrip was redeemed by the Federal treasury, as the act required; the income from these invested funds was used for endowment, support, and maintenance of the new land-grant colleges.

From this somewhat modest beginning the Federal government has expanded its contributions to the land-grant institutions. For example, the Congress, recognizing the need for research as the basis for developing agriculture, passed the Hatch Act in 1887. This act erected a system of agricultural experimental stations in connection with the land-grant colleges. In 1890 the Second Morrill Act supplemented by direct appropriation the income from land grants and reserved much of this supplemental income for instructional purposes. In 1914 the Smith-Lever Act was passed, establishing the system of cooperative extension services to bring to adults in the agricultural world the benefits of current developments in the field of agricultural art and science. Thus, these institutions, designed in the first place to foster a program of education suited to the needs of the agricultural and industrial classes, were established on a foundation of research and encompassed a program for both the youth of the campus and the adult population throughout the rural areas of the nation.

In the years after 1914, many congressional acts were passed expanding the scope and increasing the support of all three aspects of the program: research, campus instruction, and extension education. Now, in addition to the income from the original land grants, the appropriations from Federal funds to aid the states in the maintenance of land-grant institutions amount to more than 100 million dollars annually. For the year ending June 30, 1962, for example, the appropriations totaled: for experimental stations, $34,725,021; for campus instruction, $10,744,000; and for extension education, $59,590,000.[5]

These funds are distributed to the states on several different bases. Some appropriations are made in equal amounts to the states; some are made to the states on the basis of their farm population, or on their total population in relation to the population of the United States. The funds for campus instruction are distributed and administered by the Department of Health, Education, and Welfare, Office of Education. The funds for experimental stations and extension education are distributed and administered by the U.S. Department of Agriculture.

The term "land-grant college" (or university) is used in connection with any institution of higher education recognized and designated by the state legislature as qualified to fulfill the provisions and to receive the benefits of either or both the First Morrill Act of 1862 or the Second Morrill Act of 1890. The terminology has its basis in the First Morrill Act, which provided for a grant of 30,000 acres of land or its equivalent in scrip to the sev-

Figure 5.1 Nationwide Distribution of Land-grant Colleges.

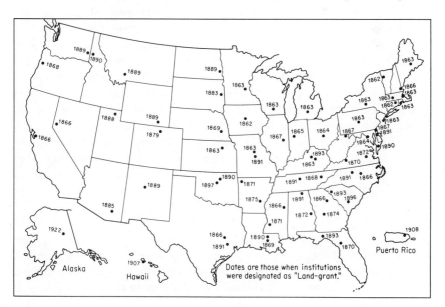

eral states for each representative and senator in Congress, to be used for ". . . endowment, support, and maintenance of at least one college . . . in each State."

There are now 68 land-grant colleges and universities. From 1929 when the Alaska Agricultural College and the School of Mines was designated a "land-grant" institution to 1957 when the "land-grant" designation of West Virginia State College was discontinued, there were 69. Among the 69 at the time of their original designation as land-grant institutions by the state legislatures, 13 were publicly supported state universities. In addition to these 13 state universities, 29 of the 69 institutions had been in operation prior to the time they were chosen to benefit from the land-grant funds. In this group we find those schools distinguished as the first established agricultural colleges: Michigan State and Pennsylvania State in 1855, Maryland in 1856, and Iowa State in 1858.

The other 27 of the 69 were established by their state legislatures as new institutions for the specific purpose of fulfilling the conditions of the Morrill Acts. During the 100-year period, 1862 to 1962, the organization and scope of operations in this nationwide system of publicly supported institutions for higher education have changed considerably. Although the present 68 land-grant colleges and universities represent only 3.4 per cent of the institutions of higher learning in this country, they enroll nearly one-fifth of the nation's college population, award 21 per cent of all bachelor's degrees, grant 25 per cent of all master's degrees, and confer 40 per cent of all doctor's degrees. It is interesting and surely significant that 33 of the institutions originally created as separate "agricultural and mechanical" colleges have grown in stature and educational affluence in their respective states and have become universities in name as well as in fact. Four institutions mentioned above as the first to be created as agricultural colleges—Michigan, Pennsylvania, Maryland, and Iowa—are now established as state universities. This means that in 1962 the land-grant college system was broad enough and strong enough to comprise 47 universities in which agriculture, engineering, and home economics represented a major part of the work; 5 major agricultural and mechanical colleges or institutes (Massachusetts Institute of Technology, Montana State College, South Dakota State College, Agricultural and Mechanical College of Texas, and Virginia Polytechnic Institute); and 16 institutions of higher education established as agricultural and technical colleges for Negroes.

The Department of Education

The movement for the creation of state superintendencies, beginning in Massachusetts in 1837, broadened by the late 1860s to include a campaign for the establishment of a department of education in the executive branch of the Federal government. The population of the country was becoming increasingly mobile: the person educated in California, for example, might live the greater part of his adult life in three or four other states. This fact, it was said, bespoke action making for greater uniformity of quality and standards among the states of the Union. The people of state A should not be made to suffer because the quality of educational opportunity in state F did not meet minimum standards. But mobility was by no means the only basis to the argument made for a Federal department of education. The educational world had witnessed a steady growth in school enrollment; a similar steady, and often spectacular, growth could have been observed in the sciences and the arts surrounding teaching and learning. The growth of educational systems was so rapid and the complexity of educational issues so challenging, it was felt they could be handled most advantageously to the nation on a national level. Finally, there was simply a willingness on the part of many educational leaders to assign a leadership role to an educational officer who would represent the entire country.

Congressional action created a Federal Department of Education in 1867.[6] Its legislative commission was to collect statistics and information showing the condition and progress of education in the states and territories and diffuse such information respecting the organization and management of schools and school systems, and methods of teaching, as would prove useful for the guidance of the people in establishing and maintaining school systems, and otherwise promoting the cause of education throughout the country.

It created, as part of the same act, the position of United States Commissioner of Education and entrusted to him the management of the new department. The original act, subsequently amended, fixed the commissioner's salary at 4,000 dollars a year and approved a table of organization for the Department of Education consisting of three clerks. Thus, in the first years the department's image before the educational world was not imposing.

The principal duty of the Commissioner of Education was to present a report to Congress embodying the results of his investigations and labors together with a statement of such facts and recommendations as would, in his opinion, serve the purpose for which the department was established. Besides, Congress directed the Commissioner to present a statement showing how Federal money and land appropriated for education had been and were being used.

In 1868 the Department of Education became the Office of Education, an agency of the Department of the Interior. In 1870 the name of the Office was changed to the Bureau of Education. Beginning in 1918 and continuing for some years, bills were introduced in Congress providing for the creation of a department of education with a secretary of education holding Cabinet rank. None of these bills were successful. In 1929 the Bureau of

Education was renamed Office of Education, and the Office remained as a subsidiary department in the Department of the Interior. In 1953 the Department of Health, Education, and Welfare—a department which had been recommended for at least twenty-five years—was created, and the Office of Education was transferred to this Department.

The 1953 reorganization was not sufficiently far-reaching to satisfy the friends of a stronger Federal Department of Education. Submerged as it is in the Department of Health, Education, and Welfare, the Office of Education is often lost in executive power struggles, and the Commissioner of Education, despite the imposing title, is largely without real authority to offer strong, effective leadership for education in the United States. In 1963 support was generated favoring an upgrading of the Office of Education to a Cabinet department and the Commissioner of Education to the rank of a Cabinet officer. Positive action in the near future is doubtful; yet justification for upgrading the office is fairly obvious: the Federal government is taking an ever-increasing interest and role in supporting education—particularly special programs related to national defense, science, and health—and prospects are good that this interest and action will be even greater in

Figure 5.2   Functions of the U.S. Office of Education.

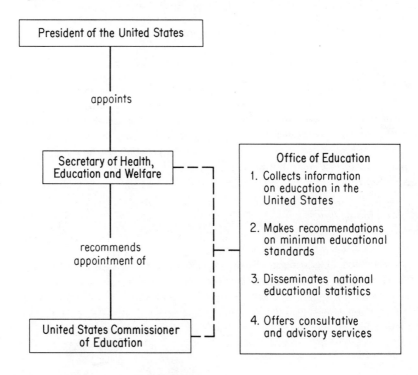

the future. The huge sums of money involved, coupled with the kind of control inevitably attaching to disbursement, would suggest an officer responsible for handling educational affairs closer to the source of national executive policy.

Despite the generally favorable context in which the Office of Education is viewed, throughout its long history the Department, Bureau, or Office of Education has been the subject of considerable debate and controversy. Its supporters have maintained that its statistical, informational, and advisory services are useful and necessary. An Office of Education in the Federal government, they insist, offers no threat to states' rights in education. These arguments, with, it would seem, abundant evidence to support them, have not always stilled the opposition. From the time the first Federal Office of Education was established in 1867, some of the following arguments have at one time or another been used against it:

1. A Federal Office of Education is unconstitutional. There is no constitutional commission empowering Congress to create such an office; and without such authority clearly stated, Congress is flagrantly usurping its authority in erecting an unauthorized office or agency.
2. A Federal Office of Education is unnecessary. The state, not the Federal government, has legal authority over education; therefore, legally it is unnecessary. Moreover, state and local governments do, in fact, perform all necessary functions in education. A Federal office is clearly superfluous. (This point of view has much less appeal today than it did twenty-five years ago.)
3. A Federal Office of Education will breed undemocratic tendencies and practices in education by encouraging standardization and inviting uniformity. There is a real danger, it was said, that the Federal government would either by control or pressure bring the state systems of education into line and make them all alike. Local option, it was maintained, would be eradicated, and democracy as well as prospects for quality learning would decrease. (Today, many responsible spokesmen for democracy support uniformity and standardization as serving both quality education and more meaningful democracy.)
4. A Federal Office of Education will lead to centralization of educational authority (Federal control) encouraging both politics and bureaucracy to intrude on pedagogy. In its first years, so the dark prediction stated, the Office would not exert excessive control, and this alone would serve to lull the people into a state of inattention and set the stage for an insidious assumption of control. Eventually, educational policies dictated in Washington, D.C., would be exposed to the exigencies of political warfare.
5. A Federal Office of Education will be inefficient. The claim was registered that no Federal office, with a spoils system dominating the selection of personnel, could be operated efficiently.

Although some of these points, or all of them, may have impressed sincere defenders of constitutional government when the Office of Education was first proposed and during the first few years of its operation, it would be difficult indeed to find that the hopes or the fears of opponents to a Federal agency for education have been realized. The Federal Office of Education has made important and impressive contributions to American education.

The United States has had sixteen Commissioners of Education since 1867. Their names and years in office are as follows: Henry Barnard, 1867–1870; John Eaton, 1870–1886; N. H. R. Dawson, 1886–1889; William T. Harris, 1889–1906; Elmer E. Brown, 1906–1911; Philander P. Claxton, 1911–1921; John J. Tigert, 1921–1928; William J. Cooper, 1929–1933; George F. Zook, 1933–1934; John W. Studebaker, 1934–1949; Earl J. McGrath, 1949–1953; Lee M. Thurston, 1953; Samuel M. Brownell, 1953–1956; Lawrence G. Derthick, 1956–1960; Sterling M. McMurrin, 1960–1962, Francis Keppel, 1962– .

EDUCATIONAL ACTIVITIES OF THE FEDERAL GOVERNMENT

The educational activities of the Federal government may be given a twofold classification: those which are concerned with education in the regular schools of the country, and those which involve special schools or special groups in the population. A discussion of the role of the Federal government in education would not be complete without touching briefly on these two types of activities.

General Educational Activities

Through its Office of Education the Federal government displays its interest in and gives its encouragement to public and private education in the United States. Of course, members of the executive departments, congressmen, and members of the judiciary may be active in educational affairs, and their activities may gain additional meaning and status because of the positions they hold, but it is through the Office of Education that Federal interests in schools in the United States and education in general are usually realized. Admittedly, the services of the Office of Education are many and varied, but its general functions may be given as follows:

1. Collecting data with respect to American and foreign education in an effort to provide the basis for comparing and evaluating educational programs both in the United States and abroad.

2. Making recommendations toward the formulation of sets of minimum educational standards for all levels of education in the United States. These recommendations are made with the cooperation of public and private educational organizations and lay groups, and such recommendations have meaning only when they are adopted by the state and local systems and by private institutions.
3. Providing services of national character that cannot be provided by state action alone. Examples of these services may easily be found in the collection, interpretation, and distribution of national educational statistics, the direction of national and regional surveys, and a convening of conferences of national stature and prominence.
4. Offering consulting services to the states, to local school systems, or to institutions on such points as financing and administering educational programs, building curricula for the schools, and giving attention and praise to progressive practices and dedicated idealism wherever they may be found in the educational complex of the United States.
5. Coordinating Federal activities in education: for example, administering certain phases of the National Defense Education Act or the Land-grant College Act.

At this point it is worth repeating that neither the Office of Education nor the Commissioner of Education has any administrative authority over the schools of the country. The law limits the activities of this agency to the collection of statistics and facts, the diffusion of educational information, and the promotion of the cause of education. In carrying out its legal responsibilities, the Office of Education has prepared many publications, circulars, and bulletins for distribution without charge or at nominal cost. It would, of course, be impossible to list here anything like a representative sample of these contributions to educational information, but two especially important Office of Education publications should be mentioned: the *Biennial Survey of Education* (formerly the *Report of the Commissioner of Education*) and *School Life*. The first is a summary of the activities of the Office of Education and of educational conditions in general. *School Life*, published monthly, is the official journal of the Office of Education. *Higher Education*, suspended in 1964, was published monthly and contained a digest of current events and issues facing America's colleges and universities.

Special Educational Activities

The Federal government has shown and continues to show interest in education generally, although its activities on broad educational fronts have been limited. We have noted the occasional, though highly significant, land and money grants made available to the states for education. Thus, the work of the U.S. Office of Education has been both inspirational and practical. In addition to these important contributions to education in the several states, the Federal government through its various departments and agencies has instituted programs for the advancement of special kinds of education or has used its good offices to organize education for special groups of people. Vocational and agricultural education, first provided for in the Morrill Act, have been extended; department training programs have been organized for Federal employees; service academies are maintained; schools are conducted for the dependents of men and women in the Federal service, both at home and abroad; educational opportunities are secured for special groups of American citizens on Federal reservations and in the territories; and extraordinary financial assistance has been accorded school districts overburdened as a result of concentration of population in certain defense areas. These are only some of the special programs engaged in by the Federal government. To them must be added the educational aspects of international cooperation, especially the role of the United States in UNESCO (United Nations Educational, Scientific and Cultural Organization) and the International Bureau of Education.

The special educational activities in which the Federal government engages are of two types: those which are related directly to a Federal responsibility, such as national defense or the training of Federal employees, and those which are associated with an objective less likely to be achieved either by independent state action or by cooperation among states than by the action of the Federal government. Some of the more prominent examples of both types of Federal activity are: 1785, the Northwest Ordinance (the land ordinance); 1787, the Northwest Ordinance (encouragement for education); 1802, United States Military Academy founded; 1845, United States Naval Academy established; 1862, the Morrill Act (land-grant colleges); 1867, the Department of Education established; 1887, the Hatch Act (agricultural experimental stations); 1914, the Smith-Lever Act (agricultural extension service); 1917, the Smith-Hughes Act (aid to vocational education); 1933, National Youth Administration, Civilian Conservation Corps, and other emergency educational grants; 1936, the George-Deen Act (additional aid for vocational education); 1944, Veterans Education Act (GI Bill); 1947, National School Lunch Act; 1952, Veterans Education Act (second GI Bill); 1958, the National Defense Education Act; and 1964, the Higher Education Facilities Act.

FEDERAL AID TO EDUCATION

For many years, at least since 1918, proposals have been made favoring a program of Federal financial aid to public education. In every recent session of Congress such legislation has been introduced, though none of the proposed measures have been enacted into law. There are, of course, many special Federal assistance-to-education programs, as we have observed above, but the general Federal aid proposal, so far unsuccessful, would make the Federal government a regular and generous partner with state and local communities in supporting public education. Some of the proposals, it should be added, have included Federal assistance to all levels of education and to private and public schools alike, but these proposals have generated a highly vocal and almost inflexible antipathy, not offering much hope for their success. It is fair to say, while there is considerable support for Federal aid to public elementary, secondary, and higher education generally, that there is apodictic sentiment and force opposing such aid to the nation's nonpublic schools.

Federal aid to education, we should begin by admitting, is a highly complex, emotion-laden, issue. Here is a place where the comment of Pliny might apply: "It is easier to be critical than to be correct." If the problem were simple, bespeaking an easy or obvious consensus, it would have been solved long ago. But it is not simple, and a consensus is neither easy nor likely in the near future. Yet, there is a general conclusion that Federal aid is both inevitable and unavoidable; a more versatile, adequate, and equitable source of support must be found for the nation's schools.

It is probably worth our time to look briefly at some of the arguments for and against Federal aid. For the affirmative, some of the following points are made: At one time, when our nation was less involved in affairs of the world and when life in the United States was simple and provincial, each state and community could be left alone and trusted with its own educational preferences. Communities wanting good schools could have them if they wanted to pay for them, but if they did not want to go to the trouble or the expense to bring quality opportunity to their children, they were left undisturbed. Today, the realist is unable to accept such an educational archaism: he believes that the nation's welfare is directly related to the quality of national education and that quality cannot be achieved without adequate financing. With this conclusion, he is brought to the threshold of Federal aid. The needs of a changing world have imposed new responsibilities on all citizens and on the national government. If these needs are to be met and our own self-interest protected, the resources of the national government must be unfettered by the fears or even the administrative procedures of the past. Despite the emphasis on internationalism and the role a nationally supported system of schools could and should play, the intranational aspects of administering programs of education are not forgotten. Proponents of Federal aid can point to the educational interrelationships among the states and between the Federal government and the states, claiming that Federal aid is a natural outcome of administrative cooperation. Finally, in this abbreviated summary, we come to what may well be the most impressive and convincing of all the allegations favoring Federal aid: There are great and undeniable variations in the ability of the several states to support education. The most obvious method of providing a broader and more adequate base for financial support of schools and at the same time equalizing the financial burden, both objectively and in terms of ability to pay, is the one implicit in Federal aid.

Even if the above points seem convincing, one should suspend judgment until he has heard the other side, which rejects flatly a declaration of states' inability to afford good schools. Some states professing poverty have actually been languid in their efforts to support schools. In brief, the fault lies with *will*, not *ability*. Even when this conclusion is not accepted uncritically, the presumption is clear: most states could expend greater effort toward school support and still not reach the point where greater effort is nullified by a paucity of resources. If zeal or effort is lacking, additional funds, irrespective of wealth, will not be forthcoming. Coupled with the charge of lethargy relative to support is the contention that Federal aid would serve not only to confirm inactivity on questions of support but would generate apathy among citizens on other important educational issues requiring their attention and demanding their support.

There may be another dimension to this phase of opposition which we have not yet explored. It has to do not so much with the actual use of Federal funds for schools as with the use of Federal funds to continue and, perhaps, consolidate educational practices considered to be undemocratic and unlawful. The taxpayer in New York State, for example, may assert his antagonism to any Federal aid-to-education program distributing money to states where school segregation is practiced. He will continue to oppose Federal aid so long as segregation is not eliminated. In somewhat the same vein, though surely not evidencing the same adherence to ideals or the same abhorrence of a lack of them, we find spokesmen pointing to the injustice of taxing the people of one state to pay the educational costs of another state. In effect, Federal aid would be doing this. Yet it is difficult to endorse such an unsophisticated approach to the doctrine of the common good.

The Federal aid problem is further complicated by a sincere fear of Federal control. Everyone, even the most fervent advocate of Federal aid, recognizes the potential dangers, for Federal control has frequently followed the Federal dollar, although, it must be admitted, this has occurred rarely in the field of education. The opponents of Federal aid, unimpressed by the lessons of specific historical illustrations, are certain any program of general and regular Federal aid to public schools will lead to Federal control.

Finally, there is opposition arising from those quarters which, while not opposed to Federal aid in principle, deplore any method of distribution excluding private schools from sharing in Federal benefits. Such methods of disbursement, and they seem at the moment to be the ones to be dealt with, would, it is alleged, violate the constitutional rights and privileges of citizens who patronize nonpublic schools. If there is to be any program of Federal aid, they assert, it must be fair and equitable; anything short of this will never receive their support. This position, for all its apparent reasonableness, is attacked by spokesmen who maintain that Federal aid to all schools, including church-related schools, would contravene the United States Constitution.

It is possible, of course, to find other arguments both pro and con on the question of Federal aid, although the ones given above are those most commonly voiced. It may be worthwhile to make a general evaluation of some of these more common views both for and against Federal aid.

It is being recognized now more clearly than ever before that it is not possible for any state to have an adequate educational program without a sound plan for financing the schools. Unsound fiscal plans result either in defective school programs or in inequities to taxpayers, or both. While it is certainly true that some communities in every state have sufficient local resources to support a satisfactory program of education, there are many other communities where such a program cannot be achieved without state assistance. As long as the funds available to support schools in some communities, *and some states,* are inadequate, there is no reasonable basis for expecting educational opportunities in these communities or states to be satisfactory.

In many states the present system of school finance evolved in haphazard fashion and has not been replaced by a systematic finance plan designed to assure equity and adequacy. Most states still distribute part of their school funds according to practices, such as the school census, which are not considered to be satisfactory. Once adopted, however, these practices tend to be continued, and they result in a great deal of educational unevenness within the states. Although a few states have made partial revisions in their fiscal programs with good results, they have at the same time continued obsolete and inequitable procedures which have minimized the good effects of the revisions. The tax base for school support is generally restricted to real property, and in many states this base is so narrow that educational needs cannot be met. In other words, although the question of willingness to support education need not be emphasized, school support policies are in need of thorough reappraisal. Before Federal aid is grasped as a solution to state and local support problems, careful studies should be made of existing finance policies.

Regardless of the findings of state studies of the structure of school finance, ability to support education is a real and serious problem. It is unlikely that modernizing state fiscal policies for education would offset completely the differences in resources from community to community and from state to state. The amount of money needed to support education has increased sharply over the past decade. This increase has been due largely to the decreased value of the dollar, but it has been due, too, to the desire of the public for more and better educational facilities. In spite of this increase in the cost of education, a smaller proportion of the national income was spent for the support of education from 1956 to 1962 than from 1950 to 1956, and during the next ten years the schools must be prepared to educate a larger proportion of the total population than ever before. Population shifts from state to state and from urban to suburban areas, and consequent shifts in wealth have made it impossible, in some places, to finance a satisfactory educational program with the resources available.

Many states and communities have never had the necessary resources for financing an adequate educational program. In states with small-district organization, differences in ability to support education range from 10,000 to 1. Even in the states with larger school districts or with the county plan, the wealthier local units may have ten to twenty-five times the ability of poorer units to support the schools from local revenue. These variations in ability to support education have made state support, or state aid, to local communities essential. But state aid has not always achieved equalization of educational opportunity within the state, and there is little hope for equalization among the states if present fiscal practices are continued. The range of ability of states to support education is about 4 to 1. New York has an income per child of school age four times greater than that of Mississippi. Current expenditures of states range from an average of slightly less than $100 per pupil in average daily attendance to an average of more than $476. Within the states the range may be greater still. These are surely striking evidences of variation in resources for the support of education, and they are perhaps the strongest argument for Federal aid, which would have the effect of equalizing support and, to some extent, equalizing educational opportunity in the United States.

We have seen that the constitutional basis of our government calls for a division of powers and authority between the states and the Federal government. Education is clearly not a Federal but a state responsibility. It has been argued that each state, therefore, can educate its citizens as it sees fit (although this view would seem to need some qualification) and that if limited resources in a state are responsible for educational inadequacies, this is the state's own concern (this view, too, is subject to some correction). In other words, whatever form Federal help for education might take—even if in the shape of completely unattached money grants—it would be intrusion on legitimate states' rights. Moreover, it is always argued by proponents of the states' rights theory applied to education that Federal aid would be followed surely and swiftly by Federal control. What are the experiences with Federal control following the Federal dollar which lead to this belief, and what are the dangers of Federal control following any general Federal aid program?

It may be fairly doubted that Federal authority would make Federal money available to the states for education without accompanying these grants with certain regulations or safeguards for spending the money. For example, proposed Federal aid for school construction has in the past restricted Federal funds to those states complying fully with the Supreme Court decision of May, 1954. It would not be easy to foresee all the possible limitations, nor would it be possible to anticipate the precedents to be built out of these limitations. Nevertheless, the history of Federal interest in and aid to education does not disclose any effort on the part of the Federal government to control education. The Ordinances of 1785 and 1787 could not be used to show that Federal grants were followed by Federal control. The Morrill Acts were intended to stimulate and encourage agricultural and technological education in colleges and universities, and as might reasonably be expected, Federal grants were made only to those states and to those schools which complied with the terms of the acts. Was this Federal control? The GI Bill of 1944, no more and no less than many other Federal enactments to give financial assistance to special educational programs, contained reasonable clauses for administering and distributing Federal funds. Did Federal control follow the Federal dollar here?

By remaining within the area of educational legislation, we may make a very strong case to prove that Federal control has not become more proximate as a result of Federal aid. In addition, it may be recalled that the fear of Federal control was the chief force behind the opposition to the Federal Department of Education. However, it is unquestionably true that, in conservation, agriculture, road construction, and many other public enterprises financed in full or in part by Federal money, Federal control has been very real. What guarantee would the states have that educational activities would be immune to Federal regulation once regular and general Federal aid to education became a reality?

One may insist, of course, that the frightful apparition of Federal control has been conjured up by those who are opposed to Federal aid. Or it may be claimed that our constitutional form of government would make Federal control of education impossible. Besides, states would be entirely free either to accept or reject Federal aid along with attendant Federal regulations: no state would have Federal aid forced on it, although its citizens would be faced with the unpleasant duty of paying Federal taxes for education which would be used in other states. Probably the best argument and the best guarantee against Federal control rest with the public mind and the public temperament. There is no disposition on the part of the public for either centralization or nationalization of education. Public policy is determined by public opinion, and as long as public opinion opposes Federal control, Federal control, regardless of the nature or form of Federal aid, is not likely. For government to control what a sovereign people does not want it to control strikes at the very heart of democracy, and to admit that government can do what the people refuses to permit it to do is a confession of democracy's failure.

Finally, let us consider briefly, and of necessity somewhat superficially, the opposition to Federal aid which arises from groups who do not expect to participate in Federal aid programs. It must be admitted, of course, that this motive in no way alters the facts of the states' ability to support education; poor states will remain poor and rich states rich—withholding Federal aid from all schools because it must be withheld from some will not bring about financial equality in education. Furthermore, it is not immediately apparent how Federal aid to public schools would hurt private schools: it would neither add to nor detract from their present resources. Nevertheless, the representatives of private and church-related schools in the United States, especially the National Catholic Welfare Conference and the National Catholic Educational Association, are noticeably cool toward Federal aid proposals and have rather consistently opposed them. It would be unfair to charge these groups with selfishness, for their opposition to Federal aid, at least those Federal aid proposals which would limit Federal aid to public schools, is not founded on selfish motives but on the sound premise that all citizens are entitled to equal justice before the law. To give financial assistance to one citizen because he attends a public school and to deny financial assistance to another citizen because he attends a private school violates all doctrines of constitutional equity. The opposition of some Catholics to Federal aid for public schools only is an attempt to prevent the Federal government from acting unjustly. Some Catholics believe they should share in Federal funds distributed for educational purposes, not as members of the Catholic Church, but as citizens of the United States and in precisely the same way as they are taxed or are called upon to perform other public duties as citizens. While many Catholics share this view, there is, it should be stated clearly, no official Catholic attitude on the Federal aid question or on the more general issue of public support for church-related schools. Catholics may, and do, differ; they are entirely free to follow their own convictions on Federal aid programs and to support proposals wherein public schools alone are scheduled to share in public money.

SUMMARY

In the United States, legal responsibility for education rests with the states, and day-to-day supervision of schools is a responsibility delegated to local communities. Even without any direct responsibility for education, the Federal government has regularly displayed a keen interest in preserving and extending the breadth and depth of educational opportunity. This interest has been made effective by land and money grants and by providing educational leadership. Beginning with the Northwest Ordinance of 1785 and continuing through the Higher Education Facilities Act of 1964, many examples of Federal interest and aid to education can be cited. Perhaps one of the most important examples of Federal aid to education was the Land-grant College Act of 1862. To provide educational leadership at a national level, Congress authorized the organization of a Federal Department of Education in 1867. This agency is known now as the U.S. Office of Education.

The educational activities of the Federal government are of two types: those activities concerned with education in the regular schools of the nation and those which involve special schools or special groups of the population.

In recent years, as the problem of financing education has become more acute, more and more attention has been given to the possibility of enacting legislation which would provide Federal financial aid to public education.

QUESTIONS AND EXERCISES

1. Can the Federal government require a state to establish and maintain a system of public education?
2. What is the constitutional basis for the United States Supreme Court decision that "separate but equal" facilities for education have no place?
3. Evaluate the significance of the Northwest Ordinance of 1785 in the development of free public education. Is there any evidence that this grant was followed by Federal control of education?
4. It is sometimes maintained that the Morrill Act of 1862 was the real origin of the state university movement in the United States. After studying the implications and influence of this act, evaluate the above claim.
5. Does your state have a land-grant college? Investigate and report on its origin and development.
6. In your opinion, is there any service that the Office of Education performs which could not be performed by the several states? Do you find any precedents for Federal control in the activities of the Office of Education?
7. In the light of your study, do you believe that Federal aid to education is necessary? Do you believe that Federal control would follow Federal aid?
8. Why did Catholics oppose the Federal Department of Education? Is there a Catholic position on Federal aid to education?

ADDITIONAL READINGS

Advisory Committee on Education: *The Federal Government and Education,* Government Printing Office, 1938. A basic document covering the role of the Federal government in education.

Allen, Hollis P.: *The Federal Government and Education,* McGraw-Hill Book Company, New York, 1950. The reader's attention is called to chapters on Federal aid to, and interest in, education.

Babbidge, Homer D., Jr., and Robert M. Rosenzweig: *The Federal Interest in Higher Education,* McGraw-Hill Book Company, New York, 1962. An up-to-date account of Federal interest in, and programs for, colleges and universities.

Blackmar, F. W.: *History of Federal and State Aid to Higher Education in the United States,* U.S. Bureau of Education Circular of Information 1, 1890. An old study giving detailed information on early programs. The chapters on Federal aid are most relevant in connection with this chapter.

Carlson, Theodore E.: *Guide to the National Defense Education Act of 1958,* U.S. Department of Health, Education, and Welfare, Office of Education, Washington, 1959. Intended to help schools and school systems in qualifying for Federal aid under the terms of this act.

Educational Policies Commission: *Federal Activities in Education,* National Education Association, Washington, D.C., 1939. Note especially the arguments advanced defending the need for Federal aid in general, not only special, school programs.

————: *Federal-State Relations in Education,* National Education Association, Washington, D.C., 1945. An interesting treatment of the states' rights theory applied to education.

Lee, Gordon C.: *The Struggle for Federal Aid: First Phase,* Bureau of Publications, Teachers College, Columbia University, New York, 1949. Few educational topics create greater controversy. Lee looks at the foundation of the movement. Pay special attention to the alleged strengths and weaknesses of Federal aid and its availability to nonpublic schools.

Little, Kenneth: *A Survey of Federal Programs in Higher Education,* U.S. Department of Health, Education, and Welfare, Office of Education, 1962. An enumeration and description of Federal programs in higher education. Especially good for those coming into existence in the decade before 1962.

Marsh, Paul E., and Ross A. Gortner: *Federal Aid to Science Education,* Syracuse University Press, Syracuse, N.Y., 1963. The enviable position of science education is made clear.

Meyer, L. S.: *Federal Aid to Education: Its Impact on Arizona,* Arizona State University, Bureau of Government Research, Flagstaff, 1962. A case study of what Federal aid can do in one state.

Munger, F. J., and R. F. Fenno: *National Politics and Federal Aid to Education,* Syracuse University Press, Syracuse, N.Y., 1962. Note particularly how national politics and politicians are not always responsible in dealing with important national questions.

Rivlin, A. M.: *The Role of the Federal Government in Financing Higher*

Education, The Brookings Institution, Washington, D.C., 1961. A careful study of educational finance and the pros and cons of Federal participation. Of particular interest are those sections dealing with local and state resources and interest in supporting education.

Ross, Earle D.: *Democracy's College: The Land Grant Movement in the Formative State,* Iowa State College Press, Ames, 1942. This thorough study of the colleges arising out of the Morrill Act of 1862 should interest the reader, especially the first chapters which see the land-grant college in its infant years.

Russell, James E.: *Federal Activities in Higher Education after the Second World War,* King's Crown Press, New York, 1951. Acceleration of Federal interest in education, especially higher education, is a phenomenon of the past twenty years. "Why the Federal interest?" is a question worth pursuing here.

Spurlock, Clark: *Education and the Supreme Court,* The University of Illinois Press, Urbana, 1955. Legislative enactment has been the chief legal determiner of educational patterns, but the courts, too, have played their role. The definitive role of the United States Supreme Court is worth tracing here.

Steel, R. (ed.): *Federal Aid to Education,* The H. W. Wilson Company, New York, 1961. See especially those chapters concerned with the economics of education.

Sufrin, S. C.: *Issues in Federal Aid to Education,* Syracuse University Press, Syracuse, N.Y., 1962. See the issues as they touch on the church-related school.

Taylor, Howard C.: *The Educational Significance of the Early Federal Land Ordinances,* Bureau of Publications, Teachers College, Columbia University, New York, 1922. Of special interest here are the effects of the Northwest Ordinances of 1785 and 1787.

PART THREE

Educational

Programs and Teachers

chapter 6

Elementary Education

The organizational structure of American education, discussed in Part Two, was developed with one objective: to provide educational opportunity for all the children of all the people. No level of the education system contributes more to the realization of this objective than the first—elementary education. More than 26.1 million children are enrolled in public elementary schools and more than 5.6 million are enrolled in private elementary schools. In all, there are 105,023 public and private elementary schools with more than 940,000 teachers to direct the learning activities in them.[1] Because elementary education is a foundational educational experience, and because basic, and often lasting, attitudes toward learning and living are formed during a student's first years in formal education, elementary education—its history, objectives, curriculum, and method—must be studied carefully and critically. No educational level is more important; none have a more pervasive influence on the child's educational future.

HISTORICAL BACKGROUND

A search for the origin of elementary education takes one back in history to a time when skills and values were transmitted to the young without the help of schools. Early societies were conscious of the needs of men and women, and the elementary or rudimentary training that was provided was almost always practical: it was oriented rather narrowly to the needs of adult society. Forming or developing the personality was incidentally and often unintentionally associated with the primary objectives, which were essentially practical. It is not easy to draw clear lines of distinction between educational levels when education is informal; it may be true that all of education during primitive periods was elementary. The teachers of the young were the parents and society itself. Skills for securing food, shelter, and personal safety were taught by example rather than by precept, and the motivation for learning was self-preservation. Life in society was simple, but in preparation for it the child was introduced to the lore and the values of those with whom he was destined by birth and circumstances to live out his life. Social education was primarily a matter of learning to conform. When did elementary education begin, and when did it end? Undoubtedly it began with birth; no definite time was set for its termination.

As man evolved in history, he slowly turned his back on the simple, primitive life of his ancestors. His talents, his hopes, and his aspirations led him to a better, though in some ways a more difficult and complex, life. He

Figure 6.1 Teachers in Public Elementary and Secondary Schools, 1870 to 1970. (Statistics of State School Systems, U.S. Office of Education, 1964.)

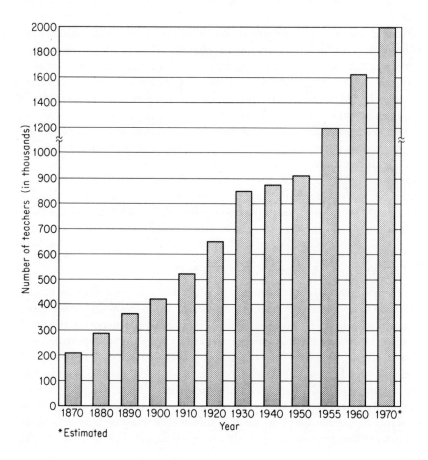

*Estimated

still needed skills to earn his daily bread, but these skills were not the skills of the hunter and the herdsman. So as man progressed, the skills needed for success, or simply for preservation, became different and sometimes more complex. Eventually, schools were established to do what parents and society could not do or did not want to do. Their purpose was to transmit to the young those skills and that knowledge which adult society believed to be elemental.[2]

So, newly formed elementary schools were charged with objectives which in earlier times had been associated with family and community living, and they organized a curriculum around a principle making knowledge an indispensable tool for life in society and for making a living. Learning, always rooted in ideals of utility, was sometimes prized as a means for social upgrading, yet few pursued it with motives inspired by disinterest and pure devotion. Arts and crafts found their way into the curriculum and stayed there because their significance could be demonstrated to anyone questioning the relevance of the school's syllabus, but their preemption was not total, and some time was set aside for superficial instruction in reading

Figure 6.2 Public and Private Elementary School Enrollment, 1900 to 1970. (Statistics of State School Systems, U.S. Office of Education, 1964.)

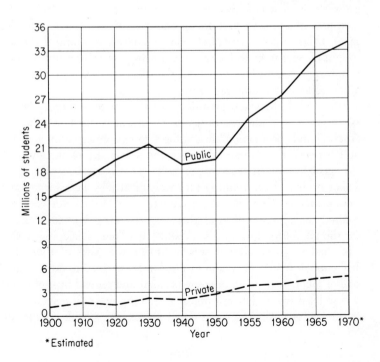

and writing. When schools were assigned elementary instruction, they were forced to operate within the boundaries of a limited commission: their objectives never went beyond those kinds of knowledge or learning clearly consistent with man's most fundamental physical needs.

It would not be accurate to say that schools assumed responsibility for all, or even most, of elementary education on what may be considered a second step in the evolution of formal education. Schooling was unusual, although it was considered useful, and children of humble origin were not offered the opportunity to benefit from it. Elementary education's practical orientation was a strange and somewhat limited orientation: practical meant economic usefulness. Preparation for life in society or citizenship—in a social, not a political, context—was not a school objective. The complexities of class-structured societies were learned, because the limitations on individual activity were as important and as binding as the taboos of the primitives. The children who attended these schools were young—sometimes only four—and they remained in school only a few years—probably not more than six. When they left the schools, they left with practical and physical skills, and the school had done its work well if it had used its resources to fashion its students as tools or as instruments for economic life.[3]

With the forward movement of history, man progressed and was encouraged by his progress to aspire to higher levels of moral, mental, aesthetic, and physical development; he began to think of elementary education as the first step away from a narrow instructional device for molding men toward a broader and deeper and more liberal learning for unraveling some of the mysteries and disclosing more of the meaning of the world. The weight of educational idealism was shifting away from utility, and in what is a barely discernible transition, the cleavage between liberal education and utilitarian training was born.

Although fathers and guardians were required, either by law or by tradition, to train their sons or wards for useful occupations, the meaning of "useful" and "occupation" was subject to new interpretations. A widening gulf between the rich and the poor, the prevalence of slavery, and increasing specialization in economic pursuits brought servile work into disrepute. Labor itself and the training for mechanical jobs were inconsistent with a new principle: "To be seeking after the useful does not become free and exalted souls." Regardless of theories pertaining to means and objectives for the good life, however, work and labor "out of keeping with the good life" had to go on. But it was not to be the work of those people who had enough wealth or station to avoid it. Leisure, then, rather than being an end of labor, became an opposite of labor and an end in itself. For the man whose lot it was to labor, a practical training was still essential, but the opportunity for this training was removed from the schools because the schools were reserved now for those who were above servile work. "Leisure" came to mean "school." The elementary schools became places where the wealthy and the freeborn could acquire culture, for culture was an obvious sign of one's station in life. These were the foundations basic to the operation of elementary education in Athens and elsewhere in Greece in the fifth and fourth centuries B.C., and they were preserved and honored as guiding principles for most education in Western civilization.

The guiding force of classical culture and values was challenged in time by Christianity. Although the classical heritage never completely lost its relationship with education in the West, Christianity had important catalytic effects on education. The value of liberal studies to a Christian view of life was challenged by some, denied by others, but liberal studies survived because they could prove their worth. But the legacy of liberal studies was not bestowed on elementary education in general. Christian elementary schools were not founded to perpetuate either class consciousness in society or classicism in culture; they returned to the practical objectives of an earlier period, but with this important difference: the practical was given a religious connotation, and elementary schools accepted otherworldly objectives. Skills for reading and writing—all the literary skills —were given less attention by Christian educators than in the classical environments of Greece and Rome. But the elementary education of the Christians was not restricted to the upper classes as Greek and Roman elementary education had been, and skills for reading and writing had a limited usefulness before the advent of movable type. Because the end of elementary education was conceived to be supernatural—as was the end of all education—and because literary skills were of little practical value to most people, the tools of education and the transmission of the social inheritance were relatively neglected in Christian elementary schools between the sixth and the sixteenth centuries.

An intellectual revolution of the sixteenth century, which had its origin in the spread of the printed word, the rise of nationalism, and a concomitant development of vernacular language and literature, and the unveiling of science, affected elementary education in many ways. In one way particularly—by making fundamental literary training almost essential—it had its greatest influence. The intellectual quickening of the sixteenth century, which owed its existence to the major movements of that period, was also indebted to the Renaissance. In time it became difficult to determine which, the Renaissance or the first of the modern centuries, had a more profound and lasting effect on elementary schools.

The educational promise of the new era was interrupted by the religious upheaval. Rather than advancing the cause of popular elementary education, as is often believed, the religious revolt and its consequences slowed educational progress throughout the next two centuries. By the time Europe learned to live in near harmony with two or more doctrinal beliefs and ritualistic practices, the old cleavages in education had returned.

Nevertheless, the modern age was not disposed to emulate the classical dualism completely, although two types of elementary education came into prominence at this time. One type was concerned with the kind of education conceived to be elemental for the common people: some training in the vernacular for reading public notices and religious materials. The second type was concerned with the kind of education believed to be consistent with the needs of an elite class: preparatory training in the languages of learning and an introduction to what was held to be upper-class culture. The former type was accepted as being socially useful, because it could be used to exercise control over the common people and keep them in their places, and it became quite generally the institutionalized type of elementary education. The latter type, although highly regarded, was only infrequently organized formally because the elite could afford private tutors, and the flexibility of tutorial arrangements permitted greater individual development. This, in general, was the evolution of elementary education until the colonization of America, and these accepted practices were transplanted to the shores of the new world without a thought of innovation.

The Evolution of Elementary Education in America

Rise of the common school. Colonial conditions varied; the New England, Middle, and Southern Colonies reflecting these variations made provisions for elementary education consistent with their special attitudes or prejudices toward the value of education.[4] More than anywhere else in the Colonies, the movement for elementary education was initiated and sustained in New England. The first elementary schools in this section of the country were called *dame schools*.

The dame school was a direct transplant from England. In colonial America, as in England, education was primarily a family or an individual responsibility, and opportunities for schooling had to be provided by private means. The dame school was usually a private-venture school: some housewife in the community would accept a few children in her home to teach them the rudiments of reading and spelling and moral and religious precepts for a modest fee. Both boys and girls were taught in these dame schools. For girls, the school's curriculum often included sewing and knitting. Although the dame school usually had its origin in the desire of some thrifty dame to earn money while she was carrying on her regular household duties, some dame schools in New York and Pennsylvania owed their origin to, or were sponsored by, religious denominations.

The town schools—sometimes called the common schools—had their origin in the Massachusetts Act of 1647,[5] but they did not immediately replace the dame schools. The most important justification for continuing the dame school was this: Towns simply did not comply with the legislation of 1647 as it was first enacted in Massachusetts, nor did the other colonies show any greater willingness to abide by the laws that were modeled after the "Old Deluder Satan Act." And after 1692 the colonies modified their compulsory school laws so that they were no longer meaningful. When town schools were established, students were usually required to display their skill in reading as a condition of admission to the town school. It is true, of course, that there were many ways for children to secure some skill in reading besides attending dame schools. They might learn from one another, or they might learn from their parents. Poor children might be taught to read in some town schools, or they might receive this instruction from their minister, from an endowed free school, or from a parochial school. Children of wealthy or at least well-to-do parents could be given the rudiments by a private tutor, or the master of the Latin grammar school (a private secondary school) [6] could usually be persuaded to teach the boys the fundamental skills of the vernacular before introducing them to Latin. Still, the dame school performed a useful service and—though not a free school—remained an established institution down to the time when publicly supported elementary education for all American children became a generally accepted ideal for American education.

The first town schools tended to be writing schools, although in some town schools arithmetic was taught. Reading, as we have suggested, was a skill the child was expected to have when he entered the town school. Eventually, however, probably by the middle of the eighteenth century, the town schools, as well as other elementary schools, began to accept reading, writing, arithmetic, and religion as the staples of an elementary curriculum. From this common practice, whether followed by public, semipublic, or private elementary schools, the typical American elementary school took its curricular form.

But the elementary schools in America before the beginning of the second quarter of the nineteenth century were not the elementary schools we know today. They were not attended by all or even a major portion of the children of school age. The children who did attend were taught individually; grading of materials of instruction and classification of students according to age, readiness, or achievement were done in a perfunctory manner or not at all. And the children were not taught as children—for there was little understanding of child nature—but as miniature adults. Whether the elementary schools were in New England or elsewhere in colonial America, they were conducted in a rigidly formalistic and somber atmosphere. The master or the dame who kept the school was invested with the authority of a tyrant and was convinced that no good teacher would hesitate to use this authority. It was a dark day, indeed, for the lad who upon being called to the teacher's desk to recite was unable to rattle off his lesson. There were no excuses for failure, but neither was there motivation for success in these deprived educational settings. Children in school did not live in a real world, nor did the teacher, but in an educational world which was considered to be something set apart from the rhythm of life. Everything to be taught and learned was placed in a narrow religious context: the children in the colonial schools and those in the schools of the early national period were exposed to one book—a religious primer—from which all useful knowledge came. In New England it was the "little Bible of New England" —the *New England Primer*—that was used. From it the child learned his ABC's and reading, but he learned, too, that God was a God of wrath, stern and cruel, and he was admonished to fear this God. After the child went through this *Primer,* or something like it in the schools of the other colonies, the Bible became his textbook. Eventually, however, some elementary textbooks were prepared, with a predominantly religious content, but containing the materials necessary for spelling and reading. History, geography, and science were given neither thought nor attention.

The following description of a New England elementary school is quoted from a student who attended such a school:[7]

> The schoolhouse chimney was of stone, and the fireplace was six feet wide and four deep. The flue was so ample and so perpendicular that the rain, sleet, and snow fell directly to the hearth. In winter the battle for life with green fizzling fuel, which was brought in lengths and cut up by the scholars, was a stern one. Not unfrequently the wood, gushing with sap as it was, chanced to let the fire go out, and as there was no living without fire, the school was dismissed, whereat all the scholars rejoiced.
>
> I was about six years old when I first went to school. My teacher was "Aunt Delight," a maiden lady of fifty, short and bent, of sallow complexion and solemn aspect. We were all seated upon benches made of slabs— boards having the exterior or rounded part of the log on one side. As they were useless for other purposes, they were converted into school benches, the rounded part down. They had each four supports, consisting of straddling wooden legs set into auger holes.
>
> The children were called up one by one to Aunt Delight, who sat on a low chair, and required each, as a preliminary, "to make his manners," which consisted of a small, sudden nod. She then placed the spelling-book before the pupil, and with a pen-knife pointed, one by one, to the letters of the alphabet, saying, "What's that?"
>
> I believe I achieved the alphabet that summer. Two years later I went to the winter school at the same place kept by Lewis Olmstead—a man who made a business of ploughing, mowing, carting manure, etc., in the summer, and of teaching school in the winter. He was a celebrity in ciphering, and

Squire Seymour declared that he was the greatest "arithmeticker" in [the] County. There was not a grammar, a geography, or a history of any kind in the school. Reading, writing, and arithmetic were the only things taught, and these very indifferently—not wholly from the stupidity of the teacher, but because he had forty scholars, and the custom of the age required no more than he performed.

Colonial elementary education reflected the colonial mind: the schools were exactly what the people wanted them to be. As long as the colonial climate remained unchanged, the schools—especially the elementary schools, because they were nearer the people—were untouched by reform. But by the middle of the eighteenth century the first signs that the old order was to be challenged began to appear. These signs may be listed as follows:

1. Religious orthodoxy began to recede. The power of an *established* religion was weakened by the rise of religious liberalism.
2. The intellectual quickening of the sixteenth century renewed man's faith in himself and fired his hopes for controlling his own fate. The claims of science came to be honored equally with the claims of religion, and the utility of knowledge as well as its power was emphasized.
3. Social and political theory began to stress the equality and worth of the individual. Poverty and misfortune, once thought of as a sign of inherent weakness or of God's justice, became the objects of humanitarian interest.

Two of the clearest evidences that these signs represented changes in the colonial mind can be found in the reforms for education proposed by Benjamin Franklin and Thomas Jefferson. Although neither Franklin nor Jefferson was concerned primarily with elementary education, their proposals relating to education—Franklin's in 1749 and Jefferson's in 1779— were far-reaching and would have affected elementary education. Both deplored the place religion occupied in education, and both advocated freeing education from the chains of religious orthodoxy. Freedom of men to think and to act in terms of rational conclusions rather than according to prescriptive doctrines was indispensable to the kind of society these two democrats envisioned. But the power of individuals to control their own destinies could be limited by ignorance as much as by religion, and so Franklin and Jefferson in their respective proposals for education advocated raising the general level of education. Without dealing with their specific proposals here, their views may be summarized as follows:

1. That without a continuous and integrated system of public education democracy would perish
2. That without religious freedom there could be no democracy
3. That the chief object of education was to teach what was useful, and that education must be conscious of its responsibilities to society

Public education, free from religious and political absolutism, and oriented toward utility, was destined to gain nearly universal theoretical and practical acceptance in the United States. But neither Franklin's nor Jefferson's educational ideas were widely accepted in their own time. Franklin was especially interested in reforming secondary education, and the academy movement, which he sponsored, fell far short of his hopes.[8] Jefferson's plan was broader than Franklin's;[9] it was directed toward reforms in elementary, secondary, and higher education, but the reception it received was a disappointing experience both for its sponsor and for all Americans interested in the welfare of the community and the nation.

Public elementary education was not entirely neglected between 1749, when Franklin first began to advocate a kind of democratic education, and 1817, when Jefferson's Bill for the Establishment of a System of Public Education was considered for the last time, but it made slow progress. This was due mainly to a general lack of understanding of the relationship between education and the great American experiment—democracy. As this relationship became clearer, it became evident that an educated electorate was essential to the effective functioning of democracy. And as men of all walks of life and all manner of circumstances began to share in affairs of government, the conclusion was generally drawn that some kind of education was necessary for everyone. With the "rise of the common man" came the growth of universal education as ideal and reality. By 1830 public men and public-spirited citizens were talking of an elementary education for this common man; in this interest and dedication to the welfare of the country we find the advent of the common school. The common school was America's most striking and perhaps most important educational achievement.

The common school of the early nineteenth century was usually a one-room elementary school. Its chief purpose, in theory, was to train loyal and responsible citizens. However, the common-school idea was supported by some educational reformers who conceived its objectives to be broader than this and who sometimes viewed the common school as an institution with higher allegiances than citizenship. The traditional dominant aim for all education in America had been religious and moral formation, and this objective was preserved in many common schools. In actual practice, the common school often remained a sectarian institution, and the retreat from orthodoxy which was characteristic of the period was not evident in its objectives or its teaching. In communities with a variety of religious preferences, the doctrines of the sect accepted by a majority of the people in the community occupied a privileged position in the school. When the religious complexion of the community changed—and sometimes it changed rapidly—it was not easy to dislodge the doctrines of this denomination from the school's curriculum.

Another educational tradition which exerted some influence on the common school was implicit in the theory of mental discipline. This theory tended to ignore the importance of the acquisition of knowledge and stressed instead the training of the faculties of the mind. Although the effect of this theory was greater in secondary and higher education than in elementary, it nevertheless tended to modify the common school's adherence to an objective which emphasized the utility of knowledge both for the individual and for society. In addition, the idealism and rationalism basic to this doctrine or theory took their toll of the school environment, which was usually dull and repressive, as well as of the curriculum and methods.

The common school's submissive attitude toward mental or formal discipline is one of the least impressive pages in its history. Neither the formal subjects, which were taught with a mechanical but uninspiring precision, the arithmetic problems, nor the spelling list bore a close relationship to the kind of world the students knew or to the realities of life. The bright child detecting this deplorable lack of relevance, given the proper opportunity, might rebel; the average or slow-learning student would not contest established authority, so he became a supporter, all unknowingly, and even perhaps unwillingly, of the educational *status quo*. Some illumination was added to what otherwise was a dull and dreary school life when a book—the reader—of quality was put in the good student's hands. In no other educational period did the book of quality play a greater or more independent role as an instructional instrument. But reading in too many schools was mechanical, and students were unable to transfer their skill: they could read from their reader but from nothing else. Unfortunately, the same thing happened in the study of grammar. Students drilled to recite the rules of grammar with all the signs of perfection were often unable to apply these rules in their own compositions. The quality of learning was low, and its breadth was limited. Studies in history and geography seldom found a place in the school's curriculum.

Some educational reformers willingly acknowledged the preeminence of citizenship as an objective for the common schools. They saw, too, that the common schools provided a general base upon which more advanced education could be built. From these higher schools, both secondary schools and colleges, the leaders of the nation would come. Besides, the common schools were effective instruments for advancing social solidarity. America was already becoming a haven for the poor, the oppressed, the strong, and the brave from most of the nations of Europe. The effect of this variety of language, culture, and national habits on the national life of the United States could be minimized through the welding influence of the common school. But, in addition to the objective of citizenship, it was often claimed that the common school should concern itself with preparing its students for useful occupations. In other words, the doctrine of utility advanced by Franklin and Jefferson came to mean for some educational reformers an inclusion of business and commercial and other skill subjects in the curriculum of the common school.

Finally, it was sometimes claimed that the common school had only one purpose, which was neither civic, religious, nor vocational. This purpose was simply to aid in achieving universal literacy.

The common school, although affected by each of these points of view, retained and eventually clarified its chief purpose—citizenship. For the most part, the clarification of the common school's objective was gained through the work of three prominent educational reformers: Horace Mann (1796–1859), Henry Barnard (1811–1900), and James Carter (1795–1849). These educational leaders and statesmen paved the way for the so-called "common-school revival" by stimulating interest in educational reform through journalism and public addresses. They introduced or caused to be introduced legislation which secured better teacher preparation and more effective state supervision of education. In dealing with other questions, such as equality, sectarianism, and support, they were both forcible and effective.

James G. Carter, sometimes called the father of the normal school,[10] was among the first to recognize that poor materials of instruction, a too narrow curriculum, myopic objectives, and incompetent teachers impaired educational progress and worked to the disadvantage of individuals and society. In his widely read *Essays on Popular Education,* Carter urged that education be considered as a science and that all the then known techniques of science be employed to improve it. He advocated the use of inductive methods of teaching—in many respects he was a disciple of Pestalozzi.[11] In 1827 he introduced the first, though unsuccessful, bill for the establishment of a state normal school—a teacher-training institution. When the legislature refused to enact his bill, he founded a private normal school in Lancaster, Massachusetts. In 1835 he drafted the bill which created the State Board of Education in Massachusetts.

Henry Barnard, who became the first United States Commissioner of Education in 1867, first attracted the attention of educational reformers when, as a member of the Connecticut Legislature, he introduced a bill creating a State Board of Education. This was in 1838. Barnard's interest in education was aroused by the plight of the common schools in Connecticut. The common schools were not being supported; most of the common schools were regarded as pauper or poor schools and were not attended; and teachers were untrained and inefficient. With Barnard's appointment as Secretary of the State Board of Education, he wrote letters, prepared reports, organized conventions, and founded and edited the *Connecticut Common School Journal* in order to describe educational conditions in the hope that information would bring reform. But reform came slowly, and before it was achieved, Barnard's office was legislated out of existence. He moved from Connecticut to Rhode Island, where he became State Commissioner of Education and where he continued his work for educational reform. In addition to his activities as a practical educational reformer, he gained recognition as an educational scholar. He studied and inspected foreign systems of education; he founded the *American Journal of Education* and edited the *Connecticut Common School Journal* and the *Journal of the Rhode Island Institute of Instruction.* In all, his written works on nearly all aspects of education filled more than thirty-two volumes of

Carter, Barnard, and others dedicated themselves to the improvement of the common school and achieved notable results. But the greatest and the more than 800 pages each.

most effective of the educational statesmen was Horace Mann.

Horace Mann and the strengthening of the common school. Few figures in the history of public education in the United States have aroused so much antagonism and suspicion as Horace Mann; on the other hand, no one has a more secure place in the annals of American education. From some writers he still receives praise for all that is good in American education; by others he is castigated as a demon, tyrant, and atheist responsible for any or all of the shortcomings in American education. Our primary interest here is not to evaluate Horace Mann. However, it would be difficult to avoid according to him a place of honor and esteem in any educational hall of fame.

Mann was a humanitarian. More than anything else, this explains his consuming interest in education. On June 30, 1837, the day Mann became Secretary to the State Board of Education of Massachusetts, his *Journal* records his feelings:[12]

> Henceforth, so long as I hold this office, I devote myself to the supremest welfare of mankind on earth. An inconceivably greater labor is undertaken. With the highest degree of prosperity, results will manifest themselves but slowly. The harvest is far distant from the seed-time, *Faith* is the only sustainer. I have faith in the improvability of the race,—on their accelerating improvability. This effort may do, apparently, but little. But mere beginning in a good cause is never little. If we can get this vast wheel into any perceptible motion, we shall have accomplished much. And more and higher qualities than mere labor and perseverance will be requisite. Art for applying will be no less necessary than science for combining and deducing. No object ever gave scope for higher powers, or exacted a more careful, sagacious use of them. At first, it will be better to err on the side of caution than of boldness. When walking over quagmires, we should never venture long steps. However, after all the advice which all the sages who ever lived could give, there is no such security against danger, and in favor of success, as to undertake it with a right spirit,—with a self-sacrificing spirit. Men can resist influence of talent; they will deny demonstration, if need be: but few will com-

bat goodness for any length of time. A spirit mildly devoting itself to a good cause is a certain conqueror. Love is a universal solvent. Wilfulness will maintain itself against persecution, torture, death, but will be fused and dissipated by kindness, forbearance, sympathy. Here is a clew given by God to lead us through the labyrinth of the world.

Mann took up the cause of education in much the same spirit that the early Christians had taken up the Cross of Christ. Education was to be mankind's savior. Mann closed his law office, offered his lawbooks for sale, severed his connection with temperance organizations, in which he had been active, and declined to seek reelection to the Massachusetts assembly. These were his sacrifices for the cause he set out to serve. He knew that his work was not going to be easy, for he was aware of the apathy and the opposition to public education, as well as the vested interests in education which had to be challenged. He made these personal sacrifices willingly because he was a humanitarian, and the true humanitarian of the early nineteenth century placed a supreme value on education and the contribution it could make to the limitless perfectibility of mankind. Although Mann overestimated the power of formal education—as all humanitarians were prone to do—he approached the responsibilities of his office with unquestioned sincerity and high devotion.

These were the important issues related to the development of the common school; these were the challenges that faced Horace Mann:

Securing public support for public education.   By 1837, when Mann became Secretary to the State Board of Education, two basic traditions with respect to school support had evolved. One was the *philanthropic* tradition, the other the *collectivistic* tradition. However, even in Massachusetts, where the collectivistic tradition was strong, schools were not always supported satisfactorily. In some communities, schools supported by public means were avoided because they had the stigma of poverty attached to them. In all communities, some rates were charged for instruction, so schools supported by public funds were by no means free schools. The principle that everyone should be taxed for the support of public education was gaining acceptance by the fourth decade of the nineteenth century, but it was not a universally accepted principle. It was accepted by parties both in the liberal and conservative camps, but these parties were, for the most part, made up of intellectuals, and this partial acceptance of taxing for the support of schools in no way led to a more general concurrence in it by the rank and file. The people were hard to convince, especially the rural people and the upper classes, for both regarded educational taxes to be confiscatory. They were adamant in their stand that education was not a public responsibility to be paid for by people of means. The members of the upper class may have taken this stand more frequently than did rural people in general because they had more to lose; rural people, while they were likely no more generous than their upper-class brethren, were little convinced by the arguments that education was a good thing and worth paying for. To a great extent, their niggardliness was an outgrowth of apathy. These negative attitudes toward education too often led to a lowering of standards in public institutions to a point where those refusing to attend them were on fairly solid ground. Refusals to support education, or effective demands for cutting expenditures, eventually resulted in lowering the quality of instruction.

Mann's responsibility was clear: By popular appeals and legal measures, the principle had to be unequivocally established that a common-school education was the birthright of every citizen and that the opportunity for this education was not to be limited by an individual's ability to pay rates or other charges. The common schools were to be made entirely free. Principally owing to the leadership of Mann, Massachusetts retained and reinforced its collectivistic tradition; by 1850 the common schools of Massachusetts were entirely free. The precedent of public support for common schools, originating in large part from the work of Horace Mann, was followed in other New England states, in the South, and in the West. Public support for public elementary education had two sources: general taxation and the income from permanent school funds.[13]

By 1850 every state except Arkansas had enacted permissive tax legislation legalizing local tax levies for the support of schools. Of course, many local communities were out of sympathy with such permissive acts and refused to take positive action. Moreover, it should be noted, a few states tired of what they regarded as ultraprogressive legislation and repealed permissive laws after a brief trial. For the most part, however, permissive tax laws laid the foundation for broad statewide systems of public education: they established the legal precedent for public school support even when no action was taken on the local level.

Establishing state supervision of the common schools. The tradition of philanthropy and collectivism applied to education influenced the formation of patterns of educational control no less than practices of educational support. The collectivistic doctrine supported a general control of education for the good of all, but general control did not always mean state control. The doctrine of philanthropy made education an individual or a local matter and resisted any kind of control that would limit individual or local freedom.

Before Mann became Secretary to the State Board of Education, some states had experimented with state control, and some had created a department of state government charged with the supervision of education. In 1812, New York provided for the first state superintendent of common schools, Gideon Hawley being the first appointee. But New York was not yet ready for state supervision and control of education, and the office of superintendent of common schools was abolished in 1821. In general, the experiments with state supervision were unsuccessful before Horace Mann made something of the office to which he was appointed in 1837. These experiments were unsuccessful because powerful elements were aligned against them. The arguments then used against state supervision and control may be listed as follows:

1. That government governs best which governs least.
2. Control of education by a government so far removed from the people as state government is certain to be inimical to the best interests of education.
3. Government control of education is the first step toward absolutism.
4. Religious formation is the end of education, and this formation cannot be supervised by a secular agency.

In addition to these arguments against state supervision of the common schools, the power of local communities and school districts was firmly entrenched.[14] This was probably the major obstacle to state control and supervision.

Mann's challenge to this jealously guarded local control and his outspoken criticisms of the district system could not have won for him many admirers among local politicians or schoolmen. Still, he persisted in his efforts to wrest from the hands of local officials this precious control over education and extend state supervision to all phases of the educational enterprise. In the long run, Mann's position was accepted, and personally he was vindicated—at least history vindicates him—but he waged the battle at great personal sacrifice. By 1850 the state had achieved a dominant position in educational matters, and a foundation was laid for a system of public schools under general state supervision. In 1850, following the leadership of Massachusetts, sixteen states had chief state school officers; twenty-eight states had established this office by 1860.

Eliminating sectarianism from the common schools. The power and influence of Horace Mann were instrumental in extending public support and in creating state control. We have seen that by giving new direction to old traditions, Mann was able to overcome a great deal of opposition and enlist new support for the cause of public education. But neither of these reforms challenged tradition or accepted practice as much as Mann's efforts to enforce the Law of 1827.

It is impossible to understand Mann's role in the sectarian issue unless one appreciates the religious situation in Massachusetts at the beginning of the nineteenth century. A spirit of religious liberalism was arising, and the historic teachings of orthodox Calvinism were being questioned and rejected. This new spirit resulted first in breaking Calvinism into two camps: the Old Calvinists and the New Lights. Then it manifested itself in the creation of many kinds of liberal religions. By 1825 the following sects or denominations had communicants or members in Massachusetts: Orthodox Congregationalists, Episcopal Methodists, Baptists, Unitarians, Universalists, Episcopalians, Roman Catholics, Christians, Friends, Freewill Baptists, Independent Methodists, Second Adventists, Wesleyan Methodists, Swedenborgians, Presbyterians, and Shakers.

The rising tide of religious liberalism coupled with the tradition that education was religious in content and purpose posed a general and a difficult problem for all the citizens of the Commonwealth of Massachusetts. Were the common schools to be religious schools? If so, which of the many denominations would be accepted as official and be privileged to have its doctrines taught by the schools? The spirit of the times was not antireligious, but neither was it generally sympathetic to an *establishment* of religion. The dilemma was resolved by the Act of 1827, in which sectarian materials were excluded from the common schools, although general religious principles upon which morality could be based were to be inculcated by the teaching and atmosphere of these schools. The important provisions in the Act of 1827 on the sectarian issue were:[15]

> It shall be, and it hereby is, made the duty of the President, Professors, and Tutors, of the University at Cambridge, and of the several Colleges in this Commonwealth, Preceptors and Teachers of Academies, and all other Instructors of Youth, to take diligent care, and to exert their best endeavors to impress on the minds of children, and youth, committed to their care and instruction, the principles of piety, justice, and sacred regard to truth, love to their country, humanity, and universal benevolence, sobriety, industry, and frugality, chastity, moderation, and temperance, and those other virtues, which are the ornament of human society, and the basis upon which the Republican Constitution is founded. And it shall be the duty of such Instructors, to endeavor to lead those under their care, as their ages and capacities will admit, into a particular understanding of the tendency of the above mentioned virtues, to preserve and perfect a Republican Constitution, and to secure the blessings of Liberty, as well as to promote their future happiness, and the tendency of the opposite vices to slavery and ruin. . . . *Provided,* also, that said committee shall never direct any school books to be purchased or used, in any of the schools under their superintendence, which are calculated to favor any particular religious sect or tenet.

It was upon this legal foundation that all Mann's efforts to remove sectarianism rested. Although the law was in effect ten years before Mann became Secretary of the State Board of Education, it had not been enforced effectively. It was the secretary's responsibility to see to it that this law was enforced, and it was easy for Mann to accept this responsibility because he was convinced that sectarianism in the common schools would destroy them. It is not our purpose here to revive the old charges that Mann's work in Massachusetts led to the creation of "Godless public schools," nor is it necessary to investigate Mann's personal religious convictions or lack of them. It is enough to indicate that the principle of nonsectarianism was contained in a legislative enactment and that Mann administered this law vigorously. From Massachusetts the principle of nonsectarianism spread throughout the Union.

Providing more effective training for teachers. The principal educational leaders of the nineteenth century were men of broad vision able to understand the complexities of public education and recognize the multiple issues to be raised in connection with it. They were able, moreover, to find the heart of the problem and appreciate both the central position and the intimate relationships in teaching and learning. The quality of a school could be reduced to the character and skill of the teacher. As it was, far too few teachers were prepared for the classroom; they happened to become teachers. "How," Mann and Carter[16] and others could ask, "is it possible to have good schools if the teachers are there not by design but by accident?" A plan for more effective teacher preparation was imperative: in its final form it provided for the founding of normal schools. More than any other public figure, James Carter was responsible for the creation of the public normal school, a school for the training of teachers.

Broadening and extending common-school experiences. We have seen that the curricular tradition in colonial elementary schools usually limited elementary subjects to the basic tools of communication. School years were brief interludes, and elementary education usually consumed no more than three years of a young person's life. The common schools of the nineteenth century perpetuated both the tradition and the practices of earlier elementary schools. Apparently, few believed that a little learning was a dangerous thing. Educational reformers, however, did not overlook the retardation of curricular development or the rigid confines of the traditional three R's curriculum. They worked hard for curricular reform, and they worked, too, to make the common school a *graded* educational experience of eight or nine years.

Presumably, this attempt at reform contained no elements which so affected men's loyalties that controversies erupted. This may be the reason why progress was so slow. For example, it was not until 1848, in Quincy, Massachusetts, that the first eight-grade elementary school was established in the United States. Grading in the common schools came about largely as a result of Horace Mann's *Seventh Annual Report,* which described grading practices in Prussian schools. The response to the reformer's common-elements curriculum—a curriculum containing knowledge necessary for broad citizenship—was anything but impressive. Nevertheless, the movement to broaden the curriculum of the common school proceeded, though slowly. It began with the preparation of elementary textbooks for the traditional three R's. From there it spread, and eventually textbooks and instructional materials began to appear in grammar, geography, and history. Readers were subject to regular improvement—and with the mention of readers, attention must be called to the famous and remarkable *McGuffey's Readers*. No schoolbook was ever more popular than these readers; probably half the children who attended school in this country between the years 1836 and 1886 used *McGuffey's Readers*.

The foundations for later developments in elementary education were laid in the common schools. From 1825 to 1850 the common schools were shaped to fit the needs and the hopes of education in the United States. At the end of this period—a period of both sharp change and gradual evolution—elementary education was publicly supported, publicly controlled, and free from sectarianism. In addition, students in the elementary schools of the country were being taught by reasonably well-qualified teachers and were being introduced to educational experiences broad enough and vital enough to challenge them.

Expansion and Consolidation of Private Elementary Education

The remarkable gains made by public elementary education in the last three-quarters of the nineteenth century should not be allowed to obscure equally remarkable developments in the field of private elementary education. The vastness of public elementary education and the essential role it plays in American democracy warrant an extensive and somewhat detailed analysis of its evolution. But in paying tribute to public education, there is a tendency to forget that some of elementary education's most effective reforms were developed in private schools.[17] The vast majority of private elementary schools have a denominational affiliation, and for most of them the affiliation is with the Roman Catholic Church. About 95 per cent of all private elementary schools in the United States are established, controlled, and supported by Catholics.

Catholic interest in education is as old as the Church itself. In colonial America, Catholic missionaries carried on educational work while performing their spiritual functions. These early Catholic ventures into education in America have little record in history. Few were permanent, and some were not very successful. The conditions of the times and the restrictive and discriminatory laws of the Colonies made Catholic foundations difficult to establish. With the formation of the United States much of this was changed, and in a more hospitable climate Catholics were able to lay a permanent educational foundation with the beginnings of Georgetown Academy (now Georgetown University) in 1786.

Catholic schools—elementary, secondary, and higher—were established because Catholics wanted to give their children a complete religious education.[18] The first formal step taken to create a system of Catholic elementary schools was taken by the First Provincial Council of Baltimore in 1829. This council enacted the following decree with respect to education:[19]

> Since it is evident that very many of the young, the children of Catholic parents, especially the poor, have been exposed and are still exposed in many places of this Province, to great danger of the loss of faith or the corruption of morals, on account of the lack of such teachers as could safely be entrusted with so great an office, we judge it absolutely necessary that schools should be established in which the young may be taught the principles of faith and morality, while being instructed in letters.

The work begun by the First Council of Baltimore was continued in the councils of this province through 1849. In the Provincial Councils of Cincinnati during the same period, the question of Catholic schools received a great deal of attention. It was the Third Plenary Council of Baltimore (1884), however, which enacted positive and final legislation with respect to Catholic education at all levels.

The council issued a decree which contained the following practical steps for creating a system of Catholic elementary schools:[20]

I.   Near each church, where it does not exist, a parochial school is to be erected within two years from the promulgation of this Council, and is to be maintained *in perpetuum*, unless the bishop, on account of grave difficulties, judge that a postponement be allowed.

II. A priest who, by his grave negligence, prevents the erection of a school within this time, or its maintenance, or who, after repeated admonitions of the bishop does not attend to the matter, deserves removal from that church.

III. A mission or a parish which so neglects to assist a priest in erecting or maintaining a school, that by reason of this supine negligence the school is rendered impossible, should be reprehended by the bishop and, by the most efficacious and prudent means possible, induced to contribute the necessary support.

IV. All Catholic parents are bound to send their children to the parochial schools, unless either at home or in other Catholic schools they may sufficiently and evidently provide for the Christian education of their children, or unless it be lawful to send them to other schools on account of a sufficient cause, approved by the bishop, and with opportune cautions and remedies. As to what is a Catholic school, it is left to the judgment of the Ordinary to define.

The legislation of the Third Plenary Council aimed at achieving ideal conditions in education, and, it must not be overlooked, was enacted more than eighty years ago, when conditions in America were considerably different. Whether or not the goal set—a parochial school in connection with every church—will ever be achieved is a point we need not debate here. Obviously, church schools did not become realities within a two-year period from the promulgation of the Council's statutes. The principle stated, and largely accepted by the Catholic people of the country, was "every Catholic child in a Catholic school." This is still the ideal; Catholics have not renounced their allegiance to basic religious education. But the realities of educational and economic life of the twentieth century would seem to be working against rather than for a positively accelerated rate of growth in Catholic elementary education.

The position is sometimes taken by responsible Catholics that the nature of elementary education—with its emphasis on skills and tools—makes it a less sensitive level than, say, secondary or higher education, and might well be deemphasized. There is nothing Catholic, it is maintained, about the teaching of reading, writing, or arithmetic; these subjects might be mastered in a public or secular school as well as in a religious school. If this advice were followed, the resources available to Catholic education could be concentrated on secondary and higher schools, where a real and effective intellectual approach can be made to teaching with a religious orientation. Too much effort, money, and personnel have been invested in elementary schools now, it is argued, and, it is insisted further, it will be impossible in the future to keep up with the demand for Catholic schools unless some decision is made to concentrate effort and resources on one or two educational levels. In fairness to spokesmen who take this position—admittedly not now a popular one—they would with adequate resources support all levels of Catholic education, but the point is, they doubt the availability or adequacy of resources, and to continue Catholic schools on all levels without them, they say, is to court disaster. The advocates of concerted effort are not enemies of Catholic elementary schools; they simply and sincerely believe in a scale of educational worth, and on it the Catholic elementary school is lighter than the Catholic high school or college.

Among Catholics willing to accept some revision of the system, not all are ready to relinquish the elementary level. There is still considerable sentiment supporting the position that basic moral habits are formed in childhood, and this opportunity once lost may never be regained. If, some defenders of the elementary level will argue, the elementary school is only a place for reading, writing, and arithmetic, there is no good reason for ever having a Catholic elementary school regardless of the resources available. If it is more than this, what constitutes the added features? They are theological and moral. The direction of a child's character formation and devotion to his religion are both products of the good, careful, and truly educative influence of the Catholic elementary school. Cost, character, theology, and personnel should swing the argument in favor of retaining Catholic elementary education, with a relative deemphasis on the two higher levels. Elementary school buildings and the instructional materials in them are less expensive than secondary school or college buildings with their libraries, laboratories, and special equipment of all kinds. Teachers for elementary schools, whether they are religious or lay, can be obtained in greater supply and in higher quality than for either of the two higher levels. It is much easier, it is argued, to prepare a person to fulfill duties demanded of an elementary teacher than it is to attract and prepare fully competent teachers for high schools and colleges.

We feel no need to resolve the question here; it is important, however, for the student to know that many Catholics are convinced the present system of Catholic education in the United States is not a fixed and unchangeable system. They expect it to evolve and adjust as the educational needs and economic abilities of the Catholic population evolve and adjust. On the other hand, Catholic educational thought is essentially conservative; extensive revisions in the structure of Catholic education, or any reduction in the degree of commitment the majority of Catholics feel to a total educational program under Catholic direction, do not seem to be imminent.

One final point might be mentioned in connection with this general discussion: It has to do with the preparation of teachers for Catholic schools. Adequacy of teacher supply is a problem—perhaps the most crucial in today's educational world—by no means singular to Catholic education. But in one respect Catholic educators have tried to solve it in a singular manner: this is the Sister Formation Movement. Started in 1950, Sister Formation has come a long way in a short time. The ever-present obstacles were lack of money, insistent pressures for larger school staffs, the lack of recruits to the Sisterhood, conservatism in viewpoint of many officials in religious women's congregations in its initial stages, and some suspicion of a central organization trying to dictate or direct policy. Throughout its short history—with efforts, accomplishments, and some minor failures—Sister Formation has stressed the need for the fusion of the spiritual and the intellectual formation. There could be no dichotomy here: nothing short of integration would do.

There are really three parts, or three emphases, in Sister Formation: an organization, an idea, and a movement. As an organization, it has done much to unite the religious communities of women in the United States in their active work for purposes of study, research, planning, and sharing of resources. As an idea, it is a recognition that Sisters doing active work in contemporary times need a long and careful spiritual formation; a general intellectual training, equipping them for a rich personal life and effective social leadership; and a precise professional formation making them equal or superior to lay people doing the same kind of work. There is the additional implication that spiritual and professional training cannot be compartmentalized, but must reciprocally enforce and strengthen each other in forming an integrated personality. Finally, as a movement, Sister Formation is a part of a worldwide effort for "renovation" and "adaptation" in the states of perfection which was begun by Pope Pius XII and the Sacred Congregation of Religious in 1950 and which has met with outstanding response from women religious in all countries and in all kinds of religious work.

The objectives of Sister Formation may be put this way: Sister Formation wants to form a woman who can think for herself, who is able to continue her education independently through reading and study, and who has a love and appreciation for things of the mind. It aims at training a Sister who has the philosophical and theological background to understand the principles of asceticism which are part of the spiritual formation program, who has enough general culture to meet and converse with professional people on their own level, and to recreate herself and her Sisters on an intellectual plane, and finally who has such a mastery of both the subject matter she teaches and the techniques of instruction as will satisfy her obligations in justice to her pupils and do credit to the Catholic educational system. Sister Formation, therefore, is the combination of spiritual and intellectual training in such a way that they positively reinforce one another, and leave in the mind of the Sister no false impression of tension or incompatability between the general and specific ends of her congregation. The aims of the Sister Formation Movement have been

TABLE 6-1
Catholic Elementary School Statistics

Year	Schools	Teachers	Students
1920	6,551	41,581	1,795,673
1924	6,867	46,322	1,947,495
1928	7,449	55,155	2,111,560
1932	7,923	58,245	2,222,598
1936	7,885	58,183	2,195,562
1940	7,916	59,701	2,086,071
1944	8,017	60,746	2,014,782
1948	8,077	59,729	2,140,840
1952	8,589	66,525	2,560,815
1956	9,568	75,000	3,544,598
1962	10,630	89,037	4,451,893
1970 (Estimated)	12,000	95,000	5,500,000

high and challenging. Yet, their accomplishment and realization thus far testify to the essential realism and practicality of the movement. Not only will the religious congregations for women reap the benefits of this movement, so also will the children who attend the Catholic schools across the country.

BROADENING THE SCOPE OF ELEMENTARY EDUCATION

At the end of the period of educational reform, the elementary curriculum of the common school was organized into a seven-, eight-, or nine-year program, depending on the section of the country in which the schools were established. But everywhere in the United States elementary education was

Figure 6.3   Broadening the Curriculum of Elementary Education.

Courses in curriculum		
		Social Studies
		Health
		Physical Education
		Play
		Cooking
		Sewing
		Manual Training
	Physical Education	Music
	Music	Drawing
	Drawing	Science
	Elementary Science	History
	History	Language
	Geography	Geography
Religious Instruction	Bookkeeping	Grammar
Bible	Arithmetic	Arithmetic
Arithmetic	Spelling	Spelling
Spelling	Writing	Literature
Reading	Reading	Reading
1635–1830	1830–1920	1920–1964

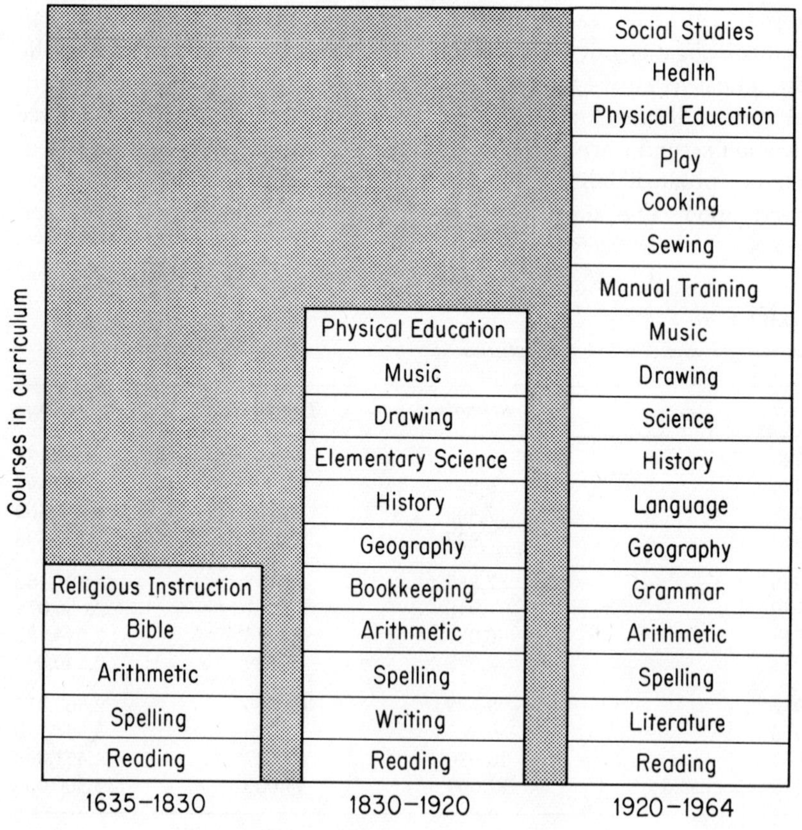

understood to have the following objectives: to inculcate citizenship, to develop some facility in spoken and written English, to teach the essentials of computation, and to encourage personal and social development. Each of these objectives was subject to some modification in the last half of the nineteenth century and during the first years of the twentieth. First, largely as a result of foreign example and the development of the science of education, history, science, literature, and geography received greater attention. Then came the methodological awakening which encouraged greater curricular attention to the development of the senses and the powers of observation. Finally, interest in child nature and the natural development of the child led to an extension of the traditional elementary school program both before the first grade and after the eighth. Before the first grade the kindergarten and the nursery school were added; the final years of elementary school were altered somewhat by the junior high school. These were the major structural broadening influences, and each will be considered briefly.

The Kindergarten

The idea of extending elementary instruction downward was given its first serious trial in Germany in 1837. The educational innovator in this instance was Friedrich Wilhelm Froebel (1782–1852). Froebel, a philosophical and educational idealist, believed children developed according to certain natural laws; certain developmental patterns were natural to them, and their unfolding was analogous to the growth, maturation, and flowering of plants. Thus, the name "kindergarten," literally, "children's garden." For the plant or flower some special nourishment, temperature, or environment leads to its greatest growth; this process inspired Froebel to say: Plants tended least flourish best. Where children rather than plants are involved, Froebel was sure their proper growth was assured naturally by activity. The principle governing all learning was applied rather exclusively by Froebel. It mattered little the direction taken by activity or the end achieved: Activity itself was important. Thus, Froebel's school can be regarded as the first activity school, a type later so highly approved by progressive educators.

The kindergarten movement, partly because it was clothed in a rather esoteric philosophical idealism and partly because it seemed to endorse activity simply for the sake of activity, was viewed with suspicion in Germany, the land of its birth, and was not embraced by educational leaders. Its European reception was cool and its progress slow.

Kindergartens were introduced to the United States by Mrs. Carl Schurz; the first made its debut in Watertown, Wisconsin, in 1855. This institution was a simple transplant preserving all the features of the German model even to the point of being German-speaking. Despite its obvious allegiances, the kindergarten was adopted in the United States and given its first trial as an English-speaking school by Elizabeth Peabody in Boston in 1860. For the next thirteen years the kindergarten movement made steady progress; by 1873 it was popular enough to be accepted as part of public education in the St. Louis school system. The influence of William T. Harris and Susan Blow, both sympathetic to the educational philosophy of Froebel, may be seen in this upgrading of the kindergarten's status. Twenty-five years after St. Louis's pioneer work with the kindergarten as a public institution, 189 United States city school systems had taken steps to incorporate this downward extension of elementary education into their school programs.

Whenever the kindergarten was added to a school system's total instructional pattern, it was given theoretical justification. There was never a case where the kindergarten was simply tacked on without debate or rationalization. It would obviously be impossible to know or to summarize all of the expressions of confidence in the kindergarten leading to its acceptance as part of public education, yet it is possible to point to two general views often employed in support of the kindergarten. One was a direct outgrowth of Froebel's plan: the kindergarten, it was maintained, provided quality opportunity for a broader and more meaningful kind of education; it was a valid educational level with untapped potential for learning. The other justification was somewhat less certain of the real educational stature of the kindergarten; at least, it was not emphasized. Rather, kindergartens would prepare children for elementary education by giving them a meaningful introduction to school life. To put it another way, the kindergarten was supported not as an integral part of elementary education, but as an articulating unit between the home and the school. Both justifications, it may be added, are still employed, and there is evidently some uncertainty as to the principal function of the kindergarten.

Junior High Schools

A second major change in the organization of elementary education was ushered in with the invention and growth of junior high schools. At the beginning of the twentieth century, the eight-grade elementary school was a firmly entrenched institution; the basic educational opportunity offered in it was supplemented in many communities by a four-year high school. By this time—1900—the conventional pattern for school organization in the United States was 8-4: an eight-year elementary school and a four-year high school.

The elementary and secondary schools of the country had hardly settled into what was recognized as the conventional pattern when proposals were made relative to revision. As early as the 1890s the Committee of Ten[21] and the Committee on College Entrance Requirements[22] recommended a reorganization of elementary and secondary education with a drastic reallocation of time given to each. In 1907, 1908, and 1909 the Committee of Five of the National Education Association (NEA) urged the adoption of the proposed reforms. Three main arguments were used to support plans for reorganization: (1) Too much time was being devoted to elementary education—grades 7 and 8 were largely a waste of time. (2) The differences between elementary and secondary education were so great that students moving from the eighth grade to the first year of high school had a difficult adjustment problem. (3) Neither the last years of elementary education nor the first years of high school took into account the natural development of the child and his special interests, needs, and adjustment problems during these critical years of his life.

Beginning in the early twentieth century, or perhaps a few years before, some communities began to reorganize their schools. Those which departed from the conventional 8-4 organization adopted 6-6, 7-5, 7-4, 6-2-4, or 6-3-3 reorganizational plans. In general the trend was toward a more nearly equal distribution of time between the two levels—elementary and secondary—and the reorganizational plan most often adopted was a six-year elementary school, a three-year junior high school comprising the seventh and eighth grades of the conventional elementary school and grade nine, the first year of a regular four-year high school.

The Nursery School

The nursery school, the last of the major changes in the structure of American elementary education, was formed by a downward extension of the kindergarten. It is a school for very young children—eighteen months to four or five years of age—that assumes many of the responsibilities of the home and, in addition, tries to provide opportunities for physical, mental, social, and emotional growth. Nursery school programs are flexible, and their daily sessions are often adapted to the schedules of the children's mothers. However, the nursery school is not intended to be merely a place where children can be left while their mothers are working. In other words, the nursery school is more than a home nursery. Both the newness of nursery schools and their rather unique objectives have retarded their acceptance as a regular part of elementary education. Although there are many private and parochial nursery schools, very few have been established as part of the public school system.

FUNCTIONS OF ELEMENTARY EDUCATION

The evolution of the elementary school in America—the broadening of its curriculum, the determination of its objectives, and the extension of its influence—has not ceased. As the needs and interests of man change in a changing world, and as society makes new or different demands of him, his education must also change. Modern elementary schools have made significant departures from practices, curricula, and objectives of the common schools of the nineteenth century. These departures, however, have not always been along a common front, for the objectives of the elementary school and the means to achieve them have been subject to different, although not necessarily antagonistic, theories of elementary education. In general, there are two prominent theories which address themselves to the question of the functions of elementary education. For want of better terms we can characterize these theories as *essentialistic* and *progressive*.

Essentialistic Elementary Education

Within the context of essentialistic theory, the functions of elementary education may be arrived at by asking the following questions: Why are elementary schools established, and what are they expected to teach? and How are they expected to teach?

Why are elementary schools established, and what are they to teach? The elementary school has always had a deep-seated practical orientation; its commitment is to learning skills and tool subjects. It is fairly easy and natural, then, for the essentialist to assign *development of the tools of education* as one of the elementary school's principal practical functions. The most obvious tools of education, although there may be others, are reading, writing, counting, and computing. These are always preliminary but highly essential skills. They stand at the doorway of intellectual development and demand mastery before students can be confident of proceeding very far along the road of academic achievement.

If developing tools of education is one of the functions of the elementary level, another must surely be *an introduction to the social inheritance*. Achieving skills to move forward toward a fuller intellectual life is an entirely worthy objective but equally important, many essentialist educators say, is an induction into the social values of the community in which students live and learn. What does education mean if it cannot contribute materially to social upgrading? And how can this upgrading be achieved? It can be done by giving elementary school students direct social experience and by equipping them with social tools equal in importance to tools of learning. But beyond this it can be supported by coordinating its objectives with those of basic literary and computational activities, perhaps even as by-products from them, exposing students to traditional social values and the evolutionary processes testing and confirming them.

The development of moral values is critical and complex, for these values are the muscles keeping societies upright. The school's acceptance of this function is based on the assumption that moral values can be taught. If they can be taught anywhere, in the home or in the church, they can also be taught in the school. The ingenuity of elementary school educators is tested regularly when this function is taken seriously. Most educators, certainly all essentialists, take it seriously.

The educational process: How are elementary schools to teach? It may very well be true that the most obvious differences in the essentialist and progressive approach to elementary education are not found in stated objectives. It is doubtful that progressive educators would disagree with many of the foregoing objectives. However, it is unlikely that they would agree with the essentialist on how to achieve these objectives. For the essentialist, the educational process consists basically of opportunities for instruction, adjustment, and discipline.

Instruction. The elementary school's first obligation to the student is to teach him what he does not know. What is to be taught and how it is to be taught depend not upon the current needs and interests of the child but upon society's best estimate of what his future needs will be. The essentialist therefore emphasizes the traditional skills and demands achievement from the students.

Adjustment. Elementary education, according to the essentialist view, is broader than skill training; it involves, also, meaningful individual and social experiences that will enable the student to live effectively in modern society. However, these adjustment opportunities are considered to be primarily content-centered or society-centered and, though activity is recognized as an essential feature of all learning, not activity-centered.

Discipline. From the essentialist point of view, discipline—both self-control and good order—is essential to any degree of excellence. For best results in learning, the school's environment must, in this view, be conducive to learning: this means that children in school must subject themselves to the authority of the teacher and that good order must be maintained. Teachers have a responsibility to teach, and students are encouraged to develop that docility so characteristic of one who is seeking to learn what he does not know. In addition, by developing habits of thought and action and by becoming systematic in their work, students achieve the discipline of mind and character which sustains them in their goal of self-development. Because there are many times when learning is not unmitigated pleasure, but difficult and onerous, discipline is essential to educational progress.

Progressive Elementary Education

Progressive elementary education, which may or may not claim close kin-ship to pragmatism as a philosophy of education, arose as a reaction—even a rejection—to elementary schools conducted with the precision and rou-tine of a learning factory. The education pattern supported by nineteenth-century idealism was regimented and unimaginative; it stood between the child and the world in which he lived. Rather than accepting learning as a meaningful experience and one in which interest and motive might play some part, the nineteenth-century elementary school too often prohibited activities which seemed to be naturally attractive to students. The curricu-lum was narrow and out of joint with the times; the methods were ar-chaic, unmindful of technique capitalizing on interest, and unwilling to adapt teaching to the level of student accomplishment. Initiative was cur-tailed; discipline, routine, silence were praised as the sign of ideal con-ditions conducive to learning.

Admittedly, every nineteenth-century elementary school was not as bad as the picture sketched above, although far too many did conform to this description. Good schools too often went unheeded, but poor ones were sufficiently obtrusive to make progressive education seem attractive and worthwhile.

Rigidity and regimentation of school environment, along with a direct emphasis on fundamentals, formalized subject matter, and drill, are, from the progressive point of view, a sure way to close the door on educational experiences. Most progressive practices in elementary education evolve from the following conclusions about the educational process:

1. Education is not a preparation for life—it is life. Therefore, the school is primarily a social rather than an intellectual institution.
2. Education is child-centered: the child is the sun about which all the activities of education revolve; he is the center around which they are organized.
3. Learning is achieved best by doing; in addition to being child-centered, the progressive elementary school is also activity-centered.
4. The school's purpose is to help the child solve *his* problems and fulfill *his* needs. The school's curriculum, therefore, will be determined essen-tially by the students, and it will not be built around subjects but around units of work or projects.
5. The school's program should be flexible and balanced. Learning periods should not be limited or determined by the clock.
6. The tools of education are to be taught functionally and incidentally. Information is acquired through a study of actual and meaningful prob-lems which arise out of the students' own experiences.
7. Measurement and evaluation of student progress should be employed to discover what pupils have accomplished, but not to determine progress

toward definite or preconceived objectives. Evaluation is to be a co-operative process in which the students have a share.

8. Students should be classified according to interests and social maturity and not according to age, mental capacity, or scholastic achievement.

9. A teacher must be a guide, not a taskmaster, a source of information, the director of the school, or the hearer of lessons.

It is not entirely accurate to say that progressive elementary education is aimless, nor is it true to claim that progressives are not interested in the development of literary, social, or economic skills. Progressives attempt to achieve what most people would agree are desirable objectives by depending upon the child's interests and motivation. They find it difficult to believe that free men, democratically educated and oriented, can be produced by machinelike and unrealistic educational processes.

Progressive elementary education, then, emphasizes wider divisions of interest and activity rather than content. This emphasis originates primarily from the theory that children's interests are really limited to the present, that their real motives are derived from the stresses and tensions of daily living, and that they are always active in meeting the problems that arise in their everyday experiences. At the same time it is believed that children who are meeting their felt needs are receiving the best training for the demands that later events will make on them. Preparation for the future is not neglected, it is said, for preparation for adult life is achieved as a result of effective participation in activities having immediate interest and value.

Contributions of Essentialism and Progressivism to Contemporary Elementary Education

The two approaches to elementary education discussed in the preceding pages have always been subject to outside influences. The major emphases in each of the approaches have often had the effect of improving programs of learning and growth in elementary schools throughout the United States. This result has been achieved because dedicated teachers and educators have been able to discover strengths in each approach. The attention given by progressive education to the education of the whole child, though somewhat distorted, has brought into closer and clearer focus the importance of child development and elementary curricula, and all elementary schools in the United States have responded by designing programs of study and programs of student activity supported by valid research and experimentation in the psychology of learning.[23] At the same time, the essentialist's determination to retain achievement and discipline as goal and means in elementary programs has had the desirable effect of minimizing what was once a progressive tendency to interpret all learning in terms of individual expression and individual action. But by laying heavy stress on self-activity as the only road to learning, progressive elementary education awakened essentialist elementary education and motivated it to return to a principle that had always been, and is still, a central feature of all learning. By emphasizing present interests and needs, the progressives have propounded a theory of learning dynamics which has been superior to that of remote goals interpreted in terms of the needs of the future. Finally, by coupling the progressive's attention to techniques and methods with a healthy respect for content, both elementary curricula and teaching have been vastly improved. Contemporary elementary education in the United States has benefited from the challenges which the two major approaches have posed for each other. Without endorsing the philosophy most often basic to progressive elementary education, it is possible to acknowledge that in many respects the practices and methods of progressive elementary education are not incompatible with fundamental systems of value basic to all types of essentialistic elementary education.

Higher quality in the learning processes of American elementary schools has been one important outcome of what may be called the "revolution" in elementary education from 1930 to 1950. Although extreme points of view are still maintained by many elementary teachers and professors of education with respect to the why, the what, and the how of elementary education, it would seem to be a fair statement to say that students who complete the curricula in elementary schools today are better prepared to continue their work in formal education and are better adjusted to the complex world in which they must live and learn than at any previous time in the history of education.

SUMMARY

Throughout most of its long history elementary education has been concerned chiefly with transmitting elemental practical knowledge. Although this objective continues to find a place in the formulation of most educational objectives, American elementary education, beginning with the reforms of the common school in the mid-nineteenth century, began to accept education for citizenship as its principal objective. This shift in emphasis was supported by important educational leaders and statesmen of the nineteenth century—Horace Mann, James Carter, Henry Barnard. But for the new emphasis to succeed, basic changes were required in the then current educational structure. These major changes may be listed as: (1) securing public support, (2) securing public control and organizing effective state supervision, (3) eliminating sectarian control and influence in public schools, (4) providing more effective teacher education, and (5) broadening and deepening the learning experiences in elementary curricula.

These changes in structure were accompanied by remarkable developments in the field of nonpublic elementary education, particularly in Catholic elementary education.

In both public and nonpublic systems, kindergartens and nursery schools were added. In both systems, also, attempts were made to make the elementary school articulate more satisfactorily with secondary schools by experimenting with six-year elementary schools and junior high schools. In addition to experiments with the organization of elementary education, educators continued to study the functions of the elementary school. The outcomes of this study led to two approaches to elementary education which often appeared to be, and sometimes were, antagonistic. Through the studies, experiments, and analyses carried on in an attempt to prove the merit of one or the other approach, strengths and weaknesses in elementary curricula and methods have been displayed. Although it may be fairly doubted that the controversy which has surrounded elementary education's purpose and content has always had the best interests of children in mind, an important by-product of this controversy has been a general improvement of learning and living in elementary schools.

QUESTIONS AND EXERCISES

1. Obtain the latest statistics on elementary school enrollment, number of schools, and teachers in the United States.
2. Summarize the early development of informal and formal elementary education.
3. Explain the features of the various colonial schools engaged in elementary education. What is your evaluation of these schools?
4. Did Franklin's and Jefferson's educational views influence elementary education in early America? When did elementary education begin to become democratic?
5. The role of religion in early elementary education is usually emphasized. From your study, do you believe this emphasis is justified?
6. Summarize the educational views and attitudes of Horace Mann, Henry Barnard, and James G. Carter. How do you rate these reformers as educational statesmen?
7. Study Horace Mann's life and educational activities, and try to answer these questions: Was he the father of American public education? Was he the founder of the secular school? What was his stand on sectarianism in the common schools?
8. Why were the elementary schools of the nineteenth century called common schools?
9. Trace the origin and development of the kindergarten in America. What in your opinion, is the kindergarten's chief value?
10. Has the reorganization movement achieved the objectives it promised? What were its chief effects on elementary education?

11. Prepare a set of objectives for elementary education. Are they essentialistic or progressive?
12. What are the strengths and weaknesses of the essentialistic and the progressive approach to elementary education?

ADDITIONAL READINGS

Beauchamp, G. A.: *Basic Dimensions of Elementary Method,* Allyn and Bacon, Inc., Boston, 1959. See chapters on organization of teaching materials and teaching-learning process.

Bramwell, R. D.: *Elementary School Work,* University of Durham Institute of Education, Durham, England, 1961. An interesting view of elementary education from an English author. Pay particular attention to the different assumptions made.

Cremin, Lawrence A.: *The American Common School,* Bureau of Publications, Teachers College, Columbia University, New York, 1951. In this connection read sections concerned with content of elementary education.

Cutts, N. E., and N. Mosley (eds.): *Providing for Individual Differences in the Elementary School,* Prentice-Hall, Inc., Englewood Cliffs, N.J., 1960. See chapters 5 and 7.

De Vault, M. V.: *Underage First Grade Enrollers,* University of Texas Press, Austin, 1959. A study of the progress of first graders who are under beginning school age.

Flanders, J. K.: *Legislative Control of the Elementary School Curriculum,* Bureau of Publications, Teachers College, Columbia University, New York, 1925. See particularly section on legislative control over language and subjects related to citizenship.

Haan, Aubrey E.: *Elementary School Curriculum: Theory and Research,* Allyn and Bacon, Inc., Boston, 1961. Attention is called to chapters on research in elementary curricula and the need for it.

Imhoff, N. M.: *Early Elementary Education,* Appleton-Century-Crofts, Inc., New York, 1959. See chapters 2 and 4.

Jameson, Marshall C., and William V. Hecks: *Elementary School Curriculum from Theory to Practice,* American Book Company, New York, 1960. This is a parent-oriented book intended to help parents understand the elementary school.

Johnson, C.: *Old-time Schools and School-books,* The Macmillan Company, New York, 1925. See especially those chapters dealing with teaching materials of colonial and early national period schools.

Jordan, William C.: *Elementary School Leadership,* McGraw-Hill Book Company, New York, 1959. An outline of what is expected of elementary school principals.

Lambert, H. M.: *Early Childhood Education,* Allyn and Bacon, Inc., Boston, 1960. See chapter on teaching techniques for young children.

Lewis, Gertrude M.: *Educating Children in Grades Four, Five, and Six,* U.S. Department of Health, Education, and Welfare, Office of Education, 1958.

Chapters on school programs for children in these grades are called to the reader's attention.

Logan, Lillian M.: *Teaching the Elementary School Child,* Houghton Mifflin Company, Boston, 1961. Read chapters on sources of opposition to current elementary school practices.

Lowrie, Jean E.: *Elementary School Libraries,* Scarecrow Press, New York, 1961. Read chapter on purpose of the elementary school library.

Meriwether, C.: *Our Colonial School Curriculum 1607–1776,* Capitol Publishing Company, Washington, D.C., 1907. The best testimony to the richness of present-day elementary curricula can be gained by examining curricula of the past. This book contains a fascinating account of early elementary schools.

Monroe, W. S.: *The Development of Arithmetic as a School Subject,* U.S. Bureau of Education Bulletin 10, 1917. This book should be of special interest to the student aiming at elementary teaching. Arithmetic was the last of the three R's to achieve status.

Reeder, R. R.: *Historical Development of School Readers and Methods of Teaching Reading,* The Macmillan Company, New York, 1900. See especially chapters on early reading methods.

Reisner, E. H.: *Evolution of the Common School,* The Macmillan Company, New York, 1930. See chapters 1 to 3.

Ross, A. M.: *Education of Childhood,* George G. Harrap Co., Ltd., London, 1960. See pages 1 to 50.

Scanlon, K. L.: *Basic Facts and Principles of Elementary Education,* Collier Books, New York, 1963. Chapters 5 to 7.

Vandewalker, N. C.: *The Kindergarten in American Education,* The Macmillan Company, New York, 1908. Read chapters on the origins of the kindergarten in America and on the present theory of kindergarten education.

Zirbes, L.: *Focus on Values in Elementary Education,* G. P. Putnam's Sons, New York, 1960. See sections on challenges facing the elementary school teacher in the area of moral or character education.

chapter 7

Secondary Education

The same forces which operated to bring about the development of elementary education contributed to the rise of the high school in America. Secondary education—which the high school of the United States came to represent—did not respond immediately to democratic influences, owing mainly to the long and deeply ingrained traditions associated with all education beyond the rudiments. Even though secondary education in America evolved less rapidly than elementary education and moved more slowly and somewhat less surely on the road to popularity, the progress of the American public high school has been remarkable (see Figure 7-1). Accompanying the growth of public high schools, private secondary schools have made similar remarkable gains in enrollment (see Figure 7-2 and Table 7-1). The magnitude of public and private secondary education warrants a study of its foundations and of the rise of the high school in the United States.

THE FOUNDATIONS
OF SECONDARY EDUCATION

As we have already said, elementary schools were established to communicate to the young skills generally recognized as being essential to life in society. Another step was added to the educational ladder, and some of the young people were encouraged to test it when life in society became more complex and greater individual competence seemed imperative. It is more difficult to discover the exact origin of secondary education than it is to determine when elementary education began, and this is due primarily to the lack of definite and clear boundaries between the two. Not infrequently secondary education is defined as that stage or level of education above elementary and below higher. Obviously, such a definition is not very helpful. But with respect to the origin of secondary education, it seems clear that it was first undertaken in a private or tutorial relationship between a teacher and a learner. The teacher was in possession of a skill or knowledge which the learner was disposed to acquire—more often than not this skill or knowledge was practical in nature and therefore useful. The kind of education or instruction—elementary or secondary—could be determined by the difficulty of what was taught and by the maturity of the learner. As was true of most early education—formal or informal—the content and purpose of secondary education were practical.

The traditional practical nature of secondary education was radically altered by the Athenians. Their political and economic life, characterized by freedom and leisure for citizens, both permitted and encouraged them to speculate about the world and their relationship to it. This led to a change in the content and purpose of secondary education: that part of the Athenian population which was free could afford a kind of secondary education whose purpose was to refine its tastes and broaden its culture. The skills of the artisan or the knowledge of the soldier were not thought important enough to be given attention by secondary educators or secondary schools. The practical orientation of a former era was distilled into

Figure 7.1 Public High School Enrollment, 1920 to 1970. (*Digest of Educational Statistics*, U.S. Office of Education, Bulletin 1964, no. 18, 1964, pp. 8 and 14–15.)

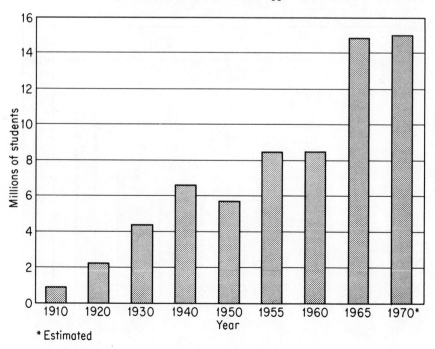

* Estimated

literary, philosophical, and cultural objectives, and the old educational objective of the Athenians—citizenship—was broadened to include individual culture.

Two types of secondary education or, rather, two emphases evolved eventually from the educational activity of the Athenians: philosophical and rhetorical. It can be said that both had the same liberating, or freeing, purpose, but the former conceived its functions in terms of the ultimate needs of man in society, whereas the latter concerned itself with practical wisdom and the development of man's capacity to make accurate temporal judgments. This division was sharpened by the subsequent educational theory and practice of the philosophers and the sophists and was bequeathed to later civilization in the intellectual tradition of the Greeks.

With the exception of certain Roman educational theorists, mainly Cicero (106–43 B.C.) and Quintilian (A.D. 35–95), separation of the speculative and the practical was continued in Rome. And Roman practices tended to accept the practical and the realistic as being proper content and objectives for secondary education. But this tradition and these practices were opposed by Quintilian:[1]

Figure 7.2 Enrollment in Nonpublic Secondary Schools, 1932 to 1970. (*Digest of Educational Statistics,* U.S. Office of Education, Bulletin 1964, no. 18, 1964, pp. 8 and 14–15.)

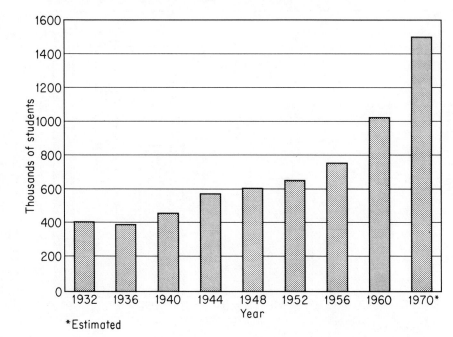

*Estimated

It is not a plodder in the forum or a mercenary pleader . . . that I desire to form but a man who being possessed of the highest natural genius stores his mind thoroughly with the most valuable kind of knowledge; a man sent by the gods to do honor to the world and such as no preceding age has known, a man in every way eminent and excellent, a thinker of the best thoughts and a speaker of the best language.

The importance of broad intellectual preparation unencumbered by a dedication to the practical was advanced also by Cicero:[2]

No man can be an orator possessed of every praiseworthy accomplishment, unless he has attained the knowledge of everything important and of all liberal arts, for his language must be ornate and copious from knowledge, since, unless there be beneath the surface matter understood and felt by the speaker, oratory becomes an empty and almost puerile flow of words.

Still, neither Quintilian nor Cicero ignored the practical, for their educated man—a public man of affairs—was well bred, cultivated in the arts, erudite, and, above all, skilled in oratory. Education, especially secondary education, could not, in their view, be divorced from life. The objective which both endorsed for education—the development of the pupil into a good man skilled in speaking—and the needs of Roman life influenced secondary schools in Rome to accept training in language and literature as their chief function. Other studies were added to the curriculum, but its

TABLE 7-1
Catholic Secondary School Statistics, 1915 to 1962

Year	Schools	Teachers	Students
1915	1,276	2,505	74,538
1920	1,552	7,915	129,848
1924	2,181	11,910	185,098
1928	2,129	13,489	225,845
1932	2,074	15,609	269,309
1936	1,984	17,016	288,864
1940	2,105	20,976	361,123
1944	2,128	24,595	420,707
1948	2,150	26,832	482,672
1952	2,189	27,770	505,572
1956	2,383	31,830	672,299
1962	2,435	34,090	945,785
1964	2,489	34,900	966,845

SOURCE: *Catholic Colleges and Schools*, Biennial Surveys, National Catholic Welfare Conference and *Digest of Educational Statistics*, U.S. Office of Education, Bulletin 1964, no. 18, 1964, pp. 32–34.

essential purpose was to furnish a linguistic-literary training as a basis for more advanced education. In the hands of the Romans, secondary education prospered and declined almost at the same time. It prospered with the organization of public grammar schools, and it declined with the change in Roman life which made the objectives of secondary education artificial and affected. The orator, or the public man, passed from the Roman political scene, but the function of the secondary school somehow remained the same; and because of its inflexibility and insensitiveness to change, it encouraged a divorce of secondary education from life itself. The kingpin of Roman education, rhetoric, became an end in itself and ceased to accept its former role as a natural instrument for expression of thought and feeling. The era of the artist and the public man was passing; that of the virtuoso was just beginning, and now we find the writer who writes not to convince, not to teach, or to move, but merely to display the versatility and the capacity of his skill. Men began to admire not the adaptation of language to thought, but the language itself.

By the end of the period of marked Roman influence on life in Europe —the early sixth century—grammar schools, those institutions that mark the awkward beginnings of modern secondary education, were still in evidence, but they were not vital either in their content or in their objectives. For the most part, they regained little of their lost favor in the centuries that separated the decline of Rome and the Renaissance. The Christian period had little need for the classical eloquence promoted by Roman secondary schools, although it did need secondary education to prepare young men for ecclesiastical and civil careers. At the same time, the public grammar schools gave way to secondary schools under religious, guild, or municipal auspices. It should be made clear that not all medieval secondary education was provided by the Church, but it should be emphasized also that the secondary schools of this period built their curricula around moral and religious literature, with an eye primarily to the needs of the Church and the education of the clergy. In this way secondary education regained both its useful character and its practical objective.

Beginning in the middle of the fourteenth century, many of the better minds of Europe turned their attention to the classics and were inspired by the humanistic lessons they contained. All of life was affected by this renewed interest in the ideals, life, and institutions of classical civilization. In education, in addition to a revival of classical language and literature in the schools' curricula, the objectives of citizenship and culture were reinstated, replacing the otherworldly outlook characteristic of most medieval studia, and the schools became places for preparing laymen for the art of living humanly rather than institutions mainly for the preparation of the clergy. Although the Renaissance had a negligible effect on elementary education, in secondary education its influence was both significant and lasting. Because of this influence, the distinction between elementary and secondary education became clearer than ever before. The distinction was one of language: secondary schools taught Latin, and elementary schools concerned themselves with the vernacular. The humanistic impress on secondary education was broad, deep, and lasting; yet it is not inaccurate to state that the clearest signs of its influence were seen first in the secondary schools of the Jesuits and those which followed the classical school model supplied by Johann Sturm in his Gymnasium at Strasbourg in 1539. There would seem to be little room for debate on this point: The foundations of all secondary education from the sixteenth century forward were laid by the Catholic Society of Jesus and the Lutheran classical scholar and schoolmaster Johann Sturm.

By defining the purpose of secondary education, by carefully organizing its curricula, and by selecting well-prepared, competent teachers, both the Jesuits and Sturm tried to blend classical language and literature with the spirit of Christianity. Their hope was to produce a broadly educated, sensitive, refined Christian. What the Jesuits and Sturm seemed to be able to do so well—for educational history unfailingly attests to the excellence of their schools—was badly mishandled in the hands of schoolmasters of lesser skill and dedication. Schoolmasters were not blameless, yet they alone were not at fault: By the end of the sixteenth century, secondary schools were available only to the children of the upper classes, and the objectives of these schools had been narrowed to the point where they were unreal. They placed an extraordinary confidence in Ciceronian eloquence. Here we have the prototype of secondary schools, transplanted to colonial America and first given institutional form in the Latin School of Boston in 1635.

SECONDARY EDUCATION
IN EARLY AMERICA

The Latin Grammar School

Pioneers who immigrated to colonial America came for various reasons: Some sought religious freedom; others were disenchanted with the political systems of their homeland and looked for a political metamorphosis in a new country; still others, unmindful of the need for religious or political refuge, came to America because the economic picture they saw was bright. Whatever the motives may have been prompting these people to uproot and look for new homes in a new land, they tried to remain true to their educational past by retaining familiar practices and patterns in secondary education. Considering the land of their origin, it is not surprising that the vast majority of colonial secondary schools were modeled after the Latin grammar schools of England. There was yet another inheritance. Because the founders of colonial secondary schools were sensitive to the religious dimension in education, their schools reflected the Reformation pattern of humanistic education common to the north of Europe rather than the liberal and aesthetic tendencies (and sometimes more human ones) of the south. Boys were sent to the Latin grammar school not so much to cultivate an aesthetic appreciation of the humanities as to prepare themselves for college and eventually, possibly, for service in church and public affairs. The main elements of the curriculum were humanistic rather than naturalistic and classical rather than scientific. They were intended to be socially useful, yet, paradoxically, Latin and Greek were usually stressed in such a narrow grammatical context that the chief advantage to be claimed for them was their formal discipline of the mind.

There was only one kind of secondary education in colonial America, although there may have been some differences in the way it was supported. Still, the essential character of the secondary schools could not be altered simply because they were supported out of philanthropy in the South or out of private, public, or church treasuries in other parts of the country. The principal features of the colonial Latin grammar school were sufficiently distinctive to warrant a summary here.

1. The general function of the Latin grammar school was made very clear in published statements and prepared prospectuses. It was to prepare young men by means of a classical curriculum for responsible positions in political and ecclesiastical society. It may be fairly doubted that the managers of these schools ever reneged on their stated purposes; on the other hand, it is seldom clear that the schools were equipped to fulfill in practice the goals set for them in theory. Most Latin grammar schools had to be satisfied with far narrower practical achievements. They began to interpret their function as one of preparation for college, and they left it to the college to finish the young man for the exigencies of the secular and ecclesiastical world. If we take into account the principal preoccupations of the colonial colleges, we begin to see the Latin grammar school as a quasi-ecclesiastical institution, a kind of minor seminary.

2. The course of studies to which the boys were exposed faithfully mirrored the school's objectives. Latin grammar and literature, Greek grammar and literature, parts of the Old and the New Testament, rhetoric, and the religious doctrines of the sect conducting the school made up the curriculum which every boy followed irrespective of his own personal interests or inclinations. The particular studies in this curriculum were carefully specified, especially in literature, where certain authors were read with almost unbelievable care. This practice was dictated by the colonial college which for one reason or another was served by a certain Latin grammar school. Entering college students were required to know

particular selections from Latin and Greek literature, and Latin grammar schools, finding no alternative to this dominance, simply complied.

3. The general routine of the school was devised without any real concern for the curricular or extracurricular interests or needs of the students. The school day was long—beginning early in the morning and continuing almost without interruption until late in the afternoon—and demanding. Discipline was severe, for schoolmasters on all levels accepted the doctrine that the teacher who taught with moderation was incompetent. Boys enjoyed few periods when, left to their own resources, they could plan their own recreation and benefit from the relaxation it could provide.

4. These schools were attended only by the sons of upper-class parents, and for this reason, mainly, were schools with small enrollments. The advantage that a small school may have in providing greater opportunity for adaptation of programs to needs and capacities was ignored, for, as we have said, the general policy governing such schools was to remain true to the educational doctrines of the past.

5. Latin grammar schools were tuition schools. In some parts of the country local communities, anxious to have a secondary school in evidence, offered financial enticements in the form of land grants or cash endowments, the latter raised out of fines or special levies. Despite indistinct signs of community generosity in these grants, it would be inaccurate to call Latin grammar schools publicly supported institutions. Throughout their long history they remained privately supported and looked to their students as the chief, and often the only, source of support.

6. Among the many masters associated with Latin grammar schools, some were dedicated, learned, skillful craftsmen, whose work advanced the status of learning in America and whose dedication paid huge dividends. These were the exceptions: for every dedicated and skillful schoolmaster, five had no real vocation, ability, or skill for teaching; they simply used teaching as a steppingstone to the ministry. The prospective master who was "sober and of good conversation" had all of the qualifications necessary for teaching in the usual Latin grammar school, provided, of course, that his denominational affiliations were appropriate and his doctrinal views sound. The prospective teachers' ability "to teach the tongues" (to teach Latin and probably Greek grammar and literature) seems to have been taken for granted.

Social change generated new educational vision, and upgraded educational opportunity supported and helped to consolidate social dynamism— the interrelationship was inevitable; religious unrest bred of discontent, with theological severity on the one hand and a revival of humanitarianism on the other, was channeled toward a greater reliance on personal confidence and competence; and a general awareness of the power of learning arising out of surprising and remarkable achievements in science led men to conclude that they needed, and should have, a kind of secondary education better suited to realities of life in their day. Traditional Latin grammar schools began to live on borrowed time. Fifty years before the advent of the nineteenth century, the *academy,* a secondary school with few ties to, and no allegiances with, the past appeared on the American scene.

The Academy

The theory of educational realism promoted by John Amos Comenius and the doctrine of utility formulated by Francis Bacon made their way across the Atlantic Ocean in the mid-eighteenth century and laid the theoretical foundations for a new kind of secondary education. Cautious educators in America were unwilling, or unable, to adopt and apply these theories to the schools of the country, but they could, and did, learn from them; and what they learned generated the basic motives for building secondary schools with curricular interests centering on English rather than Latin, applied science rather than literature, and curricular objectives committed to utility rather than culture. The theoretical conflict, by now centuries old, between learning for use, on the one hand, and learning for cultural values on the other was rejoined in America. Educators began to take sides; educational philosophies were reargued; prominent spokesmen on both sides began to emerge. The theory of utility was advocated and advanced by Benjamin Franklin, who had achieved an enviable reputation as a philosopher, author, statesman, and inventor. This man, who never tried to conceal a disdain bordering on contempt for the orthodoxies of education, as can be seen in his essay "Silence Dogood," supported a practical secondary school curriculum.[3] To further confirm his allegiance to utility, he established, in 1749, a school wherein the practical curriculum had an unrivaled status. In principle, the academy endorsed sound educational values, those esteemed by wise men and ones capable of qualifying persons to serve the public with honor both to themselves and their country. To achieve this high purpose of public service, students were entitled to the best educational opportunity public and private means could provide. As to their studies, Franklin said, it would be well if they could be taught everything useful and ornamental. "But art is long, and their time is short. It is therefore proposed that they learn those things that are likely to be most useful and most ornamental; regard being had to the several professions for which they are intended."[4]

Franklin's plan for secondary education was given both a fair hearing and thorough test throughout the nation. While the academy did not succeed in replacing the secondary schools preceding it in America, it had both a general and pervasive influence. Because of it, all secondary education was affected; old Latin grammar schools were unable to resist its influence, but they, in turn, because they were so deeply rooted in American educational life, were able to reshape the reforming institution itself. It would be a mistake to assume that the academy movement was always pure and unadulterated: academies found it impossible to remain true to the educational design of their founder and they tended to compromise; they often found some middle ground between the objectives of culture and utility to satisfy the needs of the students who came to them. Despite their willingness to compromise—to accept what in later years became the law of the educational world—they developed certain distinctive features which are identified in the following generalizations.

1. The first academy, opened by Franklin in Philadelphia, was founded without any formal preparatory objective. That this was so should not be surprising, for Franklin himself had little respect for the colleges of the country. He seemed unable to see, or to admit that he saw, any real value to the college course. Thus, the academy arose as a terminal secondary school, with objectives not going beyond the preparation of students for life in society.[5]

2. The curriculum of the academy, while not eliminating ancient and foreign languages from its course of studies, placed no special premium on them. Rather, it preferred to emphasize such practical subjects as writing, arithmetic, bookkeeping, English, history, and politics. But the institution was sufficiently flexible to alter even these curricular emphases when the needs of the students or the community justified such revisions. Thus, we find some academies teaching courses in religion, although Franklin clearly was no special friend of sectarianism in education.

3. Academies were far more successful than Latin grammar schools in identifying with the community: they tried to be community schools. This led in time to fairly generous community support—sometimes support from public sources in the form of land and money grants—followed by frequent and unwelcome efforts to exert public control over the school. In general, however, neither public support nor control was of sufficient magnitude to make the academy a genuine public institution.

4. These new secondary schools were considerably more democratic than Latin grammar schools. They sought their clientele from among the children of the middle class and, on various occasions, boasted of offering opportunities in secondary education for the common man. No doubt their doors were open to all students who could afford to attend, but since the academy always charged tuition fees, the sons of common men all too often found attendance financially impractical or impossible.

5. Throughout its long history both in Europe and colonial America, secondary education had never willingly offered girls any place in its classrooms. While in this respect the academy was not a great reforming institution, it did, nevertheless, offer parallel secondary education to girls in its feminine counterpart, the *female seminary*.

6. A secondary objective recognized by many academies, and one clearly stipulated for academies by Franklin, was educating teachers for the primary schools. In no sense were academies professional teacher-training agencies, but their curricula did contain many of the subjects—English, writing, reading, and arithmetic—found also in the curricula of elementary schools. So far as mastery of content was concerned, academy graduates were competent in elementary school subjects. How many turned to teaching and how effective they were when they did are moot questions.

Secondary education was both broadened and popularized by the influence of the academy movement. However, these schools continued to be hemmed in by tradition and did not fully achieve their purpose of providing a secondary education oriented to utility. They tended to cater to an elite clientele, and since boys who attended secondary schools usually aspired to college study, the terminal character of the early academy was redirected toward college preparation. In addition, much of the academy curriculum paralleled the curriculum of the nineteenth-century common school, rather than being built upon it. Finally, and generally, the academies were not able to maintain a level of educational democracy necessary to fulfill the requirements of a restless and growing America.

THE RISE OF THE HIGH SCHOOL

Further alterations were made in the image of secondary education as we move into the second quarter of the nineteenth century. For the second time in less than a hundred years, American ingenuity was able to develop a new approach to secondary education. Earlier, this new approach was found in the academy; now it was the turn of the high school. Founded in 1821, in Boston, the high school purported to offer educational opportunities to boys enabling them to fulfill their respective roles in the economic world of affairs. The new Boston high school, never in any sense a business institute, followed the theory that secondary education should achieve a balance between utility and culture. The new school may not have been able to fulfill its mission entirely, yet it did exert an influence strong enough both to perpetuate its kind and the Boston school itself: high schools are found the country over, and Boston English High School (originally, Boston English Classical School) still ranks among the best of the land.

Factors Contributing to the Development of the High School

The contribution of the academy. The academy was not a genuine public institution—it was not fully supported by public taxation—although some communities did contribute to its maintenance. Land grants, too, were quite common, but this limited support, when afforded, was not sufficient to motivate the academy to open its doors to all children on equal terms: it retained much of the exclusiveness of the Latin grammar school. The academy, moreover, was not directly subject to state control and did not become part of the common or public school system. By remaining essentially private schools, academies made another kind of secondary education more imperative.

Thomas Jefferson's plan for education. As early as 1779, Thomas Jefferson presented his Bill for the More General Diffusion of Knowledge to the Virginia Legislature.[6] Because Jefferson recognized the relationship between an educated electorate and self-government, his proposal contained constructive measures to eliminate political inequality by demanding that education be made available to all the children of all the people of Virginia. Although moderate when examined from the perspective of our time, Jefferson's proposal was considered far too liberal, or radical, for the lawmakers to accept. The bill provided for three years of elementary education at public expense for all the children of the commonwealth; in addition, it made secondary and higher education available for poor but able students.

Jefferson's bill embodied an ideal—one considered to be visionary and therefore unacceptable—but the ideal was sound, and in time it became a reality. It would be unfair to many other thoughtful men of the time to claim that Jefferson was alone in his demand for an extension of educational opportunity, but his position and the respect which he enjoyed contributed to the preservation of his ideal. Although Jefferson's proposal was not accepted, it marked the beginning of a movement which resulted sometime later in tax support for public education and motivated the establishment of secondary schools which concentrated on practical and secular subjects. The type of secondary education advocated by Jefferson cannot be determined clearly from the bill, but his views on the subject may be inferred from the curricular reform directed by him at the College of William and Mary. Through Jefferson's influence, the divinity school was suppressed, and legal and medical studies were raised to important positions in the curriculum.

Jefferson was not directly responsible for the creation of the American high school, but he did contribute to what it was to become. First, he called for secondary education for more people; second, he demanded that public education be practical and secular. Both positions came to be accepted in much of American public secondary education.

The influence of monitorial schools. Early in the nineteenth century, education became a subject for study in some European universities; psychology and its application to instruction were of special interest. This trend, although not strong, was noticeable, and it attracted American students, who traveled to Europe to study in European universities under professors engaged in laying the foundations of the science of education. Upon their return to America, these students, filled with zeal and a spirit of romantic humanitarianism, became educational reformers. Their general objective was an extension of educational opportunity. They regarded education, as others before and since, as the solution of, or panacea for, all individual and social problems. But they were faced from the outset with the practical problem of the cost of education. Even pioneer schools cost money to operate, and in the early nineteenth century, few taxpayers were willing to support schools with tax money.

The reformers had two immediate goals; and, typical of reformers, they pursued both with equal vigor. Popularizing education was their first objective: the people had to be convinced of the need for education if they were going to support it. In time the crusade for public support was successful. The second objective was to provide educational programs or opportunities which cost very little: this was done by importing the monitorial plan to America.

The monitorial plan was a system of instruction devised by Joseph Lancaster (1778–1838) and Andrew Bell (1753–1832) whereby one teacher could teach 200 to 1,000 students at one time in a single room. This remarkable feat was accomplished by dividing the students into groups and placing a monitor—an older student—over each group. The teacher taught the monitors, who in turn instructed their respective groups. A master promoting the monitorial plan could boast, "Give me twenty-four pupils today, and I shall give you back twenty-four teachers tomorrow."

After enjoying something resembling popularity for about a quarter of a century, monitorial schools were rejected as being unworthy of, and unsuited to, the educational needs and aspirations of America. But the schools of Lancaster and Bell were not abandoned until something better was offered; the shortcomings of the monitorial schools contributed to the creation of the American high school.

Legislation affecting high schools. The Boston English Classical School for Boys, founded in 1821, is generally recognized as America's first public high school, although the name "high school" was not used in connection with this school until 1824, and in 1832 the name of the school was changed again to English Classical School.

The immediate reason for the creation of a secondary school which included no language other than English in its curriculum and tended definitely toward practical studies was that Boston was becoming a great commercial center and young men with commercial skills were in demand. Merchants wanted the skills of clerks and bookkeepers, skills which the old classical curriculum of the usual secondary schools did not develop. The Boston high school was not narrowly vocational, but it did emphasize in its studies that training necessary for success in everyday economic activities.

State legislation did not require the establishment of the Boston English Classical School for Boys. It was permitted, even encouraged, by the Act of 1647 and subsequent educational statutes, but until 1827 no specific law pertaining to high schools was passed. In 1827 the High School Act, sponsored by James Carter, passed the Massachusetts General Assembly. This law required towns with a population of 500 families to employ a teacher competent to teach the common branches: United States history, bookkeeping, geometry, surveying, and algebra. Towns with a population of 4,000 inhabitants were required to engage a teacher for Latin, Greek, history, rhetoric, and logic.

In 1859 another law, based on the Act of 1827, but more specific than the earlier law, provided, in addition to prescribing the maintenance of, elementary schools, ". . . that every town may and every town containing 500 families or householders, shall" establish a school in which instruction would be given in general history, bookkeeping, surveying, geometry, natural philosophy, chemistry, botany, civil policy, and the Latin language. Every town with 4,000 inhabitants was required to offer instruction, in addition to the above-named subjects, in Greek, French, geology, rhetoric, astronomy, political economy, and intellectual and moral philosophy. The act permitted adjacent towns, each having less than 500 inhabitants, to create a high school district and establish a high school.

Other states became interested in high schools and provided for them by law. In New York the Union School Act of 1853 permitted the development of high schools. Michigan, in 1859, enacted a law permitting graded school districts to establish a high school or an "academical department" in a union school. The movement for high schools became general in all except the Southern states.

Encouragement implicit in the Morrill Act. The famous Land-grant College Act passed by Congress in 1862 had an indirect but important effect on the development of high schools. The agricultural college, which had its origin in this legislation, or the college which had been established earlier by the state and now gained additional financial support from the act motivated a young man to complete a high school course. Here was a college which could offer practical studies; knowledge could be used to advance farming and other useful arts. But a high school course was necessary for matriculation in almost every agricultural college. It was only natural for local school districts to establish local high schools to prepare boys for the agricultural college.

State control and the high school. Throughout most of the colonial period and for part of the national period, education was considered to be a proper and almost exclusive function of local communities. We have noted the legislative enactments during the first years and are aware that laws controlling education were rare.[7] State authority had not yet extended itself to the practical affairs of the school by the first quarter of the nineteenth century, but state control of education became a reality before the century was half over, and this control contributed to the development of high schools which were to be standardized throughout the state. State supervision and control hastened the formation of an institution which otherwise might have taken several more decades to develop. In 1859, whether in Michigan or in Massachusetts, high schools were not common. Had they been common, legislation requiring or permitting them would not have been enacted. But it is safe to say as well that legislation would not have been enacted if the people had not been sympathetic to the high school movement.

The fact that a state could require the establishment of, and prescribe much of the curriculum for, the high schools indicates that there had been a decided revision in the older concept that local government enjoyed autonomy in educational affairs; and curtailing local prerogatives in such a relatively short time testifies to the quality of educational leadership during the second and third quarters of the nineteenth century. It is not necessary, of course, to agree that the direction taken by these educational leaders was always right, but we are required to admit, after examining the record of history, that it was effective.

Integrating the High School into an Educational System

By 1821 a school for every educational level had been developed in the United States, but the establishment of these schools had been accomplished with little or no concern for preceding or succeeding educational levels. Elementary schools were charged with the development of the rudiments; colleges were usually professional schools or offered studies preliminary to professional programs. There was, however, little integration between high schools and elementary schools or between high schools and colleges. Although never completely successful in achieving an integration of the various levels, an attempt was made after 1874 to establish a general educational structure in which each level could find an acceptable relationship or articulation with the other levels. There were two significant events which gave direction to the efforts for systematizing American education: one was the Kalamazoo decision, the other the meeting of the Committee of Ten.

The Kalamazoo decision. The event marking the beginning of a period dedicated to educational systematization was the Kalamazoo decision, a decision favorable to the extension of the high school. Had the court's decision been the reverse of what it was, the death knell of the high school as a public institution might well have been sounded then and there. The case brought before the courts in 1872, in Kalamazoo, Michigan (*Stuart v. School District No. 1*), had several minor issues, none of which need our attention here. But the large question, the one on which the fate of the high school depended, was the constitutionality of the Michigan High School Act of 1859.

It will be recalled that the law of 1859 permitted the establishment of a high school in graded school districts and implied that funds collected for school support could be used for high schools. The legal issue, then, which the courts were called upon to interpret was: May public funds be used for the support of high schools?

The citizens responsible for initiating litigation contended that the high school was part of higher education—a private matter to be cared for by personal means—and that the constitution did not provide for its support out of tax money. It may be of some interest to interpolate here that the suit was a friendly suit: that is, Charles Stuart and the other people who joined with him in contesting the legality of the Michigan law of 1859 were not opposed to the practice of supporting high schools with public money; they merely wanted the constitutionality of the law clarified. Such concern was certainly reasonable and commendable, for as good citizens they were reluctant to see a vast system of public high schools destroyed if, at some later date, the law of 1859 was declared unconstitutional.

The case passed through the lower courts until it reached the Supreme Court of Michigan. The supreme court decided that not only was a high school a legal institution within the context of Michigan's constitution but it was the intention of the constitution that a system of public education from the elementary school through the state university be supported by public funds. The opinion of the court as to the legality of high schools was stated as follows: [8]

> . . . These facts . . . demonstrate clearly and conclusively a general state policy, beginning in 1817 and continuing until after the adoption of the present constitution, in the direction of free schools in which education, and at their option the elements of classical education, might be brought within the reach of all the children of the State. . . . We might follow the subject further and show that the subsequent legislation has all concurred with this policy, but it would be a waste of time and labor. We content ourselves with the statement that neither in our state policy, in our constitution, or in our laws, do we find the primary-school districts restricted in the branches of knowledge which their officers may cause to be taught, or in the grade of instruction that may be given, if their voters consent in regular form to bear the expense and raise the taxes for the purpose.

The legislation of 1859 was upheld by this legal victory for high schools in Michigan.

Obviously, the constitution of Michigan or any interpretation of it by a Michigan court could not be binding on any other state. But as it developed, the Kalamazoo decision was accepted as a general precedent, and the position of the high school as part of the structure of public education was made secure. The right of high schools to share in public funds was not again open to serious legal question. The court's decision did not establish high schools or require that they be established. This was still a matter for the school districts to decide. The court's decision did, however, provide a solid legal foundation upon which high schools could be built. It may be noted, too, that high schools in and out of Michigan had been receiving public support for many years prior to the Kalamazoo case. The use of tax money for high schools was not a practice instituted by the court; the decision was merely an interpretation of the Michigan constitution which held such practices to be legal. Nevertheless, although admitting the limitations of the court's decision, the clarification of the legal issue surrounding support served as an impetus to the establishment of high schools everywhere. Probably more than any other single event, the decision in the Kalamazoo case served to accelerate the high school movement, and by 1890 there was every indication that it was to become a popular institution.

The Committee of Ten. The National Education Association appointed a Committee of Ten on Secondary School Studies in July, 1892. For some years prior to 1892, college administrators were concerned with the variety of entrance requirements which the different colleges imposed on prospective students. The majority of the colleges were privately controlled and supported, and each was accustomed to going its own way. For some years the requirements for college admission were surprisingly high, although there was an amazing lack of uniformity among them. Quite possibly, a student who could fulfill admission requirements for Harvard would not be qualified for admission to any other college.

In the interests of contributing to some semblance of uniformity, the presidents of several Eastern colleges held informal meetings to discuss the possibility of arriving at a code for college entrance requirements. Charles W. Eliot, president of Harvard, and Nicholas Murray Butler, president of Columbia, were key figures in these meetings. The meetings resulted eventually in the formation of the College Board, a forerunner of the Committee on College Entrance Requirements, and the College Board attempted to resolve the problems of admission which were resulting from the variety of high school offerings and the rigidity of college admission policies. At this time, about 1880, the majority of applicants for college had taken their secondary studies in preparatory schools, not public high schools.

But the number of high school graduates seeking admission to college was sufficiently large to warrant some consideration. There was some indication, too, that high schools were resisting the "strangle hold" that the colleges had consistently maintained on the high school curriculum. High schools were intended, of course, to prepare students for the practical world of affairs and not for college, but in actual practice the curriculum of the high school was preparatory rather than terminal.

At the same time, colleges were undergoing a marked change in their objectives and curricula.[9] They were retreating from the tradition, long and fairly honorably maintained, that within their walls a liberal education could be obtained. In place of a liberal curriculum they were directing their attention, as the high schools were intended to do from the beginning, to the demands of the society which surrounded them. In other words, by refusing to liberalize their entrance requirements, the colleges were asking the high schools to continue a curriculum which the colleges were no longer sure was important. Certainly the position of the colleges was untenable in demanding preparation which they, for the most part, did not really value. To resolve the problems arising out of a confusion of aims and curricula, the Committee of Ten was appointed. It should be understood that the Committee of Ten was a body without any real authority in a legal sense: it could make recommendations, but it had no power to demand compliance with any of its recommendations.

Five of the ten members of the committee were college presidents. They could speak for the colleges which they represented, and because these colleges were prominent and powerful academically, there was the implication, though no official commitment, that these members spoke for most of the other colleges also. The committee was weighted heavily with the college point of view.[10]

As the first order of business, the committee defined the purpose of the high school. In its definition the committee refused to acknowledge the position so long assumed by the colleges and apparently accepted by many high schools that the function of the high school was college preparation. The committee recognized the high school's function in relation to college preparation but identified its primary function as terminal—preparing students for life. More specifically, the committee's report contained recommendations which contributed to the integration of the high school into the educational system:

1. The foundation for high school studies should be laid in the elementary school.
2. All high school pupils should be taught in the same way, and distinctions should not be made in curricula for students planning to enter college.
3. Programs of study should be organized in which the several subjects would be approximately equivalent.

4. The high school program, for purposes of college entrance, should be evaluated quantitatively.

Reorganizing secondary education. Educational consciousness was both keen and general in nineteenth-century America; but whenever this consciousness fermented, the secondary level was most directly affected. By 1900 the accepted pattern for education consisted of an eight-year elementary school, a four-year high school, and a four-year college. American school organization had evolved slowly and indecisively; now the 8-4-4 system was accepted. Its acceptance, however, was extremely short-lived, for either just before or just after the advent of the twentieth century, plans were advanced for reorganizing the schools. The new plans usually called for a shorter period assigned to elementary education, the creation of a new unit standing between the elementary school and the high school, an abbreviated senior high-school course, and a two-year college program pursued either in a local or a regional junior college. Of the many plans advanced for school system reorganization, the one given most attention and eventually the one most widely accepted was 6-3-3-2: a six-year elementary school, a three-year junior high school, a three-year senior high school, and a two-year junior college.

The theoretical justification for reorganization can be expressed in a single word—articulation. Articulation really pointed in two directions and hoped to accomplish good results by going both ways. First, the theory of articulation was concerned with the student as a growing and maturing social person. His emotions, his social growth, as well as his maturing mentality were increasingly recognized, and educational opportunity following the 8-4-4 plan was found wanting. Transfers from elementary to secondary and from secondary school to college were made, according to educators who put articulation on its psychological bases, at precisely the wrong time for optimum emotional and personality development. Support was found for reorganized schools from psychologically oriented educators. Another justification for reorganization came in the form of curricular articulation. In this context, it was argued, experiences of the student and his upward movement on the educational ladder are both broadened and accelerated by a school arrangement capitalizing on student experiential growth and interest. Curricular articulation suggested, or was sympathetic to, an educational ladder endorsed by proponents of the 6-3-3-2 plan.

Without ever clearly demonstrating its validity, defenders of the reorganized school regularly adopted the view that the 8-4-4 plan militated against social, emotional, and curricular articulation. Even today we look in vain for convincing evidence of greater curricular or social articulation in reorganized schools; nor are we certain of the reorganized school's greater success in attaining its objectives; on the other hand, there is no evidence that reorganized schools are less capable of fulfilling broad educational needs than traditionally organized schools. Now almost sixty-five years old, reorganized schools have had their greatest influence on structure rather than content or outcomes. They represent another way to organize formal educational experiences.

DETERMINING THE PURPOSES OF SECONDARY EDUCATION

In 1635 the Boston Latin Grammar School, the first secondary school founded in the English Colonies, opened its doors to students. What was the principal motive contributing to this school's founding? In general it reflected the long-standing tradition that secondary schools should be preparatory institutions. The school had the principal purpose of preparing boys for college. There were no colleges in the Colonies in 1635, but colleges were anticipated, and until they were established, boys wanting a college education were expected to get it in one of the English colleges. After 1635 many Latin grammar schools were established throughout the Colonies, especially in New England. With not a single exception, Latin grammar schools conceived their objectives to be intimately associated with college preparation. After 1751 the academy began to compete with the Latin grammar school and eventually became more popular than its older competitor. But the academy, too, although its original purpose was to prepare students for practical, worldly activities, became a college preparatory institution. Undoubtedly the program of studies offered by the academy was broader than that of the old Latin grammar school; but regardless of the enlarged scope of its curriculum, the academy was, in fact, a preparatory school for college. This did not mean that everyone who attended the academy continued into college—everyone who studied at the Latin grammar school did not go to college—but it did mean that the school's program was geared to the demands of a college curriculum.

Even the first high school—Boston, 1821—and those which followed tended to pattern a program after that which had been common in the earlier secondary schools. For about 250 years the secondary schools in the Colonies and the United States accepted, almost without question, the preparatory function of secondary education. This was neither strange nor unusual. A vast majority of students in secondary schools were there because they intended to go to college; the secondary school accepted its preparatory function and did its best to give a specific foundation for college studies. From another point of view, it was almost impossible for secondary education to do anything else. Colleges had strict entrance requirements, although they were not always high. There was a great variety in the specific preparation demanded from college to college, but each college, before

1870, demanded a preparatory course of every student who applied for admission. If most students in secondary schools wanted to enter college, and if colleges without exception demanded preparatory programs of applicants, the secondary school was without an alternative. It had to concentrate on college preparatory curricula. Thus, the major objective of secondary education came to be preparation of students for college.

The liberalizing influences of American life, the apparent need for expanded educational opportunity beyond the elementary school, and the induction of the high school as part of the public school system were factors which caused educators and interested citizens to study the purposes of high schools. Besides, in the late nineteenth century, when the high school began to take shape as a popular institution, a majority of high school students were not going on to college. Did these considerations warrant a reorganization of high school objectives and curricula? Answers to this question began to emerge as early as 1893 in the *Report of the Committee of Ten.*

The Influence of the Committee of Ten

The Committee of Ten dealt with many problems concerning secondary education, but here we are interested in its findings having a bearing on the objectives of secondary education. It may be noted again that the membership of the Committee of Ten had strong college ties. It would have been surprising indeed had the committee resolved that secondary education abandon college preparation as its primary function. However, the committee did this very thing. It proposed that secondary education have a dual purpose: that of readying students for college and preparing them for life. Since, in 1892, there were more secondary or high school graduates who were not going on to college than who were, the committee suggested that preparation for life be given first place as the objective for secondary education. The implication became rather apparent, moreover, that specific preparatory studies were not essential to success in college, although it was recognized that at that time some such subjects were necessary for admission to college.

The *Report of the Committee of Ten* was the first serious break with tradition. Throughout most of its history in America, secondary education had been committed to one goal: preparation for college. After 1893 it became committed to two goals: college preparation and preparation for life. The latter goal was accepted as the more important. The authors of the report maintained that the secondary schools of the United States, taken as a whole, did not exist for the purpose of preparing boys and girls for college. Only an insignificant percentage of the graduates of high schools, they pointed out, went on to colleges or scientific schools. The main function of the secondary school, the report continued, is to prepare for the duties of life that small proportion of all the children in the country—a proportion small in number, but very important to the welfare of the nation—who show themselves able to profit by an education continued through the secondary school and whose parents are able to support them while they remain in school for that length of time. The authors of the report did not ignore the private and endowed secondary schools of the United States that made it their principal objective to prepare students for colleges and universities, but neither did they fail to notice that the number of such schools was small. The general view was stated succinctly: A secondary school program intended for national use must be made available to children whose education would not extend beyond the secondary school. The preparation of a few pupils for college or university studies should in the ordinary secondary school be an incidental objective. At the same time, it was pointed out, all college and university courses should be accessible to boys and girls who had completed creditably the high school course. Parents often do not decide as early as four years before college age is attained whether or not they want their children to attend college, and students themselves may not know until they are about ready to complete the high school course whether they want to continue their education. To assure successful high school graduates of a fair hearing on their college applications, the colleges, the committee wrote, should be ready to accept to appropriate courses of instruction every graduate of a solid high school course. This principle guiding admissions was believed to be valid and operative regardless of the subjects pursued by the student in high school. The committee anticipated the college's response on its admissions proposal and in its *Report* summarized the reaction it believed most acceptable. The gist of the committee's view was as follows: [11]

A college might say: We shall accept for admission any groups of studies taken from the secondary school program, providing the sum of the studies taken in each of the four years amounts to at least sixteen periods a week, and that in each year at least four of the subjects presented shall have been pursued at least three periods a week and that at least three of the subjects shall have been pursued three years or more.

The recommendations of the Committee of Ten marked the beginning of a new era in the determination of high school objectives and curricula. In addition to redefining the high school's principal purpose, the *Report* clearly established a quantitative measure of secondary education and endorsed the principle of equivalence of studies. The committee's work, however, was only a beginning: later committees, conferences, commissions, and studies built upon the foundation laid in the *Report* and continued the examination of high school objectives and studies.

The Committee on College Entrance
Requirements and Others

The trend toward liberalization of the studies in secondary education was continued in the resolutions of the Committee of Fifteen, in 1895; the Committee on Six Year Courses, 1907, 1908, 1909; and the Committee on Economy of Time in Education, 1909 to 1913. Liberalizing studies meant, of course, freeing secondary curricula from the domination of the colleges and permitting secondary schools to determine for themselves their programs of study. Freedom for secondary education was an objective made quite explicit in the "Resolves" of the Committee on College Entrance Requirements in 1899.[12]

Still, with all this apparent desire for freedom, and with all these proposals for liberalization of high school studies, the high schools continued to be guided in the formation of their curricula by the colleges that some of their students would attend. Until 1918 there was every indication that secondary schools as a group were caught between two fires: they wanted to throw off the domination of the colleges, but they wanted to be sure that their students would be acceptably prepared for college.

The Committee on Reorganization
of Secondary Education

By 1918, when the Committee on Reorganization of Secondary Education met, secondary education had made noteworthy progress in America. From the end of the Civil War to the turn of the century, steady progress had been made in popularizing the high school, but it was the rapid, almost phenomenal heightening in popularity of secondary education from 1890 to 1918 which enabled the Committee on Reorganization to complete the work begun by the Committee of Ten and bestow a new character on the high schools of the United States. The liberalization of secondary education, although undertaken first by the Committee of Ten and furthered by the work of other committees, was not complete by 1918. The Committee on Reorganization, noting the modifications taking place in secondary education and particularly in the secondary school population—1 pupil for every 210 of the total population attended the secondary school in 1889–1890; 1 for every 121 in 1899–1900; 1 for every 89 in 1909–1910; and 1 for every 73 in 1914–1915—proposed that there be a further broadening of the scope of secondary education. The *Report* of the committee called attention to the wide range and varying capacities of pupils who were then attending high schools and admitted that a large number of those who entered the school could not complete the full course. It was estimated that of 9 students entering the four-year high school only 1 would be successful in completing the four-year program. In many cases, but not all, this high mortality rate was due to lack of ability; equally important was the lack of challenge that the high school curriculum contained for students without college aspirations.

After reviewing the changes which had taken place and those which were taking place in society, the committee examined the character of the secondary school population. From there it moved on to explore changing educational theory. It recognized individual differences and commended them to the attention of secondary educators; asked for a reinterpretation and reexamination of subject values, this in view of the declining importance of the theory of formal discipline; reasserted the importance of determining the value of knowledge by testing all knowledge in terms of life activities; and endorsed the theory, then and now the basis for the reorganized secondary school, of continuity in the development of children.

The committee believed that the changes in society, the changes in school population, and the changes in educational theory required a drastic reform of secondary education. This reform was to begin, according to the committee's *Report,* with the acceptance of the *Seven Cardinal Principles,* which were developed by the committee and presented in its *Report.*[13]

The committee's function, as defined by its parent organization, the National Education Association, was to:

1. Formulate statements of valid aims, efficient methods, and kinds of material whereby each subject might best serve the needs of high school pupils
2. Enable the inexperienced teacher to secure at the outset a correct point of view
3. Place the needs of the high school before all agencies that were training teachers for positions in high schools
4. Secure college entrance recognition for courses that would meet the needs of high school pupils

The committee conceived of democratic education, both in and out of school, as having the objective of developing in each individual the knowledge, interests, ideals, habits, and powers whereby he would be able to find his place in society and direct both himself and society toward noble ends. In the high school this objective was to be secured, according to the committee's report, by organizing the curricula of secondary education to achieve (1) health, (2) command of the fundamental processes, (3) worthy home membership, (4) vocational efficiency, (5) citizenship, (6) worthy use of leisure, and (7) ethical character. These objectives, the Seven Cardinal Principles of secondary education, gained immediate and general acceptance as goals for American high schools.

The Eight Year Study

In 1932, thirty-nine years after the *Report of the Committee of Ten* was issued, the Eight Year Study was undertaken. Almost as soon as the *Report of the Committee of Ten* was published, college entrance requirements were liberalized. These liberalizations—actually attempts to make the college articulate more closely with the high school—continued to be achieved in practice down through the years, and the doctrine of equivalence of studies contained in the *Report of the Committee of Ten* received more and more sympathetic attention. But colleges continued to state some requirements for admission in terms of units of subject matter, and these requirements limited the freedom of some high schools. The spread of progressive education into the field of secondary education gave rise to even greater impatience with these requirements for college entrance.

Progressives were not very much interested in subject matter; their main interest was with the ongoing experiences of young people. Subject matter was only one way, and often not a very important way, for enriching these experiences. With a curriculum based on students' experiences, progressive secondary schools were unable to fulfill college entrance requirements exactly. Still, though they could not fulfill the letter of these requirements, they felt that they were able to more than fulfill their spirit. To prove this, the Eight Year Study was undertaken.

Two hundred and fifty colleges agreed to participate with thirty progressive high schools in an eight-year study. The purpose of the study was to determine whether conventional college preparatory curricula were more useful to a student's achievement in college than progressively organized high school curricula. Upon the principals' recommendation, students from the thirty high schools were admitted to the cooperating colleges without the usual entrance requirements. At the end of eight years, the achievement of the students from the thirty high schools was compared with that of college students who had been prepared for college by other, more conventional curricula. The results of this study were published in 1942.[14] They suggest that the conventional college preparatory curriculum does not contribute so much to a student's success in college as was generally thought and that success in college does not depend on study of certain subjects for a prescribed length of time in the secondary school.

Statements of the Educational
Policies Commission

In 1938 the Educational Policies Commission of the National Education Association prepared a report called *The Purposes of Education in American Democracy*. This report listed four large objectives for education: (1) self-realization, (2) good human relationships, (3) economic efficiency,

(4) civic responsibility. Each of the large objectives was capable of further subdivision, self-realization, for example, having the subitems of the inquiring mind, speech, reading, writing, numbering, sight and hearing, health knowledge, public health, recreation, intellectual interests, aesthetic interests, and character.

Continuing its work toward defining goals for education, and particularly for secondary education, the Educational Policies Commission, in a report entitled *Education for All American Youth,* 1944, presented a list of ten imperative needs of young people. The needs, as listed, are intended to serve as a basis for educational planning and for the formulation of policies for secondary education:[15]

1. All youth need to develop saleable skills and those understandings and attitudes that make the worker an intelligent and productive participant in economic life. To this end, most youth need supervised work experience as well as education in the skills and knowledge of their occupations.
2. All youth need to maintain and develop good health and physical fitness.
3. All youth need to understand the rights and duties of a citizen of a democratic society and to be diligent and competent in the performance of their obligations as members of the community and citizens of the state and nation.
4. All youth need to understand the significance of the family for the individual and society and the conditions conducive to successful family life.
5. All youth need to know how to purchase and use goods and services intelligently, understanding both the values received by the consumer and the economic consequences of their acts.
6. All youth need to understand the methods of science, the influence of science on human life, and the main scientific facts concerning the nature of the world and of man.
7. All youth need opportunities to develop their capacities to appreciate beauty in literature, art, music, and nature.
8. All youth need to be able to use their leisure time well and to budget wisely, balancing activities that yield satisfaction to the individual with those which are socially useful.
9. All youth need to develop respect for other persons, to grow in their insights into ethical values and principles, and to be able to live and work cooperatively with others.
10. All youth need to grow in their ability to think rationally, to express their thoughts clearly, and to read and listen with understanding.

Purposes of Catholic Education

Catholic secondary schools, consistent with the general objectives of Catholic education, have been established to provide broad educational opportunities for Catholic youth. They are grounded on the theological and philosophical principle that men live in three worlds—the physical, the human, and the spiritual—and are not adequately instructed or realistically educated unless they have intellectual contact with these worlds. Contrary to some popularly held opinions, Catholic secondary schools are not concerned exclusively with the development of moral and theological virtues, although they are understandably impatient with schools and educators who refuse to value these virtues. Catholic secondary schools try to be value-centered, but they accept a clear commitment to intellectual development; for if they are not concerned primarily with what can be taught, they are not good schools. The first requirement of the Catholic school, the first requirement of any school, is that it be an intellectual agency: it must be concerned with graduating boys and girls who will be good citizens, effective members of family and other social units, and intelligent and devoted Catholics. The fact that all of the graduates of Catholic secondary schools do not fulfill the expectations of Catholic education in no way weakens the Catholic school's position or detracts from the worth of the objectives it accepts. Individual responsibility cannot be replaced by instruction, although it can be strengthened by instruction when there is good will, and the free will of the human person can reject and refuse to accept validly presented objective ideals. The role played by Catholic secondary schools is in many respects more demanding than those assigned public secondary schools, for it represents a broad education which can be organized only by drawing on the resources of man's three worlds.

The Catholic secondary school, then, is first of all an intellectual agency devoted to teaching; it accepts responsibility for laying an intellectual foundation upon which a value system may be built. Beyond this, its concern is with preparing students for later social, economic, and political responsibilities.

Catholic secondary schools have experienced an internal evolution far more remarkable than their external growth. In their first years after transplantation to the United States, they honored European education precedents and geared their objectives to those of ecclesiastical seminaries. Thus, their curricula and objectives were clerically and professionally centered. Liberalization came slowly, but it came; eventually, parish secondary schools were built on the foundations of existing elementary schools and became a regular part of the parochial school system. In assuming this new status, they found it necessary to offer attractive and meaningful educational opportunities to boys and girls of varying interests and abilities. In its educational and instructional program, the Catholic secondary school tries to offer the comprehensive and varied opportunities now so common in public high schools. But there are differences between the two schools —the public and the Catholic—and where differences are found, they are real and essential. These differences are based on the Catholic conception of man's nature and the meaning of education.

What are the principal educational purposes generally accepted by Catholic secondary schools?

1. *Mastery of the tools of Education.* Because of its traditional devotion to high intellectual performance, Catholic education naturally places a premium on excellence. The Catholic secondary school, therefore, willingly accepts the challenge with respect to mastery and tries to graduate students who are adept in the important skills of reading, writing, and computing. When these skills are mastered earlier, there is no need for the high school to concentrate on them; but the experience of teachers in all kinds of secondary schools runs counter to the belief that these skills do not need constant and unrelenting attention. There are, moreover, good reasons for developing courses in which these skills may be offered again to students who for reasons of lack of ability or lack of interest could not master them in the elementary school. Today's high school is a multipurpose institution: it maintains a regular academic pace for average students; it offers special programs—honors and advanced placement, etc.—for above average students; and it organizes remedial courses for students who have learned slowly in the past and have a definite need for remedial curricula.

2. *Assimilation of a tested social inheritance.* Catholic secondary schools are essentially conservative in their approach to curricular objectives. They acknowledge values inherent in the social, cultural, literary, and scientific inheritance of mankind and hope to preserve and perpetuate them. To answer the question: What should the curriculum contain? Curriculum directors of Catholic schools respond by organizing the curriculum around a common core of basic culture. They include in their courses not only the best literature, but tested scientific knowledge, and authentic and acknowledged social and cultural values as well. The curricular philosophy of Catholic secondary education endorses teaching the student what he does not know and in so doing concentrating—because of the great accumulation of knowledge, everything cannot be taught—on content tested by time and experience. Students leaving schools should have reasonably well-informed minds; the most efficient way of achieving this goal is by putting them in contact with curricula built on the stored wisdom of the ages. Because of its conservative approach to curricular content, Catholic secondary education is sometimes labeled anachronistic; yet despite the claims of its detractors, Catholic secondary education is not unmindful of the present or the future. The best way to form minds, it assumes, is to expose them to, and inspire them by, experiences of high quality.

3. *Continued development of moral and theological virtues.* In its total educational program, including everything done in the classroom as well as everything else that falls under the school's jurisdiction, Catholic

secondary education accepts a responsibility for creating a climate or a social and educational environment wherein its students may perfect both their moral and religious life. All of the school's cocurricular functions are really laboratories for moral formation: these activities, when properly guided and supervised, make it easier for students to accept objective ideals and incorporate them into their personal value systems. In addition, religious observances and devotions intimately related to the school's life set a tone and provide an example for a healthy spiritual life. In accepting the development of moral and theological virtues as authentic purposes for secondary education, Catholic schools make undeniable contributions to the common good by helping to form patriotic and effective citizens and intelligent and practical Catholics.

4. *Satisfaction of individual needs.* Catholic educators have always recognized students as God's creatures, and have understood the divine quality to their talents and aspirations. These God-given capacities, intended for actualization, really define the ultimate purpose of the school. Thus, Catholic secondary schools are especially conscious of their responsibility for developing broad programs of instruction wherein students may find opportunity most suited to their needs. Unfortunately, it has not always been possible for the Catholic secondary school to achieve all of the goals it sets for itself. Pressure of enrollments, lack of adequate funds (a not uncommon complaint in all secondary schools), difficulties in assembling versatile faculties with the talents to educate youth in diverse fields of interest have all retarded the complete attainment of educational breadth. Yet Catholic secondary education, despite these critical problems, has always recognized the student as a person, has dealt with him accordingly, and has offered all its resources for the development of his individual capacities.

5. *Guidance.* Catholic education has a broad and profound interest in the student, encompassing his academic, social, emotional, economic, and spiritual life. Either in a formal guidance program or in informal and everyday contacts with students, teachers and administrators in Catholic secondary schools willingly accept the responsibility of helping students form their life goals. To this end, means are now available to explore students' interests and capacities, and individual attention is given to aid them in achieving autonomy: helping them direct their energies and determine their goals. The Catholic secondary school, more than any other secondary school, is guidance-centered; its broad commitment is always one of helping students achieve an interesting, productive, and satisfying life.

Other Statements

In addition to the statements of purposes for secondary education in the United States which are reviewed in the preceding pages, many other statements of purpose have been made. The Committee on the Orientation of Secondary Education produced its *Functions of Secondary Education* in 1937. In 1938 the New York Regents Study of High Schools prepared four books pertaining to the functions of high schools: *High School and Life, Education for Citizenship, When Youth Leave School,* and *Education for Work.* The American Youth Commission, appointed by the American Council on Education, released studies in 1939 entitled *How Fare American Youth, Youth Tell Their Story, Matching Youth and Jobs,* and *Equal Educational Opportunity for Youth.* The North Central Association of Colleges and Secondary Schools appointed a commission to study high school curricula. In 1942 *General Education in the American High School,* the report of this commission, appeared. Added to the foregoing are the Harvard Report, *General Education in a Free Society;* the report of the John Dewey Society, *The American High School;* the reports of the Commission on Life Adjustment for Youth; and the James B. Conant report, *The American High School Today.* Some of these reports have emphasized the high school's function as being one of *general education,* while other reports have established the high school's chief role in the area of *special* or *vocational education.* It has been remarked that the work that has been done in defining the purposes of secondary education in the United States will suffice for years to come and that "fully ample statements of purpose are posted on the schoolhouse door, as a challenge to all teachers who would enter there." The important question, then, once the purposes have been arrived at, is how to achieve any or all of these purposes.

ACHIEVING THE GOALS OF SECONDARY EDUCATION

Since 1958, when the Western world was rudely awakened and shaken by the spectacular achievements of Soviet Russia's scientific and technological community, American education, but especially American secondary schools, has been the object of intensive, though not especially widespread, criticism. Critics of the high schools have pointed accusing fingers at the schools while voicing the manifesto that schools exist for one purpose only: to teach organized and disciplined subjects. They have insisted that schoolmen and textbook publishers have been brainwashed by exponents of a life adjustment educational philosophy and have in a way betrayed the youth of America, and the nation itself, by permitting schools to be nonintellectual institutions with social rather than academic objectives. They have argued that the fads and the frills of high school programs have siphoned off intellectual inspiration from the best students and have confused the scholastic intentions of entirely capable but average students. In addition, they seem convinced that the cost of education is everywhere too great, that teachers are incompetent, and that parents are indifferent to the quality of education. The panacea, according to the most outspoken and intransigent of these critics, is to be found in going back—in being conservative revolutionists—to the rigid curriculum and the approved methods of a century ago.

Part of the ammunition for castigating American high schools is gathered by comparing the performances—to the extent they are known—of Soviet and American secondary school students. In most of these comparisons the American student is made to appear second best; and irrespective of the validity of the judgment made, the practices and programs of American high schools are denounced. Little if any attention is given to the fact that most secondary school education outside the United States is reserved for the few; in most countries popular secondary education is still a long way off. Thus, there is no urgency about developing educational programs for students without a definite academic orientation, or who are unable by reason of capacity, interest, or money to pursue a scientific high school curriculum. Such school systems, moreover, are not democratic; they are not based on the ideal of universal education and often have no reverence for the student as a human person. American secondary schools are unwilling to sacrifice ideals of democracy in order to make a good appearance on the balance sheet prepared by these critics. Besides, it is by no means clear that American secondary schools are inferior or that they are not achieving the goals set for them. Obviously, all high school students are not taking college preparatory courses, but they are being prepared for life in society; and the school is offering to them, and to all its students, comprehensive educational opportunity so necessary to democratic life. To introduce an additional dimension of fairness, it must be agreed, few American secondary school educators are so obtuse as to refuse to acknowledge the real possibility for an improvement of high schools. Yet, they do not want to sacrifice fundamental ideals of democratic education in order to obtain short-term gains in the competition for scientists in the market place.

What are the constituent elements in a secondary school program helping it achieve broad and well-conceived objectives? In other words, when we scrutinize American high schools—assuming necessary means for achieving generally acknowledged goals—what should we expect to find?

One item often considered, not for its essential character but because it attracts attention, is size. How many teachers are on the faculty? What is the total enrollment? A rule of thumb sometimes accepted recommends, if the school is to offer educational opportunity at the lower limit of acceptability, a graduating class of at least 100 students. Taking into account dropouts and transfers, this figure suggests for mere adequacy a total high school enrollment of about 500. Although there may be some merit to the contention that size alone—enrollment and faculty—is not important, size does support an assumption of the presence of other necessary conditions for high-quality instruction. Small high schools may have entirely adequate resources, variety of programs, and competent teachers, yet they are faced with the dogmatic standard making them inferior to larger schools.

Regardless of the number of students a high school enrolls or the size of its faculty, its program may be assigned high marks for adequacy if it is able to score well on these items: How extensive are curricular offerings in *English literature and composition,* and what sequences are observed in connection with this part of the total program? How broad is the social studies program and how are courses in *American history* related to it? Are courses in economics, sociology, and government available to interested and advanced students?

With the wide range in abilities found in the high school population, it is essential for high schools today, if they are conducting programs wherein students may exploit their talents, *to group students according to ability,* especially in required courses.

One evidence of adequacy may be found in the *general education* program; another is the school's *elective curriculum.* How extensive are elective offerings and do they include vocational and commercial courses for boys and girls? Such courses may adopt a program of work experience, although there is no reason to insist on experience, or to suppose that quality can be guaranteed with it.

Reading remains the chief tool of formal education: with poor reading skill otherwise highly capable students are unable to achieve their potential; even good readers can improve themselves. The evidence gathered over many years seems conclusive; both reading rate and comprehension can be increased for most students by special instruction. The question, then, is Does the high school program include *remedial reading courses for slow readers* and *special reading courses for talented students?*

Besides special courses in reading, are there other curricular provisions for *gifted students?* Does the school cooperate with colleges on *advanced placement* programs for college-bound students, or other programs, such as honors courses, that recognize superior achievement and accelerate outstanding students? Accelerated courses may be made available during the summer, although it is probably unrealistic to expect every high school to have summer programs. Yet, clearly, high schools organizing summer courses are keenly aware of the motivation good students have for making progress up the educational ladder.

If curriculum directors in high schools are serious in their commitment to general education, they will construct core curricula of varying intensity for all students. Building on this foundation of a core program, they will provide instructional opportunities tailored to students' strengths, weaknesses, interests, and needs. This is what is meant by *individualized instruction,* a feature indispensable to high-quality secondary education.

We move next to physical facilities. Is the school plant equipped to conduct an extensive and well-balanced cocurricular program? Are laboratories and classrooms designed to meet instructional demands? Is the *library well-selected and accessible,* and is it staffed by persons able to help students use its resources?

Finally, we come to *guidance and personnel services.* Does the program offer students educational, vocational, and personal guidance? Are guidance and counseling services staffed with qualified persons, and does the philosophy of guidance recognize the goal of helping the student help himself toward personal autonomy, the broad objective of all education?

SUMMARY

Secondary education, like other levels of education in early America, was imported from Europe. Progress in grafting indigenous characteristics to secondary schools was slow. One of the first attempts to revise secondary education and to make it respond more fully to the needs and aspirations of American life was undertaken by Benjamin Franklin. However, Franklin's academy, for all the brief popularity it enjoyed, was unable to maintain a curriculum essentially different from that of the Latin grammar schools which had preceded it. By the end of the first quarter of the nineteenth century, it became clear that a new type of institution was needed. This new type of secondary school began to evolve with the establishment of the Boston English Classical High School—the first American high school—in 1821.

But the high school, too, was faced with problems that had curtailed the promising influences of the academy. High schools—their purposes, curricula, and activities—were dominated by the overarching principle that secondary education's only purpose was to prepare students for college. Besides, questions were raised as to whether the high school really belonged to public education and whether public support could be bestowed on it.

The question of the place of the high school in public education was decided by the people. The right of the high school to receive public support was settled for the state of Michigan in the famous Kalamazoo decision (1874), and this decision served as a decisive precedent for the other states. The purposes for the high school were broadened as a result of the *Report of the Committee of Ten.* With these changes in secondary education, it became possible for nearly everyone who wanted a high school education to receive it, either in a public or in a nonpublic high school.

But popularization was attended by new problems, and high schools felt compelled to design curricula to meet the needs and interests of students who had wide ranges of ability and motivation.

Junior high schools, senior high schools, and junior colleges were organized as part of secondary education to meet the requirements of a new psychology of instruction and new, or altered, purposes for secondary education. Curricula, too, were experimented with; core and subject curricula were offered to blend content and experience to meet a wider objective— life in American society. Most public and nonpublic high schools tried to build their programs around the goals contained in the Seven Cardinal Principles.

Contemporary life has led the high schools to reconsider their organization and reorganization of the past. Old solutions do not always apply to new problems. The high school was mainly a terminal institution from 1800 to 1940. In recent years it stands again between the elementary school and the college. The part the high school must play in offering liberal and general studies as foundations for life is probably the most pressing concern facing secondary education today.

QUESTIONS AND EXERCISES

1. Name the educational practices and types of institutions which were transplanted from the mother country to the Colonies. Give the chief characteristics of the schools which were transplanted.
2. Compare the Latin grammar school with the academy, with the high school.
3. Summarize Jefferson's educational plan for Virginia. Why was it rejected?
4. List and explain the importance of the "battles" for American public education.
5. What effect did the Kalamazoo decision have on high schools in the United States?
6. Summarize the findings of the Committee of Ten.
7. Criticize monitorial instruction. Did monitorial schools make any contribution to American secondary education?
8. Articulation is the key to the reorganized schools. Give the meaning of articulation, and show how it has been achieved in reorganized schools.
9. Evaluate the Seven Cardinal Principles as objectives for secondary education.
10. Investigate the Eight Year Study. Evaluate its findings.
11. Discuss Conant's proposals for secondary education made in *The American High School Today*.
12. Do you believe that comparisons made between American and Soviet secondary education are valid? Develop arguments pro and con.

ADDITIONAL READINGS

Aikin, W. M.: *The Story of the Eight Year Study,* Harper & Row, Publishers, Incorporated, New York, 1942. This volume contains the general conclusions of the Eight Year Study and supports the position that college students from the progressive high schools were better equipped for college work than students from college preparatory programs.

Alberty, Harold B., and Elsie J.: *Reorganizing the High School Curriculum,* 3d ed., The Macmillan Company, New York, 1962. Chapter 1 sets the general dimensions of reorganization.

Austin, David B., Will French, and J. Dan Hull: *American High School Administration,* Holt, Rinehart and Winston, Inc., New York, 1961. See chapters on organization and administration of the curriculum.

Brown, B. Frank: *The Nongraded High School,* Prentice-Hall, Inc., Englewood Cliffs, N.J., 1963. This Florida experiment provides greater flexibility for student progress. See especially those sections which set forth the rationale of the nongraded high school.

Coleman, James S.: *The Adolescent Society,* The Free Press of Glencoe, New York, 1961. The author takes a close look at adolescent culture, value climates, and the role of sport and study in student school life.

Conant, James B.: *The American High School Today: A First Report to Interested Citizens,* McGraw-Hill Book Company, New York, 1959. The author is concerned about the quality of the high school course. After visiting a number of high schools across the country, he makes several recommendations for their improvement.

————: *The Child, the Parent, and the State,* Harvard University Press, Cambridge, Mass., 1959. This book undertakes to explain to interested citizens the principal theses of public education.

———— *Recommendations for Education in the Junior High School Years,* Educational Testing Service, Princeton, N.J., 1960. This commentator on American education makes recommendations for policy making in junior high schools and explains their implications for the instructional program.

————: *The Revolutionary Transformation of the American High School,* Harvard University Press, Cambridge, Mass., 1959. Look especially at the reasons offered for reshaping the American high school.

Everett, Samuel: *Growing Up in English Secondary Schools,* The University of Pittsburgh Press, Pittsburgh, Pa., 1959. It is broadening to know how schools in other countries see their goals in relation to the needs of youth and society. Read especially for an understanding of the philosophy of British secondary education.

Grizzell, E. D.: *Origin and Development of the High School in New England before 1865,* The Macmillan Company, New York, 1923. The foundations of the American high school were molded in New England. Consult those sections which touch on legislation affecting the first high schools.

Honeywell, Roy J.: *The Educational Work of Thomas Jefferson,* Harvard University Press, Cambridge, Mass., 1931. See especially Jefferson's educational plan of 1779 and its provisions for secondary education.

Inglis, A. J.: *The Rise of the High School in Massachusetts,* Bureau of Publications, Teachers College, Columbia University, New York, 1911. See chapters 1 to 3.

Kandel, I. L.: *The History of Secondary Education,* Houghton Mifflin Company, Boston, 1930. Read chapters on the academy and measure its relationship to the high school.

Koerner, James D.: *The Case for Basic Education,* Little, Brown and Company, Boston, 1959. See pages 3 to 17 and 240 to 251, which deal with the case for, and prospects of, basic education. This is a conservative approach to secondary education.

Krug, Edward A.: *The Secondary School Curriculum,* Harper & Row, Publishers, Incorporated, New York, 1960. The author is concerned with the organization of the curriculum from grades seven through twelve. Chapter 1 contains the author's philosophy of curriculum.

Latimer, John F.: *What's Happened to Our High Schools?* Public Affairs Press, Washington, D.C., 1958. This is an attempt to assign responsibility for the failure of high schools to meet the demands of the post-Sputnik I era.

Lull, H. G.: *Inherited Tendencies of Secondary Instruction in the United States,* University of California, Berkeley, 1913. A careful, scholarly study of the debt American secondary education owes to the past. See especially chapter on secondary education's preparatory responsibilities.

Mallery, David: *High School Students Speak Out,* Harper & Row, Publishers, Incorporated, New York, 1962. A view of the high schools from the students' position; problems from value commitments to divisiveness in the community are examined.

Perdew, Philip W.: *The American Secondary School in Action,* Allyn and Bacon, Inc., Boston, 1959. The author combines an analysis of hypothetical but realistic narratives of incidents in secondary schools with discussions of various important features of secondary education in the United States.

Stabler, Ernest (ed.): *The Education of the Secondary School Teacher,* Wesleyan University Press, Middletown, Conn., 1962. See chapters on collegiate preparation of the high school teacher.

Stiles, Lindley H., Lloyd E. McCleary, and Roy C. Turnbaugh: *Secondary Education in the United States,* Harcourt, Brace & World, Inc., New York, 1962. The last section treats of current and important issues in secondary education.

Van Til, W. A., G. F. Vars, and J. H. Lounsbury: *Modern Education for Junior High School Years,* The Bobbs-Merrill Company, Inc., Indianapolis, 1962. See part I on the history of the junior high school movement.

Wiles, K.: *The Changing Curriculum of the American High School,* Prentice-Hall, Inc., Englewood Cliffs, N.J., 1963. This book is designed to help parents, teachers, and administrators understand school programs and their inevitable evolution.

Woody, Thomas: *Educational Views of Benjamin Franklin,* McGraw-Hill Book Company, New York, 1931. Note especially how the academy and Franklin's doctrine of utility affected American secondary education.

chapter 8

Higher Education

The third general level on the American educational ladder is higher education. Before we examine the foundations, trace the developments, discuss the purposes, and explore important current issues, a word should be said concerning the scope of contemporary higher education in the United States. In 1964 the United States had 2,139 institutions of higher education of all types, including colleges, universities, technological schools, theological schools, other professional schools, and junior colleges. Of this total, 762 or about 35 per cent were publicly controlled. The remaining 1,377 or approximately 65 per cent were under ecclesiastical, philanthropic, or other nongovernmental control.

Enrollment statistics for higher education fluctuate more sharply from year to year than the number of institutions. For this reason, it is not possible to give representative figures for total college enrollment. All indications are, however, that enrollment in higher institutions will continue to grow. It is possible, nevertheless, while recognizing the need for an almost daily revision of statistics, to make a few generalizations about college enrollment. The 1963–1964 total college enrollment was 4,528,516. Of this total, 2,789,527 or 61.6 per cent were men, and 1,738,989 or 38.4 per cent were women. And although only 35 per cent of the institutions of higher education were publicly controlled, 64.4 per cent of the students were enrolled in publicly controlled schools. Higher institutions were attended by 4,810,000 students in 1964–1965, and the estimates for the 1970 college enrollment range from 6 to 7 million (see Table 8-1).

For the 1964–1965 school year, the total number of faculty members in higher institutions was 351,500; 263,625 or about 75 per cent were men, and 87,875 or about 25 per cent were women. In this same year, 52 per cent or 182,780 were in institutions under public control; 48 per cent or 168,720 were in private institutions. According to the President's Committee on Education beyond the High School,[1] somewhere between 180,000 and 270,000 new college teachers must be recruited in the next twelve to fifteen years—between 15,000 and 22,500 annually. Less conservative estimates indicate a considerably higher need.[2]

THE FOUNDATIONS OF HIGHER EDUCATION IN AMERICA

The first schools transplanted to colonial America were mission schools. These schools were established by French and Spanish Catholic missionaries for the purpose of educating the children of the colonists and the natives in the rudiments of learning and the essentials of religion. However, neither French nor Spanish colonies had broad or lasting effects in shaping the character of American life or institutions. The schools founded and conducted by the missionaries who accompanied French and Spanish expeditions, though important, were not permanent. It was in English colonial America that the cornerstones were laid for American education. The first of the transplanted institutions was the Latin grammar school; the second was the colonial college. The American foundation for higher education, therefore, began with Harvard College in 1636, but this college was modeled on a constituent college of Cambridge University (England) and in its purposes, curriculum, and general atmosphere accepted a heritage which had its beginnings in medieval universities. A brief review of the development in higher education prior to the seventeenth century may indicate more clearly how early American colleges were influenced by the universities which preceded them.

TABLE 8-1

Higher Education: Enrollment and Faculty, 1890 to 1970

Year	Enrollment	Faculty
1890	156,756	15,809
1900	237,597	23,868
1910	355,213	36,480
1920	597,880	48,615
1930	1,100,737	82,368
1940	1,494,203	146,929
1950	2,659,021	246,722
1960	3,980,000	350,554
1970	6,500,000 *	500,000 *

* Estimated.

SOURCE: *Digest of Educational Statistics,* U.S. Office of Education, Bulletin 1964, no. 18, 1964, pp. 70–80.

Medieval Universities

Sometme between 1140 and 1170 a band of scholars formed a guild for the purpose of pursuing their common interests in higher education. This was the beginning of the University of Paris—the mother of universities. To achieve goals consistent with advanced teaching and learning the members of the masters' guild, who could be addressed as professors, masters, or doctors, gave their *studium* a distinct and unique scholastic character: they incorporated the institution according to the laws governing guilds to ensure perpetuity for their undertaking, and they organized the various branches of learning then available into a broad curriculum called faculties. Their motivation was never on the level of mere whim, for with corporate status they were able to gain for themselves and to offer to their students some protection from outside forces and interferences which ranged from physical encounters with townspeople to the encroachments of civil and ecclesiastical authorities. By building a curriculum and separating it into faculties, they could offer a course of studies broad enough to meet the needs of a versatile student body and at the same time respect the content and objectives of ever-expanding bodies of knowledge. Paris and other early medieval universities tried to maintain four faculties—or four branches of university studies—styled, respectively, arts, law, medicine, and theology. Each of these faculties was distinct within the university structure; each had its own teachers and students; but in concert the faculties of medieval universities sought to provide a base for universal teaching and learning.

The European universities that followed the University of Paris sometimes departed slightly from the original plan. That is, some did not establish four faculties or did not regularly offer instruction in each of the four faculties, but, in general, the *studium generale* (what we today would call a university) had a faculty of arts—the *inferior* faculty—and one of the *superior* faculties—law, medicine, or theology.

Before the University of Paris was organized, teachers and students were unquestionably interested in what we might call higher studies. The Egyptians, Assyrians, Babylonians, Hebrews, Greeks, Romans, and Moslems made important contributions to art, science, law, medicine, and philosophy. Socrates, Plato, Aristotle, and others studied, experimented, and taught, but they did so without the external and internal organization which was first applied to higher education by medieval masters.

A satisfactory sketch of the medieval university is not easy to draw: it was a complex institution, and it tended to adapt itself to the country or the city in which it happened to carry on its work.[3] However, while recognizing the difficulties of generalization when dealing with the subject, the following points will disclose its chief characteristics:

1. Initiative for organizing universities came from the masters, yet the masters were never entirely free agents. The corporate life of a university and the boundaries of its academic commission were contained in a *charter* granted by a king, prince, or pope. The power of the chartering authority determined the influence and strength of the university. The type of charter a university might boast—royal or papal—was of no small significance to students who earned their degrees at that institution: degrees from a university with a royal charter were recognized in the kingdom; those from a papal university were valid everywhere in Christendom.
2. A charter provided the legal bases for university organization, and upon these bases the masters constructed a system of internal government and control. Except in medieval universities of the south of Europe where students managed the schools they attended, masters were responsible for university government. They made policies with respect to curriculum, degrees, student decorum, and everything else coming within the ambit of university life. And doing what today would be regarded as a tour de force, they elected their own deans and university presidents.
3. The language of medieval learning was Latin, so naturally the official language of the university was Latin. Although students and masters might resort to native tongues when congregating in clubs (nations), vernacular languages were not yet strong enough to bear the weight of scholarship; all lectures, disputations, and resumptions were conducted in Latin, and all theses were written in Latin.
4. Degrees from medieval universities were licenses to teach or practice. The master of arts degree was perhaps the first formal teacher's license, and the faculty of arts was likely the first teacher's college. Masters' degrees in law, medicine, and theology were normally recognized as authorizations to practice or preach.
5. Medieval universities were conducted with a remarkable degree of permissiveness. Apart from oaths students took when matriculating, few rules, codes, or disciplinary proscriptions confined them. Generally speaking, they were free to attend lectures or not as they saw fit; no course examinations plagued them; no marks buoyed them up at the end of the semester or dashed their hopes for academic success. When they felt prepared for final examinations, they presented themselves to boards of examiners and were held responsible for the entire college course. From a successful outcome on this examination they could proceed to the preparation of a masterpiece—a thesis—which, if accepted by the masters, authorized the conferral of a master's degree.

By 1500, seventy-nine universities had been established in Europe, each conforming more or less exactly to the points listed above. But life in Europe was altered in the sixteenth century. The Protestant revolt, the influence of humanism, and the Catholic reforms had far-reaching effects which the universities could not escape. These effects were directed chiefly at the university's purpose. Where the old universities had devoted themselves to the perfection of intellectual life, they were now in the sixteenth century called upon to serve the interests of religion, religious controversy, or humanism. By the close of the sixteenth century the universities of Europe had lost what they needed most: independence and clearness of purpose. Their independence was lost to civil or ecclesiastical officials, and their purpose was defined by these authorities.

The time was ripe for university reform, but reform came slowly and was not especially effective until the end of the seventeenth century. Even then its effects were confined mainly to Germany and had little or no impress on the infant colleges in colonial America. The internal revitalization of higher learning was expressed along six main lines. (1) Modern philosophy with its principle of the independence of reason and based on the blossoming modern sciences, especially of mathematics and physics, supplanted Aristotelian-scholastic philosophy as the intellectual center around which university curricula revolved. (2) Freedom became an important condition to scholarship and found its way into the context of research and instruction; the rigidly supervised and controlled curriculum capitulated to the stronger claims of academic freedom. (3) Systematic lectures, now personal interpretations or actual reports on professors' research, replaced the *lectio* of the earlier university, a turn of events not altogether surprising considering the impression printing was making on intellectual affairs and institutions. (4) The older universities had employed the *disputation,* a device for presenting, defending, and discussing intellectual questions, to good advantage, but time was running out for this technique, too. Its place was taken by the university seminar, wherein advanced students carried out and reported on research. (5) Ancient language and literature were not eliminated from the new-type university, but their role was changed; no longer was there a tendency to imitate the classics; instead, a concerted effort was made to capture the spirit of the classical age and build upon it. (6) Finally, the language of the university became the vernacular of the country in which the school was located. The modern university was no longer a Latin-speaking school.[4]

Early American Colleges

Before 1800, twenty-six permanent colleges were established in what is now the United States. These colleges, with their dates of founding and religious affiliation, if any, are given in Table 8-2.

The colonial colleges, it is true, were representatives of an earlier tradition in higher education, but their inheritance from medieval universities was screened through universities affected by the Renaissance and the Protestant revolt and was therefore indirect. They were influenced more directly by the universities of England, and particularly by Emmanuel College at Cambridge University. This influence affected Harvard College first, but to some extent it affected all America's colonial colleges. The most important characteristic of Harvard—a transplanted characteristic—was its purpose of training ministers. The purpose of the college was expressed in this way:[5]

> After God had carried us safe to New England, and wee had builded our houses, provided necessaries for our livelihood, rear'd convenient places for Gods worship, and setled the Civill Government: One of the next things we longed for, and looked after was to advance *Learning* and perpetuate it to Posterity; dreading to leave an illiterate Ministery to the Churches, when our present Ministers shall lie in the Dust.

Of the twenty-six colleges founded before 1800, twenty-three had predominantly religious purposes, and the three state colleges—Georgia, North Carolina, and Vermont—although they were not officially affiliated

TABLE 8-2

Permanent Colleges Established before 1800

Present name	Date	Religious affiliation
Harvard University	1636	Congregational
College of William and Mary	1693	Episcopal
Yale University	1701	Congregational
Princeton University	1746	Presbyterian
Columbia University	1754	Episcopal
University of Pennsylvania	1755	Episcopal
Brown University	1765	Baptist
Rutgers University	1766	Dutch Reformed
Dartmouth College	1769	Congregational
Washington College	1782	Episcopal
Washington and Lee University	1782	Presbyterian
Hampden-Sidney College	1783	Presbyterian
Transylvania College	1783	Presbyterian
Dickinson College	1783	Presbyterian
St. John's College	1784	Episcopal
University of Georgia	1785	None
College of Charleston	1785	Episcopal
Georgetown University	1786	Catholic
Franklin and Marshall College	1787	German Reformed
University of North Carolina	1789	None
University of Vermont	1791	None
Williams College	1793	Congregational
Bowdoin College	1794	Congregational
Tusculum College	1794	Presbyterian
University of Tennessee	1794	Presbyterian
Union University	1795	Presbyterian

with a religious denomination came under definite religious influences. Even the University of Pennsylvania, an outgrowth of Franklin's academy, was controlled by religious interests. For the most part these schools were presided over by clerical presidents, and the colleges themselves, although they may not have been just theological seminaries, were interested primarily in preparing an educated or a learned clergy. The religious denominations which were doctrinal in theology and ritualistic in devotion wanted a "learned clergy," a clergy having the advantages of a classical education plus specialized study in sectarian theological doctrine. Evangelical sects, while avoiding both dogma and ritual, were unwilling to accept an ignorant and illiterate clergy, so they established colleges to provide their sects with an "educated clergy." They had decided preferences for classically trained clergymen. It is easy to understand the motivation of Congregationalists and Presbyterians for creating schools to preserve a learned ministry. However, it is somewhat more difficult to appreciate the motives of the Baptists and other evangelical sects in founding colleges; for them the source of truth was inspiration and intuition, not reason, and the doctrine of justification by faith contained at the very least the suggestion of repudiating learning with impunity. It was unquestionably hard for unsophisticated laymen to understand their need for ministers skilled in science, rhetoric, logic, and philosophy to hear and understand the words of the Bible. The word of God, they had been led to believe, was uttered in clear, simple, and unmistakable dicta, and man's natural mind, they had been taught, was really incapable of refinement. Thus, they could argue against education both for laymen and clergymen, regarding it as a trap for unsuspecting victims, possibly a guise invented by Satan, and accept the Holy Ghost as their only teacher. Within this context of a naïve but plausible rejection of mental sophistication, Protestant theologians were forced to defend the proposition of justification by faith without allowing it to become a justification for illiteracy.

The colleges established by evangelical sects were intended to prepare ministers in polite learning, thereby enabling them to achieve the prestige and position expected of ministers in colonial society. Clerically minded students could get a polite education in other denominational colleges but not without some danger to their sectarian beliefs or zeal. In a friendlier religious climate they could avoid the ardent proselytism so characteristic of the colleges of the time. In addition, missionary objectives and denominational rivalry prompted the evangelical sects to repress their deep-seated and active animosities toward educated ministers and create colleges for their preparation. However, the chronicle of colonial college development is mainly one of college founding by dogmatic sects; only about 15 per cent of the permanent colleges founded before the Civil War were established by evangelicals.

With the exception of one permanent college founded before 1800—Georgetown University—colonial colleges were designed to prepare an educated or learned ministry. Georgetown's purpose was slightly different from that of the other colleges, for Catholic clergymen received their theological training in seminaries, not colleges. Georgetown was to prepare boys for the seminary, and in 1799 St. Mary's Seminary in Baltimore was opened to accept students from Georgetown. Because Georgetown was not immediately engaged in the training of clergymen, both her objectives and curriculum were somewhat broader than those of the colleges which preceded her on the American scene.

Apart from the great design to educate ministers in their own way, what were these colonial colleges like? What were the most prominent features of seventeenth- and eighteenth-century American colleges?

The students who appeared at the gates of a colonial college were usually the sons of ministers, well-to-do merchants, or others who could afford the cost of a college course. They were being sent to college because their parents expected that in college they would receive an education to fit them for leadership in the church or state. But beyond the common purpose which parents had in sending their sons to college, the boys who attended were hardly a homogeneous group. Some were as young as seven or eight, while others were as old as twenty-five. Most had attended some Latin grammar school, but for a few the college course was to be their first experience with formal education. Whether prospective college students had ever attended school before was not in itself a matter to concern the college admissions officer—usually the college president—very much. He simply tested the boys' ability to read and translate elementary Latin and Greek. Toward the close of the colonial period arithmetic became one of the subjects tested in the entrance examination. It is doubtful, however, that many boys were refused admission to a college because they could not pass the examination. The college could prescribe extra work or institute special classes for the boys who were deficient in their preparation.

If there were wide differences in the ages, abilities, and interests of the students, there was also some lack of uniformity in religious affiliation. Religious tests were not applied officially, and it was possible, it is claimed, for any student, whatever his sectarian beliefs, to enroll at one of the colonial colleges. Nevertheless, while the claims of college tolerance and liberality may be valid, every student was expected to conform to the religious discipline of the college, and this meant that he attended church services, morning and evening prayers, and whatever other religious observances were common to the sectarian belief officially held by the college. During later periods of college development a surprising degree of tolerance was present in each institution, but during the colonial period it was the rare student indeed who ventured into the college of a sect whose creed he did not accept. And it would have been extremely unusual for sects to establish and maintain colleges for the purpose of preparing ministers in their own way and then admit students to these colleges without any thought of the students' religious commitments.

Few lawful amusements were mentioned in the codes regulating student life. Puritans always detected the prized virtues in an environment of hard work and feared idleness believing it led to sin. Physical recreation was apparently misunderstood or taken for idleness, for in school programs boys had no time for enjoyable relaxation or diversions from their books. We should not, of course, expect to find well-defined cocurricular activities in these colleges, nor should special criticism be directed at their indifference to them, but descriptions of colonial colleges would be misleading if they neglected this climate of austerity regularly regarded as a singular strength of college life. Any comparison on this point of student life between the colonial colleges and their European counterparts must call attention to a decided regression in the social milieu of higher education. The colonial college tried to maintain a social regimen too severe even for the most ascetic monastic establishment. Students spent their free time in talking and walking; nothing else seemed quite orthodox in a colonial college community.

Yet boys remained boys, even when enrolled at Harvard, Yale, or other early schools, and bowed to repressive rules only when means to violate them were unavailable. On several notable occasions they challenged the established order and their disciplinary taskmasters, upset the tranquil setting of learning, and broke the bonds of college restraint by becoming wanton and disorderly. Among other things, they brawled with townspeople and played dangerous practical jokes on college officers and tutors. At one college they showed only a mild display of temper, or of fun, by painting the president's horse. Whenever the culprits were detected and apprehended, punishment took the form of imposition of fines, confinement in a special room (sometimes called the "jug") without food, extra prayers or studies, or the rod applied by the sturdy arm of the college disciplinarian. For especially severe breaches of discipline, or when college officers felt they were dealing with an unsalvageable delinquent, expulsion was the supreme punishment.

The college's curriculum may give us deeper insight into its personality. The curriculum of a college, or of any school, reveals the expectations society has for its educational institutions and the youth who attend them. It contains an explicit endorsement of the values of character and mind judged to be most essential in an educated community. By examining curricula, one is able to sense the cultural pressures affecting and, to a very large extent, directing the work of schools.

The colonial college curriculum was an adaptation of the course of study common in medieval universities; it was prescribed and inflexible. Students were required to spend three-fourths of their time on Latin and Greek; the rest of the time they were engaged with mathematics, natural philosophy (the rudiments of physics and chemistry), and rhetoric. All these studies were subordinated to a religious objective. This curriculum promised to train ministers, educate gentlemen, and develop all the powers of the mind through discipline. It was the only avenue to the degree of bachelor of arts.

Most American colleges adopted a four-year course of study with the respective classes styled freshman, sophomore, junior, and senior; but a few colleges departed from this plan to devise a seven-year program including high school as well as college studies.

The first Catholic colleges in the United States did not follow the older non-Catholic colleges of the country in the organization of curricula: they were either six- or seven-year schools. The academic nomenclature designating the various classes sounds strange to modern ears, and, though it has no special relevance now, is sufficiently unique and interesting to merit brief treatment here. If a Catholic college organized its classes according to a six-year plan, the classes were probably listed as Rudiments, Third Grammar, Second Grammar, First Grammar, Humanities, and Rhetoric. The seven-year course was often styled Rudiments, Third Humanities, Second Humanities, First Humanities, Poetry, Rhetoric, and Philosophy. Contrary to the general practice of the day and to a current assumption as well, Catholic colleges made no inflexible or exclusive commitment to the classical curriculum; English studies always occupied a position of some importance. A prefect of studies at early Georgetown instructed the teachers at the college to emphasize and cultivate English. "It surely cannot be doubted," he said, "that the vernacular language is always the most important. Without this knowledge every other branch of education would be almost useless." [6] Catholic colleges retained their somewhat distinctive curricular arrangement and the long course until about 1890. From that year to 1920 curricular reorganization became common, and Catholic colleges adopted the four-year course.

The chief, sometimes the only, teacher at these colleges was the president. In addition to his instructional duties he conducted the college's religious exercises, administered the school, raised money, recruited students, and often served as the pastor of the neighboring church. When conditions warranted, the colleges tried to add other teachers (seldom more than two or three), each teacher being assigned a class of students to whom he imparted knowledge on all subjects. These teachers were usually young men who had just finished the college course and who accepted a position on the school's faculty as a steppingstone to an appointment as a minister. Although brilliant and cultivated men sometimes graced college faculties, most teachers were equipped neither by their education nor their interests to guide the intellectual development of their students. Considering these deficiencies, we should not be surprised to know that college students were often displeased with their college experience. They found the course of studies sterile and the techniques of teaching repressive and unimaginative. They were required to prepare lines of Latin and Greek, to work problems in mathematics, and to prepare a certain number of pages in a textbook; in the classroom the exercises seldom went beyond the routines of recitation and drill, all of which reminded students too much of elementary school and the subordination it demanded to the teacher's will. The more perceptive student wondered when he was to be given an opportunity to think for himself.

Control of these colleges was vested in external, usually self-perpetuating boards of trustees. The college president was expected to enforce the policies enacted by the board. Clergymen were in the majority on every board before the nineteenth century, including those controlling early state universities. College government in America departed noticeably from what it had been in European universities, where the faculties themselves formulated all academic policies. The American college was not governed by its faculty.

The college of colonial days was a small institution. In its infant years its enrollment seldom exceeded a dozen students, and during the entire period before the Revolution a college with one hundred students was considered to be unusually prosperous. Because so few students attended, the colleges did not need more than one or two multipurpose buildings, wherein the boys studied, worshiped, slept, ate, and, on occasion, took their recreation. All the colleges were poor, depending almost entirely on student fees for their income. Their greatest problem, therefore, was to remain solvent, and while they were concerned with financial questions, they could not provide much beyond rather rude instructional facilities. Their greatest handicap in this respect was probably their libraries. By 1775 the best of the college libraries was Harvard's, with about 4,000 volumes, but in some institutions libraries were nonexistent.

THE DEVELOPMENT OF HIGHER EDUCATION IN THE UNITED STATES

In spite of attempts by Benjamin Franklin, at the University of Pennsylvania, and Thomas Jefferson, at the College of William and Mary and the University of Virginia, to reform the narrow orthodoxy of the colleges, few significant changes were effected in college objectives or curriculum before the end of the first quarter of the nineteenth century. But after 1825 the colleges became somewhat more responsive to the need of American society. They relaxed their orthodoxy, broadened their objectives, and embraced curricula in keeping with the intellectual influence of the European Enlightenment and the practical values of American life. Although it would be a mistake to think that American higher education became secular in the first few decades of the nineteenth century, it did become less openly sectarian. The age was an age of ferment, and higher education, subjected to all kinds of economic, social, and democratic pressures, was reformed and developed. The most prominent changes are identified and discussed below.

Liberalization of Purpose and Curriculum

One of the strongest challenges to the accepted eighteenth-century pattern of American higher education was offered by the Dartmouth College controversy. While the state of New Hampshire was dominated by Congregational interests, few complaints were made that Dartmouth College, in accepting the educational theory of mental discipline and in concerning itself mainly with the education of gentlemen and embryo clergymen, was unresponsive to the public interest and the public will. But when religious liberalism dissolved the power of the Congregationalists, liberal and democratic elements in the state began to question Dartmouth's right to retain its charter and at the same time continue its narrow denominational approach to higher education. In 1816 the Legislature passed a law creating a board of overseers composed of certain state officials and appointed members to control Dartmouth College. Dartmouth's self-perpetuating board of trustees declared this interference by the state to be an infringement of its colonial charter of 1769 and appealed to the courts to protect the college's charter. The Supreme Court of the state of New Hampshire upheld the Legislature's right to alter the original charter and exercise control over the college. However, in an appeal to the United States Supreme Court in 1819 the decision of the state court was reversed. The Court held that the charter was a contract between the state and the college and that the New Hampshire Legislature had acted unconstitutionally in impairing the obligations of a contract.

Undoubtedly the Dartmouth College decision established an important and lasting precedent with respect to the inviolability of a contract, and it gave private colleges a sense of security. However, it would be unhistorical to interpret the decision as a kind of doctrine of immunity for private colleges. So far as higher education was concerned, the importance of the Dartmouth College question lay not in the court's decision but in the challenge to private colleges to become the kind of institutions the people of America wanted. While it is true that the decision did not result immediately in the establishment of publicly controlled colleges, neither did it protect the private colleges from society's demands that higher education be freed from narrow denominational interests and broadened to include practical and scientific knowledge for the material improvement of mankind. Many private colleges were founded after 1819 and before the Civil War, but each foundation was motivated not by the relative guarantee of permanence to be found in the Dartmouth College decision but by the hope that in its purpose and curriculum it could satisfy some of the needs of a growing America.

The Dartmouth College controversy was a rallying point from which college liberalization and democratization movements proceeded to challenge (1) the theory of mental discipline and (2) the prescribed curriculum. Eventually, and largely as a result of these challenges, the college curriculum was broadened to include parallel courses, technical, practical, and scientific curricula; and the prescribed curriculum of the old college gave way to electivism in the college of the nineteenth century.

The growth of private colleges in America as well as the growth of state universities may be attributed to the development of new ideas and new ideals with respect to higher education. While higher education concerned itself with preparing boys for a career in the ministry, many denominations displayed only mild interest in the founding of colleges, and the states remained relatively inactive. By 1860, for example, the Methodists had established 34 permanent colleges, although none of their colleges were opened before 1800, and the Baptists had founded 15 colleges, whereas they had opened only 1 before 1800. Before 1850, Catholics founded 42 colleges, 10 of which were permanent, but from 1850 to 1900, 152 Catholic colleges were founded, of which 45 were permanent. In addition to the marked increase in the number of private colleges—180 in 1860, 406 in 1870, and 977 in 1900—the liberalization movement brought increases in enrollment ranging from 500 to 1,000 times greater than before the colleges broadened the scope of their curricula and expanded the range of their objectives. And financial problems, constant sources of worry in private colleges, were relieved somewhat because the colleges were able to attract a broader base of support.

Professional Education

Although all America's first colleges may not have been theological institutes exclusively, it would not be difficult to build a strong argument for the claim that the first colleges were essentially professional schools. However, as the colleges tended to relinquish their predominantly sectarian purposes, their curricula became less directly related to professional pursuits. Where the old curriculum, supported by the theory of mental discipline, purported to be a direct preparation for any profession or occupation, new curricula of the early nineteenth century were more properly regarded as preparatory to further study in theology, law, medicine, engineering, and business. But the colleges did not move immediately, or on a broad scale, into professional curricula, for much of professional education was accounted for by the apprenticeship system. As the century wore on, it became increasingly apparent that science, technology, and research had contributions to make to professional education and that the apprenticeship system was not equal to the task of integrating these contributions to the current body of professional skill and knowledge. To fill what appeared to be a vacuum, professional institutes for law, medicine, and business began to flourish and for a time dominated professional education. For the most part, these institutes were not associated with colleges or universities. Their courses were superficial and short; the majority were useless, and worse, for the purpose of systematic study. Of all the professional institutes that arose during the early decades of the nineteenth century, those of law and medicine were the weakest. Despite the fact that law could boast of the famous Litchfield School and the Philadelphia School of Medicine could claim the famous Dr. Benjamin Rush, institutes of law and medicine reflected a general decline in the professional standards surrounding such studies. Twenty-six new schools of medicine were opened between 1810 and 1840, and forty-seven more between 1840 and 1876. The majority of these places were schools only in name; in fact they were profit-making ventures, without laboratories or hospital connections, in which teaching

TABLE 8-3

Catholic Colleges in the United States: Enrollment and Faculty

Year	Number of colleges	Students	Faculty
1920	130	33,798	3,697
1924	139	60,169	4,715
1928	163	87,031	6,829
1932	172	113,658	8,968
1936	184	128,362	10,778
1940	193	161,886	13,142
1944	196	148,515	12,499
1948	208	293,656	17,065
1952	213	298,000	17,998
1956	254	241,709	18,501
1960	267	314,259	24,918
1962	293	342,660	27,512
1964	303	372,726	29,012

SOURCE: *National Catholic Almanac*, 1920–1964.

was carried on according to the lecture method dressed up on occasion by a dissection. The program of instruction lasted only one year; examinations were perfunctory affairs which any fee-paying student could take in easy stride, for the payment of fees really guaranteed success. Competition with such academic charlatanism tended to depress the standards of the university-related medical schools. Even at Harvard during the early presidency of Charles W. Eliot, the regulation stated that any degree candidate acceptable to five out of nine examiners was passed. And at this time state boards did not exercise control over standards.

The colleges entered or reentered the field of professional education to correct the abuses that had been permitted to creep in. Those colleges not having the means to establish professional schools developed preprofessional curricula. Better-placed or more generously endowed colleges created graduate or undergraduate professional schools with fairly rigid entrance requirements and reasonably high standards. In these preprofessional and professional curricula the attempt was sometimes made —not always successfully—to integrate humanism and science and produce a professional man whose human interests included literature, philos-

TABLE 8-4

First Permanent Catholic Colleges in the United States

Name	Location	Date	Founder	Present control
Georgetown University	Washington, D.C.	1786	Bishop John Carroll	Jesuit
Mt. St. Mary's College	Emmitsburg, Md.	1808	Father John Dubois	Diocesan
St. Louis University	St. Louis, Mo.	1818	Bishop Louis Dubourg	Jesuit
Spring Hill College	Mobile, Ala.	1830	Bishop Michael Portier	Jesuit
Xavier University	Cincinnati, Ohio	1831	Bishop John Purcell	Jesuit
Fordham University	New York, N.Y.	1841	Bishop John Hughes	Jesuit
University of Notre Dame	Notre Dame, Ind.	1842	Father Edward Sorin, C.S.C.	Congregation of the Holy Cross
Villanova University	Villanova, Pa.	1842	Father Patrick Moriarity, O.S.A.	Augustinian
Holy Cross College	Worcester, Mass.	1843	Society of Jesus	Jesuit
St. Vincent College	Latrobe, Pa.	1846	Boniface Wimmer, O.S.B.	Benedictine

ophy, and art and whose scientific knowledge and skill formed a professional man of excellence and integrity. With or without culture, collegiate
professional schools came in time to be the only gateway to the professions,
and by accepting responsibility for professional education, American higher
education achieved greater development and a more secure position in
American life.[7]

Public Higher Education

Before the Civil War twenty-seven public and semipublic colleges were
founded. Although these colleges were recognized as public institutions,
they were not always controlled by public or elected officials. For example,
the University of North Carolina, chartered in 1789 and opened to students in 1795, was controlled by a self-perpetuating board of trustees until
1821. Most of the first public colleges, whether they were state or municipal institutions, either were dominated by denominational interests or were
effectively influenced by them. The factors which contributed to the rise
of public higher education may be listed as follows:

1. A desire to extend public control over all levels of education
2. A hope that in public colleges sectarianism might be avoided
3. An interest in scientific and vocational curricula which prompted the
   public to establish their own colleges
4. A wish to create a kind of higher education which would fulfill the needs
   and expectations of a democratic society (a factor especially evident in the
   land-grant college movement [8])

These factors hastened the organization of state universities in every
state, the founding of at least one land-grant college in every state, and the
establishment of ten municipal colleges throughout the country.

Public higher education was largely an achievement of the last half of
the nineteenth and the first half of the twentieth century. Before the Civil
War the following public colleges were founded:[9] University of Georgia,
1785; University of North Carolina, 1789; University of Vermont, 1791;
University of Tennessee, 1794; Ohio University, 1802; University of
South Carolina, 1805; Miami University (Ohio), 1809; University of
Maryland, 1812; University of Virginia, 1816; University of Alabama,
1821; Indiana University, 1828; University of Delaware, 1833; University
of Kentucky, 1837; University of Michigan, 1837; University of Missouri,
1839; University of Mississippi, 1844; State University of Iowa, 1847;
University of Wisconsin, 1848; University of Minnesota, 1851; Louisiana
State University, 1853; University of California, 1855.

Higher Education for Women

Throughout the seventeenth and eighteenth centuries in America, educational opportunity was restricted almost solely to boys. If a girl obtained even the rudiments, her study was usually done privately, for there was a good deal of public sentiment to support the belief that "a woman without ability is normal." Although the academy movement was concerned chiefly with providing boys with a practical education, a few academies for girls, or "female seminaries," were established in the early nineteenth century, and some of these schools developed into colleges for girls in the last half of the century. By 1860 about sixty so-called colleges for women were in existence.

Girls' academies were concerned with practical studies, but not the same kind of practical studies common to the academies for boys: girls did not need to study surveying, although they could have found profit in domestic science or home economics. For a time the colleges that grew out of such girls' schools, such as Troy Seminary and Mount Holyoke, retained the curricula of their academy days, but eventually—especially after the Civil War—most colleges for women modeled their programs of study on those of colleges for men.

Perhaps the most important single factor which led to the spread of higher education for women was popular elementary education. Teaching opportunities were opened for women in elementary schools throughout the country, and colleges or academies for women began to adjust their studies to prepare their students for elementary teaching. Between 1860 and 1890 the elementary schools of the country did not actively seek either women teachers or college-trained teachers, but teaching was an activity in which women could engage, and most colleges for women were able to attract students by promising to offer professional or semiprofessional curricula.

Accompanying the growth of women's colleges was the movement for coeducation. Colleges for men had been successful in excluding women down to the third decade of the nineteenth century. In 1833 Oberlin College admitted women, as did Antioch in 1853, Indiana University in 1868, and the University of Michigan in 1870. Some Eastern private colleges for men experimented with what were called "coordinate" colleges, or colleges for women affiliated with colleges for men, for example, Harvard-Radcliffe, Columbia-Barnard, and Brown-Pembroke. In Catholic colleges coeducation proceeded even more slowly than in the other colleges of the country. Residue from earlier views that women could not possibly profit from higher learning served as something of a brake on progress, but the larger question seemed to have had a moral base: Catholic schools were afraid of coeducation. In 1909 Marquette University in Milwaukee, Wisconsin, made the first break with tradition and, as an experiment, opened a summer school for women. This was not, strictly speaking, coeducation, because male students were not on the campus during the summer months, but in a way it was coeducation, because women were admitted to university halls heretofore reserved exclusively for men. In 1914 DePaul University in Chicago went several steps beyond the Marquette experiment by admitting women to all its regular session courses.

Most public and many private colleges and universities now admit women and men on an equal basis. The most obvious effect higher education for women has had on higher education generally is in enrollment: In 1870 approximately 11,000 or about 21 per cent of the higher-education enrollment was accounted for by women; in 1964 the percentage of women in higher-education institutions was 39. Not only did the proportion of women in attendance at college increase during the ninety-three year period; there was also a great increase in the proportion of degrees conferred on women. In 1869–1870 approximately 1 degree in 7 was conferred on a woman; in 1964 this proportion was 1 in 2.7.[10]

The University Ideal

Although American colleges had been successful in broadening both their objectives and their curricula, the colleges of the nineteenth century quite generally believed that their general functions were (1) to communicate knowledge to students, (2) to exercise and develop their mental faculties, and (3) to form their religious and moral characters. The elective system was introduced, the theory of mental discipline was challenged, and the sectarian character of higher education was modified; nevertheless, the colleges were extremely conservative, and they were reluctant to make too sharp a break with tradition. Scientific study and research made some inroads—inspired mainly by the example of German universities—but the educated opinion of the day continued to preserve the ideal which associated college training with the education of a gentleman. Professional education, it is true, was embraced, and an attempt was made to use positive scientific knowledge in professional curricula. Still, the colleges were not responding to the scientific spirit of the age; they were giving every indication of being content to communicate what was known rather than dedicating themselves to widening the boundaries of knowledge.[11] The time for decision was at hand: The age of the college was passing; the age of the university was hovering over the horizon. A new kind of American educational leader, a leader with academic and scientific credentials rather than religious allegiances, assumed control and redirected the energies of the academic world. The years of transition—years when the college ideal was subordinated to the university ideal—were dominated by Andrew D. White of Cornell University and Charles William Eliot of Harvard. By

1876, with the founding of the Johns Hopkins University in Baltimore, the American university world had come into being.

The sponsorship for the university ideal was to be found in the profound changes taking place in American life and in the new demands that these changes made on higher education. An agricultural economy was giving way to an industrial economy, and industry not only was willing to support but insisted upon supporting a kind of higher education that would emphasize scientific and technological knowledge. Industrial growth was dependent upon the transmission of knowledge, but even more so on its extension: research became the distinctive feature of the new American universities. The institutions which led the way in accepting science and research as the most prominent objectives for higher education were Harvard, Cornell, Johns Hopkins, Michigan, Wisconsin, and Minnesota.

Schools which adopted a university character received the support of men of wealth, and some new institutions dedicated to science and research were the recipients of money grants so large as to stagger the imagination. For example, Cornell received $500,000, Vanderbilt $1,000,000, Johns Hopkins $3,500,000, Stanford $20,000,000, and the University of Chicago $30,000,000.

Scientific schools did not require the guardianship of clerical presidents, and even the old denominationally related colleges began, in this new era, to replace clerical personnel with secular and scientific men. Although this emphasis on scientific training, wide experience, and broad interests affected the faculties at all the "new" universities, it had its most noticeable effect on the selection of presidents: by 1870 the age of the minister-president had passed, especially in the major universities.

New purposes for higher education led to other changes, also: The institutions were reorganized to include graduate schools, and in some universities all academic activities centered in the graduate school; the curriculum was pruned of most subjects which did not have a rather apparent relevance to scientific inquiry; laboratory work and research were emphasized and classroom lectures and recitations deemphasized; professors were appointed because they had made a name for themselves in research and publication and because they were the most prominent men available in their fields of specialization; undergraduate curricula were pushed aside, not because they were unimportant, but because they were considered to be inferior or preparatory. It was the rare university man who did not regard undergraduate work as a training ground leading almost inevitably to graduate study.

Some universities—Johns Hopkins is the best example—did not admit students for an undergraduate education. Universities at this time— 1870–1900—were concerned with science and applied science primarily:

the key characteristic of the American university was "independent inquiry."

The University ideal spread rapidly throughout the land, and in time university status became synonymous with academic respectability. Both old and new colleges tried to become universities; some did so prematurely by adding graduate work and assuming a research character before they were ready. For the colleges not responding to the drive for upgrading and expansion, two courses of action seemed open. A college could, without altering its earlier commitments to undergraduate studies, build a reputation on the quality of its collegiate program. The decision to accept this alternative led some schools into elite college circles. The other alternative permitted colleges to become quasi-vocational schools with specialized curricula preparing young men and women for life in society and to be democratic institutions in which all knowledge was welcomed and used for the education of the proverbial common man rather than for the education of gentlemen or scholars.

Junior Colleges

The most far-reaching and significant innovation in American higher education in the late nineteenth century was the upward extension of the college organization to include graduate work. While this change was being accomplished, some university educators suggested that the first two years of college—grades 13 and 14—be transferred to the high schools in order that the colleges and universities might be able to pursue their educational goals without the inconvenience of teaching freshman and sophomore college students. However, these views seemed to have little effect on high school or college organization until around 1900. In that year, William R. Harper, president of the University of Chicago, reorganized the college of the University of Chicago into two divisions: the junior college, grades 13 and 14; and the senior college, grades 15 and 16. He also urged the founding or organization of junior colleges either in connection with universities or independent of them.

According to Harper, the junior college would be a valuable new unit in American education because:[12]

1. Some junior college curricula could be terminal and educate students who could not gain much profit from a regular college course.
2. The two-year junior college course would be attractive to students who could not afford to spend more than two years in college.
3. The junior college curriculum could serve as an introduction to students who were uncertain of their ability to complete a longer college course.

4. In communities where junior colleges were added to the local high school, the atmosphere of the high school would be improved.
5. Many students could not afford to leave home to attend college, and local junior colleges would make higher education more democratic by making it more available to the young men and women of America.
6. Many four-year colleges had limited resources to continue as complete colleges, but they could become excellent two-year, or junior, colleges.

After 1900 many educational leaders endorsed the junior college idea, and public and private junior colleges were established by (1) making the first two years of a four-year college a distinct unit, (2) extending the high school curriculum to include the first two years of college work, (3) establishing independent junior colleges, and (4) reducing four-year colleges to junior college status. The growth of the junior college as part of American higher education is reflected in the following summary: In 1918, 14 public and 32 private junior colleges were in operation. In 1938, twenty years later, 209 public and 244 private junior colleges had been established. In the twenty-year period following 1938, 68 new junior colleges were founded, bringing the total in late 1957 to 295 public and 226 private junior colleges. In 1964, 372 public and 210 private junior colleges were active in the United States. These institutions enrolled 504,-000 or about 15 per cent of all students in higher education in the United States.

Since 1947 the place and purpose of junior colleges have been the subject of study and debate. The junior college, now usually called the community college, is supported and defended in circles that a half century ago could see no need for such institutions. Up to 1940 most state universities regarded junior colleges as nuisances infringing on their prerogative in higher learning; but with today's demands made on them, these same state universities are seeking relief and are hoping to find it in the community college. These lower colleges, they hope, will attract students who would otherwise seek admission to the state university. Of course, only one dimension of a community college's function is directed at conventional or traditional college work; in other words, only some community colleges or certain phases of their program include vocational and terminal studies which serve both useful social and economic purposes. Stated succinctly, their basic purpose is to offer terminal and preprofessional education in community centers of learning. Another attractive feature is their ability to remove or deemphasize geographic and economic barriers to higher learning: young men and women attend these free public colleges without leaving home.

CONTEMPORARY ISSUES
IN HIGHER EDUCATION

Since 1900, American colleges and universities have assumed a large task in liberalizing their purposes, curricula, and structure and in opening their doors to many more young men and women. The change in the complexion of the colleges themselves and the increasing complexity of society have created new problems or emphasized old ones which higher education must try to solve. In this section our purpose is merely to present some of the more critical issues facing American higher education.

Purpose of Higher Education

In addition to establishing curricula for scientific, professional, semiprofessional, and vocational education and training and rightfully recognizing their place in higher education, colleges and universities have been encouraged to show an increasing concern for the education of free men. It is often claimed that present college programs, because they lack unity and are overspecialized, do not do as much as they should by way of providing a general or liberal education for their students. The number of college courses has increased so much that a student could spend a lifetime taking all the courses that some colleges offer. This tendency to diversify the college curriculum has contributed to the technical or professional competence of the student but has not prepared him better for fulfilling his role as a parent, a citizen, or a man. The important problem for colleges and universities today is to find the right relationship between special and general education—between training for thousands of vocational and professional careers and educating for a basic culture and a common citizenship.

Opportunity for Higher Education

As American higher education faces the future, it is confronted with the problem of providing educational opportunities for larger and larger numbers of qualified students. Even the most conservative estimates indicate that the college enrollment in 1970 will be 6 million. It is estimated, also, that 49 per cent of the population of the United States has the mental ability to complete fourteen years of schooling and that 32 per cent of the population has the mental ability to complete an advanced or specialized professional program of education. Although some of these otherwise qualified students will have neither the motivation nor the interest to attend college, others who are qualified or potentially qualified will be unable to enroll because of artificial barriers or discrimination.

In order to equalize opportunity for higher education, the following steps should be taken by American schools:

1. The general quality of high school education must be improved to guarantee all youth, regardless of their geographic location or the high school they attend, a foundational education enabling them to enroll in, and profit from, a college course of studies.
2. Guidance and counseling services in high schools should be provided where they do not now exist and generally upgraded in schools where they are presently available. The Federal government has stimulated activity in this field in recent years and the net result, it is hoped, will be a generation better prepared to meet the uncertainties of the future and more confident in the knowledge that they are pursuing reasonable academic and vocational goals.
3. Both public and private colleges must broaden their programs of study to enable students of diverse talents to profit from schooling beyond the high school. The tendency on the part of some colleges to seek only the best students (those who score exceptionally well on College Board Examinations) and to neglect the others, if imitated by any large portion of American colleges, will close the door of college opportunity on capable but not brilliant students. It is at this point particularly that public colleges below university rank can perform an outstanding educational service: They can conduct a variety of programs; or one school can offer courses in one type of program attracting a certain clientele while another college takes another curricular direction. Diversity in programs and diversity in colleges seem to be highly desirable.
4. Additional public financial aid should be made to students and colleges. Scholarships, grants-in-aid, state or Federal guarantees backing student loans, Federal appropriations for additional physical facilities in private colleges are all important to liberalizing opportunities for higher learning.
5. Programs of adult education should be expanded considerably, and more of them should be made the responsibility of colleges and universities.
6. Public education at all levels should be made equally accessible to all, without regard to race, creed, sex, or national origin.

Financing of Higher Education

Financing higher education in the United States follows a complex pattern. As the enrollments increase and as the facilities for instruction are enlarged proportionately, the sources of support for higher education will be called upon to make larger sums of money available. These sources are private individuals, corporations, church groups, college alumni, students and their families, and government—local, state, and Federal. Institutions privately controlled are supported mainly by student tuition and fees and gifts received from donors, including income from endowed funds. Public institutions are supported by public funds and student tuition and fees.

It is sometimes argued that students should pay a larger share of the cost of their education and that public money should be appropriated only to pay for those costs which the student himself cannot bear. In most private colleges and universities tuitions and fees finance about 60 per cent of the total operating cost; this same proportion should be maintained in public universities and colleges, according to this point of view. On the other hand, it is claimed that opportunity for higher education should be made available to all qualified students at public expense. In addition to these arguments, the point is sometimes made that higher education on the scale that we may expect by 1970 *cannot* be financed; America, it is said, does not have the resources to support higher education for all students who may want to attend higher institutions in the next ten to twenty years.

These different points of view cannot be reconciled here. However, general recommendations may be made concerning the financing of higher education in the United States. In the first place, higher education must rest on the educational and financial bases of the elementary and secondary levels. Unless these lower educational levels are adequately supported, neither a soundly financed nor an effective system of higher education is likely to be attained. Beyond this, both the place and purpose of higher education and its relevance to the nation's good must be recognized if reasonable and regular financial support is to be forthcoming. Cost and character are complementary features: adequate programs of support for higher education will not be shaped until the character (and the social significance) of higher learning is thoroughly understood and appreciated. Understanding the relationship of science and technology to the national interest has not caused anyone any special concern in recent decades, and colleges and universities have no trouble whatever in relating these parts of their curricula either directly or indirectly to national defense goals. Thus, certain types of colleges, or special parts of their programs, have been the fortunate recipients of financial assistance, while other colleges without any special scientific orientation, or parts of college programs concerned with humanistic or philosophical objectives, have been neglected by foundations and government agencies with money to spend on programs in higher learning. The Higher Education Facilities Act of 1964 may alleviate some of the inequities among institutions on the level of Federal assistance. But, it should be noted, facilities only are affected by this act.

Even the state university may have its problems, for surely the education committee in the legislature can see and appreciate the social benefits accruing from a research laboratory for physics; there may be some note of acerbity to the tone of its response denying a request for funds to build a special center for humanistic studies. This brings us to another point in connection with fiscal principles governing higher schools: All elements and all levels of higher education should be given adequate support, or at best the general program of higher education will meet with limited success.

Finally, principles basic to the financing of higher education should include a plan of finance committed to assuring equality of opportunity. Economic barriers to equal opportunity should be nullified in favor of making ability and interest the only criteria for an institution of higher learning. In addition, the plan of finance should recognize public responsibilities for higher education, but it should allow for private support in both public and nonpublic colleges and universities. The educational interests of this nation can best be served by the continuous and vigorous expansion of private as well as public support for institutions of higher education. The total program of higher learning for America must be founded upon the principle of dualism, a principle wherein the need for partnership must be emphasized. The role of each partner should be established in terms of the social, economic, and educational welfare of the nation. There are apodictic proofs that fiscal policy should be correlated with objectives in social and educational policies.

Staffing Higher Education

In 1957 the President's Committee on Education beyond the High School estimated a need for from 15,000 to 25,000 Ph.D.s each year for ten years; in that year the universities of the United States were producing only about 9,000 Ph.D.s, of whom slightly over one-half were entering college or university teaching. Every year the deficit has become larger; the decline in the proportion of Ph.D.s available for filling college and university positions has accelerated. The belief is quite general among university people that unless unusual and successful efforts are made to check this cumulative deficit, higher education will be in a precarious position. The plight of the colleges may be only part of the picture: business, industry, and government have a brisk demand for trained personnel. They may be able, through financial and other incentives, to draw an even larger portion of Ph.D.s to their plants and laboratories, and they may attract people who are now in college teaching to more lucrative positions than they now occupy. The research dimension alone is enough to cause real concern whenever the question of trained personnel is raised: Expenditures for research in the United States amounted to 12 billion dollars in 1959 and went up to 16 billion in 1961. Of these amounts, the universities account for less than 4 per cent; the research responsibility is borne by government and industry.

Thus, the demand for highly educated personnel capable of contributing to the advancement of knowledge and the development of technology is even greater in government and industry than it is in the collegiate community. The crisis of supply—a crisis felt especially in the academic agency responsible for preparing highly educated persons (the graduate school)—arises out of the needs of both university and nonuniversity agencies.

A variety of efforts have been made to correct or, at least, to alleviate this serious situation. The Woodrow Wilson Fund of nearly 25 million dollars was established to attract able students to graduate study and then to teaching in the college classroom. The National Defense Education Act of 1958 had the same general purpose: aiding capable students to continue their studies through the graduate school with the understanding, or the implication, that they would spent at least the first few years of their professional lives in college teaching. Financial assistance to students entering graduate study has been given over the past several years by universities, foundations, institutes, councils, and scholarly and professional societies as well as by state and Federal governments, industrial and commercial organizations, individual donors, and other agencies.

Even with these widespread efforts to induce qualified students to pursue graduate study and then to accept appointments to college and university faculties, the deficit in the production of Ph.D.s and other qualified postgraduates, compared to the need, appears to be growing. The question we are faced with now is this: What means may colleges and universities employ to alleviate the crisis surrounding staffing? Some of the following recommendations may be made:

1. Make college teaching more attractive financially by offering higher salaries, enabling colleges to compete with government and industry for qualified people.

2. Upgrade the present members of the college community through programs of sabbatical studies and research; reduce teaching loads to free the teacher for study, and provide him with clerical and mechanical aids minimizing the drudgery of routine tasks connected with teaching.

3. Stimulate the interest of all undergraduate students in professional educational activities, and urge promising students to prepare for college teaching. They should be apprised of the financial assistance available in the form of fellowships, scholarships, grants-in-aid, grants, and student loans.

4. Build professional attitudes among present members of college faculties by making available all the conditions for professionalizing rather than unionizing college teaching. Capable young men and women will not be attracted to a career in college teaching unless it is apparent that college faculties now have a professional spirit and enjoy a professional status.

5. College and university governing boards and administrations must make teaching conditions generally more attractive and offer teaching staffs realistic opportunities to share in the building of academic policies. Colleges must do more than pay lip service to democracy; the college must become the true home of democracy, and democratic procedures must be observed in its government.

6. Prepare students for college teaching by making available graduate studies and programs giving insights into the requirements of college teaching and some of the knowledge and skill necessary to success in teaching. It may not be true that college teaching is the one profession for which training is unnecessary, and explicit preparation for a career in higher education has been badly neglected. Fortunately, there are now more than a dozen major universities with programs of study in higher education intended to prepare students for careers in colleges and universities. The following universities grant doctor's degrees in higher education: Boston College, University of Buffalo, The Catholic University of America, University of California, University of Chicago, University of Denver, Florida State University, George Peabody College for Teachers, University of Maryland, Michigan State University, University of Michigan, University of Minnesota, New York University, Pennsylvania State University, Southern Illinois University, Stanford University, Syracuse University, and Teachers College, Columbia University.

SUMMARY

During the half century after 1850, elementary education was popularized in the United States. The period 1900 to 1950 may be described as the age of the high school, for it was during these years that the high school realized, and in many instances more than realized, the hopes of its founders. The next half century promises to be the age of higher education, although it will undoubtedly be true that both elementary schools and high schools will be affected by this new emphasis and will be called upon to adjust their programs and their purposes to changing education in a changing world.

The college movement began for English America with the founding of Harvard College in 1636. For almost two hundred years this type of higher education—privately controlled and supported—prevailed in America. Experiments with publicly controlled and supported higher education began late in the eighteenth century, but it was not until college curricula became more practical in objectives and less classical in scope that public higher education began to flourish. In addition to this, it was commonly believed that higher education was not a public responsibility. One of the major factors contributing to the rise of public colleges and universities was the Morrill Act of 1862. This act granted land to the states for the purpose of establishing colleges of agriculture and mechanical arts.

Until 1876 most colleges in the United States were concerned chiefly with the communication of knowledge rather than with its discovery through research. But scientific knowledge as a basis for technology grew more and more important to American social and economic life. This pressure led the colleges to reconstruct their curricula, modify their purposes, and expand the area of their endeavors. Research became the distinctive feature of the American university that followed the example of the Johns Hopkins University at Baltimore, the first American university to devote its resources almost fully to research and the training of graduate students.

Higher education was narrowed somewhat when it accepted research and scientific specialization as its principal mission. And this was done just as higher education began to attract larger and more diversified student bodies. To accommodate students who were interested in, and qualified for, some education beyond the high school, the junior college was introduced. More recently the junior college idea has been broadened, and a new name has been given to a kind of higher education that will offer terminal and preparatory programs of study to students in their local communities—the community college.

The impending age of higher education presents many crucial issues: Who shall attend college? How shall college programs be designed to accommodate the interests and needs of students? How will popular higher education be financed? Where will college teachers be recruited to guide and direct the learning activities of an estimated 6 to 7 million college students by 1970?

QUESTIONS AND EXERCISES

1. Investigate and discuss the origin of universities.
2. What were the objectives of the first American colleges, and how did they differ from those of the European universities of that time?
3. How were American colleges affected by the scientific movement? What effect did science have on the college curriculum of the later nineteenth century?
4. Why were the early American colleges for men only?
5. Discuss the importance of the Dartmouth College decision.
6. What role do community colleges have in American higher education today? Do you favor the extension of the community college movement?
7. How would you distinguish between junior colleges and community colleges?
8. What do you consider the major problems facing higher education today? How would you resolve these problems?
9. Is higher education in the United States popular? If not, should it be?

ADDITIONAL READINGS

Brown, E. E.: *The Origin of American State Universities,* University of California Press, Berkeley, 1903. An old but valuable study of state action in higher education. The reasons for state action are both interesting and pertinent.

Brubacher, John S., and Willis Rudy: *Higher Education in Transition,* Harper & Row, Publishers, Incorporated, New York, 1959. See chapter 12: "Articulation of Secondary and Higher Education."

Carmichael, Oliver C.: *Universities: Commonwealth and American,* Harper & Row, Publishers, Incorporated, New York, 1959. Read the chapters on Commonwealth universities. The author discusses seven systems of higher education.

Chambers, M. M.: *Chance and Choice in Higher Education,* The Interstate Printers and Publishers, Danville, Ill., 1962. Addresses, essays, and lectures on higher education form this volume.

Ducret, Bernard (ed.): *The University Today: Its Role and Place in Society,* World University Service, Geneva, Switzerland, 1960. A description of the cultural function of the university.

Fehl, Noah E.: *The Idea of a University in East and West,* Chung Chi College, Hong Kong, 1962. Read chapters on the universities of the East.

Fields, Ralph R.: *The Community College Movement,* McGraw-Hill Book Company, New York, 1962. An interesting discussion of the community college. Notice particularly the promise of the institution.

Fisher, Margaret B., and Jeanne L. Noble: *College Education as Personal Development,* Prentice-Hall, Inc., Englewood Cliffs, N.J., 1960. This book is concerned with three principal aspects of higher education: the student and his personal values, the student and his life plan, and the college community and its resources.

Frankel, Charles: *Issues in University Education,* Harper & Row, Publishers, Incorporated, New York, 1959. A general treatment of American higher education.

Garrison, Roger H.: *The Adventure of Learning in College,* Harper & Row, Publishers, Incorporated, New York, 1959. See especially chapters pertaining to freshman and sophomore students' expectations for higher learning.

Harris, Seymour E.: *Higher Education: Resources and Finance,* McGraw-Hill Book Company, New York, 1962. A searching analysis by an economist of higher education's resources. The sections on financing may be of special interest to the student who is looking forward to a career in college teaching.

Havighurst, Robert J.: *American Higher Education in the 1960's,* Ohio State University Press, Columbus, 1960. A discussion of modern challenges to higher schools.

Henderson, Algo D.: *Policies and Practices in Higher Education,* Harper & Row, Publishers, Incorporated, New York, 1960. Read the section on policies.

Hofstadter, Richard, and C. DeWitt Hardy, *The Development and Scope of Higher Education in the United States,* Columbia University Press, New York, 1952. Part I, "The Development of Higher Education," is brief but excellent. See especially the section, "Age of the College."

McConnell, Thomas R.: *A General Pattern for American Public Higher Education,* McGraw-Hill Book Company, New York, 1962. Note especially the author's discussion of college admissions and the doctrine of the "right to fail."

Medsker, Leland L.: *The Junior College: Progress and Prospect,* McGraw-Hill Book Company, New York, 1960. See chapter on the prospects for the junior college.

Millett, John D.: *The Academic Community: An Essay on Organization,* Mc-Graw-Hill Book Company, New York, 1962. A competent treatment of the distinctiveness of college organization. The author argues that principles of business or political organization do not necessarily apply to the academic community. Chapter 4 contains a discussion of students' roles.

Orlans, H.: *The Effect of Federal Programs on Higher Education,* The Brookings Institution, Washington, D.C., 1962. Gives special attention to the effect Federal programs may have on the quality of higher learning.

Power, Edward J.: *A History of Catholic Higher Education in the United States,* The Bruce Publishing Company, Milwaukee, 1958. See especially chapter 2, "The American Scene and the Founding of Catholic Colleges."

Rosecrance, F. C.: *The American College and Its Teachers,* The Macmillan Company, New York, 1962. Chapters 2 to 4 should be of special interest.

Ross, Earle D.: *Democracy's College: The Land Grant College Movement in the Formative Stage,* Iowa State College Press, Ames, 1942. See sections on the popularization of higher education brought about largely by inaugurating vocational programs in agriculture and mechanic arts.

Rudolph, Frederick: *The American College and University,* Alfred A. Knopf, Inc., New York, 1962. A general history of American higher education. Especially good for colonial colleges.

Sanford, Nevitt (ed.): *The American College,* John Wiley & Sons, Inc., New York, 1962. A huge volume with several contributors covering many facets of contemporary college life.

Schmidt, George P.: *The Liberal Arts College,* Rutgers University Press, New Brunswick, N.J., 1957. A competent, general history of the liberal arts college.

Shuster, George N.: *Education and Moral Wisdom,* Harper & Row, Publishers, Incorporated, New York, 1960. See especially chapters on education's relationship to moral wisdom.

Storr, Richard J.: *The Beginning of Graduate Education in America,* The University of Chicago Press, Chicago, 1953. Shows how graduate schools were superimposed on undergraduate colleges.

Tewksbury, Donald: *The Founding of American Colleges and Universities before the Civil War,* Bureau of Publications, Teachers College, Columbia University, New York, 1932. Read for an interpretation of the influence of the Dartmouth College decision on public and private colleges.

Thwing, C. F.: *A History of Higher Education in America,* Appleton-Century-Crofts, Inc., New York, 1906. A general history of higher education. Interesting mainly because it was perhaps the first book to deal with American higher education from the perspective of history.

Veblen, Thorstein: *The Higher Learning in America,* B. W. Huebsch, Publisher, New York, 1918. A caustic discussion of the fault and the fraudulence in American higher learning.

Workman, John R.: *New Horizons of Higher Education,* Public Affairs Press, Washington, D.C., 1959. Where can higher education go from here? This book tries to capture visions of the future.

chapter 9

Learning and Teaching

Several years ago a prominent educator remarked that neither educators nor schools showed a vital interest in the *raison d'être* of education: learning and teaching. Teachers, he maintained, were exerting their best energies on educational tangents; and superintendents, principals, and school boards were preoccupied with budgets, buildings, and public relations. They were too busy, he said, to attend to issues of curriculum, methods of teaching, motivation of students, and relevant and quality learning opportunites.[1] We shall not pause here to engage in debate or to undertake a reinforcement or a refutation of this broad criticism. Yet, despite these and other charges made relative to the central interests of educators, the record attests to the attention given essential features of formal education—teaching and learning.

The inspiration for this attention to pedagogic realities may not have originated with Socrates, for teachers who preceded him were intensely interested in basic educational issues; yet Socrates, because of his preeminent reputation as the greatest of Western teachers, offers a good starting point. If we attempt to find his greatness in the field of theory and systematic philosophy, we shall either concede him too much and Plato too little or else end in disbelieving in him altogether. Aristotle is very likely correct in believing that the theoretical structure of the philosophy Plato puts in Socrates's mouth was essentially the work of Plato himself. But Socrates is much more than a collection of stimulating ideas which is left when we subtract the theory of ideas and the rest of the dogmatic doctrine from Plato's picture of him. His importance lies in another direction. He is neither the continuator of a scientific tradition nor the inheritor of an assortment of philosophical doctrines. He was a man of his time: a teacher, who tried to upgrade the intellectual values of Athens. He sought this goal by rejecting democratic processes and opportunities and concentrating instead on curricula and methods for the education of an elite class.

234 The true Socratic method may be reduced to two essential ele-

ments: exhortation and examination. On the level of practice, both elements employed the question. Socrates taught by exhortation when, by means of the skillfully posed question and his own ethical standards, he led students closer to truth and virtue; and by examination, still employing the question, he introduced them to critical techniques whereby they could refute error and reject superficial intellectualism. Plato makes Socrates, the teacher, speak like a doctor, only the patient is not the physical but the spiritual man.

Plato himself and Aristotle, too, were alert to the psychological foundations of learning, and they argued with philosophic passion and extraordinary astuteness for more skillful and honest teaching. Plato's preferences for philosophical idealism led him and his faithful followers to a doctrine of infused or intuitive knowledge. In such idealistic categories, teaching and learning retained their significance, but the direction of learning was reversed. Scant heed was paid the world of experience, from which, in many traditional views, learning proceeds; instead, interest centered on ideas stored in the mind, unwilling captives waiting to be released by effective teaching.

Aristotle rejected Plato's idealistic dogmatism, but in so doing, he strengthened rather than weakened the role of learning. His theory, moreover, with laws of association, on the one hand, and his emphasis on habit and education on the other, set the theoretical stage for psychological and pedagogic speculation for centuries to come.

There are intermediate figures between Aristotle and Quintilian who could testify to preoccupations with teaching and learning, but we must ignore them here, with only that word of recognition, because of limitation of space and time. The record of their achievements is dimmed by the incomparable Quintilian, whose theories of teaching, built on a more basic theory of learning, guided schoolmasters for a thousand years. *The Education of the Orator* contains a reservoir of psychological and methodological insights rediscovered hundreds of times by modern educational theorists.[2]

Vittorino da Feltre, in his court school at Mantua, was devoted to effective teaching and quality learning, and, if the accounts of his work are at all objective, he was never distracted from education's chief purpose. Comenius and his natural method; Vives and Locke; Rousseau and Pestalozzi; Herbart and Dewey all were determined to find a more meaningful relationship between learning and teaching.[3]

The litany of names, if complete, would be long; from ancient to contemporary times schoolmen displayed a keen interest in the essential features of education. Because of it, we now have many different, often opposing, theories of learning, and teachers often feel compelled to accept one theory in preference to others. Of course, theories of learning have intimate relationships to theories or interpretations of man: man's abilities depend on his nature. Philosophies of man are the general foundations supporting theories of learning.

THE MEANING OF LEARNING

The general question What is learning? is subject to two interpretations: One is broad and includes many, or all, types of learning; the other, somewhat more specialized, is directed at the problem of learning how to learn. Both have profound meaning for educators; perhaps the latter belongs especially to the teacher's province, for he is concerned not only with communicating knowledge but with inculcating skills of learning as well. Yet learning how to learn is a subject with implications extending beyond the classroom. In contemporary society, especially, we are constantly impressed by the realization that today's learner is often tomorrow's teacher —the corpus of knowledge is expanding so rapidly—and either for learning or teaching, knowing how to learn, itself a product of learning, is indispensable.

Rather than embarking on a theoretical discussion of the nature of learning here, we shall be content with a descriptive approach. Neither the value nor the relevance of theory is doubted or dismissed; our interests are in another direction. We may begin by hypothesizing two essential features of learning: First, activity is imperative; second, learning modifies behavior. On the most basic level, certain conditions are part of all learning. First is the context, of which the learner is clearly a part, with opportunities or threats motivating action toward satisfying goals. The range of responses varies among learners. If identical contexts could be devised for two learners, with the sole variable being intrinsic personal qualities, we should no doubt discover that responses depend to a great extent on personal characteristics of attitude, skill, and ability. Before the person acts, before he directs his energies toward a goal, he tries to anticipate the outcome of his action. There is a predictive element here: the person tries to foresee some of the possible consequences of his action. Having considered the possible results of various kinds and degrees of action, the learner acts. Now he is faced with acceptance or rejection of results. If they are acceptable, additional possibilities or opportunities arise for consolidation and incorporation as well as progressive modification and fixation. But if the results are dissatisfying and frustrating, the person must try again and perhaps continue this process until satisfaction is attained.[4]

The most significant conditions mentioned above are problem (thinking begins with a problem), motivation, action, and consequences. With these conditions, learning is possible; if it occurs, what has happened? What is learning? Learning is a change in behavior as a result of experience.

THE MEANING OF TEACHING

The importance of teaching must be clear to anyone giving thought to the multiple issues confronting education. Yet, not all learning requires teaching. When the person faced with a problem either thinks through the problem or solves it in some acceptable way, we say he has learned. At least, he has altered his behavior. When a cat in a puzzle box escapes, we say he has learned to release himself. It is possible, of course, for persons to seek and obtain help in solving problems; it may be given in the form of explanations, descriptions, demonstrations, or analyses. In the cat's situation, it can be helped to find the way to freedom, thereby reducing expenditure of time and energy.

The learning process may be aided or unaided: When aided, the dimension of teaching is introduced; when unaided, it is proper to speak simply of learning by discovery. Yet even here there is lack of precision, because in all learning, even when teaching is most effective, discovery is fundamental; in its elemental meaning, all learning is self-learning, all education is self-education.[5]

Learning by unaided discovery is a part of learning where teaching considerations do not arise. Learning by instruction, however, introduces the element of aid from others respecting matters to be learned. Learning by instruction is always education by another (teaching), involving the employment of some art cooperatively to facilitate the natural learning process.

In a somewhat restricted sense, teaching means directing learning activities in classrooms or laboratories. This implies that the teacher, the person who occupies the center of the educational stage, possesses the knowledge, skill, and habit he is trying to lead another to acquire. It is futile or worse for the teacher to try to communicate what he himself does not know. Yet, there are broad areas open to teachers in which they may succeed in stimulating others to acquire knowledge or habits which they themselves do not possess. An important phase of the teacher's task, then, must surely be helping create conditions favorable to learning, and playing a part in spurring student learning to range beyond formal curricular boundaries.

At the very least, teaching implies knowledge and art. Knowledge is indispensable, and is generally acknowledged, but so is art. What is to be taught must be organized or artistically planned and intentionally executed. In the absence of pedagogic artistry or intention there is no real teaching, although the possibility is not eliminated of some learning's resulting not from what is done but in spite of it.

Teaching is a human activity combining or bridging theory and practice; in combining knowledge and art, one expedites human learning.

THEORIES OF LEARNING

The organization of teaching-learning activities may or may not follow theories advanced to explain the principal elements in learning situations. In general, most of us would probably agree, the more we know about the nature and conditions of learning, the better able we shall be to formulate theories and methods of teaching. In the long history of teaching, methodologists have prospected for insights into natural learning, and some, claiming success, built teaching processes on a foundation of natural methods. The great difficulty surrounding these assertions, however, was the stubborn refusal of their authors to reveal their discoveries to the waiting educational world. Secret theories or methods have no place in education.

There is a more basic problem here than infrequent and probably invalid claims of having discovered the philosopher's stone of learning: Are learning theories really important to teachers? On this point there are two schools of thought. One, maintaining the importance of theory, questions the quality of teaching procedures not clearly and solidly grounded on principles of learning. The other dismisses theory, seeing little relationship between it and effective teaching and, further, offers examples of excellent teachers having little or no knowledge of theory, or of significant theoretical metamorphoses being ignored in teaching practice. While proponents of the second school may profess an interest in theory and admit to the mere possibility of its leading to versatility in teaching techniques, they adamantly deny any intrinsic or necessary relationship between learning theory and pedagogic practice.

There are, in other words, educators and teachers who accept a theory of human nature and a theory of learning based on it and relate both to successful classroom procedures. But this position is challenged by others who refuse to participate in alliances between theory and practice, believing, undoubtedly, that allegiances to theory impair judgments or limit freedom on practical educational issues.

In searching for a theory of learning to embrace, what alternatives do we have? There are theories of association, field theories, and theories emphasizing purposive behavior. We may discuss each briefly.

Association

The most common name for this theory is connectionism, but modern associationism, functionalism, and stimulus-response psychology are terms sometimes used to identify it. To avoid confusing modern associationism with the older Aristotelian brand, we shall use the term connectionism. Connectionism, as a modern and more mechanistic development of associationism, tries to explain learning largely in terms of a learner's reaction to his environment.

It is impossible to spend any amount of time on connectionism without mentioning the name of its principal architect, Edward L. Thorndike. The work of Thorndike, first at Harvard under the famous William James, and then at Columbia, was inspired by two sources. Alexander Bain, an English associationist, provided him with the basic "laws" which he reworked and refined. Evolution was the other source. Darwin's theory led to a controversy over the capacity of animals to reason, and biologists engaged in experiments to gather evidence one way or another. These biological experiments opened new psychological vistas, and from them psychologists hoped to learn something more about human psychological functions.

Departing from two rather diverse sources—along with some bewilderment over the awkwardness of assumptions made in traditional associationism—armed with some knowledge of the reflex arc and the neural impulse, Thorndike began to observe the pecking actions of chicks.

Traditional associationism seemed too cumbersome for explaining how chicks learned to peck, and it involved an elaborate set of questionable assumptions regarding mental processes. These objections led Thorndike to modify conventional associationism. Instead of the traditional association between ideas (an association compatible with the laws of contiguity, contrast, or similarity), he introduced a more direct association between situation and response. In pecking, the situation, S, is presented by food; the response, R, is the act of pecking.

Stimulus-response psychology, in the hands of Thorndike and his followers, was used to explain not only the activities of chicks but the behavior of people as well. Of course, the behavior of persons, being highly complex, necessitated the introduction of mental associations to support mere physiological connections. Yet mental associations, when introduced, were fitted into the S-R formula: each new idea was a response to a preceding idea or sensation. All human action, Thorndike maintained, was susceptible of stimulus-response description and analysis.

Good teaching, according to this theory, is really a matter of creating situations wherein learners may respond. The effectiveness of their response will depend to a large extent on how carefully the principal laws of connectionism—effect, readiness, and exercise—are honored in the scholastic setting. In its simplest terms, the law of effect states that organisms are attracted by pleasurable situations and responses and are repelled by painful ones. Broadly interpreted, effect could be motivation. Readiness implies an ability or a degree of maturity in the nervous system to convey neural impulses arising in S-R experiences. In formal education the law of readiness, readiness to learn, is universally understood, although not always in a connectionist context. The law of exercise, or stamping in, states that repetition will reduce resistance on neural avenues and make responses to given situations more effective. Many teachers have interpreted the law of exercise as meaning drill; it is not easy to avoid this conclusion entirely.

Connectionism was transplanted from the level of theory to practice with relative ease. For many years, especially in the United States, its prestige in educational circles was high because it contained accepted doctrines of educational psychology. Although this position of prominence has deteriorated somewhat in recent years, the theory is still widely honored, and teachers still follow its educational directives. In general, connectionism puts great stress on learning—learning is the central psychological process, and all other phenomena are incidental—and makes learning almost solely a reaction to man's environment.[6]

Field Theories

Associationist theories, especially connectionism and behaviorism, tend to emphasize the discreteness of the environment; field theories, on the other hand, are supremely confident that the key to learning is found in relationships between organization, structure, and experience. Two prominent field theories are gestalt and topological.[7]

Gestalt psychology arose largely as a reaction to associationism. This reaction or revolt was inspired mainly by the German psychologists Wertheimer, Koffka, and Kohler. According to these gestalt psychologists, and those who follow them, experience is always structured. Whenever we are aware of anything, we are aware of it as part of a complex pattern or structure or organization. We never perceive a mere mass of separate details. Some of these details will assume a prominent position in experience; others will occupy a subordinate role. In ordinary experience there is always something standing out, while other things, at least for the moment, recede into the background. Even when the external environment has, or seems to have, no structure, learners try to find some principle of organization. This tendency may go so far, that is, structure may so completely dominate an experience, that details not actually present will be experienced. There are many examples of this: rough sketches of rectangles or triangles where corners are imperfectly joined are seen as rectangles or triangles. Familiar words in print are understood even though letters are transposed. Proofreading is especially difficult for persons familiar with the subject and an almost impossible task for authors.

Perception and learning are critical problems in gestalt psychology. Perception entails our awareness of the world and involves efforts to explain how our experiences of situations remain relatively constant while the physical events responsible for them are subject to intense fluctuations. Learning is a matter of seeing relations. Its effectiveness rests on creating a pattern within the learner containing at the same time the problem to be solved and the means of solving it. Once the pattern is formed, the critical phase of learning is over. Luster, speed, and efficiency may be added in a variety of ways, but a major breakthrough in learning is achieved with the establishment of a pattern.

Topological and gestalt theories meet on common ground when they assert the significance of pattern and field, and both share the view that they contain the determinants of experience, although topological theory departs somewhat from the classical gestalt in stressing behavior over experience and depends more upon individual motivation. In other words, topological theory is somewhat more sophisticated than gestalt because its structures are psychological as well as physical. It has led methodologists into broad questions involving dynamic processes in learning, especially the employment of group processes. This learning theory has room for goals, forces, and structure. Within the structure there may be negative and positive forces, but neither have permanent value. The negative force in a learning situation today may be the chief incentive to learning tomorrow. The obstacles that once kept a child confined to a limited area may later become attractive objects to jump or climb.

Purposive Theories

The S-R may explain some of life's actions, gestalt may explain others, but behind all of these explanations, the purposivist asserts, stand phenomena of goal and need. There is wide variety in the tools or the actions a person may use to reach his goal. And from this point of view, what really counts is neither the synapse nor the structure, but the determination of the person to achieve some special objective.

No theory of learning ignores motivation, but with purposivists motivation is central, and the chief problem in formal education is supplying and clarifying motives. The teacher may be faced with the task of creating incentives first; when this is done, content and methodology fall naturally into place.

Purposive psychology, or one of its major branches, psychoanalysis, is keenly aware of goal-seeking behavior. It sees goal-directed behavior as a constant competition among attractive and worthwhile goals. So far, psychoanalysis has not shown any special interest in learning, but it has given a great deal of attention to the general conditions surrounding learning experiences. It has much to say about mental hygiene, about the significance of early childhood experiences, and about personal adjustment.[8]

Learning is only one aspect of behavior, and most theories pertaining to it treat of other aspects of behavior as well. In any case, what we have reviewed so quickly are theories proposed to explain general behavior; some among them show a lively preoccupation with learning and its attendant features. Gestalt psychology recognizes learning largely as a by-product, as a change in the structure of experience, while most connectionists and some purposivists regard learning as the central psychological issue, although, understandably, their analyses of its psychological and physical foundations differ greatly.

MOTIVATION

The need for stimulation as a basis for human action has long been recognized. Motivation is behind whatever we do. Sometimes our motives, or reasons for doing something, are clear; perhaps too often they are obscure both to our associates and ourselves. Motives have been interpreted as the initial impulse, the push starting us in one direction or another, and somehow we carry on from there. They have also been regarded as nothing more than good will, a proper disposition toward action. In still other interpretations, motives are either entirely intrinsic or extrinsic, or motives may include not only the initiation of action but directing and sustaining it toward a goal as well.

The Importance of Motivation

Despite many obscurities surrounding the general problem of motivation, the powerful influence of motivation on behavior is universally admitted. Of all the devices available to teachers, perhaps the most important is motivation. If, for example, we do nothing more than make it important for a child to learn a certain thing, the chances of his learning it are excellent.

Learning is a complex psychological phenomenon with many mechanisms, none of which alone, not even motivation, produces learning. Yet motivation may be the force setting other mechanisms in motion, thereby producing conditions necessary for learning. Motivation may trigger the process leading to learning, but both it and the ensuing process need direction and care. Motivation must be stressed as part of learning, not to indicate that it alone may be relied upon to produce results, but to point to its unique and central role in the entire learning process.

Motivation in Formal Education

Motives playing a vital role in life generally—the basic physical urges—do not seem to find their way directly into the school. Students are prompted to action, are stimulated to learn, by a variety of other motives. In the religiously oriented school, some motives are supernatural. One need do no more than visit an elementary or secondary school where religious perspectives are prominent to have this demonstrated to him. The skillful teacher is able to capitalize on such motivation and at the same time reinforce these strong supernatural motives. In the school where the supernatural dimension is excluded, and even in the religious school, there are other motives initiating, directing, and sustaining activity. In general, these motives have a social and intellectual foundation. The learner's need to be with people, his need to attract and hold the attention of others, his need to be of service to them, all may be utilized by teachers. In addition, there are powerful motives to be exploited in the learner's hope to be liked by people, in his desire for self expression, and in his persistent need to have a good opinion of himself.

Motivation to Learn

Some students appear to be naturally motivated to learn, and their teachers experience no difficulty in translating their basic motives into effective learning exercises. But the converse of this state of affairs is also real with unwilling and indifferent students avoiding learning opportunities. The most a teacher can assume, perhaps the minimum with which he can work, is the student's good will toward learning. From basic good will, he can proceed to tell students what is expected of them, both in virtue and knowledge. These, then, become educational or learning objectives and, as such, are clearly motives, for students learn more effectively when they are aware of standards set for them.

Despite the importance generally attached to intention in learning, we should be aware of the possibility, at least the possibility, of learning's taking place even when no apparent effort is made to learn. This is called incidental learning. A great deal of attention is now being given to it, and some experimentation is being carried on. There is, for example, an unusual amount of interest regarding the possibility of learning while asleep, but profound doubt is also cast on this kind of incidental learning.

Whatever may be said about learning in the absence of deliberate intention, there is no question whatever that intention is a great boon to learning. Learning seems to be improved by a simple announcement attaching importance to the material presented. On a lower level, it may be improved by simply stating what is self-evident, viz., students are in school to learn. Such spurs to motivation are never enough, yet few teachers have ever remained totally indifferent to them.

In general, we think of motives coming from two sources: internal and external. Other terminology is also used: extrinsic and intrinsic motives. The internal or intrinsic motive originates within the learner. It grows and flowers with experience and thus may not be an entirely original datum, yet it attaches to the life of inner rather than outer experience. Internal or intrinsic motives seem to have greater force and are not so subject to redirection or interruption. Most teachers think of intrinsic motivation as a superior kind.

Extrinsic motives are formed out of the pressures of living. For example, a boy may learn to read because he wants to please his mother. In spite of the general feeling that extrinsic motives lack the purity, directness, and simplicity of intrinsic motives, there are times in teaching-learning processes when no intrinsic motivation is apparent, and neither teachers nor students seem to be able to wait for it to appear. Classes may be motivated by fear of punishment or of low marks, and while we recognize these motives as being on a lower plane than, say, the sheer love of learning, or knowledge for its own sake, we are forced to admit their effectiveness.

Attitudes toward Learning

We know relatively little about the acquisition of attitudes in general; perhaps we know even less about attitudes toward learning. Some children come to school with a keen desire to learn. No learning tasks are drudgery for them; they are enthusiastic about everything. Other children, perhaps brothers or sisters of the ones so interested, show none of this apparently native desire or curiosity for learning. They find school life almost unbearable and wait with signs of impatience until compulsory attendance statutes permit freedom from the confinements of the academic world.

Attitudes toward learning are products both of environment and reason. The cultural milieu has an influence on young intellects and wills; the social environment is unquestionably one factor helping form attitudes and ideals relative to learning. Once these attitudes are formed, they are altered only with considerable difficulty; and forming or reforming attitudes toward learning is surely one of the important responsibilities of schools. They stand either as important incentives to learning or as ominous obstacles to motivation and achievement.

In broad terms, attitudes toward learning reflect one of two convictions: knowledge is desirable and learning is a natural, even necessary, act of man; or knowledge is useful, and learning is but a means to an end. These basic attitudes affect not only the kinds of learning attractive to students but their drive and dedication as well.

The Relationship between Motivation and Knowledge of Results

Knowledge of results has a definite effect on physical and mental performance. Clearly, knowledge of results leads to greater expenditures of effort, but we are not yet certain of a high positive correlation between the efforts spent and the quality of learning. Teachers' contacts with students, however, reinforce their confidence in the close relationship between diligent practice and improved learning.

If motivation in the form of knowledge of results does prove to be highly effective, its employment would be easy to recommend, because we should really be competing against ourselves, against our own past performances. There would be no danger, for a student would not be asked to attain an ideal standard of performance or even to compete with the more able members of his class. He would merely be asked to improve his performance.

In addition to being safe, this motive is easily manipulated. Teachers could use it in many different ways in regular classrooms, although its most explicit use would be in connection with examinations or quizzes. It is desirable to make the results of examinations known to students as soon as possible. Oftentimes, students will be able to correct their own drills and quizzes and thus be almost immediately aware of the quality of their work. Younger students may need the sustaining effects of this kind of motivation more than do older, more mature students, yet on every educational level knowledge of results is important.

If tests are effective means for informing students of their progress, the question might be asked: How frequently should tests be given? Should they be given daily? Such frequency may interfere with, rather than accelerate, progress. There is no general agreement on the value of frequent tests. On the college level, for example, there is no definite advantage to frequent tests over tests given once or twice a term. On the elementary or secondary level, more frequent tests are often recommended. In general, it is hard to defend the practice of surprise tests. If the test itself is a motive, i.e., if students know a test is to be given, they prepare for it. The surprise test provides no such opportunity and may, in addition, give students an impression of learning as a game in which teachers try by hook or crook to outwit students. Such attitudes are bound to destroy rather than build motivation.

Rewards and Censure

Under ordinary circumstances, students receive information indicating the quality of their work, but only rarely do these reports include statements of praise or blame. Marks or achievement reports may, of course, have implicit implications of praise or reproof. However, over the years, teachers have sometimes tried to accelerate learning by praising or blaming students publicly. Students who do well are praised and are motivated to continue high-level performance; students who fail are praised for their accomplishments —failure is not mentioned—and thus are led to work harder and more effectively in the future. Or the student who has done well is censured for his mistakes and the student whose work is inferior is likewise blamed or punished. Every school with an honor roll, every college with a dean's list or an honors program is praising superior performance. And there are regular academic debates concerning the merits of these devices and their total effect on the life of an academic community.

Both praise and blame seem to be motives to greater effort. At the present state of our knowledge, however, it is not possible to say which is more effective. Regardless of claims made for stimulating the superior student to greater performance by publishing glowing reports of his accomplishments, or putting him in a special group, these very devices may undermine the confidence, the community spirit, and the motivation of the average or, at least, less gifted students who do not achieve such laurels.

Other fairly basic issues are involved in the use of praise and blame. They have to do with teachers' and students' personalities. Teacher A may use censure effectively with students B and C, but ineffectively with students D and F. One person needs praise to keep going; another is indifferent either to praise or censure. From the point of view of personal adjustment, a series of uninterrupted failures can be harmful. For some students regular experiences of success may be boring and unchallenging. The threat or the possibility of failure should be present for them. A series of successes followed by a serious failure can be disturbing and even dangerous.[9]

MEANING

Learning of many kinds takes place by employing motivation, drill, and reinforcement. We have all met children who are able to recite lines of prose or poetry. Although they may astound us by what are often truly precocious feats, it is usually easy to detect their lack of understanding. Even in formal learning, students learn many things in an arbitrary way. Doubtless, some of this arbitrariness is necessary. The need to save time discourages teachers from waiting for a level of student maturity leading to meaning and understanding. Yet, meaning is the most important dimension in learning; it is, in fact, the goal of learning.

If, therefore, teachers are to capitalize on learning opportunities, they must seek to reveal and utilize meaningful relations. It is natural for learners to seek meanings, structures, and patterns in their subjects, and one of the important features of learning how to learn must always be a consistent effort on the part of teachers—this is the intentional phase of teaching as a cooperative art—to help students develop their ability to perceive structure and meaning. This was the direction taken by the theory of mental discipline: What students learned was not as important as the perfection of skill in learning. This archaic educational theory did not always furnish instruments for achieving this goal, but there was, nevertheless, a certain validity to the goal. Detailed defenses for classical curricula of schools of the past century were not always prompted by convictions of the usefulness of the classical course. By exposure to such a course, the habits or the disciplines of learning were sharpened and these disciplines supported all learning activities in the future. Exponents of the theory of mental discipline could argue for this course as a preparation for any future learning or work.

Meaning as the *sine qua non* of education needs no further emphasis here. Every teacher acknowledges this goal, although in actual practice, it must be admitted, it is sometimes missed by a wide margin, swamped in detail, drill, routine, or accumulation of knowledge. The latter, sometimes accepted because its results can be assessed, has inspired the retort: A cultivated mind is a sharp instrument not a full box.

The following generalizations may be made relative to meaning in learning:

1. To realize the most from teaching opportunities, consistent use must be made of meaningful relations.
2. Structure or organization is extremely useful to all learning experiences. General ideas or general patterns are grasped more easily than details of an idea or experience. In addition, general structures are easier to learn; and when the meaning in the general structure is clear, learning is accelerated even further. A meaningless or artificial structure is grasped with considerable difficulty; and when there is no apparent structure to the material to be learned, learning is retarded even further. A simple, easily devised experiment with nonsense syllables, on the one hand, and meaningful words, on the other, will supply ample proof of this to the reader.
3. In presenting a lesson, the general structure should be presented first. From a knowledge of the general pattern, students may move more readily to a mastery of the details. There is no suggestion here that details are unnecessary or unimportant, but when they can be attached, related, or associated with a general pattern and infused with meaning, learning proceeds more rapidly and attains a higher quality. Techniques of teaching built on the principle of identifying structures first must recognize the need for clarity and simplicity in developmental lessons to avoid eluding students' mental grasp. Teaching an entire lesson based, say, on two or three general principles may require a mental sophistication not yet achieved by students. Besides, it is important for the structure to be in the material to be learned and not merely in the mind of the teacher. It is possible, of course, for students to act as if they see structures simply to please the teacher.
4. After a general pattern has been established, and this is the justification for methodological instruments such as prelection and orientation, additional material—the details—may be used to fill it out. Details fit more neatly into the background of experience whenever there is a frame of reference.

5. At every possible juncture, teachers should underline meaningful relations within the material taught. Relations apprehended may then be built upon, and the entire learning pattern may be constructed analogously to working a jigsaw puzzle. New experiences should be anchored in meaning and in the life experiences of students. To this end, analogies and illustrations have usually proved most helpful.

6. A method of learning by wholes or parts should be adopted only after its suitability to the type of learning involved is apparent. It is by no means clear that whole learning is always superior to learning by parts. The better approach for one student may not be the better approach for another, and the method a student says he prefers may not always be suited to him.

7. Meaning is the primary goal of all good teaching. If the question is the universal instrument of all good teaching, answers must have meaning, organization, and insight. Besides being a goal for teaching, meaning is also a means to more and better learning. A rich background of meanings —understanding, a step on the way to wisdom—and of deep and functioning insights is the best intellectual legacy any school can give its students. Knowledge is important and must not be downgraded or abused, but knowledge if organized into a general structure dominated by clearly understood principles is far more valuable than undominated and unrelated facts. It may, of course, not always be possible to fit all of a student's learning experiences into a nice structure. Something is almost always left over or left out; there are always loose ends. There is nothing wrong with loose ends—they are even signs of dynamism—if they are not dead ends.

TEACHING FOR TRANSFER

For several years now educators have studied, talked, and written about the subject of transfer of training: whether or not, and to what degree, things learned in school will affect students' out-of-school life, or whether things learned in one class will affect the learning required in another class. There are really three questions to be asked about transfer: one, if there is transfer from one situation to another, does this transfer aid in the performance of a subsequent task? Two, will what is transferred interfere with later learning? Three, is the effect of one learning situation on another neutral?

On the level of common sense, we have always assumed transfer from formal education to real-life situations, although we have not always devised curricula with lifelike qualities. If people were not convinced of formal schooling's direct relevance to life, they would be extremely reluctant to support schools. At various times in the history of education, theories have emphasized one or another element to be transferred; relatively few theorists have denied the possibility of transfer. Outstanding among elements eligible for transfer are process and product. If process is to be transferred, this is how it is supposed to occur: A student is exposed to a curriculum intended to dispose, habituate, and discipline his mind. With mental strength, the real object of schooling, the student is prepared to meet the exigencies of life regardless of their source.[10]

If product is to be transferred, conditions are altered considerably: the student leaving school is armed with knowledge and skills. This knowledge and these skills may be applied in the world outside the school in a specific way. There is transfer, of course, but only to the degree products possessed by this young mind are applicable in a changing world.

We have heard a great deal in recent years about the general purposes of elementary and secondary education: to develop thinkers or to teach people how to think. If this goal can be reached, the salutary influence on society will be inevitable. In this conception, thinking is a transferable general ability. Anyone who learns to think by taking courses in philosophy, for example, ought to give evidence of thinking facility in mathematics courses and even in social and political discussions on the community level. This is analogous to driving an automobile: if you can drive make X, make Y should be easy to drive. The general pattern of skill and action needed for driving the two cars is similar.

Evidence preferred by many observers on this point of transfer is implied in the remarkable predictability classical high school curricula have for success in college. There are considerable data showing, for example, that students who take Latin in high school perform better in college. The success of these students may be attributed to the disciplining qualities in the study of Latin; in the study of Latin, students may learn to think. But this may miss the point: Quite possibly, the better minds are attracted to the study of Latin in the first place, and students with good minds, whether or not Latin is studied, make better college records than average or poor students.[11]

Much remains to be learned about transfer. For example, the origin and incidence of negative transfer needs study; for when previous skill or knowledge interferes with later learning, schools cannot feign indifference. Yet, on the other hand, positive transfer occurs so frequently, it must be more thoroughly understood as it pertains to the school life of young people. What should interest us most is not how transfer takes place—this would seem to be an argument to be resolved by psychologists more than by teachers—but how we may exploit this phenomenon to the fullest and make learning experiences generally rich and widely applicable. We must be interested in transfer in school situations from one school subject to another, as well as in transfer from school to college and from college to life. Study and experience suggest factors which affect the amount of transfer taking place, and teachers should be aware of these. Transfer may be increased by deliberate teaching for it, and methods adopted depend on the material being taught and the parts of the subject applicable in other fields. At least two practices may be advanced as general rules for teachers:

1. Give particular attention to features of the material learned which may be applied to other fields. If the teacher is teaching Latin, he may make relevant applications of this teaching to English; if he is teaching history, he may indicate causes or effects in political philosophy. Some observers believe desirable results of this technique are due to insights students have of the material studied, and with insight, they say, there is no longer a specific question of transfer. Apart from disputes or varying interpretations of transfer and its efficacy, we should be willing to admit of the reality of direct teaching. Teachers who advise students to study Latin in order to improve their knowledge of English might better advise students to study English.
2. Provide opportunities for application of and practice with material to be applied or transferred to other fields. Not only should the element to be transferred be brought clearly into the picture, but it should also be applied to fields outside the subject matter of the lesson. If the teacher intends to test his students with a problem-centered test in which they are to apply general principles, he should give them practice in doing this in class. If the teacher of educational psychology hopes to have his teaching applied by students when they become teachers, he must find a way to formulate methodological principles and apply them.

A final word may be said concerning the two presently prevailing general transfer theories: generalization and identical elements. According to the former, transfer takes place on a level of general principles; the latter allows for transfer only when elements in the two learning or acting situations are identical. The former theory was advanced by Charles Judd, the latter by Edward Thorndike.[12] Neither, today, is considered to contain a satisfactory explanation of how transfer takes place.

THEORIES OF TEACHING

We have given about as much attention to learning as space allotments permit, yet we have only skimmed the surface of the subject. Many interesting aspects of learning were not mentioned at all. No doubt, students shall have additional opportunity in other professional courses to pursue points merely mentioned here. Any preoccupation educators have with learning is entirely legitimate, for learning is the center of education and the only conceivable justification for the existence of schools. If one shows an interest in learning, he must also be aware of the significance of its complement, teaching. We have already said something about the meaning of teaching, so here we shall try to explore some theories of teaching.

Depending somewhat on their conception of the essentials of formal education, and somewhat on examples of teaching they themselves have seen, teachers select general methods for presenting material and conducting classes. The variety is almost infinite. We have seen exceptional teachers whose methods are highly formal proceeding almost exclusively with the lecture method. They try to incorporate what they know of the dynamics of learning in this technique, one that recognizes presentation of material as the principal responsibility of teachers. Other teachers find such an emphasis repugnant either to their personalities or to their theory of teaching. They urge students toward activity and encourage participation from the members of the class. Teaching and learning are for them dialogues in which the friction of mind on mind produces desirable results. Still other teachers try to balance their method between presentation and participation.

Great, even good, teachers differ among themselves; poor teachers have many features in common. Unquestionably, there are factors representing training, skill, and personality in the private arsenal of a teacher, and we have yet to discover which of these is most important. Of all the teachers in history whose reputation for greatness has persevered, personality was the critical feature. The famous Abelard was a man of genius, but who really believes that his knowledge of philosophy alone made him the most popular teacher of the twelfth century? Still, teachers alone do not make a highly attractive learning situation: Where would Abelard have been with an unmotivated or indifferent class? There is no denigration of teaching in an assertion that what students bring to school with them—both knowledge and motive—is probably as important to their development as any instruction given by teachers.

In a sense everyone is a teacher, but such teaching, conceived in a broad context, is informal and incidental. It may be highly effective, but few theories have been formulated or few rules or methods have been devised for it. We are not concerned with informal education; our attention here centers on schools; what teachers do when they stimulate, guide, and direct learning activities in the classroom.

Of all the theories of teaching so far proposed, the most widely heralded and probably the most carefully developed were those of Johann Herbart (1776–1841) and Henry Morrison (1871–1945). Herbart is famous for the Formal Steps of Method; Morrison is remembered for his Cycle Concept of Teaching.

Herbart, a careful student of philosophy and psychology, became interested in pedagogy and tried to formulate scientific bases for teaching and learning. The teaching procedures developed from his psychological doctrine were preparation, presentation, association, generalization, and application. This is clearly a teacher-centered approach wherein a definite, almost unalterable structure to the teaching process is assumed. Based on this point of view, the Herbartian methodology became highly formal and tended to ignore the variables of the teaching situation: the personality and background of the teacher, the personalities and experiences of the students, the content of instruction, the context in which instruction is carried on, and the specific technique of teaching most naturally related to the material to be taught.

Henry Morrison's teaching cycle, though less centered on the teacher, is nevertheless an approach placing the primary responsibility for administering teaching with the teacher. The steps—not essentially different, it would seem, from Herbart's, although there are differences in emphasis—involve exploration, presentation, assimilation, organization, and recitation. Unquestionably, the key to both Morrison's and Herbart's teaching theories is organization of content for presentation to the learner.

Teacher-centered approaches, represented best in Herbart's steps and Morrison's cycle, have commanded the field of teaching theory for decades, yet they do not stand alone. Learner-centered theories are also prominent, and in recent years have achieved reasonably high standing. In such a theory the entire academic emphasis is placed on the learner, his personality, his interests, and his needs. And the educational process is built around the kinds of experiences he wants or feels he needs. The student-centered schoolroom need not, perhaps cannot, eliminate the teacher or his influence, but it can take him out of the educational spotlight. In the teacher-centered school the teacher comes close to creating the educational environment for students; he is the hub around which all learning experiences revolve. But the student-centered school, which under certain circumstances may be the activity school, alters the balance between teacher and student; and when the learning process is engaged, there is a dynamic yet equal involvement of all participants.

Neither theory anticipates sharply different learning outcomes. In general, any theory of teaching and most teachers are confident that information, adjustment, and discipline are goals toward which the teaching process should aim. The theory emphasizing the central role of the teacher as an indispensable element in this process is unable to understand how quality learning can take place without clear guidance and constant direction. On the other hand, a theory which puts the learner in the center of the educational stage is unable to see how learning is possible if the teacher is always in the way. In the final analysis an impasse is reached: there is little likelihood of consensus being achieved on these points. To complicate the matter still further, apparently good teachers have adopted both techniques. Outstanding teaching performances are given by persons representing the teacher-centered philosophy, and the quality of learning from such teaching is high. Similarly high quality demonstrations and results may come when the teacher carefully avoids centering activities on himself and places the burden on the learner instead. With such evidence, where does the educational observer go, and what conclusions is he entitled to draw? We discover what we have always known: art and personality are unavoidable constituents, and, irrespective of theories or special techniques, artistic teachers are effective. In one case the teacher may assert himself; in another he may practice the art of withdrawal along with providing a general framework in which students may learn.

The success of any particular method depends upon the eagerness of the students to learn. As much as teachers may like to teach only students who are anxious to learn, most teachers are aware that not all of their students have a deep interest in what is being taught. One of the primary problems, then, and one that is a part of, or related to, any teaching technique is motivating students. Some motivation may be counted on: students are taught by their parents to want to do well in school; they are influenced by their peers, and, depending upon the climate of the school, this peer influence may strengthen or weaken motivation. Students want to be liked, and, to be certain of acceptance by their classmates, it may be important to avoid any display of academic achievement; on the other hand, acceptance may depend upon high academic performance. In addition to the influence of parental teaching and student attitudes, students are motivated by grades. They want to do well enough to succeed; for many students success means passing grades. Much as teachers like to resist emphasis on grades, they are still the most effective motivators. The tendency to apologize for accepting such apparently artificial motives should be avoided, for these and other motives are simply the tools used to stimulate learning. As far as learning and retention are concerned, the motives employed seem to be inconsequential. The presence of motivation is the important thing.

We sometimes hear the complaint: "The more we teach, the less our students learn." The greater the emphasis on detail in learning, the less adequate the command of essentials seems to be. If there is any truth to this view, and professional opinion tends to support it, the teaching technique adopted must stress organization. Techniques enabling students to find a framework into which to fit the products of learning are more effective than those merely communicating masses of information without pre-arrangement or design.

There are undoubtedly intimate relationships between teaching techniques, motivation, and structure. But there is an additional point to be made. Knowledge of results is important to the learner and therefore bears directly on techniques of instruction. The most effective teaching methods appear to be those where knowledge of results is built in, or is contiguous with, the learning process itself, and where learners are able to use—practice in a very general sense—what they have learned. Practice may not lead to perfection, but practice does strengthen method whenever the learner learns the results of his practice. At first such an assertion would seem to strengthen the case for nondirective techniques, such as discussion, or some other type of student-centered teaching. Actually, however, in such approaches the learner does not become aware of results, and normally they are far from being apparent.

Selecting a Teaching Method

"I want to be a successful teacher, respected by my colleagues and reverenced by my students. What teaching method (tool of teaching) should I choose if I am to achieve success?" Choosing from among available methods of teaching would appear at the outset to be simple. By now, we should think, the science of education has determined which teaching method is clearly superior, or, if this is too much to ask, then which method works best in a given teaching situation. How effective is the lecture method? Is it superior or inferior to discussion methods? Is it not possible to demonstrate the superiority of student-centered over teacher-centered instruction? How effective are laboratory teaching, project methods, and automatic techniques?

Arriving at an index of teaching effectiveness in connection with various methods is far from simple. It is complicated by student reactions, teachers' personalities, the selection of an adequate sample, and the educational objectives being sought. The teacher who is effective with one class of students may not be effective with another; or the teacher who is effective in achieving one objective in a course, using a particular method, is not necessarily effective in achieving others. So there is, as yet, no simple answer, no patent advice to be given a teacher who is seeking the one best method. However, comments may be made relative to the various methods available.

Lecturing has long been associated with teaching, especially on the more advanced levels of education, and is widely used when teachers are intent on transmitting knowledge. When this is the objective of the class period, or when this is the principal objective, when the material is not too difficult, when the teaching is of concepts where knowledge of results is immediately important, and when the teaching of problem-solving skills is not involved, the lecture rather than being a handicap to learning may be a great boon. A quick comparison may be made between the lecture and the discussion method when communication of knowledge is the goal of instruction. Since the rate of transmission is slow in a discussion group, and since in such groups it is not easy to remain on the point, we should expect the lecture to be superior for such purposes. Yet, it must be remembered, teachers lecture with varying degrees of effectiveness: a good discussion may produce far better results even for transmission of knowledge than a poor lecture. The length of the lecture period, the size of the class, the interests, backgrounds, and attitudes of the students may all have some effect on the over-all outcomes.

"The lecture method is obsolete and should have been replaced, along with other archaic educational devices, when movable type was developed." How valid is this criticism? Is lecturing a waste of time for students who can read? Students can probably read a book faster than it can be read to them, and they can read, ponder, and digest it at their own pace. But if we move from a book to books, the case is altered; even though lectures are slower than reading, a good lecturer may be able to give his students what they need from several books in much less time than it would take to read the same material. In a lecture, moreover, possibilities for integrating knowledge are more prominent than through reading in isolation. And, of course, depending on the size of the class, the lecture may be tailored to its needs, a dim prospect with books; in addition, there is some opportunity for interchange between the teacher and his students.

There are liabilities associated with lecturing: the learner has a passive role; and if we are trying to emphasize application, critical thinking, or some higher-level cognitive responses, a group discussion would provide better opportunity. Yet the results of the research on student-centered vis-à-vis teacher-centered instruction are not impressive. They tend to support the assumptions with which this discussion began. Discussion methods are not immune to the vagaries of student interests, attitudes, anxieties, and motivations. There are many factors which affect the effectiveness of discussion methods. The buzz session, a subgroup small enough for ease of discussion, depends for its success on the attitudes of the students, and their abilities, too. There are unquestionably leadership opportunities for students when discussion methods are employed, but interest in leadership may quickly give way to interest in grades, and this rechanneling of interest may cause the discussion technique to lose its dynamic qualities. The size of the class is certainly another factor. Large classes are seldom effectively taught by this method, and even buzz sessions do not compensate for the unwieldy character of a large class. Or if class size is not a major consideration, the quality of the members of the group may be. One of the common criticisms of discussion classes is the time wasted on problems raised by good students which are too abstruse for others, or of those raised by poor students which are too simple for the majority. Even with a student-centered approach, the teacher and his skills must not be neglected: one teacher is adept at leading discussions, others are not.

Studies of project methods and independent study plans do not point clearly to any conclusion. They may be used to achieve desirable ends, but they are not the methods our hypothetical teacher is looking for. At least there is no methodological panacea in them. Nor, for that matter, are automated techniques the miracle drugs of learning. There is an ever-growing body of literature detailing the strengths and weaknesses of TV teaching, films, test and teaching machines, and programed textbooks. Almost daily, reports of research pour in with pros and cons on the effectiveness of these aids to teaching. Here we shall try to suggest rather than conclude.

Television is not a method of instruction in the sense of lecture and discussion. It is, rather, a means of giving the student a clear view of what is going on. We should expect the effectiveness of TV teaching to vary depending upon the importance of being able to see clearly. This technique of presentation should have little advantage when the communication is primarily verbal. In addition, the attitudes of the students will count for a great deal: if they dislike being instructed through this medium, or if they place value on contact and two-way communication with a live teacher in the classroom, they will not respond well; and whatever other benefits there may be, learning will be adversely affected.

Research data indicate that television, films, teaching machines, and programed books can be used to facilitate the achievement of educational goals. Their usefulness varies, of course, and depends upon the educational objectives desired, the attitudes, interests, and capacities of students, and the refinement of the materials used. This same research reveals no danger of these aids eliminating the need for face-to-face interaction between teachers and students.

GUIDANCE IN LEARNING AND TEACHING

Guidance has always been a part of education. Even when we are dealing with informal or incidental education, we see the need for helping learners formulate and achieve their goals. In formal education the need for and the role of guidance are accentuated, for the formulation of life or educational goals and the achievement of skills and the development of knowledge and understanding to meet them have become increasingly difficult as education and the life it serves have become more complex. Today there is no need to offer proofs for what is already obvious: Guidance is an essential element of an educational program. Students on all levels—elementary, secondary, and higher—can profit from the assistance offered by well-conceived and effectively administered guidance programs. Undoubtedly, some students have greater need than others for the good offices of psychometrists and counselors, but probably all students can profit from mature, experienced, and sympathetic aid from persons with special training and profound insight into vocational, educational, and personal problems.

Ideally understood and organized guidance programs accept objectives intimately related to instructional and cocurricular goals; but viewed from a slightly different perspective, they make a concerted effort to individualize educational opportunity. Programs have the following clearly understood goals: They are interested in helping students plan their futures; they are involved in studying the needs, interests, and abilities of students by collecting and interpreting data; they are deeply concerned with issues of adjustment and try to aid students in understanding institutional pressures and developing the skills or tools needed to cope with them; and, of course, they are determined to use every means at their disposal to help students succeed on their present level. The breadth of guidance objectives is great and could hardly be an exclusive responsibility of a school's guidance office or department. To be sure, guidance officers—school psychologists, counselors, psychometrists—have a primary involvement, but so do teachers. Neither common sense nor the sciences so close to guidance would exclude teachers from the guidance functions; regardless of the differences in roles, all school personnel share in the total guidance program, and all contribute to its effectiveness.

In general, one may refer to guidance as a part of the educational program which accepts the commission to help students understand their capacities and their aspirations, to help develop them within reasonable limits, to relate them to life objectives, and, ultimately, to direct students toward a level of maturity from which self-determination may proceed.[14]

Types of Guidance

For the sake of convenience in presentation, guidance may be classified as educational, vocational, and personal. This is not the only classification possible; many others have appeared in the literature. Specialists in guidance and counseling do not always distinguish between educational and vocational guidance. They see educational guidance being funneled upward toward vocational objectives and are reluctant to make a theoretical delineation whose validity cannot be clearly demonstrated on the level of practice. It is easy to show how vocational objectives arise from education and training; unquestionably, educational guidance does contribute directly or indirectly to vocational objectives. Yet, if one chooses to classify types of guidance according to distinct emphases or special direction rather than following a logical part-whole approach, no serious distortion, either in the purpose of guidance or the technique or materials involved, should arise. In making the foregoing threefold classification, we are aware of the intimate relationship between the various types and proceed with it only to underline the important emphases to be made in a total approach to guidance.

Educational guidance.   The general purpose of educational guidance is to help students attain highly personal goals in their academic careers. Its functions may extend into three important areas: helping students succeed at their present educational level, helping students choose a course of study which is geared to their capacities and their interests, and helping students make decisions concerning further education. The idea to be stressed here, and in all of the operations of the guidance program for that matter, as it is stressed in the terminology we have used, is *helping* students arrive at competent decisions.

Helping students succeed at their present educational level is chiefly the responsibility of the teacher. And here is where the teacher comes directly into the guidance program or, it may be said, is simply involving himself fully in good teaching. At this point there is no easy formula for discovering where teaching starts and stops and where guidance begins and ends. The best teachers have always taken a keen interest in the special qualities of each of their students; they have polished their strengths and have nursed their weaknesses; they have probed for their interests and have tried to direct or redirect their best energies. But even the best teachers have not always been able to do this effectively, because they have not had the knowledge of their students that such complex teaching reflexes demand. At this point the special resources of guidance officers comes into play; testing and counseling, records, and reports give the teacher a profile of the student far more complete and considerably more precise than one he would normally be able to draw depending solely upon his contacts in the teaching-learning situation.

In past decades it was common to emphasize the help teachers could give students who were not achieving minimum standards. This is still important and will always remain so, but there is another dimension presently being given more and more attention. It is the one of giving special educational opportunities to superior or gifted students. In many ways, we have learned, the problems involved in genuine success for the superior student are more complex than those with slow learners. One of the functions of guidance is to make available to teachers the kind of information they must have if they are to first identify the students needing special attention or special opportunity and then to exploit fully the native capacity of their students. This objective should not be superseded by others in the school's educational program.

Decisions relative to selecting a course of study must still be fresh in the minds of most college students. They made a choice when entering college and are faced with reaffirming or altering this choice at the beginning of every new semester. Such choices are important and can be made wisely only after the student has gained insight into his abilities and interests, only after he has some understanding of the goals he wants to achieve. In choosing a personally meaningful course of study, effective guidance depends upon the student's knowledge of himself, his goals, an accurate assessment of his capacities, and the interpretation of these in the light of the challenges inherent in the course of studies he hopes to pursue. A student should be warned to avoid educational goals which are out of his reach, but the heart of the counseling situation here is to aid him in clarifying personal and vocational goals and then to help him select a course of study enabling him to attain these goals. An early choice of career, or arriving at personal educational objectives—and this is usually desirable—will simplify the counseling situation and make favorable outcomes for the student more likely.

Helping a student decide his future in terms of higher education is one of the important functions of educational guidance. In view of the increasing opportunities for higher education in colleges, universities, and professional and technical schools and institutes this may very well be a phase of guidance to which high schools will have to devote more attention in the future. But here, as elsewhere where decisions concerning an individual must be made, the responsibility rests finally with the student himself; a counselor's role must be defined with this limitation in mind. Students and parents make the final decision; guidance helps them make the right decision.

Special problems in educational guidance. The three areas or phases of educational guidance reviewed briefly above are the major ones, but there are other, perhaps more special, problems which are part of educational guidance: athletics and health education, gifted students, and students with special abilities or creative talents.

Health education and physical development are given a place in most statements of educational objectives, and most schools have programs for the preservation of health, both personal and community, and the advancement of physical development. It is not instruction in these areas which concerns guidance directly, but, rather, the help which can be given to students in making decisions regarding health problems and athletic interests or physical development. Health education, of course, is one of the school's curricular offerings, and athletics are usually an important part of the cocurricular program. The guidance role is to encourage students to participate in these programs and to help them make judgments concerning problems which may arise as a result of their participation. The responsibility for this phase of guidance depends upon the organization for guidance in each school.

Whenever possible, gifted students should be given curricular opportunities commensurate with their talents, but when this cannot be done, the school's responsibility to the gifted bears more heavily on guidance. The first duty which teachers or guidance specialists have with respect to the gifted is to discover them. Many potentially superior students are unrecognized to the extent that their progress is actually retarded. Once gifted students are identified, it is the function of guidance to secure special opportunities for them and to stimulate and encourage them. Much of this may be done by classroom teachers.

Over and above a general superior capacity which some students may possess, there is the question of special talent to be considered. One student may have a special interest in dramatics, while another may be interested in music. Any number of special interests and apparently special capacities are possible. While these may not be, and usually are not, provided for in the curriculum, the school must be interested in the development of special talents, and it gives evidence of this interest in the cocurricular program and in counseling students with respect to their capacities and the opportunities for their development. It is not the principal object of the school to develop students in these so-called "special-ability" fields, but this does not mean that the school cannot serve the student, largely through guidance, in the development of special abilities.

Vocational guidance. What is vocational guidance? It is helping students select a vocation and, once it is selected, advising them about the best preparation for the career they have chosen. A summary of the aims of vocational guidance may be given quickly. To some extent, it may be said, they involve character formation. There is, at the very least, an obvious concern with the development of an oriented moral man and, in specific vocational terms, the fostering of healthy attitudes toward work. Beyond this, such guidance programs will include informational aspects or, to use a more common expression, will find a point of departure in occupational information. Knowledge of the kinds of careers possible has a necessary relationship to career development. Then there is a responsibility for assessing the student's interests, skills, and aptitudes and helping him form career goals. It may even be desirable at certain times and at certain educational levels to give students some firsthand experience with the vocation they are preparing for. In some cases school programs can be devised to give this kind of information; in others out-of-school experience, visits, on-the-job training, or cooperative work-and-study programs may be arranged. Finally, where preparing for a specific career involves education beyond the high school, the guidance department must assume some responsibility for two additional things: It must guide students toward the proper prerequisite education for their future formal preparation, and it must offer information, and some evaluation of it, to enable students to choose the place of this additional education or training. Trustworthy information and sound counseling procedures are imperative at all points in the guidance program, but at no point can their value be stressed more than here.

Personal guidance. Although the discussion so far has emphasized planning for the future, either educationally or in terms of career development, guidance is really concerned with total personality development, social behavior, and problems connected with learning. To some degree, therefore, when guidance is approached in its broadest meaning, vocational motives occupy something short of a major role; it is man in all his relations, not just the economic man, that guidance services hope to assist.

In any school community some persons may require the kind of therapy administered by neither the school psychologist nor the counselors. Deep-seated emotional disturbances demand the attention of psychiatrists or other highly trained therapists, spiritual counselors, or confessors. When such cases do arise, the officers of the guidance department refer them to the agency, person, or clinic best qualified to handle the case. Large school systems may have the services of school psychiatrists or specially prepared clinical psychologists, and certain types of cases may be treated by them in school. In religious schools, spiritual counselors on the staff are prepared to deal with certain types of emotional or religious problems. In most public schools, however, the therapy required for emotional and mental disturbances or spiritual distress is available only outside the school. In these instances the schools' guidance departments act as referral agencies.

In many school systems specialists including psychiatrists, psychologists,

Figure 9.1 Organization for Guidance.

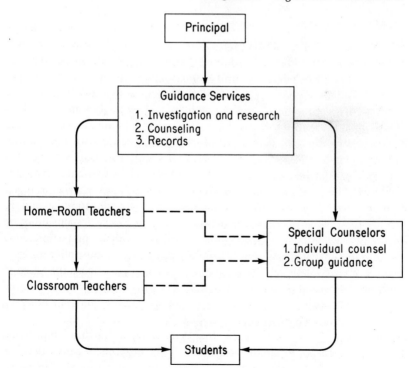

nurses, vocational and placement counselors, attendance officers, social workers, and visiting teachers function on a full-time basis, and under such conditions the school's guidance program may give the appearance of being autonomous, a special program largely unrelated to the instructional purposes of the school. In small school systems, where none of these specialists can be employed on a full-time basis, the intimate relationship between guidance and teaching is obvious. Whether a school is large or small, and irrespective of the complexity or simplicity of the school's organization for guidance, teachers have a definite and important role in any guidance program. Guidance, learning, and education may be distinguished for purposes of analysis, but they cannot be separated in any school's educational program. Every day and everywhere, when teachers come in contact with students, guidance is going on.

Teachers may not always have the qualifications to deal with every student who may need help. Where the school is large and when guidance specialists are members of the school's regular faculty, teachers have specialized assistance in helping their students. In small schools teachers may have to refer special cases to qualified persons, perhaps medical or spiritual advisers, outside the school.

SUMMARY

Schools exist to offer opportunities for teaching and learning; all other school activities are properly subsumed to these essential functions. If learning could take place effectively and economically without teaching, schools would be inhabited only by students. But we have discovered after more than twenty centuries of experience with teaching and learning that though unaided learning is possible and oftentimes extraordinarily productive, it is normally tedious and wasteful. Teaching implies knowledge, art, and intention; learning suggests as a minimum both discovery and modified responses on the learner's part.

Theories of learning, e.g., connectionism, field, and purposive, have been advanced to explain the way human learning proceeds. The application of these theories to teaching varies. All, however, touch on such important considerations as motivation, meaning, and transfer.

Not only are there theories of learning to be considered, there are also theories of teaching which favor various approaches to the basic problem of directing and guiding learning activities. Directing learning brings us to the level of method, and here, too, we have a variety of techniques from which to choose. The particular teaching tool to be used in any teaching situation depends in part upon personality—both the students' and the teacher's—partly on what is being taught, and partly on the context in which teaching is conducted. It is hardly ever possible to endorse a single technique for all types of teaching. At the same time it is impossible to endorse new teaching aids—TV, automated devices, etc.—as methodological panaceas.

Wherever teaching is taking place, guidance is present too. The organization into which guidance fits may vary from school to school: in one school guidance may be handled by teachers; in another, guidance may be set aside for specialists. The range of guidance and counseling is also broad, from educational guidance in which a student is helped toward success on his present level to personal guidance where students may be treated for deep-seated emotional problems.

QUESTIONS AND EXERCISES

1. What are the essential features of learning? To put the same question another way, How do we know when learning has taken place?
2. How would you distinguish between mastering subject matter and learning how to learn? Does the latter have special significance for teachers?
3. Use an example from your own experience and show how a goal influences learning. Do you think that teachers are always in a position to capitalize on students' goals?
4. Examine the assertion: All education is self-education. What qualifications or disclaimers would you add?
5. Explain how the "laws" of readiness, exercise, and effect may be applied to classroom learning.
6. Report on the development of field theory as a learning theory, and compare its principal doctrines with those of connectionism.
7. Is there any adequate explanation for the high motivation of one student vis-à-vis the low motivation of another student?
8. What part does knowledge of results play in motivation? Do you think frequent tests are helpful to you?
9. Discuss the role of meaning in effective teaching and learning.
10. Report on the two principal theories explaining transfer of training.
11. Can effective teaching become an obstacle to learning?
12. How should teachers select a teaching technique? Should a teacher's method vary from one educational context to another?
13. Distinguish between teacher-centered and student-centered techniques.
14. What, in your opinion, is the future of educational TV?
15. What are the guidance dimensions in teaching?

ADDITIONAL READINGS

Alexander, William A.: *Are You a Good Teacher?* Holt, Rinehart and Winston, Inc., New York, 1959. A brief work intended to help teachers evaluate and improve their work in the classroom.

Bruner, Jerome S.: *The Process of Education,* Harvard University Press, Cambridge, Mass., 1960. The idea of structure in learning is stressed and implications are drawn for organizing materials of instruction before teaching begins.

Chandler, B. J.: *Education and the Teacher,* Dodd, Mead & Company, Inc., New York, 1961. A general introduction to teaching as a profession.

Craig, Robert C.: *The Transfer Value of Guided Learning,* Bureau of Publications, Teachers College, Columbia University, New York, 1953. Contains reports of experiments and indications for methodology of transfer.

Davis, Allison: *Social Class Influences upon Learning,* Harvard University Press, Cambridge, Mass., 1955. A study of social-class status and its effect on motivation and behavior.

Dewey, John: *How We Think,* D. C. Heath and Company, Boston, 1910. Dewey develops the thesis that the fundamental principle of education is the establishment of scientific attitudes and habits of thought.

Guzie, Tad W.: *The Analogy of Learning,* Sheed & Ward, Inc., New York, 1960. A book that essays to integrate Thomistic philosophy and educational psychology.

Harris, T. L., and W. E. Schwann: *Selected Readings on the Learning Process,* Oxford University Press, Fair Lawn, N.J., 1961. See the first four articles dealing with the learning process.

Highet, Gilbert: *The Art of Teaching,* Alfred A. Knopf, Inc., New York 1950. The author discusses the qualities and abilities of good teachers and the methods they use in and out of the classroom. One of the best books on teaching ever written.

Kingsley, H. L., and R. Garry: *The Nature and Conditions of Learning,* 2d ed., Prentice-Hall, Inc., Englewood Cliffs, N.J., 1957. See chapters 6, 7, 10, 12, and 13, dealing with basic issues in learning.

McClelland, D. C. (ed.): *Studies in Motivation,* Appleton-Century-Crofts, Inc., New York, 1955. Chapter 9, treating of the origins of the achievement motive, is most relevant here.

Meenes, Max: *Studying and Learning,* Random House, Inc., New York, 1954. A book containing practical advice to the college student about effective methods of study.

Sharp, D. Louise (ed.): *Why Teach?* Holt, Rinehart and Winston, Inc., New York, 1957. A collection of short articles written by prominent figures on the satisfactions to be derived from teaching.

Smith, Mary H.: *Using Television in the Classroom,* McGraw-Hill Book Company, New York, 1961. An anthology intended to help teachers use instructional television more effectively.

Stacey, C. L., and M. F. De Martino: *Understanding Human Motivation,* Howard Allen, Inc., Cleveland, 1958. Another anthology dealing with various aspects of motivation. Helpful for understanding why pupils behave as they do.

Thorpe, Louis P., and A. M. Schmuller: *Contemporary Theories of Learning,* The Ronald Press Company, New York, 1954. See the last two chapters, which treat of areas of agreement among the more prominent theories of learning.

Tilton, J. W.: *An Educational Psychology of Learning*, The Macmillan Company, New York, 1951. The leading theories of learning are compared. The author himself takes an eclectic position.

Wernick, Robert: *They've Got Your Number*, W. W. Norton & Company, Inc., New York, 1956. A book which is critical of what is thought to be an overemphasis on testing in contemporary society.

chapter 10

Teachers and Their Profession

"The school system in our town is outstanding" and "The schools in our city are poor" are statements made daily by proud or interested citizens. Families move from one community to another because the schools they leave have a poor reputation and the schools in their new community are supposed to be good. Schools do get reputations, and, in a sense, they have personalities, too. Yet even with optimum conditions the rating of schools or colleges is most hazardous. Despite our suspicion of rank order ratings of schools and colleges, it cannot long be doubted that some schools are truly outstanding and others are extremely poor. Some provide excellent educational opportunity for genuinely interested and ambitious students; others hardly offer minimal opportunities, and students are placed in the unenviable position of having to learn in spite of the school and its environment rather than because of it. Why is one school good and another weak? It is possible to point to money of course, and there is the ever-present temptation to ascribe a high correlation between adequate financial resources and academic quality. But money doesn't educate; it may simply make available more of the conditions necessary for quality learning. One of the essential conditions, and money may be of some help here, is good teaching. The answer to the question: What makes schools good? is easy to find. Good teachers make schools good. There is no reason to doubt the validity of this assertion.[1]

THE EVOLUTION OF THE AMERICAN TEACHER

The Teacher in Colonial America

Anyone who has read Washington Irving's *Legend of Sleepy Hollow* and is familiar with the antics of Ichabod Crane has some appreciation of the

266

conditions which were prevalent in education during the colonial and early national period. Of course, there were many teachers who would not have fitted into the "Ichabodian" mold, but the conditions which are implied in Irving's famous story are certainly more fact than fiction. The unfortunate and often humorous circumstances which surrounded education, and particularly the teacher, have frequently found their way into print. Naturally many of these accounts are exaggerated, but in each exaggeration there is a particle of truth.

What were the qualifications of these early teachers? Our first reaction might be to answer, "None." But such a conclusion is too hastily drawn. Actually, there were criteria which they had to meet, although, in all but the rarest cases, requirements or qualifications were very low when judged by the standards of our own day. The qualifications were not solely in terms of a teacher's educational record or schooling, as indeed today's qualifications should not be. But the particular weakness in any early set of requirements was that the prospective teacher's ability to teach was hardly ever considered. For example, the Society for the Propagation of the Gospel in Foreign Parts, an English missionary society interested in education in America, published a set of qualifications in 1711 which all the teachers of the society were expected to meet. Notably absent from this standard was any mention of the candidate's grasp of the subjects he was to teach or his skill in teaching them. Knowledge and skill, it was naïvely assumed, were always present as part of a teacher's tools, and nothing needed to be prescribed relative to them, or, it was believed, these were mere details to be mastered along the way or as the need arose. In any case the qualifications skirted these points and stressed instead such things as age, marital status, moral and religious habits, political views, and church membership. When the examiners were satisfied with the candidate's "sober and pious conversation" and with his doctrinal and disciplinary orthodoxy in the Church of England, he presented himself for an interview before a board of ministers who made some perfunctory inquiry into his skill as a schoolmaster, especially his ability to teach the catechism of the Established Church. This examination, if it may be so labeled, was better than nothing, though it did not ensure the recruitment of good teachers, nor was it an efficient check upon the possibility of ignorant and inexperienced persons swelling their ranks.[2]

Frequently, the best qualification a prospective teacher could offer when appearing before his interrogators was that he had no other employment and could therefore devote his time to keeping school without detracting in any way from the economy of the colony. Because the attitude was prevalent that the teacher was a worthless fellow, the occupation of teaching tended to attract worthless fellows. Many of the early schoolmasters were itinerants, wandering from locality to locality, offering their services as teachers when sober, but making themselves unfit for keeping school when they had reaped some of the meager benefits of their efforts. The tutor of Horace Mann is reported to have been an exceptionally capable scholar for his time, but "demon rum" made him ineffective throughout the greater part of the year.

The teachers during this early period can be divided into two main classes: those who offered their services to individual students or to families, and those who presented themselves to town school committees seeking a position in the local schools. In general, the former were more competent than the latter, and the position of tutor carried with it considerably more prestige than that of the schoolmaster of a town school. In addition, the tutorial situation often provided a larger remuneration, for those who had the means and desired the services of a tutor regarded learning more favorably than the general public and displayed a greater willingness to pay for it.

A schoolmaster in a town school in the half century after 1640 could expect the equivalent of $3 a week for his work, while the schoolmistress, though rarely employed in the town school during this period, seldom received more than $1.75 a week. The schoolmistress received a smaller stipend than the schoolmaster because it was assumed that a young woman could find employment in one of the households of the community and thus supplement her income.

Although it is true that the schoolmistress was seldom employed for teaching in the town school, women played an important role in education during these early years. One of the most common means for imparting the rudiments of education during the colonial period was the dame school. The dame school, which flourished in the Colonies, especially in Massachusetts, was an importation from England; it was in this school that most boys received their preparation for the town school.[3] The dame school was a kind of neighborhood school and was usually conducted by one of the housewives of the community. More often than not the children would assemble for their lessons in the dame's kitchen.

In most of the colonies membership in the Established Church was a qualification which the teacher would have to meet. In South Carolina a statute was passed in 1712 requiring:[4]

> . . . that the person to be master of the said school shall be of the Church of England, and conform to the same, and shall be capable to teach the learned languages, that is to say, Latin and Greek tongues, and to catechise and instruct the youth in the principles of the Christian religion, as professed in the Church of England.

In addition, an oath was demanded of those who applied for teaching positions:[5]

I do sincerely promise and swear, That I will be faithful, and bear true allegiance to his majesty King George. So help me God.

I do swear, that I do from my heart abhor, detest and abjure, as impious, and heretical, that damnable doctrine and position. That princes excommunicated or deprived by the Pope, or any authority by the see of Rome, may be deposed or murthered by their subjects, or any other whatsoever. And I do declare, that no foreign prince, person, prelate, state or potentate, hath or ought to have any jurisdiction, power, superiority, pre-eminence or authority, ecclesiastical or spiritual, within this realm. So help me God.

The general view that teachers were not well qualified is expressed in the statement of the purposes for the establishment of Benjamin Franklin's academy in 1751:[6]

That a number of the poorer Sort will be hereby qualified as Schoolmasters in the Country, to teach Children Reading, Writing, Arithmetic, and the Grammar of their Mother Tongue, and being of good morals and known character, may be recommended from the Academy to Country Schools for that purpose; The Country suffering at present very much for want of good Schoolmasters, and obliged to employ in their Schools, vicious imported Servants, or concealed Papists, who by their bad Examples and Instructions often deprave the Morals or corrupt the Principles of the Children under their Care.

Several teachers during this early period were little more than slaves; many were indentured servants; some were petty criminals from European prisons. But each, regardless of his background, had to obtain a license to teach, and in many of the colonies this license was granted by the Bishop of London. In 1758 New Jersey, for example, required masters to hold such licenses:[7]

We do further direct that . . . no Schoolmaster be henceforth permitted to come from England and to keep School in the said province without the License of the said Bishop of London, and that no other person now there or that shall come from other parts, shall be admitted to keep School in that Our said province of New Jersey, without your License first obtained.

In 1760 New Jersey demanded further qualifications, which were set forth in the following proclamation:[8]

New York, November 5. On the 21st Instant, his Excellency Thomas Boone, Esq., Governor of New Jersey, issued a proclamation setting forth, that whereas the Education of Youth is a Matter of great Consequence, and ought not to be trusted but to Persons of good Character, and loyal Principles, and professed Protestants; therefore he requires all Magistrates to inform themselves sufficiently of the Character of the Schoolmasters in the

Province; to administer Oaths to them, and give them, under the Hands of two, a Certificate of Approbation, by which they may obtain a License; and forbidding all Persons, after the 31st of December, to execute the Office of Schoolmaster without such License first obtain'd.

In spite of some enactments designed to regulate teaching, colonial teachers were not distinguished for their quality. There were a few exceptions. Catholic and Protestant missionaries conducted schools in the Colonies, and their schools were often manned by competent scholars and excellent teachers. For some of the other schoolmasters, this can be said of them: They may not have had a great deal of formal education, but they were sincere and had that dedication to the service of youth we seek in our teachers today.

The Demand for Better Teachers in the Nineteenth Century

Although a majority of the inhabitants of the New World remained oblivious to the needs of youth and the necessity of providing a sound education for children under the direction of a professional body of teachers, there were a few farsighted men who understood the intimate but too often elusive relationship between democracy and education. The Colonies had made considerable progress in teaching the mother country their lack of need for her; if the lesson was not fully mastered, the promises of the New World were at least becoming clearer and more than matched the expectations nurtured in the hearts of venturesome and hardy pioneers. The New World was a world of almost limitless resources; included among these resources waiting to be utilized—one might even say, exploited—was the youth of the country. In concert with many other nations learning the same lesson, this youthful land recognized the precious nature of human talent and set about the hazardous but promising task of bringing it to fruition. Some people balked at offering educational opportunity to youth, either because they doubted the value of education or feared it's power. Ultimately the more progressive view prevailed, and democratic educational opportunity was given a chance to find a place in the history of American pedagogy.

Yet despite all of this hope the colonial teacher's position was an unenviable one, partly because of the natural chaos which accompanies the settlement of virgin lands and partly because of the unwillingness or inability of most colonists to recognize the real value of education. Perhaps they confused the memorizing of a few prayers and a passing acquaintance with the Bible with education. If education was nothing more than this, they saw little reason to concern themselves with qualifications for teachers which were academically and not religiously oriented. An inability or an unwillingness to recognize the value of good teachers was an attitude which stemmed directly from a misunderstanding of education's role, and in large part this attitude was responsible for many of the faults of colonial education.

Before the advent of the nineteenth century the attention of the public was being directed to the importance of a kind of education which would serve the new nation and contribute directly to the great democratic experiment. More particularly, these efforts to revive an interest in education were centered on the teacher—his role and qualifications. In 1790 Benjamin Rush injected new life into what were until then somewhat sterile discussions of school keeping. He emphasized the dignity of the occupation and opined, with what may have been greater hope than conviction, that next to mothers, teachers were society's most influential persons. Why, then, if this were true, he could go on, are teachers held in such low esteem, and what is more, why do they themselves rank the prestige of their occupation even lower than those who have no intimate attachment to it? Or why do so many people simply refuse to take teaching seriously? They do not rank it on a low level of the ladder of social prestige; they simply remain indifferent to it or are contemptuous of it and refuse to rank it at all. Rush's answer, perhaps somewhat naïve, but understandable nevertheless when viewed in the context of his day, emphasized the need for disassociating ideas of violence and despotism from teaching. His formula, for all the good it contained, was too simple: "Let schoolmasters cease to be tyrants, and they will soon enjoy the respect and rank, which are naturally (sic) connected with their profession." [9] From this beginning he could go on to endorse the rise of an attitude which conceived of education in social terms as well as a matter of private good. Besides, he refused to allow the responsibility for superintending education to be assigned to any agency of government; it was a role to be filled by the people of the country acting more or less directly with their schools. His interest in social betterment was as intense, and even more general, than his interest in education—though neither could be separated from the other—and the principal instruments for achieving these humanitarian goals were "Mothers and schoolmasters [who] plant the seeds of nearly all the good and evil which exists in our world." [10]

Around the end of the first quarter of the nineteenth century James Carter was more incisive in his criticisms of teachers, schools, and teaching and more demanding with respect to the preparation and skill of persons assigned the responsibility of guiding and directing the learning of children. He asked: To whom do we assign the functions of disciplining and instructing our children from four to twelve years of age? Who take upon themselves the trust of forming those principles and habits upon which future social and professional actions will be based? In a word, who are the moral educators of youth?

He could go on to inquire whether or not the teachers of his day really understood their importance or influence on the character of youth. Carter's answers to these questions may not have brought about any immediate revolution in teacher preparation or employment, but they did focus attention on one of the essentials in this dimension of formal education. The education of many teachers, he charged, ceased in the very school where they began teaching, and their subsequent educational attainments were modest or nonexistent. But bad as this might be, there was something worse: They were often very young, constantly changing employment, equipped with little experience, and totally deprived of any direct preparation for the work they were expected to perform. This is the only service, Carter was prompted to remark, "in which we venture to employ young and, often, ignorant persons, without some previous instruction in their appropriate duties. . . ." [11] Carter's complaints, and his suggestions for improvement, too, rested upon three propositions: (1) The preparation of prospective teachers is inadequate and is totally devoid of any standard for guaranteeing reasonable competence; (2) the remuneration for employment is so trifling, it is hardly possible to expect well-educated people to waste themselves in such an occupation; (3) the certification of teachers—a way of attesting to their skill in the profession and a method, too, of licensing them for employment—is a farce. (In Carter's time teacher certification was controlled by local ministers whose standards were highly personalized.)

So James Carter, in his *Essays on Popular Education* and in other public utterances, preached an educational crusade leading to an upgrading of teaching. This outcome, he knew, could be accomplished only by improving the preparation of persons aspiring to the profession of teaching. A refinement of the quality of teaching could move the educational world away from what Carter called *school keeping* to *teaching school*, which were, he insisted, two quite different things.

While James G. Carter was campaigning in Massachusetts for better teachers, Samuel R. Hall, in Vermont, had opened in 1823 what was perhaps the first teacher training institution in the United States. "Prepare students for the business of teaching and then pay them well" was the theme underlying Hall's endeavor to provide more efficient teachers for the schools of the country. Seven years before Hall opened his teachers' seminary, Denison Olmsted of Connecticut proposed the establishment of a school which would have provided students with a practical preparation for the management of schools. Several other public-spirited men accepted the general proposition that teachers be more carefully and thoroughly prepared for teaching, and a few institutes were opened where candidates for teaching could obtain some instruction.

Considerable impetus was given to the teacher training movement by individuals who traveled to Europe for the purpose of inspecting the conditions of education there. During the first half of the nineteenth century several Americans visited Europe with the hope of obtaining ideas for the improvement of education in the United States. One of the more prominent of these European travelers was Henry Barnard. Barnard visited Europe in 1835 and found in Germany—in German school regulations—certain practices which he was sure would improve American education. Barnard's report on education abroad placed special emphasis on the preparation and work of German teachers. His report was given a great deal of attention in this country, and it seems likely that it was instrumental in stimulating legislators to enact laws both for regulating the licensing of teachers and for the establishment of institutions where candidates for the teaching profession could receive some preparation.

Barnard thought the German school system's excellence was due to provisions in German law maintaining high-quality teaching. These provisions included:

1. An explicit recognition of the true dignity and importance of the teacher's office.
2. The establishment of teacher education schools in which persons interested in teaching could prepare for their first position and where continuous study was given to the elusive relationships involved in teaching and learning.
3. The inauguration of a system of certification and evaluation for all teachers. Certification was a prerequisite to teaching, but even with certification, if evaluations proved incompetence, certification could be revoked.
4. The organization of a system of promotion wherein successful teachers received professional and economic rewards.
5. Cognizance of teachers' year-round financial obligations vis-à-vis their part-time employment relating to annual employment or compensation.
6. Opportunities for testing interest and skill in teaching early in a student's educational career. This was not only a screening device for removing unacceptable candidates; it was also a way of attracting exceptional persons to teaching.
7. Regular associations of teachers providing ample occasions for learning, sharing, and interchange on a professional level.
8. A system whereby teachers were freed from military service in times of peace.
9. A program of benefits including sick leave and health and life insurance.
10. Systematic encouragement for teachers to keep abreast of their fields and developments in pedagogy. Books and periodical literature were made available to all teachers.[12]

Barnard's recommendations, based on the foregoing ten points, were accepted slowly. As a matter of fact, some have not yet been fully accepted in all parts of the United States. It is indeed remarkable that the German law made references to these points as early as the fourth decade of the nineteenth century.[13]

The German plan, introduced by Barnard, was adopted hesitantly and selectively. Probably inspired by the progress in Germany and increasingly hopeful for success in this country, James Carter, Henry Barnard, and Horace Mann backed the founding of a state normal school in Lexington, Massachusetts, by the General Court in July, 1839. This school was later relocated in Framingham, Massachusetts, where it operates today as a state college, a living symbol of the first public effort to professionalize teaching and upgrade its quality. Yet the public (speaking through its legislators) may not have acted so early, or at all, had it not been for a donation of $10,-000 accompanied by the condition that the state match this amount and establish a school for teachers. Within a year, two other normal schools were established in Massachusetts. Mann's interest in the first normal school was intense; some of this interest can be detected in his letter to the Legislature which informed it of the donation and the conditions:[14]

Gentlemen,

Private munificence has placed conditionally at my disposal the sum of Ten Thousand Dollars, to promote the cause of Popular Education in Massachusetts.

The condition is, that the Commonwealth will contribute the same amount from unappropriated funds, in aid of the same cause;—both sums to be drawn upon equally, as needed, and to be disbursed under the direction of the Board of Education, in qualifying Teachers of our Common Schools.

As the proposal contemplates that the State, in its collective capacity, shall do no more than is here proffered to be done by private means, and as, with a high and enlightened disregard of all local, party and sectional views, it comprehends the whole of the rising generation in its philanthropic plan, I cannot refrain from earnestly soliciting for it the favorable regards of the Legislature.

Very respectfully,
Horace Mann
Secretary of the Board of Education
Boston, March 12th, 1838.

The movement for the establishment of state normal schools, begun in Massachusetts in 1839, was followed by many of the other states. By 1870 twenty-two states had provided for normal schools, and many private normal schools were founded. However, although normal schools may have contributed to the improvement of the common schools, they did little to raise the position of the teacher. For example, teachers' salaries were not much higher than they had been in 1700. It is not likely that the most able people were being attracted to the profession. In 1879 the average monthly salary for a male teacher was $29 in Michigan's rural schools, $32 in Massachusetts, and $37 in New York. In each instance the salary for a female teacher was lower.

The Effect of European Theory on Teacher Education

Although public men had commented on the training of teachers and the benefits which could be obtained from a good education, there were few attempts to formulate theories of education or theories of teacher training before the Civil War. Some of the more prominent and able state school officers, Horace Mann, for example, were aware of the current educational trends in Europe. Others—scholars and public men——became interested in European educational theories and movements, and many of them traveled to Europe to see for themselves the innovations that were being tested in educational practice. In most instances the travelers were impressed by what they saw and, when they returned to America, brought with them the ideals and plans of European educational reformers.

Pestalozzianism. Johann Heinrich Pestalozzi (1746–1827) followed, in general, the basic precepts of educational naturalism.[15] He was not essentially a theorist—in fact, he showed little interest in theory. He was interested in the development of a natural method of instruction. The work of Pestalozzi was both extensive and important, and many of his views had a permanent value. Most of his personal ventures were failures.

Without going into a detailed discussion of Pestalozzi's life and work, it may be said that the basic principles of his method were formulated while he was conducting schools in Southern Europe. He founded his method upon three main principles: (1) the reduction of all subjects to their unanalyzable ements and the teaching of these subjects by carefully graded steps; (2) the use of the object lesson, wherein an attempt was made to appeal directly to sense experience rather than learning to manipulate words; (3) the oral teaching of all subjects.

It is necessary to indicate, although not essential to elaborate, that the results of Pestalozzi's method were not always satisfactory. But the results of application of any new theory or method take some time. Pestalozzianism was still too new in the late eighteenth and early nineteenth centuries to have had a thorough testing and a complete evaluation. Because it was new and because it did have some attractive features, some of Pestalozzi's disciples wanted to have his method adopted by all the normal schools in the United States. Joseph Neef, a coworker of Pestalozzi, came to America in 1808, some years before normal schools became popular here, and founded a school in Philadelphia. In this school he hoped to follow the precepts and practices of his "master." To promote his school, he published a book wherein he outlined in considerable detail the ideas of Pestalozzi on the teaching of speech, geometry, numbers, writing, reading, grammar, natural history, ethics, natural philosophy, chemistry, gymnastics, music, poetry, languages, lexicology, and geography. This book was entitled *Sketch of a Plan and Method of Education, Founded on an Analysis of the Human Faculties, and Natural Reason, Suitable for the Offspring of a Free People and for All Rational Beings.* He wrote other books in an attempt to stimulate interest in methods of teaching.

The work of Pestalozzi began to bear fruit: Textbooks were published following his principles—perhaps the best known was Colburn's *First Lessons in Arithmetic on the Plan of Pestalozzi,* 1821—and teachers' associations, institutes, lyceums, and some normal schools popularized the object lesson. In spite of the attention which the new method was given, it must be said that it did not affect American education to any great degree before 1860. Many teachers' journals and the reports of Calvin Stowe, Henry Barnard, and Horace Mann had taken a clear and forcible stand in favor of the techniques of Pestalozzi, but most teachers neither read the journals nor heard of the reports. Pestalozzianism was an effective instrument only among the initiated few. However, late in the nineteenth century, interest in these methods was revived, and Pestalozzianism was received with enthusiasm, even fervor, by teachers, normal schools, and teachers colleges. In its revived form it was called American Pestalozzianism or the Oswego movement.

The Oswego movement. Pestalozzianism in a more or less undiluted form did not, as we have indicated above, make a profound impression on the majority of American teachers before 1860. While the principles of Pestalozzi's method were being spread in America during the first half of the nineteenth century, they were also being circulated in England. English Pestalozzianism was introduced to America, in Canada, shortly before the Civil War; and in 1861 Edward A. Sheldon (1823–1897) established a normal school in Oswego, New York, which embodied the principles and methods of Pestalozzi.

The Oswego movement spread rapidly and soon influenced the training of teachers throughout the United States. It was a poor normal school which did not boast one or more Oswego-trained teachers on its staff. Teacher training became much more "scientific." The time was fast going by when a teacher could find employment without having had some exposure, in a normal school, to the precepts of the object lesson. Not only did Sheldon present new ideas concerning the education of teachers, but he taught a method which teachers generally quickly accepted. This method involved the careful selection and arrangement of materials of instruction, the skillful use of questions, and diligence in conducting learning exercises. Along with these points, the development of perception and individual judgment was emphasized, and generalization was cultivated; textbooks were accorded a subordinate position in the educational process.

The Oswego movement readily adhered to Pestalozzi's emphasis on observation: "Observation is the absolute basis of all knowledge. The first object, then, in education, must be to lead a child to observe with accuracy; the second, to express with correctness the result of his observations." Although this was not a new idea, it was a new methodological emphasis, and it had an important influence on both teacher training and classroom management. It would not be an exaggeration to claim that the Oswego movement was largely responsible for the development of a new type of teacher in America.

The theory of evolution.   Naturalism, exemplified best in the doctrines of Rousseau, ushered in a new and extreme interpretation of the nature of man. But it did not result in immediate or radical educational changes, for men were not inclined to take it seriously until the question was answered, "How does man become man?" This question was given a positive answer in the evolutionary theory of Charles Darwin (1809–1882). With the theory of evolution, naturalism was completed: man's origin, nature, and destiny were explained naturally.

The theory of evolution had profound effects on education. Where education had long been thought to have religious purposes and was mainly religious in content, naturalism, supported by the theory of evolution, denied these age-old objectives and replaced them with an exclusive concern for the temporal. Now man stood alone, without relationship or devotion to anything above or below him. Because he had already traveled such a long road of progress, with such marvelous results, there was no reason to suppose that he could not travel even further. Man could, in time, become something far greater, for implicit in the theory of evolution, especially as it applied to education, was the doctrine of indefinite perfectability.

It was no longer sufficient for teachers to present the social and religious inheritance to their students. At its best this educational diet was considered to be inadequate for man as he was conceived in evolutionary theory. The child was living in a world characterized by one main principle—change. A doctrinaire or dogmatic curriculum would not do; neither would traditional teaching methods. Prospective teachers were imbued with the notion that the child had to be free: freedom was tantamount to development. A philosophy of permissiveness invaded teacher training institutions—not immediately translated into practice—and with this philosophy a concerted effort was made to develop a science of education as a worthy corollary to the theory of evolution.

Humanitarianism.   Although the theory of evolution exerted a powerful influence on education in the nineteenth century, it would be somewhat inaccurate to suggest that it was responsible for popularizing education and making it the desire of nearly every man, woman, and child in the United States during the half century before 1900. The theory of evolution had deep and lasting effects on the philosophy, psychology, and methodology of education, but it was humanitarianism which raised education to almost dizzy heights of popularity.

When men no longer believe in God, the only alternative remaining is to believe in man. To put it briefly, this is humanitarianism. For the humanitarian there is no reality greater than man, but man can be made more perfect than he is. In this cult, education was given a place of first importance. The educational views of the humanitarians need not be totally condemned; neither may they be approved without reservation. It is to the credit of the humanitarians of the nineteenth century that they carried on and won the battle for the cause of free public education. But it is hardly to their credit that they looked upon education as a panacea for all man's and society's ills and evils. It may be remarked that education can perform the service of making men good, but formal education does this only as a by-product and not as a primary goal. Humanitarianism predicted with confidence that a good school would make good citizens, and good citizens would make a good society. Humanitarians, therefore, turned their attention to making schools good by directing their objectives toward social reform.

The common school was a great boon to America, but the common-school philosophy formulated by the humanitarians of the mid-nineteenth century demanded that teachers and students be cast from one mold. In order to achieve a high level of individual, political, and social morality, the humanitarians tried to create a uniform school environment by planning for and regulating all the activities of teachers and students. The idealism of their outlook paved the way for the educational *laissez faire* of the twentieth century.

THE EVOLUTION
AND IMPROVEMENT
OF TEACHER EDUCATION

Normal Schools

"Normal school" is a name seldom used by educational institutions today. Schools so designated in their early years have in the past half century preferred to use some other form of identification. They have been prompted to do so for two reasons: In fact, they have outgrown their normal-school period—in many respects a period of academic childhood and immaturity—and have appealed to legislatures or boards of control for modification of charter or new or amended statutes permitting them to appear before the public with new titles; and they have become sensitive to the trend for curricular broadening which in today's educational world leads an institution closer to academic respectability. Normal schools long stood in the shadow of liberal arts colleges and universities; too often they were regarded as inferior or were held in the public mind to be educationally unreliable. Much of this unfavorable image they blamed on their name. These schools became tired of being reminded, or having their name remind them, of their past. So steps were taken to become, first, teachers colleges, then, successively, colleges of education, state colleges, and finally, in some states, universities. Generalizations about quality of educational institutions must be made with extreme caution if they are to be made fairly, so a conclusion relative to these efforts at upgrading and renaming is hazardous. In too many of these schools the changes have been nominal only; in others the changes in title are accurate reflections of internal academic growth.

If we look at the record of normal-school evolution from infant years to periods of greater maturity, we see some of the developmental steps. The pre-1860 normal school, although its objective of teacher training was explicit, was set in an atmosphere of chaos. There was nothing precise about its organization—it wavered between public, semipublic, private, and semi-private control. It admitted students without setting any standards relative to their educational attainments; it allowed them to remain at the institution to take the full course—in time somewhat precariously set at two years —or leave when they had absorbed what they thought they wanted. The curriculum was disjointed; there was no accepted course of studies; and the students, when their studies were finished, were endowed with extremely superficial educational accomplishments. Even the best justification for its existence was none too good. One commentator on the period remarked: "Their only excuse as a class, for being, was that the facilities for the training of teachers were as yet inadequate, and even the training that the poorest of them gave was better than none."

The enthusiasm generated for such schools by educational leaders began to wane even before the schools, poor as they were, had a fair chance to strengthen themselves. Massachusetts, the home of the first state normal school, expected too much too soon, but this did not deter the Legislature from trying to suppress its normal school in 1850, when the school was only eleven years old. Dissatisfaction with the record of the school's accomplishments contributed to the movement to close the school, but action arose out of something more basic than disenchantment with an institution. Legislators challenged schools promising to create a teachers' profession.

We have, they said, academies and high schools that are fully competent to supply teachers for the lower schools. And what is more, they argued, district schools are in session only three or four months of the year. It is, therefore, obviously impossible and perhaps undesirable that "the business of keeping the schools should become a distinct and separate profession, which the establishment of Normal Schools seems to anticipate." [16]

The full circle was almost complete: back to the starting point where doubts were expressed about the quality of talent needed for common-school teaching and, also, about the need for, even the desirability of, a discrete profession of teaching. Such attitudes must have been a source of great dismay and anxiety both for teachers committed to their vocation and for educational leaders devoted to elevating the standards of education in the United States. In any case, the opposition did not prevail; the school in Massachusetts was retained, and other normal schools, both in Massachusetts and in other states, appeared on the scene.

After 1860 the normal schools gained more definite public acceptance and support. Their steady progress is marked by the increase in the number of normal schools from 12 state and about 24 private in 1860 to approximately 350 public and private normal schools in 1895. After 1860, moreover, normal schools gained the confidence of the public, and to the extent that they did, they increased in number and importance in response to the demands which were made on them. The normal schools came to be accepted as the chief agency for the education of teachers for the common schools. In many respects the normal schools of this period were not colleges or universities, and they did not pretend to be. They were equipped to *train* teachers for the elementary schools, and they achieved a fairly good reputation in this work.

Teachers Colleges

A normal school fulfilling its stated purpose presented an instructional program including a review of common-school subjects and an introduction to the skills of pedagogy. Perhaps the more ambitious normal school tried to link theory and practice and therefore added a few preliminary lectures on the theory of teaching. The limits of its professional goals were reached quickly and usually did not include the granting of a college degree. There were normal-school certificates of course, but in no sense did they correspond to the bachelor's degree of the college or university. The teachers college appeared on the American scene as a mature relative of the normal school. Why it came at all is a long and involved story, which would take us far afield here, but we can point to a few of the more important reasons.

Normal schools, as we have said, experienced constant internal pressures to grow larger and become more respectable. Some moved up the ladder of quality and, in time, outgrew the purposes of their past. Then, too, pedagogy, teaching, education, became more scientific, and a body of knowledge about the science and art of teaching was accumulated. A stronger and more respectable academic structure was believed to be necessary to support the weight of a new academic discipline. By the advent of the twentieth century, with the great increase in high schools, relatively few prospective teachers were not high school graduates. And a high school graduate would have felt out of place in the old normal school, with its nonacademic, almost anti-intellectual, atmosphere; with a new and better educated clientele, teacher education schools felt intense pressures for upgrading and broadening their professional programs. Moreover, if these schools really wanted to prepare teachers for all the schools, both elementary and secondary, and there was a growing demand for high school teachers, they would obviously have to move toward a curriculum which educated students along with training them, a curriculum which dealt with the content of learning as well as the techniques or skills connected with guiding it. Finally, there were institutional pressures perilous to ignore. The public mind required demonstrations of meaning from the new science of education, and it wanted assurances of its incorporation in academic agencies cast from the traditional mold of higher learning. Other higher schools had hardly noticed the coming of the normal school, but eventually their social sense motivated them to take a closer look at the schools involved in teacher preparation. What they saw sometimes disturbed them. They were almost uniformly skeptical of the normal school's ability to prepare a competent teacher, and they translated this skepticism into an agency or accrediting group which forced normal schools to strengthen themselves or submit to a public recounting of their weaknesses. The public generally, school boards who hired teachers, and students interested in preparing for a career in education wanted the kinds of assurances accrediting of institutions could give them. Naturally, the normal school could ignore accrediting, although to do so was simply a gateway to oblivion; but when it did not, it began to move in the direction of collegiate status.

All of these factors stimulated the growth of college-level teacher training, which came in some instances by the growth of the normal schools and in others by the founding of four-year teachers colleges. Examples of the former are found in the designation, in 1897, of the Ypsilanti Normal School as the Michigan State Normal College, and in the reorganization of the state normal school in Albany, New York, in 1890, as a teachers college. Perhaps the best illustration of the latter development is to be found in the establishment, in 1888, of the New York College for Teachers. This school was renamed Teachers College in 1892 and in 1898 was incorporated in Columbia University. The fact that Teachers College became part of a great university did not alter its professional purposes or commitments, and since its founding it has maintained a position of leadership in the professional study of education. But, it should be stated, not every new teachers college looked for or was granted intimate structural association with a university. As a matter of fact, most of the new teacher training schools, all of them four-year degree-granting institutions (in 1913 there were nine, by 1920 there were forty-six), preferred to avoid entangling alliances.

Teacher Training in Colleges and Universities

Despite the interest shown in the cause of popular education in the nineteenth century, colleges and universities were not disposed to assume the responsibility of the education of teachers. It was true, of course, that the distribution of education, although becoming more generous, did not extend much beyond the primary school before 1870. Colleges and universities were reflecting the generally accepted view when they dismissed elementary teaching as a temporary activity for which little, if any, special training was necessary. Liberal arts colleges tended to oppose the intrusion of professional or vocational courses into their programs.

Although this was the general reaction, some teacher training programs were introduced in the colleges and universities. New York University established a chair of the philosophy of education in 1832. On the recommendation of President Francis Wayland, Brown University established a normal department in 1850. Normal classes or departments were instituted at Indiana University in 1852, the University of Iowa in 1855, the University of Wisconsin in 1856, the University of Missouri in 1868, and the University of Kansas in 1881. A chair of the science and art of teaching was established at the University of Michigan in 1879. By the time the University of Michigan organized its course for teachers, the requirements for teaching were somewhat different from what they had been thirty years earlier. High schools were rapidly becoming part of the educational experience of an increasing number of young people. The methodological indoctrination of the teachers' short course or that of the normal school was insufficient preparation for the high school teacher. Teachers needed a better education, and many colleges and universities followed the lead of the University of Michigan and established chairs of education, pedagogy, or didactics as part of some existing department; in other colleges teachers' courses were organized as independent units, such as teachers colleges, colleges of education, or schools of education.

Professional Organizations

One of the striking facts about the educational profession is its traditional rejection of broad-scale organization. Medieval masters formed associations (their famous guilds) in order to protect themselves and the integrity of knowledge. But the master's guild was a local affair without any connection with any other guild in the academic world. Its extreme localism permitted cooperation among teachers within a faculty and encouraged an attitude of indifferentism toward academic occurrences in other faculties. Thus we find guilds of medicine, law, theology, and arts at some of the great medieval centers of teaching and learning. Both the legal and medical professional continued this tradition of professional association outside the school and broadened it to include almost every phase of their activity and almost all of the personnel associated with the field. Teachers, however, despite the repeated admonitions and warnings of their leaders, preferred to ignore the lessons of history and refused to organize for professional purposes, or simply remained indifferent to professional associations. There may be good reasons for this attitude among teachers: e.g., public enterprises are not the most fertile places for unions or associations; teachers often fear potential professional degradation from overaggressive organizations; private bargaining somehow befits professional persons; and academicians are determined to preserve their individuality—men must not be lost in groups. Whatever the reasons, and there must be almost as many as there are teachers, teachers are not good joiners. This may be a weakness for teachers who must contend with the complexities of control and administration in contemporary education.

Yet with all this perceptible resistance to joining, teachers' organizations are so numerous we should never think of trying to list them here. And teachers who do become *active* members of one, or several, professional groups do so because (1) they are convinced the organization will be instrumental in raising the standards of the profession, (2) they believe the group will make an important contribution to the professional growth of teachers, and (3) they hope their actions will lead to total professional upgrading.

Of all the national, state, regional, and subject-matter organizations for teachers, the most powerful is the National Educational Association of the United States, founded in 1857 as the National Teachers Association, and chartered by Congress in 1906. It takes an active interest in national issues touching on education, while its subgroups—state National Educational Associations—try to exert educational leadership on the state level. General appraisals of the NEA's effectiveness are seldom free from bias. It would be surprising indeed if any organization so large were devoid of friends or free from enemies. Still, there is something misleading about the numerical strength of the NEA and something illusory about its claim of speaking for the teaching profession: some classroom teachers are members of the association because they have been victimized by an overzealous principal who insists on having a perfect record of NEA representation from his school.

Thousands of teachers listed on membership rolls are merely nominal members; they assume no role in the proceedings of the group as a whole or its many subgroups and may not endorse the policy positions of the association. There are, moreover, several NEA critics among private school teachers, who see the NEA as anti-private school or so pro-public school in its attitude that it ignores or, what is worse, undermines the stature of private education. Although many teachers and administrators from private schools do participate in the affairs of the association, its image is publicly centered.

As the NEA has grown over the years, it has embarked on ventures going considerably beyond representing the profession to the public. Its bulletins and research reports especially have contained highly significant data for understanding the educational enterprise and following its progress. In addition, there are many services offered by the national and state organizations for schools and teachers. Members of the association, believing improvement of economic conditions to be its principal purpose, oppose the extension of these services. They say there is no real need for many of the activities of the association, that other agencies can offer them more efficiently. The association, they insist, has become conservative when it should be militantly active in improving the economic position of teachers. This attitude, as might be expected, has fostered the creation of other types of associations, for example, the American Federation of Teachers, which has allied itself with the American Federation of Labor.

The counterpart of the NEA in private education, although it represents only Catholic schools and their personnel (and the latter with their nominal membership have little or no voice in association policies), is the National Catholic Education Association, founded in 1904. The various departments and commissions of the NCEA have worked effectively to provide quality educational opportunities in all Catholic schools from the elementary through the university levels. And the NCEA itself has taken an active part in influencing national educational policies (Federal aid to education, child-welfare benefits, etc.), in encouraging greater and better education for all of the children of the nation, and in promoting and protecting the interests of the students in the schools and the teachers themselves.

THE TEACHER TODAY

Teaching as a Profession

We have seen something of the development of the teaching profession in the United States. From what has been said, it is apparent that the teacher's position has not always been an enviable one. There was a time when teachers were regarded as the most unproductive group in the community—they were teaching, it was felt, because there was nothing else they could do. Because teaching was considered to be unimportant, capable individuals who might otherwise have entered the profession were not attracted to it. What are the attractions of teaching? A discussion of the conditions which are now prevalent will be given later in the chapter, but here we are interested in the appeal which is inherent in teaching, and not the conditions which, somewhat belatedly, have given the profession some prestige, stability, and remuneration. These latter are important and necessary considerations, but they are not the heart of the teacher's ideal, and alone they do not invite high-minded and well-qualified individuals to become teachers.

If we look back on the history of education, we notice that among the ancient Hebrews, for example, the work of the teacher was regarded as being a work of God. Nothing was considered to be more important than the formation of young people; and in undertaking this, the teacher undertook a serious obligation. In this society, teachers were respected for their work and for the dedication they brought to it. Before accepting such a high social trust, prospective teachers searched their minds carefully in an attempt to discover whether they had the proper attitude toward the duties they were undertaking and whether they had the ideals necessary to sustain them in their work. Although teachers were not paid, teaching enjoyed unusual respect and remarkable prestige.

There is no way for teaching to obtain a high status if the society which teachers serve does not value their work. A society which does not value learning will not value teaching. Many people seem to have some difficulty in evaluating or placing a value on a product or activity unless it is tangible. Although the product of teaching is certainly tangible and unquestionably real, it is a deferred product. At a given time it is not always possible to determine just what the outcomes are; nor is it always possible to predict just what the results will be. Much of a teacher's work must be taken on faith: development can only be hoped for—it cannot be guaranteed. Teaching is a *cooperative art,* and its outcomes cannot be weighed and measured by the usual measurements of quantity; nor can its effectiveness be evaluated adequately on a day-to-day basis. Because teaching and learning are such complex, involved processes, it is not surprising that their values are sometimes misjudged.

Teachers must have patience and prudence, but above all they must have ideals. A teacher must hold learning in reverence and value it for its own sake; he must be able to form a vision of what his students will be. The teacher must be at the same time a visionary and a practical man— some would say an idealist and a realist. But the two must be balanced: if the teacher becomes too practical, he will lose the significance of his mission; if he becomes too much of a visionary, he will lose sight of the world in which he and his students must live and learn.

Recruitment and Preparation

A great deal has been written in the past decade about the shortage of qualified teachers on all levels of the educational ladder. We know our schools do not have all the fully qualified teachers needed, and the shortage may become more acute in the years just ahead. Nearly ninety thousand teachers presently employed in public elementary and secondary schools do not possess qualifications for state minimum certification. If they are replaced by qualified teachers and, in addition, if qualified teachers are appointed to fill vacancies occurring by reason of increased enrollment, and retirement and withdrawal of teachers from the profession, thousands of new teachers will be needed. Precisely how many new teachers will be needed to meet the demand is something of an open question. An estimate here is pointless, for all estimates are based on certain assumptions, and can easily be outdated in a year or less. We have means available for keeping abreast of the teacher-demand picture: publications of the U.S. Office of Education, reports of the NEA, reports of state educational agencies, and publications of private foundations.

Opportunities in teaching are as good or better than they have ever been before. If the prospective teacher is mobile, the entire United States can be the scene of his search for a position. No well-qualified candidate should experience much difficulty in obtaining an attractive teaching position, although, it is true, the demand for teachers varies somewhat from subject to subject. Prospective secondary school teachers may find more positions available in science and mathematics than in English, but the qualified English teacher will not experience unusual difficulty in finding a promising position.

The crucial point is not a shortage of good positions for candidates but a shortage of qualified candidates for positions. Perhaps the profession has not recruited effectively. Unlike physicians and theologians, teachers seem to ignore the issue of professional perpetuation. There may be many excellent reasons for this apparent indifference to recruitment, but this must not obscure the need for accelerated recruitment. Such organizations as the Future Teachers of America, the student NEA, and other preteaching clubs in high schools and colleges are active, and the National Defense Education Act contains provisions for attracting college students to a career in public school teaching.

What are we able to tell interested students about teaching, and about preparation for it? In broad terms there are two parts to this issue: (1) knowing what to teach and (2) knowing how to teach.

Knowing how to teach is the problem of professional education. What kind of preparation must the prospective teacher have? First, teachers must know something of the general system of education and the traditions of that system. Then, they must understand and appreciate the purposes of education and the objectives formal education is attempting to achieve. They must understand children and young people and the nature of learning. Finally, they must be craftsmen who can guide and direct learning experiences effectively. The number and nature of professional college courses needed to achieve this kind of knowledge and skill depend on the organization of a college's teacher education program and also on the state requirements for teacher certification.

Besides professional, theoretical, and technical preparation, prospective teachers need supervised experiences in which they are actually engaged in directing learning activities. But even the best professional preparation is no guarantee of a candidate's effectiveness, for teaching is essentially an art, not a science. In addition to professional courses and experiences, the studies of candidates for teaching should include general education as well as thorough preparation for the field or area in which they expect to teach.

Of course, the major part of any prospective teacher's college education must be—and today is—liberal or general. However, even ardent supporters of strict liberal education are admitting nowadays that a definite part of the future teacher's preparation must be devoted to those professional courses whose aim is to make teachers out of scholars.

Teacher education undergraduate programs in teachers colleges, colleges, and universities are usually organized according to one of the following plans:

1. Four-year general and professional program. This program is structured to introduce the student to his professional studies early in his college course along with other studies in general or liberal and special education. Individual programs differ, but it is not unusual for a student to take one professional course each of the eight semesters he devotes to college study.

2. Two-two general and professional program. According to this plan, one becoming decidedly less popular, college students preparing to teach spend the first two years of college study in general or liberal curricula. Their junior and senior years are reserved for concentration on professional courses. The obvious weakness in this program is the amount of time spent in purely professional study—one-half of the college course or approximately sixty semester hours. Whatever critics of professional education may say, few college officers or teachers responsible for organizing teacher-preparation programs are convinced of the desirability of heavy concentrations of professional study on the undergraduate level.

3. Four-year program with a professional sequence. The college curriculum in which this plan operates allows students to elect a professional sequence

in education in the same way a major or a minor in another field of study is selected. Majors and minors are usually chosen and completed in the junior and senior years; similarly, the professional courses are elected in these years.

4. Five-year program. The five-year program for teacher preparation places professional courses in the last year after requirements for the bachelor's degree have been met. Three states now require a fifth year of college for full initial certification for secondary school teachers; no state has enacted this requirement for elementary school teachers, although several states have enacted legislation requiring a master's degree or its equivalent for all teachers after a specified date in the future. It seems reasonable to expect five-year programs to eventually become as common as today's four-year programs.

In-service Teacher Education

The preliminary preparation of candidates for teaching is given in teachers colleges, liberal arts colleges, or universities. With this preparation students are able to obtain state teacher's certificates and may begin their careers as teachers. But the teacher's education must not cease with his induction into a school system. The beginning teacher is not a "finished product." No teacher education program can prepare a teacher completely: the teacher himself and the school system which appoints him must be concerned with in-service education and professional growth. A word may be said concerning the means available to teachers to aid them in continuing their education and improving themselves in their profession.

The values of self-directed study and reading should not be overlooked in this connection, although in-service education is usually conceived in terms of a formal program. College graduates have had broad intellectual vistas opened to them, and in-service teachers have many opportunities for achieving self-directed self-development. It is a common experience, however, and teachers share it, that goals of self-improvement may more nearly be attained if motivation is provided by a formal program. There are many possibilities for in-service education of teachers:

1. Self-directed study
2. Supervisory programs for beginning teachers conducted by the local school system
3. Teachers' seminars and discussion groups organized within the local school system
4. Summer school programs conducted by colleges and universities
5. Teachers' institutes conducted by teachers' organizations, state departments of education, colleges or universities, private corporations, the National Science Foundation, of the U.S. Office of Education

6. Continuing education programs made available through university extension departments or correspondence courses
7. School centers established by colleges and universities in cooperation with local school systems

Teacher Certification

During the later medieval period (ca. 1150–1500) and for much of the early modern period (ca. 1500–1700), a degree from a university was the traditional license to teach. But in the United States, with the popularization of education and the increasing demands for teachers during the nineteenth century, the supply of university graduates was not sufficient to meet the needs of education. As we have indicated earlier in the chapter, the practice of licensing teachers or issuing certificates to teachers is not new. Teacher licensing and certification throughout the eighteenth century and much of the nineteenth century were often a token attempt to determine a candidate's fitness for teaching: their real purpose was usually to exclude certain defined "religious undesirables" from teaching. The public's demand for better schools was eventually translated into state laws which established definite and normally somewhat higher qualifications for teachers. The practice of state teacher certification has been introduced throughout the United States and has tended to replace local certification. However, a few states still permit, in addition to state certification or in place of it, county or city certification.

While state certification was still in its infancy, and before teacher education institutions had clearly established their positions in professional preparation, the candidate for a teachers' license was required to pass an examination before the issuance of a certificate. Contemporary practices in certification seldom include teachers' examinations administered by the state, although a few city and county systems continue to require candidates for teaching positions to pass such examinations. And some school districts have initiated testing programs for teachers in an attempt to rate and screen them for promotions either in salary or position. What may be the most recent development on this level is the use in some school systems of the National Teachers Examination; the results of the test are used to guide administrators in appointments, promotions, and salary adjustments. At this point, in reference to state examinations for certification, the fact that such examinations are seldom, if ever, now administered is not an indication of any relaxation of standards. It is, rather, an expression of confidence in teacher education institutions preparing and recommending candidates for teachers' certificates. In most states, colleges and universities preparing teachers for certification must have their programs approved by the state department of education, and they simply recommend successful students who have followed the approved program. This is hardly a sign of abdication of responsibility for preserving quality; the control over quality is simply being exercised from another source.

The minimum requirements for certification in each state may be obtained by consulting abstracts of these codes appearing in various publications, such as R. C. Woellner and M. A. Wood: *Requirements for Certification of Teachers, Counselors, Librarians, Administrators for Elementary Schools, Secondary Schools, and Junior Colleges.* General noneducational requirements usually include most of the following: United States citizenship, the ability to take an oath of allegiance to the Constitution of the United States or the constitution of the state, or both, a recommendation from the college or university attended, and a certificate of health.

Without going into all the details of kinds of certification, it is possible to indicate, in general, the more important points.

1. Where is the certificate valid? The validity of a certificate depends upon the authority of the agency by which it is granted. If a certificate is issued by the state, it is usually possible for the teacher to teach anywhere in the state. However, certificates issued by intermediate or local school units are valid only for the school unit by which they are issued.

2. What are the educational levels for which a certificate is valid? There are nursery school, kindergarten, elementary, junior high, senior high, and junior college certificates, as well as certificates for special subjects, for special education (the blind, deaf, crippled, etc.), and for administration and supervision. However, there is some overlapping. For example, an elementary certificate may authorize its holder to teach in the junior high school or through grade 9, and a teacher with a secondary certificate may teach grades 7, 8, and 9.

3. What subjects may be taught? Some certificates entitle a teacher to teach all the subjects at the level for which the certificate is valid. Others specify the subjects which may be taught.

4. For what length of time is the certificate valid? Certificates are temporary, limited, or permanent. A temporary certificate is issued in emergency cases to individuals who are not fully qualified and is valid usually for only one year. These certificates are sometimes called "substandard." They may be renewed when the need for teachers is acute, but they may not be converted into a higher or standard certificate unless the holder fulfills all the requirements for the higher certificate. In a sense, temporary certificates are limited. However, the limited certificate is usually, though not always, a provisional certificate which the teacher obtains when he graduates from college. Its term of validity is stipulated—often five years —and if certain conditions are met within that time, the provisional certificate may be converted into a permanent certificate. Permanent certificates are issued only after applicants for them have demonstrated a high degree of proficiency under actual teaching conditions. Normally there is

an educational requirement to be fulfilled—college credits beyond the bachelor's degree—before the permanent certificate will be issued.

As we have indicated before, a teachers' license or certificate does not have general validity. A fully certified teacher in Montana, for example, is not entitled to teach in the schools of Maine without first obtaining a Maine certificate. The same is true of most other states. In other words, there is little reciprocity in teacher certification, a fact which has led the National Education Association and the National Commission for the Accrediting of Teacher Education (NCATE) to argue against restrictive state policies as contrary to the best interests of education. NCATE maintains its accreditation of teacher education institutions is a way of breaking down state barriers in teacher certification. It seems reasonable to anticipate reciprocal certification arrangements between several of the states within the next decade or two.

WORKING CONDITIONS FOR TEACHERS

Employment

Appointment of teachers is a function of local boards of education and cannot be delegated. Although superintendents, principals, or individual board members may recommend the appointment of teachers, only the school board, as such, may contract with them. Teachers' contracts are normally reduced to a single document to be signed by the teacher and members of the board, but letters, telegrams, and board resolutions taken together may actually contain the terms of the agreement between a teacher and the board of education. State law often requires that contracts be written and that they follow a definite and uniform form. Teachers' organizations have often recommended that a contract meet the following conditions:

1. It should be written.
2. It should contain a definite statement as to the length of the school term.
3. It should specify the salary to be paid.
4. It should specify a date for notification of reappointment.

Teaching Load

"Teaching load" is defined as the number of hours spent in the classroom each week. There are, of course, additional duties which all teachers are expected to accept, and these may not be part of actual teaching. It is becoming more popular, therefore, to refer to a teacher's "work week," rather than to "class" or teaching load. There seems to be some agreement that forty-five hours is a normal work week for teachers.

Implicit in any consideration of teaching load or work week is the question of teacher-pupil ratio, or the size of the classes which are the instructional responsibility of teachers. Most professional teacher organizations and many accrediting associations currently favor the practice which maintains a maximum of 30 pupils to each class, with a daily limit to the number of a teacher's class contacts. For example, the National Education Association has recommended a maximum of 25 pupils per class, with a daily pupil load for each teacher not exceeding 100.

Tenure

The first state teacher tenure law was passed in New Jersey in 1909. Since then thirty-nine states have enacted such statutes, and those states which do not have tenure laws often have passed permissive laws which make legal tenure possible in certain types of school units. It has been estimated that approximately two-thirds of the nation's teachers have some form of tenure. Tenure laws were not passed without opposition, for it was sometimes believed that tenure would give teachers too much power and that with it they could wrest control of the schools from boards of education and superintedents. The strongest opposition to tenure came from people who were unable to understand that teachers, as everyone else, must have some security if they are to do their work effectively.

"Tenure" is synonymous with "permanency" or "stability." Normally, a teacher must complete a probationary period before being given tenure. This probationary period may last for one, two, three, or more years. After a teacher is placed on tenure, it is difficult for the local school system to dismiss him. In order to do so, specific charges must be made against him in testimony before a tenure commission. After all the testimony is taken, the commission renders its verdict, and the teacher may be either dismissed or retained. In many states, an unfavorable verdict for the teacher may be appealed to the state commissioner of education or to the courts. Some state tenure laws are so rigid that it is almost impossible to dismiss even a patently inefficient teacher.

It is undoubtedly possible that tenure has led some teachers into an early and unwarranted "retirement" from the duties they are obligated to perform. On the other hand, tenure makes it possible for the majority of teachers to do their work free from the fear that they may displease someone in the community and as a result lose their positions. Although there are some disadvantages to it, the advantages of tenure tend to outweigh its shortcomings.

Salaries

In recent years attention has been given to problems of recruitment and retention of teachers. The schools of the nation cannot obtain and retain highly qualified people unless the remuneration is adequate and, in addition, is comparable to the position teachers must maintain in the community. The possible rejoinder here is that in comparison with other learned professions, teaching has always been underpaid, and somehow the schools have managed to employ and retain teachers of satisfactory competence. But is this rejoinder entirely convincing? Have the schools always been able to employ teachers whose competence was at least satisfactory? Idealism has regularly been part of the equipment of dedicated teachers, and dedicated teachers, often unmindful of their material needs, have graced our classrooms. Yet are we to believe their idealism would somehow be deflated if their material needs were cared for more generously? "Idealism is hard to spend at the local supermarket, and the local banker never recognizes it as legal tender" is the incisive reply of the teacher asked to sacrifice too many of the legitimate economic wants of his family. The teacher does not need just a living wage; he needs a professional salary, one enabling him to live for twelve months, although he teaches only nine, and one making it possible for him to withdraw from the world of care and economic insecurity to one containing conditions important to a selfless pursuit of profound knowledge and professional skill. Men do not live by bread alone; teachers especially, if they are to attain optimum effectiveness, need to be free from the nagging worries of making economic ends meet. They cannot live without "bread."

Why should communities give special consideration to teachers' economic security? First, because the teacher's vocational success demands it; second, because of today's competition for talent, and the talented teacher or prospective teacher will have difficulties in resisting attractive opportunities in business, industry, and government. If communities want good teachers, they must pay for them.

What has been said about the economic dimension in teaching is valid, but it does not tell prospective teachers about teachers' salaries today. Who determines salaries? What are the opportunities for advancement after employment? Are there regional or geographic salary differentials? What are the criteria for salary increases?

Boards of education make final decisions on salary questions. What a beginning teacher earns depends to some extent on the state—thirty-four states have legal minimums—but the final determination above legally established minimums is made on the local level. Professional teachers' organizations, local finance committees, and other noneducational groups make recommendations both for local communities and on a national level, but these proposals are suggestions only. The school system's financial ability is really the controlling factor—it overrides even the good will of a community to compensate its teachers—and, as we have seen in earlier chapters, this ability varies greatly from community to community and from state to state. One community may pay teachers only $2,000 a year, while another offers salaries of $10,000. The maximum salary is always determined on the local level; states have taken no action with respect to legal maximums.

A teacher's opportunities for salary increases are usually predetermined by a salary schedule. The most common salary schedule today is the *single salary*. A single-salary schedule provides equal compensation for all teachers in a school system, men and women, married and unmarried, elementary and secondary, alike, based on years of training and experience.

The mobile teacher or prospective teacher may be especially interested in geographic salary differences. These change, of course, so interested persons should obtain the latest averages. At this writing, the average annual salary for instructional staff, by region, looks something like this: Far West, $6,900; Northwest, $4,800; Southwest, $5,300; Middle West, $5,800; Southeast, $4,500; Middle Atlantic, $6,300; New England, $5,800.

Teachers' salaries, and salary increments, are based on education, experience, and merit. The teacher with a bachelor's degree normally will not receive as large a salary as the teacher with a master's degree, assuming that both have the same experience. Thus, education, or preparation, is taken into account, and preparation increments are built into the salary schedule to compensate the teacher for his master's or doctor's degree. Some salary schedules provide preparation increments for semester-hour or quarter-hour credit toward either of these advanced degrees. In addition to formal education, travel and other broadening experiences sometimes count for a preparation increment.

TABLE 10-1
Illustration of Steps on the Single-salary Schedule

Step	B.A.	M.A.
1	$4,150	$4,400
2	4,450	4,700
3	4,750	5,000
4	5,050	5,300
5	5,350	5,600
6	5,650	5,900
7	5,950	6,200
8	6,250	6,500
9	6,550	6,800

Experience counts; it counts especially on salary schedules. Single-salary schedules are constructed with a certain number of annual steps, often nine, to a maximum with an annual experience increment of, say, $300. The teacher is given a salary increase based on the previous year's experience. Table 10-1 illustrates the application of an experience increment for teachers with different preparation. Besides preparation and experience increments, some salary schedules make provisions for merit increments. This involves merit rating, always a sensitive topic when related to salaries. Who is to judge the effectiveness of teachers A and B? How are we able to say one is better than another, if both are fully competent, and, furthermore, how can we translate this judgment into dollars and cents? We are not against merit increments, nor are we opposed to merit rating. Yet, at best, merit determinations are difficult to make and often lead to morale problems on a faculty.

Teachers' Benefits

Retirement plans. Retirement plans for teachers are presently available in all the states, although there are great variations among them. Some plans are quite adequate, whereas others, even when supplemented by social security payments, provide for such small payments that the retired person is bound to be economically insecure in his old age. The vast majority of these state plans must be classified as annuities rather than pensions. That is, financial returns made from retirement funds are made on the basis of the teacher's contribution. The usual retirement plan today requires participation of all contract personnel who must contribute part of their income—about 5 per cent—and this sum is matched by the state or the school district. If a person leaves teaching, many of the retirement plans permit withdrawal of the individual contribution. Administration of retirement funds and distribution of benefits vary from state to state and often from district to district. Thirty years of service covered by a retirement plan normally qualifies a teacher for the full benefits of the plan.

Sick leave. Most school districts make contractual provisions for a specified number of days of sick leave. These days—usually ten or twelve—may be taken without loss of pay. The terms of sick-leave arrangements vary; the plan considered ideal by teachers permits them to accumulate leave indefinitely and not lose it when it is not used.

Disability pay. In instances where illness is prolonged and where sick leave is not adequate, disability programs insure the teacher and make payments proportional to his regular salary.

Hospitalization insurance. Insurance covering all or part of hospital and medical costs is now available to teachers in almost every school district. In addition, such policies are sometimes available through teachers' organizations. Premium payments are often made by the school district.

Leave with pay. Many districts now allow teachers a specified number of days each year for personal leave without loss of pay. In larger and somewhat more progressive school systems sabbatical leaves, usually at half pay, are available to enable teachers to pursue advanced graduate study or otherwise seek professional improvement, such as exchange teaching, research, or living and travel in foreign countries.

SUMMARY

The importance of the role of the teacher as a mediator in the educational life of youth—though always understood by some—is more generally recognized today than in any previous period in the history of American education. In preceding periods, attention and emphasis were given to organization, administration, curriculum, and objectives. In contemporary America, though these phases of the educational enterprise are not ignored, it is teaching and the teacher that command the attention of educators and the general public. The central position of teachers and teaching in the contemporary scene is the result of the natural evolution of teaching as a profession.

The teacher's essential function—to guide and direct learning activities —is not subject to change; the teacher's responsibility to his students is probably broader than ever before. Qualified and dedicated teachers are indispensable to the formation of youth and the future of America. To attract and retain teachers of quality for the rapidly increasing numbers who are entering and will enter schools at all levels, the profession has been made more attractive in terms of opportunities and rewards, and more and more persons of distinction and dedication are now selecting teaching as a career.

QUESTIONS AND EXERCISES

1. What qualifications were demanded of teachers in your state during the nineteenth century? Investigate the evolution of teacher certification in your state.
2. When and why did women become more numerous than men as teachers in American schools?
3. How did European influence bear upon teacher preparation in the United States?
4. Discuss the place of the normal school in the preparation of teachers in the United States.
5. Review the development of teachers colleges in the United States.

6. List those characteristics or qualities which you consider most essential in a teacher.
7. Prepare arguments for and against teacher tenure. What is the status of tenure in your state? Do teachers in private schools have tenure?
8. What are the advantages and the disadvantages of a single-salary schedule?
9. As a teacher, how would you react to the twelve-month school year?
10. What is meant by reciprocity in teacher certification? Would it be a good thing?

ADDITIONAL READINGS

Anderson, T., et al.: *The Education of the Secondary School Teacher,* Wesleyan University Press, Middletown, Conn., 1962. Note the two-dimensional approach to teacher education. The views on the place of professional education are interesting.

Barzun, Jacques: *The Teacher in America,* Little, Brown and Company, Boston, 1945. An idealistic portrait of teaching compared with the American teacher as Barzun sees him.

Brighton, Stayner F., and Cecil J. Hannan: *Merit Pay Programs for Teachers,* Fearon Publishers, San Francisco, 1962. A summary of merit salary programs for teachers. Contains responses to frequently asked questions and persistently raised objections to merit salary schedules.

Burrup, Percy E.: *The Teacher in the Public School System,* Harper & Row, Publishers, Incorporated, New York, 1960. Read especially chapters on the teacher in the school community and professionalism of the teacher.

Conant, James B.: *The Education of American Teachers,* McGraw-Hill Book Company, New York, 1963. Among the twenty-seven recommendations the author makes, see those on student teaching and continuing education for teachers.

Dearborn, N. H.: *The Oswego Movement in American Education,* Bureau of Publications, Teachers College, Columbia University, New York, 1925. The Oswego Normal School led all the other nineteenth-century normal schools in prestige and prominence. Follow the course of Pestalozzianism as it came to America and was spread by this school.

Elsbree, Willard: *The American Teacher,* American Book Company, New York, 1939. A broad approach to the evolution of teaching as a profession in America. See particularly for the colonial beginnings.

Faunce, Roland C., and Morrel J. Clute: *Teaching and Learning in the Junior High School,* Wadsworth Publishing Co., San Francisco, 1961. See chapter on integration of curricular and cocurricular activities in the junior high school.

Gauerke, Warren E.: *Legal and Ethical Responsibilities of School Personnel,* Prentice-Hall, Inc., Englewood Cliffs, N.J., 1959. This book is intended to help educators and other interested persons become acquainted with some minimum legal obligations and rights and acquire a deeper understanding of ethical choices.

Gordy, J. P.: *Rise and Growth of the Normal School Idea in the United States,* U.S. Bureau of Education Circular of Information 8, 1891. An old but interesting book on the spread of the normal-school idea. Read for an understanding of the place and purpose of the normal school in American education.

Harper, C. A.: *A Century of Public Teacher Education,* National Education Association, Washington, D.C., 1939. This book begins with the founding of the first state normal and covers the next 100 years of teacher education. See especially for the development of the teachers college.

Hodenfield, G., and T. M. Stinnett: *The Education of Teachers,* Prentice-Hall, Inc., Engelwood Cliffs, N.J., 1961. This is a review of the work of three national conferences on problems in teacher education.

Kershaw, J. A., and Roland McKean: *Teacher Shortages and Salary Schedules,* McGraw-Hill Book Company, New York, 1962. Reviews the relationships between teachers' salaries and the supply of teachers for American schools.

Klausmeier, Herbert J., and Katharine Dresden: *Teaching in the Elementary School,* Harper & Row, Publishers, Incorporated, New York, 1962. A survey of academic and psychological dimensions in elementary school teaching.

Marshall, Max S.: *Two Sides to a Teacher's Desk,* The Macmillan Company, New York, 1951. An interesting and somewhat original analysis of teaching-learning processes.

McGlothlin, William J.: *Patterns of Professional Education,* G. P. Putnam's Sons, New York, 1960. A study of several distinctive approaches to the education of teachers.

Pangburn, Jessie M.: *The Evolution of the American Teachers College,* Bureau of Publications, Teachers College, Columbia University, New York, 1932. A pertinent account of the role of the teachers college in the education of secondary school teachers.

Peterson, Dorothy G., and Velma D. Hayden: *Teaching and Learning in the Elementary School,* Appleton-Century-Crofts, Inc., New York, 1961. Present practices and future trends in psychology and methodology as they apply to the elementary school are reviewed.

Riccio, Anthony C., and Frederick R. Cyphert: *Teaching in America,* Charles E. Merrill Books, Inc., Columbus, Ohio, 1962. The editors have compiled provocative statements on teaching in the schools of the United States.

Ryans, David G.: *Characteristics of Teachers,* American Council on Education, Washington, D.C., 1960. This book undertakes to define and appraise the qualities of good teachers.

Sarason, Seymour B., Kenneth S. Davidson, and Burton Blatt: *The Preparation of Teachers,* John Wiley & Sons, Inc., New York, 1962. This volume contains many challenges to the accepted views on the preparation of teachers. It calls for a reexamination, based on evidence and research, of programs for the preparation of teachers.

Smith, Elmer R.: *Teacher Education: A Reappraisal,* Harper & Row, Publishers, Incorporated, New York, 1962. The need for more effective programs in student teaching is emphasized.

Stinnett, Timothy M., and Lawrence D. Haskew: *Teaching in American Schools,* Harcourt, Brace & World, Inc., New York, 1962. A perceptive analysis of the origin, development, and purpose of America's system of free schools.

PARENTS WHO BELIEVE
IN
DEMOCRACY
SEND THEIR CHILDREN
TO SCHOOL
DO NOT BOYCOTT

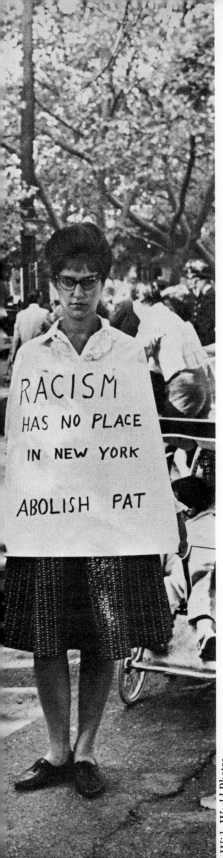

PART FOUR

*Contemporary
Issues and Special Problems*

chapter 11

Education and Democracy

THE MEANING OF EDUCATION

What Is Education?

Education, the cynic says, enables you to go through life without intelligence, and intelligence enables you to go through life without education. Even though cynics are not always entirely wrong, we should find it extremely difficult to distill any general theoretical or practical positions from such a view. The important point is not whether or when education and intelligence may be interchanged or replaced, but what is the correlation between them? The answer to this depends somewhat on prior assumptions or definitions. Education is imparting truth and knowledge, it is molding people to be like each other, or it is the art of forming differences of mind. Plato saw education as a process of conversion, where eyes that could see, but were looking in the wrong direction, were helped to select new goals for vision. Aristotle interpreted education as a means of promoting the happiness and the welfare of the state. For John Dewey education became a process of remaking experience in which experiences were socialized, or their social value was emphasized, by broadening the range of experience and accentuating the degree of control each learner should have over his own powers. Johann Herbart set a tone for modern education, one not ignored by Dewey, seemingly out of keeping with his great attachment to scientific progress in teaching and learning, when he wrote: Morality, universally acknowledged as the highest goal of humanity, must be the ultimate objective of education. Herbart's definition raised educational issues transcending the school, although, unfortunately, his views have been understood largely within the context of school learning. Thomas Henry Huxley regarded education as the instrument of intellect in the laws of nature, and the fashioning of the affections and the will into an earnest and living de-

303

sire to move in harmony with those laws. William James saw it as a way of organizing acquired habits of action to fit a person to participate in physical and social environments. Transcendental implications appear naturally in Immanuel Kant's statement that education's purpose is to train children to fix their attention on an ideal conception of humanity, a conception encouraging society to achieve higher standards of humaneness. John Locke's view of education leads to an illusion of breadth: It is not the business of education, Locke maintained, to make the young perfect in any one of the sciences, but it is its business to open minds and dispose them toward scientific study. There is more than a hint of mental discipline here, although it is offset when Locke sets attainment of a sound mind in a sound body as the end of education. If we take Locke seriously, we may be left with two apparently contradictory interpretations of education. A strong mind may have been the general capability which Locke prized most, or it may have been the healthy mind, the one able to withstand the shock of civilization in general or contemporary culture in particular. We could stop to debate with these thinkers, or we could pause in search of elaborations of their meanings, but to do so would have questionable value here. We shall add a few more general views of education simply for the sake of balance. The majestic tones of John Milton seem to gain in majesty when he refers to a complete and generous education fitting man to perform justly, skillfully, and magnanimously all the offices both public and private, of peace and war. Johann Pestalozzi, a long-time disciple of Rousseau, believed education's real meaning could be found in the natural, progressive, and systematic development of all the powers of the person. Socrates was somewhat less inclusive—perhaps he did not have the same optimistic glow of some of his followers when he, speaking through the mind and pen of Plato, set the aim of education as one of dispelling error and discovering truth.[1]

More recent reactions to the meaning of education, and ones without the authority commanded by wise men, range from an emphasis on training youth in the tools of knowledge, or the cultivation of character, or the art of awakening curiosity, to preparation for economic life, for citizenship, or just for life. The last, despite its ring of realism, is a particularly meaningless conception of the role education must or may play. Established as a goal, preparation for life admits a context so broad and undefinable as to eliminate points of convergence or so narrow as to be archaic.

Is there any help to be derived from looking at the word itself? Etymologically, education is derived from the Latin word *educare*: to make a plant grow. There is a philological relationship to the word *educere*—to lead out—although the two words are distinct. Making plants grow was in Froebel's mind when he began his famous kindergarten, and the gardening metaphor, if we are alert to its limitations, may be illuminating. The comparison is clear in the fact that no gardener has ever made a plant grow: he may help it by putting it in good soil, he may water, feed, and cultivate it, and he does all of this to help the plant realize its inner potentialities for growth. Perhaps the greatest lesson implied in the metaphor is the one of wholeness or individuality: the gardener does not treat one part of the plant, cultivate one side, or nurse one pretty flower. He gives his attention to the plant as a whole and tries to help it grow. One plant grows faster than the rest; another is taller; still others have brighter flowers; and none of these differences are deplored or discouraged by the gardener. Each plant is allowed to grow, to develop in its own way. Deliberate education either in home or in school takes us away from the garden, and analogies become less satisfying. Yet part of education must surely be phrased in terms of duty: the duty of parents and teachers to discover the needs of children, as distinguished from wants, and their potentialities, and then to help those potentialities grow. All of this implies a versatility and flexibility on the part of teachers, for if we reject the want of the student as being tantamount to legitimate need, we must be prepared to reject personal goals of teachers as being valid objectives for students. Essentially the meaning is this: Good education is not teacher-dominated; a principal educational fallacy gave unchallenged appropriateness and meaning to teacher-formulated objectives. Its cultivation, moreover, led to the determination of institutional objectives in a highly irrelevant way: the character of schools was determined by teachers—justifiable when teachers are excellent but dangerous when they are ungraded—and education's image was teacher-made.[2]

So now we may ask again, what is education? Throughout man's long history many answers have been given to this question. And the answers have been broad or narrow, normative or descriptive, complete or incomplete, depending upon various interpretations of man's nature and needs. "What is man?" is the first question to be asked in any attempt to determine the meaning of education. This question may be answered by dealing with human nature in its essential being and by taking into account its phenomenal characteristics, or it may be answered by depending entirely upon what is known of man from the modern sciences of observation and measurement. The first approach is philosophical-empirical; the second is purely empirical. Empirical expressions of education's meaning are often based on the belief that man is constantly evolving and that education, if it is to satisfy his needs, must be subject to continuous reconstruction. Some of the goals of education are subject to change, but neither the primary ends nor the essential meaning of education is determined by the ephemeral needs of man or society.

Some caution must be exercised in accepting empiricism when it is not tempered by philosophic insights into human nature in its essential meaning. What schools recognize as their functions at a given time may not be entirely valid objectives; and to honor empirically oriented objectives without reviewing them in the light of man's essential nature may result in erroneous educational emphases. A willingness to survey, to experiment, to measure, and to describe may be indicative of lack of certainty with respect to education's general objectives. Still, experimentation is essential to progress in education, though its contribution may not be very useful unless the general answer to the meaning of education is based on the unavoidable preamble of man's essential nature. But if one must be cautious in using empirical guides in dealing with the meaning of education, one must be cautious, too, in being dominated by philosophy, that is, in using only man's essential nature to determine the meaning and goals of education. Men and societies change in history, and education must recognize and keep abreast of these changes.[3]

The Changes in Meaning

We may begin by assuming that education has not always meant the same thing to everyone. However convincing the philosopher may be when he deals with education in its essential meaning and argues for the timeless and unchanging character of it, all men do not see its meaning in precisely the same way. One need only glance at the views of the famous men to whom we have referred above to see this, and one may, if he needs more proof, examine educational opportunities in the context of cultural development to discover that what today is called training, or wasted energy in some instances or sheer frivolity in others, was once a prized activity for which most people developed some facility. Today, moreover, it would be meaningless to talk of education solely in terms of preservation of self; at least it would be meaningless in most parts of the Western world, particularly if such preservation implied an active engagement in the skills of the chase, from which, in former ages, food and clothing were procured. But meaning must be distilled from a context. It was not aimless activity for the American Indian when he learned the skills of tracking and hunting; he would not have been thought well educated, indeed he would not have survived for long, if his attention had centered on a literary kind of learning so common in other parts of the world. He learned what he needed to know, and this was intimately related to survival. Is this really different from what happens in American society when youth are immersed in a kind of learning enabling them to make a living? No serious student of education believes such goals are unimportant. And who can afford to ignore health education which is education for preservation on another level of sophistication.

But these points need little emphasis—they need not be belabored—for obviously the content of education, training, or whatever term one uses, is different from what it was in the past and probably from what it will be in the future, too. Are we convinced, though, simply because the content was or will be different, that the goal or the fundamental meaning of education will be different, too? Education is too closely related to life for such a conviction to go for long unchallenged. It is not to be expected that a satisfying philosophy of education (an understanding or interpretation of education) can be formulated apart from a philosophy of life. Philosophies of life mature and are enriched by experience and learning; what a boy believes important, an operational insight into his value system, may change drastically before he becomes a man. Even in his mature years these values are subject to modification; it is most difficult to think of a total philosophy of life as a fixed, unyielding dogma driving men to action or turning them toward inaction. Reconstruction, far from being an unrealistic view of experience, is most important to men; they cannot live well unless they are ready and able to adapt to and learn from their experiences.

Whatever education may mean for a teacher, and his conception of it is important, we cannot be certain of the student's ability to share it with him at any given time. The teacher's vision of the learner's goals is usually very different from the student's aspirations. Teachers may seek conversion to their vision of education, but they should not be disappointed if it does not occur at once. A third-grade student sees education on any level of formality or informality as important or unimportant depending on his previous experience and the kind of impression society has been able to make on him. Simple computation is interesting and meaningful or meaningless and dull to the third grader. It is the former if he sees the skills involved as somehow fitting usefully into his value system. No third grader has ever admitted to a pursuit of study from purely liberal motives; he is hardly ever seeking knowledge for its own sake. So part of the business of education is to convert the learner to accept a larger vision of himself; to help him understand his human character and his capacities of intellect and will. There may be real, uncontested value in the skills youth learn without instruction, or the knowledge they master under direct tutelage. We should be willing to say, for example, that no one in contemporary society can lead a full and satisfying life without elemental skills, such as reading, writing, and computing (these skills are not in themselves so worthwhile, but they are bridges to later important growth), and we should be able to say also, and this brings us much nearer the meaning of education, that these skills are but rungs on a ladder up which the person will climb. The goal when the uppermost part of the ladder is reached is mental and moral autonomy. Freedom, or freeing, is a feature most interpretations of education have in common. Plato's conversion was a conversion to freedom, and Herbart looked forward to an autonomous life in which a framework of morality was respected and accepted on the level of action.[4]

The point is, however, despite our willingness to accept autonomy as the key to education, its end and its real meaning, we should be aware of the difficulty of translating this real and meaningful but highly abstract purpose to make it an effective and constant motive for us all, for we are all involved in the educational process. A satisfying philosophy of education, by which we mean one serving as a directive force from the day we begin deliberate education until human life is no longer meaningful, can never be achieved apart from a satisfying philosophy of life. [5] And to complicate the issue further, a philosophy of life is itself a product of education. We learn our values, or we see them, understand them, at least on our own terms, and then accept them as supports to be strengthened, moved, altered, or re-shaped. These philosophical values, firmly or tentatively held, give life a sense of direction. However, a defective or immature philosophy of life blurs the sense of direction and deprives education of its clearer meanings. Societies without a sense of direction supplied by an underlying philosophy of value, something seldom found in a gross pragmatism, are never in a position to infuse education with determined purposes or a real sense of mission.

Sense of direction, or basic purpose, is imperative, but it does not guarantee either broad or humane learning. Totalitarian governments communicate a sense of purpose to, or force one on, their people. Their educational systems are clearly dominated by this overall purpose, and the quality of the entire process, if one is to judge by results alone, is high. Whatever was accomplished by the schools of the Nazi regime in Germany and whatever is achieved under the Communists in Russia, regardless of the economic or social or military or scientific consequences, is not education in the best or broadest meaning of the term, because there is neither freedom in such processes nor autonomy at the end of the process.[6]

We have then a cyclical process wherein social value is a directive force for all institutions of society and educational values affect the process at some points. A sovereign people govern themselves and define the purposes of their schools, but the schools have, and ought to have, a direct influence on these people and an indirect effect on the future through the youth educated in the schools. To point to what appears to be a highly confused social complex may lead some persons to feelings of despair. There is a fear at the middle of the twentieth century generated by the sociologists who seem to be demonstrating that we are all patterned and largely determined by our social groups and that the laws of social development are as inexorable as the laws of chemical change. If we believe this, value seems to be excluded from education: it is truly caught not taught. But if we become as detached as the scientists to whom these views are attributed, and if we regard enthusiasm, vision, commitment, and faith with a cynical eye, we shall be unable to understand our own doubts and uncertainties.

Hope and faith may not be the products of formal education, but both may be cultivated in home, in school, and in society. With hope and faith, life can be lived and not merely endured, or, in one ingenious way or another, escaped from. For without faith and hope, there is no future worth talking about and no education really worth seeking.

To have beliefs generated or sustained and supported by educational experiences and to have a sense of purpose is to live in harmony with the nature of life. To wish to escape for long from purposes and commitments and beliefs is like wanting to escape to an atmosphere where there is no air.

We should try here to face some elemental facts about education. Every child is affected greatly by the society in which he is brought up, by its habits and conventions and the values it simply assumes are important and takes for granted. Professional educators quite often, and the general public, too, have underestimated the subtlety and unconscious character of much of the educative process and the extent to which education is the product of forces within society generally. Because of this, there has been a tendency to identify it too much with what goes on in school. The school today is an indispensable institution, but it has not yet shown itself to be the most powerful educative factor in the lives of those who attend it. The moribund school can hinder some vital kinds of learning or even block them entirely; the viable school can cultivate talent which otherwise would be lost. In the history of culture and education, some homes and schools have undoubtedly been as successful in placing effective talent in jeopardy as they have been successful in bringing it to a state of realization. And a great deal of fundamental education, whether received in or out of school, must have the character of indoctrination, although these doctrines will not be passed on at a conscious level.

Education of a more or less formal sort may be indispensable, but it is not inevitable: indoctrination is. Societies would never be formed were it not for indoctrination and, once formed, could not survive without it. The value system with which we begin and seldom alter fundamentally, although we have the capacity for doing so, is a product of indoctrination, a worthy, wholesome, and serious effort to perpetuate values in which we believe (and in some cases for which men have fought and died) and to transmit them to the young as effective means for choosing or making value judgments. Indoctrination may sometimes be blind, and when it is, it is not recommended; but indoctrination which has the support of a major segment of any society cannot be totally blind. It can be erroneous, or evil, but not blind. The Communist child is indoctrinated as is the democratic child, but the process, whatever its content may be, is not lacking in ideals or fundamental commitment to them. Eventually, of course, if education follows indoctrination and if this education seeks freedom for the person, the values implanted by indoctrination will be reinforced or revised or destroyed by learning.[7]

To recognize indoctrination as a corollary of social living is not the same as defending all indoctrination or accepting it as a substitute for or synonym of education.

Neither fears of indoctrination nor social determinism should deter us for long; for the former, as we have said, may often be put to good use, and the latter, as we shall now contend, is somewhat unreal. Society, when it is considered apart from persons who make it up, is an abstraction without roots. There is a social consciousness, a spirit of the age, there are social values, views, hopes, and fears because persons hold to them and believe in them. In any society complexities, conflicts, and ideals of many different strands and brands are held together. The same is true of the person who lives in this society: he too binds together in one more or less unified personality many divergent and inconsistent ideals, aspirations, and opinions. Unwavering consistency is almost too much to ask of men. So a society is open to change and modification by those who live in it, and probably most effectively by those who belong to it in a most central sense and yet somehow are eccentric: they hold views somewhat different from the ones commonly accepted. These differences, these eccentricities, offer no special immunity to education; in fact they may often touch the very core where education's most precious and persistent issues are settled. Which potentialities are to be developed by formal education will, in fact, depend to a great extent on the traditions of society. A number of characteristics, and this is easy to appreciate, which might have been developed in a man may not come into functional existence because of the particular race or society or class to which he belongs. Education today cannot escape a social dimension, and this social dimension demands that education, so far as it is under our control, must be especially concerned with which of the variants within the main currents of our society shall be allowed greater scope in those we educate. In the past we have shown less concern for, perhaps we have been less conscious of, the selective processes employed in the schools by control of "climate," choice of staff, philosophies of teacher education, building of curricula, and preferences in schedule than we can afford to any longer.

The end of education is not "happiness," which is most difficult to translate, but the development of a capacity of awareness; to deepen personal understanding and wisdom; to awaken and discipline a sensitive power of reason; and to make right action perfectly natural. Education is a human enterprise. In its broadest meaning education is the intellectual, moral, social, and physical development of boys and girls, men and women. Broadly conceived, education's goals are skill, information, and formation, and the end of education, therefore, can be limited neither to the making of minds nor the building of character. Its primary end is the formation of men. Secondary but essential ends for education—citizenship, making a living, and preparation for family life are examples—arise out of man's life in society.

Formal and Informal Education

When life in society was considerably less complex than it is today, the moral, intellectual, and physical formation of young people was left to the family and to society generally. Schools were created when the effects of informal and incidental education no longer fulfilled the expectations of society. In other words, the school is a social institution created to fulfill functions which other institutions in society—for example, the home and the church—and society itself cannot fulfill at all or cannot fulfill so well as a special education institution. Because the school was created by society and was given general institutional objectives, it is sometimes easy to misinterpret its relationship to education. It is becoming more and more common to identify education and instruction in school. Though it is not a mistake to associate education and learning, it is inaccurate to think of all education and learning as being institutionalized or an exclusive responsibility of the school's. The school is one place where children may be educated, but it is not the only place, and sometimes it is not even the best place. Even excellent schools cannot be expected to provide all the educational opportunities, supply all the individual needs, or control every educational experience. The school's limited influence on individuals and society has been the theme of many writings.

Although the influence of the school may be limited, its responsibility is fairly clear, and its contributions are important. The school must be shaped into a functioning community in a living relationship with the larger community which it serves. It should make cooperation a reality by seeking to give to every individual a feeling of responsibility for the entire community. And the school should prepare its pupils to be articulate and capable in helping to determine the community life of the people. Habits of independent thought must be fostered, and discussion of important issues should be encouraged, in order that disciplined attitudes may be formed with respect to the functioning of democratic societies. Every pupil must be respected; individuality must not be ignored. Only in this way can the profound truths and aspirations of democracy be realized and become part of the life ideals of the children who attend educational institutions.

It is relatively easy to make a verbal distinction between schooling and education in the larger sense, which is lifelong and life-wide, but it is probably impossible to be certain whether the formation of an individual, or what part of that formation, was achieved in school or by the total social environment. In any case, schooling is referred to as formal education, and all the educative experiences and opportunities outside the school make up informal education. This distinction does not provide the basis for a value judgment, nor does it decide the relative importance of formal and informal education. It is nevertheless a useful distinction, and it will be employed in this book whenever it is necessary to distinguish between schooling and education in its broadest meaning.

Our discussion of formal and informal education may be carried on at a more practical level. We may look, for example, at almost any set of educational objectives and identify in them the part expected of formal education and speculate concerning the role informal education has in helping achieve the same objectives. The Seven Cardinal Principles—health, command of the fundamental processes, worthy home membership, vocational efficiency, citizenship, worthy use of leisure, and ethical character[8]—were formulated as guides for the school, but it is impossible to believe that out-of-school experiences which are truly formative can be ignored as progress is made moving toward these objectives. The universal human needs proposed by Cunningham—education (by which is meant intellectual development), health, human companionship, economic security, leisure, civic security, and divine security[9]—are clearly to be achieved by a dual process including the work of the school and all other agencies and experiences outside the school.

If we begin with health, we can see there is a great deal the school can do to instruct youth in habits of health, in providing an environment conducive to the development of health, in detecting and correcting certain threats to good health, and in generating wholesome attitudes relative to individual and community health. Communities would not tolerate schools refusing to acknowledge their responsibility toward health. On the other hand, schools are not established to be hospitals or clinics or health centers; other community agencies assume direct and primary responsibilities in this area. But the home is, first of all, the place where habits pertaining to health are established and where fundamental attitudes toward health are built. What the home does is hardly ever on the level of conscious instruction; much of its health education is incidental; it is education by example and is informal. The great advances in the sciences of physiology and hygiene over the past several decades make imperative the formal status of health education. Too much scientific knowledge is available to allow health education to be left solely in the hands of the home, or other informal avenues of education. This is where the school's role must be emphasized. It is not only a question of scientific knowledge; it is also a question of unscientific, inaccurate, sometimes dangerous information being circulated as if it were valid, when a responsible agency like the school is not involved. Exercise, diet, mental and physical health, all have a place in education, and the school, we should think, would be the most appropriate place for disseminating knowledge about such important topics. Yet, the school is not alone, for alone it is inadequate.

Whether we take "command of the fundamental processes," an objective of the Cardinal Principles, or Cunningham's "education" as a point of departure, the school's inherent responsibility is apparent. The general function of formal education is the making of minds, not the making of men (this is the purpose of education in its totality), and the school must begin with the most elemental kinds of learning to lead the learner up the ladder of intellectual development. Despite our willingness to accept the school as an agency concerned primarily with the making of minds, we admit to a great deal of important learning going on outside the school. The home is the first "school" to contact the child; in the home he learns to speak and listen; there he is introduced to a value system which may remain with him for life; there he learns some of the most basic skills of family living; and there, too, he is instructed in his relationship to spiritual and divine forces. The home may go beyond this in tutoring the child and preparing him for the world. It may, as a matter of fact, assume full responsibility for his intellectual education. During America's first years it was not unusual for a young man to come to a university without ever before having attended a school and without ever having had the services of a professional tutor.

Formal education includes private education, by which Aristotle, Quintilian, and Locke, to mention only three educational theorists, meant tutorial arrangements whereby a child was educated at home by a professional teacher. Although this method of teaching was considered superior, especially among certain classes of the population, because it protected the learner from distractions, these theorists demurred. Education under public auspices, they held, was superior because it gave the learner many more opportunities for experience and, in addition, introduced him to the social dimension of learning.

The school's part in providing opportunities for mental formation is discussed later under "intellectual education." Now we shall be content to reassert the contributions informal education may make to mental development. The life of man and the life of the mind are not easily separated even for purposes of discussion. It is not possible, therefore, to say with precision just what products of learning are due to formal and what to informal education. Study may be accomplished under formal auspices, but motivation may come from the froth and the foam of informal experiences. The first meanings of a proposition may be seen in the classroom; the significance of the proposition and its deeper meaning may be exposed only in the formality of experience and day-to-day applications of the products of learning. In spite of all the difficulties and dangers in trying to separate, or even to distinguish, things that cannot be separated or distinguished, we should like to leave this point in the discussion with an awareness of the contribution made by both formal and informal education to a richer and more versatile intellect. Even if life outside the school is not richer than life inside the school, we should be prepared to accord to informal education an important place in the total education of men.

Cunningham's "human companionship" and "worthy home membership" of the Cardinal Principles are prime examples of informal education at work. The curriculum on later educational levels may contain sound principles around which social living may be understood, and students may come to have a keen intellectual awareness of the importance of both on the level of human action. But this is a level where the intellectual approach is not enough. No one has ever learned to live worthily in a family by examining the sociological principles supporting family life, and no one has ever made lasting friendships or firm and satisfying human contacts purely on the theoretical level. Good homes are the best social educators, and the laboratories for the social principles absorbed there are the playgrounds of the neighborhood. There may, of course, be a theoretical dimension which the school must not ignore, and its support of the family as the primary social agency and "heart" of society must be unequivocal, yet the formal approach here does not seem to be the most promising or the most rewarding. Beyond this, however, the school itself does have a social climate, and the school may set the tone of its own society. Of special significance at this point is the cocurricular program of the school. The values of cocurricular or out-of-class activities—morale, loyalty, and responsibility—are values that should not be dismissed. And activities with a social flavor—homeroom functions, civic clubs, school social activities, student government, and athletic activities are all important enough to command the attention of school administrators. In connection with these activities the school's social life comes into full play, and under proper guidance and supervision the skills learned and the values formed are of the first order of significance. It is a mistake for schools to put undue emphasis on social education—as some critics have charged—but a greater error is to expurgate social education or give it only lip service. Being a good member of society and a good member of a family, a good husband or a good wife, a good son or a good daughter are surely as important in the long run as being fluent in languages or skilled and profound in mathematics and science.

So long as the school does not put social formation first on its list of objectives, no one should object, for who can gainsay its permanent value both to the individual and society. There is a dangerous naïveté in assuming the essentials of social education can come from outside the school.

Out-of-school forces are present and persistent and may be clearly superior in providing opportunities for social education, but this is not a valid reason for excluding social education from the school.

Nor is it valid to argue, because the school must be interested in developing the minds of its students, against its concern for their vocational futures. For many years now the educational literature has contained hundreds of articles and books deploring the invasion of vocationalism into the schools. School is a place for learning, it is said, not for job training. But how can valid distinctions be made between "pure" learning and learning for use. What is pure, or liberal, learning for one student is vocational learning for another. And, to look at the matter from another direction, how is it possible to be certain that so-called pure learning has greater merit than learning undertaken with utilitarian motives?[10]

Fortunately, the school is not charged with the vocational preparation of its students, unless, of course, it is a school which accepts the vocational product as its principal objective, and this puts it in the category of a special school. The usual elementary or secondary school is not a vocational institution, although it may have vocational curricula intended to help students find their places in a world where economic security cannot be ignored. Other agencies in society must accept responsibility for helping young people find economic security; the school need not give special or primary attention to this objective. But if there are such agencies, the school has a right to work with them; and if there are not such agencies, the school must do what needs doing. How futile it is to argue for the purity of the school when the school, an agency created by man to be of service to him, must and will respond to the demands made on it. If we are convinced of the need for vocational courses and are determined students should leave school knowing something very well and being able to do something very well, the purity of the school is hard to defend. Any school in contemporary American society ignoring totally the economic security of its students is a poor school and should be altered or closed, but, again, economic instruments should not be the sole or the most important objectives.

Informal education makes its impression on vocations, too. We know of hobbies growing into principal occupations, and we know of the skills learned in nonscholastic environments. Although we have passed from a domestic economy, and have departed somewhat, too, from the apprenticeship system which often had its roots in a home, much vocational learning still takes place on this level. Some of the most persistent vocational motives and career selections come from, or are generated by, the influence of the home or from other, incidental relationships in society.

Leisure was once thought to be found in school (a view no longer held except by the undergraduate who has not yet taken his first term examination) or was, at least, a condition which made attending school possible.

Some philosophers have regarded leisure as being the goal of work: we work in order to command conditions necessary to leisure. Whether or not these philosophical positions are acceptable is irrelevant here, although gross observation would seem to confirm them. But a correlation between work and leisure need not be causal. In any event, leisure is regarded as a universal human need: Scripture may be quoted along with philosophers, psychologists, and sociologists to stress man's need for distractions from his work and the need for recreation for both mind and body.

Today we do not associate the school and leisure, except in adult education programs which may be regarded as leisure-time activities for participants; rather, we expect the school to provide tools for the profitable and interesting use of leisure. And the schools have generally accepted the challenge; in accepting it, they say: "We shall give you an opportunity to develop skills making informal education richer." If formal and informal education are competitors, here one competitor is voluntarily strengthening its adversary. But, of course, formal and informal education are not foes in any real sense; they have competed for the interests of the student without ever having learned to capitalize on mutual relationships.

"Ethical character" of the Cardinal Principles and "divine security" of Cunningham's universal human needs have some common elements, although in stressing the religious dimension in education for character, Cunningham's divine security clearly goes beyond the objective of ethical character. Despite its apparent inadequacy, ethical character as a stated objective recognizes the part schools may play in forming the total man and their voice in shaping the values accepted or rejected by young people. Far from removing the school from the realm of moral formation, the objective of ethical character as stated by the Commission on the Reorganization of Secondary Education puts the schools squarely behind any effort to improve moral sensitivity. How effective schools are in teaching values is another question; trying to communicate or inculcate values is surely within the limits of the commission society has given them.

However much one may doubt the ability of the school to teach virtue—this is only one part of an age-old question raised at least as early as Socrates, when he inquired into the possibility of teaching virtue under any or all auspices—there is really little doubt that learners come to accept a set of values on an objective level and then, by some process not yet fully understood, convert it into a set of values subjectively acceptable to be used as a guide for action. Values, one may theorize, are taught in a formal way or, at the very least, are the products of a structured situation, a situation consciously created by someone in order to inculcate value or impress certain value considerations on persons in the situation. Or one may see merit in the claim that values are not really taught at all: they are caught somehow in the multiple activities of life. But the terminology "taught" and "caught" in this context may actually be misleading. To catch a value suggests an accidental quality to a process we should like to think is infused with meaning and responsibility. Better phrases can be employed: Some values become known (acceptance may still be another step) through aided discovery, and others are discovered without the help, at least without obvious help. So we have, finally, values recognized intellectually as a result of a teaching process, where the intention of the teacher becomes the controlling factor, and we have the same outcome as a result of a process of unaided discovery. The unanswered question is, of course, how, by what means, is the objectively held value translated into an ideal, a guide to action staying with a person in all the vagaries of life. This is not the place to probe the problem further, and it is not the point where we should expect an answer to questions raised concerning it. It is possible, however, to point to the important role all out-of-school learning processes play in building a set of values. Family contacts have nearly indelible qualities to them: do we ever really forget the lessons taught at home; is the permanence attributed to these lessons the result of good albeit informal teaching, or is it the outcome of the natural impressionableness and pliability of the young mind and the nondirected will?

But the family, powerful as it is and should be in forming basic ideals, is not alone: the natural gregariousness of the child brings him into contact with others, and out of the froth and the foam of human relationships certain value hypotheses can be arrived at. These hypotheses, recognized or unrecognized, understood or misunderstood, are retested again and again and are finally accepted, rejected, revised, or retested. The social environment must be reckoned with in the formation of values; the school's part in the face of the power of the social environment may be puny and weak indeed. Possibly it is powerless; on the other hand, the school can be a factor in teaching values, in forming ideals, if it rethinks its role and is alert to necessary program adaptations. If the school's purpose is to reform or rebuild value systems, so one theory goes, it will surely fail, because these value systems are too securely established, too indelibly defined, to admit of revision or substantial rebuilding. There is another way of looking at the matter: The school may recognize the futility of attempted reforms— some would insist the sooner the school sees this the better—but it may recognize also the possibility of overlaying old values with new ones or conditioning persons to act in a socially acceptable manner while still retaining the old value system. The school may be engaged in an art of concealment, where basic values, apparently somewhat unacceptable on an objective level, are not changed but where the person holding such values or embracing such ideals is sensitized to act according to a planned pattern. The role of the school is not a reformer's role; it is, rather, a way of raising the level of personal sophistication to make responses conventional.

From what we have seen by briefly exploring the formal and informal functions of education in connection with certain stated educational objectives, education does not begin or end at the schoolhouse door. Who can really weigh the strength of informal education or assess its quality? We need no such exact evaluation here to recognize the significance of informal and formal education or to recommend to teachers and students a constant awareness of this dualism.

Intellectual, Moral, and Physical Education in the School

Schools are successful in accomplishing their principal mission when all members of the school staff are conscious of the direction of education and are conscious also of their colleagues' contribution to it. Success, then, depends upon an active and deliberate measure of collaboration. But even in the most favorable circumstances, this position, as it is generally understood in the contemporary educational world, suffers from two serious weaknesses. These are seen in a double tendency toward disassociation. The first is a tendency to dissociate the intellectual from other facets of the personality, from interests, sentiments, desires, moods, and attitudes, and from all physical concomitants. The second is to dissociate what is known as the purely intellectual from other kinds of intellectual activity, to recognize only one kind of intelligence, the academic, and to refuse recognition to other kinds, which may manifest themselves in manual dexterity or in other ways. Both these positions are commonly held, and neither is defensible. Those who hold the first position have allowed a fictitious analysis to become first an unexamined assumption and then a matter of fact. The analysis is the traditional division of a human being into body, mind, and spirit, a convenient and useful analysis but dangerous, too, when these three parts are separated in the educational process. It is always hazardous to elevate unreal abstractions to the level of real being. And in the school situation the only real being is the whole child, whose intellectual needs must be regarded as aspects of the need and potentiality of a whole and undivided person, intimately related to and interacting with other needs, and often modified and changed in character in the very process of interaction: some of these needs are physical, some are emotional, some contain a need for security, for confidence, or for significance. Formal education is always on the verge of separating the inseparable, a body-mind. Failing to distinguish various approaches to childhood education is a sign of weakness, too. While there is undoubtedly a strong attraction to the eternal saying "truth sets men free," education is fully human only when it recognizes that the gulf between certain kinds of education (physical and intellectual, for example) has no metaphysical necessity: it is a product of education.

Education is fully human when it is broad enough to admit the whole man, yet the admission of the whole man requires certain attachments, certain distinctions, and certain emphases. We may deal briefly with some of these.

Because the school must deal essentially with what can be taught, its primary aim is the formation of intelligence—this is intellectual education. As a process, intellectual education is both individual and social. It is individual, since the development and cultivation of personal capacities can be achieved only through self-activity. One cannot learn for another. The old Egyptian adage "Thoth [the god of learning] has placed the rod on earth; educate the stubborn with it" may have initiated activity, but learning has never been achieved as a direct result of the activity of anyone other than the learner himself. Although it is logically correct to say that one cannot teach himself, it is not accurate to claim that one cannot educate himself. Strictly speaking, all education is self-education; there is no other kind.

The formation of intelligence or the attainment of intellectual virtue in some degree, then, depends upon two things: first, the willingness of the learner to strive for intellectual virtue; second, the capacity which he has. Willingness to learn, or motivation, may compensate for some lack of intellectual capacity. In other words, students of limited or low native capacity may actually achieve considerably more than is expected of them because they are unusually well motivated. On the other hand, capable but unwilling students will not be active; they will not engage their best energies in the pursuit of truth; and their achievement, therefore, will not be commensurate with their capacities.

Intellectual education is social, too, for it is largely because of the contributions of man's vast social inheritance that there are opportunities for cultivating the human abilities, and the cooperation of society in providing educational opportunities is an essential feature.

The process of acquiring knowledge is necessary but is also slow and arduous. All indications are that only the human person is capable of such an achievement; yet even he with all his great power is faced with hazards: his life is short; no sooner does he gain some insight into his powers and into the nature of the world surrounding him than he dies. His place is taken by others who make concerted efforts to absorb the essential activities of the community and its guiding knowledge. Unless this is done expeditiously, the community will fall into chaos and ignorance and end up submitting to internal decay or external force. The essential activities of the community are transmitted, and this transmission is one of the principal tasks of education. Without education no human society can maintain itself, and, in this sense, it is both natural and essential to human life. Historically no community, no matter how primitive, has ever failed to develop some means of communication by which this vital problem of transmission of knowledge was met.

Transmission of knowledge, values, and ideals is a vital part of the educational process. Much of it is the work of instruction, and learning from and with others is a preeminent social relationship in formal education. Undoubtedly and ultimately all education is self-education, but learning often requires the assistance of another—in school, the teacher. What is learned is discovered, whether the discovery is aided or unaided; and aided discovery need not be and should not be either a coercion or an indoctrination of the student, but positive guidance for him to learn what he does not know.

Although formation in moral life and virtue is an important and essential part of the primary aim of education, the school has not the means to secure moral education fully and completely and therefore may not accept moral development as its primary objective. The school is bound, however, to contribute as positively and completely as it can to the moral formation of its students. The objective of moral education is the development of habits of thought and action which will consistently and constantly dispose the individual to accept personal and social values which conform to the moral law. It is not intended that the discussion of moral education given here be complete; yet it must be said that moral development is concerned more with action than it is with knowledge. To be well versed in ethics or to know objectively what is good or what should be done in a given case is not moral virtue. It is inaccurate to believe that teaching or preaching can make men good or moral or that right knowledge is a guarantee of right action. But at the same time it would be hard to believe that an individual who knew the truth would not be guided by it to a greater extent than the person who did not know the truth. Still, there can be no guarantee that knowledge will lead to virtue. Although knowledge of what is right does not flow automatically into right action, the school may not replace its principal function of intellectual formation with moral objectives. No one doubts that schools have definite and grave responsibilities for the development of character, but even with a fully justified interest in character building, the school's function as an intellectual agency must not be permitted to deteriorate. Moral education is a function which the school shares with other social institutions, and because the school must deal essentially with that which can be taught, its function is directed to the formation and education of intelligence more than of the will.

The proper functioning of the body is an important preliminary to intellectual and moral formation. Most educational theories, and especially Christian educational theories, recognize the values of physical culture and health education. Perhaps physical education is more important today, or has a special emphasis not evident several years ago. With modern forms of transportation and with varieties of creature comforts installed in our homes, we simply do not get the kind or the amount of exercise needed for good health. The benefits derived from physical education are so obvious, a prolonged discussion could not be justified. Even though health is not recognized as a primary objective for schools and physical education is usually granted lower-level priority than intellectual or moral education, all schools must try to prepare their students for community life and for a full and satisfying personal life. As part of this preparation, basic skills and knowledge relative to individual and community health and physical well-being must be communicated.

Social Education

Sociology has made many exciting contributions to our knowledge of human limitation, of human possibility, and the mechanism of social change. These seem destined to have profound effects upon educational practices both inside and outside the school. The findings of sociology, it may be maintained, are as seminal in their influence upon the study and organization of education as the findings of psychology are on teaching and learning. In the next fifty years sociology may have an effect on education reminiscent of psychology's effect over the past fifty. The sociological approach has brought into the open the permeating—and, to a large extent, the predictable—effects upon the unconscious mind of living and learning in one society rather than in another. To some extent, of course, all of this was known before, but on a different level of awareness. We simply did not reckon with our knowledge.

It is impossible to think of any human child, surviving from infancy simply as an individual. From the moment he comes into the world he is a member of a group, in most cases of a family—and is helped through difficult formative years when he has few dependable skills. The immense influence of the group or society upon the individual is more easily seen in primitive society, but this influence is far from being obscured by the complexities of modern society.

The authority of custom and tradition is extraordinarily powerful and permeating; to challenge entrenched authority requires remarkable individual courage, and even then successful challenges cannot be guaranteed. Brought up in a primitive society, we should all be primitives, or brought up in a Communist society, most of us would be Communists. At no stage in the growth of the human person to maturity can the considerable educational significance of group influences—despite their often unconscious character—be ignored. In the first months and years they are the chief formative influences. And, we should know by now, it is simply not possible to remain a nationally unbiased child for very long or to remain free from the prejudices of the period into which one has been born. Essentially there is little differentiation between the child born in the thirteenth century and the one born in the twentieth, or between the babies born in Alaska, London, and Moscow. But all kinds of loyalties blossom early and are endowed with a highly permanent quality.

For children born in any country the most powerful educative force is the home. The child's home is his most intimate environment, there development begins, and there, eventually, his life comes to flower. In the home he finds freedom, an imperative condition for growth, and an environment of affection and regard in which growth becomes a wholly natural thing; he finds creature needs cared for, but most of all his education is nourished, and his mental and emotional outlook is secured with a background of trust and interest. The home is very largely responsible for the development of emotional as well as physical health; in the home the child gets the emotional experiences leading to emotional maturation. It is a sad thing that so many homes in modern times have not contained the kinds of experiences making for good emotional formation.

At home or in school much of the child's education is a process of growing into fuller and deeper membership of the society and culture of which the school and the home are themselves products. Much of the education of men is made possible, or entirely impossible, simply by environment. The most direct means of modifying education is direct and compulsory modification of the environment. In this connection the physical environment is not the only one that counts. A change in physical surroundings has its effects, but changes in the moral environment are more penetrating. For example, think how difficult it would be to be energetic and hard-working in a society which values and approves laziness, or to be creative and inventive in a society committed to the status quo.

We have known for a long time, although this knowledge is only now making a strong impression, that children do not come into the world with personalities already formed; they need time for the seeds of personality development to germinate, grow, and blossom. All children, we may assume, have to be given a great part of their character before it can be developed, and society has many subtle ways of giving people the characters they end up having. It is a pure assumption, without very solid support, that if you leave persons to themselves, they will develop characters in the context of their society. The point is, they cannot be left to themselves, for society will not leave them alone, so what they do become depends to a large measure on the ideals contained in the principal philosophy subserving society.

Faced with all this evidence of the power of society, its impressive educative force and its control over the habits and the outlook of its members, contemporary man may feel deprived of freedom and accept society's force as a determining one. He may come to believe in socially determined learning, and, though he may regard it as elemental and subtle, he will accept it as immensely important. But this picture is somewhat too bleak and places too great a stress on the combined productions of the sciences of sociology and psychology. Even in this deterministic frame of mind, however, it is possible to salvage a great deal: the sociological approach to the study of education makes us once again strongly aware of the power of environment. Until fairly recent years there was a tendency to emphasize the overriding importance of heredity in life and education. It is now clear, environmental factors can be decisive in producing certain kinds of behavior in certain kinds of societies. And this, we might suggest, is encouraging, for it is obviously easier to control and modify an environment directive of education than it is to change the inherited characteristics of persons to be educated.

The Education of the Whole Man

It is sometimes assumed that the theory of whole-man education is something new. To some extent this misapprehension arises from the emphasis which modern pragmatism has given to the development of the whole man or the whole child. Before examining any of the views either for or against the theory of whole-man education, it is important to note that the term does not mean the same thing to everyone: some educational theorists speak of the education of the whole child and mean that the school is responsible for the child's complete development, while others who are interested in the subject observe that education continues during one's entire lifetime and that the school is only a partial and inchoative agency with respect to the education of the whole man.

The traditional Christian concept of education has always included this emphasis: All of man's capacities should be developed. It has recognized individual differences in capacity, and it has understood that variations in interest and motivation may demand both adaptation and experiment in the educational process. But the traditions of Christian education do not commit the school to the education of the whole man; schools are not the only educative agencies in society. By using or utilizing all human and social institutions, education may achieve the development of the whole man; but to say that the education of the whole man is desirable or that broadly conceived this is education's primary aim does not mean that whole-man education is either the school's chief function or its sole responsibility.

If the school is to contribute to the education of the whole man, it should be recognized as the central educative agency in society. In addition to its general function of dealing primarily with what can be taught, the school may seek to integrate the educational outcomes of other social institutions and in this way help a child attain his full formation or his completeness as a man. In speaking of the education of the whole man, we are not assigning responsibility for this broad education to the school. Yet the school, despite its inability to operate effectively on all levels of education and in all facets of learning, must maintain a vital interest in the total development of the learner. The school may not be able to take an active part in the religious formation of the school child, but the school must be sympathetic to this formation and must try to supplement the efforts made by outside agencies toward it. In the same vein, the school may not be in a position to accept the full responsibility for moral education, but this should not deter the school from using every means at its disposal to help students become good men. What we have said about the development of personality and the formation of character puts the school in the position of a constant and interested supporter of a good cause but neither the principal expediter nor initiator of the cause. But if the school does not take an active part, can we affirm the education of the whole man as either desirable or possible?

First, total education, we must recognize, is an ongoing process whose limits are defined by the length of a man's life. Not all education is formal, and much of a person's most important learning does not take place in school at all. There is moral formation in the home and in the church; physical education on the summer playground and in the recreation league; and personality development whenever children get together to play. All of this is educational, although there are no books or teachers in the conventional sense. The family is an educational agency in every meaningful sense of the word; the church is an educational agency; so is the political club and ladies social club. In these and hundreds of other human associations, education is constantly taking place. The proponents of "whole man education" ask the school to be conscious of these various avenues of development, to be sympathetic to them, and willing to help them flourish. There is nothing very mysterious or aggressive about advocating secondary school educational programs broad enough to include meaningful preparation for citizenship, family living, economic life, moral relationships, intellectual responsibilities, social and physical development, and spiritual insight. Schools are not fully responsible for these objectives, although they may be expected to contribute to the attainment of each objective.

This interpretation of the education of the whole man is almost above debate. When, however, the school is asked to do more than it can or should, many serious objections are raised. The most serious danger in establishing the school as the sole educational agency is that children will not have an opportunity to develop in a many-sided way. What assurances can the school give, as the only educative agency, of working positively toward many-sided teaching and learning opportunities necessary to the optimum development of youth?

DEMOCRATIC EDUCATION

After having gained at least a partial understanding of the meaning of education, it is possible now to consider democratic education. Does democracy influence education, and, conversely, does education affect democracy? One way to approach this question is to divide it into three parts and try to find the meaning of democratic education by an analysis of each of the parts: the educational system, the student, and the needs of the society in which the school exists and which the school is expected to serve. Democratic education is broader than formal education. To study democratic education in all its aspects, one would have to deal with every human relationship in society. Although the relevance of democratic education in this broad sense is recognized here, the analysis to be made will be limited to democratic education in schools.

The System

If democratic privileges in education are permitted and encouraged by government, the educational system should be democratic. But what do we mean when we say that the system should be democratic? The meaning is relatively simple, and it includes the following: the extent of the system, the availability of the opportunities of the system to all who desire them, and the relationships among the system's component parts.

An educational system cannot be truly democratic unless schools are established and maintained in every part of the country. In a sense, schools should be ubiquitous. A rich or generous distribution of schools makes educational opportunity universal. But universal opportunity for education does not mean equality of educational opportunity, as has often been mistakenly suggested and more often mistakenly believed. Nor can one be sure that equality of educational opportunity is implied in the concept of democratic education. This is especially true if equality of educational opportunity is interpreted to mean the existence of uniform educational advantages and opportunities throughout an entire country. Legislated uniformity is inconsistent with democratic ideals and practices. It is unwise and probably futile to expect educational opportunity to be maintained uniformly. There are diversities of resources and needs from one part of the country to another, and though the mobility of a population may justify the establishment of certain minimum standards, the citizens of the one community may not want and therefore will not seek the same kind of education that other citizens in other communities may want.

It is not possible to claim that the several states of the United States are equally capable of providing minimum essentials for a good education; such a claim could not be supported. A practical objective of a democratic educational system would be to encourage schools everywhere to meet certain minimum standards and to try to eliminate all financial obstacles which block progress toward the attainment of minimum essentials. But this is probably not the same thing as equality of educational opportunity. Equality of opportunity does not apply to the system, but to individuals. It is the person in a democracy who counts, and the individual, not the system, is to be guided toward temporal and eternal ends. Opportunity must exist if individual needs are to be provided for, but it does not follow that every school within a system must have facilities and programs to provide for particular and special educational needs.

Implicit in the concept of universal opportunity, which may, of course, become universal education (this depends on compulsory-education legislation and the people themselves), is the basic democratic ideal that discriminatory practices have no place in education and that artificial barriers concerning race, creed, and color must not be used to exclude any member of society, except legally defined undesirables, from the schools. Once schools are established, the people must have the right to use them. On the other hand, although the system must be neither arbitrary nor discriminatory in providing educational opportunities, every member of society must be free to choose between public and private schools. Almost 90 per cent of elementary and secondary school students in the United States attend public schools, but the vastness of the public educational enterprise should in no way limit the freedom of students to attend nonpublic schools if they want to. Of course, the common good requires some education for everyone, but compulsory attendance does not mean that every child must attend public schools. Public schools must be available—this is an essential feature of democratic education—but equally essential to democracy is the nonpublic school or the freedom of nonpublic schools to exist and the right of students to attend them. This is an important part of democratic education, and democracy is being strengthened wherever public and private schools exist as partners.

Within the educational system, democracy must be evident in the relationships among the members of the teaching profession. School personnel may represent different parts of the educational system, and as result of their varying responsibilities to education, they may seek to assert the prerogatives which are, or which are thought to be, identified with their positions. The specific duties and responsibilities of administrators, supervisors, and teachers need not concern us here. It is sufficient to suggest that the fundamental relationship in the educational system must be between teachers and students and that all the other parts of the educational system must be directed toward the improvement of this relationship.

The teacher's function is one of helping students to become articulate, free, and autonomous. Democracy in the classroom is not the same as majority rule with minority rights. Teachers must have genuine authority to teach and to be respected and listened to. But they must love and understand their students. A teacher assumes definite obligations to his students and to society, and these obligations are met or not depending upon the way the teacher conducts himself. The teacher requires competence, which includes both scholarly ability and insight into the nature of the pupil and the nature of learning, but as an indispensable supplement to his intellectual qualifications the teacher must have unquestioned moral stature. Without the latter the teacher's work will be defective.

If we agree that the moral virtues are not taught and learned in the usual way, or at least not in the same way in which reading and writing and arithmetic are taught and learned, then they are incorporated into the pupil's system of values through practice, example, and emulation. With respect to moral formation, the role of the teacher may not be minimized, for he is the chief creator of the student's educational environment and the main source of his inspiration. His influence on the moral development of his pupils is challenging and important, although he need not assume responsibility for the complete moral education of children any more than he need assume responsibility for their complete intellectual education. The home, the church, society itself have obligations to the learner which are as clear and demanding as those of the school.

A student's contribution to educational democracy is mainly the desire to learn and a willingness to follow the teacher's instruction and example. This is especially true at the lower educational levels, where the pupil, because of his limited experience and immaturity, must necessarily be a follower. But as he matures, he can contribute in many ways to the functioning of educational democracy. By adopting a cooperative attitude and by assuming appropriate responsibilities in the school, the student can best advance democratic ideals.

The Student

If education is democratic and if the ends of society are implemented by education, students must have an opportunity to actualize their potentialities. If education is democratic in practice as well as in theory, the possibility of individual progress will not be restricted by artificial and arbitrary barriers. This can be the only view of education in a functioning democracy, and it is the only way in which a democratic society can really profit from the educational system it supports. More specifically, the individual must be provided with sufficient educational means to enable him to prepare for life in society and for good citizenship and to secure the knowledge and skill required for implementing a particular function in the social whole, for meeting family responsibilities, and for making a living. Moreover, the challenge of education should be commensurate with the student's capacities, and his opportunities in school should enable him to discover, express, and preserve basic values or ideals.

Education is a process whereby individuals achieve their dignity and their rights as men, but it is a process, too, whereby men come to understand their duties. Neither rights nor duties should be considered alone; neither should be taught or studied separately. They are correlative terms, and when they are correctly understood, it is apparent that disregarding one may shortly result in abrogating the other. If the student has the right to an education, the school as society's agent has the duty to provide some of the means. If the student is to receive a good education, schools must be designed to form individuals for their places in the world and to live as humanly and fully as possible. Education without this objective and schools without means to achieve it are not democratic and are not the kind of schools for a democracy.

With these conditions for learning it is possible to keep alive in students their curiosity; in this way it is possible to stimulate their imaginations, and to foster in them a desire to understand and dominate their experiences and not be dominated by them. This process, if started properly at school, will never end. Much depends on the teacher's recognition of the many different types of intelligence students possess, of the different ways they learn, and of the different material they need for learning. For some, the order of learning is to grasp an abstract principle from a book, and follow it with an application and use of the principle in novel situations; for others, the order of learning is experiencing many particulars leading eventually to the discovery of the principle and its subsequent application. This distinction is intended when we speak of the practical versus the theoretical approach in teaching and learning. It is, in fact, a distinction between two ways of learning or, to speak more exactly, two orders of learning. If students are to become good learners in the context of democratic life, we must avoid the mistake of imposing the wrong order on a pupil. This is the real ground for supporting different types of schools with various curricular emphases and flexible standards. But wherever students attend school, schools must instill in them a sense of mystery about learning and a feeling of affection, or love, for it. This latter is not so easy today when the range of human knowledge is so vast, but we must be conscious of it and try, in addition, to kindle in them the spirit of dedication to learning: our students should be impressed less by what we know and more by how much is yet to be learned.

The Needs of Society

A free society is held together by practical and theoretical agreements concerning the fundamental bases of life in common. Without these agreements we should have anarchy, and the well-ordered society where people pursue their individual and social objectives would be impossible. But to make these agreements is one thing; to perpetuate and to obtain common consent on them from generation to generation is another. They must be perpetuated if society is to be preserved. There are, then, certain agreements which a genuine democratic society must neither impose nor coerce upon its members, yet the basis of its structure must not be and cannot be left to chance. In a democracy, education must seek to preserve the tenets upon which democracy is based.

For education to do its work well, at least two conditions must be met: First, the agreements which either practically or theoretically are basic to society must be understood and retained in a form making possible their transmission or communication. Second, a climate of opinion must be generated for teaching these agreements in a way most conducive to their acceptance. Indoctrination is neither inevitable nor impossible, but propagandizing is proscribed as being unworthy of a democratic society. One thing stands out clearly here: The democratic society has the right and should develop the means to preserve and protect itself. The most powerful means at its disposal is education, for again we meet with the eternal saying: Truth frees men and keeps them free.

The socially responsible school serves society best by seeking to preserve its essential form. Even in this setting the school may be reform-minded, but as an instrument of society it must never be allowed to destroy its social creator. Nor may it abort social and political tranquillity to bring about agreements on the theoretical bases for the democratic charter. The school tries to promote the democratic charter not by seeking agreement on the level of theory, but by seeking agreement on the level of practice. This, it may be objected, is not going to the heart of the issue, for there are better bases upon which a democratic order can rest than practical agreements. All of this is true, of course, but does it follow, because there are theoretical agreements among some men as to the fundamental meaning and application of democracy, that these fundamental meanings can be presented to all men and accepted by them? A pluralistic society, with a variety of interpretations as to man's nature and needs, cannot help but have a variety of theoretical convictions on the nature of democracy. But on the practical level, where democracy is at work in the day-to-day lives of men, agreement —consensus or compromise—is possible and does work. The principal function of the school is to serve this end and create an intellectual and moral climate in which democracy can be accepted and flourish.

SUMMARY

In order to understand democratic education, it is necessary first to understand the meaning of democracy and the meaning of education. After many experiments with democracy, beginning with loose tribal associations among primitive peoples, certain fundamental principles of democracy evolved as bases for modern democracy: personal worth and dignity, equality of opportunity, civil and political liberty, and dedication to truth. On these principles social, political, and educational democracy rest; and with the acceptance of these principles education in its full meaning—the complete formation of men—may be achieved.

In its broadest meaning education applies to all life's activities, throughout life. In this broad meaning no distinction need be made between formal and informal education. But narrower meanings may be given to education: for example, intellectual education, moral education, and social education. The school—an institution engaged in formal education—is chiefly responsible for intellectual education, although it may contribute to the development of character and social effectiveness, for example, which are primary objectives for the church and the home.

In its clearest and most definite form, democratic education means that social and political democracy, which are basic to it, have created a climate or social atmosphere in which there is agreement that an educational system be constructed to make schooling available to everyone in order that everyone with interest and motivation have the opportunity to pursue the amount of formal education equal to his ability. Democratic education, moreover, must seek to promote understanding and acceptance of the theoretical and practical principles on which modern democracies rest.

QUESTIONS AND EXERCISES

1. Formulate your own definition of democracy, and give an explanation of it.
2. What does democracy mean in politics, economics, society, and religion? From your own experience discuss practices in the foregoing activities which are not democratic.
3. What is the core of the concept of democracy? Do you think citizens of democratic countries ever stop to consider what the foundations of their democracy are?
4. How does representative democracy differ from the type of democracy practiced in ancient Athens? Do you believe that a representative of the people should vote according to his own mind, or should he vote the way his constituents want him to vote?
5. Evaluate Plato's provisions for democracy in *The Republic.* Describe Plato's plan for education.
6. Investigate and report on the influence of Rousseau on modern democracy.
7. "Christianity and organized religions are inconsistent with democracy." Comment on this statement.
8. Define education in your own words. Then select ten definitions of education proposed by others, and compare them with your own.

9. Distinguish formal and informal education. Give some examples from your own experience of informal education.
10. What is the difference between training and education? Do you think that principles of education and principles of training are the same?
11. Is change essential in education? Is education possible without change?
12. Distinguish between intellectual and moral education. Are both achieved in the same way? What is your interpretation of the education of the whole man?

ADDITIONAL READINGS

Barnett, George, and Jack Otis: *Corporate Society and Education*, The University of Michigan Press, Ann Arbor, 1962. The authors discuss the crises of modern society and propose a radically revised idea of men, institutions, and the state.

Bayles, Ernest E.: *Democratic Educational Theory*, Harper & Row, Publishers, Incorporated, New York, 1960. The author examines the major tenets of a genuinely democratic educational program.

Chalmers, Gorden Keith: *The Republic and the Person*, Henry Regnery Company, Chicago, 1952. A highly competent treatment of the role of the person in a complex modern society.

Cox, Philip W., and Blaine E. Mercer: *Education in Democracy: Social Foundations of Education*, McGraw-Hill Book Company, New York, 1961. A survey of the major social foundations of education.

Curti, Merle: *The Roots of American Loyalty*, Columbia University Press, New York, 1946. An examination of a highly volatile and complex issue—loyalty—by a respected social historian.

Dewey, John: *Democracy and Education*, The Macmillan Company, New York, 1961. A contemporary educational classic which contains directive doctrines for progressive educators. Note especially the emphasis on relevance of learning and the need for a closer relationship between learning and living.

Gabriel, Ralph H.: *The Course of American Democratic Thought*, The Ronald Press Company, New York, 1947. The author explores evolution of democratic thought but leaves educational doctrines practically untouched.

Lerner, Max: *Education and a Radical Humanism*, Ohio State University Press, Columbus, 1962. Read especially for the author's interpretation of radical humanism and for his new program in creative education.

Lippmann, Walter: *The Public Philosophy*, Atlantic Monthly Press, Little, Brown and Company, Boston, 1955. An incisive analysis of democratic institutions by an unusually competent commentator on the American scene.

Livingstone, Richard: *On Education*, Cambridge University Press, New York, 1944. Essentialism in education is the theme of this theoretical analysis of education.

Mason, Robert E.: *Educational Ideals in American Society*, Allyn and Bacon, Inc., Boston, 1960. A treatment of American traditions, science and democracy, humanistic culture, and critical intelligence and their influence on education.

Meiklejohn, A.: *Education between Two Worlds,* Harper & Row, Publishers, Incorporated, New York, 1942. Education can be, and often is, used as a tool for the advancement of conflicting political ideologies. Notice how totalitarianism can use education to serve its own ends.

Montagu, Ashley: *Education and Human Relations,* Grove Press, Inc., New York, 1958. The thesis is offered that education must consist principally in a training in the theory and art of human relations.

Morris, Van Cleve: *Philosophy and the American School,* Houghton Mifflin Company, Boston, 1961. Pay particular attention to philosophy's role as a practical instrument in the construction of a system and program of education.

National Society for the Study of Education: *Modern Philosophies and Education,* Fifty-fourth Yearbook, Chicago, 1955, part I. See chapter by Jacques Maritain.

Sayers, Ephraim V., and Ward Madden: *Education and the Democratic Faith,* Appleton-Century-Crofts, Inc., New York, 1959. This book essays to isolate those principal issues dividing Americans with respect to purposes in life and education and thus enable students to clarify and appraise these issues.

Shields, Curran V.: *Democracy and Catholicism in America,* McGraw-Hill Book Company, New York, 1958. Read chapter 8, "Catholicism and Democracy Today." It should be noted that the author is not a Catholic.

Ulich, Robert: *Fundamentals of Democratic Education,* American Book Company, New York, 1940. See especially chapters 6 to 9: "Education and Society," "Education and the State," "Education and Religion," and "The Mission of American Education."

Wales, J. N.: *Schools of Democracy,* The Michigan State University Press, East Lansing, 1962. An Englishman's impression of secondary education in the American Middle West.

chapter 12

Conflicting Theories of Education

In Chapter 11 we were concerned with the meaning of education and especially the relationship between education and democracy. During the course of the chapter it became clear that education does not have the same meaning for everyone: there are different interpretations, theories, or philosophies of education. It is the purpose of this chapter to discuss the prominent contemporary theories, or philosophies, of education and to show how these theories may make a difference in how schools are administered, how curricula are selected and organized, how teachers teach, and how educational objectives and values are determined. The basic educational questions which immerse us at once in theory may be phrased as follows:

Who? Who is to be educated? This question may, of course, be asked in a variety of contexts. It is one thing to inquire into the fundamental nature of man—and this must be done at some point in the philosophy of education or we shall never really know with whom we are dealing in the educational enterprise—and it is another thing to make the inquiry in the light of current controversies respecting the issues dividing men. The question should be asked both ways, for the *who* in education is broad and complicated, but as we shall see later in the chapter, man's nature is the permanent guide to the educational process and the question "who?" is raised here in this context.

Why? Why are schools conducted; what are the goals, objectives, or purposes of education? Once we know something about the nature of man and the nature of society, it is possible for us to say something about the kind of education he should have. The question "Why?" is always asked and answered within the context of a philosophy of life and a philosophy, or theory, of education. Goals for education depend upon a philosophy of education, and philosophy of education depends, in turn, upon more basic life values. These values give a sense of direction to the educational

333

enterprise: they may be a directive force in the assignment of goals for any educational process. For example, one does not begin a journey to a distant and unknown destination without the aid of a guide, a set of directions, or a map. But even before questions of route arise, before any decisions are made respecting the "how" of the journey, one must be satisfied that his reasons for making the trip are good. Why am I seeking schooling? This is a fundamental theoretical question, and the direction of education depends upon the answer. In other words, educators cannot really begin to educate —to build schools, organize curricula, employ teachers, and admit students —until they establish, first, the reason for education and, second, the outcomes or goals expected.

How are goals for education determined? Must everyone work out his own goals? And if everyone does, can all the ends, or goals, be valid? In response to the first question, it is from the philosophy of education, or rather in it, that knowledge is obtained concerning the direction education should take. But philosophies of education differ, and some affirm certain goals that others reject. From what sources may educational philosophers obtain information which will be helpful to them in answering basic educational questions? Because as a discipline the philosophy of education is an applied, not a speculative or normative, philosophy, it can and must use evidence presented by revelation (theology), philosophy (especially metaphysics, epistemology, and ethics), biology, sociology, psychology, or any other source—phenomenological or theoretical—which will contribute to knowledge concerning man's nature, the objectives of education, and the educational process.

What? "What" in education is clearly a question of content, a question of means: what means are to be used for achieving the goals of education? The school's curriculum contains the principal means used to achieve the ends agreed upon. If we emphasize intellectual formation, the principal educational means may be the subject-centered curriculum; if, however, we think principally of man in his social relationships, we may construct a curriculum having its main roots in society: the society-centered curriculum. We may go beyond this, to set an educational goal built around a breadth of experience, experience prompted by the inner drives or interests of the student. This would lead us to the activity-centered curriculum. In any event, we are concerned with the means used to arrive at valid and worthwhile ends.

Once the goals for education are agreed upon (and such agreements are rare), we should think the means could be arrived at quickly and without dissent. But this is too often wishful thinking. Let us begin by assuming that educational theorists accept liberal education as a kind of education proper to all men. The next step incumbent on these theorists is to determine and order or arrange the means leading to the realization of the goal they have set. At this point educational theory becomes practical and differences come to light, because now educational theorists are asked to determine procedures and practices to be followed in man's education. This is no ivory-tower occupation; it belongs on the level of utmost practicality. Now we begin to observe different interpretations of the meaning of liberal education: the theorists have said liberal education is good, but each has largely reaffirmed his own private view of its meaning. Even where there is agreement on meaning, a curriculum aiming toward liberal objectives awaits selection. What is the role of the classics in such a curriculum; what is the role of Latin and Greek? Is it possible in this modern world for physics to be more liberalizing than Latin? Despite theoretical agreements on the value of liberal culture as a desirable educational outcome, we are faced, nevertheless, with real issues in trying to determine means for obtaining liberal culture.[1]

How?   The how of education is a question of method. It makes itself felt in the classroom, where techniques are employed in connection with teaching and learning, and in administration of schools, where the principal consideration is creating and conducting situations favorable to learning. Whether or not "how?" is always a philosophical question is moot. Where, for example, is the theoretical dimension in selecting a method for teaching reading? If the goal is teaching the child to read efficiently and economically, the reading teacher's philosophy of education would seem to have little bearing on his choice of method. The method or methods selected should be based on empirical evidence. The philosophical dimension arises, not on the level of methodology, but on the level of human relationships: Who and what are these children who are being taught to read?

Where?   Where are teaching and learning taking place? And what contribution to the total educational process is made by the environment? Is education to be public or private? This is a point with possible far-reaching effects on the goals and the content of formal education. If the public school is unable to admit religious instruction to its classrooms, if prayer and Bible reading are proscribed by the Constitution of the United States and by the statutes of individual states, its horizons may be too limited for some theories of education.[2] Do schools differ, and do these differences affect students? They do differ, and students are affected not only in the kind of education open to them but by its breadth and depth also. The quality of public and private schools is not under scrutiny, usually questions of quality do not arise, but the breadth of opportunity offered is. Some schools—usually religiously oriented schools—believe their curricula contain wholly adequate instructional experiences, while they doubt the curricular adequacy of public schools. The *where* of education, the institution attended, may not in itself belong to the realm of theory, but it surely reflects a theory at work.

There remains, however, the problem of selecting or accepting a philosophy of education. This is a perplexing problem, one more controversial than any other in education. Yet it is not accurate to say that the problem of selecting a philosophy of education is too difficult to solve. Some difficulty arises, no doubt, when one realizes not merely that there are many philosophies of education but that among the many, and not a few of them conflicting, there may be only one that is correct.

A philosophy of education which is accepted and judged to be true is or may be true not because the educator is attracted to it, not because it appeals to his opinions, prejudices, or emotions, but because it conforms to the real nature of man and the real nature of society and correctly relates man to his society. Why, then, if what has been said above is true, do philosophies of education differ? It is because there are different, and sincerely held, views concerning man's nature, the nature of reality, possibilities of knowledge, and determinations of value. These differences make for conflict in educational theory, and, more importantly, they are the foundations for different interpretations of educational goals, content, and method.

The contemporary prominent educational theories may be classified as follows: Christian humanism, pragmatism, and realism. The agreements and differences among these philosophies of education may be discussed in reference to the following points: the role of educational theory, the nature of reality, knowledge, and value, the nature of man, the objectives of education, and educational practice.

The Role of Educational Theory

Some years ago at a philosophy of education meeting a member stated bluntly that too much time was spent arguing about educational theories. He said: "Why should we spend our time discussing various theories when we all do the same thing in the classroom?" If, despite theoretical differences, all teachers teach alike, all schools are administered in precisely the same way, and all curricula are intended to minister to educational goals without reference to theoretical positions, educational theory is faced with a serious indictment. If the charge is true, educational philosophy can hardly be justified unless, of course, it is preserved for mental gymnastics, Francis Bacon's justification for retaining deductive logic.[3]

Throughout this chapter we shall attempt to point not only to differences in theory but to the difference theory makes in practice as well. We shall try to show how objectives differ among various educational theories, and, on the level of practice, where it is not always possible to find distinctiveness or uniqueness, we shall acknowledge the critical significance of the teacher's conception of the pupil. In addition, there are subconceptual values formed out of a view of life and of man. These, we shall insist, are always meaningful; if they do not originate in a philosophy of education, they at least flow through it. Theory, as we shall try to show, does make a difference: educational philosophers are not wasting their time. What, then, is the role of educational theory? Once we acknowledge the propriety of the role, we must explore its points of relevance for educational practice. First, we should be precise about the scope of educational theory, for questions of role and adequacy are more easily understood when educational theory is not limited merely to policies and practices devised for schools. Educational theory must be broader in its outlook than this: it must take into account not only formal education but informal education as well; and so far as formal education is concerned, its principles must be applicable to the highest as well as the lowest levels. After having set the limits in which educational philosophy may be expected to operate, we may now return to our original question: What is the role of educational theory? Educational theory or philosophy is a tool or instrument used to manage education; it helps educators decide how to educate men. The important issues in educational theory are practical, not theoretical, because they are issues of policy, and the general principles upon which they are based constitute the philosophy of education as a set of answers to the most general practical questions to be asked about education in action.

Some philosophies of education stand as directive doctrines; their role is one of determining educational objectives and guiding educational practice toward these objectives. Other educational philosophies are somewhat less ambitious: they try to be liberal disciplines providing a forum for the discussion of perennial educational questions. In this view educational philosophy is expected to follow rather than lead educational practice; it becomes quite frequently a rationalization of current educational practices which have arisen in a random informal fashion. These practices seem not to be the natural consequences of a general educational plan; but by using logic and imagination, the educational philosopher is able to supply both the foundation for such practices and an intellectual structure into which they may fit. In this way, and being as consistent as possible, the philosopher develops what appears to be a common theory underlying diverse educational practices. The kind of educational philosophy is retrospective rather than prospective: it follows, but it does not lead.

From one point of view, the function of educational philosophy is to dominate and superintend education; from another, its function is to provide a forum for checking, discussing, and evaluating educational policies and procedures. Thus, the Christian humanist sees the philosophy of education as an application of tested theological and philosophical principles and phenomenological knowledge to educational issues. "When we use the phrase 'Philosophy of Education' we are referring, first of all, to the purposes of education in the life of man; and secondly, to the procedures which are to be followed in the achievement of those purposes. . . . [Such a philosophy] is an inquiry into end and means." [4]

The pragmatist is hardly ever content to accept this position. He is more concerned with avoiding directives in educational philosophy than he is with finding the role of the educational philosopher. There is usually a willingness to declare indebtedness to general philosophy, for many general principles of educational philosophy come from it, and in a sense educational philosophy has the same general function as general philosophy: where educational philosophy ought to help men manage their educational affairs, general philosophy ought to help men manage their lives. But even for the pragmatist, who dislikes being limited in a role, there are special ways in which educational philosophy may be helpful: In the first place, it may be useful as a way of criticizing or evaluating the assumptions made by all educational philosophers; in the second place, it may bring the various educational aims into focus and give them validity and meaning; finally, it may be charged with evaluating the various educational techniques as they bear on selected aims for education. Since this final objective could hardly ever be meaningfully achieved apart from some overall evaluation of the results of application of methodology, the educational philosopher may be put in the position of having to say whether, first, the aims of education seem to fit the circumstances of the day and, second, assuming the aims are valid, whether or not the means (methods or techniques) are adequate to fulfill their assigned function.

The realist is less sure than the Christian humanist but more certain than the pragmatist of the role of educational theory. The realist educational philosopher is assigned a place between the Christian humanist and the pragmatist. Sometimes he tries to lead education by shaping his theory as a directive doctrine; at other times he tries to create an environment conducive to discussion and evaluation. In other words, he tries to make educational theory a liberal discipline; he tries to convert what was formerly, and appropriately, a directive doctrine into a clearinghouse for discussing educational problems—educational philosophy leads education, but it also follows. In his recent book, *Building a Philosophy of Education*, Harry Broudy, who seems to be comfortable with a realist label, expresses the view that educational philosophy is really a place where a systematic discussion of educational problems may be conducted at a philosophical level.[5] He assumes, validly or otherwise, that every educational question can be resolved on the philosophical level; educational problems are really problems of ethics, logic, metaphysics, epistemology, or aesthetics.

Reality

Educational practices reflect many things, but in particular they reflect what an educator thinks reality is. In educational theory two major positions are apparent with respect to the nature of reality: (1) Only matter is real; there is no reality above or beyond matter. (2) Both matter and spirit are real. Within these two major points of view there is both a reluctance and an enthusiasm for dealing with metaphysical questions—questions of reality. Educational theorists who adhere to the first position—only matter is real—may regard questions of reality as basic to a philosophy of education, or they may argue that no general theory of reality is possible, in other words, that outside a specific context nothing scientifically meaningful can be said about reality. Educational philosophers who subscribe to a dualistic view of reality—that both matter and spirit are real—may not be enthusiastic about discussing metaphysical questions as part of educational theory, but they regard these questions, nevertheless, as basic to their interpretations of man's nature and his educational needs.

Because metaphysics necessarily deals with the existence and nature of God, Christian humanism bases its educational theory on metaphysical principles as well as on the knowledge of man's origin, nature, and destiny which comes from revelation. The realities of the spirit are as impressive to the Christian humanist as are the realities of matter; it is possible and important to know both.

Pragmatism shows little interest in providing a metaphysical basis for education mainly because, at least for the followers of John Dewey, such a metaphysical basis cannot be formulated. There is in pragmatism, however, a willingness to accept the evolutionary hypothesis, which in itself is a kind of theory of reality. Most books on educational theory written from a pragmatist perspective tend to avoid discussion of such things as the essential being of the universe, for to raise such questions assumes that something can be known about essential nature, which is contrary to the position usually taken. More exactly, it is to raise a meaningless question, for it is impossible for us to know anything more about the world than our contacts with it disclose. Yet the works of John Dewey, John L. Childs, Sidney Hook, and others reveal pragmatists themselves making some general assumptions about the nature of reality.[6] It is more important for us, they believe, to know, or to examine, the social dimensions of life than to look for ultimate causes in the life of men and the world of nature. They show considerably greater preoccupation with social science than with natural or physical science, although they have been known to borrow the terminology of physical science and apply it both to social science and the philosophy of education.

For the noninitiated, the principal metaphysical doctrine in pragmatism appears to be this: The world is characterized throughout by process and change. Everything is in flux and movement. Some things may change more slowly than others, and for the observer the change may be so slow as to be hardly perceptible, but change, nevertheless, so this confident assumption goes, is taking place. Moreover, the ends or the objectives men seek—the really important things toward which they strive—are ends confined to this process of change. The values men accept or come to believe worthwhile belong to the process or are formed in it and do not arise out of some moral imperative outside the world of contact and immediate context. And finally, the world may be understood, or better, managed, without any appeal to theism, mysticism, or spiritualism. Man does not stand apart from the world and ponder or wonder at its mystery or its meaning; he is one with it; he is part of nature and continuous with it.

To regard reality as fixed or stable and then to try to discover and describe it is, according to the pragmatist, to engage in arbitrary and meaningless speculations. The world of the pragmatist is one of experience and can be understood only in terms of the here and now: no absolute principles or doctrines of reality can be applied to a constantly changing and relativistic world. Although their lack of metaphysics may make them philosophical heretics, the pragmatists, nevertheless, rely upon experience and refuse to construct any general theory of reality.

It is not easy to present the general metaphysical view of pragmatism; as we have seen, some pragmatists doubt the possibility or necessity of a general theory of reality. But this denial of theory, or better, a retreat from a general theory of reality, may in itself be a kind of metaphysic. In any case, it is one with which the pragmatists have been able to live. No less complex is the metaphysical position of realists, although the complexity is to be found not in the absence of theory, or the reluctance to form one, but in the variety of theories offered. Their metaphysical beliefs run all the way from naturalism to theism; it is almost impossible to distill from the statements any common metaphysical ground on which all realists willingly stand. What would appear to be a common starting point may be phrased as follows: The universe is made up of real, substantial entities, existing in themselves and related to one another by material bonds. These entities and these relations among them do in fact exist, whether or not we know or are aware of them. For a thing to exist is not the same as to be known. Men and the world actually exist, and our desire or opinions have nothing to do with this existence. In realist terminology, this is called the thesis of independence.[7]

Apart from their common view that the qualities of experience are real, independent facts of an external world, there is considerable divergence in the metaphysical views of realists. In fact, realists could not be grouped together if it were not for their common assent to the principle of independence. Some, for example, are pluralists, others are dualists, and a few are monists. Pluralism means, in this context, there are many ultimate, or final, substances which comprise the cosmos; dualism means there are but two, matter and spirit; and monism means there is only one, matter or spirit. To continue for a moment with the variety in realist beliefs, some realists are convinced of man's freedom and his capacity for making choices in a complex but orderly world, whereas others (they are probably in the majority) are certain, despite the order in the world, that man is subject to outside forces determining his course of action. The mind-body problem attracts their attention, too. And here we find some realists seeing mind as simply a function of the organism whereby the person is related to his environment; for them mental life is unequivocally rooted in bodily existence. Others, however, see mind activity as being definitely above physical functioning and do not believe that any conception of mind can be adequately presented by using physical terms. Mental activity, they would probably agree, does depend to some extent on physical foundations, but they attribute to mind a quality raising it above any mechanistic explanation of brain functions. Mind, in this interpretation, although it may not have the spiritual qualities attributed to it by the Christian humanist, is definitely unique as compared to physical things. Finally, they hold different views concerning a transempirical reality: God. These views go all the way from a thoroughgoing naturalism, where no God is needed or wanted, through pantheism, a conception of God in which the phenomenal world is simply a manifestation of His spirit, to a complete and orthodox theism. Wherever their final views come to rest, they tend to have a unique conception of the place religion should occupy in the lives of men and a unique conception, too, as to religion's place in education. They begin, not with a belief in God, but with a recognition of such beliefs. To approach the matter in this way does not require any test of the belief's validity; some people have these beliefs, and they are real. Real beliefs, regardless of what contrary beliefs others may have, should be respected in an orderly society of intelligent men; and because these beliefs are real, they may have a place claimed for them in the school's curriculum.

From this preview of realist metaphysics we see the common ground on which realists stand: There is a real world which we may come to know; it stands apart from us; and our knowledge of it or our hopes for it do not change the substantial entities contained in it. This world is a world of order and law; we may not be able to change it, but we can come to know it. The latter is the supreme task of education.

Knowledge

Although it may be possible to theorize about education without first accepting a general view of reality—the pragmatist seems to do this—a philosophy of knowledge must be accepted, either consciously or unconsciously, before a philosophy of education can be constructed. This is because the first steps in education cannot be taken until a decision—tentative or final—concerning the following points is made:

1. Is knowledge possible?
2. Does knowledge have some stability and dependability?
3. Is knowledge valid?
4. What is the nature of the knowledge process?

If knowledge is not possible, that is, if it is impossible to know reality as it is, the educational task would seem to be futile, unless it is conceived to be an exercise in having experiences. At best these experiences would be lacking in objectivity, for their essentials could not be stated in terms of content that others could also experience, but only in terms of an individual's activity. If knowledge were neither stable nor dependable, the educational task would not be centered on teaching *truth* but would be geared to various activities in which the students showed some interest. It would be indefensible, indeed, to teach as truth a curricular content which is subject to continuous change or reconstruction. If, moreover, the validity of knowledge cannot be established, it would seem useless to insist that students master content that might or might not be true. Finally, the basic features of educational methodology must depend on the teacher's understanding of the knowledge process. If the process involves only a development of the senses in order that they may be more sensitive in their contacts with the world of reality, the techniques employed by teachers will differ in important ways from what they would be if the knowledge process were understood to involve a difference in nature between the senses and the intellect.

The theories of learning discussed in Chapter 9 enable us to see how the learning process might be affected by learning theory. It is impossible to know the reaction of all teachers, but two extremes seem to be represented in the following examples: teacher A is convinced that whatever is worth knowing is already discovered and waiting to be learned. There is, of course, an element of discovery in a person's trying to master what he does not know. But at this point the teacher is not thinking of the learner's discovery; he is thinking, rather, of knowledge as a product of someone else's discovery or research, assembled in the curriculum and properly arranged for learning. For teacher A, learning is a process culminating in a knowledge product. On the other hand, the content of the curriculum may not matter to teacher B; it is merely a starting point for further experience, to deeper, possibly more profound, but surely more personal learning. Perhaps one would not be entirely wrong in equating this latter approach with the English gentleman's conception that what counts is not "whether or not you win, but how you play the game," or that gaining knowledge is much less an intellectual experience than the quest for it. In its approach to learning the class-room directed by teacher A has an air of finality, whereas the other class-room appears to be more a workshop for experiences. There is no reason, of course, why both approaches cannot be applied to the same general learning situation. We are firmly convinced of the validity of some of our knowledge and are prepared to teach it with art and conviction. Yet, at the same time, there is room for broadening horizons, for developing intellectual self-reliance, and for raising learning far above the level of a rote process. Quality learning ignites a spark of individuality and ingenuity, and this spark may easily be snuffed out if all learning is approached in a catechetical way.

Visits to elementary and secondary school classrooms convince us of teachers' extraordinary confidence in and dependence on knowledge collected in textbooks or anthologies. If one of the extremes rather than the other is captivating, it is the one where knowledge is conceived to be ready-made and the pupil, as a sponge, need only absorb it.

The teacher whose philosophy of knowledge has room for certitude would try to teach what he believes to be true. But to take the position that truth is possible is not quite the same as assuming that knowledge is ready-made, waiting to be absorbed; it is rather evidence of a belief that reality may be known—not always fully, not always accurately—and that certitude is possible. Furthermore, it is undoubtedly an over-statement of the position of educators who believe that truth is possible to represent them as believing that everything that needs to be known or can be known is already in the storehouse of knowledge. And the activity and meaningfulness of the learning process need not be interfered with in any way by a philosophy of knowledge that holds that "Without trust in truth, there is no human effectiveness." On the other hand, the teacher who does not believe that knowledge is possible or that truth consists in the conformity of the mind with reality will try to provide opportunities for experiences leading students to individual and social effectiveness. But if knowledge is not possible, it is somewhat difficult to understand how teachers who accept this point of view can be so certain of the validity of their point of view. And in this way of looking at the world and man, it would seem that the only way skepticism can be avoided is by avoiding questions which would open the gates to skepticism. A philosophy of knowledge which attributes the label of "absolute" to all curricular content provides as little direction and balance for the educational task as the philosophy of knowledge which removes all objective bases for the construction of curricula.

Where do the prominent contemporary philosophies of education stand in relation to the knowledge problem? Christian humanism begins by maintaining that truth is possible, that it can be tested in various ways, and that, once validated, it has qualities of both stability and dependability. In this point of view a distinction is made between the senses, and the kind of knowledge of which they are capable, and the intellect, which is capable of probing the essential features of things. Sense knowledge is not undervalued, but human knowledge is not limited to the experience of the senses —rather, it is with the senses that it begins. Reason and sense knowledge are not the same, and it is this basic point that is denied by empiricism.

One should hardly expect a philosophy of man which sees no essential difference between man and other forms of life to concern itself with differences between reason and sense knowledge. This lack of concern points directly to the difference between a Christian dualism and a monistic empiricism: What is man? What is he capable of doing? How should he be treated? What is his destiny? It is not always easy to see the differences between theories of education, especially when these theories have been translated into educational practice. This has led astute observers to deny real differences among philosophies of education. It is said: "All of us do the same things in the classroom anyway, so why should we be concerned with theoretical differences which are more apparent than real? Even if they are real, they make no real difference on the level of practice." Let us assume a pragmatist educator has just made this statement. According to his educational theory, or more importantly following his practices, teaching and learning opportunities will be broad enough to cover the whole development of youth and be interested in the cultivation of the rational and spiritual powers of his mind, but in doing so will be ignorant of the very nature of these powers, and will have a disregard for their needs and their hopes, and will reduce everything to the ambiguous level of the education of a man in terms of the simple, material life of an animal. Classroom teachers may not vary greatly in the practices they employ, but what they do in the classroom, despite the similarity of technique, does reflect their basic view of the child's essential nature.

Yet the difference, however great on this level, does not stop at this level. Who could gainsay the importance to the teacher, to education, of the question: What is man? But beyond this there is an additional question every teacher must sometimes ask: What is truth? For the relativist, and most pragmatists fall into this category, the term "truth" either falls out of the vocabulary or is subjected to drastic redefinition. Even with redefinition there is considerable difficulty, for purging meanings from lexicons is easier than purging minds. When the pragmatist describes apparently dependable and stable knowledge as meaningless outside a given context, the uninitiated mind begins to rebel. Why does it rebel? Is it because there is a necessary correlation between dependability and utility? Unless knowledge is dependable it can hardly be useful. Is truth a kind of psychological need; is it like beauty, as some say, in the eye of the beholder? These questions are answered in a context, and in the context of empiricism, with its unfortunate tendency to define human thought in terms of animal knowledge and reaction, trust in truth is lacking; where there is no trust in truth, there is no human effectiveness.

Christian humanism views formal education as having the primary responsibility of creating learning situations where youth can be prepared to exercise their human abilities. This means that the educational process must emphasize the training of the senses—for nothing reaches the intellect except through the senses—as well as the natural interests which the child brings to school—for these natural interests are the beginning of motivation. In addition, the principle of activity must also be emphasized, for without activity there will be no preparation for students to exercise their distinctively human powers.

The pragmatist philosophy of knowledge is instrumental. This means that the knower does not stand apart from reality—as a spectator—and identify it and give it a label such as "knowledge" or "truth." Reality, meaningless in itself, derives its sense from the aims whose attainment it promotes. Knowledge, then, or truth—in a very limited sense—has meaning only in a particular context. And the senses, rather than being gateways to knowledge, are but stimuli to action. Saying that knowledge has an instrumental character is just another way of saying that knowledge is relative, that it is not an event within nature: it is a tool—an instrument. Knowing is a natural process like eating or digesting, and no essential distinction is made between sensation and reason. The way to make ideas clear is not to subject them to rational analysis but to test their consequences: in its simplest form this means that if an idea works, it is true. Before this crucial test is made, however, there is no knowledge, and after it is made, there is no reason to believe that the consequences of a previous test will also be the consequences of a subsequent test.

For the pragmatist there is no problem of knowledge in general, as there is no problem of reality in general. This would seem to leave the pragmatist without an epistemology or a philosophy of knowledge in the conventional sense, and this is where he wants to be left, for he feels that to begin inquiry by raising the usual epistemological questions is to stop meaningful inquiry before it starts. Preserving traditional epistemology, moreover, is not the pragmatist's goal—he conceives a philosophy of knowledge as having the function of describing the way problems are solved. Knowledge is not a quest for certainty; it does not disclose reality to the learner. It is, rather, an operational and contextualistic enterprise, or, in the words of John Dewey, a *transaction*.

What generalizations may be made, by way of summary, of the pragmatic view of knowledge, and how does this view of knowledge affect man in his search for security, or truth, or conviction, in a world that seems sometimes to be out of sympathy with his hopes and aspirations? It may not be possible to make such generalizations with the clarity we should like, but this is because we cannot go beyond the positions taken by pragmatists, the authors of the theory. If their views are rendered in a form less than either clear or satisfying, we may ask them for clarification and amplification, but we cannot do more without coming perilously close to violating the positions they hold. It is not our purpose to challenge or refine, but only to present. In the first place, the pragmatist does not believe knowledge is discovered or disclosed to a knower. To look at the knowledge problem this way would suggest a dualism between the knower and the object, and this dualism is surely not encouraged by pragmatists. Knowing is a joint action of the knower and the environment; the knower as well as the perceived environment are part of knowledge. Second, the human element to knowledge cannot be overlooked or replaced, and individual differences in knowledge cannot be eliminated although they may be controlled. Finally, what is called scientific knowledge is relative to knowers in a given context, for whatever a thing may be when independent of any observer or frame of reference is scientifically meaningless.

In this point of view "knowledge" is social as well as individual, but it is preeminently social in its consequences; it is a product of activity; and it grows. For formal education the consequences of such a conception of knowledge are both dramatic and profound. Predetermined curricula with carefully selected and carefully organized content are replaced with the problem-operational approach. Knowing is an outcome of an immersion in the immediate problems of life; knowledge is never fixed or absolute but, like James's universe, is open at both ends.

The realist theory of knowledge is a revolt against the theory of knowledge of idealism, which holds that the qualities of experience depend upon a knower for their existence and do not subsist in themselves. Since the beginning of the twentieth century, realists have been refuting the idealist reasoning and have formulated an epistemology of their own. The principle that above all others unites realists is "the principle of independence," which we took as our common starting point toward the beginning of this discussion: Realists claim that the qualities of experience are real, independent facts of the external world. They are unchanged when they enter the mind of the knower and do not depend upon any mind for their existence.

In addition, following the indications of experience, the realist believes in the intentional or relational character of all knowledge. Every concept is a concept of something; every judgment is a judgment about something. The act of knowing is an act whereby the knower becomes united, in a nonmaterial sense, or directly identified with the thing, a really existent thing, standing as the object of knowledge. The mind, of course, does not become physically identified with its object, for as realists say: to know an explosion is not to explode. Yet knowing something is a matter of becoming relationally identified with an existent entity as it is: the intrusion of subjectivism is an obstacle to valid knowledge, and the realist makes every effort to avoid it; rather than avoiding subjectivism, the pragmatist would seem to make it a condition, an essential element, of the knowledge transaction.

In general, realism acknowledges the possibility of truth and maintains that certain truths are subject only to minor change or are unchangeable. The truths which could gain admission to these categories would have to be carefully validated, and generally they would have to have the support of tested experimental evidence. In areas of human activity or inquiry outside the scope of positive experimental methods truth probably could not be achieved.

Value

Questions of value are questions of what man will accept as guides for human action. Two major positions seem to be apparent in contemporary value theory: (1) That values have no meaning in themselves; they are meaningful when they serve as means to some desirable end. For example, driving on the right side of the street can be considered a value. However, this practice is valueless in itself, though as a means to save travel its value is immediately apparent. (2) That some values have an intrinsic worth which does not depend upon convention or social acceptability. In other words, some values, or guides to human action, have their origin in God or in man's nature, and they dominate values which can be experimentally determined. These two points of view may be stated in another way: (1) Primary values are objective. (2) All values are subjective, and their worth is determined by their utility. A theory of value which asserts that some values are absolute need not, and usually does not, maintain that all guides for action are unalterable. On the other hand, a theory of value which defines values exclusively in terms of usefulness is relativistic.

What meaning does value theory have for educational philosophy? Christian humanism finds ultimate value in a personal God. Without God there is no ultimate purpose in life and no ultimate purpose in education. God made man "to know, love, and serve Him in this life and to be happy with him forever in the next." Value is found first, then, in God's law, but it is found also in the law of man's nature—the natural law. Values which arise out of these two sources are absolute, and they are the major guides for all of life. There are, however, social, political, economic, and other values which may be determined in terms of contemporary life and its needs, and these values are subordinate and subject to the domina-

tion of God's law and the law of nature. A Christian humanist interpretation of value permits of many kinds of values—intrinsic and instrumental
—but it requires a hierarchal arrangement of these values. Men have
naturally many loyalties which compete for time, attention, and affection.
The question of value is really a fairly simple one: What is most worth
doing? Man's worlds—physical, human, spiritual—have their own values
or value systems. A hierarchy of values is not a product of authority; it
does not come by fiat, but rather arises out of man's nature and his world
relationships. But it is cumbersome and dangerous to avoid making a
hierarchy of values known to the young; it is one of the principal businesses of education to educate the moral as well as the intellectual man.
These values, then, and the hierarchy on which they are arranged are
goals worthy of moral formation.

What would appear to be the essentials of pragmatist value theory may
be stated briefly. As with knowledge, values have an operational or instrumental character. What is good or useful depends not upon what one
thinks or says, much less upon what someone else thinks or says, but upon
how one acts. According to pragmatism, to hem man in with absolute
guides is not only to destroy freedom but to destroy the very meaning of
life as well. What is desirable is not preconceived or separated from action
but arises in the continuum of experience.

Values do not have an independent status; they are not always in evidence and do not always mean the same thing. What is most worth doing?
is a question about which one can be ambivalent. There is really no way
of telling until the opportunity to act presents itself, and then it may be
too late; for when one acts, who can guarantee the quality of his choice?
And what, after all, is success? It may have a variety of meanings and
appear in obscure forms. At best the pragmatist sees it as something helping man adapt his behavior to the natural order. Nonpragmatists are wary
of blindly following nature and allowing it to be the final arbiter. Yet
the pragmatist will defend the natural by asking whether it may not be
as natural to be "good" as it is to be "bad." [8] Finally, the pragmatist
regards the natural order as an intimate existence of which he is an integral
part. So the value which is disclosed in action, whatever the theory may
be, is regarded as natural and therefore justifiable, although it may have
no part in forming a code of values or a hierarchy of value objectives.

The foundation of realist value theory may be described in terms borrowed from social philosophy. There is no general appeal to the natural,
although all men, it is acknowledged, share common traits responsible for
determining the general direction that children will take in their actions.
It is the business of education to clarify the meaning of these common
traits and to help persons construct a personal code for guiding action. The
realist believes that it is unreasonable to expect the determinants of

action to come to the surface unaided, for men are not animals and do not have an endowment including inflexible instincts dictating appropriate action. In place of an elaborate set of instincts, man has flexible tendencies which become more deeply rooted with knowledge and practice; or to put it another way, man can rationally understand his essential needs and freely determine the action to be taken in connection with them. Human nature is unfinished and is in need of completion; this is one of the basic meanings of life. If completion is to be achieved in a meaningful and desirable way, men must follow a moral or natural law. All men by employing introspection and self-observation have a basic moral knowledge which can by disciplined study be expanded into a more profound understanding

TABLE 12-1

Synoptic View of Prominent Contemporary Theories of Education

Theory	Role of educational theory	Nature of reality	Nature of knowledge	Nature of value
Christian humanism	To arrive at ends and means for education; expected to lead educational practices.	God is the Author of all nature. The world of matter and the world of spirit are real.	Truth is possible; man may know the world in which he lives.	Ultimate value originates with God; some values have intrinsic worth; some values arise out of man's actions. Primary values are objective, not relative.
Realism	A clearinghouse for educational questions. Theory sometimes leads educational practices, but it may also follow practices.	Realists differ with respect to the number of final substances: monism, dualism, pluralism.	Principle of independence (see p. 340).	Value is based on natural law. Knowledge is the only trustworthy guide for human action.
Pragmatism	To formulate theoretical justification for practices that are believed to be sound. Theory follows educational practice.	A theory of reality in general is not possible. What may be outside the context of which the learner is a part is scientifically meaningless.	Truth or knowledge is relative and therefore instrumental (see p. 345).	Values, like truth, are operational and instrumental in character.

of man and his evolution in history. The natural law, the realist concludes, is the only trustworthy guide for human action; knowledge leading to a fuller compliance with this law, and a happier and more complete life, is one of the inevitable and unavoidable concerns of education.

The realist is determined to find an objective basis for action and he is anxious, too, to assert the possibilities of knowing a world consisting of real, knowable entities that are always independent of the knower. Here there are universal goals toward which men may strive; these goals, moreover, may become norms or standards for value. The point not to be missed is this: By exercising his reason and striving for self-realization, self-determination, and self-integration, man discovers his ultimate goals and fundamental obligations. These become as real, and in time as inflexible, as the fact of life itself.

The Nature of Man

Why do philosophies of education differ? They differ because different positions are taken with respect to reality, knowledge, and value. Because these philosophical bases center finally in man, they lead to different interpretations of man's nature. The question "What is man?" is the starting point for every philosophy of education, and thus different interpretations of man's nature lead naturally to different, and sometimes conflicting, theories of education. It is possible to classify every philosophy of education according to its starting point: philosophies of education are either naturalistic or supernaturalistic in their view of man.

The theory of Christian humanism is built upon a supernatural view of man. Its answers to questions concerning man's origin, nature, and destiny may be stated as follows:[9]

1. Man was created by God. Since God is infinitely wise and infinitely good, He must have created man for a purpose. That purpose is man's happiness, a happiness to be realized only perfectly in God.
2. Man is composed of body and soul, united in essential unity. Thus, it is not the mind that thinks—it is the person that thinks. It is not the body that feels—it is, again, the person that feels.
3. The soul of man is nonmaterial, spiritual. It is intrinsically independent of matter, although necessarily united to the body to form a composite.[10]
4. Man has an intellect. With it he is capable of understanding, forming judgments, and drawing conclusions.
5. Man has free will—the ability to make free choices. I ought, therefore I can, although I need not. Free will does not mean that we act without a motive, and it does not mean that all human acts are free. In an individual's day there may be very few fully free acts.
6. Because man has an intellect and free will, he is essentially different

from the highest form of brute life. Man is an animal, but a rational animal. No mere animal thinks or wills.

7. Since the soul of man is nonmaterial or spiritual, it can be destroyed only by God. Annihilation can blot it out of existence; and to annihilate belongs solely to God. On the other hand, there is in human nature everywhere and at all times a craving for perfect happiness, so universal that it can have been put into human nature only by the Author of that nature itself. Since this perfect happiness is unattainable in this life even by those who keep God's law, we can have no reasonable doubt of the immortality of man's soul. Otherwise, we have a natural craving that can never be fulfilled.

8. There are certain human acts that are of their very nature good and deserving of praise, and therefore independent of all human law; other actions are of their very nature, that is, intrinsically, bad and deserving of blame. There is a norm to determine the good act and the bad act.

Implicit, also, in the Christian humanist view of man is the doctrine of the Fall of Man—original sin. Man, as created by God, was endowed with supernatural gifts but lost these gifts because he disobeyed God's law. Because of man's disobedience, God withdrew the supernatural gifts and wounded man's nature by darkening his intellect and weakening his will. In the Christian humanist view of man, therefore, man is not naturally good—neither is he naturally evil. His natural powers are not destroyed—they are weakened. He is not killed, only wounded. He is not depraved, but deprived. Through Redemption man's union with God was restored, and because man is redeemed by Christ, the Son of God, he is able to share in the supernatural life. From this starting point the Christian humanist develops his educational theory.

Pragmatism is naturalistic. From this point of view all that the Christian humanist says about man's nature is meaningless. Man is a product of the evolutionary process, not a creature of God; his destiny cannot be found outside the world of experience. Man is neither good nor bad—he is just man. There is no dualism of mind-body. Although mind is a unique function, it is not a mysterious or spiritual entity; it can be explained in the realm of nature. Neither is it an independent entity; it exists in activity and ways of behaving; it is what it does. There is nothing essential or unchanging about man's nature; all of nature, including man, is constantly being reshaped by the dynamic forces of change or evolution. Still, man is capable of having experiences, that is, of coming in contact with his environment; but it is a moving, shifting environment that he contacts, and he, being part of it, is moving and shifting, too. But it is this contact with a novel and changing environment which leads to a reconstruction of man's experiences, and this is learning.

Where does the pragmatist stand on the question of freedom of choice?

Can man freely choose the direction he will take, the kind of experiences he will have, or is he determined by forces beyond his control? Actually neither freedom nor determinism would seem to represent pragmatism. Pragmatism takes a position somewhere between freedom and determinism. Man, in other words, does not stand above his environment and choose from among several possible alternatives; neither is he subordinated to and directed by his environment. He is one factor in the continuum of experience, and the alternative that he "takes" is not chosen by him or dictated by his environment but is an outcome of man's influence on his environment and of the environment on him. The weight of these influences will direct action. And the richer and the more vital the environment, the "better" and the fuller will man's life be. This view of man, along with the philosophical bases discussed earlier, sets the stage for the pragmatist's kind of education.

Realism is usually, though not always, naturalistic. And modern realists seem to be able to write books and articles on educational theory without ever setting down precisely their views of man's nature. This is probably not an oversight or a pose. It would seem that the realist prefers to begin theorizing about education in search of a definition or description of man rather than to begin with such a definition. What man is depends upon what he is capable of doing; his capacities must be examined carefully before the answer can be given. Implicit in the realist educational theory is the view that man has capacities that can be realized, although these capacities—for example, memorizing or thinking—may not be essentially different from other organic functions. Yet man has a potentiality for mental life which sets him apart from other kinds of nature, and for the perfection of this mental life both *activity* and *content* are important. In the realist conception reality has an independent existence, and reality may be known by man. For realism the educational task is essentially that of putting man in a proper relationship with his environment. Man's highly complex nervous system makes him capable of having and holding effective relationships with his environment.

Realism reflects some ambiguity in its interpretations of God. The Christian humanist might say, "Realism is clothed in an understandable language and presents a fairly coherent system. Its agnosticism is puzzling." Even when some realists are certain of the existence of God, their reflections do not lead to an active and orthodox theism but rather to a conventional deism. Man's soul, which they acknowledge, is merely the principle of life, but they are confident, nevertheless, of man's matchless intellectual abilities. These abilities, the realist asserts, are not the products of the revolutionary process: men are not simply highly developed animals. In addition, norms of conduct prescribed by the law of man's nature are perilous to violate. At this point we are entitled to wonder how the laws of nature can demand compliance—this is a way of setting a tone of individual responsibility—and punish violations, unless there is a quality of freedom in man permitting him to choose. But again we detect diffidence: realism does not go all the way with freedom. Some realists accept as a fact the capability of man to freely choose; believing in freedom, they see any denial of freedom as a shrinking of the stature of human personality.

Educational Objectives

The determination of goals for education is an application of value theory to a practical human problem. But values are intimately bound up with other philosophical issues which find their climax in man's nature. What man is will determine what education can do for him. By knowing man, educational theorists can formulate educational objectives that will satisfy his needs. To be adequate, it would seem that an educational theory would have to state its objectives in terms that include all education, not just formal education, and all of life, not just a preparation for part of life. Regardless of the adequacy of any educational theory, it answers questions related to the objectives of life and formal education within the context of its philosophy of man. If man is conceived to have an essential nature, the goals of education, in so far as they are directed at perfecting his essential nature, will be unchanging—although it does not follow necessarily that the process of achieving these goals would have to remain fixed. But philosophies of education that see in man a quality of permanence often see, also, certain characteristics of his nature that are subject to change. To the extent that man may change, the goals of education may change, too.

Philosophies of education which do not detect any qualities of permanence in man's nature will obviously not be sympathetic to any attempt to formulate definite educational objectives. Rather than stating goals in advance, such philosophies are usually inclined to think of educational objectives in terms of outcomes. Consistent with this point of view is the claim that there can be no precise dualism or dichotomy of *means* and *ends*. The educational theory which fixes goals and then organizes means to achieve these goals accepts a distinction between ends and means; but in doing so, it may recognize that ends often become means to subsequent ends. The opposition to fixed goals is usually based on the fear that a goal, end, or objective carries with it a connotation of finality. To state an end is, in other words, to limit the possibilities of experience, and educational objectives, then, rather than advancing the cause of education, actually serve as a menace to its effectiveness. Besides, definitely stated educational objectives are, in this view, at the same time artificial and limitations on freedom. They are artificial because the content of experience cannot be prescribed: value follows experience; what should be or what should be done must arise out of a context, or experience will be meaningless. Freedom is restricted by authority. Although some limitations on freedom may be freely accepted in the interests of the social whole, the child in school should not be put in a position where he will have to surrender any of his freedom to have a personally meaningful life. Goals imply authority, and if authority is exercised in education, someone will prescribe the kind of experiences formal education should offer on the basis of *his* needs, not the child's. Too frequently, it is contended, decisions concerning what education should be are made by persons who have little or no contact with young people and know little about their interests or their needs.

Where do the major philosophies of education stand on the matter of educational objectives?

Christian humanism understands the aim of education, in the broadest meaning of the term "education," to be the formation of a man. This means that education is concerned with the physical, social, religious, and mental development of human beings. But, in a more limited sense, education in school—formal education—is concerned *primarily* with mental development. Secondarily, the school is concerned with moral life, citizenship, social education, and practical preparation for making a living. The primary aim, then, of formal education is fixed, although the means—the curriculum, the methods, and the administrative practices in which educators engage—must be flexible, for to be effective means they must be adjusted to the changing circumstances of man in society. The secondary aims of formal education, however, are not fixed, for the Christian humanist acknowledges that man's relationships to the world in which he lives, and that world, too, change.

At this point it is probably important to say that while a large, representative body of educational opinion among Christian humanists accepts the school as primarily an intellectual agency, complete unanimity is lacking. For some Christian humanists the school's primary function is moral not intellectual; a principle directing the school to deal essentially with what can be taught does not exclude morality. Why must schools refrain from trying to teach morality when so many other agencies of society are charged with inculcating it? Perhaps morality is not taught in precisely the same way as arithmetic or some other conventional school subject, but this is all irrelevant. In other words, the principle "a school must deal essentially with what can be taught" is valid only if its application is broad enough to include moral formation.

Pragmatist educational theory, more than avoiding stated educational aims, actually opposes them. To do otherwise would be inconsistent with the philosophical ideas pragmatists entertain. In its simplest and clearest form the pragmatist concept of education is this: Education is not a preparation for life—it is life. The aims in life are pluralistic, and their hierarchy is arrived at in a specific context. The ends which children may seek in formal education are as many and varied as those of life itself and just as valid as the children's needs. The purpose of education, therefore, from this point of view, could be said to be social and individual efficiency, and the school, rather than creating ends toward which students would strive, provides or tries to provide opportunities for effective experiencing.

One of the difficulties educational reforms always face is the simple but highly effective inertia reflected clearly in this attitude: What is now being done is about as effective as anyone has a right to expect. This is one of the obstacles keeping many of the pragmatist's theories on the philosopher's shelf, or has led the pragmatist to respond after the manner of Kant, who acknowledged "leaving his philosophy in the office" when he ventured into the world of actual living. Many pragmatists have deplored their inability to apply their theories fully; but at the same time they realize society's unreadiness for the full impact of their educational plan. If it is not possible to organize a school wherein experience in effective experiencing can be the principal objective and where the emerging curriculum, a customized curriculum for each student, will be available, where does the pragmatist stand? Are his hands tied, or is it possible for him to offer some substitute, or second best, suggestions, while waiting for the time when his plans can be put fully into operation? In trying to lay bare some of the pure theory of pragmatism, it would be a mistake to emphasize theory and ignore practice. In actual fact pragmatists are concerned with learning, although they would not like to approve the current order of learning which puts artificial objectives ahead of the learner's interests. Pragmatism does see the school as an intellectual agency wherein the quality of experience is dependent on the school's ability to make its environment a place for fine living. Fine, quality living leads to the best learning, not directly but indirectly. The school is an educational unit involved with living and learning, regarded in this theory as correlative terms, but it is an intellectual agency only to the extent that intellectual development is a by-product of quality living.

Because of this stress on living, and a constant fear, if the school is too conventional, that its spirit will be killed, moral education is given considerable support. It may come as something of a surprise, but the pragmatist is is considerably more interested in moral formation than he is in intellectual development. He is interested in all of life, which includes, of course, physical and social formation and skill. But above all he stresses the possibilities, so far seldom realized, of functional learning. He speaks disdainfully of the old-line school and the old-line subjects in it, but he advises his opponents that their fears are groundless: The old-line subjects will still be taught, but in a different way. He goes beyond this, claiming old-line subjects taught in different ways are taught more effectively. Whether or not this can be proved is doubtful, but modern day pragmatists assert that the students of their schools are as capable in all of the usual informational and skill subjects as any other students and are distinctly superior in those areas where initiative and problem solving are the *sine qua non* of success.[11] All of this, the devotee of pragmatism argues, is simply another way of underlining his desire to promote quality living: The excellence and exactness supposed to be associated with more rigid forms of education, but not exclusively associated with them, are desirable, and we must try to give students ample quantities of these qualities, too.

For the realist the ultimate aim of education is the good life: educational values and objectives are stated only after the values of life are determined. There is no hesitancy here in assigning objectives to education and specifying the means to achieve them. Realists do not see how it is possible to create a social institution—the school—and refuse or be unable to say what is expected of it. They prod the pragmatists to action, the activity about which they are always so certain and so confident, hoping they too will assign some firm goals to their educational process. But if the pragmatist does not act, the realist finds in this inaction no warrant for impreciseness on his part. The school, he says, has four essential civilizing functions:

1. It has the function of discovering the theoretical bases for life and for stating these bases in understandable and communicable terms. In a word, the school has the important responsibility of finding the truth about the world. This may not be easy, but easy or not it is important, for if the school does not do it, there is no assurance of any action. Inaction on this level is more damaging than anarchy in political life, for a refusal to look for the bases of life restricts its meaning and eliminates the possibility of achieving the good life.

2. Once the school has arrived at truth—there is a remarkable, perhaps excessive, stressing of the research function of the school—it has the responsibility for extending, interpreting, and applying it to all reality. The school, in this view, is a central agency with uncommon power; it deals with things of the mind, which, after all, are really the things used to manage the world and control affairs of men. We could assign to the school, then, not only the role of discovery but the roles, too, of teaching (disseminating) and preserving knowledge. Perhaps because so many realists do their own teaching at the university level, the functions assigned to the school are similar to the functions usually assigned to the university.

3. The school is to exercise indirect control over the society it serves. It serves best when it creates a climate infecting men with ideas or one

where ideas are contagious. The realist is convinced of the controlling, reforming, uplifting power of ideas; he is aware, moreover, of man's limitations and of more complete knowledge as a generative force leading to the best of possible worlds: a world of structure and design where the power of mind is clearly revealed.

4. It is the duty of the school to formulate principles of law and order, morality and duty, and to teach these principles, eliciting zeal and devotion. The teacher is charged, first of all, with communicating knowledge in a clear and authoritative manner. But he must not stop there. His teaching should take possession of the student. Education, says the realist, is the art of communicating truth. It has not been fully achieved until this truth not only lies within but actually possesses the mind and heart of the student.[12]

The Educational Process

The discussion so far has dealt with practical educational questions, but little has been said about what teachers and students will do in school, that is, about what is usually called the "educational process." What this process will be depends upon the answers which have been given to previous educational questions. Elements which need to be mentioned as part of the process are curriculum, interest, motivation, discipline, effort, measurement, evaluation, individual differences, and methods. It is not our purpose here to examine the elements of the educational process in any detail, but only to make a general statement as to how distinctive processes are distilled out of philosophies of education.

In general there are two major points of view with respect to what should be done in the classroom. For want of better terms these points of view may be described as *essentialistic* and *experimentalistic*.

The essentialist approach, to which both Christian humanism and realism subscribe, maintains that the school is a place where students are encouraged to learn what they do not know. The content of education— the curriculum—contains knowledges and skills and opportunities for development that are consistent with previously determined educational aims. Although this content will be adjusted whenever possible to the interests and needs of the students and opportunities will be coordinated to individual differences, the student's main responsibility is to master the content of the curriculum. This achievement, or lack of it, will be measured or tested and evaluated in terms of stated aims rather than in terms of his needs. It is not expected that the learner will be passive, but his activity will be directed toward ends that are accepted as valid by adult society. To assure achievement, the teacher's responsibility is to direct and guide learning, to interest, motivate, and teach; as an essential condition for achievement, discipline will be maintained. Particular techniques of teaching to be employed by teachers are not given a privileged position in the essentialist-oriented school: the effectiveness of a technique is judged in terms of the results it achieves. For this reason techniques often thought to belong to the experimental approach to the educational process are used, but when they are used, the essentialist says, they are given a special direction. In this respect techniques are like a carpenter's hammer: they can be used either to build or to destroy.

The experimental approach to the educational process which is in keeping with the pragmatist outlook sees no dualism between the learner and what is to be learned. What is to be learned is not stated in advance. In other words, there are no subject matter requirements, for the experimentalist believes there is little or nothing worth holding up for the examination of every student. Students differ; they come to school with their own interests; these interests must be attended to. Not only is there no predetermined set of experiences to be offered to all, there is no uniformity in presenting educative experiences. In conventional terminology it is hard for the pragmatist to see why anyone should want all students to begin reading in the second grade or all students to take long division in the fifth or sixth. Despite all kinds of disclaimers about stating the kinds of knowledge students should have, the pragmatist nevertheless agrees to a considerable body of common knowledge and skills necessary to a decently educated group. They object, however, to naming this knowledge and these skills in advance. At best, it is difficult to see, especially for those not initiated into this system of thought, how we should expect competence in common knowledge and skill unless we let students know what skills and what knowledge we want them to master and will help them learn.

The curriculum may be described as an emerging curriculum: one which is conceived in terms of child activity and interests instead of formal subject matter. In it the child can seek answers to his own problems and can share in formulating plans for the attention of the group. Interest will arise out of the meaningfulness of the problems devised by students and not out of the cleverness of the teacher. Discipline will be an outcome of the independence and freedom experienced in solving problems. The steps common to laboratory experimentation and the techniques of science will be employed—hence, experimentalism. The student's vision, intelligence, and reflective thinking will be enriched by following the experimental approach to learning and living.

The ideal educational process as the pragmatist conceives it may be best described by a pragmatist.[13]

I would have the school start with its children wherever they are and help them, first, to get wholesome and vigorous living under way. Then, I should have the school work at all times, in season and out, (1) to raise as best it could the quality of living at each age level; (2) to make this actual living grow up into all-round living—including the growing up into the best phases of current social life—as all-round as the school can manage, not to interfere with the high quality of living otherwise; and (3) to develop the creative aspect of living as the finest single test of success, that these children may grow in the actual ability to think up good new things to do, in the wish to do, and in the effective ability to do them wisely, all things considered. If we can get our schools to work honestly and zealously along these lines, I believe we shall get better results of every defensible kind that can be attained on any other basis. Such a program may be called the *emerging curriculum*. . . . For myself I would group children according to social age. The word *promotion* and what it stands for would drop out. I strongly oppose X, Y, Z grouping as unnecessary and as cruelly degrading to the Z group. I would have no separate subjects taught, as such, in the elementary school

TABLE 12-2

Summary of Philosophies of Education and Their Meaning in Educational Practice

Philosophy	Nature of man	Educational objectives	Educational practices
Christian humanism	Man is the creature of God, with the defect of original sin, but possessing intellect, free will, and an immortal soul.	In its most general meaning education is intended to form man. Formal education has intellectual development as the primary objective.	To interest, motivate, and teach; achievement and discipline emphasized.
Realism	What man is depends on what he is capable of doing.	To achieve truth, apply what is discovered, inspire students to intellectual effort, elicit zeal and devotion to truth.	To teach the child what he does not know, discipline being essential to any degree of excellence.
Pragmatism	Man is a product of the evolutionary process. Mind is explained within the realm of nature.	Social and individual efficiency.	Achievement and discipline are encouraged, but freedom, problem solving, and experimentation on the learner's part are part of the educational process.

and, accordingly, no departmentalized work there. Such divisions in operation so cut across living at that level as to sadly deaden it. . . . I would use no textbooks as such, but instead all sorts of reference books. . . . I would give no marks in either elementary or secondary school, and would send no regular report cards, especially of a kind intended to compare one pupil with another. I think all such seriously hinder the kind of living the school exists to foster.

The experimentalist educational process will be evaluated and measured by standards which are not independent or outside of the process but which are continuous with the process.

SUMMARY

Three prominent contemporary philosophies of education are engaged in dealing with fundamental educational questions. These questions—the why, what, and how of education—can be answered only within the framework of a theology and philosophy of life; a general philosophy—theories of reality, knowledge, and value; and scientific knowledge of man and the world in which he lives. This knowledge is synthesized in a philosophy of man, for it is with man—his origin, nature, and destiny—that every philosophy of education begins. The different philosophies ascribe different meanings to education because they take different positions with respect to man's nature. Each philosophy of education must be evaluated in terms of its starting point, and with each philosophy of education this starting point is *man,* but man viewed in a different way.

The philosophies, or theories, of education discussed in this chapter are Christian humanism, realism, pragmatism. Basic philosophical positions on reality, knowledge, and value and their meaning for education are analyzed. (For a summary of these positions see Tables 12–1 and 12–2.)

QUESTIONS AND EXERCISES

1. What is the function of educational theory or educational philosophy?
2. Why is a philosophy of education important?
3. Can you show how general philosophy and educational philosophy are related?
4. What do you consider the principal strengths and weaknesses of each of the philosophies of education discussed in Chapter 12?
5. Is educational philosophy really relevant? Does it make any difference to teachers who are actually teaching children?
6. Some educators claim that the best educational philosophers representing all points of view could get together and arrive at one acceptable

philosophy of education. Do you think this kind of consensus on fundamental questions is really possible?

7. The points of view of many prominent men are touched on in this chapter. Make a list of the names of these men, indicate their past and
present academic connections, and try to place each man according to the
educational theory he represents.

8. How would a school conducted according to realist educational theory
differ from a Christian humanist's school?

9. What relationship does a theory of reality have for education?

10. What is the place of epistemology, or a theory of knowledge, in educational philosophy?

11. Can you show how values are related to educational objectives?

12. It is sometimes claimed that it is better to philosophize about educational problems than to come to definite conclusions about education and
finally accept a theoretical position. What is your reaction to this?

ADDITIONAL READINGS

Avalos, B.: *New Men for New Times,* Sheed & Ward, Inc., New York, 1962.
This is an attempt to construct a Christian philosophy of education.

Brameld, Theodore: *Education for the Emerging Age: Newer Ends and
Stronger Means,* Harper & Row, Publishers, Incorporated, New York, 1961.
See the sections on "indoctrination" and "defensible partiality."

Broudy, Harry S.: *Building a Philosophy of Education,* rev. ed., Prentice-Hall,
Inc., Englewood Cliffs, N.J., 1961. See chapter 1, which treats of the
meaning and function of educational philosophy.

Brubacher, John S.: *Modern Philosophies of Education,* McGraw-Hill Book
Company, New York, 1962. Read the final chapter on consensus in educational theory.

Burns, H. W., and C. J. Brauner (eds.): *Philosophy of Education,* The Ronald Press Company, New York, 1962. A book of readings on educational
theory containing varieties of educational theories.

Butler, J. Donald: *Four Philosophies and Their Practice in Education and
Religion,* Harper & Row, Publishers, Incorporated, New York, 1957. The
section on the history of pragmatism is excellent.

Childs, John L.: *American Pragmatism and Education,* Holt, Rinehart and
Winston, Inc., New York, 1956. An expression of a pragmatic educational
creed by an author who can claim to be an orthodox pragmatist.

Cunningham, William F.: *The Pivotal Problems of Education,* The Macmillan
Company, New York, 1940. See chapter 17, "A Philosophy of Catholic
Education."

Dewey, John: *Democracy and Education,* The Macmillan Company, New
York, 1961. Read chapter 1 in connection with the commentary on Dewey
in Butler's *Four Philosophies and Their Practice in Religion and Education.*

Fitzpatrick, Edward A.: *How to Educate Human Beings,* The Bruce Publishing Company, Milwaukee, 1953. A book that sets forth a theology of education.

Gruber, F. C.: *Foundations for a Philosophy of Education,* Thomas Y. Crowell Company, New York, 1961. This book essays to offer the student the means for building his own philosophy of education by giving him a vocabulary, presenting some contemporary views on education, and exposing him to the main currents in educational theory.

Johnston, Herbert L.: *A Philosophy of Education,* McGraw-Hill Book Company, New York, 1963. Read chapter 9, which presents and analyzes the views of several contemporary educational theorists.

Kilpatrick, William H.: *Philosophy of Education,* The Macmillan Company, New York, 1963. The author tries to consider critically and constructively the principal problems of educational theory as they touch today's schools.

Maritain, Jacques: *Education at the Crossroads,* Yale University Press, New Haven, Conn., 1943. The entire book is worth careful study. Note especially the basic theses in chapter 1.

———: *The Education of Man,* Doubleday Press, Toronto, Canada, 1962. An updated presentation of Maritain's basic ideas on education.

Mayer, Frederick: *Man, Morals, and Education,* College and University Press, New Haven, Conn., 1962. A discussion of the relationship of philosophy to life and education.

Morris, Van Cleve: *Philosophy and the American School,* Houghton Mifflin Company, Boston, 1961. See chapters 3 and 7.

National Society for the Study of Education: *Philosophies of Education,* Forty-first Yearbook, Chicago, 1942, part I. See Adler's chapter, "In Defense of the Philosophy of Education."

———: *Modern Philosophies and Education,* Fifty-fourth Yearbook, Chicago, 1955, part I. See chapter on realism by John Wild.

Park, Joe: *Selected Readings in the Philosophy of Education,* The Macmillan Company, New York, 1963. Read part I, "The Place of Philosophy in the Study of Education."

Price, K.: *Education and Philosophical Thought,* Allyn and Bacon, Inc., Boston, 1962. Another study of the relationship between philosophy and education.

Redden, John D., and Francis A. Ryan: *A Catholic Philosophy of Education,* The Bruce Publishing Company, Milwaukee, 1956. An interpretation and application of philosophical principles to educational theory by Catholic authors.

Smith, Vincent E.: *The School Examined: Its Aim and Content,* The Bruce Publishing Company, Milwaukee, 1960. A highly readable book on current theoretical issues facing the schools.

Ulich, Robert: *Philosophy of Education,* American Book Company, New York, 1961. See chapters 1 and 2.

Wynne, John P.: *Theories of Education,* Harper & Row, Publishers, Incorporated, New York, 1963. Attention is called especially to the section on educational perennialism.

chapter 13

The Role of Religion
in Democratic Education

In a sample of public opinion one would learn that education separated from religion is often believed to be basic education for democracy. It is not strange, of course, to find that the man who does not believe in God does not place much confidence in religion. However, many Americans having both a positive and an active religious affiliation feel that religion's place is in the church; secular knowledge and citizenship, not faith and piety, are the work of the school. There is, besides, a significant portion of the population of the United States who believe in God and are devoted to religion and to whom any education not religiously oriented is not the best kind of education for democracy.

Most educators endorse morality and ethical character as worthwhile objectives for American schools. But it is not unusual for them to claim that morality and ethical character can be achieved in school without any help from religion. Although good morals and ethical character are always praised, religion and denominationalism are sometimes labeled as divisive forces in education and democracy.[1]

The argument for religion in education is simple but fundamental: If there is a God, and if He has revealed truth, man's most important life task and education's most fundamental objective is to understand and follow God's truth. In this view, education without religion will not fulfill its most basic responsibility. But there is nothing explicit or implicit here demanding the destruction of the system of public schools. Responsible people do not denounce public education. Those who advocate the essential role of religion in education are not enemies of public education, and they do not favor placing public education under denominational control. To argue that religion is essential to education is not the same as endorsing the doctrine of identification of church and state. All Americans, even those most ardent in their religious affiliations and convictions, would probably oppose any attempt to replace civil officials with ecclesiastical authorities. To advocate religion in education is not part of a sinister plot to turn the civil government over to one denomination or another.

Public education in the United States is committed by law to the principle that denominational doctrines may not be taught as part of the official school program. Public policy, moreover, has moved to the point where neither nondenominational prayers nor Bible reading, without comment, may form any part of a public school program. Despite these recent, but clear, legal interpretations and proscriptions, the problem of religion's place in education remains. To outlaw prayer and Bible reading is a way of avoiding not answering the problem, it is said, yet at this time even those elements of the American public most convinced of the need for closer cooperation between religion and education are not certain of the means to obtain this cooperation and integration. Apart from means, on which there is much disagreement, are there any propositions to which supporters of religion in public education can agree? The following summary may be an adequate representation of these propositions at this time:

1. There is a problem: Religion is needed for a complete education; religious illiteracy is dangerous to men and societies.
2. However religion is brought into the school, by whom and in what form, adequate safeguards must be erected to maintain the separation of church and state. Although there is a general willingness to defend the principle of separation, there is uncertainty about labeling every religious activity a violation of it. Witness, for example, the concern expressed when the New York State practice of prayer in public schools was declared unconstitutional by the United States Supreme Court in 1962.
3. Proponents of closer ties between religion and education do not see the principle of nonsectarianism, initiated in the early nineteenth century, as an attempt to exclude all religious teaching and religious commitment from the schools.
4. Throughout much of modern history the divisive qualities of denominationalism have been accentuated. What is needed to replace archaic denominationalism, it is said, is a common religion of mankind, a creed of humanism or a deistic doctrine with no relationship between God and man. Only relationships between men and codes (a religion) to govern them are recognized. Such views lead naturally to an advocacy of teaching a common core of religious beliefs. Most groups sympathetic to religious education would oppose this. On the same level of unacceptability is the proposal for teaching "moral and spiritual values" totally devoid of religious foundations.
5. There is some anxiety, considering recent court decisions, that opposition to religion, often under the guise of neutrality, or atheism, is protected, whereas theism is excluded from education. Antireligious teaching, it is

pointed out, is as illegal as sectarian teaching, and both should be treated equally and fairly as legal proscriptions.

6. The school, it is agreed, should not become a church; the role of the school in religious education is factual, informational, intellectual, but not devotional. The rituals of denominations should not proceed beyond the steps of the public school.

7. Although the school is not a devotional agency, it must be concerned with moral formation. It should encourage youth to closer contacts with organized religion and an intelligent understanding of religion's place in man's life. It may encourage also zeal and devotion to a religious ideal. In other words, the school is asked to aid the church in the recruitment of members, not in an active or obvious or partisan way but in a way conducive to the development of healthy and sympathetic attitudes toward denominational religion.

To favor religion in public education reflects a basic attitude, a fundamental philosophy of life; to oppose religion in public education does not imply a denunciation of religion, nor is it an expression of religion's inadequacy, but it does establish religion as an entirely private matter barred from a public institution. Those who are committed to keeping education and religion apart—or to keeping religion in its place—argue that by promoting religion, religious controversy is encouraged. The best way to avoid such controversy, such disruptive and divisive forces, is to keep religion and public education at safe distances.

Anyone who has read the history of the past 400 years with any degree of perceptiveness agrees that religious controversy has been an abrasive in social relations; this controversy has invaded political relations; it has involved families and close friends. Who could gainsay the disruptiveness of religious quarreling? So one of the questions raised by opponents of religion in public education is: Whose creed is to be taught? There is no agreement among the various creeds on the doctrine to be taught in the schools, so which set of religious truths takes precedence? Which is to find its way into the schoolroom? Perhaps these conflicts led thoughtful men to nonsectarianism in the first place.

Answers to questions of character formation, this group asserts, are not found in denominational practices or creeds but in a foundational morality independent of denominational beliefs. The Bible, it is claimed, is a book of great moral value; its real value does not, however, depend upon a particular version, and no one should fight for one or another version.[2] But even more basic is the view that the school is the place for supporting moral and spiritual values; the home and the church are the places for inculcating them.

Opposition to religion in education, religion in public education and even in nonpublic schools, may find its origin in an interpretation of American traditions. There is in this tradition, it is claimed, a "wall of separation" between church and state, and this "wall" prevents the teaching of religion under any form in schools supported by public funds. Government is more than neutral in its dealings with religion; in this interpretation it appears to be antagonistic.

The separation of church and state and antagonism to religion are not the only bases for maintaining that education should be separated or shut off from religion. It is also argued that religious freedom means freedom from religion. In a democracy the citizen must go out of his way if he wants religion, religious instruction, or religious education. It would be undemocratic, it is said, to offer religious instruction in public education, because students who take advantage of such curricular offerings would be receiving something from the school which students who do not accept this instruction would not receive.

Despite all the arguments and counterarguments, evidence of recent history shows how public education has tried to fit religious instruction, or religious literacy, into its program. Prayer was permitted as an opening or closing school exercise in some states until the summer of 1962, when in *Engel v. Vitale* (370 U.S. 421) the United States Supreme Court declared the practice unconstitutional. The Bible was read without comment in many states until the summer of 1963, when the United States Supreme Court declared both Bible reading and the recitation of the Lord's Prayer unconstitutional practices (*School District of Abington Township v. Schempp,* 374 U.S. 203).[3] Some public schools offer Bible study. Plans for releasing students from school to attend special classes for religious instruction often receive school support; and special teachers have been invited to give denominational instruction during the school day. In a few communities compromise plans have been developed whereby denominational schools become part of the public school system without losing their distinctive character as denominational schools.

A fuller exploration of the major points touched on in this brief introduction will be made in subsequent sections of this chapter.

RELIGION AND MORALITY IN AMERICAN EDUCATION

Before approaching the issue of religion and morality in American education, it seems necessary to make a distinction between *religious instruction* and *religious education*.

Religious Instruction

By religious instruction is meant the teaching of the principal tenets, doctrines, and beliefs of a denomination; in other words, students receive catechetical instruction. Religious instruction can be given anywhere and at almost any time. The school, of course, is one place, but not the only place, where it may be offered. Further, there may be some reason to doubt that religious teaching of the catechetical type needs to be continued at every level of formal education. After students have learned the principal doctrines of their denomination, it seems unnecessary to continue catechetical instruction.

Religious Education

Religious education is based on fundamental religious doctrines. To deny this would be tantamount to taking the heart out of religious education. But religious education goes beyond instruction in essential denominational beliefs. What are the criteria for religious education? These, perhaps, may be illustrated best by taking one of the levels of the educational ladder and discussing how its education may be distinctively religious or Christian. The level chosen here for purposes of illustration is the college; this level is selected because it is assumed that the reader will be more fully aware of and directly concerned with college experiences, although it is clear that the illustration may be applied without essential changes to elementary and secondary schools as well. What, then, is a religious or a Christian college?

A Christian college, like any college, is a place of higher learning. It is not doing its work unless it imparts higher learning. It is a misconception to conceive the essential purpose of a Christian college to be character training, to be a guardian of youth's intelligence and freedom against materialistic philosophy, to be the education of the whole man, to be a sort of layman's diluted imitation of novitiate or seminary training, to be the formation of Christian charity, to be the formation of Christian social leaders, and so on. Such a statement of objectives sets too big a job before the Christian college and so makes it risk failure in doing the one limited thing that it could and ought to do, or designates as objectives various goals which are incomplete because they are silent about the mental formation of another Christ, or makes indirect results and later lifetime achievements the primary, immediate, specific end which the college is trying to accomplish.

The college, of course, is only one educative force at work on students. Other educators have preceded it. Other educators—formal and informal —are active in stimulating and molding students, in their homes, in their parishes, among their friends, in their leisure hours, in the books and daily papers they read, and in the radio and television programs they are exposed to.

The Christian college is mainly concerned with students' minds. It wants these minds to grow straight, to be exact in fundamental information, clear, inquiring, and orderly, and rich in intelligent Christian convictions and habits. If these minds are Christian minds, there will be a natural —though not necessarily an inevitable—tendency for attitudes, ideals, and virtues to correspond to convictions and wisdom. The college can point the way to its students and give them an opportunity to apply their knowledge; but they can still refuse to go Christ's way in their conduct, even as anti-Christian minds do at times refuse to run on anti-Christian highways. It is only through minds that the Christian or religiously oriented college can aid in moving wills. These wills are free only when they themselves, because they themselves wish it, choose to act in accordance with the principles of right reason and of Christ's teaching.

We have said that it is the primary concern of the Christian college to form minds; and we have emphasized the need, if the college is really Christian, for a formation of the mind in a special way. How can the mind be formed in a special way? To answer, we turn to a discussion of means that the Christian college may adopt. These may be grouped under three main headings:

1. A *Christian climate* in the college. To this everyone in the school— teachers, administrators, and students—can contribute.
2. In particular subjects and courses of instruction, the *Christian viewpoint*.
3. In subjects for which there is no special Christian viewpoint, a *pro-Christian setting* and a *pro-Christian manner of handling*.

It must be emphasized that formal curricular means are not being discussed under the headings listed above. A science is no less a science, nor is its area of knowledge restricted or mutilated, when it is taught in a Christian college. An art in the curriculum, intended to develop human capacities for expression, is neither curtailed nor violated by the Christian frame of reference in which it is presented. The legitimate and necessary content of fields of knowledge remains unaltered when a college adopts these means.

A Christian climate.   The truly Christian climate is one which stresses the supernatural. It is one in which the realities, truths, and values of the supernatural order are made familiar and in which the goods of the order of grace are prized as the best treasuries of man. The ways in which Christian schools may build a supernatural climate are:

1. There is no compromise on distinctively Christian ends or on distinctively Christian means. Compromise here tends to secularize a Christian school.
2. Religion or theology classes are given a central role in the curriculum.
3. The technique of suggestion is used. Totalitarian governments have

shown what results can come from this technique. But the Christian college uses it for the good of its students. What is said, the firmness and sureness with which it is said, what is taken for granted in opinions and judgments, what is praised and blamed—all are reducible to suggestion. In religion and philosophy various truths must be formally explained and proved; in other courses, these proofs may be taken for granted. The teacher mentions them, reasons from them, illustrates by them, freshens students' imaginations and memories in regard to them, and renews and strengthens motivations based on them. Although suggestion does not create genuine convictions, it does create attitudes, predispositions, and renewal of convictions.

4. Using models is another way of creating or contributing to a school's Christian climate. Where the models are persons, they have a singularly strong appeal to students. Teachers are the primary and most evident models for supernatural cultured living.

5. The use of physical things and symbols also contributes to the supernatural climate. Such religious decorations are found in chapels, halls, classrooms, and recreation rooms. In the Catholic school a crucifix symbolizes Christ the Teacher on His Cross, and for the students Christ crucified must be the judge of what takes place in the classroom.

In regard to religious practices, these points seem to be most important for college students: They should be led to understand the character and purpose of the religious exercises in which they share. They should no longer just go to church but should have some insight into the meaning to their lives of the practice of their religion.

The Christian point of view. The Christian point of view is a theological, supernatural, or religious point of view. It accepts the Divine as real, and it accepts the truths, the orders, and the gifts of God. Especially in everything that immediately touches the welfare of persons or of human societies there is an essential theological constituent. There is a theological view of history, of man, and the same theological point of view has its own specific attitude to natural knowledge and natural goods. It accepts the universal presence of God in His creatures, the universal government of God over His creatures, and God's providence over men. The Christian point of view regards the moral aspect of any question as always being relevant.

There is also a special Christian wholeness which gives greater vision and completeness to knowledge. The intelligent Christian cannot know everything—every detail of fact—but he must accept truth from all orders and sources: from right reason, experience, tradition, and faith; from the order of nature and from the realm of grace. He will not have reason without faith, nor faith without reason. His attitude to the natural will be this: (1) All that is natural—reality, knowledge, art, virtue—is good in itself. (2) The natural alone is not enough for the Christian; the supernatural is indispensable for fullness of reality, for fullness of knowledge, for true virtue, for the attainment of the destiny of the person and of society. (3) The supernatural alone is not enough for the Christian. Grace presupposes and perfects nature; it does not wound, destroy, or eliminate it. The two orders, of nature and grace, have mutual implications, exert a mutual effect on man, and interact in man. Grace, or the supernatural, must be emphasized because of its superior importance and its greater value; on it the Christian must primarily rely in accomplishing the main tasks of life. But nature must be emphasized, too, in the Christian's efforts and for practical self-helpfulness and achievements.

The Christian viewpoint challenges everything opposed to Christian first principles. This often puts the Christian at a disadvantage by seeming to make him critical rather than constructive. He cannot agree with most of the *isms* which are current: rationalism, materialism, idealism, pantheism, totalitarianism, mere empiricism, or mere pragmatism. But he must try to oppose these with a constructive view of reality.

Pro-Christian setting and manner of handling topics. If the Christian college is to be a college in the real sense, it follows that natural knowledge must be taught and that such knowledge and the accompanying goodness in the natural order must not be despised. Natural knowledge must be taught in the Christian college, and it must be taught according to its specific nature. Mathematics is mathematics; statistics is statistics; chemistry is chemistry; the force of gravity is the same whether it is holding Christians or pagans on the earth. Although there is no particular place for a Christian attitude on these things and no immediately relevant Christian premise, these subjects must be taught with the same excellence in a Christian college as in a secular college. For example, a Christian engineer must be a good engineer, just as a Christian mother must be a good mother and not just a good woman.

Yet man and his sciences, his arts, his recreations have, when rightly ordered or oriented, a certain leaning to Christianity. There is in the soul of man and in his most natural activities a certain disposition toward the Christian and the supernatural. The Christian college or school can create in its students dispositions favorable to Christianity and exclude, weaken, or eliminate unfavorable conditions.

Antagonism or mere indifference to religious education is often accompanied by the conviction that by using the means given above, the religiously oriented college or school violates or mutilates both art and science. This conviction sometimes extends to the point where students educated in denominationally related schools are regarded as being biased and lacking in objectivity. There is, moreover, an all too common prejudice that religious faith makes scholarship impossible. Anyone who has had a religious education, it is assumed, has somehow forfeited his reason and cannot be a competent or an objective scholar. The pagan and the Christian investigator may not find the same meaning in the facts of nature, but both are able to find the same facts.

Religious education seeks to create the opportunity for students to study the three worlds in which they live—the physical, social, and spiritual—and to apply their knowledge to the critical problems of living. Opposition to religious education usually comes from people who deny the reality of the spiritual world or the possibility of knowing about it. In either case, study of the spiritual world is excluded from the school's curriculum.

Religion and Education in Early American Schools

We have already seen something of the close relationship that existed between religion and education during the formative years of our nation. The colonial schools, for example, were religious in both content and purpose; they were established to serve the ends of institutionalized religion.[4] Where there was an established religion, and this was the case in most of the colonies, the schools taught the doctrines of that religion. That there was an official religion and that this religion was being taught in the schools stimulated few complaints. Neither the period of social and educational transplantation (1635–1750) nor the period of social and educational transition (1750–1820) contained strong movements to divorce religion from education. However, during these same two periods there was a slow but definite trend away from "the establishment of Bible commonwealths, with the maintenance of an ecclesiastical social order firmly buttressed by the civil authority and by a class-structured society."[5] In the seventeenth century every colony in New England, except Rhode Island, supported an established religion, and in Massachusetts especially, but to some extent in all the colonies, the state was only the handmaiden of the church. According to Parrington, the church-state in Massachusetts was an oligarchy of Christian grace:[6]

> The minister was the trained and consecrated interpreter of the divine law, and the magistrate was its trained and consecrated administrator; and both were chosen by free election of the Saints. If unfortunately the Saints were few and the sinners many, was not that a special reason for safeguarding the Ark of the Covenant from the touch of profane hands? Hence all legislative experiments by annually elected deputies, no matter how exactly those experiments might fall in with the wishes of the majority, were sternly frowned upon or skillfully nullified. Not only were such popular enactments, it was held, too often prompted by the carnal desires of the natural man, but they were no better than an insult to God, as implying the insufficiency of the Scriptures to every temporal need. Unregenerate and

sinful men must have no share in God's work. The Saints must not have their hands tied by majority votes. This explains, quite as much as mere love of power, the persistent hostility of the leaders to every democratic tendency. Such institutions as grew up spontaneously out of the necessities of the situation, were sharply hedged about by restrictions. The town meeting, which was extra-legal under the charter, was safeguarded by limiting the right of voting to freemen, except in a few trivial matters; and the more popular deputies, who inclined to become self-willed, were forced to accept the principle of magisterial veto on their actions.

As the years wore on and as the character of the country began to change perceptibly, the practice of the official church in using the state and considering it a mere adjunct was not so generally approved. There were many attempts—some more successful than others—to take from the church and its ministers the power they exercised over civil affairs. The First Amendment to the Constitution of the United States may be considered the most successful and lasting of these attempts. However, the First Amendment —"Congress shall make no law respecting an establishment of religion, or prohibiting the free exercise thereof; or abridging the freedom of speech or of the press; or the right of the people peaceably to assemble, and to petition the government for a redress of grievances"—limited the action of Congress, not the action of the states. In addition, neither the First Amendment nor the Bill of Rights applies, as such, to religion in education, and it can hardly be claimed that this amendment was the culmination of a tradition which erected a wall of separation between religion and education.

The Fourteenth Amendment, proclaimed July 28, 1868, made the Bill of Rights applicable to the states. Section I of the amendment reads as follows:

> All persons born or naturalized in the United States and subject to the jurisdiction thereof, are citizens of the United States and of the State wherein they reside. No State shall make or enforce any law which shall abridge the privileges or immunities of citizens of the United States; nor shall any State deprive any person of life, liberty, or property, without due process of law; nor deny to any person within its jurisdiction the equal protection of the laws.

There is no question that the Fourteenth Amendment applied the First Amendment to the states, but it may be fairly doubted that this application can be understood as evidence of a preconstitutional tradition disassociating public education from religious or denominational influences. It is not easy to see how the framers of the First Amendment could have had insight into the problems of public education, for public education of the nineteenth century was maintained, if at all, only as a vision in the minds of public men of the eighteenth century. But the eighteenth century knew the meaning of "an establishment of religion." The Fourteenth Amendment applied a constitutional principle; it did not create a tradition.

In an effort to reinforce arguments claiming that the First Amendment was intended to outlaw religious teaching in public education, the statements and known views of outstanding public men of the later colonial and early national periods have been given considerable prominence.[7] The leading spokesmen opposing religion in education during these years were Benjamin Franklin and Thomas Jefferson. Franklin had little interest in religion, and he excluded it from the curriculum of his academy. However, many schools modeled on Franklin's academy did have religious instruction, and some attempted to offer a real religious education. Jefferson, although a constant friend of programs and plans to distribute education more widely and generously, was consistent in his opposition to church-sponsored and church-controlled education. He believed that if the general level of education was to be raised, the people would have to be freed from coercion in religious matters; there would be no democracy, he reasoned, without religious freedom. But his proposed reform was intended to establish religious freedom and not to erect an insurmountable barrier between religion and education. His Act for Establishing Religious Freedom was passed by the Virginia Assembly:[8]

> That the impious presumption of legislators and rulers, civil as well as ecclesiastical, who, being themselves fallible and uninspired men, have assumed dominion over the faith of others, setting up their own opinions and modes of thinking as the only true and infallible, and as such endeavoring to impose them on others, hath established and maintained false religions over the greatest part of the world, and through all time; that to compel a man to furnish contributions of money for the propagation of opinions which he disbelieves, is sinful and tyrannical. . . .

Whether the views of Franklin, Jefferson, and others may be taken as representative of the time and whether these views contributed to the formation of a tradition are questions worth considering. However, it should be remarked that for every Franklin and Jefferson making pronouncements against religion as an orthodox creed or religious education as a limitation on democratic freedom there were dozens of public men, perhaps not great historical figures, but influential in their own place and time, who were defending the intimate relationship that existed between religion and education.

Jefferson and Franklin were influential; but as great men their principal imprint was not on their own but a later time. Seldom do we take the personal views of men, however great they may be, as reflecting the attitude of a period or as constituting the origin of a tradition. In our own day the personal views of public men are often unacceptable. If, as a matter of fact, Franklin and Jefferson reflected so clearly the mind of the time, why were religion and education so closely related in their period? Their views, frequently respected and often worthy of respect, represented a minority view; and minority views can hardly be counted as traditions or representative of the general practices of a period.

Evidences of Decline in Religious Control of Education

We have argued that the constitutional and traditional briefs for religion separated from education make something less than a convincing case. It would be unrealistic, however, to take the position that from about 1750 to 1825 denominational control over education was not declining. Academies were relatively popular after 1750, and they emphasized practical curricula; higher education was certainly giving, or was being made to give, more attention to science and secular programs and less to divinity courses.

During their early years colonial colleges offered little other than vocational programs for prospective ministers, but by the third quarter of the eighteenth century attempts were made to abridge the divinity course and expand the curriculum in favor of law and medicine. The historic control that religious denominations had had over education was waning.

That this is true is undebatable, but historical facts do not interpret themselves. Why was the type of educational control which formerly had been so secure now being challenged? The answer is not too difficult. The realization was becoming more and more general that learning was good, desirable, and necessary to the needs of life in America. Learning was no longer thought of as an exclusive privilege of the upper classes—although in practice education was still mainly for the well to do—but was considered to be a birthright. Religious control over education was neither flexible nor imaginative enough to meet the challenges of the new demand for education. Because it could not do so, a different form of control was instituted.

Attempts by civil government to establish a more general educational base were not always successful. Numerous plans, Jefferson's for Virginia being perhaps the best example,[9] were offered for universalizing education. However, the essential motivation behind these plans was not opposition or antagonism to religion. Jefferson proposed his Bill for the More General Diffusion of Knowledge because of the great confidence he had in education's political and social values, not because he opposed religious control over schools. His plan and others were offered because denominational schools and religious control could not perform the task that was considered to be necessary.

To read antagonism toward religion and religious education into attempts made during the national period to organize education for the opportunity of all the people is to read into them something that was not there. Had the movement against religion in education been as general and widespread as it is sometimes believed to have been, it is unlikely that charity, philanthropic, and private-venture schools, most of them denominationally controlled and supported, would have been as popular as they were, especially in the Middle States and in the South.

Higher education, too, needed some reform. The old schools were reluctant to change their ways or to open their curricula to scientific and professional study. In some instances the old colleges—most of them denominationally controlled—lost some of their independence to the states, and with this loss of independence there were additions to the curriculum. But this is clear evidence not of hostility to religion, but of impatience with the conservatism of these colleges and the indifference they were showing for scientific, technical, and professional education.

The influence of realism and the Enlightenment, spread by its champions in Europe and America, became stronger. The colonial colleges were ill-suited to the new emphases and resisted the sciences in their new experimental form in an effort to retain the old tradition that higher education and divinity studies were equivalent. After 1800 the beginning of the state-university movement relaxed some of the pressure on the older denominational colleges to provide scientific instruction, but pressure was continued by the students, and to some extent by the states, until the old colleges capitulated to popular demand rather than have their independence further jeopardized by state intervention and control.

The struggle for the control of higher education was unquestionably real. This struggle is depicted most clearly in the Dartmouth College case,[10] in which the college was victorious, but neither the Dartmouth College controversy nor the general struggle for control over the colleges can be demonstrated to have been a challenge to religious control or religious education in the colleges. The basis for the friction at Dartmouth was political, but in other schools, where political factions did not seek partisan satisfaction by gaining control over the colleges, the issue was curricular: the public wanted a more practical college course of studies.

Public Funds and Church Schools

The contemporary scene contains some evidence that the issue of using public funds for church-related and other nonpublic schools is not settled.

There is often a good deal of acrimony in these debates, and neither side can be completely exonerated when charges of rashness and imprudence are made. However, our concern here is not with present-day activities which either support or oppose public support for nonpublic education. We are concerned with types of educational support during the periods of transplantation (1636–1750), transition (1750–1820), and awakening (1820–1870). It is sometimes maintained that the traditions of American education strongly opposed the use of public money for nonpublic schools. In addition, the claim is often made that the First Amendment to the Federal Constitution was enacted to protect these traditions.

Although every private school may not have received public money, it would seem that practices of support between 1635 and 1870 established some precedent for using public money for nonpublic education. Institutions ranging from private and denominational Latin grammar schools to private and, in their origin, nonsectarian academies were permitted to share in public funds and public land grants. Even after laws were passed prohibiting sectarian teaching in public or common schools, private schools continued to receive, although perhaps not quite so regularly, some support from public funds. In some cases where private educational foundations did not receive such funds, it was not always because they were denominational or nonpublic. For example, a Massachusetts law prohibited academies from receiving public land grants if other schools were operating within a reasonable distance from the academies seeking public aid. The famous Massachusetts Law of 1827 did not prohibit the use of public funds for church-related schools: it forbade the teaching of sectarian doctrines in the common schools of the state.

Although the First Amendment may now mean that public funds cannot be used for nonpublic or church-related schools, it did not convey this meaning to President Ulysses S. Grant, who twice urged the adoption of an amendment to the Federal Constitution which would prohibit the use of public money for church-related or church-sponsored schools. In 1876 this proposed amendment was offered to Congress:

> No state shall make any law respecting the establishment of religion or prohibiting the free exercise thereof; and no money raised by taxation in any state for the support of public schools or derived from any public fund therefor, nor any public lands devoted thereto, shall ever be under the control of any religious sect or denomination, nor shall any money so raised or lands so devoted be divided between religious sects or denominations.
>
> This article shall not vest, enlarge, or diminish legislative power in the Congress.

The proposed amendment was passed by the House of Representatives but failed in the Senate. Although never becoming part of the Constitution, the amendment, even in defeat, was effective in calling attention to a practice long in operation and eventually in forming a large and vocal body of public opinion in opposition to the practice of using tax money for nonpublic schools. It may be argued that the tradition so often referred to by opponents of publicly aided nonpublic education received definite form about 1880 and that it was not at all a clearly enunciated or general policy from the first years of the nation's existence.

NONSECTARIANISM AND TENDENCIES TOWARD SECULARISM

Sectarianism does not present any educational problems for a denominationally homogeneous people. There was, for example, considerable religious uniformity in the American Colonies, and attempts to establish some base for public support for education were not thwarted by the sectarian issue. However, along with the increased demands for education in the nineteenth century, the religious outlook and religious affiliation of large numbers of the population began to change. The spirit of religious liberalisms was strong by 1820, and orthodox religions were required to relinquish preeminent positions of influence and control." In many of the states, nevertheless, orthodoxy continued to claim the schools as special adjuncts of the church.

These attempts by orthodox religions to maintain or retain a hold on education were consistent neither with the spirit of the time nor with the tenor of the new democracy. Men with religiously liberal tendencies were in complete accord on one point: Orthodox control over social and political institutions had to be broken. Agreement was easily reached among the liberal sects when the cause was opposition to orthodoxy, but when orthodoxy was finally stripped of some of its power, this question became important: "Which of the liberal sects shall take its place?" There was little unanimity in answering this question. Although orthodox doctrines were removed from education, what was to take their place?

The liberals were not opposed to religion; they sought it as eagerly as, sometimes more eagerly than, their orthodox brethren. But they could not overlook many fundamental differences among liberal sects, and they refused to give one liberal sect the same position in education which the orthodox had held for so many years. Apparently the only answer possible was the one finally arrived at: Sectarian doctrines shall not be part of the official teachings of any public school. This was far from being a denial of the worth of religious education, and there was a concerted effort on the part of all the sects to keep religion in education, but it was to be some kind of nonsectarian religion.

Proponents of nonsectarianism had no thought of taking religion out of education. They believed morality was best inculcated by religious instruction, and they deemed it proper, even necessary, for the Bible to be read in school. In some states the Bible was read without explanation; in others Bible study was judged to be nonsectarian religious instruction. Yet, however honorable the intentions of the liberals may have been, they failed to see that nonsectarianism is only a short step from secularism. In many cases it led to secularism, and it is not uncommon now to regard nonsectarianism as the origin of secularism.

Although the source of secularism is not clearly nonsectarianism, secularism did gain some hold on American education. Over a period of years educational practices have been followed in public schools which tend to ignore man's relationship to God. These practices, however, are not always approved or followed, and though some legal opinions have emphasized the neutrality of public education in matters of religion, they have not achieved a definitive legal status. Before 1963 some states prohibited while many states required or permitted Bible reading or prayer as part of public education. But these practices were often formulas without appeal or effectiveness.

It is evident that the schools cannot be turned over to any one sect. The recapturing of American public education by sectarianism would not advance the cause either of religion or of education. It is equally evident that secularism will not only limit the effectiveness of education but will weaken the foundations of society.

PLANS TO RETURN RELIGION TO PUBLIC EDUCATION

Prayer in Public Education

Beginning the day's work with prayer has long been a Christian practice. The early schools of America, having as they did a close relationship with organized Christianity, followed the practice of opening and closing the school day with prayer. Much of the content of education in these early schools was moral or religious in nature, and in the nineteenth century, education gained some moral inspiration from *McGuffey's Readers*. But with the establishment of the code of nonsectarianism for public education, most states began to regard prayer when part of a school's program as a violation of law. Prayer in public schools was thereafter an uncommon rather than a common practice. By the early twentieth century even nonsectarian prayers were thought to be out of keeping with the mission of public education.

More recently there have been sporadic and local attempts to reestablish the practice of opening and closing the school day with prayer, but, in general, these attempts cannot be considered to be either religious instruction or religious education. For example, in November, 1951, the New York State Board of Regents proposed that a nonsectarian prayer be recited in all the public schools of the state. Although this proposal met with a fairly favorable reaction from the public, only about 10 per cent of the school districts in New York instituted such a practice. The prayer was simple and short: "Almighty God, we acknowledge our dependence upon Thee, and we beg Thy blessings upon us, our parents, our teachers, and our country," yet in 1962 it was judged unconstitutional. According to the decision, the practice constituted an establishment[11] of religion by government, impermissible under the First Amendment to the Federal Constitution. The immediate reactions to the decision were that the Supreme Court had barred the practice because the prayer in question had been composed by an agency of the state government and in so doing the state was invading the neutral ground of religious conscience. By now, however, there is no mystery about what the Court decided in *Engel v. Vitale:* It excluded official prayers because they constitute official religious practices, not just official prayers, to say nothing of official prayers composed by government officers.

The practice in New York, it should be remarked, left any school district free to adopt or not adopt the prayer plan. Relatively few did, as we have noted above. Pupils in the schools who did not desire to recite the prayer were permitted to remain silent or, if they wished, to be excused from the room. But this freedom of the pupils to pray or not pray did not impress the Court. It regarded official prayers, regardless of their origin or their composers, as violations of the First Amendment.

Study about Religion in Public Education

Since 1930 or earlier, public education has been subjected to some criticism for producing religiously illiterate students. In order to correct this deficiency, the Committee on Religion and Education[12] and the Educational Policies Commission[13] as well as many other interested groups, have suggested that religion and its cultural influences be treated as part of the content of such courses as history, psychology, sociology, economics, philosophy, literature, music, and fine arts. Courses in the history of religion have also been suggested. The content of a course in the history of religion would probably consist of a treatment of the origin, development, and chief doctrines of the major religions of the world. The approach in such courses would not be sectarian. Still, they would provide students with some knowledge of the forces which have played an important role in shaping Western civilization.

It is possible, of course, to go beyond this and teach about religion—

teaching *about* is to be distinguished from teaching *it*—as a legitimate part of secular knowledge. The pupil in such a course would learn about religion, and religions, in a way analogous to the way he learns about politics and nations. But such an approach, although it has won and likely will win considerable support, is not entirely free from danger. In an ideal conception and an ideal execution of the plan, where beliefs, histories, controversies, personalities, and practices are presented within the limits of strict neutrality, important benefits could result. But is ideal execution within the reach of public education? Are teachers available with a thorough knowledge of the various religions enabling them to present fundamental doctrines and practices without favoring one religion or slighting others; is it possible to obtain the kind of objectivity needed? In other words, this hoped-for objectivity, versatility, and neutrality on the part of teachers is a most elusive thing. Values, it could be said, are as important in religious perception as knowledge, and a teacher who does not believe in the Catholic doctrine of Transubstantiation or the Sacrament of Penance could not possibly give an adequate presentation of either, to say nothing at all about a sympathetic treatment.

But if attribution, or teaching about religion, will not do, and many religious spokesmen say it will not, what course of action is open to free us from the dilemma of religion in the schools? Is some teaching about religion, fraught as it is with difficulties and obstacles, not superior to no teaching about religion? For persons who are convinced that the educational process in a democratic country should be able to accord to each citizen, as an integral part of the process, those value foundations most closely congruent to his own conscientious goals, it clearly is not. Basic beliefs are too important to be dealt with lightly; intrusions of prejudice and ignorance are much too likely; religious doctrines which stand upon a foundation of faith cannot be trusted to teachers without knowledge, sympathy, or belief.

Bible Reading and Bible Study in Public Education

In June, 1963, the United States Supreme Court declared Bible reading and recitation of the Lord's Prayer in public schools a violation of the "establishment clause" of the First Amendment. Up to this date the states had followed a variety of practices with respect to Bible reading: Thirteen states required daily reading from the Bible, but proscribed any comment or discussion of what had been read; twenty-five states permitted Bible reading, leaving it up to the local school districts to determine whether or not the Bible would be read in the local schools; eight states, regarding the Bible to be a sectarian document, prohibited Bible reading in the public schools; four states remained silent on the issue. This state action suggests a variety of opinions about the Bible and suggests, too, that the people of eight states felt their schools could provide needed moral teaching without Bible reading.

In the June, 1963, decision, two cases were adjudicated: One involved the law of the Commonwealth of Pennsylvania, requiring "at least ten verses from the Holy Bible shall be read, without comment, at the opening of each public school on each school day. Any child shall be excused from such Bible reading, or attending such Bible reading, upon the written request of his parent or guardian"; the other involved a regulation of the Board of School Commissioners of Baltimore, providing for the holding of opening exercises in the schools of the city consisting primarily of the "reading, without comment, of a chapter in the Holy Bible and/or the use of the Lord's Prayer."

According to the Court, schools following the law, in the instance of Pennsylvania, and the regulation, in the instance of Baltimore, were prescribing exercises as curricular activities for students attending school under the requirements of compulsory attendance, and these exercises were held in school buildings under the direct supervision of teachers employed in the schools. Further, the Court wrote, these opening exercises were and were intended to be religious ceremonies. The Bible, it found, is an instrument with a definite religious, even sectarian, character. In both cases, the Court concluded, the law required religious exercises conducted in direct violation of the rights of the initiators of the suits. These required exercises were in no way mitigated because students could absent themselves on parental request, for in itself this could furnish no defense to a claim of unconstitutionality under the establishment clause.[14]

While the Court clearly struck down the practice of Bible reading in public education in this decision, it left untouched, as it definitely intended to, the curricular practice of Bible study. It even commended this practice along with the study of comparative religion by pointing to the incompleteness of an education not including studies in comparative religion or the history of religion and its relationship to the advancement of civilization. The Bible, the Court wrote, is worthy of study for its literary and historical qualities; its decision was not intended to effect any changes in school programs including study of the Bible or of religion when presented objectively as part of a secular program.

Bible study is, of course, nothing new. It has been part of the school's program for decades, if not for centuries, although it is not now an especially popular curricular offering. But Bible study of the past was not the study endorsed by the Supreme Court for contemporary schools: it was not required to find a secular context into which it could be safely put, or where it could be studied in say the same way as one might study Homer's *Iliad* or Shakespeare's *Hamlet*. It is not easy to see how the Bible could be put in such a context in the first place, or how it could be so placed without doing some violence to its integrity. How can the very foundation of Christianity be studied as a secular book? And if it can, what, then, does it become, and what are the meanings to be derived from it? It is not easy either to appraise or to approve a secular approach to the Bible, nor is it easy to predict the values from such a study.

Compromise Plans

A compromise plan is effected in a community when a church-related school is incorporated into the public school system or becomes the public school for the community but retains its distinctive features as a denominational school. Where state law forbids the teaching of sectarian doctrines in institutions supported by public money, religious instructions are offered either before or after the *legal school day*. Although many communities have adopted compromise plans, these plans, owing to their peculiar, almost extralegal nature, have received little publicity. Usually, too, they are found in communities where religious preferences are relatively homogeneous.

Although there have been, and still are, a number of compromise plans in operation, the best-known attempts at compromise were organized in Lowell, Massachusetts (1831–1852), Poughkeepsie, New York (1873–1898), and Faribault and Stillwater, Minnesota (1891–1893).[15] A summary of the common essentials of each of these plans will not be out of place here:

1. Each of these plans involved an agreement between the local Catholic clergy and the public board of education.
2. The Catholic school building was rented to the board of education for a nominal fee.
3. The building was controlled by the board of education during the school day but reverted to the parish at the end of the school day.
4. Teachers were employed by the board of education with the approval of parochial authorities.
5. Textbooks and other instructional materials were supplied by the board of education.

No provisions were made for selecting students for these Catholic-public schools, but it was probably understood that only Catholic students would attend.

There was little local opposition to these three well-known compromise plans, as there is generally little local opposition to such plans as are now being conducted. However, when they receive publicity, opposition is usually generated on a statewide basis, and the attempts at compromise must be abandoned.

Released Time

Of the several attempts to return religion to education, released time is currently the most popular. Released-time programs are not part of public education. The only relationship that the public school has to religious instruction in a released-time program is this: Students are permitted to attend classes for religious instruction during part of the regular school day. But religious instruction is provided under private rather than public auspices, and neither public funds nor public buildings are used. The sole contribution made by the public school is to release students from school during some part of the regular school day.

A New York law which permits the public schools to release students during school hours, on written request of their parents, so that they may leave the school buildings and grounds and go to religious centers for religious instruction or devotional exercises, was subjected to a constitutional test in *Zorach v. Clauson* before the United States Supreme Court in 1952. The Supreme Court held that the released-time practice which the law permitted did not violate the First Amendment in that it neither prohibited the "free exercise" of religion nor made a law "respecting an establishment of religion" within the meaning of the First Amendment. In its majority opinion the Supreme Court did not mention the "wall of separation" metaphor used in the McCollum decision. It explained instead that the separation of the state from religion must bring about not a relationship that is "hostile, suspicious and . . . unfriendly" but rather one which has been described as a "symbiosis," a biological term meaning the living together in intimate association of two dissimilar organisms.

The accent and emphasis of the Zorach decision are almost totally different from the tone of the McCollum opinion. Writing for the majority, Justice Douglas went so far as to say: "When the state encourages religious instruction . . . it follows the best of our traditions." But while the state may "encourage" religion, it cannot aid it; the government should, however, "sponsor an attitude that lets each religious group flourish." [16]

So-called Released Time

Another plan for returning religion to public education is *so-called* released time. According to this plan, classes in religion are taught for those who elect to attend, by denominational teachers in school buildings during regular school hours. Released time differs from this practice in that, with released time, students actually leave the school, and religious instruction is not given on public property. So-called released-time plans retain students in the school, and teachers representing various religious denominations instruct the students who attend.

So-called released time was the issue in *McCollum v. Board of Educa-*

tion, 1948. In this litigation the Supreme Court of the United States over-ruled the lower courts and held the practice unconstitutional because it violated the First Amendment and was in effect an establishment of religion.[17]

Shared Time

As a formal approach to the problem of religion in education, shared time is relatively new. It dates from around 1961. However, as an informal, *ad hoc* plan for striking some balance between secular and sacred studies and for reducing the financial burden on church-related schools, shared time is a quarter century or more old. It aims at bringing public-private dualism down to an operational level, where institutional cooperation extends into the curriculum: students attend a Catholic parochial school (elementary or secondary) for their courses in religion, English, and social studies—those which have a superior commitment to teaching values—and take courses in mathematics, science, art, mechanical and industrial arts, and home economics in the public school. In other words, the student shares his time between the two schools.

Shared time is now in its experimental stages. Some public education officers welcome it; others, as might be anticipated, are opposed. State laws in many states seem to permit the practice, although constitutional and statutory obstacles may exist in some states. Some nonpublic educators are anxious to extend shared-time experiments and see shared time as the solution to private school (especially financial) problems. But the financial dimension is by no means the sole attractive one: Shared-time plans widely dispersed throughout the country would make Catholic educational facilities available to many Catholic children who cannot use them now. Yet, despite the attractive features to the plan, some Catholic educators are adamantly opposed to it, fearing it spells the demise of a system of Catholic education. Others see difficulties in control, discipline, curriculum, social education, etc., which appear to them to be insurmountable.

At the present time, shared time is in its embryonic stage. What it will become, if anything, remains to be seen. On the operational level, the actual involvement ranges all the way from Catholic schools' teaching religion only—all else being taught in the public school—to an entirely nonscientific curriculum with all of the sciences being taught in public schools. The grade levels where shared time is now most popular are 7 to 9, the junior high school years.

The Child-welfare Doctrine

Although the United States Supreme Court held that so-called released time was unconstitutional in *McCollum v. Board of Education* (1948) and that released time was constitutional in *Zorach v. Clauson* (1952), neither decision disturbed the precedent recognized by the Court in *Everson v. Board of Education* (1947) that legislation is not void if it achieves a public purpose even though in so doing a private end is incidentally aided. In 1930 the Court had unanimously ratified this precedent when it allowed the state of Louisiana to furnish textbooks for children in religious schools.[18] It was affirmed again in the Everson, or the New Jersey bus, case, when the Court declared that the "wall of separation between Church and State" was not breached by a New Jersey law which authorizes district boards of education to pay transportation costs for children attending private non-profit schools. In other words, according to the child-welfare doctrine, the state is obliged to ignore the child's creed, but not his need. And this interpretation permits states to make auxiliary services available to children in public and private schools alike.

In the Everson case the Court declared that New Jersey could not contribute tax-raised funds to the support of any institution which teaches the doctrines and faith of a religious sect. But the Court observed also that according to the First Amendment:[19]

New Jersey cannot hamper its citizens in the free exercise of their own religion. Consequently it cannot exclude individual Catholics, Lutherans, Mohammedans, Baptists, Jews, Methodists, Non-believers, Presbyterians, or the members of any other faith, because of their faith or lack of it, from receiving the benefits of public welfare legislation. While we do not mean to intimate that a state could not provide transportation only to children attending public schools, we must be careful, in protecting the citizens of New Jersey against state-established churches, to be sure that we do not inadvertently prohibit New Jersey from extending its general state law benefits to all of its citizens without regard to their religious belief. . . .

Measured by these standards, we cannot say that the First Amendment prohibits New Jersey from spending tax-raised funds to pay the bus fares of parochial school pupils as a part of the general program under which it pays the fares of pupils attending public and other schools.

The Court noted that with this public aid children are helped in attending church schools. But it points out that the same possibility exists where the state requires a local transit company to provide reduced fares to all children or where a city-owned transportation system carries all school children free of charge. The same principle applies in the case of traffic policemen, fire protection, sewage disposal, public highways, and sidewalks, all of which, to some extent, contribute to nonpublic institutions. Cutting off church schools from these services, so separate and so clearly marked off from a religious function, would make it far more difficult for these schools to operate.[20]

But such is obviously not the purpose of the First Amendment. That Amendment requires the state to be neutral in its relations with groups of religious believers and non-believers; it does not require the state to be their

TABLE 13-1

The Supreme Court and Religious Education

Case	Date	Issue	Decision
Cochran v. Board of Educ., 281 U.S. 370	1930	Constitutionality of Louisiana law permitting the state to supply textbooks for children in private schools	Louisiana law constitutional; state may act to achieve a public good even though in doing so a private end is aided.
Everson v. Board of Educ., 330 U.S. 1	1947	Constitutionality of New Jersey law permitting the use of public money to pay transportation costs for children in non-public schools	Constitutional; the state must ignore the child's creed, but not his need.
McCollum v. Board of Educ., 333 U.S. 203	1948	So-called released time	Permitting the teaching of sectarian religion on public school property during hours set aside for public education is a violation of the First Amendment.
Doremus v. Board of Educ., 342 U.S. 429	1952	Constitutionality of New Jersey law requiring reading from the Old Testament in public schools	The Supreme Court held that the constitutional question could not be decided because appellants had not shown enough direct injury by the law.
Zorach v. Clauson, 343 U.S. 306	1952	Released time	Released-time practice, by which children leave the public school during regular school hours to receive denominational religious instruction, is not a violation of the First Amendment.
Engel v. Vitale 370 U.S. 421	1962	Prayer in public schools	Prayer in any form in public schools is an official part of the curriculum and violates the First Amendment.
School District of Abington Township v. Schempp, 374 U.S. 203	1963	Bible reading in public education	Reading the Bible is a sectarian practice and cannot be accepted as constitutional in public schools.

adversary. State power is no more to be used so as to handicap religions than it is to favor them.

The Court then goes on to point out that the parochial schools which may have profited from the law appear to meet the requirements of New Jersey's educational code, that the state contributes no money to the schools, and that it does not support them. The law, therefore, does no more than provide a general program to help parents get their children, regardless of their religion, safely and expeditiously to and from accredited schools. The decision concludes:[21]

> The First Amendment has erected a wall between church and state. That wall must be kept high and impregnable. We could not approve the slightest breach. New Jersey has not breached it here.

SUMMARY

Although there are differences of opinion as to the place religion should have in American democratic education, everyone is agreed that public schools should not become official representatives of one or another sect or denomination. The problem, then, which faces American education today —religious instruction for children who want it—has really nothing to do with the often-quoted doctrine of separation of church and state. Religion in education need not mean and should not imply an "establishment of religion" in public schools. There is, however, a general and fairly well documented belief that public school students should be given an opportunity to study about religion during regular school hours and that those who elect it should be given instruction in the tenets of the denomination to which they belong. According to this view, there is no reason why public education need accept a kind of neutrality in religious matters which borders on hostility or antagonism.

American traditions do not support practices which make public education secular. The American heritage is one deeply oriented to religion, and America's schools of the seventeenth, eighteenth, and much of the nineteenth century were religious in content and purpose. Although it is easy to find opposition to religious or denominational control over education in the history of education in the United States, this opposition arose primarily from the conviction that ideals of universal education and democratic opportunity could not be achieved with a system of denominationally controlled schools. This conviction notwithstanding, public support for church-related schools was both general and regular down through the first three-quarters of the nineteenth century.

From 1875 onward, proposals have been made for returning religion to public education, and in most cases the proposals have been consistent with the American principle that public education may not be sectarian. The most recent plans proposed or tried to provide religious literacy, at least, in public education have included Bible reading (now illegal), Bible study, released time, and so-called released time.

Auxiliary benefits, for example, the furnishing of textbooks and public transportation, to children in nonpublic, nonprofit schools are tangentially related to the general problem of the role of religion in democratic education. Recent legal interpretations with respect to religious teaching in public education and auxiliary services are summarized in Table 13-1.

QUESTIONS AND EXERCISES

1. Give and discuss the arguments for and against religion in public education.
2. Did your state permit or require either prayer or Bible reading in the public schools? Try to find the laws of your state that pertained to this issue.
3. Are you convinced that the American tradition opposes religion in public education? What do you believe the tradition is?
4. Investigate and report on how some other countries have handled the issue of public support for nonpublic church-related schools.
5. What are auxiliary services? May nonpublic schools or students attending nonpublic schools share in these services?
6. Distinguish between religious instruction and religious education.
7. What is the First Amendment to the United States Constitution? Does the First Amendment prohibit the use of public funds for nonpublic schools?
8. It is sometimes claimed that a school which is not supported by public money does, nevertheless, perform a public service and is, in that sense, a public institution. Comment.

ADDITIONAL READINGS

Aubrey, Edwin E.: *Humanistic Teaching and the Place of Ethical and Religious Values in Higher Education,* University of Pennsylvania Press, Philadelphia, 1959. A study of ethical and religious values in humanistic teaching at the University of Pennsylvania.

Blum, Virgil C.: *Freedom of Choice in Education,* The Macmillan Company, New York, 1958. Read for Father Blum's analysis of freedom of choice in education.

Brickman, William W., and Stanley Lehrer (eds.): *Religion, Government, and Education,* Society for the Advancement of Education, New York, 1961. The editors have compiled a variety of views on the issue of government aid for religious schools.

Buttrick, George A.: *Biblical Thought and the Secular University,* Louisiana State University Press, Baton Rouge, 1960. Assumptions and presumptions related to religious education are reviewed within the contexts of reason and revelation.

Butts, R. Freeman: *The American Tradition in Religion and Education,* Beacon Press, Boston, 1950. The author argues that the traditions in American education are fundamentally opposed both to religious teaching in public schools and to public financial support for nonpublic schools.

Carter, Gerald E.: *The Modern Challenge to Religious Education,* William H. Sadlier, Inc., New York, 1961. Modern techniques and special modern instructional problems in religious education are reviewed.

Committee on Religion and Education: *The Relation of Religion to Public Education: The Basic Principles,* American Council on Education, Washington, D.C., 1947. See pages 19 to 30 for the important conclusions drawn in this study.

Conover, Charles E.: *Moral Education in Family, School, and Church,* The Westminster Press, Philadelphia, 1962. Contemporary moral values are studied for their implications for moral education.

Cully, Iris V.: *The Dynamics of Christian Education,* The Westminster Press, Philadelphia, 1958. The author attempts to develop means for making Christian principles relevant in the lives of young children and to incorporate these principles in curricular materials.

Doescher, Waldemar O.: *The Church College in Today's Culture,* Augsburg Publishing House, Minneapolis, 1963. A statement of the place of Christian education in an age of technology.

Drinan, Robert F.: *Religions, the Courts, and Public Policy,* McGraw-Hill Book Company, New York, 1963. An authoritative study by a priest-lawyer of the role of the courts in forming public policy vis à vis religion and education.

Dunn, W. I.: *What Happened to Religious Education?* The Johns Hopkins Press, Baltimore, 1958. The author documents the decline of religious teaching in public elementary schools from 1776 to 1861.

Educational Policies Commission: *Moral and Spiritual Values in the Public Schools,* National Education Association, Washington, D.C., 1951. A document that recommends including religion and its cultural influences in such courses as history, psychology, sociology, economics, philosophy, literature, music, and fine arts.

Gordis, Robert, et al.: *Religion and the Schools,* The Fund for the Republic, Inc., New York, 1959. The authors are concerned with defining the role of parochial schools in our society and with the place of religion in the nation's public schools.

Hartford, Ellis F.: *Moral Values in Public Education,* Harper & Row, Publishers, Incorporated, New York, 1958. Another look at the position to be accorded moral values in public education.

Hay, C. L.: *The Blind Spot in American Education,* The Macmillan Company, New York, 1950. Religion is the blind spot in American education. The author's views are stimulating.

Healey, Robert M.: *Jefferson on Religion in Public Education,* Yale University Press, New Haven, Conn., 1962. Jefferson's views have often been accepted as prescriptive in the American educational establishment. This would appear to be a definitive study of the positions taken by Jefferson on religion in education.

Henry, Virgil: *The Place of Religion in Public Schools,* Harper & Row, Publishers, Incorporated, New York, 1950. Note especially for the challenges made to religion in education.

McCluskey, Neil G.: *Public Schools and Moral Education,* Columbia University Press, New York, 1958. The author examines the influence of Horace Mann, William T. Harris, and John Dewey on moral and religious elements in public schools.

Niblett, William R.: *Christian Education in a Secular Society,* Oxford University Press, London, 1960. An examination of the influence a Christian teacher may have on adolescents in the intellectual, moral, and spiritual climates of today's world.

O'Neill, James M.: *Religion and Education under the Constitution,* Harper & Row, Publishers, Incorporated, New York, 1949. A critical study of the United States Supreme Court's decision on so-called "released time" (*McCollum v. Board of Education*).

Phenix, Philip H.: *Education and the Common Good,* Harper & Row, Publishers, Incorporated, New York, 1961. The author explores the relationships between moral philosophy and the curriculum.

Russell, Bertrand: *Education of Character,* Philosophical Library, Inc., New York, 1961. This controversial philosopher treats educational goals in the light of modern psychology and concludes that character formation is the mission of early elementary education.

Taylor, Marvin J.: *Religious Education: A Comprehensive Survey,* Abingdon Press, New York, 1960. The principles of religious education are reviewed for their relevance to educational programs, materials, and methods.

Thayer, Vivian T.: *Religion in Public Education,* The Viking Press, Inc., New York, 1947. Another study of the proper role of religion in public education.

chapter 14

The Dilemma of
Democratic Education

What is a dilemma? And how does a dilemma arise in democratic education? A dilemma is a situation involving a choice between equally unsatisfactory alternatives. In American education the dilemma becomes apparent when one recognizes that a choice must be made between *quality* and *quantity*. In other words, education in America cannot avoid deciding whether to design schools' programs suited to the abilities and needs of more intellectually mature and able students or to ignore qualitative differences in ability and educational opportunity and be content with conducting schools geared to the abilities and needs of average and less than average maturity and intelligence.

In countries with dual systems of education—systems which provide one set of schools for the upper classes and another set of schools for the common people—there is no dilemma of quality versus quantity. The issue does not arise because there is no commitment in such systems, as there is in American education, to the principle of equality of educational opportunity, and there is no commitment, as there is in educational organization in the United States, to a single-ladder organization.[1]

In dual systems some children, for any one of a number of reasons, are sent to a school where they are prepared for leadership. Their interests and abilities are developed without any immediate regard for, or without any clear attempt to cultivate, social consciousness. The products of such schools are not necessarily introverts or social isolates, for there is always some opportunity in any human society for the development of one's social nature. But what is the purpose of the schools which these students attend? Their aim is to develop the student as an individual and not primarily as a citizen of society.

Other groups of children, not of high social or economic standing, are

391

sent to schools where they are given little opportunity for cultivating the arts of the mind—thought and expression—but are encouraged to understand their position as members of a social unit. These children are sent to school for the purpose of welding them more securely into their social unit. If they have any talents, there is a tendency to overlook them, for social unity is somehow believed to be inconsistent with individual development. The upper-class children, or the elite, are in the kind of schools they are precisely because they are being encouraged to develop talents and bring forth abilities unrestrained by the limitations a heterogeneous group might impose on them. Their education disposes them to remain outside of, or at least on the fringe of, the large social group.

In such social and educational systems the dilemma of democratic education does not exist, for a dilemma may exist only when there are possibilities for choosing between alternatives. However, in a democratic society, where each individual is respected and valued as a creator of the society in which he lives and at the same time is encouraged to develop his capacities to the fullest degree possible, the dilemma is very definitely present.

Social experiences and the possibilities for social development are as real in school as they are outside of school. Education for democracy implies a development of the social nature of the child even when such an emphasis may hinder or retard the development of individual and perhaps somewhat specialized talents. There is a strong suggestion of *communityism* when social education is accepted as the primary goal of education and toward *individualism* when individual development is accorded a position of pre-eminence. The attempt to secure both communityism and individualism and to achieve both at the same time and in the same educational environment raises the question of quality versus quantity and is another way of stating the dilemma of democratic education.

The dilemma is this: Individualism without a tempering of communityism is unsatisfactory, but how can both be achieved? The student who cultivates his talents with regard only for his own goals and success will often, especially in the democratically organized school, disturb or detract from the opportunities available to other students who are not endowed with equivalent talents. Such educational practices, regardless of any dispositions we may have for endorsing programs which make for excellence in achievement, tend to violate the democratic principle of educational cooperation. On the other hand, students who are prepared solely for membership in the group or for life in society and whose educational opportunities are organized with this objective dominating the educational program are being denied opportunities to separate themselves from group objectives and cultivate their own talents. They are, moreover, being deprived of equality of educational opportunity, and society loses the benefits of contributions which such students might make.

In the United States today the dilemma extends into all schools and serves to create questions of appropriate educational opportunities for three classes of students: the gifted, the above average (bright), and the retarded (slow learners). The breadth of the issues involved in the education of the definitely superior, the bright, and the slow learners makes it impossible to treat all of them fully, but the more important considerations relating to the education of each class should be touched on.

THE EDUCATION OF GIFTED CHILDREN

This part of the general problem can be introduced by pointing to the growth of the American high school, both in the number of its pupils and in the concept and scope of secondary education. Many instructional problems have attended this growth. The number of high schools in the United States has increased approximately ten times and the number of students fourteen times since 1890. The magnitude of the public high school as an institution may be more adequately indicated with the presentation of the following comparison: From 1890 to 1930 the total high school enrollment increased 1,900 per cent, while the total population of the United states increased slightly more than 100 per cent.[2]

This rapid increase in secondary school enrollment has been accompanied by heterogeneity in the school's population. The range of intellectual capacity, for example, is wider, and the number of pupils of lower levels of intelligence in our schools today has increased greatly. Likewise, the range of interests, abilities, aptitudes, and other characteristics has broadened. The result is that secondary education today is faced with problems of adapting methods and materials of instruction, as well as educational objectives, to widely different types of students. These are real problems.

·If we accept the distinctions of normal distribution, we may assume that a small percentage of the schools' population will show unusual ability in general academic work or in some special field, or possibly in both. The experiences of professional educators and laymen tend to support this assumption. During the period when experiments with reorganization were so common, it was felt that special capacities and interests could be cared for better in reorganized schools.[3] This promise, however, has not been uniformly realized. If a child is endowed with a special disposition for the fine or the mechanical arts, attention should be given in school to these interests. If a student has rare qualities for intellectual achievement, it is only reasonable to anticipate great and good things from him. However, he may never be able to attain the educational or intellectual goals for which his native capacity fits him, because informal and formal educational opportunities do not always contain challenges commensurate with his capacities. "A man cannot achieve eminence without possessing a great intellect, but he can possess a great intellect and yet fail to achieve eminence." [4]

Before 1890, American secondary schools were rather highly selective and were expected to give superior students appropriate developmental opportunities. In some foreign countries secondary schools were concerned only with those students who had superior intellectual qualifications. But the ideals and programs of the past are not the ideals and programs of the present. The American elementary and secondary schools are neither class nor select schools; yet, as a group, teachers show much greater concern for the inabilities of the retarded or dull child than they do for the potentialities of the bright student. To the extent that this type of sentimental concern is both dominant and current, the problems surrounding the education of gifted children and gifted children themselves may be ignored, with the result that gifted students cannot expect inspired and challenging educational opportunities.

Democracy in education is sometimes interpreted to mean that all the children of all the people will have educational opportunity and that they may attend schools without regard for those social distinctions which, in some educational systems, are barriers on the ladder of educational progress.[5] If the foregoing interpretation is accurate, democracy in education may be said to rest on the principle of attendance or the availability of schools. Accordingly, if the facilities of schools are not open to all who desire to attend, the school may be labeled undemocratic. In recent years it has been contended that an educational system that does not provide equally for the various needs of a group to be educated is undemocratic. But this claim is usually made from a rigid social context, and it seldom takes into account the student who has special academic interests. Following a philosophy of need, the result has too often been the expansion of school curricula to the extent that many schools have approached the extreme where their identity as academic institutions is very nearly lost.

One may note with some satisfaction the tendency among many educators today to reemphasize the school's intellectual function while maintaining programs for students who have neither the interest nor the ability to follow an academically centered curriculum. Equality of educational opportunity, in the best sense, offers students equal opportunities to achieve in accordance with their capacities.

Perhaps one should argue that democratic education must be concerned as much with the development of talent as with maintaining equal opportunity for all who come to school. The point so often stressed in democratic education is equality of opportunity, and it merits all the attention and support it has received, but while equality of opportunity is being extolled as a solid democratic principle, it is in constant danger of becoming uniform or identical opportunity. Uniformity, of course, is a bitter enemy of and a serious obstacle to the realization of special talent; the school adopting uniformity rather than equality as its guiding policy is an uninteresting place for unusually capable boys and girls. The school should be concerned first with the education of academically talented students when it offers special opportunities in its program, but it should not ignore talented students whose special abilities are in nonacademic areas. Whenever schools have the means, they should offer quality instruction to students with special though nonscholastic talents.[6]

There is nothing undemocratic about utilizing social and human resources for the betterment of society. Certainly no society can afford to ignore individual differences and individual talents. American education became keenly aware of the social values to be defended by intellectual astuteness when the Soviet Union launched its first space vehicle. The scientific community has received rather generous support since then, and scientific education has been examined and reexamined many times since Sputnik I soared into space. Talented students with interests in science have been given exceptionally fine opportunities to pursue their interests, and for many students these opportunities extend well beyond high school years. There is no good reason why one should criticize sponsorship of science, although there is something unfortunate about a great and sensitive nation's being officially oblivious to human talent until challenged by threat of war, and annihilation, but criticism is bound to come unless studies related to other human values, values having a claim to our allegiance at least equal to that of science, begin to receive more generous support. There is much to be said for aiding special talent in science, but there is also much to be said for supporting extraordinary talent and interest in history, literature, and sociology. We are prepared to develop special talents to defend ourselves; is it any less important for us to prepare students of superior ability for social and intellectual leadership? This assertion seems sound from two points of view: First, students have a right to expect developmental opportunities in the school. Second, in the interests of serving the common welfare, schools have an obligation to society to prepare students who possess potentialities and qualities for leadership. If our schools do not prepare the best minds of the country, what institution is going to do so?

In general, it can be maintained, the curriculum and standards of American schools are geared for average students. But American schools of the past decades, in an almost exclusive concern for the average, neglected the exceptionally bright, the above average, and the exceptionally dull students. Students who are above average usually complete their regular schoolwork with little or no effort; because they fulfill minimum requirements, they seldom require the teacher's attention. In some instances, however, potentially superior students may actually be retarded, and this may be true even when they are doing better than average work. Unless the school is able to identify its superior students, they will, in many cases, pass through the school without having attained educational goals commensurate with their native capacities. On the other hand, students who are below average in mental abilities cannot maintain the pace set for the average class; they cannot be expected to fulfill the standards of achievement set for the average at the same rate at which average students fulfill them.

Providing Educational Opportunities for Academically Gifted Students

Teachers' sensitivity to talent is an educational commonplace; for centuries they have recognized the ability of some children to learn more quickly than others, but on the instructional level they have not always responded to what they knew. Provisions for educating gifted students have usually been inadequate. Only in relatively recent years have concerted and persevering efforts been brought to bear on the issue. We are now reacting more intelligently to a longstanding crucial issue. How many children in the schools are truly gifted? How big will be the job of educating these students if schools make a full commitment to special programs for the talented? These questions take on a somewhat different meaning as their contexts are altered. What is more, how much difference does it make in a practical way how many gifted students are in American schools? What is important is how many gifted students are in the local school and what is done for them.

To turn our backs on the problem of the talented student is to effectively deny him the democratic privilege of equality of educational opportunity. The principle is violated as much by giving a superior student opportunities geared to the talents of the average as it is by giving average students opportunities devised for slow learners. Variety of opportunity and distinctiveness in talent must be recognized and related in truly democratic education.

But, of course, before anything can be done for the gifted—the same is true for superior students—we must find them; they must be identified. Today this should not be difficult. Many tests of general and special aptitude are available, and, in addition, we have the valuable testimony, even in the face of relatively unsatisfactory test scores, from the teachers and other persons who have recognized students with unusual ability. Even parents may be helpful, though parents are seldom very objective about the talents of their offspring. Instruments are available, and if they are used, it should not be necessary to defend the school for missing students with talent. But all of this assumes that the search for talented students begins early in the school years: a child who is discovered to be talented when he is in high school was talented in the elementary school and should have been discovered then. There is an ever-present danger for talented students missed on the early rungs of the educational ladder to become retarded by being exposed to the usual curriculum and thus being permanently lost to the company of talented youth.

Once the gifted student has been identified, the goals for his program must be determined. In other words, what kind of person do we want this gifted student to become, and what set of educational objectives will help? A disclaimer should be entered here: The educational objectives for gifted, superior, average, and slow learners do not differ. The curriculum for one of these groups may place greater emphasis on creative effort, critical thinking, or responsibility and have greater confidence in the individual initiative and leadership qualities of its students than other programs, but even when this is done, while programs are being tailored, they are all aimed, or should be aimed, at the same goals.

The important questions, then, are really questions of means: How do we get where we want to go, and what do we use to get there? This is always an important educational question; it assumes added significance where gifted students are concerned.

Several theories have been advanced, many studies have been made, and much experimentation has been undertaken in an attempt to devise suitable programs for the advanced capacities of superior pupils. The plans advanced for the resolution of this most important part of the dilemma of democratic education may be given a fourfold classification: acceleration, enrichment, enlargement, and entertainment.

"Acceleration" is a commonly used term in education. It means students are promoted more rapidly than normal. "Enrichment" provides for essential adjustments in the curriculum. In other words, the course of study designed for superior students has opportunities for greater breadth and depth of development than may be found in the school's regular curricula. Enrichment plans are sometimes called "major work" classes or honors programs. "Enlargement" or independent study means gifted students are challenged to range beyond the regular course of study for library or other individual work or are given special direction or additional work. "Entertainment," in this connection as elsewhere, means recreation and extracurricular activities.

Schools may follow one plan while ignoring others, but more commonly schools today combine two or more plans in an attempt to give gifted students more appropriate opportunities. A combination of these plans, or some of them, may be advisable, for acceleration, for example, without some kind of enrichment is an inadequate approach to improved instructional opportunities for bright children.

In colleges throughout the country special curricula and special programs are being arranged to care for the intellectual needs of the best students. Some of these programs have been in existence for as many as forty years. Elite colleges, often without designated programs for exceptionally able students, announce their entire course as one for academically talented youth. Still others, believing it difficult to manage a special program within the conventional college organization, have created special honors colleges for gifted students. But in general, despite the age of a few programs, college plans for the talented youth are relatively recent in origin. About fifty new honors courses or other special programs have been organized in the nation's colleges each year for the past six years. They range all the way from reciprocal agreements with selected high schools for advanced placement to independent study programs. A brief description of the more common types of programs for the talented is relevant to our discussion here.

1. Advanced Placement: The gifted high school student pursues advanced courses in high school for which he receives college credit, or, in those cases where college credit is not given, he is advanced when he reaches college. In other words, he is anticipating some of the college courses, and may be admitted to the sophomore class.
2. Early Admission: Because they have followed an accelerated high school course and because they are endowed with a high degree of native ability, selected students are admitted to college after 2½, 3, or 3½ years in high school.
3. Independent Study: Students of demonstrated academic ability are freed from some of the requirements of class attendance and are allowed to study at their own pace. They are subjected to examinations and may be required to submit reports or term or research papers, but they enjoy freedom to study to the depth and breadth their capacity and interest dictate.
4. Honors Programs: It is almost impossible to give a valid general description of honors programs because almost every recent program has its own distinctive character. There are science honors programs, arts honors programs, programs beginning with the freshman year in college and others open only to seniors, cooperative honors programs which exploit the resources of several geographically proximate colleges, and honors programs for professional schools of universities. The general idea is clear: Academically talented college students are segregated into special programs from which it is hoped they may more fully utilize the opportunities of the college and perfect their own intellectual capacities.[7]

In the adaptation of curriculum, methods, and materials to the capacities of gifted children, it is important to remember that gifted children differ from other children only in degree. Consequently, many of the principles and practices underlying and contributing to the education of gifted children are basic also to a superior education for average children. Educators and laymen are becoming more and more conscious of the great asset the country has in its superior children. The problem of the superior, and indirectly the dilemma of democratic education, is constantly being studied. Schools are trying to provide for the gifted in a number of ways, but the important thing is not the specific program they have devised but, rather, that they are doing something for the gifted justifiable in terms of outcome.

Once the program for the gifted has been founded, special issues arise, and they seem to arise whether the program for the gifted is in a high school or a college. The first, and probably the most obvious, is the recruitment of a faculty. If the gifted student needs an enriched curriculum, he probably needs enriched teachers, too. But talking about the need for teachers for the talented is easier than finding good ones. On occasion, exceptional teachers refuse to take part in such programs; they find gifted students annoying, disturbing, and unduly taxing, or they may sincerely prefer to deal with average or slow-learning students, believing greater personal satisfaction is possible from teaching such groups. We see the converse of this when poorly qualified teachers—that is, poorly qualified for teaching gifted students—attach prestige to being associated with special programs and clamor for appointments. Staffing programs for the gifted is a difficult administrative problem even when funds for faculty appointments are plentiful, which is an unusual, but happy, circumstance in most high schools and colleges.

Another issue associated with programs for the gifted is evaluation. Is the program achieving its stated purposes? Evaluation of these special programs must be constant and searching. Too much is at stake to allow a poor program to continue unrevised or to permit an excellent program to deteriorate.

Finally, we come to issues surrounding neither organization nor teachers, but the students themselves. Despite our best efforts, they sometimes fail. Why do gifted students fail? There are probably as many reasons for failure as there are gifted students, so one should be cautious rather than positive in supplying answers. There are, nevertheless, some general answers to which we can point and still avoid any charge of dogmatism in an area where so much is obscure. Low motivation is one reason why gifted students fail. The lack of motivation for these students—the whole phenomenon of motivation itself—may be analyzed in the same way as for any student. There are differences only because with gifted persons failure is so much more dramatic. Poor work habits or never having developed good work habits may be another reason. Exceptionally able students have not had to extend themselves when competing with average students. Thus, we can more easily appreciate the significance of lack of study skill and scholastic discipline when they compete for excellence with their peers. The capacity of gifted students is seldom tested in a regular school program, so when they are forced to compete with students equally talented, it is sometimes just too much for them: they are unwilling to expend the necessary effort.

Occasionally, gifted students seek and gain satisfaction and prestige from simply being "brilliant" rather than from pleasure in mastering the knowledge of a particular academic discipline. Coupled with this is the danger that gifted persons have learned to manipulate people, and their experience in doing so allows them to misplace values or misunderstand them. Neither their peers nor their teachers on advanced levels will be easy to manipulate. Finally, too much is often expected from even some gifted students. If parents or others set unrealistic, unattainable goals, failure becomes imminent even for the gifted.

Failure, we must realize, is possible among gifted students, although they are no more prone to failure than anyone else. They may become emotionally disturbed, also, yet experience has shown these assumptions to be false: brilliant students are easily broken down emotionally, highly capable students do not have as good judgment or character as the solid middle group, genius is usually accompanied by eccentricity or even frank mental illness, or neurosis promotes creativity. On the contrary, the need —which all students have—for some guidance and the incidence of emotional disturbance or illness is no greater among the gifted than any other segment of the school population.

SUPERIOR EDUCATION
FOR BRIGHT STUDENTS

Although there is every justification for attempting to plan the right kind of education for gifted children, attention must also be directed to the kind of educational opportunity available for students who in terms of their ability are not gifted (genius or near genius) but are clearly above average. In other words, students who in their maturity and ability rank in the upper one-third of the school population need an educational program which will be meaningful and worthwhile. Perhaps it is for this group more than for the gifted that the dilemma of democratic education is particularly damaging. The above-average student is educated, in most cases, as if he were average or below average, and the pace that is set in learning is too slow to keep him well motivated. His abilities are being sacrificed to the interests of quantity. Quantity in education is, of course, essential to the democratic outlook and the democratic program, for every American child must be given educational opportunity, but quantity here, in the case of the above-average student, is a choice that is wasteful.

It seems unnecessary to pursue the point at any greater length, and much of the discussion given the problem of the education of the gifted applies to the bright child as well. The upper one-third of the student population in elementary schools, high schools, and colleges should be offered superior education. How may this be done without sacrificing the objective of social solidarity which all democratically oriented schools must seek to achieve? Over the years since 1900 it was hoped that the reorganization of the schools and the introduction of junior high schools, senior high schools, and junior colleges would help achieve the desired results. There is little reason to believe now, however, that the hope for greater educational quality will be fulfilled in the reorganized school. It has been suggested that elementary and secondary schools in a community be reserved for special types of students: above-average students would go to school A, average students to school B, and slow learners to school C. This proposed solution to the dilemma, if put into actual operation, might very well solve some of the issues of quality that now plague contemporary education in the United States, but it might serve also to dissolve the strong bonds of social solidarity, cooperation, and citizenship that are so securely formed in the schools as they are at present organized.

Cosmopolitan high schools or differentiated high schools with their wide ranges of curricular offerings are often praised for the good they accomplish in having curricula for all classes of interests and intellectual maturity. But the high school does not come into the picture until students are about fourteen years of age, and for gifted and bright children a great deal of valuable time is already lost: some of these students will never be able to retrieve high motivation and keen intellectual curiosity, and others will have missed fundamental skills and knowledge.

Among the plans, suggested solutions, and constructive criticisms which have been advanced for changing both the traditional and the reorganized schools in an attempt to resolve the dilemma of democratic education, the common characteristic seems to be flexibility in both grading and curricula. This characteristic of flexibility applied to groups was introduced to American education in the Batavia (New York) plan in the early years of the present century. Rather than continuing the rigidly graded system of elementary education, this plan provided for two groups of students for each elementary grade: those making normal progress and those making less than normal progress. If the number of students in the class was fewer than fifty, the teacher was directed to give special attention to the slow learners. If the class was over fifty, an assistant teacher was assigned to work with the slow-learning group. A further development of the idea of flexibility was applied in Cambridge, Massachusetts. The Cambridge plan divided the elementary school program into two parallel courses—one of six, the other of eight years. The two programs maintained identical curricula, but the six-year course was intended for brighter children. Variations of the Cambridge plan have been tested by organizing three elementary courses in which, instead of mastering identical curricula at different rates, the rate is held constant and the curriculum is broadened for the brighter children. The better-known experiments with this varation of the Cambridge plan were in Santa Barbara, California, and Baltimore, Maryland.

A few school systems, like that of Pueblo, Colorado, in 1888, allowed even greater flexibility and permitted each child to proceed at his own rate without regard for his age or grade. But this freedom for the individual child created so many administrative problems that it has been encouraged only infrequently in the twentieth century. Still, this concept of flexibility was adopted, at least partially, in the famous Winnetka plan. In 1919, at Winnetka, Illinois, the elementary school was divided into two parts. One part consisted of achievement units, the other of self-expression and socializing activities. Children were encouraged to progress according to their ability in the achievement units, their progress being limited only by their achievement. In the other part of the program all children participated in the same curricular experiences. Another plan to achieve the same objective of progress in terms of ability and break the lock step in elementary education was developed in Dalton, Massachusetts. According to the Dalton plan, students would enter into contracts with their teachers for a specified amount of work. The plan was to have all students cover the regular curriculum, but each student could do so at a rate which his motivation and ability dictated.

In recent years, ideas and techniques for reintroducing flexibility in the school's program have been given some attention, and a few school systems have developed basic primary or elementary school units wherein the principle of flexibility is accepted. In addition, suggestions have been made to apply this principle throughout the entire educational system. Such a proposal was made by Paul Woodring in his book, *A Fourth of a Nation*.[8] In Woodring's plan the old age-grade relationship—too often thought to be sacred—is discarded. More mature and able students proceed at a pace natural to them. Less mature and less able students (the slow learners) make the kind of progress they are equipped to make.

A brief survey of the employment of flexibility in the elementary grades indicates the refreshing attempts that have been made, and are being made, to relate instruction and ability. Whether the plans mentioned above, which in recent years have received renewed attention, or other plans that have been offered, such as Woodring's, have the answer to the crucial dilemma facing American education remains to be seen. But one of these plans, or some other not yet devised, which incorporates the principles of equality and quality in educational opportunity must one day replace the present organization with its apparent commitment to a downgrading of ability and an upgrading of inability.

THE EDUCATION OF SLOW LEARNERS

The general objectives of education are the same for slow-learning students as they are for average or superior children. It is a fact, of course, that with slow learners not only is the rate of learning decreased but the scope may be sharply restricted and the depth drastically curtailed. With some children, slow learning may be due to a lack of readiness or immaturity rather than actual lack of capacity to learn. Whatever the cause of his retardation, the slow learner is faced with goals of achievement which are usully not realistic when he is placed in competition with average students in a regular classroom. His achievement deficiencies are even more obvious when his performance is compared with students who are above average. For all students in a classroom of which the distinctive feature is heterogeneity there is bound to be some inequity—too slow for the fast, too fast for the slow—and in trying to accommodate one or both extremes, the needs, interests, and abilities of the average are missed.

Standards in the schools are not the point at issue when one considers the slow learner's problems. At least there is no question that the standards are too high, though they may be inappropriate. The issue, rather, is this: how to design an educational program that, in being fully adapted to the students' abilities, will enable them to attain some mental formation, to acquire social habits and attitudes and manual skills, and finally to make a satisfactory adjustment to the home, the community, and the vocational world.

With the schools as now organized, that these goals can be achieved at all satisfactorily may be subject to debate. On the face of it, it would seem that the schools of today, with all their interest in slow learners, are not equipped to give the kind or the quality of education that slow learners really need and, in the interests of the common good, the kind of education they should have.

THE PLACE OF THE TEACHER

It would be too much to expect that teachers alone can resolve the dilemma of quality versus quantity—that with the resources available to them adequate provisions can be made for the education of superior, bright, and slow-learning children, as well as all the other kinds of the atypical who may enter the schools. On the other hand, the place of the teacher—his inspiration, guidance, and understanding of the principal agent in the educational process, the student—is so important that it cannot be neglected. And for the teaching of what we might call exceptional children, teachers need not only special preparation for but also special understanding of the students whom they are to guide, encourage, inspire, and teach.

Before 1940 the opinion was prevalent that teachers of exceptional children should first be prepared for and have actual teaching experiences with normal children. Then with additional specialized preparation they might qualify for their new duties. This opinion is no longer firmly held, although a broad background of teaching experience is always considered to be desirable. Successful teachers of normal children may not want to leave the kind of teaching in which they have achieved success and in which they feel secure. School administrators, moreover, may be reluctant to transfer their most skillful teachers from regular programs. Preparation for teaching some groups of exceptional children (mentally or physically handicapped, for example) may consist in two or more years of specialized college study, and to add this time to the regular teacher-education program plus a number of years of teaching experience with normal children may discourage rather than encourage interested and qualified people. Finally, successful teachers of regular classes do not always experience similar success in special programs. For these reasons especially, the tendency is now to accept candidates for teaching exceptional children on the basis of their general and specialized preparation in teacher-education programs.

There are more than 150 colleges and universities in the United States which offer some program or course to acquaint prospective teachers with the general field of the education of exceptional children. About half these schools have at least one program in which prospective teachers may specialize in some phase of this type of special education. With the more general awareness that now prevails concerning the whole issue of the education of the exceptional, new and attractive opportunities are opening for qualified teachers. Specialization for teaching in this area is a choice many candidates for teaching may be encouraged to make. The satisfaction a teacher may find in seeing gifted students develop in knowledge and understanding or in sharing the slow learner's sense of accomplishment as he masters the solution to a problem may equal or exceed satisfactions to be gained in dealing with regular classes. But these are decisions to be made by prospective teachers after they have explored their interests and assessed their qualifications. In general, the personal qualities believed to be necessary for success in the teaching of exceptional children are no different from those necessary for success in regular classroom teaching.

SUMMARY

The present system of American education developed largely by accident; it resulted from the extension of free public education in common schools up through the high school and the college. The purposes of the common school were citizenship and the welding together of society into a democratic and cooperating whole. When other levels were added to public education—the high schools and public colleges—the purposes of the common school were transferred to them. Public education, whether in the elementary school, the high school, or the college, was too often conceived to be a political, social, or vocational excursion and not one in which a certain kind of intellectual formation might be considered essential. Although this philosophy of public education always caused some difficulty for men who were alert to and concerned with the utilization of America's most precious resource—intellectually talented youth—the problem did not become acute while half and more of the secondary school students of the country attended private academies and high schools and more than 80 per cent of the college students were in private colleges. But as public education attained a completely commanding position, the problem did become acute, and more problems were added. All these problems may be summarized as follows: How are American schools at all levels going to offer educational experiences of high quality while they are committed to the education of all the people? By high-quality education we mean appropriate opportunities for the gifted, bright, average, and slow-learning. In the absence of any clear resolution of the various phases of democracy's educational dilemma, the contribution that qualified, effective, and dedicated teachers can make, especially with exceptional children, must be emphasized.

QUESTIONS AND EXERCISES

1. What is the dilemma of democratic education? Express it in your own words.
2. Why is the dilemma not found where dualism in education is practiced?
3. It is sometimes claimed that the retarded child should be given first consideration in special educational programs. Do you agree that the retarded or slow-learning child should be given preference over superior children or bright children?
4. Summarize the issues involved in the education of gifted children. How would you organize education to accommodate the gifted?
5. Make a list of the opportunities for teachers in special education or the education of exceptional children.
6. How is it possible to maintain that slow learners have the same general objectives in education as the bright or the average?
7. Analyze Paul Woodring's plan for reorganizing American schools. How would present school organization have to be modified to establish this plan?
8. In your reading try to find other plans that are intended to resolve democratic education's dilemma. Report on these plans.

ADDITIONAL READINGS

Baker, Harry J.: *Introduction to Exceptional Children,* The Macmillan Company, New York, 1959. A basic book for understanding the qualities and needs of exceptional children.

Bowers, J. E., et al.: *Exceptional Children in Home, School and Community,* Dent & Sons, Ltd., Publishers, London, 1960. The care and training of exceptional children is especially important during their formative years in the home. See particularly the chapters treating of the exceptional child in the home.

Cleugh, M. F.: *Teaching the Slow Learner in the Secondary School,* Methuen & Co., Ltd., 1961. An excellent treatment of the student who is too often neglected in today's secondary school programs.

———: *Teaching the Slow Learner in the Special School,* Philosophical Library, Inc., New York, 1961. This volume touches day schools and other special schools concerned with the teaching of slow learners.

Copley, F. O.: *The American High School and the Talented Student,* The University of Michigan Press, Ann Arbor, 1961. The author examines educational issues surrounding academically talented students and offers suggestions on inaugurating and sustaining advanced-placement programs.

Cruickshank, William, and Orville Johnson: *Education of Exceptional Children and Youth,* Prentice-Hall, Inc., Englewood Cliffs, N.J., 1959. An anthology of literature on the education of a typical youth.

DeHaan, R. F., and R. J. Havighurst: *Educating Gifted Children,* The University of Chicago Press, Chicago, 1961. The book was written to stimulate and guide interested persons toward improving the scope and adequacy of the education of gifted children.

Endicott, F. S.: *Guiding Superior and Talented High School Students,* Lund Press, Inc., Minneapolis, 1961. Contains suggestions for developing a guidance program for talented children.

Fleege, U. H.: *Educating the Gifted,* DePaul University Press, Chicago, 1959. An anthology of studies on the teaching of gifted youth.

Fliegler, L. A.: *Curriculum Planning for the Gifted,* Prentice-Hall, Inc., Englewood Cliffs, N.J., 1961. The theme of the volume is to settle the issue: What shall the gifted be taught?

Freehill, M. F.: *Gifted Children,* The Macmillan Company, New York, 1961. A survey of psychology and education in relation to gifted children.

Garrison, K. C.: *Psychology of Exceptional Children,* The Ronald Press Company, New York, 1959. An introduction to the field of exceptional and physically handicapped children and a survey of the problems of, and desirable attitudes toward, educational retardation.

Getzels, Jacob W., and Philip W. Jackson, *Creativity and Intelligence,* John Wiley & Sons, Inc., New York, 1962. A fascinating study of the origins of creativity and the correlation between high intelligence and creativity.

Johnson, G. Orville: *Educating Slow Learners,* Prentice-Hall, Inc., Englewood Cliffs, N.J., 1963. A broad approach to the problems surrounding the education of slow learners.

Kephart, N. C.: *The Slow Learner in the Classroom,* Charles E. Merrill Books, Inc., Columbus, Ohio, 1960. A book containing many important ideas on the day-to-day teaching of slow learners.

Magery, James F., and John R. Eichorn: *The Exceptional Child,* Holt, Rinehart and Winston, Inc., New York, 1960. A collection of statements on the exceptional child and his educational requirements.

Magnifico, L. S.: *Education for the Exceptional Child,* Longmans, Green & Co., Inc., New York, 1958. Contains an educational program for exceptional children.

Paschal, Elizabeth: *Encouraging the Excellent,* Fund for the Advancement of Education, New York, 1960. A survey of educational programs for talented students.

Riessman, Frank: *The Culturally Deprived Child,* Harper & Row, Publishers, Incorporated, New York, 1962. A pioneer study of the underprivileged, containing imaginative proposals for bringing about more effective adjustment in their education and life.

Sumption, M. R., and E. M. Luecking: *Education of the Gifted,* The Ronald Press Company, New York, 1960. See chapters 1 to 3.

Tannenbaum, A. J.: *Adolescent Attitudes toward Academic Brilliance,* Bureau of Publications, Teachers College, Columbia University, New York, 1962. Contains the results of a study investigating the effect of mental superiority on social status.

Tansley, A. E., and R. Guillinford: *Education of Slow Learning Children,* Routledge & Kegan Paul, Ltd., London, 1960. The aims, principles, and organization of special programs are reviewed.

Torrance, E. P.: *Guiding Creative Talent,* Prentice-Hall, Inc., Englewood Cliffs, N.J., 1962. The book is designed to help counselors guide children with wide ranges of creative talent at all age and educational levels.

Ward, V. S.: *Educating the Gifted,* Charles E. Merrill Books, Inc., Columbus, Ohio, 1961. The author develops a systematic theory of differential educational experiences for gifted students.

Woodring, Paul: *A Fourth of a Nation,* McGraw-Hill Book Company, New York, 1957. See especially chapter 4, "Toward a New Synthesis."

chapter 15

Liberal and General Education

Throughout the history of education men have wondered whether education should fit them for the daily tasks of living or whether it should be concerned primarily with their activities in their leisure time. The choice of emphasis in different historical periods has depended essentially on men's needs or on the needs of those who were offered the advantages of education. Thus, in periods in which human goals were centered in economic and political security, education tended to be ordered by the principle of utility. Francis Bacon (1561–1626) in characterizing knowledge as power emphasized for succeeding generations the usefulness of learning. With it men could control their environment more effectively. And knowledge that had no apparent or immediate relevance for promoting this end was labeled wasteful. But another tradition both preceded and accompanied the doctrine of utility. In class-structured societies the class that had little or no need for preparation in the practical pursuits of life received an education that was oriented toward culture and manners; rather than being based on the doctrine of utility, this education was based on the doctrine of courtesy. One kind of education, therefore, was considered to be appropriate for that part of society which was already in a position to enjoy leisure; the other part of society was educated or trained for work.

Yet, with an apparent dichotomy between education in "manners and morals" and vocational education, the former was often valued more highly. It was not at all uncommon, then, when nations began to take the first steps in distributing education more generously to a larger percentage of their citizens, for cultural objectives in education to take precedence over citizenship, making a living, and family responsibilities. Because liberal education had been associated with the kind of education appropriate for the Athenian free man and citizen, and generally throughout history with a leisure class, liberal education was unfortunately identified with ornamentation. Whether owing simply to inertia or to design, both the identification and the type prevailed as acceptable educational currency.

A philosopher and educational theorist such as Herbert Spencer (1820–1903) could point to the deficiencies of education in his own day. It was a time when advocates of liberal education were more interested in the ornamental than the useful, when knowledge capable of contributing to personal comfort and happiness was set aside in favor of acquirements bringing praise or glory. According to Spencer these topsy-turvy attitudes on education had roots in the schools of Greek antiquity where knowledge bearing little on action was prominent, whereas knowledge relevant to real life was either ignored or given a subordinate place. English secondary schools and universities, he wrote, were guilty of the same errors, and were engaged in the same fraudulent practices. They regularly defended their curricular preoccupation with Latin language and literature, but they could never point to more than a few students who made any use of these studies in the actual commerce of life. If any of this so-called liberal knowledge was used in later life, it was for effect, for ornamental purposes having nothing whatever to do with the really important questions of life. The attachment to classical education—for Spencer synonymous with liberal education—was based neither on insight, illumination, nor mental acumen but on blinded public opinion. The case was analogous, Spencer said, to fashion, where conventions preserve out-of-date dress uncomplimentary to thinking men. Latin and Greek find their way into education and stay, Spencer argued, not because they have any intrinsic value but because boys feel disgraced to be ignorant of them. With such an attitude toward liberal education, as he understood it and as it often was, the only course open was to reject it.[1]

In rejecting liberal studies as being nothing more than mere ornamentation, Spencer was reflecting educational views which grew out of the intellectual and scientific revolutions of the sixteenth and seventeenth centuries. In addition, he was underlining the association that liberal education had long had with a social elite; in this way he prefigured the distrust that democratic education developed for so-called liberal studies. Whether Spencer and others who opposed liberal education as they knew it would have opposed liberal education if its scope had been broader and its ideals higher—as they should have been—is difficult to say. The point is, however, that liberal education in its nineteenth-century form was not accepted by scientifically minded educational theorists. The answer to the question "What knowledge is of most worth?" was given in a utilitarian context. "Scientifically useful knowledge, never liberal knowledge," was the answer.

The narrowness of liberal education was directly a responsibility of educational theorists and practitioners of the Renaissance. With few exceptions, the revived classical theories—concerned with educating laymen for citizenship—fell far short of that promise and instead educated gentlemen for the kind of life their social positions warranted. If not an actual mutilation of the classical concept of liberal education, this was at least an acceptance of the Platonic attitude that utilitarian training has nothing to do with education in its essential sense. Our conventional wisdom would uphold knowledge as being both powerful and good; dedicated defenders of liberal learning would establish priorities: before knowledge is powerful it is good. Even though the liberal may be good in and of itself—it is learning completed in itself and needs nothing outside itself—and worth seeking, nothing in general can be said about its meritoriousness. Plato's quick dismissal of the illiberal from the realm of education could not have made friends for liberal education, for, it is easy to see, useful knowledge may at times be more important than liberal knowledge. Newman's example is a good one: He alludes to the student who, having studied medicine, is able to set broken bones, and compares this illiberal knowledge with knowledge or skill in fox hunting, which is liberal. Which has greater worth? Plato, intent upon keeping the vulgar and the unreasonable out of education, became righteous and exclusive.[2]

Plato's educational ideas were not representative of classical practices. Although they were basic to the Renaissance conception of liberal studies, Plato's notions of liberal education were too narrow for the fourth century B.C. because they were too exclusive in their concern for the education of an elite. Aristotle's views on education were broader; and had they formed the seeds from which modern liberal education grew, the dichotomy between the liberal and the illiberal would not have been so sharp and the distrust of liberal education would not have been so great.

Aristotle approved teaching the necessary useful arts as a regular part of formal and informal education while withholding approval from teaching all useful arts—far fewer in his day than in ours—for such teaching he feared would render persons vulgar who participated in it. Any task was deemed vulgar if it restricted the body or the mind or made them impotent to attain the employments and actions of virtue. Tasks were not alone capable of inducing such servility: the liberal sciences, too, if they were pursued too far—perhaps to the point of specialization—could generate a vulgar manner. In this view of liberal learning, Aristotle injects a novel note. He calls attention to the motive of the learner, the object a person has in mind when he undertakes a study. One action or study undertaken by a person because of an intellectual or moral drive may be liberal; the same action or study pursued by another person for purposes of gain or fame could be judged menial or servile. It is, at any rate, action unbefitting a free man. Wrestling, for example, a highly prized skill in the classical world, might, if practiced for skill and enjoyment, be a liberal activity. If, however, this athletic skill were perfected not for itself but to defeat opponents in the prize ring, it would then be a servile action inconsistent with ideals of liberal citizens. The same could be said for singing, flute playing, or dancing, all honored skills among Aristotle's fellow citizens.[3]

Expressing a theory is easier than accomplishing its practical objectives. On the long road between the ancient and the modern world many worthwhile and many worthless interpretations came to attach themselves to liberal learning. But the history of liberal learning is not part of our object here. We touch on it only to alert the reader to the impressive traditions standing behind it. For our purposes we can pick up the threads of its history in the early nineteenth century.

Despite its emphasis on utility and science, the nineteenth century did see some value in forming and disciplining the mind. In other words, though it was regarded as being far too narrow, liberal education did have some useful purposes. And these useful purposes were incorporated in a reconstructed view of liberal education which was described best by Thomas Henry Huxley (1825–1895): [4]

> That man, I think, has had a liberal education who has been so trained in youth that his body is the ready servant of his will, and does with ease and pleasure all the work that, as a mechanism, it is capable of; whose intellect is a clear, cold, logic engine, with all its parts of equal strength, and in smooth working order; ready, like a steam engine, to be turned to any kind of work, and spin the gossamers as well as forge the anchors of the truths of nature, and of the laws of her operations; one who, no stunted ascetic, is full of life and fire, but whose passions are trained to come to heel by a vigorous will, whether of Nature or of art, to hate all vileness and to respect others as himself. Such an one, and no other, I conceive, has had a liberal education; for he is, as completely as man can be, in harmony with Nature.

A naturalistic emphasis, evident in Huxley, began to turn the content of liberal education away from the classics and toward science; and with this emphasis the purpose of liberal education, for some, came to be a harmonious adjustment to nature. Freeing and forming a man, making him more fully human, were replaced as liberal objectives; machinelike efficiency and responsiveness to nature's laws were substituted for linguistic ideals. Although the arguments for liberal education were generally isolated and ineffective, mainly because they were committed to the theory of mental discipline,[5] the nineteenth century did produce a clear and forcible interpretation of liberal education intimately related to a complete philosophy of education. This interpretation was made by Cardinal Newman (1801–1890) in his widely quoted and generally respected *The Idea of a University*.

However, neither the preciseness nor the conciseness of Newman's ideas made them more acceptable, although through his writings liberal education was more clearly understood.[6] Intellectual excellence—Newman's end for liberal education—became suspect because too many people believed that this was an aristocratic notion. In America, therefore, liberal education was vulnerable and was judged to be out of keeping with the social, economic, and political principles of democracy. Besides, in the late nineteenth and early twentieth centuries John Dewey's writings proposed and popularized a new conception of mind: Intellectual excellence, in itself, was meaningless. The mind was not something that could be disciplined and cultivated, for, like all of man, it was ever growing, experiencing, and evolving.[7] Dewey, however, did not reject liberal education outright; he redefined it so that all learning, without regard for the traditional distinctions of servile and liberal, became liberal.

Dewey's educational views were timely: their widespread acceptance was due undoubtedly to the intellectual climate of the day as well as to the promise they seemed to contain, not only for higher-quality education, but also for a better society and a higher life. But Dewey's Darwinian conception of liberal education, though it may have had an element of effectiveness in it for the first thirty years of the twentieth century, seems to fall short of the challenges implicit in mid-twentieth-century America. Social and economic changes have renewed the need for a kind of education that, while furnishing students with indispensable vocational and professional skills, will lay a foundation for continued participation in the intellectual life—for knowledge is man's first object after he provides for his physical needs, and contemplation is the highest of human acts. The old, and to some extent valid, objection that liberal education was concerned with a preconceived aristocracy and therefore dealt with "a class to be educated" may no longer have much merit: today's liberal education must be directed to everyone, and its immediate, though surely not its ultimate, purpose must be to prepare men in order that they may reap intellectual benefits from the many hours of leisure which industrial technology has assured them in the world of today and tomorrow. All of technology, but principally automation, has relieved or will relieve the citizen of today and tomorrow from many menial and servile tasks. The chief challenge facing American education is to provide educational opportunities which will free man intellectually, as the machine has freed him physically. This important work must be done in programs of liberal and general education.

Liberal Education for Today and Tomorrow

The term "liberal" employed in connection with education was first used in Athens about five centuries before the birth of Christ. There the term denoted not the studies which students pursued but the position they held in society. Only free men could study in Athenian schools, and the education or learning pursued there was thus called liberal. This interpretation of liberal studies obtained throughout the ancient world; it was common in Rome after Greek influence became pronounced, and it continued into the medieval and modern world of life and letters.

In time, however, rather than denoting political freedom, liberal studies came to be accepted as those studies or that education proper to the ruling or the leisure class. But liberal studies need not be associated with class education, and in a democratic society they must not be. In the best sense, liberal education is not the free-man idea of the Greeks—not at least in any political or physical understanding of freedom—nor is it the "class to be educated" concept. Liberal education is "education directed toward wisdom, centered on the humanities, aiming to develop in people the capacity to think correctly and to enjoy truth and beauty." [8] This is education for freedom, or liberal education. It is the kind of education to which everyone is entitled regardless of the special kind of training or skill that particular vocations may require.

Liberal education considered in the light of contemporary human needs retains its traditional affinity for things of the mind. It is concerned with the formation of men—their humanness—and not principally with the practical requirements of making a living or even with laying a foundation upon which vocational or professional training may rest.

In the accepting of liberal education as a basic rather than a preparatory study, there is no necessary or unavoidable commitment to those disciplines or studies which, in the past, were conceived to be the only avenue to intellectual awakening. Nor is there any reason to believe that an education which makes liberal learning a primary aim must isolate itself from that kind of knowledge which is essential to life in society, citizenship, and making a living. The effectiveness of liberal education may depend upon the degree of association that schools are able to effect between a primary aim that is liberal and secondary aims that are appropriate to technical, professional, preprofessional, or vocational study. It is not a matter of saying that liberal studies must depend for their content on the Latin and Greek classics; it is not even necessary to concede that liberal education needs Latin or Greek at all. Latin and Greek, once widely used as languages of learning, were undoubtedly indispensable tools of education and vehicles for scholarly communication at one time, but it would be hard indeed to show why a man today could not be liberally educated without these classical tools. On the other hand, it would be hard to show how a man today could be liberally educated without some broadening of the humanities and the liberal arts to include the knowledge produced through the investigations of modern science.

The classic statement pertaining to liberal education was made by John Henry Cardinal Newman in connection with the launching of the Catholic University of Ireland in 1851. Newman's purpose was to lay a philosophical foundation upon which could be built the university he was to head. The laying of this foundation was begun in a series of lectures delivered by Newman to persons interested in the welfare of the university venture, and in these lectures we find the initial expressions of Newman's ideas on liberal learning. The lectures were by no means definitive: Newman worked and reworked his ideas and cultivated his phraseology for a period of over twenty years. In 1873 the refined and highly polished—perhaps we could say the definitive—version of *The Idea of a University* appeared. It has always been highly regarded as a careful statement worthy of universal respect; its prescriptions have not always been applied to university education even by those educators who assert their right to be classed in the tradition of Newman, and who applaud and approve his philosophical statements about education.

The Idea of a University consists of nine discourses (or chapters): The first is introductory, and in it Newman discusses his reasons for considering the subject of university education at all; the second undertakes an exposition and defense of theology as a branch of knowledge, a position Newman wanted to make very clear. Discourses 3 and 4 are concerned with the relationship theological knowledge has to other kinds of knowledge and the bearing other kinds of knowledge may have on theology. In discourse 5 we find Newman's essential views on liberal education. The discourse is entitled "Knowledge Its Own End." Discourses 6 to 9 deal, respectively, with knowledge viewed in relation to learning, to professional skill, and to religious duty, and the duties of the Church toward knowledge.

Although one must be especially careful in taking into account only part of a work having such essential unity, our principal interest at this point is in discourse 5: "Knowledge Its Own End," for it is in this section of the book that Newman handles the issue of liberal education. But to preserve the internal integrity of the work, it may be well to present the major theses underlying Newman's thought. These theses, it would seem, are the integrating features; they were the principal positions Newman tried to elucidate. In the first place, Newman wanted to clarify the place of theological knowledge in an institution of higher learning. He argued that a university—a school concerned with universal knowledge—could not be what it professed to be unless it included complete theological study in its curriculum. The second thesis, one which has troubled many directors of Christian colleges, one which, as a matter of fact, was something of a source of discontent and imprecision in the early years of Christian education, may be understood as an assertion that the purpose of the university is neither to inculcate virtue nor to prepare for a vocation, but to train the mind. The university is not a place, Newman never tired of saying, where men come to be made good. This, at least, is not the principal object of a university, although surely it will not be a good social institution if it tries to pervert them. And it is not a place with a primary interest in making men skillful in one of multiple trades, skills, or professions. Its purpose is to make minds: to train and help perfect them. At first blush, it might seem, this thesis would need some defending, for, if for no other reason, so many people to whom Newman was addressing himself believed the principal business of church-related higher education to be forming good Catholics. Newman did not have to be a mind reader to know this, so for his third thesis he affirms that the values served by mental formation are not absolute; they are not the ultimate objectives of education broadly conceived, nor are they to be equated with the ultimate goal of life, but they are good in themselves. The highly trained mind may not win in competition with the good will, but this does not underrate the trained mind as a worthy value in itself. Finally, Newman assumes, one of the major worths of university education, properly conceived, is the formation of a philosophical temper, an attitude toward man and the world that cannot avoid being of great service to society.

At this point the student of Newman may be entitled to wonder whether this liberally formed mind, this liberally educated man, is, after all, using his knowledge or his disposition? Can it really be said, and defended, as Veblen and others have done,[9] that liberal learning is useless learning? Is Newman taking the position that whatever is learned and whatever arts of mind are developed in the liberally oriented course may never be used for any purpose outside of themselves? This is not what Newman said. What he did claim, however, was that knowledge gained out of liberal motives might lose its distinctive character as liberal knowledge by having its end divided from itself. Knowledge said to be liberal might cease to be liberal by being applied, but to make any value judgment on the basis of this transformation is absurd. On the level of merit, the illiberal or servile may be greater than the liberal.

It would be easy to continue an exploration of the more general themes expressed by Newman apropos of university education, but we must guard against being led away from our principal purpose which is to investigate the meaning, or meanings, of liberal education. According to Newman, the university was to be a universal seat of learning, a community of scholars—students and teachers—in which there would be ample opportunity for students to immerse themselves in the pure and clear atmosphere of thought. In this environment, though no student would be able to study everything, an intellectual tradition would be perpetuated which would serve as a guide and an inspiration for all students. In this university atmosphere the student could apprehend the great outlines of knowledge and come to understand the principles on which it rests. All of this would lead, or could lead, to habits of mind—something Newman liked to call the philosophic habit—of which the principal features were freedom, equitableness, calmness, moderation, and wisdom. This is what Newman meant by a liberal education, and, in broad outline, this is the general means for achieving it. It is another question, one which Newman could ask, and answer: What is the use of it?

The answer was: Knowledge can be its own end. Newman believed, and many readers agree, that he succeeded in proving liberal knowledge had a tangible, real, and sufficient end. He was quick to add, however, that the end could never be divided from liberal knowledge itself. In other words, knowledge is capable of being its own end, for such is the constitution of the human mind, and any kind of knowledge is capable of being its own reward. At this point Newman does not go into the matter of the worth of liberal acquirements, but he does maintain, and later demonstrates, that liberal knowledge is an object of its own nature, really and undeniably good, that it has been the compensation for a great deal of thought in the compassing and a great deal of trouble in the attaining. Nowhere, however, does Newman deny to philosophy, science, or liberal knowledge, when impregnated by reason, an end external to itself. It is possible for this kind of knowledge to be an instrument as well as an end; but before it is an instrument, it is good.[10]

Modern liberal education—the kind defined by Newman—is not concerned primarily with preserving the past. It is, in fact, concerned with the past, as such, only as the record of the past may help to guide man and illuminate the issues and the problems of life today. Nor is it concerned with creating an exclusive abode in which some men and some women may live out their lives without ever facing present-day realities. Although George R. Geiger's criticisms of what he calls traditional liberal education may still be applicable to some interpretations of the objectives and content of liberal education—that the traditionalist "would prepare the adolescent by steeping him in historical materials of classic dimensions, and in the grand style, and then turn him loose, as an adult, on modern problems" [11] —it cannot be applied validly to the view of liberal education presented above.

Education for freedom must be an objective of all democratic education, and all education must be liberally oriented if it is to meet the contemporary needs of democratic life in a democratic society. In high schools and colleges basic liberal education should occupy a primary position; elementary schools and higher education must at the very least be friendly or sympathetic to the purposes of liberal formation. But liberal education today need not be and probably cannot be confined to schools, at least not to the schools that make up the conventional three-step educational ladder. Promising possibilities for liberal education seem to lie in the opportunities men and women have to continue their intellectual growth after their formal schooling has been completed. Liberal education's relationship to leisure, then, is still evident, although it is not the same kind of relationship cultivated in previous eras. In the first place, by being concerned with furthering basic liberal education, schools can lay the foundation for continuing liberal education in the leisure hours of adult life. This is not to imply that liberal education can always be carried on without direction or guidance or that it is leftover education, but it does mean that the content of liberal education is so broad and so deep that it cannot be confined to four or eight years of formal education. In the second place, the humanistic and liberal formation of man will provide him with interests, understandings, and ambitions which can be fulfilled, deepened, or satisfied in a society where leisure hours have been multiplied both by phenomenal technological advances and the effectiveness and the stability of contemporary economic institutions. In previous historical periods liberal education could have been labeled accurately as a luxury; today it is nothing less than a corollary of a free, full, interesting, and useful life.

General Education for American Schools

Since 1930 more than usual interest has been shown in general education. The early schools in America, beginning with the schools in colonial New England, had established some precedent for training the mind. Although these early schools and those which followed were not always successful in achieving their stated objectives, the tradition of mental training was strong enough to maintain itself until the last quarter of the nineteenth century. Then educational objectives were disassociated from mental training—especially from mental or formal discipline—and specialized or vocational training received greater attention. Premature specialization has always been a natural foe of general education.

After fifty years of specialization, or at least strong tendencies toward it, and after more or less thorough experiments with electivism, educational theories began to return again to broader, and older, ideas of human development while retaining newer and somewhat more progressive ideas with respect to the means for achieving it. Since 1930 the literature has contained many studies, analyses, and interpretations of general education.

Perhaps one of the most widely used and generally respected documents dealing with the subject was the Harvard report, *General Education in a Free Society*, published in 1948. Nine years earlier the general education movement was formally presented in the Thirty-eighth Yearbook of the National Society for the Study of Education, part II, under the title *General Education in the American College*. Again in 1952 the National Society for the Study of Education showed its interest in general education in its Fifty-first Yearbook, part I, *General Education*. Where the Thirty-eighth Yearbook had been concerned chiefly with the growing disunity in college programs, the Fifty-first Yearbook centered its attention on "fundamental aspects of the social and intellectual needs, the interests and responsibilities of youth and the objectives and procedures of the educational programs which the higher institutions are continuously endeavoring to adapt to the requirements these youth must meet for the achievement of their goals." [12] In addition to the attention given to general education in educational literature, most of which has related to college programs, trial or pilot programs for general education have been organized in both secondary schools and colleges.

Meaning of General Education

Earlier in the chapter the meaning of liberal education was discussed. In what way does general education differ from liberal education, or does general education embody the meaning of liberal education? The committee which drafted the Harvard report, *General Education in a Free Society*, explained that it adopted the term "general education," rather than the traditional term "liberal education," for three principal reasons:[13]

1. Because of "the invidium which, rightly or wrongly, attaches to liberal education in the minds of some people"
2. Because the basic issue is the difference and relationship between general and special education
3. Because a successful democracy must find the answer to the question "How can general education be so adapted to different ages and, above all, differing abilities and outlooks that it can appeal deeply to each, yet remain in goal and essential teaching the same for all?"

It has been said that the Harvard report established the respectability of the term "general education." Still, it seems clear, for the Harvard committee general education meant liberal education, reorganized so as to suffuse all special education and give meaning and relevance to the specialty. Yet this reorganization, on the one hand, and the effort to suffuse a speciality, on the other, may have deprived the new general education of much true liberality.

If we return to the early definitions of general education, we can at least understand what its original purposes were, and we can get some partial view of how they were to be achieved in the school's program of studies. Over the years, general education has had at least three principal meanings; a fourth meaning has attached itself more recently. General education was based, first, on the assumption of a neglected heritage of knowledge about the ideals and institutions, the arts and literature of Western civilization that any reasonably well educated person should have an opportunity to investigate. Following this assumption, the school's program should include courses giving students a substantial opportunity to probe the foundations of our institutions and investigate the common core to basic culture. While not made explicit in theory, in practice students would choose whether or not to take advantage of the opportunities the school offered along these lines. A second assumption supported a requirement of students, irrespective of their academic goals or professional or life goals, to take certain courses designed to expose them to the principal foundations in the cultural inheritance. Apparently, a certain sense of urgency generated this assumption—the necessity would seem to be obvious —for now the student was not free to determine his need for such cultural immersions.

In the third place, the level of competence expected in cultural or general courses was gratuitously supposed to be lower than for specialized or ordinary department courses. In the former, mere exposure would do; in the latter, appropriateness involved more profound understanding. Considering the breadth of many of these courses, it is easy to understand why so many educators felt that real meaning or understanding, to say nothing of scholarly discipline, was almost totally precluded. The real purpose of the general education course was to present students with an interesting array of ideas about persistent human and social problems—moral, political, philosophical, religious, economic—and to be content with presentation; an agenda of important human issues would do, and now the students would be sensitive to some of the agonies through which an evolving civilization had to pass. Perhaps later courses, not in the fold of general education, would serve incidentally to broaden and deepen some of the surface insights gained in the general survey; but whether or not this ever came to pass, it would still be possible to point to students who had been exposed to general education courses and to praise the generalizations they were privy to concerning the big ideas of all time. More recently, the idea has been advanced that general education courses should involve all of the major disciplines and, in the actual instruction of the students, departmental lines be ignored. This theory has given rise to the general education course in the humanities, social studies, and the natural sciences.

Although the objective of exposing students to opportunities for learning about the foundations of Western culture are to be praised, it is not easy to see what general education as interpreted above has in common with liberal education as defined by Newman in *The Idea of a University*. General education seems to lack the most essential feature Newman assigned to liberal education: disinterested learning. This alone should not be enough to condemn general education, for disinterest by itself neither validates nor guarantees meritoriousness. Yet despite this lack of a liberalizing quality, perhaps an essential liberalizing feature, general education is not usually thought to be greatly different from liberal education. General education is frequently accepted as a phrase identifying nonspecialized and nonvocational education, or a kind furnishing a common experience to all educated men and women. In this conception general education is not sharply distinguished from liberal education; the difference is one of degree rather than kind. Following this line of reasoning, then, general education movements are really movements to redefine liberal education, update its content, and make its academic context realistic and relevant for students exposed to it. In the words of the President's Commission on Higher Education, general education is liberal education "with its matter and method shifted from its original aristocratic intent to the service of democracy." General education's purpose is to make available to all the benefits of a liberating education.

In other interpretations general education is regarded as a preparation for young people to deal with persistent contemporary problems: foreign policy, political leadership, philosophies of life. These are problems, or opportunities, faced by everyone; some preparation for facing them cannot be gainsaid. Or it may be education consisting of those knowledges and skills that are useful and profitable for all students; it will help students to balance their general knowledge against their special knowledge. Neither, it seems, should outrun the other by far. It is not necessary here to do more than point to the obvious differences between general and liberal education in these latter interpretations. Is the difference between liberal and general education a difference of degree or of kind?

At the risk of oversimplification, it may be said that there are two common interpretations of the meaning and purpose of general education. In one view general education must transmit the tested ideas and values of civilization's cultural inheritance; its objective is the formation of human beings. This is the view of the humanist, and according to this view general education has a great deal in common with liberal education. The humanist believes that above all man should be given an opportunity to perfect his rational qualities and develop his human abilities of thought and expression. To do this, the humanist claims, education must proceed on a broad and profound cultural front and not on a narrow and professional or vocational one.

According to this interpretation general education is the foundation for man's intellectual and social and moral life. The humanist doubts that man can be really and fully human without this foundation. However, although the beliefs of the humanist may be emphasized, they must not be misrepresented; he would not demand that all education always be non-specialized. After the foundation in general education has been securely laid, the humanist is sympathetic to detailed and thorough professional and scientific studies. Humanistic general education would not always be accepted as liberal education, but it would not be easy to make a clear and definite distinction between the two.

In another interpretation general education is considered to have little in common with the humanist's education or liberal education. Where the humanist thinks first in terms of individual values and outcomes and of intellectual excellence, the proponents of this view think in terms of social values and social outcomes. For them general education means, to put it a bit too simply, to be educated generally. To be educated generally implies some acquaintance with a number of studies or disciplines but little depth in any one of them. Now what value can there be in superficial preparation? For those who endorse this kind of general education, value cannot be isolated and judged independently of its social consequences. That knowledge which the student gains—superficial or profound is only a means to an end, and the end is social competence and social grace. The content of general education becomes, then, whatever will enable individuals to achieve these objectives. In other words, the ends of education are sociological.

THE EDUCATIONAL SYSTEM AND GENERAL EDUCATION

In leaving our consideration of the different interpretations of general education, we may now turn to the question "What provisions are made for general education in American schools?" All levels of the educational system make or may make a contribution to the objectives of general education. The elementary school, the secondary school, and the college all have a part.

The Elementary School and General Education

If the objective of general education is to provide the knowledge, skill, and understanding necessary to man living in society, it is difficult to see how the place of elementary education and the part it plays in general education can be ignored. As a matter of fact, most elementary education is general education, or as it has been said: "General education at the elementary level is the elementary school, and the elementary school is general education." All elementary schools which are concerned with a development of the tools of education (reading, writing, and arithmetic) and an introduction to the social inheritance are contributing to the goals of general education. Even progressive elementary education, although it does not emphasize achievement in predetermined goals, claims to lay a foundation for general education. In such schools social experiences are considered to be of greater importance than laying a foundation for subsequent learning and living: from this point of view the child is experiencing life, not preparing for it. It should be remarked, however, that essentialistic elementary education does not ignore social education, although social skills are not considered to be the primary and special function of the elementary school.

General education is concerned with giving children an opportunity to learn the fundamentals in all the great fields of knowledge. If this is to be accomplished at all, for certainly it cannot be accomplished fully in the elementary school, the tools of education or skills in learning necessary to this goal must be developed. Traditionally the place and the time for developing some competence in the rudiments of education is the elementary school. More than at any other educational level, elementary education offers opportunities for general education. In addition to the development of educational tools, an introduction to the social inheritance is made with materials of instruction which are useful and meaningful to the student at that time but are also essential to him throughout his life. The sciences and the arts—into which the fields of knowledge may be classified—are normally represented in the curriculum of the elementary school. Elementary science, social studies, and, in some schools, religion are coordinated with introductions to the liberal and the fine arts. Each of these studies can be presented within the context of students' needs, interests, and maturity, and in this way elementary schools share a role in both general and liberal education.[14]

Secondary Schools and General Education

Throughout most of its history in America secondary education has concerned itself with preparatory rather than liberal or general objectives. Whereas the common or elementary schools of the country were established with the purpose of educating all the children for citizenship, secondary schools—even as late as 1893, when the *Report of the Committee of Ten* appeared [15]—catered to a select group. The expansion of secondary education from 1890 onward was accompanied by a conviction that the secondary school should recognize the need for a wide variety of learning activities and that general subjects should be taught and evaluated in terms of social behavior, attitudes, and understandings rather than in terms of knowledge of subject matter or of intellectual formation, as such.

When secondary education so conceived came to be called general education is subject to debate, but this kind of secondary education owes a great deal to John Dewey, who proposed a synthesis between culture and utility: [16]

> Social efficiency as an educational purpose should mean cultivation of power to join freely and fully in shared or common activities. This is impossible without culture, while it brings a reward in culture, because one cannot share in intercourse with others without learning—without getting a broader point of view and perceiving things of which one would otherwise be ignorant. And there is perhaps no better definition of culture than that it is the capacity for expanding in range and accuracy one's perception of meanings.

Dewey defined the scope of general education: "Everything that makes a man a man" is to be found not in a few favored subjects or special curricular arrangements but in all those interests and activities that are of social significance.

General education in today's secondary school centers in social processes and social techniques. Its curricular approach is mainly functional in that commonly it disregards subject-matter lines and organizes content around practical life activities, needs, and problems, such as personal and community health, marriage and family adjustment, vocational orientation, social adjustment, and other such everyday practical goals. Because contemporary secondary education is terminal education for about four out of five students in American secondary schools, general education at the secondary level is popularly understood to include the processes and experiences concerned with developing in all students those knowledges, skills, habits, attitudes, and appreciations which are most likely to cause them to be better members of their families and to be informed, law-abiding, and active citizens of local, state, national, and world communities.

Colleges and General Education

The interest shown by American colleges in the general education movement is due largely to the following factors:

1. More than 65 per cent of the freshmen who enter college do not graduate, and more than 50 per cent never enter the junior year.

2. College curricula have tended more and more toward overspecialization.
3. The breadth of college programs has attracted students to college for a multiplicity of reasons.
4. The objectives of college education have been subjected to important changes.
5. A lack of unity in college curricula has increased the desire for integrated programs of study.

The general education movement at the college level began with the Experimental College organized at the University of Wisconsin in 1928. This college was founded on two basic assumptions: that a college is a place where students and teachers form a community of learning; and that their learning should be centered in contemporary life. The Wisconsin experiment lasted five years. It was followed by other experimental programs at other colleges and universities: the General College at the University of Minnesota in 1932, the General College at the University of Florida in 1935, the College at the University of Chicago in 1931, and the General College at the University of Houston in 1934 received the greatest attention. In addition to the foregoing institutions, fifty-three liberal arts colleges reported that they had instituted some kind of general education program before the Second World War. In recent years the universities of Iowa, Denver, Southern California, Iowa State, Drake, Michigan State, Notre Dame, Florida State, Boston, Minnesota, Wisconsin, Michigan, Oregon, Harvard, Princeton, Columbia, Wayne State, Kansas, and many others have organized programs in general education. Most of the programs established at these schools have recognized the following goals:

1. To prepare students for citizenship
2. To provide a foundation for continuing general or professional education.
3. To provide opportunities for students to make satisfactory adjustments to college life and to life after leaving college
4. To provide a common core to basic culture
5. To provide terminal programs in general or technical education that may be completed in less than four years

Although among the colleges and universities which have organized programs of general education there is considerable agreement as to its purposes, the same cannot be said for the means employed by the various colleges to attain these goals. Six different approaches to general education in the college may be listed.

The distribution system. The purpose of a distribution system is to provide opportunities for students to study in all the major fields of knowledge. However, this plan does not require all students to pursue the same curriculum. For example, social science may be studied by taking courses in any of the social science areas, or physical science may be studied by enrolling for a course in any of the physical sciences. These studies, as part of a program of general education, could be pursued at any time during a student's college course and, though elementary in nature, would be expected to supplement and complement a specialized program of studies.

The core system. The core system for general education at the college level has been organized in two different ways: related subjects or fields of knowledge are taught in a "core course" by a "core teacher"; or individual courses are retained but are taught in such a way that their unity, or the relationship between courses, is always apparent.

The basic-curriculum system. When the basic-curriculum system is followed, all students in the general education program are required to take the same courses during their first two college years. In these courses the major fields of man's interests and endeavors are presented.

The time-and-area system. Programs of general education organized according to the time-and-area system require students to study a particular culture or civilization at a particular period of history. In this approach the literature, art, history, politics, philosophy, etc., of a particular time and area become the content of general education.

The great-books system. Another plan that probably belongs to the initial phase of the general education movement is the great-books system. Its ground plan was drawn at Columbia College by John Erskine as an honor's course for juniors and seniors. But the great-books curriculum most closely associated with the general education movement is that which was begun at St. John's College, Annapolis, Maryland, in 1937–1938. An important difference between the great-books approach and other plans for general education is that the great books are the complete college curriculum and are completely prescribed.

The block-and-gap system. The block-and-gap system is to some extent a variation of the great-books approach. It is an attempt to organize the content of general education around the great events or great discoveries of civilization. The block is the great event; the gap is the intervening period between great events.

SUMMARY

In its broadest meaning education is the full formation of man; in a narrower, though entirely legitimate, meaning education is concerned with man's intellectual formation. By definition, it would seem, formal education should be concerned chiefly with liberal purposes, that is, freeing or liberating man's mind, giving him the intellectual tools for expression and thought, and ultimately enabling him to perform the highest function of the intellectual life—contemplation. In ascribing to formal education objectives which are primarily intellectual, there is no thought of excluding from formal education such necessary and important objectives as citizenship, vocational preparation, and preparation for family life, but these objectives are secondary to education's first goal—the making of minds—and must always be dominated and superintended by it.

American education in the past has not been devoted to the objectives of basic liberal education as they are summarized above. There has been, rather, a strong tendency to think of vocational preparation, specialization, and professional goals as the most essential of education's purposes and to set liberal studies aside entirely or to inject them when nothing more important needs to be done. Though it would be unfair to insist that all American education always and in every school has neglected basic liberal education, the generalization that American education has been dominated by the "doctrine of utility" is not open to serious question.

New problems of international and domestic import and new and attractive opportunities for education in contemporary life have led to a reexamination of education's purposes and a reconsideration of fundamental human values to be served only through liberal education. It may not be too much to say that there is a general feeling that education of the past century, oriented as it was to practical and utilitarian goals, failed to fulfill the great expectations for it. Without analyzing the factors which have brought this change in attitude about, it is fair to say that contemporary education is searching for ways and means to restore intellectual formation as the fundamental educational goal.

The means selected to achieve this restoration have been labeled *liberal,* or *general,* education. At times the terms liberal and general are used interchangeably to identify that kind of education which is concerned with the development and cultivation of man's human abilities—thought and expression. In other contexts general education and liberal education are not used synonymously and have little in common: general education is regarded as a broad, preparatory study upon which later specialized study may be based.

Many elementary, secondary, and higher schools are designing curricula intended to achieve the goals set for liberal, or general, education.

QUESTIONS AND EXERCISES

1. Distinguish the two views of general education discussed in the chapter.
2. What is liberal education? Can you summarize the traditions of liberal education?
3. Why is the elementary school important to general education?
4. What provisions would you make in a general education program for the educational development of atypical children?

5. Discuss the objectives of general education in secondary schools.
6. If you were given the opportunity to reform American higher education, what major changes would you make?
7. Liberal education is sometimes thought to be undemocratic. Why? Do you believe that it is undemocratic? Why or why not?

ADDITIONAL READINGS

Cunningham, William F.: *General Education and the Liberal College*, B. Herder Book Co., St. Louis, 1953. A philosophy of general education wherein the author commits general education in the liberal college to developing the human abilities of thought and expression.

Dressel, Paul L.: *Liberal Education and Journalism*, Bureau of Publications, Teachers College, Columbia University, New York, 1960. A study of the need for liberal education of journalists and the extent to which that need is presently fulfilled in professional schools of journalism.

Fisher, J. A.: *The Humanities in General Education*, W. C. Brown Company, Publisher, Dubuque, Iowa, 1960. The author reviews the changes in general education in the humanities.

Glass, H. B.: *Science and Liberal Education*, Louisiana State University Press, Baton Rouge, 1960. How genetics serve man, liberal education in a scientific age, and Darwinian evolution and human values are the principal topics discussed.

Griswold, Alfred W.: *Liberal Education and the Democratic Ideal and Other Essays*, Yale University Press, New Haven, Conn., 1959. A statement of how liberal education contributes to the major tenets of democracy.

Harvard Committee on the Objectives of Education in a Free Society: *General Education in a Free Society*, Harvard University Press, Cambridge, Mass., 1945. A statement of principles for general education. General education is herein regarded as liberal education with a new title.

Hock, Louise E., and Thomas J. Hill: *The General Education Class in the Secondary School*, Holt, Rinehart and Winston, Inc., New York, 1960. The authors use case studies and personal experiences to propose a theory and a method for general education in the secondary school.

Holstein, Edwin J., and Earl J. McGrath: *Liberal Education and Engineering*, Bureau of Publications, Teachers College, Columbia University, New York, 1960. A study of the present status of liberal studies in professional schools of engineering.

Mayhew, Lewis B.: *General Education*, Harper & Row, Publishers, Incorporated, New York, 1960. A presentation of tested theories, programs, and practices for general education.

McConnell, T. R.: *A General Pattern for American Public Higher Education*, McGraw-Hill Book Company, New York, 1962. See chapter 9, "The Individual and the System."

McGrath, Earl J.: *The Graduate School and the Decline of Liberal Education*, Bureau of Publications, Teachers College, Columbia University, New York,

1959. A former United States Commissioner of Education argues that present-day emphases in graduate schools may militate against liberal education in the undergraduate school.

Morse, Horace T., and Paul L. Dressel: *General Education for Personal Maturity,* W. C. Brown Company, Publisher, Dubuque, Iowa, 1960. The role of courses in personal adjustment, preparation for marriage, and vocational planning are discussed.

Rudy, Willis: *Evolving Liberal Arts Curriculum,* Bureau of Publications, Teachers College, Columbia University, 1960. A history of the liberal arts curriculum in American colleges.

Van Doren, Mark: *Liberal Education,* Holt, Rinehart and Winston, Inc., New York, 1959. The meaning of and need for liberally educated men is stressed and cogently defended.

Wager, Willis J., and Earl J. McGrath: *Liberal Education and Music,* Bureau of Publications, Teachers College, Columbia University, New York, 1960. A report on certain phases of professional education along with their relationships to particular areas of music study.

Woody, Thomas: *Liberal Education for Free Men,* University of Pennsylvania Press, Philadelphia, 1951. A theory of liberal education for a society devoted to the freedom of the person.

STUART V. SCHOOL DISTRICT NO. 1

Decided: July 21, 1874
Mr. Justice Cooley delivered the opinion of the Court.

. . . The more general question which the record presents we shall endeavor to state in our own language, but so as to make it stand out distinctly as a naked question of law, disconnected from all considerations of policy or expediency; in which light alone are we at liberty to consider it. It is, as we understand it, that there is no authority in this state to make the high schools free by taxation levied on the people at large. The argument is that while there may be no constitutional provision expressly prohibiting such taxation, the general course of legislation in the state and the general understanding of the people have been such as to require us to regard the instruction in the classics and in living modern languages in these schools as in the nature not of practical and therefore necessary instruction for the benefit of the people at large, but rather as accomplishments for the few, to be sought after in the main by those best able to pay for them, and to be paid for by those who seek them, and not by general tax. And not only has this been the general state policy, but this higher learning of itself, when supplied by the state, is so far a matter of private concern to those who receive it that the courts ought to declare it incompetent to supply it wholly at the public expense. This is in substance, as we understand it, the position of the complainants in this suit.

When this doctrine was broached to us, we must confess to no little surprise that the legislation and policy of our state were appealed to against

* The documents in this section have been edited to eliminate inessential technical data.

the right of the state to furnish a liberal education to the youth of the state in schools brought within the reach of all classes. We supposed it had always been understood in this state that education, not merely in the rudiments, but in an enlarged sense, was regarded as an important practical advantage to be supplied at their option to rich and poor alike, and not as something pertaining merely to culture and accomplishment to be brought as such within the reach of those whose accumulated wealth enabled them to pay for it. As this, however, is now so seriously disputed, it may be necessary, perhaps, to take a brief survey of the legislation and general course, not only of the state, but of the antecedent territory, on the subject.

It is not disputed that the dissemination of knowledge by means of schools has been a prominent object from the first, and we allude to the provision of the ordinance of 1787 on that subject, and to the donation of lands by congress for the purpose, only as preliminary to what we may have to say regarding the action of the territorial authorities in the premises. Those authorities accepted in the most liberal spirit the requirement of the ordinance that "schools and the means of education shall forever be encouraged," and endeavored to make early provision therefor on a scale which shows they were fully up to the most advanced ideas that then prevailed on the subject. The earliest territorial legislation regarding education, though somewhat eccentric in form, was framed in this spirit. It was "an act to establish the Catholepistemiad, or University of Michigania," adopted August 26, 1817, which not only incorporated the institution named in the title, with its president and thirteen professors, appointed by the governor, but it provided that its board of instruction should have power "to regulate all the concerns of the institution, to enact laws for that purpose," "to establish colleges, academies, schools, libraries, museums, atheneums, botanic gardens, laboratories and other useful literary and scientific institutions consonant to the laws of the United States of America, and of Michigan, and to appoint officers and instructors and instructrices, in, among, and throughout the various counties, cities, towns, townships and other geographical divisions of Michigan." To provide for the expense thereof the existing public taxes were increased fifteen per cent., and from the proceeds of all future taxes fifteen per cent. was appropriated for the benefit of this corporation. . . . The act goes but little into details, as was to be expected of a law which proposed to put the whole educational system of the commonwealth into the hands and under the control of a body of learned men, created and made territorial officers for the purpose of planning and carrying it out; but the general purpose was apparent that throughout the territory a system of most liberal education should be supported at the public expense for the benefit of the whole people. The system indicated was prophetic of that which exists to-day, and is remarkable in this connection mainly, as being the very first law on the subject enacted in the territory, and as announcing a policy regarding liberal instruction which, though perhaps impracticable in view of the then limited and scattered population of the territory, has been steadily kept in view from that day to the present.

This act continued in force until 1821, when it was repealed to make way for one "for the establishment of an university," with more limited powers, and authorized only "to establish colleges, academies and schools depending upon the said university," and which, according to the general understanding at the time and afterwards, were to be schools intermediate the university and such common schools as might exist or be provided for. . . . In 1827 the educational system was supplemented by "an act for the establishment of common schools," which is also worthy of special attention and reflection, as indicating what was understood at that day by the common schools which were proposed to be established.

The first section of that act provided "that every township within this territory, containing fifty families or householders, shall be provided with a good schoolmaster or schoolmasters, of good morals, to teach children to read and write, and to instruct them in the English or French language, as well as in arithmetic, orthography, and decent behavior, for such term of time as shall be equivalent to six months for one school in each year. And every township containing one hundred families or householders, shall be provided with such schoolmaster or teacher for such term of time as shall be equivalent to twelve months for one school in each year. And every township containing one hundred and fifty families or householders shall be provided with such schoolmaster or teacher for such term of time as shall be equivalent to six months in each year, and shall, in addition thereto, be provided with a schoolmaster or teacher, as above described, to instruct children in the English language for such term of time as shall be equivalent to twelve months for one school in each year. And every township containing two hundred families or householders shall be provided with a grammar schoolmaster, of good morals, *well instructed in the Latin, French and English languages,* and shall, in addition thereto, be provided with a schoolmaster or teacher, as above described, to instruct children in the English language, for such term of time as shall be equivalent to twelve months for each of said schools in each year." And the townships respectively were required under a heavy penalty, to be levied in case of default on the inhabitants generally, to keep and maintain the schools so provided for. . . .

Here, then, was a general law, which, under the name of common schools, required not only schools for elementary instruction, but also grammar schools to be maintained. The qualifications required in teachers of grammar schools were such as to leave it open to no doubt that grammar schools in the sense understood in England and the Eastern states were intended, in which instruction in the classics should be given, as well as in such higher branches of learning as would not usually be taught in the schools of lowest grade. How is it possible, then, to say, as the exigencies of complainants' case require them to do, that the term common or primary schools, as made use of in our legislation, has a known and definite meaning which limits it to the ordinary district schools, and that consequently the legislative authority to levy taxes for the primary schools cannot be held to embrace taxation for the schools supported by village and city districts in which a higher grade of learning is imparted.

It is probable that this act, like that of 1817, was found in advance of the demands of the people of the territory, or of their ability to support high schools, and it was repealed in 1833, and another passed which did not expressly require the establishment or support of schools of secondary grade, but which provided only for school directors, who must maintain a district school at least three months in each year. . . . The act contains no express limitations upon their powers, but it is not important now to consider whether or not they extended to the establishment of grammar schools as district schools, where, in their judgment, they might be required. Such schools would certainly not be out of harmony with any territorial policy that as yet had been developed or indicated.

Thus stood the law when the constitution of 1835 was adopted. The article on education in that instrument contained the following provisions:

> 2. The legislature shall encourage by all suitable means the promotion of intellectual, scientifical and agricultural improvement. The proceeds of all lands that have been, or hereafter may be, granted by the United States to this state for the support of schools, which shall hereafter be sold or disposed of, shall be and remain a perpetual fund, the interest of which, together with the rents of all such unsold lands, shall be inviolably appropriated to the support of schools throughout the state.
> 3. The legislature shall provide for a system of common schools, by which a school shall be kept up and supported in each school district at least three months in every year; and any school district neglecting to keep up and support such a school may be deprived of its equal proportion of the interest of the public fund.

The fifth section provided for the support of the university, "with such branches as the public convenience may hereafter demand for the promotion of literature, the arts and sciences," etc. Two things are specially noticeable in these provisions: *first,* that they contemplated provision by the state for a complete system of instruction, beginning with that of the primary school and ending with that of the university; *second,* that while the legislature was required to make provision for district schools for at least three months in each year, no restriction was imposed upon its power to establish schools intermediate the common district school and the university, and we find nothing to indicate an intent to limit their discretion as to the class or grade of schools to which the proceeds of school lands might be devoted, or as to the range of studies or grade of instruction which might be provided for in the district schools.

In the very first executive message after the constitution went into effect, the governor, in view of the fact that "our institutions have leveled the artificial distinctions existing in the societies of other countries, and have left open to every one the avenues to distinction and honor," admonished the legislature that it was their "imperious duty to secure to the state a general diffusion of knowledge," and that "this can in no wise be so certainly effected as by the perfect organization of a uniform and liberal system of common schools." Their "attention was therefore called to the effectuation of a perfect school system, open to all classes, as the surest basis of public happiness and prosperity." In his second message he repeated his admonitions, advising that provision be made for ample compensation to teachers, that those of the highest character, both moral and intellectual, might be secured, and urging that the "youth be taught the first principles in morals, in science, and in government, commencing their studies in the primary schools, elevating its grades as you approach the district seminary, and continue its progress till you arrive at the university." This message indicated no plan, but referred the legislature to the report of the superintendent, who would recommend a general system.

The system reported by superintendent Pierce contemplated a university, with branches in different parts of the state as preparatory schools, and district schools. This is the parent of our present system, and though its author did not find the legislature prepared to accept all his views, the result has demonstrated that he was only a few years in advance of his generation, and that the changes in our school system which have since been adopted have been in the direction of the views which he then held and urged upon the public. And an examination of his official report for 1837 will show that the free schools he then favored were schools which taught something more than the rudiments of a common education; which were to give to the poor the advantages of the rich, and enable both alike to obtain within the state an education broad and liberal, as well as practical.

It would be instructive to make liberal extracts from this report did time and space permit. The superintendent would have teachers thoroughly trained, and he would have the great object of common schools "to furnish good instruction in all the elementary and common branches of knowledge, for all classes of community, *as good, indeed, for the poorest boy of the state as the rich man can furnish for his children with all his wealth.*" The context shows that he had the systems of Prussia and of New England in view, and that he proposed by a free school system to fit the children of the poor as well as of the rich for the highest spheres of activity and influence.

It might also be useful in this connection to show that the Prussian system and that "of the Puritans," of which he speaks in such terms of praise, resemble in their main features, so far as bringing within the reach of all a regular gradation of schools is concerned, the system of public instruction as it prevails in this state to-day. But it is not necessary for the purposes of the present case to enter upon this subject. It must suffice to say that the law of 1827, which provided for grammar schools as a grade of common schools, was adopted from laws which from a very early period had been in existence in Massachusetts, and which in like manner, under heavy penalties, compelled the support of these grammar schools in every considerable town. . . .

The system adopted by the legislature, and which embraced a university and branches, and a common or primary school in every school district of the state, was put into successful operation, and so continued, with one important exception, until the adoption of the constitution of 1850. The exception relates to the branches of the university, which the funds of the university did not warrant keeping up, and which were consequently abandoned. Private schools to some extent took their place; but when the convention met to frame a constitution in 1850, there were already in existence, in a number of the leading towns, schools belonging to the general public system, which were furnishing instruction which fitted young men for the university. These schools for the most part had been organized under special laws, which, while leaving the primary school laws in general applicable, gave the districts a larger board of officers and larger powers of taxation for buildings and the payment of teachers. As the establishment and support of such schools were optional with the people, they encountered in some localities considerable opposition, which, however, is believed to have been always overcome, and the authority of the districts to provide instruction in the languages in these union schools was not, so far as we are aware, seriously contested. The superintendent of public instruction devotes a considerable portion of his annual report for 1848 to these schools, and in that of 1849 he says: "This class of institutions, which may be made to constitute a connecting link between the ordinary common school and the state university, is fast gaining upon the confidence of the public. Those already established have generally surpassed the expectations of their founders. Some of them have already attained a standing rarely equaled by the academical institutions of the older states. Large, commodious, and beautiful edifices have been erected in quite a number of villages for the accommodation of these schools. These school-houses frequently occupy the most eligible sites in the villages where they are located. I am happy in being able to state in this connection that the late capitol of our state, having been fitted up at much expense, was, in June last, opened as a *common school-house;* and that in that house is maintained a free school which constitutes the pride and ornament of the city of the straits." This *common* free school was a union school equivalent in its instruction to the ordinary high school in most matters, and the report furnishes very clear evidence that the superintendent believed schools of that grade to be entirely competent under the primary school law.

It now becomes important to see whether the constitutional convention and the people, in 1850, did anything to undo what previously had been accomplished towards furnishing high schools as a part of the primary school system. The convention certainly did nothing to that end. On the contrary, they demonstrated in the most unmistakable manner that they cherished no such desire or purpose. The article on education as originally reported, while providing for free schools to be kept in each district at least three months in every year, added that "the English language and no other shall be taught in such schools." Attention was called to this provision, and it was amended so as to read that instruction should be "conducted in the English language." The reason for the change was fully given, that as it was reported it might be understood to prohibit the teaching of other languages than the English in the primary schools; a result that was not desired. Judge Whipple stated in the convention that, in the section from which he came, French and German were taught, and "it is a most valuable improvement of the common school system." The late superintendent Pierce said that in some schools Latin was taught, and that he himself had taught Latin in a common school. He would not adopt any provision by which any knowledge would be excluded. "All that we ought to do is this: we should say the legislature shall establish primary schools." This, in his opinion, would give full power, and the details could be left to legislation. . . .

The instrument submitted by the convention to the people and adopted by them provided for the establishment of free schools in every school district for at least three months in each year, and for the university. By the aid of these we have every reason to believe the people expected a complete collegiate education might be obtained. The branches of the university had ceased to exist; the university had no preparatory department, and it must either have been understood that young men were to be prepared for the university in the common schools, or else that they should go abroad for the purpose, or be prepared in private schools. Private schools adapted to the purpose were almost unknown in the state, and comparatively a very few persons were at that time of sufficient pecuniary ability to educate their children abroad. The inference seems irresistible that the people expected the tendency towards the establishment of high schools in the primary school districts would continue until every locality capable of supporting one was supplied. And this inference is strengthened by the fact that a considerable number of our union schools date their establishment from the year 1850 and the two or three years following.

If these facts do not demonstrate clearly and conclusively a general state policy, beginning in 1817 and continuing until after the adoption of the present constitution, in the direction of free schools in which education, and at their option the elements of classical education, might be brought within the reach of all the children of the state, then, as it seems to us, nothing can demonstrate it. We might follow the subject further, and show that the subsequent legislation has all concurred with this policy, but it would be a waste of time and labor. We content ourselves with the statement that neither in our state policy, in our constitution, or in our laws, do we find the primary school districts restricted in the branches of knowledge which their officers may cause to be taught, or the grade of instruction that may be given, if their voters consent in regular form to bear the expense and raise the taxes for the purpose.

Having reached this conclusion, we shall spend no time upon the objection that the district in question had no authority to appoint a superintendent of schools, and that the duties of superintendency should be performed by the district board. We think the power to make the appointment was incident to the full control which by law the board had over the schools of the district, and that the board and the people of the district have been wisely left by the legislature to follow their own judgment in the premises.

It follows that the decree dismissing the bill was right, and should be affirmed.

The other justices concurred.

THE CARDINAL PRINCIPLES OF SECONDARY EDUCATION*

The goal of education in a democracy. Education in the United States should be guided by a clear conception of the meaning of democracy. It is the ideal of democracy that the individual and society may find fulfillment each in the other. Democracy sanctions neither the exploitation of the individual by society, nor the disregard of the interests of society by the individual. More explicitly—

The purpose of democracy is so to organize society that each member may develop his personality primarily through activities designed for the well-being of his fellow members and of society as a whole.

This ideal demands that human activities be placed upon a high level of

---

* *A Report of the Commission on the Reorganization of Secondary Education, Appointed by the National Education Association,* Washington, 1918.

efficiency; that to this efficiency be added an appreciation of the significance of these activities and loyalty to the best ideals involved; and that the individual choose that vocation and those forms of social service in which his personality may develop and become most effective. For the achievement of these ends democracy must place chief reliance upon education.

Consequently, education in a democracy, both within and without the school, should develop in each individual the knowledge, interests, ideals, habits, and powers whereby he will find his place and use that place to shape both himself and society toward ever nobler ends.

The main objectives of education. In order to determine the main objectives that should guide education in a democracy, it is necessary to analyze the activities of the individual. Normally he is a member of a family, of a vocational group, and of various civic groups, and by virtue of these relationships he is called upon to engage in activities that enrich the family life, to render important vocational services to his fellows, and to promote the common welfare. It follows, therefore, that worthy home membership, vocation, and citizenship demand attention as three of the leading objectives.

Aside from the immediate discharge of these specific duties, every individual should have a margin of time for the cultivation of personal and social interests. This leisure, if worthily used, will recreate his powers and enlarge and enrich life, thereby making him better able to meet his responsibilities. The unworthy use of leisure impairs health, disrupts home life, lessens vocational efficiency, and destroys civic-mindedness. The tendency in industrial life, aided by legislation, is to decrease the working hours of large groups of people. While shortened hours tend to lessen the harmful reactions that arise from prolonged strain, they increase, if possible, the importance of preparation for leisure. In view of these considerations, education for the worthy use of leisure is of increasing importance as an objective.

To discharge the duties of life and to benefit from leisure, one must have good health. The health of the individual is essential also to the vitality of the race and to the defense of the Nation. Health education is, therefore, fundamental.

There are various processes, such as reading, writing, arithemetical computations, and oral and written expression, that are needed as tools in the affairs of life. Consequently, command of these fundamental processes, while not an end in itself, is nevertheless an indispensable objective.

And, finally, the realization of the objectives already named is dependent upon ethical character, that is, upon conduct founded upon right principles, clearly perceived and loyally adhered to. Good citizenship, vocational excellence, and the worthy use of leisure go hand in hand with ethical character; they are at once the fruits of sterling character and the channels through which such character is developed and made manifest. On the one hand, character is meaningless apart from the will to discharge the duties of life, and, on the other hand, there is no guaranty that these duties will be rightly discharged unless principles are substituted for impulses, however well-intentioned such impulses may be. Consequently, ethical character is at once involved in all the other objectives and at the same time requires specific consideration in any program of national education.

This commission, therefore, regards the following as the main objectives of education: 1. Health. 2. Command of fundamental processes. 3. Worthy home membership. 4. Vocation. 5. Citizenship. 6. Worthy use of leisure. 7. Ethical character.

The naming of the above objectives is not intended to imply that the process of education can be divided into separated fields. This can not be, since the pupil is indivisible. Nor is the analysis all-inclusive. Nevertheless, we believe that distinguishing and naming these objectives will aid in directing efforts; and we hold that they should constitute the principal aims in education.

The role of secondary education in achieving these objectives. The objectives outlined above apply to education as a whole—elementary, secondary, and higher. It is the purpose of this section to consider specifically the role of secondary education in achieving each of these objectives.

For reasons stated in Section X, this commission favors such reorganization that secondary education may be defined as applying to all pupils of approximately 12 to 18 years of age.

1. *Health.* Health needs can not be neglected during the period of secondary education without serious danger to the individual and the race. The secondary school should therefore provide health instruction, inculcate health habits, organize an effective program of physical activities, regard health needs in planning work and play, and cooperate with home and community in safeguarding and promoting health interests.

To carry out such a program it is necessary to arouse the public to recognize that the health needs of young people are of vital importance to society, to secure teachers competent to ascertain and meet the needs of individual pupils and able to inculcate in the entire student body a love for clean sport, to furnish adequate equipment for physical activities, and to make the school building, its rooms and surroundings, conform to the best standards of hygiene and sanitation.

2. *Command of fundamental processes.* Much of the energy of the elementary school is properly devoted to teaching certain fundamental processes, such as reading, writing, arithmetical computations, and the elements of oral and written expression. The facility that a child of 12 or 14 may acquire in the use of these tools is not sufficient for the needs of modern life. This is particularly true of the mother tongue. Proficiency in many of these

processes may be increased more effectively by their application to new material than by the formal reviews commonly employed in grades seven and
eight. Throughout the secondary school, instruction and practice must go
hand in hand, but as indicated in the report of the committee on English,
only so much theory should be taught at any one time as will show results
in practice.

3. *Worthy home membership.* Worthy home membership as an objective
calls for the development of those qualities that make the individual a
worthy member of a family, both contributing to and deriving benefit
from that membership.

This objective applies to both boys and girls. The social studies should
deal with the home as a fundamental social institution and clarify its
relation to the wider interests outside. Literature should interpret and
idealize the human elements that go to make the home. Music and art
should result in more beautiful homes and in greater joy therein. The co-
educational school with a faculty of men and women should, in its organization and its activities, exemplify wholesome relations between boys and
girls and men and women.

Home membership as an objective should not be thought of solely with
reference to future duties. These are the better guaranteed if the school
helps the pupils to take the right attitude toward present home responsibilities and interprets to them the contribution of the home to their development.

In the education of every high-school girl, the household arts should have
a prominent place because of their importance to the girl herself and to
others whose welfare will be directly in her keeping. The attention now
devoted to this phase of education is inadequate, and especially so for girls
preparing for occupations not related to the household arts and for girls
planning for higher institutions. The majority of girls who enter wage-
earning occupations directly from the high school remain in them for
only a few years, after which home making becomes their lifelong occupation. For them the high-school period offers the only assured opportunity to
prepare for that lifelong occupation, and it is during this period that they
are most likely to form their ideals of life's duties and responsibilities. For
girls planning to enter higher institutions: "our traditional ideals of preparation for higher institutions are particularly incongruous with the actual
needs and future responsibilities of girls. It would seem that such high-
school work as is carefully designed to develop capacity for, and interest in,
the proper management and conduct of a home should be regarded as of
importance at least equal to that of any other work. We do not understand
how society can properly continue to sanction for girls high-school cur-
riculums that disregard this fundamental need, even though such curricu-
lums are planned in response to the demands made by some of the colleges

for women." In the education of boys, some opportunity should be found to give them a basis for the intelligent appreciation of the value of the well-appointed home and of the labor and skill required to maintain such a home, to the end that they may cooperate more effectively. For instance, they should understand the essentials of food values, of sanitation, and of household budgets.

4. *Vocation.* Vocational education should equip the individual to secure a livelihood for himself and those dependent on him, to serve society well through his vocation, to maintain the right relationships toward his fellow workers and society, and, as far as possible, to find in that vocation his own best development.

This ideal demands that the pupil explore his own capacities and aptitudes, and make a survey of the world's work, to the end that he may select his vocation wisely. Hence, an effective program of vocational guidance in the secondary school is essential.

Vocational education should aim to develop an appreciation of the significance of the vocation to the community, and a clear conception of right relations between the members of the chosen vocation, between different vocational groups, between employer and employee, and between producer and consumer. These aspects of vocational education, heretofore neglected, demand emphatic attention.

The extent to which the secondary school should offer training for a specific vocation depends upon the vocation, the facilities that the school can acquire, and the opportunity that the pupil may have to obtain such training later. To obtain satisfactory results those proficient in that vocation should be employed as instructors and the actual conditions of the vocation should be utilized either within the high school or in cooperation with the home, farm, shop, or office. Much of the pupil's time will be required to produce such efficiency.

5. *Civic education* should develop in the individual those qualities whereby he will act well his part as a member of neighborhood, town or city, State, and Nation, and give him a basis for understanding international problems.

For such citizenship the following are essential: A many-sided interest in the welfare of the communities to which one belongs; loyalty to ideals of civic righteousness; practical knowledge of social agencies and institutions; good judgment as to means and methods that will promote one social end without defeating others; and as putting all these into effect, habits of cordial cooperation in social undertakings.

The school should develop the concept that the civic duties of men and women, while in part identical, are also in part supplementary. Differentiation in civic activities is to be encouraged, but not to the extent of loss of interest in the common problems with which all should cope.

Among the means for developing attitudes and habits important in a democracy are the assignment of projects and problems to groups of pupils for cooperative solution and the socialized recitation whereby the class as a whole develops a sense of collective responsibility. Both of these devices give training in collective thinking. Moreover, the democratic organization and administration of the school itself, as well as the cooperative relations of pupil and teacher, pupil and pupil, and teacher and teacher, are indispensable.

While all subjects should contribute to good citizenship, the social studies —geography, history, civics, and economics—should have this as their dominant aim. Too frequently, however, does mere information, conventional in value and remote in its bearing, make up the content of the social studies. History should so treat the growth of institutions that their present value may be appreciated. Geography should show the interdependence of men while it shows their common dependence on nature. Civics should concern itself less with constitutional questions and remote governmental functions, and should direct attention to social agencies close at hand and to the informal activities of daily life that regard and seek the common good. Such agencies as child-welfare organizations and consumers' leagues afford specific opportunities for the expression of civic qualities by the older pupils.

The work in English should kindle social ideals and give insight into social conditions and into personal character as related to these conditions. Hence the emphasis by the committee on English on the importance of a knowledge of social activities, social movements, and social needs on the part of the teacher of English.

The comprehension of the ideals of American democracy and loyalty to them should be a prominent aim of civic education. The pupil should feel that he will be responsible, in cooperation with others, for keeping the Nation true to the best inherited conceptions of democracy, and he should also realize that democracy itself is an ideal to be wrought out by his own and succeeding generations.

Civic education should consider other nations also. As a people we should try to understand their aspirations and ideals that we may deal more sympathetically and intelligently with the immigrant coming to our shores, and have a basis for a wiser and more sympathetic approach to international problems. Our pupils should learn that each nation, at least potentially, has something of worth to contribute to civilization and that humanity would be incomplete without that contribution. This means a study of specific nations, their achievements and possibilities, not ignoring their limitations. Such a study of dissimilar contributions in the light of the ideal of human brotherhood should help to establish a genuine internationalism, free from sentimentality, founded on fact, and actually operative in the affairs of nations.

6. *Worthy use of leisure.* Education should equip the individual to secure from his leisure the recreation of body, mind, and spirit, and the enrichment and enlargement of his personality.

This objective calls for the ability to utilize the common means of enjoyment, such as music, art, literature, drama, and social intercourse, together with the fostering in each individual of one or more special vocational interests.

Heretofore the high school has given little conscious attention to this objective. It has so exclusively sought intellectual discipline that it has seldom treated literature, art, and music so as to evoke right emotional response and produce positive enjoyment. Its presentation of science should aim, in part, to arouse a genuine appreciation of nature.

The school has failed also to organize and direct the social activities of young people as it should. One of the surest ways in which to prepare pupils worthily to utilize leisure in adult life is by guiding and directing their use of leisure in youth. The school should, therefore, see that adequate recreation is provided both within the school and by other proper agencies in the community. The school, however, has a unique opportunity in this field because it includes in its membership representatives from all classes of society and consequently is able through social relationships to establish bonds of friendship and common understanding that can not be furnished by other agencies. Moreover, the school can so organize recreational activities that they will contribute simultaneously to other ends of education, as in the case of the school pageant or festival.

7. *Ethical character.* In a democratic society ethical character becomes paramount among the objectives of the secondary school. Among the means for developing ethical character may be mentioned the wise selection of content and methods of instruction in all subjects of study, the social contacts of pupils with one another and with their teachers, the opportunities afforded by the organization and administration of the school for the development on the part of pupils of the sense of personal responsibility and initiative, and, above all, the spirit of service and the principles of true democracy which should permeate the entire school—principal, teachers, and pupils.

Specific consideration is given to the moral values to be obtained from the organization of the school and the subjects of study in the report of this commission entitled "Moral Values in Secondary Education." That report considers also the conditions under which it may be advisable to supplement the other activities of the school by offering a distinct course in moral instruction.

MEYER V. STATE OF NEBRASKA

Decided: June 4, 1923
Mr. Justice McReynolds *delivered the opinion of the Court.*

Plaintiff in error was tried and convicted in the District Court for Hamilton County, Nebraska, under an information which charged that on May 25, 1920, while an instructor in Zion Parochial School, he unlawfully taught the subject of reading in the German language to Raymond Parpart, a child of ten years, who had not attained and successfully passed the eighth grade. The information is based upon "An act relating to the teaching of foreign languages in the State of Nebraska," approved April 9, 1919, which follows:

> Section 1. No person, individually or as a teacher, shall, in any private, denominational parochial or public school, teach any subject to any person in any language other than the English language.
> Sec. 2. Languages, other than the English language, may be taught as languages only after a pupil shall have attained and successfully passed the eighth grade as evidenced by a certificate of graduation issued by the county superintendent of the county in which the child resides.
> Sec. 3. Any person who violates any of the provisions of this act shall be deemed guilty of a misdemeanor and upon conviction, shall be subject to a fine of not less than twenty-five dollars ($25), nor more than one hundred dollars ($100) or be confined in the county jail for any period not exceeding thirty days for each offense.
> Sec. 4. Whereas, an emergency exists, this act shall be in force from and after its passage and approval."

The Supreme Court of the State affirmed the judgment of conviction. . . . It declared the offense charged and established was "the direct and intentional teaching of the German language as a distinct subject to a child who had not passed the eighth grade," in the parochial school maintained by Zion Evangelical Lutheran Congregation, a collection of Biblical stories being used therefore. And it held that the statute forbidding this did not conflict with the Fourteenth Amendment, but was a valid exercise of the police power. The following excerpts from the opinion sufficiently indicate the reasons advanced to support the conclusion.

The salutary purpose of the statute is clear. The legislature had seen the baneful effects of permitting foreigners, who had taken residence in this country, to rear and educate their children in the language of their native land. The result of that condition was found to be inimical to our own safety. To allow the children of foreigners, who had emigrated here, to be taught from early childhood the language of the country of their parents was to rear them with that language as their mother tongue. It was to educate them so that they must always think in that language, and, as a consequence, naturally inculcate in them the ideas and sentiments foreign to the best interests of this country. The statute, therefore, was intended not only to require that the education of all children be conducted in the English language, but that, until they had grown into that language and until it had become a part of them, they should not in the schools be taught any other language. The obvious purpose of this statute was that the English language should be and become the mother tongue of all children reared in this state. The enactment of such a statute comes reasonably within the police power of the state. . . .

It is suggested that the law is an unwarranted restriction, in that it applies to all citizens of the state and arbitrarily interferes with the rights of citizens who are not of foreign ancestry, and prevents them, without reason, from having their children taught foreign languages in school. That argument is not well taken, for it assumes that every citizen finds himself restrained by the statute. The hours which a child is able to devote to study in the confinement of school are limited. It must have ample time for exercise or play. Its daily capacity for learning is comparatively small. A selection of subjects for its education, therefore, from among the many that might be taught, is obviously necessary. The legislature no doubt had in mind the practical operation of the law. The law affects few citizens, except those of foreign lineage. Other citizens, in their selection of studies, except perhaps in rare instances, have never deemed it of importance to teach their children foreign languages before such children have reached the eighth grade. In the legislative mind, the salutary effect of the statute no doubt outweighed the restriction upon the citizens generally, which, it appears, was a restriction of no real consequence.

The problem for our determination is whether the statute as construed and applied unreasonably infringes the liberty guaranteed to the plaintiff in error by the Fourteenth Amendment. "No State shall . . . deprive any person of life, liberty, or property, without due process of law."

While this Court has not attempted to define with exactness the liberty thus guaranteed, the term has received much consideration and some of the included things have been definitely stated. Without doubt, it denotes not merely freedom from bodily restraint but also the right of the individual to contract, to engage in any of the common occupations of life, to acquire useful knowledge, to marry, establish a home and bring up children, to worship God according to the dictates of his own conscience, and generally to enjoy those privileges long recognized at common law as essential to the orderly pursuit of happiness by free men. . . . The established doctrine is that this liberty may not be interfered with, under the guise of protecting the public interest, by legislative action which is arbitrary or without reasonable relation to some purpose within the competency of the State to effect. Determination by the legislature of what constitutes proper exercise of police power is not final or conclusive but is subject to supervision by the courts. . . .

The American people have always regarded education and acquisition of knowledge as matters of supreme importance which should be diligently promoted. The Ordinance of 1787 declares, "Religion, morality, and knowledge being necessary to good government and the happiness of mankind, schools and the means of education shall forever be encouraged." Corresponding to the right of control, it is the natural duty of the parent to give his children education suitable to their station in life; and nearly all the States, including Nebraska, enforce this obligation by compulsory laws.

Practically, education of the young is only possible in schools conducted by especially qualified persons who devote themselves thereto. The calling always has been regarded as useful and honorable, essential, indeed, to the public welfare. Mere knowledge of the German language cannot reasonably be regarded as harmful. Heretofore it has been commonly looked upon as helpful and desirable. Plaintiff in error taught this language in school as part of his occupation. His right thus to teach and the right of parents to engage him so to instruct their children, we think, are within the liberty of the Amendment.

The challenged statute forbids the teaching in school of any subject except in English; also the teaching of any other language until the pupil has attained and successfully passed the eighth grade, which is not usually accomplished before the age of twelve. The Supreme Court of the State has held that "the so-called ancient or dead languages" are not "within the spirit or the purpose of the act." . . . Latin, Greek, Hebrew are not proscribed; but German, French, Spanish, Italian and every other alien speech are within the ban. Evidently the legislature has attempted materially to interfere with the calling of modern language teachers, with the opportunities of pupils to acquire knowledge, and with the power of parents to control the education of their own.

It is said the purpose of the legislation was to promote civic development by inhibiting training and education of the immature in foreign tongues and ideals before they could learn English and acquire American ideals; and "that the English language should be and become the mother tongue of all children reared in this State." It is also affirmed that the foreign born population is very large, that certain communities commonly use foreign words, follow foreign leaders, move in a foreign atmosphere, and that the children are thereby hindered from becoming citizens of the most useful type and the public safety is imperiled.

That the State may do much, go very far, indeed, in order to improve the quality of its citizens, physically, mentally and morally, is clear; but the individual has certain fundamental rights which must be respected. The protection of the Constitution extends to all, to those who speak other languages as well as to those born with English on the tongue. Perhaps it would be highly advantageous if all had ready understanding of our ordinary speech, but this cannot be coerced by methods which conflict with the Constitution—a desirable end cannot be promoted by prohibited means.

For the welfare of his Ideal Commonwealth, Plato suggested a law which should provide: "That the wives of our guardians are to be common, and their children are to be common, and no parent is to know his own child, nor any child his parent. . . . The proper officers will take the offspring of the good parents to the pen or fold, and there they will deposit them with certain nurses who dwell in a separate quarter; but the offspring of the inferior, or of the better when they chance to be deformed, will be put away in some mysterious, unknown place, as they should be." In order to submerge the individual and develop ideal citizens, Sparta assembled the males at seven into barracks and intrusted their subsequent education and training to official guardians. Although such measures have been deliberately approved by men of great genius, their ideas touching the relation between individual and State were wholly different from those upon which our institutions rest; and it hardly will be affirmed that any legislature could impose such restrictions upon the people of a State without doing violence to both letter and spirit of the Constitution.

The desire of the legislature to foster a homogeneous people with American ideals prepared readily to understand current discussions of civic matters is easy to appreciate. Unfortunate experiences during the late war and aversion toward every characteristic of truculent adversaries were certainly enough to quicken that aspiration. But the means adopted, we think, exceed the limitations upon the power of the State and conflict with rights assured to plaintiff in error. The interference is plain enough and no adequate reason therefor in time of peace and domestic tranquility has been shown.

The power of the State to compel attendance at some school and to make reasonable regulations for all schools, including a requirement that they shall give instructions in English, is not questioned. Nor has challenge been made of the State's power to prescribe a curriculum for institutions which it supports. Those matters are not within the present controversy. Our concern is with the prohibition approved by the Supreme Court. *Adams v. Tanner* . . . pointed out that mere abuse incident to an occupation ordinarily useful is not enough to justify its abolition, although regulation may be entirely proper. No emergency has arisen which renders knowledge by a child of some language other than English so clearly harmful as to justify its inhibition with the consequent infringement of rights long freely enjoyed. We are constrained to conclude that the statute as applied is arbitrary and without reasonable relation to any end within the competency of the State.

As the statute undertakes to interfere only with teaching which involves a modern language, leaving complete freedom as to other matters, there seems no adequate foundation for the suggestion that the purpose was to protect the child's health by limiting his mental activities. It is well known that proficiency in a foreign language seldom comes to one not instructed at an early age, and experience shows that this is not injurious to the health, morals or understanding of the ordinary child.

The judgment of the court below must be reversed and the cause remanded for further proceedings not inconsistent with this opinion.

Reversed

PIERCE V. SOCIETY OF SISTERS

Decided: June 1, 1925
Mr. Justice McReynolds *delivered the opinion of the Court.*

These appeals are from decrees, based upon undenied allegations, which granted preliminary orders restraining appellants from threatening or attempting to enforce the Compulsory Education Act* adopted November 1,

---

* *Be it Enacted by the People of the State of Oregon:*

Section 1. That Section 5259, Oregon Laws, be and the same is hereby amended so as to read as follows:

Sec. 5259. *Children Between the Ages of Eight and Sixteen Years*—Any parent, guardian or other person in the State of Oregon, having control or charge or custody of a child under the age of sixteen years and of the age of eight years or over at the commencement of a term of public school of the district in which said child resides, who shall fail or neglect or refuse to send such child to a public school for the period of time a public school shall be held during the current year in said district, shall be guilty of a misdemeanor and each day's failure to send such child to a public school shall constitute a separate offense; provided, that in the following cases, children shall not be required to attend public schools:

(a) *Children Physically Unable*—Any child who is abnormal, subnormal or physically unable to attend school.

(b) *Children Who Have Completed the Eighth Grade*—Any child who has completed the eighth grade, in accordance with the provisions of the state course of study.

(c) *Distance from School*—Children between the ages of eight and ten years, inclusive, whose place of residence is more than one and one-half miles, and children over ten years of age whose place of residence is more than three miles, by the nearest traveled road, from a public school; provided, however, that if transportation to and from school is furnished by the school district, this exemption shall not apply.

(d) *Private Instruction*—Any child who is being taught for a like period of time by the parent or private teacher such subjects as are usually taught in the first eight years in the public school; but before such child can be taught by a parent or a private teacher, such parent or private teacher must receive written permission from the county superintendent, and such permission shall not extend longer than the end of the current school year. Such child must report to the county school superintend-

1922, under the initiative provision of her Constitution by the voters of Oregon. . . . They present the same points of law; there are no controverted questions of fact. Rights said to be guaranteed by the federal Constitution were specially set up, and appropriate prayers asked for their protection.

The challenged Act, effective September 1, 1926, requires every parent, guardian or other person having control or charge or custody of a child between eight and sixteen years to send him "to a public school for the period of time a public school shall be held during the current year" in the district where the child resides; and failure so to do is declared a misdemeanor. There are exemptions—not specially important here—for children who are not normal, or who have completed the eighth grade, or who reside at considerable distances from any public school, or whose parents or guardians hold special permits from the County Superintendent. The manifest purpose is to compel general attendance at public schools by normal children, between eight and sixteen, who have not completed the eighth grade. And without doubt enforcement of the statute would seriously impair, perhaps destroy, the profitable features of appellees' business and greatly diminish the value of their property.

Appellee, the Society of Sisters, is an Oregon corporation, organized in 1880, with power to care for orphans, educate and instruct the youth, establish and maintain academies or schools, and acquire necessary real and personal property. It has long devoted its property and effort to the secular and religious education and care of children, and has acquired the valuable good will of many parents and guardians. It conducts interdependent primary and high schools and junior colleges, and maintains orphanges for the custody and control of children between eight and sixteen. In its primary schools many children between those ages are taught the subjects usually pursued in Oregon public schools during the first eight years. Systematic religious instruction and moral training according to the tenets of the Roman Catholic Church are also regularly provided. All courses of

---

ent or some person designated by him at least once every three months and take an examination in the work covered. If, after such examination, the county superintendent shall determine that such child is not being properly taught, then the county superintendent shall order the parent, guardian or other person, to send such child to the public school the remainder of the school year.

If any parent, guardian or other person having control or charge or custody of any child between the ages of eight and sixteen years, shall fail to comply with any provision of this section, he shall be guilty of a misdemeanor, and shall, on conviction thereof, be subject to a fine of not less than $5, nor more than $100, or to imprisonment in the county jail not less than two nor more than thirty days, or by both such fine and imprisonment in the discretion of the court.

This Act shall take effect and be and remain in force from and after the first day of September, 1926.

study, both temporal and religious, contemplate continuity of training under appellee's charge; the primary schools are essential to the system and the most profitable. It owns valuable buildings, especially constructed and equipped for school purposes. The business is remunerative—the annual income from primary schools exceeds thirty thousand dollars—and the successful conduct of this requires long time contracts with teachers and parents. The Compulsory Education Act of 1922 has already caused the withdrawal from its schools of children who would otherwise continue, and their income has steadily declined. The appellants, public officers, have proclaimed their purpose strictly to enforce the statute.

After setting out the above facts the Society's bill alleges that the enactment conflicts with the right of parents to choose schools where their children will receive appropriate mental and religious training, the right of the child to influence the parents' choice of a school, the right of schools and teachers therein to engage in a useful business or profession, and is accordingly repugnant to the Constitution and void. And, further, that unless enforcement of the measure is enjoined the corporation's business and property will suffer irreparable injury.

Apellee, Hill Military Academy, is a private corporation organized in 1908 under the laws of Oregon, engaged in owning, operating and conducting for profit an elementary, college preparatory and military training school for boys between the ages of five and twenty-one years. The average attendance is one hundred, and the annual fees received for each student amount to some eight hundred dollars. The elementary department is divided into eight grades, as in the public schools; the college preparatory department has four grades, similar to those of the public high schools; the courses of study conform to the requirements of the State Board of Education. Military instruction and training are also given, under the supervision of an Army officer. It owns considerable real and personal property, some useful only for school purposes. The business and incident good will are very valuable. In order to conduct its affairs long time contracts must be made for supplies, equipment, teachers and pupils. Appellants, law officers of the State and County, have publicly announced that the Act of November 7, 1922, is valid and have declared their intention to enforce it. By reason of the statute and threat of enforcement appellee's business is being destroyed and its property depreciated; parents and guardians are refusing to make contracts for the future instruction of their sons, and some are being withdrawn.

The Academy's bill states the foregoing facts and then alleges that the challenged Act contravenes the corporation's rights guaranteed by the Fourteenth Amendment and that unless appellants are restrained from proclaiming its validity and threatening to enforce it irreparable injury will result. The prayer is for an appropriate injunction.

No answer was interposed in either cause, and after proper notices they were heard by three judges . . . on motions for preliminary injunctions upon the specifically alleged facts. The court ruled that the Fourteenth Amendment guaranteed appellees against the deprivation of their property without due process of law consequent upon the unlawful interference by appellants with the free choice of patrons, present and prospective. It declared the right to conduct schools was property and that parents and guardians, as a part of their liberty, might direct the education of children by selecting reputable teachers and places. Also, that these schools were not unfit or harmful to the public, and that enforcement of the challenged statute would unlawfully deprive them of patronage and thereby destroy their owners' business and property. Finally, that the threats to enforce the Act would continue to cause irreparable injury; and the suits were not premature.

No question is raised concerning the power of the State reasonably to regulate all schools, to inspect, supervise and examine them, their teachers and pupils; to require that all children of proper age attend some school, that teachers shall be of good moral character and patriotic disposition, that certain studies plainly essential to good citizenship must be taught, and that nothing be taught which is manifestly inimical to the public welfare.

The inevitable practical result of enforcing the Act under consideration would be destruction of appellees' primary schools, and perhaps all other private primary schools for normal children within the State of Oregon. These parties are engaged in a kind of undertaking not inherently harmful, but long regarded as useful and meritorious. Certainly there is nothing in the present records to indicate that they have failed to discharge their obligations to patrons, students or the State. And there are no peculiar circumstances or present emergencies which demand extraordinary measures relative to primary education.

Under the doctrine of *Meyer v. Nebraska,* 262 U.S. 390, we think it entirely plain that the Act of 1922 unreasonably interferes with the liberty of parents and guardians to direct the upbringing and education of children under their control. As often heretofore pointed out, rights guaranteed by the Constitution may not be abridged by legislation which has no reasonable relation to some purpose within the competency of the State. The fundamental theory of liberty upon which all governments in this Union repose excludes any general power of the State to standarize its children by forcing them to accept instruction from public teachers only. The child is not the mere creature of the State; those who nurture him and direct his destiny have the right, coupled with the high duty, to recognize and prepare him for additional obligations.

Appellees are corporations and therefore, it is said, they cannot claim for themselves the liberty which the Fourteenth Amendment guarantees.

Accepted in the proper sense, this is true. . . . But they have business and property for which they claim protection. These are threatened with destruction through the unwarranted compulsion which appellants are exercising over present and prospective patrons of their schools. And this court has gone very far to protect against loss threatened by such action. . . .

The courts of the State have not construed the Act, and we must determine its meaning for ourselves. Evidently it was expected to have general application and cannot be construed as though merely intended to amend the charters of certain private corporations, as in *Berea College v. Kentucky,* 211 U.S. 45. No argument in favor of such view has been advanced.

Generally it is entirely true, as urged by counsel, that no person in any business has such an interest in possible customers as to enable him to restrain exercise of proper power of the State upon the ground that he will be deprived of patronage. But the injunctions here sought are not against the exercise of any *proper* power. Plaintiffs asked protection against arbitrary, unreasonable and unlawful interference with their patrons and the consequent destruction of their business and property. Their interest is clear and immediate, within the rule approved in *Truax v. Raich, Truax v. Corrigan* and *Terrace v. Thompson,* . . . and many other cases where injunctions have issued to protect business enterprises against interference with the freedom of patrons or customers. . . .

The suits were not premature. The injury to appellees was present and very real, not a mere possibility in the remote future. If no relief had been possible prior to the effective date of the Act, the injury would have become irreparable. Prevention of impending injury by unlawful action is a well recognized function of courts of equity.

The decrees below are

Affirmed

EVERSON V. BOARD OF EDUCATION

Decided: February 10, 1947
Mr. Justice Black *delivered the opinion of the Court.*

A New Jersey statute authorizes its local school districts to make rules and contracts for the transportation of children to and from schools.* The

* "Whenever in any district there are children living remote from any schoolhouse, the board of education of the district may make rules and contracts for the transportation of such children to and from school, including the transportation of school children to and from school other than a public school, except such school as is operated for profit in whole or in part.

"When any school district provides any transportation for public school chil-

appellee, a township board of education, acting pursuant to this statute, authorized reimbursement to parents of money expended by them for the bus transportation of their children on regular busses operated by the public transportation system. Part of this money was for the payment of transportation of some children in the community to Catholic parochial schools. These church schools give their students, in addition to secular education, regular religious instruction conforming to the religious tenets and modes of worship of the Catholic Faith. The superintendent of these schools is a Catholic priest.

The appellant, in his capacity as a district taxpayer, filed suit in a state court challenging the right of the Board to reimburse parents of parochial school students. He contended that the statute and the resolution passed pursuant to it violated both the State and the Federal Constitutions. That court held that the legislature was without power to authorize such payment under the state constitution. . . . The New Jersey Court of Errors and Appeals reversed, holding that neither the statute nor the resolution passed pursuant to it was in conflict with the State constitution or the provisions of the Federal Constitution in issue. . . .

Since there has been no attack on the statute on the ground that a part of its language excludes children attending private schools operated for profit from enjoying State payment for their transportation, we need not consider this exclusionary language; it has no relevancy to any constitutional question here presented. Furthermore, if the exclusion clause had been properly challenged, we do not know whether New Jersey's highest court would construe its statutes as precluding payment of the school transportation of any group of pupils, even those of a private school run for profit. Consequently, we put to one side the question as to the validity of the statute against the claim that it does not authorize payment for the transportation generally of school children in New Jersey.

The only contention here is that the state statute and the resolution, insofar as they authorized reimbursement to parents of children attending parochial schools, violate the Federal Constitution in these two respects, which to some extent overlap. *First.* They authorize the State to take by taxation the private property of some and bestow it upon others, to be used for their own private purposes. This, it is alleged, violates the due process clause of the Fourteenth Amendment. *Second.* The statute and the resolution forced inhabitants to pay taxes to help support and maintain schools which are dedicated to, and which regularly teach, the Catholic Faith.

---

dren to and from school, transportation from any point in such established school route to any other point in such established school route shall be supplied to school children residing in such school district in going to and from school other than a public school, except such school as is operated for profit in whole or in part. . . ."

This is alleged to be a use of state power to support church schools contrary to the prohibition of the First Amendment which the Fourteenth Amendment made applicable to the states.

First. The due process argument that the state law taxes some people to help others carry out their private purposes is framed in two phases. The first phase is that a state cannot tax A to reimburse B for the cost of transporting his children to church schools. This is said to violate the due process clause because the children are sent to these church schools to satisfy the personal desires of their parents, rather than the public's interest in the general education of all children. This argument, if valid, would apply equally to prohibit state payment for the transportation of children to any non-public school, whether operated by a church or any other non-government individual or group. But the New Jersey legislature has decided that a public purpose will be served by using tax-raised funds to pay the bus fares of all school children, including those who attend parochial schools. The New Jersey Court of Errors and Appeals has reached the same conclusion. The fact that a state law, passed to satisfy a public need, coincides with the personal desires of the individuals most directly affected is certainly an inadequate reason for us to say that a legislature has erroneously appraised the public need.

It is true that this Court has, in rare instances, struck down state statutes on the ground that the purpose for which tax-raised funds were to be expended was not a public one. . . . But the Court has also pointed out that this far-reaching authority must be exercised with the most extreme caution. . . . Otherwise, a state's power to legislate for the public welfare might be seriously curtailed, a power which is a primary reason for the existence of states. Changing local conditions create new local problems which may lead a state's people and its local authorities to believe that laws authorizing new types of public services are necessary to promote the general well-being of the people. The Fourteenth Amendment did not strip the states of their power to meet problems previously left for individual solution. . . .

It is much too late to argue that legislation intended to facilitate the opportunity of children to get a secular education serves no public purpose. . . . The same thing is no less true of legislation to reimburse needy parents, or all parents, for payment of the fares of their children so that they can ride in public busses to and from schools rather than run the risk of traffic and other hazards incident to walking or "hitchhiking." . . . Nor does it follow that a law has a private rather than a public purpose because it provides that tax-raised funds will be paid to reimburse individuals on account of money spent by them in a way which furthers a public program. . . . Subsidies and loans to individuals such as farmers and home-owners, and to privately owned transportation systems, as well as many other kinds of businesses, have been commonplace practices in our state and national history.

Insofar as the second phase of the due process argument may differ from the first, it is by suggesting that taxation for transportation of children to church schools constitutes support of a religion by the State. But if the law is invalid for this reason, it is because it violates the First Amendment's prohibition against the establishment of religion by law. This is the exact question raised by appellant's second contention, to consideration of which we now turn.

Second. The New Jersey statute is challenged as a "law respecting an establishment of religion." The First Amendment, as made applicable to the states by the Fourteenth, *Murdock v. Pennsylvania,* 319 U.S. 105, commands that a state "shall make no law respecting an establishment of religion, or prohibiting the free exercise thereof. . . ." These words of the First Amendment reflected in the minds of early Americans a vivid mental picture of conditions and practices which they fervently wished to stamp out in order to preserve liberty for themselves and for their posterity. Doubtless their goal has not been entirely reached; but so far has the Nation moved toward it that the expression "law respecting an establishment of religion," probably does not so vividly remind present-day Americans of the evils, fears, and political problems that caused that expression to be written into our Bill of Rights. Whether this New Jersey law is one respecting an "establishment of religion" requires an understanding of the meaning of that language, particularly with respect to the imposition of taxes. Once again, therefore, it is not inappropriate briefly to review the background and environment of the period in which that constitutional language was fashioned and adopted.

A large proportion of the early settlers of this country came here from Europe to escape the bondage of laws which compelled them to support and attend government-favored churches. The centuries immediately before and contemporaneous with the colonization of America had been filled with turmoil, civil strife, and persecutions, generated in large part by established sects determined to maintain their absolute political and religious supremacy. With the power of government supporting them, at various times and places, Catholics had persecuted Protestants, Protestants had persecuted Catholics, Protestant sects had persecuted other Protestant sects, Catholics of one shade of belief had persecuted Catholics of another shade of belief, and all of these had from time to time persecuted Jews. In efforts to force loyalty to whatever religious group happened to be on top and in league with the government of a particular time and place, men and women had been fined, cast in jail, cruelly tortured, and killed. Among the offenses for which these punishments had been inflicted were such things as speaking disrespectfully of the views of ministers of government-established churches, non-attendance at those churches, expressions of non-belief in their doctrines, and failure to pay taxes and tithes to support them.

These practices of the old world were transplanted to and began to thrive in the soil of the new America. The very charters granted by the English Crown to the individuals and companies designated to make the laws which would control the destinies of the colonials authorized these individuals and companies to erect religious establishments which all, whether believers or non-believers, would be required to support and attend. An exercise of this authority was accompanied by a repetition of many of the old-world practices and persecutions. Catholics found themselves hounded and proscribed because of their faith; Quakers who followed their conscience went to jail; Baptists were peculiarly obnoxious to certain dominant Protestant sects; men and women of varied faiths who happened to be in a minority in a particular locality were persecuted because they steadfastly persisted in worshipping God only as their own consciences dictated. And all of these dissenters were compelled to pay tithes and taxes to support government-sponsored churches whose ministers preached inflammatory sermons designed to strengthen and consolidate the established faith by generating a burning hatred against dissenters.

These practices became so commonplace as to shock the freedom-loving colonials into a feeling of abhorrence. The imposition of taxes to pay ministers' salaries and to build and maintain churches and church property aroused their indignation. It was these feelings which found expression in the First Amendment. No one locality and no one group throughout the Colonies can rightly be given entire credit for having aroused the sentiment that culminated in adoption of the Bill of Rights' provisions embracing religious liberty. But Virginia, where the established church had achieved a dominant influence in political affairs and where many excesses attracted wide public attention, provided a great stimulus and able leadership for the movement. The people there, as elsewhere, reached the conviction that individual religious liberty could be achieved best under a government which was stripped of all power to tax, to support, or otherwise to assist any or all religions, or to interfere with the beliefs of any religious individual or group.

The movement toward this end reached its dramatic climax in Virginia in 1785–86 when the Virginia legislative body was about to renew Virginia's tax levy for the support of the established church. Thomas Jefferson and James Madison led the fight against this tax. Madison wrote his great Memorial and Remonstrance against the law. In it, he eloquently argued that a true religion did not need the support of law; that no person, either believer or non-believer, should be taxed to support a religious institution of any kind; that the best interest of a society required that the minds of men always be wholly free; and that cruel persecutions were the inevitable result of government-established religions. Madison's Remonstrance received strong support throughout Virginia, and the Assembly postponed consideration of the proposed tax measure until its next session. When the proposal came up for consideration at that session, it not only died in committee, but the Assembly enacted the famous "Virginia Bill for Religious Liberty" originally written by Thomas Jefferson. The preamble to that Bill stated among other things that "Almighty God hath created the mind free; that all attempts to influence it by temporal punishments or burthens, or by civil incapacitations, tend only to beget habits of hypocrisy and meanness, and are a departure from the plan of the Holy author of our religion, who being Lord both of body and mind, yet chose not to propagate it by coercions on either . . . ; that to compel a man to furnish contributions of money for the propagation of opinions which he disbelieves, is sinful and tyrannical; that even the forcing him to support this or that teacher of his own religious persuasion, is depriving him of the comfortable liberty of giving his contributions to the particular pastor, whose morals he would make his pattern. . . ." And the statute itself enacted "That no man shall be compelled to frequent or support any religious worship, place, or ministry whatsoever, nor shall be enforced, restrained, molested, or burthened in his body or goods, nor shall otherwise suffer on account of his religious opinions or belief. . . ."

This Court has previously recognized that the provisions of the First Amendment, in the drafting and adoption of which Madison and Jefferson played such leading roles, had the same objective and were intended to provide the same protection against governmental intrusion on religious liberty as the Virginia statute. . . . Prior to the adoption of the Fourteenth Amendment, the First Amendment did not apply as a restraint against the states. Most of them did soon provide similar constitutional protections for religious liberty. But some states persisted for about half a century in imposing restraints upon the free exercise of religion and in discriminating against particular religious groups. In recent years, so far as the provision against the establishment of a religion is concerned, the question has most frequently arisen in connection with proposed state aid to church schools and efforts to carry on religious teachings in the public schools in accordance with the tenets of a particular sect. Some churches have either sought or accepted state financial support for their schools. Here again the efforts to obtain state aid or acceptance of it have not been limited to any one particular faith. The state courts, in the main, have remained faithful to the language of their own constitutional provisions designed to protect religious freedom and to separate religions and governments. Their decisions, however, show the difficulty in drawing the line between tax legislation which provides funds for the welfare of the general public and that which is designed to support institutions which teach religion.

The meaning and scope of the First Amendment, preventing establishment of religion or prohibiting the free exercise thereof, in the light of its history and the evils it was designed forever to suppress, have been several times elaborated by the decisions of this Court prior to the application of the First Amendment to the states by the Fourteenth. The broad meaning given the Amendment by these earlier cases has been accepted by this Court in its decisions concerning an individual's religious freedom rendered since the Fourteenth Amendment was interpreted to make the prohibitions of the First applicable to state action abridging religious freedom. There is every reason to give the same application and broad interpretation to the "establishment of religion" clause. The interrelation of these complementary clauses was well summarized in a statement of the Court of Appeals of South Carolina, quoted with approval by this Court in *Watson v. Jones,* 13 Wall. 679, 730: "The structure of our government has, for the preservation of civil liberty, rescued the temporal institutions from religious interference. On the other hand, it has secured religious liberty from the invasion of the civil authority."

The "establishment of religion" clause of the First Amendment means at least this: Neither a state nor the Federal Government can set up a church. Neither can pass laws which aid one religion, aid all religions, or prefer one religion over another. Neither can force nor influence a person to go to or to remain away from church against his will or force him to profess a belief or disbelief in any religion. No person can be punished for entertaining or professing religious beliefs or disbeliefs, for church attendance or non-attendance. No tax in any amount, large or small, can be levied to support any religious activities or institutions, whatever they may be called, or whatever form they may adopt to teach or practice religion. Neither a state nor the Federal Government can, openly or secretly, participate in the affairs of any religious organizations or groups and *vice versa.* In the words of Jefferson, the clause against establishment of religion by law was intended to erect "a wall of separation between church and State." . . .

We must consider the New Jersey statute in accordance with the foregoing limitations imposed by the First Amendment. But we must not strike that state statute down if it is within the State's constitutional power even though it approaches the verge of that power. . . . New Jersey cannot consistently with the "establishment of religion" clause of the First Amendment contribute tax-raised funds to the support of an institution which teaches the tenets and faith of any church. On the other hand, other language of the amendment commands that New Jersey cannot hamper its citizens in the free exercise of their own religion. Consequently, it cannot exclude individual Catholics, Lutherans, Mohammedans, Baptists, Jews, Methodists, Non-believers, Presbyterians, or the members of any other faith, *because of their faith, or lack of it,* from receiving the benefits of public welfare legislation. While we do not mean to intimate that a state could not provide transportation only to children attending public schools, we must be careful, in protecting the citizens of New Jersey against state-established churches, to be sure that we do not inadvertently prohibit New Jersey from extending its general state law benefits to all its citizens without regard to their religious belief.

Measured by these standards, we cannot say that the First Amendment prohibits New Jersey from spending tax-raised funds to pay the bus fares of parochial school pupils as a part of a general program under which it pays the fares of pupils attending public and other schools. It is undoubtedly true that children are helped to get to church schools. There is even a possibility that some of the children might not be sent to the church schools if the parents were compelled to pay their children's bus fares out of their own pockets when transportation to a public school would have been paid for by the State. The same possibility exists where the state requires a local transit company to provide reduced fares to school children including those attending parochial schools, or where a municipally owned transportation system undertakes to carry all school children free of charge. Moreover, state-paid policemen, detailed to protect children going to and from church schools from the very real hazards of traffic, would serve much the same purpose and accomplish much the same result as state provisions intended to guarantee free transportation of a kind which the state deems to be best for the school children's welfare. And parents might refuse to risk their children to the serious danger of traffic accidents going to and from parochial schools, the approaches to which were not protected by policemen. Similarly, parents might be reluctant to permit their children to attend schools which the state had cut off from such general government services as ordinary police and fire protection, connections for sewage disposal, public highways and sidewalks. Of course, cutting off church schools from these services, so separate and so indisputably marked off from the religious function, would make it far more difficult for the schools to operate. But such is obviously not the purpose of the First Amendment. That Amendment requires the state to be a neutral in its relations with groups of religious believers and non-believers; it does not require the state to be their adversary. State power is no more to be used so as to handicap religions than it is to favor them.

This Court has said that parents may, in the discharge of their duty under state compulsory education laws, send their children to a religious rather than a public school if the school meets the secular educational requirements which the state has power to impose. . . . It appears that these parochial schools meet New Jersey's requirements. The State contributes no money to the schools. It does not support them. Its legislation, as applied, does no more than provide a general program to help parents get their children, regardless of their religion, safely and expeditiously to and from accredited schools.

The First Amendment has erected a wall between church and state. That wall must be kept high and impregnable. We could not approve the slightest breach. New Jersey has not breached it here.

Affirmed

McCOLLUM V. BOARD OF EDUCATION

Decided: March 8, 1948
Mr. Justice Black *delivered the opinion of the Court.*

This case relates to the power of a state to utilize its tax-supported public school system in aid of religious instruction insofar as that power may be restricted by the First and Fourteenth Amendments to the Federal Constitution.

The appellant, Vashti McCollum, began this action for mandamus against the Champaign Board of Education in the Circuit Court of Champaign County, Illinois. Her asserted interest was that of a resident and taxpayer of Champaign and of a parent whose child was then enrolled in the Champaign public schools. Illinois has a compulsory education law which, with exceptions, requires parents to send their children, aged seven to sixteen, to its tax-supported public schools where the children are to remain in attendance during the hours when the schools are regularly in session. Parents who violate this law commit a misdemeanor punishable by fine unless the children attend private or parochial schools which meet educational standards fixed by the State. District boards of education are given general supervisory powers over the use of the public school buildings within the school districts. . . .

Appellant's petition for mandamus alleged that religious teachers, employed by private religious groups, were permitted to come weekly into the school buildings during the regular hours set apart for secular teaching, and then and there for a period of thirty minutes substitute their religious teaching for the secular education provided under the compulsory education law. The petitioner charged that this joint public-school religious-group program violated the First and Fourteenth Amendments to the United States Constitution. The prayer of her petition was that the Board of Education be ordered to "adopt and enforce rules and regulations prohibiting all instruction in and teaching of religious education in all public schools in Champaign School District Number 71, . . . and in all public school houses and buildings in said district when occupied by public schools."

The board first moved to dismiss the petition on the ground that under Illinois law appellant had no standing to maintain the action. This motion was denied. An answer was then filed, which admitted that regular weekly religious instruction was given during school hours to those pupils whose parents consented and that those pupils were released temporarily from their regular secular classes for the limited purpose of attending the religious classes. The answer denied that this coordinated program of religious instruction violated the State or Federal Constitution. Much evidence was heard, findings of fact were made, after which the petition for mandamus was denied on the ground that the school's religious instruction program violated neither the federal nor state constitutional provisions invoked by the appellant. On appeal the State Supreme Court affirmed. . . .

The appellees press a motion to dismiss the appeal on several grounds, the first of which is that the judgment of the State Supreme Court does not draw in question the "validity of a statute of any State" as required by 28 U.S.C. § 344 (a). This contention rests on the admitted fact that the challenged program of religious instruction was not expressly authorized by statute. But the State Supreme Court has sustained the validity of the program on the ground that the Illinois statutes granted the board authority to establish such a program. This holding is sufficient to show that the validity of an Illinois statute was drawn in question within the meaning of 28 U.S.C. § 344 (a). . . . A second ground for the motion to dismiss is that the appellant lacks standing to maintain the action, a ground which is also without merit. . . . A third ground for the motion is that the appellant failed properly to present in the State Supreme Court her challenge that the state program violated the Federal Constitution. But in view of the express rulings of both state courts on this question, the argument cannot be successfully maintained. The motion to dismiss the appeal is denied.

Although there are disputes between the parties as to various inferences that may or may not properly be drawn from the evidence concerning the religious program, the following facts are shown by the record without dispute. In 1940 interested members of the Jewish, Roman Catholic, and a few of the Protestant faiths formed a voluntary association called the Champaign Council on Religious Education. They obtained permission from the Board of Education to offer classes in religious instruction to public school pupils in grades four to nine inclusive. Classes were made up of pupils whose parents signed printed cards requesting that their children be permitted to attend; they were held weekly, thirty minutes for the lower grades, forty-five minutes for the higher. The council employed the religious teachers at no expense to the school authorities, but the instructors were subject to the approval and supervision of the superintendent of schools. The classes were taught in three separate religious groups by Protestant teachers, Catholic priests, and a Jewish rabbi, although for the past several years there have apparently been no classes instructed in the Jewish religion. Classes were conducted in the regular classrooms of the school building. Students who did not choose to take the religious instruction were not released from public school duties; they were required to leave their classrooms and go to some other place in the school building for pursuit of their secular studies. On the other hand, students who were released from secular study for the religious instructions were required to be present at the religious classes. Reports of their presence or absence were to be made to their secular teachers.

The foregoing facts, without reference to others that appear in the record, show the use of tax-supported property for religious instruction and the close cooperation between the school authorities and the religious council in promoting religious education. The operation of the State's compulsory education system thus assists and is integrated with the program of religious instruction carried on by separate religious sects. Pupils compelled by law to go to school for secular education are released in part from their legal duty upon the condition that they attend the religious classes. This is beyond all question a utilization of the tax-established and tax-supported public school system to aid religious groups to spread their faith. And it falls squarely under the ban of the First Amendment (made applicable to the States by the Fourteenth) as we interpreted it in *Everson v. Board of Education,* 330 U.S. 1. There we said: "Neither a state nor the Federal Government can set up a church. Neither can pass laws which aid one religion, aid all religions, or prefer one religion over another. Neither can force or influence a person to go to or to remain away from church against his will or force him to profess a belief or disbelief in any religion. No person can be punished for entertaining or professing religious beliefs or disbeliefs, for church attendance or non-attendance. No tax in any amount, large or small, can be levied to support any religious activities or institutions, whatever they may be called, or whatever form they may adopt to teach or practice religion. Neither a state nor the Federal Government can, openly or secretly, participate in the affairs of any religious organizations or groups and *vice versa.* In the words of Jefferson, the clause against establishment of religion by law was intended to erect 'a wall of separation between church and State.'" . . . The majority in the *Everson* case, and the minority . . . agreed that the First Amendment's language, properly interpreted, had erected a wall of separation between Church and State. They disagreed as to the facts shown by the record and as to the proper application of the First Amendment's language to those facts.

Recognizing that the Illinois program is barred by the First and Fourteenth Amendments if we adhere to the views expressed both by the majority and the minority in the *Everson* case, counsel for the respondents challenge those views as dicta and urge that we reconsider and repudiate them. They argue that historically the First Amendment was intended to forbid only government preference of one religion over another, not an impartial governmental assistance of all religions. In addition they ask that we distinguish or overrule our holding in the *Everson* case that the Fourteenth Amendment made the "establishment of religion" clause of the First Amendment applicable as a prohibition against the States. After giving full consideration to the arguments presented we are unable to accept either of these contentions.

To hold that a state cannot consistently with the First and Fourteenth Amendments utilize its public school system to aid any or all religious faiths or sects in the dissemination of their doctrines and ideals does not, as counsel urge, manifest a governmental hostility to religion or religious teachings. A manifestation of such hostility would be at war with our national tradition as embodied in the First Amendment's guaranty of the free exercise of religion. For the First Amendment rests upon the premise that both religion and government can best work to achieve their lofty aims if each is left free from the other within its respective sphere. Or, as we said in the *Everson* case, the First Amendment has erected a wall between Church and State which must be kept high and impregnable.

Here not only are the State's tax-supported public school buildings used for the dissemination of religious doctrines. The State also affords sectarian groups an invaluable aid in that it helps to provide pupils for their religious classes through use of the State's compulsory public school machinery. This is not separation of Church and State.

The cause is reversed and remanded to the State Supreme Court for proceedings not inconsistent with this opinion.

Reversed and remanded

DOREMUS V. BOARD OF EDUCATION

Decided: March 3, 1952
Mr. Justice Jackson *delivered the opinion of the Court.*

This action for a declaratory judgment on a question of federal constitutional law was prosecuted in the state courts of New Jersey. It sought to declare invalid a statute of that State which provides for the reading, without comment, of five verses of the Old Testament at the opening of each public-school day. . . . No issue was raised under the State Constitution, but the

Act was claimed to violate the clause of the First Amendment to the Federal Constitution prohibiting establishment of religion.

No trial was held and we have no findings of fact, but the trial court denied relief on the merits on the basis of the pleadings and a pretrial conference, of which the record contains meager notes. The Supreme Court of New Jersey, on appeal, rendered its opinion that the Act does not violate the Federal Constitution, in spite of jurisdictional doubts which it pointed out but condoned as follows:

> No one is before us asserting that his religious practices have been interfered with or that his right to worship in accordance with the dictates of his conscience has been suppressed. No religious sect is a party to the cause. No representative of, or spokesman for, a religious body has attacked the statute here or below. One of the plaintiffs is "a citizen and taxpayer"; the only interest he asserts is just that and in those words, set forth in the complaint and not followed by specification or proof. It is conceded that he is a citizen and a taxpayer, but it is not charged and it is neither conceded nor proved that the brief interruption in the day's schooling caused by compliance with the statute adds cost to the school expenses or varies by more than an incomputable scintilla the economy of the day's work. The other plaintiff, in addition to being a citizen and a taxpayer, has a daughter, aged seventeen, who is a student of the school. Those facts are asserted, but, as in the case of the co-plaintiff, no violated rights are urged. It is not charged that the practice required by the statute conflicts with the convictions of either mother or daughter. Apparently the sole purpose and the only function of plaintiffs is that they shall assume the role of actors so that there may be a suit which will invoke a court ruling upon the constitutionality of the statute. Respondents urge that under the circumstances the question is moot as to the plaintiffs-appellants and that our declaratory judgment statute may not properly be used in justification of such a proceeding. . . . The point has substance but we have nevertheless concluded to dispose of the appeal on its merits.

Upon appeal to this Court, we considered appellants' jurisdictional statement but, instead of noting probable jurisdiction, ordered that "Further consideration of the question of the jurisdiction of this Court in this case and of the motion to dismiss or affirm is postponed to the hearing of the case on the merits." On further study, the doubts thus indicated ripen into a conviction that we should dismiss the appeal without reaching the constitutional question.

The view of the facts taken by the court below, though it is entitled to respect, does not bind us and we may make an independent examination of the record. Doing so, we find nothing more substantial in support of jurisdiction than did the court below. Appellants, apparently seeking to bring themselves within *Illinois ex rel. McCollum v. Board of Education,*

333 U.S. 203, assert a challenge to the Act in two capacities—one as parent of a child subject to it, and both as taxpayers burdened because of its requirements.

In support of the parent-and-school-child relationship, the complaint alleged that appellant Klein was parent of a seventeen-year-old pupil in Hawthorne High School, where Bible reading was practiced pursuant to the Act. That is all. There is no assertion that she was injured or even offended thereby or that she was compelled to accept, approve or confess agreement with any dogma or creed or even to listen when the Scriptures were read. On the contrary, there was a pretrial stipulation that any student, at his own or his parents' request, could be excused during Bible reading and that in this case no such excuse was asked. However, it was agreed upon argument here that this child had graduated from the public schools before this appeal was taken to this Court. Obviously no decision we could render now would protect any rights she may once have had, and this Court does not sit to decide arguments after events have put them to rest. . . .

The complaint is similarly niggardly of facts to support a taxpayer's grievance. Doremus is alleged to be a citizen and taxpayer of the State of New Jersey and of the Township of Rutherford, but any relation of that Township to the litigation is not disclosed to one not familiar with local geography. Klein is set out as a citizen and taxpayer of the Borough of Hawthorne in the State of New Jersey, and it is alleged that Hawthorne has a high school supported by public funds. In this school the Bible is read, according to statute. There is no allegation that this activity is supported by any separate tax or paid for from any particular appropriation or that it adds any sum whatever to the cost of conducting the school. No information is given as to what kind of taxes are paid by appellants and there is no averment that the Bible reading increases any tax they do pay or that as taxpayers they are, will, or possibly can be out of pocket because of it.

The State raised the defense that appellants showed no standing to maintain the action but, on pretrial conference, perhaps with premonitions of success, waived it and acquiesced in a determination of the federal constitutional question. Whether such facts amount to a justiciable case or controversy is decisive of our jurisdiction.

This Court has held that the interests of a taxpayer in the moneys of the federal treasury are too indeterminable, remote, uncertain and indirect to furnish a basis for an appeal to the preventive powers of the Court over their manner of expenditure. . . . The latter case recognized, however, that "The interest of a taxpayer of a municipality in the application of its moneys is direct and immediate and the remedy by injunction to prevent their misuse is not inappropriate." . . . Indeed, a number of states provide for it by statute or decisional law and such causes have been entertained in federal courts. . . . Without disparaging the availability of the remedy by taxpayer's action to restrain unconstitutional acts which result in direct pecuniary injury, we reiterate what the Court said of a federal statute as equally true when a state Act is assailed: "The party who invokes the power must be able to show not only that the statute is invalid but that he has sustained or is immediately in danger of sustaining some direct injury as the result of its enforcement, and not merely that he suffers in some indefinite way in common with people generally."

It is true that this Court found a justifiable controversy in *Everson v. Board of Education,* 330 U.S. 1. But Everson showed a measurable appropriation or disbursement of school-district funds occasioned solely by the activities complained of. This complaint does not.

We do not undertake to say that a state court may not render an opinion on a federal constitutional question even under such circumstances that it can be regarded only as advisory. But, because our own jurisdiction is cast in terms of "case or controversy," we cannot accept as the basis for review, nor as the basis for conclusive disposition of an issue of federal law without review, any procedure which does not constitute such.

The taxpayer's action can meet this test, but only when it is a good-faith pocketbook action. It is apparent that the grievance which it is sought to litigate here is not a direct dollars-and-cents injury but is a religious difference. If appellants established the requisite special injury necessary to a taxpayer's case or controversy, it would not matter that their dominant inducement to action was more religious than mercenary. It is not a question of motivation but of possession of the requisite financial interest that is, or is threatened to be, injured by the unconstitutional conduct. We find no such direct and particular financial interest here. If the Act may give rise to a legal case or controversy on some behalf, the appellants cannot obtain a decision from this Court by a feigned issue of taxation.

The motion to dismiss the appeal is granted.

ZORACH V. CLAUSON

Decided: April 28, 1952
Mr. Justice Douglas *delivered the opinion of the Court.*

New York City has a program which permits its public schools to release students during the school day so that they may leave the school buildings and school grounds and go to religious centers for religious instruction or devotional exercises. A student is released on written request of his parents. Those not released stay in the classrooms. The churches make weekly reports to the schools, sending a list of children who have been released from public school but who have not reported for religious instruction.

This "released time" program involves neither religious instruction in public school classrooms nor the expenditure of public funds. All costs, including the application blanks, are paid by the religious organizations. The case is therefore unlike *McCollum v. Board of Education,* 333 U.S. 203, which involved a "released time" program from Illinois. In that case the classrooms were turned over to religious instructors. We accordingly held that the program violated the First Amendment which (by reason of the Fourteenth Amendment) prohibits the states from establishing religion or prohibiting its free exercise.

Appellants, who are taxpayers and residents of New York City and whose children attend its public schools, challenge the present law, contending it is in essence not different from the one involved in the *McCollum* case. Their argument, stated elaborately in various ways, reduces itself to this: the weight and influence of the school is put behind a program for religious instruction; public school teachers police it, keeping tab on students who are released; the classroom activities come to a halt while the students who are released for religious instruction are on leave; the school is a crutch on which the churches are leaning for support in their religious training; without the cooperation of the schools this "released time" program, like the one in the *McCollum* case, would be futile and ineffective. The New York Court of Appeals sustained the law against this claim of unconstitutionality. . . .

The briefs and arguments are replete with data bearing on the merits of this type of "released time" program. Views *pro* and *con* are expressed, based on practical experience with these programs and with their implications. We do not stop to summarize these materials nor to burden the opinion with an analysis of them. For they involve considerations not germane to the narrow constitutional issue presented. They largely concern the wisdom of the system, its efficiency from an educational point of view, and the political considerations which have motivated its adoption or rejection in some communities. Those matters are of no concern here, since our problem reduces itself to whether New York by this system has either prohibited the "free exercise" of religion or has made a law "respecting an establishment of religion" within the meaning of the First Amendment.

It takes obtuse reasoning to inject any issue of the "free exercise" of religion into the present case. No one is forced to go to the religious classroom and no religious exercise or instruction is brought to the classrooms of the public schools. A student need not take religious instruction. He is left to his own desires as to the manner or time of his religious devotions, if any.

There is a suggestion that the system involves the use of coercion to get public school students into religious classrooms. There is no evidence in the record before us that supports that conclusion. The present record indeed tells us that the school authorities are neutral in this regard and do no more than release students whose parents so request. If in fact coercion were used, if it were established that any one or more teachers were using their office to persuade or force students to take the religious instruction, a wholly different case would be presented. Hence we put aside that claim of coercion both as respects the "free exercise" of religion and "an establishment of religion" within the meaning of the First Amendment.

Moreover, apart from that claim of coercion, we do not see how New York by this type of "released time" program has made a law respecting an establishment of religion within the meaning of the First Amendment. There is much talk of the separation of Church and State in the history of the Bill of Rights and in the decisions clustering around the First Amendment. . . . There cannot be the slightest doubt that the First Amendment reflects the philosophy that Church and State should be separated. And so far as interference with the "free exercise" of religion and an "establishment" of religion are concerned, the separation must be complete and unequivocal. The First Amendment within the scope of its coverage permits no exception; the prohibition is absolute. The First Amendment, however, does not say that in every and all respects there shall be a separation of Church and State. Rather, it studiously defines the manner, the specific ways, in which there shall be no concert or union or dependency one on the other. That is the common sense of the matter. Otherwise the state and religion would be aliens to each other—hostile, suspicious, and even unfriendly. Churches could not be required to pay even property taxes. Municipalities would not be permitted to render police or fire protection to religious groups. Policemen who helped parishioners into their places of worship would violate the Constitution. Prayers in our legislative halls; the appeals to the Almighty in the messages of the Chief Executive; the proclamations making Thanksgiving Day a holiday; "so help me God" in our courtroom oaths—these and all other references to the Almighty that run through our laws, our public rituals, our ceremonies would be flouting the First Amendment. A fastidious atheist or agnostic could even object to the supplication with which the Court opens each session: "God save the United States and this Honorable Court."

We would have to press the concept of separation of Church and State to these extremes to condemn the present law on constitutional grounds. The nullification of this law would have wide and profound effects. A Catholic student applies to his teacher for permission to leave the school during hours on a Holy Day of Obligation to attend a mass. A Jewish student asks his teacher for permission to be excused for Yom Kippur. A Protestant wants the afternoon off for a family baptismal ceremony. In each case the teacher requires parental consent in writing. In each case the teacher, in order to make sure the student is not a truant, goes further and requires a report from the priest, the rabbi, or the minister. The teacher in other words cooperates in a religious program to the extent of making it possible for her students to participate in it. Whether she does it occasionally for a few students, regularly for one, or pursuant to a systematized program designed to further the religious needs of all the students does not alter the character of the act.

We are a religious people whose institutions presuppose a Supreme Being. We guarantee the freedom to worship as one chooses. We make room for as wide a variety of beliefs and creeds as the spiritual needs of man deem necessary. We sponsor an attitude on the part of government that shows no partiality to any one group and that lets each flourish according to the zeal of its adherents and the appeal of its dogma. When the state encourages religious instruction or cooperates with religious authorities by adjusting the schedule of public events to sectarian needs, it follows the best of our traditions. For it then respects the religious nature of our people and accommodates the public service to their spiritual needs. To hold that it may not would be to find in the Constitution a requirement that the government show a callous indifference to religious groups. That would be preferring those who believe in no religion over those who do believe. Government may not finance religious groups nor undertake religious instruction nor blend secular and sectarian education nor use secular institutions to force one or some religion on any person. But we find no constitutional requirement which makes it necessary for government to be hostile to religion and to throw its weight against efforts to widen the effective scope of religious influence. The government must be neutral when it comes to competition between sects. It may not thrust any sect on any person. It may not make a religious observance compulsory. It may not coerce anyone to attend church, to observe a religious holiday, or to take religious instruction. But it can close its doors or suspend its operations as to those who want to repair to their religious sanctuary for worship or instruction. No more than that is undertaken here.

This program may be unwise and improvident from an educational or a community viewpoint. That appeal is made to us on a theory, previously advanced, that each case must be decided on the basis of "our own prepossessions." . . . Our individual preferences, however, are not the constitutional standard. The constitutional standard is the separation of Church and State. The problem, like many problems in constitutional law, is one of degree. . . .

In the *McCollum* case the classrooms were used for religious instruction and the force of the public school was used to promote that instruction. Here, as we have said, the public schools do no more than accommodate their schedules to a program of outside religious instruction. We follow the

McCollum case. But we cannot expand it to cover the present released time program unless separation of Church and State means that public institutions can made no adjustments of their schedules to accommodate the religious needs of the people. We cannot read into the Bill of Rights such a philosophy of hostility to religion.

Affirmed

BROWN V. BOARD OF EDUCATION

Decided: May 17, 1954
Mr. Chief Justice Warren *delivered the opinion of the Court.*

These cases come to us from the States of Kansas, South Carolina, Virginia, and Delaware. They are premised on different facts and different local conditions, but a common legal question justifies their consideration together in this consolidated opinion.

In each of the cases, minors of the Negro race, through their legal representatives, seek the aid of the courts in obtaining admission to the public schools of their community on a nonsegregated basis. In each instance, they had been denied admission to schools attended by white children under laws requiring or permitting segregation according to race. This segregation was alleged to deprive the plaintiffs of the equal protection of the laws under the Fourteenth Amendment. In each of the cases other than the Delaware case, a three-judge federal district court denied relief to the plaintiffs on the so-called "separate but equal" doctrine announced by this Court in *Plessy v. Ferguson,* 163 U.S. 537. Under that doctrine, equality of treatment is accorded when the races are provided substantially equal facilities, even though these facilities be separate. In the Delaware case, the Supreme Court of Delaware adhered to that doctrine, but ordered that the plaintiffs be admitted to the white schools because of their superiority to the Negro schools.

The plaintiffs contend that segregated public schools are not "equal" and cannot be made "equal," and that hence they are deprived of the equal protection of the laws. Because of the obvious importance of the question presented, the Court took jurisdiction. Argument was heard in the 1952 Term, and reargument was heard this Term on certain questions propounded by the Court.

Reargument was largely devoted to the circumstances surrounding the adoption of the Fourteenth Amendment in 1868. It covered exhaustively consideration of the Amendment in Congress, ratification by the states, then existing practices in racial segregation, and the views of proponents and opponents of the Amendment. This discussion and our own investigation convince us that, although these sources cast some light, it is not enough to resolve the problem with which we are faced. At best, they are inconclusive. The most avid proponents of the post-War Amendments undoubtedly intended them to remove all legal distinctions among "all persons born or naturalized in the United States." Their opponents, just as certainly, were antagonistic to both the letter and the spirit of the Amendments and wished them to have the most limited effect. What others in Congress and the state legislature had in mind cannot be determined with any degree of certainty.

An additional reason for the inconclusive nature of the Amendment's history, with respect to segregated schools, is the status of public education at that time. In the South, the movement toward free common schools, supported by general taxation, had not yet taken hold. Education of white children was largely in the hands of private groups. Education of Negroes was almost nonexistent, and practically all of the race were illiterate. In fact, any education of Negroes was forbidden by law in some states. Today, in contrast, many Negroes have achieved outstanding success in the arts and sciences as well as in the business and professional world. It is true that public school education at the time of the Amendment had advanced further in the North, but the effect of the Amendment on Northern States was generally ignored in the congressional debates. Even in the North, the conditions of public education did not approximate those existing today. The curriculum was usually rudimentary; ungraded schools were common in rural areas; the school term was but three months a year in many states; and compulsory school attendance was virtually unknown. As a consequence, it is not surprising that there should be so little in the history of the Fourteenth Amendment relating to its intended effect on public education.

In the first cases in this Court construing the Fourteenth Amendment, decided shortly after its adoption, the Court interpreted it as proscribing all state-imposed discriminations against the Negro race. The doctrine of "separate but equal" did not make its appearance in this Court until 1896 in the case of *Plessy v. Ferguson*, . . . involving not education but transportation. American courts have since labored with the doctrine for over half a century. In this Court, there have been six cases involving the "separate but equal" doctrine in the field of public education. In *Cumming v. County Board of Education*, 175 U.S. 528, and *Gong Lum v. Rice*, 275 U.S. 78, the validity of the doctrine itself was not challenged. In more recent cases, all on the graduate school level, inequality was found in that specific benefits enjoyed by white students were denied to Negro students of the same educational qualifications. . . . In none of these cases was it necessary to re-examine the doctrine to grant relief to the Negro plaintiff. And in *Sweatt v. Painter*, . . . the Court expressly reserved decision on the question whether *Plessy v. Ferguson* should be held inapplicable to public education.

In the instant cases, that question is directly presented. Here, unlike *Sweatt v. Painter*, there are findings below that the Negro and white schools involved have been equalized, or are being equalized, with respect to buildings, curricula, qualifications and salaries of teachers, and other "tangible" factors. Our decision, therefore, cannot turn on merely a comparison of these tangible factors in the Negro and white schools involved in each of the cases. We must look instead to the effect of segregation itself on public education.

In approaching this problem, we cannot turn the clock back to 1868 when the Amendment was adopted, or even to 1896 when *Plessy v. Ferguson* was written. We must consider public education in the light of its full development and its present place in American life throughout the Nation. Only in this way can it be determined if segregation in public schools deprives these plaintiffs of the equal protection of the laws.

Today, education is perhaps the most important function of state and local governments. Compulsory school attendance laws and the great expenditures for education both demonstrate our recognition of the importance of education to our democratic society. It is required in the performance of our most basic public responsibilities, even service in the armed forces. It is the very foundation of good citizenship. Today it is a principal instrument in awakening the child to cultural values, in preparing him for later professional training, and in helping him to adjust normally to his environment. In these days, it is doubtful that any child may reasonably be expected to succeed in life if he is denied the opportunity of an education. Such an opportunity, where the state has undertaken to provide it, is a right which must be made available to all on equal terms.

We come then to the question presented: Does segregation of children in public schools solely on the basis of race, even though the physical facilities and other "tangible" factors may be equal, deprive the children of the minority group of equal educational opportunities? We believe that it does.

In *Sweatt v. Painter*, . . . in finding that a segregated law school for Negroes could not provide them equal educational opportunities, this Court relied in large part on "those qualities which are incapable of objective measurement but which make for greatness in a law school." In *McLaurin v. Oklahoma State Regents*, . . . the Court, in requiring that a Negro admitted to a white graduate school be treated like all other students, again resorted to intangible considerations: ". . . his ability to study, to engage in discussions and exchange views with other students, and, in general, to learn his profession." Such considerations apply with added force to children in grade and high schools. To separate them from others of similar age and qualifications solely because of their race generates a feeling of inferiority as to their status in the community that may affect their hearts and minds in a way unlikely ever to be undone. The effect of this separation on their educational opportunities was well stated by a finding in the Kansas case by a court which nevertheless felt compelled to rule against the Negro plaintiffs: "Segregation of white and colored children in public schools has a detrimental effect upon the colored children. The impact is greater when it has the sanction of the law; for the policy of separating the races is usually interpreted as denoting the inferiority of the negro group. A sense of inferiority affects the motivation of a child to learn. Segregation with the sanction of law, therefore, has a tendency to [retard] the educational and mental development of negro children and to deprive them of some of the benefits they would receive in a racial[ly] integrated school system." Whatever may have been the extent of psychological knowledge at the time of *Plessy v. Ferguson,* this finding is amply supported by modern authority. Any language in *Plessy v. Ferguson* contrary to this finding is rejected.

We conclude that in the field of public education the doctrine of "separate but equal" has no place. Separate educational facilities are inherently unequal. Therefore, we hold that the plaintiffs and others similarly situated for whom the actions have been brought are, by reason of the segregation complained of, deprived of the equal protection of the laws guaranteed by the Fourteenth Amendment. This disposition makes unnecessary any discussion whether such segregation also violates the Due Process Clause of the Fourteenth Amendment.

Because these are class actions, because of the wide applicability of this decision, and because of the great variety of local conditions, the formulation of decrees in these cases presents problems of considerable complexity. On reargument, the consideration of appropriate relief was necessarily subordinated to the primary question—the constitutionality of segregation in public education. We have now announced that such segregation is a denial of the equal protection of the laws. In order that we may have the full assistance of the parties in formulating decrees, the cases will be restored to the docket, and the parties are requested to present further argument on Questions 4 and 5 previously propounded by the Court for the reargument this Term. The Attorney General of the United States is again invited to participate. The Attorneys General of the states requiring or permitting segregation in public education will also be permitted to appear as *amici curiae* upon request to do so by September 15, 1954, and submission of briefs by October 1, 1954.

It is so ordered.

ENGEL V. VITALE

Decided: June 25, 1962
Mr. Justice Black *delivered the opinion of the Court.*

The respondent Board of Education of Union Free School District No. 9, New Hyde Park, New York, acting in its official capacity under state law, directed the School District's principal to cause the following prayer to be said aloud by each class in the presence of a teacher at the beginnings of each school day: "Almighty God, we acknowledge our dependence upon Thee, and we beg Thy blessings upon us, our parents, our teachers and our Country." This daily procedure was adopted on the recommendation of the State Board of Regents, a governmental agency created by the State Constitution to which the New York Legislature has granted broad supervisory, executive, and legislative powers over the State's public school system. These state officials composed the prayer which they recommended and published as a part of their "statement on Moral and Spiritual Training in the Schools," saying: "We believe that this Statement will be subscribed to by all men and women of good will, and we call upon all of them to aid in giving life to our program."

Shortly after the practice of reciting the Regents' prayer was adopted by the School District, the parents of ten pupils brought this action in a New York State Court insisting that use of this official prayer in the public schools was contrary to the beliefs, religions, or religious practices of both themselves and their children. Among other things, these parents challenged the constitutionality of both the state law authorizing the School District to direct the use of prayer in public schools and the School District's regulation ordering the recitation of this particular prayer on the ground that these actions of official governmental agencies violate that part of the First Amendment of the Federal Constitution which commands that "Congress shall make no law respecting an establishment of religion"—a command which was "made applicable to the State of New York by the Fourteenth Amendment of the said Constitution." The New York Court of Appeals, over the dissents of Judges Dye and Fuld, sustained an order of the lower state courts which had upheld the power of New York to use the Regents' prayer as a part of the daily procedures of its public schools so long as the schools did not compel any pupil to join in the prayer over his or his parents' objection. We granted certiorari to review this important decision involving rights protected by the First and Fourteenth Amendments.

We think that by using its public school system to encourage recitation of the Regents' prayer, the State of New York has adopted a practice wholly inconsistent with the Establishment Clause. There can, of course, be no doubt that New York's program of daily classroom invocation of God's blessings as prescribed in the Regents' prayer is a religious activity. It is a solemn avowal of divine faith and supplication for the blessings of the Almighty. The nature of such a prayer has always been religious, none of the respondents has denied this and the trial court expressly so found:

> The religious nature of prayer was recognized by Jefferson and has been concurred in by theological writers, the United States Supreme Court and State courts and administrative officials, including New York's Commissioner of Education. A committee of the New York Legislature has agreed.
> The Board of Regents as amicus curiae, the respondents and intervenors all concede the religious nature of prayer, but seek to distinguish this prayer because it is based on our spiritual heritage. . . .

The petitioners contend among other things that the state laws requiring or permitting use of Regents' prayer must be struck down as a violation of the Establishment Clause because that prayer was composed by governmental officials as a part of a governmental program to further religious beliefs. For this reason, petitioners argue, the State's use of the Regents' prayer in its public school system breaches the constitutional wall of separation between Church and State. We agree with that contention since we think that the constitutional prohibition against laws respecting an establishment of religion must at least mean that in this country it is no part of the business of government to compose official prayers for any group of the American people to recite as a part of a religious program carried on by government.

It is a matter of history that this very practice of establishing governmentally composed prayers for religious services was one of the reasons which caused many of our early colonists to leave England and seek religious freedom in America. The Book of Common Prayer, which was created under governmental direction and which was approved by Acts of Parliament in 1548 and 1549, set out in minute detail the accepted form and content of prayer and other religious ceremonies to be used in the established, tax-supported Church of England. The controversies over the Book and what should be its content repeatedly threatened to disrupt the peace of that country as the accepted forms of prayer in the established church changed with the views of the particular ruler that happened to be in control at the time. Powerful groups representing some of the varying religious views of the people struggled among themselves to impress their particular views upon the Government and obtain amendments of the Book more suitable to their respective notions of how religious services should be conducted in order that the official religious establishment would advance their particular religious beliefs. Other groups, lacking the necessary political power to influence the Government on the matter, decided to leave England and its established church and seek freedom in America from England's governmentally ordained and supported religion.

It is an unfortunate fact of history that when some of the very groups which had most strenuously opposed the established church of England found themselves sufficiently in control of colonial governments in this country to write their own prayers into law, they passed laws making their own religion the official religion of their respective colonies. Indeed, as late as the time of the Revolutionary War, there were established churches in at least eight of the thirteen former colonies and established religions in at least four of the other five. But the successful Revolution against English political domination was shortly followed by intense opposition to the practice of establishing religion by law. This opposition crystallized rapidly into an effective political force in Virginia where the minority religious groups such as Presbyterians, Lutherans, Quakers and Baptists had gained such strength that the adherents to the established Episcopal Church were actually a minority themselves. In 1785–1786, those opposed to the established Church, led by James Madison and Thomas Jefferson, who, though themselves not members of any of these dissenting religious groups, opposed all religious establishments by law on grounds of principle, obtained the enactment of the famous "Virginia Bill for Religious Liberty" by which all religious groups were placed on an equal footing so far as the State was concerned. Similar though less far-reaching legislation was being considered and passed in other States.

By the time of the adoption of the Constitution, our history shows that there was a widespread awareness among many Americans of the dangers of a union of Church and State. These people knew, some of them from bitter personal experience, that one of the greatest dangers to the freedom of the individual to worship in his own way lay in the Government's placing its official stamp of approval upon one particular kind of prayer or one particular form of religious services. They knew the anguish, hardship and bitter strife that could come when zealous religious groups struggled with one another to obtain the Government's stamp of approval from each King, Queen, or Protector that came to temporary power. The Constitution was intended to avert a part of this danger by leaving the government of this country in the hands of the people rather than in the hands of any monarch. But this safeguard was not enough. Our Founders were no more willing to let the content of their prayers and their privilege of praying whenever they pleased be influenced by the ballot box than they were to let these vital matters of personal conscience depend upon the succession of monarchs. The First Amendment was added to the Constitution to stand as a guarantee that neither the power nor the prestige of the Federal Government would be used to control, support or influence the kinds of prayer the American people can say—that the people's religions must not be subjected to the pressures of government for change each time a new political administration is elected to office. Under that Amendment's prohibition against governmental establishment of religion, as reinforced by the provisions of the Fourteenth Amendment, government in this country, be it state or federal, is without power to prescribe by law any particular form of prayer which is to be used as an official prayer in carrying on any program of governmentally sponsored religious activity.

There can be no doubt that New York's state prayer program officially establishes the religious beliefs embodied in the Regents' prayer. The respondents' argument to the contrary, which is largely based upon the contention that the Regents' prayer is "non-denominational" and the fact that the program, as modified and approved by state courts, does not require all pupils to recite the prayer but permits those who wish to do so to remain silent or be excused from the room, ignores the essential nature of the program's constitutional defects. Neither the fact that the prayer may be denominationally neutral nor the fact that its observance on the part of the students is voluntary can serve to free it from the limitations of the Establishment Clause, as it might from the Free Exercise Clause, of the First Amendment, both of which are operative against the States by virtue of the Fourteenth Amendment. Although these two clauses may in certain instances overlap, they forbid two quite different kinds of governmental encroachment upon religious freedom. The Establishment Clause, unlike the Free Exercise Clause, does not depend upon any showing of direct governmental compulsion and is violated by the enactment of laws which establish an official religion whether those laws operate directly to coerce nonobserving individuals or not. This is not to say, of course, that laws officially prescribing a particular form of religious worship do not involve coercion of such individuals. When the power, prestige and financial support of government is placed behind a particular religious belief, the indirect coercive pressure upon religious minorities to conform to the prevailing officially approved religion is plain. But the purposes underlying the Establishment Clause go much further than that. Its first and most immediate purpose. rested on the belief that a union of government and religion tends to destroy government and to degrade religion. The history of governmentally established religion, both in England and in this country, showed that whenever government had allied itself with one particular form of religion, the inevitable result had been that it had incurred the hatred, disrespect and even contempt of those who held contrary beliefs. The same history showed that many people had lost their respect for any religion that had relied upon the support of government to spread its faith. The Establishment Clause thus stands as an expression of principle on the part of the Founders of our Constitution that religion is too personal, too sacred, too holy, to permit its "unhallowed perversion" by a civil magistrate. Another purpose of the Establishment Clause rested upon an awareness of the historical fact that governmentally established religions and religious persecutions go hand in hand. The Founders knew that only a few years after the Book of Common Prayer became the only accepted form of religious services in the established Church of England, an Act of Uniformity was passed to compel all Englishmen to attend those services and to make it a criminal offense to conduct or attend religious gatherings of any other kind—a law which was consistently flouted by dissenting religious groups in England and which contributed to widespread persecutions of people like John Bunyan who persisted in holding "unlawful (religious) meetings . . . to the great disturbance and distraction of the good subjects of this kingdom. . . ." And they knew that similar persecutions had received the sanction of law in several of the colonies in this country soon after the establishment of official religions in those colonies. It was in large part to get completely away from this sort of systematic religious persecution that the Founders brought into being our Nation, our Constitution, and our Bill of Rights with its prohibition against any governmental establishment of religion. The New York laws officially prescribing the Regents' prayer are inconsistent both with the purposes of the Establishment Clause and with the Establishment Clause itself.

It has been argued that to apply the Constitution in such a way as to prohibit state laws respecting an establishment of religious services in public schools is to indicate a hostility toward religion or toward prayer. Nothing, of course, could be more wrong. The history of man is inseparable from the history of religion. And perhaps it is not too much to say that since the beginning of that history many people have devoutly believed that "More things are wrought by prayer than this world dreams of." It was doubtless largely due to men who believed this that there grew up a sentiment that caused men to leave the cross-currents of officially established state religions and religious persecution in Europe and come to this country filled with the hope that they could find a place in which they could pray when they pleased to the God of their faith in the language they chose. And there were men of this same faith in the power of prayer who led the fight for adoption of our Constitution and also for our Bill of Rights with the very guarantees of religious freedom that forbid the sort of governmental activity which New York has attempted here. These men knew that the First Amendment, which tried to put an end to governmental control of religion and of prayer, was not written to destroy either. They knew rather that it was written to quiet well-justified fears which nearly all of them felt arising out of an awareness that governments of the past had shackled men's tongues to make them speak only the religious thoughts that government wanted them to speak and to pray only to the God that government wanted them to pray to. It is neither sacrilegious nor antireligious to say that each separate government in this country should stay out of the business of writing or sanctioning official prayers and leave that purely religious function to the people themselves and to those the people choose to look to for religious guidance.

It is true that New York's establishment of its Regents' prayer as an officially approved religious doctrine of that State does not amount to a total establishment of one particular religious sect to the exclusion of all others—that, indeed, the governmental endorsement of that prayer seems relatively insignificant when compared to the governmental encroachments upon religion which were commonplace 200 years ago. To those who may subscribe to the view that because the Regents' official prayer is so brief and general there can be no danger to religious freedom in its governmental establishment, however, it may be appropriate to say in the words of James Madison, the author of the First Amendment:

> [It] is proper to take alarm at the first experiment on our liberties. . . . Who does not see that the same authority which can establish Christianity, in exclusion of all other Religions, may establish with the same ease any particular sect of Christians, in exclusion of all other Sects? That the same authority which can force a citizen to contribute three pence only of his property for the support of any one establishment, may force him to conform to any other establishment in all cases whatsoever?

The judgment of the Court of Appeals of New York is reversed and the cause remanded for further proceedings not inconsistent with this opinion.

Reversed and remanded.

SCHOOL DISTRICT OF ABINGTON TOWNSHIP V. SCHEMPP

Decided: June 17, 1963
Mr. Justice Clark *delivered the opinion of the court.*

Once again we are called upon to consider the scope of the provision of the First Amendment to the United States Constitution which declares that "Congress shall make no law respecting an establishment of religion or prohibiting the free exercise thereof. . . ." These companion cases present the issues in the context of state action requiring that schools begin each day with readings from the Bible. While raising the basic questions under slightly different factual situations, the cases permit of joint treatment. In light of the history of the First Amendment and of our cases interpreting and applying its requirements, we hold that the practices at issue and the laws requiring them are unconstitutional under the Establishment Clause, as applied to the states through the Fourteenth Amendment.

I

The Facts in Each Case: . . . The Commonwealth of Pennsylvania by law . . . requires that "At least ten verses from the Holy Bible shall be read, without comment, at the opening of each public school on each school day. Any child shall be excused from such Bible reading, or attending such Bible reading, upon the written request of his parent or guardian." The Schempp family, husband and wife and two of their three children, brought suit to enjoin enforcement of the statute, contending that their rights under the Fourteenth Amendment to the Constitution of the United States are, have been, and will continue to be violated unless this statute be declared unconstitutional as violative of these provisions of the First Amendment. They sought to enjoin the appellant school district, wherein the Schempp children attend school, and its officers and the Superintendent of Public Instruction of the Commonwealth from continuing to conduct such readings and recitation of the Lord's Prayer in the public schools of the district pursuant to the statute. A three-judge statutory District Court for the Eastern District of Pennsylvania held that the statute is violative of the Establishment Clause of the First Amendment as applied to the States by the Due Process Clause of the Fourteenth Amendment and directed that appropriate injunctive relief issue. . . . On appeal by the District, its officials and the Superintendent . . . we noted probable jurisdiction. . . .

The appellees Edward Lewis Schempp, his wife Sidney, and their children, Roger and Donna, are of the Unitarian faith and are members of the Unitarian Church in Germantown, Philadelphia, Pennsylvania, where they, as well as another son, Ellory, regularly attend religious services. The latter was originally a party but having graduated from the school system pendente lite was voluntarily dismissed from the action. The other children attend the Abington Senior High School, which is a public school operated by appellant district.

On each school day at the Abington Senior High School between 8:15 and 8:30 A.M., while the pupils are attending their home rooms or advisory sections, opening exercises are conducted pursuant to the statute. The exercises are broadcast into each room in the school building through an intercommunications system and are conducted under the supervision of a teacher by students attending the school's radio and television workshop. Selected students from this course gather each morning in the school's workshop studio for the exercises, which include reading by one of the students of 10 verses of the Holy Bible, broadcast to each room in the building. This is followed by the recitation of the Lord's Prayer, likewise over the intercommunications system, but also by the students in the various classrooms, who are asked to stand and join in repeating the prayer in unison. The exercises are closed with the flag salute and such pertinent announcements as are of interest to the students. Participation in the opening exercises, as directed by the statute, is voluntary. The student reading the verses from the Bible may select the passages and read from any version he chooses, although the only copies furnished by the school are the King James version, copies of which were circulated to each teacher by the school district. During the period in which the exercises have been conducted the King James, the Douay and the Revised Standard versions of the Bible have been used, as well as the Jewish Holy Scriptures. There are no prefatory statements, no questions asked or solicited, no comments or explanations made and no interpretations given at or during the exercises. The students and parents are advised that the student may absent himself from the classroom or, should he elect to remain, not participate in the exercises.

It appears from the record that in schools not having an intercommunication system the Bible reading and the recitation of the Lord's Prayer were conducted by the home-room teacher, who chose the text of the verses and read them herself or had students read them in rotation or by volunteers. This was followed by a standing recitation of the Lord's Prayer, together with the Pledge of Allegiance to the flag by the class in unison and a closing announcement of routine school items of interest.

At the first trial Edward Schempp and the children testified as to specific religious doctrines purveyed by a literal reading of the Bible "which were contrary to the religious beliefs which they held and to their familial teaching." . . . The children testified that all of the doctrines to which they referred were read to them at various times as part of the exercises. Edward Schempp testified at the second trial that he had considered having Roger and Donna excused from attendance at the exercises but decided against it for several reasons, including his belief that the children's relationships with their teachers and classmates would be adversely affected.

Expert testimony was introduced by both appellants and appellees at the first trial, which testimony was summarized by the trial court as follows:

> Dr. Solomon Grayzel testified that there were marked differences between the Jewish Holy Scriptures and the Christian Holy Bible, the most obvious of which was the absence of the New Testament in the Jewish Holy Scriptures. Dr. Grayzel testified that portions of the New Testament were offensive to Jewish tradition and that, from the standpoint of Jewish faith, the concept of Jesus Christ as the Son of God was "practically blasphemous." He cited instances in the New Testament which, assertedly, were not only sectarian in nature but tended to bring the Jews into ridicule or scorn. Dr. Grayzel gave as his expert opinion that such material from the New Testament could be explained to Jewish children in such a way as to do no harm

to them. But if portions of the New Testament were read without explanation, they could be, and in his specific experience with children Dr. Grayzel observed, had been, psychologically harmful to the child and had caused a divisive force within the social media of the school.

Dr. Grayzel also testified that there was significant difference in attitude with regard to the respective Books of the Jewish and Christian Religions in that Judaism attaches no special significance to the reading of the Bible per se and that the Jewish Holy Scriptures are source materials to be studied. But Dr. Grayzel did state that many portions of the New, as well as the Old, Testament contained passages of great literary and moral value.

Dr. Luther A. Weigle, an expert witness for the defense, testified in some detail as to the reasons for and the methods employed in developing the King James and the Revised Standard Versions of the Bible. On direct examination, Dr. Weigle stated that the Bible was non-sectarian. He later stated that the phrase "non-sectarian" meant to him non-sectarian within the Christian faiths. Dr. Weigle stated that his definition of the Holy Bible would include the Jewish Holy Scriptures, but also stated that the "Holy Bible" would not be complete without the New Testament. He stated that the New Testament "conveyed the message of Christians." In his opinion, reading of the Holy Scriptures to the exclusion of the New Testament would be a sectarian practice. Dr. Weigle stated that the Bible was of great moral, historical and literary value. This is conceded by all the parties and is also the view of the court. . . .

The trial court, in striking down the practices and the statute requiring them, made specific findings of fact that the children's attendance at Abington Senior High School is compulsory and that the practice of reading 10 verses from the Bible is also compelled by law. It also found that:

> The reading of the verses, even without comment, possesses a devotional and religious character and constitutes in effect a religious observance. The devotional and religious nature of the morning exercises is made all the more apparent by the fact that the Bible reading is followed immediately by a recital in unison by the pupils of the Lord's Prayer. The fact that some pupils, or theoretically all pupils, might be excused from attendance at the exercises does not mitigate the obligatory nature of the ceremony for . . . Section 1516 . . . unequivocally requires the exercises to be held every school day in every school in the Commonwealth. The exercises are held in the school buildings and perforce are conducted by and under the authority of the local school authorities and during school sessions. Since the statute requires the reading of the "Holy Bible," a Christian document, the practice . . . prefers the Christian religion. The record demonstrates that it was the intention of . . . the Commonwealth . . . to introduce a religious ceremony into the public schools of the Commonwealth. . . .

. . . In 1905 the Board of School Commissioners of Baltimore City adopted a rule pursuant to Art. 77, 202 of the Annotated Code of Maryland. The rule provided for the holding of opening exercises in the schools of the city consisting primarily of the "reading, without comment, of a chapter in the Holy Bible and/or the use of the Lord's Prayer." The petitioners, Mrs. Madalyn Murray and her son, William J. Murray, III, are both professed atheists. Following unsuccessful attempts to have the respondent school board rescind the rule this suit was filed for mandamus to compel its rescission and cancellation. It was alleged that William was a student in a public school of the city and Mrs. Murray, his mother, was a taxpayer therin; that it was the practice under the rule to have a reading on each school morning from the King James version of the Bible; that at petitioners' insistence the rule was amended to permit children to be excused from the exercise on request of the parent and that William had been excused pursuant therto; that nevertheless the rule as amended was in violation of the petitioners' rights "to freedom of religion under the First and Fourteenth Amendments" and in violation of "the principle of separation between church and state, contained therein. . . ." The petition particularized the petitioners' atheistic beliefs and stated that the rule, as practiced, violated their rights

> . . . in that it threatens their religious liberty by placing a premium on belief as against non-belief and subjects their freedom of conscience to the rule of the majority; it pronounces belief in God as the source of all moral and spiritual values, equating these values with religious values, and thereby renders sinister, alien and suspect the beliefs and ideals of . . . Petitioners, promoting doubt and question of their morality, good citizenship and good faith.

The respondents demurred and the trial court, recognizing that the demurrer admitted all facts well pleaded, sustained it without leave to amend. The Maryland Court of Appeals affirmed, the majority of four justices holding the exercise not in violation of the First and Fourteenth Amendments, with three justices dissenting. . . . We granted certiorari. . . .

II

It is true that religion has been closely identified with our history and government. As we said in *Engel v. Vitale,* 370 U.S. 421, . . . "The history of man is inseparable from the history of religion. And . . . since the beginning of that history many people have devoutly believed that 'More things are wrought by prayer than this world dreams of.'" In *Zorach v. Clauson,* 343 U.S. 306, . . . we gave specific recognition to the proposition that "[w]e are a religious people whose institutions presuppose a Supreme Being." The fact that the Founding Fathers believed devotedly that there was a God and that the unalienable rights of man were rooted in Him is clearly evidenced in their writings, from the Mayflower Compact to the Constitution itself. This background is evidenced today in our public life through the continuance in our oaths of office from the Presidency to the Alderman of the final supplication, "So help me God." Likewise each House of the Congress provides through its Chaplain an opening prayer, and the sessions of this Court are declared open by the crier in a short ceremony, the final phrase of which invokes the grace of God. Again, there are such manifestations in our military forces, where those of our citizens who are under the restrictions of military service wish to engage in voluntary worship. Indeed, only last year an official survey of the country indicated that 64% of our people have church membership, Bureau of Census, U.S. Department of Commerce, Statistical Abstract of the United States, 48 (83d ed. 1962), while less than 3% profess no religion whatever. Id., at p.45. It can be truly said, therefore, that today, as in the beginning, our national life reflects a religious people who, in the words of Madison, are "earnestly praying as . . . in duty bound, that the Supreme Lawgiver of the Universe . . . guide them into every measure which may be worthy of his . . . blessing. . . ." . . .

This is not to say, however, that religion has been so identified with our history and government that religious freedom is not likewise as strongly imbedded in our public and private life. Nothing but the most telling of personal experiences in religious persecution suffered by our forebears . . . could have planted our belief in liberty of religious opinion any more deeply in our heritage. It is true that this liberty frequently was not realized by the colonists, but this is readily accountable to their close ties to the Mother Country. However, the views of Madison and Jefferson, preceded by Roger Williams, came to be incorporated not only in the Federal Constitution but likewise in those of most of our States. This freedom to worship was indispensable in a country whose people came from the four quarters of the earth and brought with them a diversity of religious opinion. Today authorities list 83 separate religious bodies, each with memberships exceeding 50,000, existing among our people, as well as innumerable smaller groups. Bureau of Census, *op. cit., supra,* at 46–47.

III

Almost a hundred years ago in *Minor v. Board of Education of Cincinnati,* Judge Alphonzo Taft, father of the revered Chief Justice, in an unpublished opinion stated the ideal of our people as to religious freedom as one of

. . . absolute equality before the law of all religious opinions and sects . . .

The government is neutral, and, while protecting all, it prefers none, and it disparages none.

Before examining this "neutral" position in which the Establishment and Free Exercise Clauses of the First Amendment place our government it is well that we discuss the reach of the Amendment under the cases of this Court.

First, this Court has decisively settled that the First Amendment's mandate that "Congress shall make no law respecting an establishment of religion, or prohibiting the free exercise thereof" has been made wholly applicable to the states by the Fourteenth Amendment. Twenty-three years ago in *Cantwell v. Connecticut*, 310 U.S. 296, this Court, through Mr. Justice Roberts, said:

> The fundamental concept of liberty embodied in that [Fourteenth] Amendment embraces the liberties guaranteed by the First Amendment. The First Amendment declares that Congress shall make no law respecting an establishment of religion or prohibiting the free exercise thereof. The Fourteenth Amendment has rendered the legislatures of the states as incompetent as Congress to enact such laws. . . .

In a series of cases since *Cantwell* the Court has repeatedly reaffirmed that doctrine, and we do so now. *Murdock v. Pennsylvania*, 319 U.S. 105 . . . ; *Everson v. Board of Education* . . . ; *Illinois ex rel. McCollum v. Board of Education*, 33 U.S. 203; . . . *Zorach v. Clauson*; . . . *McGowan v. Maryland*, 366 U.S. 420; . . . *Torcaso v. Watkins*, 367 U.S. 488; . . . and *Engel v. Vitale*. . . .

Second, this Court has rejected unequivocally the contention that the establishment clause forbids only governmental preference of one religion over another. Almost 20 years ago in *Everson*, . . . the Court said that "[n]either a state nor the Federal government can set up a church. Neither can pass laws which aid one religion, aid all religions, or prefer one religion over another." And Mr. Justice Jackson, dissenting, agreed:

> There is no answer to the proposition . . . that the effect of the religious freedom Amendment to our Constitution was to take every form of propagation of religion out of the realm of things which could directly or indirectly be made public business and thereby be supported in whole or in part at taxpayers' expense. . . . This freedom was first in the Bill of Rights because it was first in the forefathers' minds; it was set forth in absolute terms, and its strength is its rigidity. . . .

Further, Mr. Justice Rutledge, joined by Justices Frankfurter, Jackson and Burton, declared:

The [First] Amendment's purpose was not to strike merely at the official establishment of a single sect, creed or religion, outlawing only a formal relation such as had prevailed in England and some of the Colonies. Necessarily it was to uproot all such relationships. But the object was broader than separating church and state in this narrow sense. It was to create a complete and permanent separation of the spheres of religious activity and civil authority by comprehensively forbidding every form of public aid or support for religion.

The same conclusion has been firmly maintained ever since that time, . . . and we reaffirm it now.

While none of the parties to either of these cases has questioned these basic conclusions of the Court, both of which have been long established, recognized and consistently reaffirmed, others continue to question their history, logic and efficacy. Such contentions, in the light of the consistent interpretation in cases of this Court, seem entirely untenable and of value only as academic exercises.

I V

The interrelationship of the Establishment and the Free Exercise Clauses was first touched upon by Mr. Justice Roberts, for the Court in *Cantwell v. Connecticut,* . . . where it was said that their "inhibition of legislation" had

. . . a double aspect. On the one hand, it forestalls compulsion by law of the acceptance of any creed or the practice of any form of worship. Freedom of conscience and freedom to adhere to such religious organization or form of worship as the individual may choose cannot be restricted by law. On the other hand, it safeguards the free exercise of the chosen form of religion. Thus the Amendment embraces two concepts—freedom to believe and freedom to act. The first is absolute but, in the nature of things the second cannot be.

A half dozen years later in *Everson v. Board of Education,* . . . this Court, through Mr. Justice Black, stated that the "scope of the First Amendment . . . was designed forever to suppress" the establishment of religion or the prohibition of the free exercise thereof. In short, the Court held that the Amendment "requires the state to be a neutral in its relations with groups of religious believers and non-believers; it does not require the state to be their adversary. State power is no more to be used so as to handicap religions than it is to favor them." . . .

And Mr. Justice Jackson, in dissent, declared that public schools are organized

. . . on the premise that secular education can be isolated from all religious teaching so that the school can inculcate all needed temporal knowledge and also maintain a strict and lofty neutrality as to religion. The assumption is that after the individual has been instructed in worldly wisdom he will be better fitted to choose his religion. . . .

Moreover, all of the four dissenters, speaking through Mr. Justice Rutledge, agreed that

> Our constitutional policy . . . [D]oes not deny the value or necessity for religious training, teaching or observance. Rather it secures their free exercise. But to that end it does deny that the state can undertake or sustain them in any form or degree. For this reason the sphere of religious activity, as distinguished from the secular intellectual liberties, has been given the two-fold protection and, as the state cannot forbid, neither can it perform or aid in performing the religious function. The dual prohibition makes that function altogether private. . . .

Only one year later the Court was asked to reconsider and repudiate the doctrine of these cases in *McCollum v. Board of Education.* It was argued that "historically the First Amendment was intended to forbid only government preference of one religion over another. . . . In addition they ask that we distinguish or overrule our holding in the *Everson* case that the Fourteenth Amendment made the 'establishment of religion' clause of the First Amendment applicable as a prohibition against the States." . . . The Court, with Mr. Justice Reed alone dissenting, was unable to "accept either of these contentions." . . . Mr. Justice Frankfurter, joined by Justices Jackson, Rutledge and Burton, wrote a very comprehensive and scholarly concurrence in which he said that "[s]eparation is a requirement to abstain from fusing functions of government and of religious sects, not merely to treat them all equally." Continuing, he stated that:

> . . . the Constitution . . . prohibited the government common to all from becoming embroiled, however innocently, in the destructive religious conflicts of which the history of even this country records some dark pages. . . .

In 1952 in *Zorach v. Clauson,* Mr. Justice Douglas for the Court reiterated:

> There cannot be the slightest doubt that the First Amendment reflects the philosophy that Church and State should be separated. And so far as interference with the "free exercise" of religion and an "establishment" of religion are concerned, the separation must be complete and unequivocal. The First Amendment within the scope of its coverage permits no exception; the

prohibition is absolute. The First Amendment, however, does not say that in every and all respects there shall be a separation of Church and State. Rather, it studiously defines the manner, the specific ways, in which there shall be no concert or union or dependency one on the other. That is the common sense of the matter. . . .

And then in 1961 in *McGowan v. Maryland* and in *Torcaso v. Watkins* each of these cases was discussed and approved. Chief Justice Warren in *McGowan,* for a unanimous Court on this point, said:

> But, the First Amendment, in its final form, did not simply bar a congressional enactment establishing a church; it forbade all laws respecting an establishment of religion. Thus this Court has given the Amendment a "broad interpretation . . . in the light of its history and the evils it was designed forever to suppress. . . ."

And Mr. Justice Black for the Court in *Torcaso,* without dissent but with Justices Frankfurter and Harlan concurring in the result, used this language:

> We repeat and again reaffirm that neither a State nor the Federal Government can constitutionally force a person "to profess a belief or disbelief in any religion." Neither can constitutionally pass laws or impose requirements which aid all religions as against non-believers, and neither can aid those religions based on a belief in the existence of God as against those religions founded on different beliefs. . . .

Finally, in *Engel v. Vitale,* only last year, these principles were so universally recognized that the Court without the citation of a single case and over the sole dissent of Mr. Justice Stewart reaffirmed them. The Court found the 22-word prayer used in "New York's program of daily classroom invocation of God's blessings as prescribed in the Regents' prayer . . . [to be] a religious activity." . . . It held that "It is no part of the business of government to compose official prayers for any group of the American people to recite as a part of a religious program carried on by the government." In discussing the reach of the establishment and free exercise clauses of the First Amendment the Court said:

> Although these two clauses may in certain instances overlap, they forbid two quite different kinds of governmental encroachment upon religious freedom. The Establishment Clause, unlike the Free Exercise Clause does not depend upon any showing of direct governmental compulsion and is violated by the enactment of laws which establish an official religion whether those laws operate directly to coerce non-observing individuals or not. This is not to say, of course, that laws officially prescribing a particular form of religious worship do not involve coercion of such individuals. When the power, pres-

tige and financial support of government is placed behind a particular religious belief, the indirect coercive pressure upon religious minorities to conform to the prevailing officially approved religion is plain. . . .

And in further elaboration the Court found that the "first and most immediate purpose [of the Establishment Clause] rested on a belief that a union of government and religion tends to destroy government and to degrade religion." When government, the Court said, allies itself with one particular form of religion, the inevitable result is that it incurs "the hatred, disrespect and even contempt of those who held contrary beliefs."

V

The wholesome "neutrality" of which this Court's cases speak thus stems from a recognition of the teachings of history that powerful sects or groups might bring about a fusion of governmental and religious functions or a concert or dependency of one upon the other to the end that official support of the State or Federal Government would be placed behind the tenets of one or of all orthodoxies. This the Establishment Clause prohibits. And a further reason for neutrality is found in the Free Exercise Clause, which recognizes the value of religious training, teaching and observance and, more particularly, the right of every person to freely choose his own course with reference thereto, free of any compulsion from the state. This the Free Exercise Clause guarantees. Thus, as we have seen, the two clauses may overlap. As we have indicated, the Establishment Clause has been directly considered by this Court eight times in the past score of years and, with only one Justice dissenting on the point, it has consistently held that the clause withdrew all legislative power respecting religious belief or the expression thereof. The test may be stated as follows: what are the purpose and the primary effect of the enactment? If either is the advancement or inhibition of religion then the enactment exceeds the scope of legislative power as circumscribed by the Constitution. That is to say that to withstand the strictures of the Establishment Clause there must be a secular legislative purpose and a primary effect that neither advances nor inhibits religion. . . . The Free Exercise Clause, likewise considered many times here, withdraws from legislative power, state and federal, the exertion of any restraint on the free exercise of religion. Its purpose is to secure religious liberty in the individual by prohibiting any invasions thereof by civil authority. Hence it is necessary in a free exercise case for one to show the coercive effect of the enactment as it operates against him in the practice of his religion. The distinction between the two clauses is apparent—a violation of the Free Exercise Clause is predicated on coercion while the Establishment Clause violation need not be so attended.

Applying the Establishment Clause principles to the cases at bar we find that the States are requiring the selection and reading at the opening of the school day of verses from the Holy Bible and the recitation of the Lord's Prayer by the students in unison. These exercises are prescribed as part of the curricular activities of students who are required by law to attend school. They are held in the school buildings under the supervision and with the participation of teachers employed in those schools. None of these factors, other than compulsory school attendance, was present in the program upheld in *Zorach v. Clauson.* The trial court in No. 142 has found that such an opening exercise is a religious ceremony and was intended by the State to be so. We agree with the trial court's finding as to the religious character of the exercises. Given that finding the exercises and the law requiring them are in violation of the Establishment Clause.

There is no such specific finding as to the religious character of the exercises in No. 119, and the State contends (as does the State in No. 142) that the program is an effort to extend its benefits to all public school children without regard to their religious belief. Included within its secular purposes, it says, are the promotion of moral values, the contradiction to the materialistic trends of our times, the perpetuation of our institutions and the teaching of literature. The case came up on demurrer, of course, to a petition which alleged that the uniform practice under the rule had been to read from the King James version of the Bible and that the exercise was sectarian. The short answer, therefore, is that the religious character of the exercise was admitted by the State. But even if its purpose is not strictly religious, it is sought to be accomplished through readings, without comment, from the Bible. Surely the place of the Bible as an instrument of religion cannot be gainsaid, and the State's recognition of the pervading religious character of the ceremony is evident from the rule's specific permission of the alternative use of the Catholic Douay version as well as the recent amendment permitting nonattendance at the exercises. None of these factors is consistent with the contention that the Bible is here used either as an instrument for nonreligious moral inspiration or as a reference for the teaching of secular subjects.

The conclusion follows that in both cases the laws require religious exercises and such exercises are being conducted in direct violation of the rights of the appellees and petitioners. Nor are these required exercises mitigated by the fact that individual students may absent themselves upon parental request, for that fact furnishes no defense to a claim of unconstitutionality under the Establishment Clause. . . . Further, it is no defense to urge that the religious practices here may be relatively minor encroachments on the First Amendment. The breach of neutrality that is today a trickling stream may all too soon become a raging torrent and, in the words of Madison, "it is proper to take alarm at the first experiment on our liberties." . . .

It is insisted that unless these religious exercises are permitted a "religion of secularism" is established in the schools. We agree of course that the State may not establish a "religion of secularism" in the sense of affirmatively opposing or showing hostility to religion, thus "preferring those who believe in no religion over those who do believe." . . . We do not agree, however, that this decision in any sense has that effect. In addition, it might well be said that one's education is not complete without a study of comparative religion or the history of religion and its relationship to the advancement of civilization. It certainly may be said that the Bible is worthy of study for its literary and historic qualities. Nothing we have said here indicates that such study of the Bible or of religion, when presented objectively as part of a secular program of education, may not be effected consistent with the First Amendment. But the exercises here do not fall into those categories. They are religious exercises, required by the States in violation of the command of the First Amendment that the Government maintain strict neutrality, neither aiding nor opposing religion.

Finally, we cannot accept that the concept of neutrality, which does not permit a State to require a religious exercise even with the consent of the majority of those affected, collides with the majority's right to free exercise of religion. While the Free Exercise Clause clearly prohibits the use of state action to deny the rights of free exercise to anyone, it has never meant that a majority could use the machinery of the State to practice its beliefs. Such a contention was effectively answered by Mr. Justice Jackson for the Court in *West Virginia Board of Education v. Barnette*, 319 U.S. 624:

> The very purpose of a Bill of Rights was to withdraw certain subjects from the vicissitudes of political controversy, to place them beyond the reach of majorities and officials and to establish them as legal principles to be applied by the courts. One's right to . . . freedom of worship . . . and other fundamental rights may not be submitted to vote; they depend on the outcome of no elections.

The place of religion in our society is an exalted one, achieved through a long tradition of reliance on the home, the church and the inviolable citadel of the individual heart and mind. We have come to recognize through bitter experience that it is not within the power of government to invade that citadel, whether its purpose or effect be to aid or oppose, to advance or retard. In the relationship between man and religion, the State is firmly committed to a position of neutrality. Though the application of that rule requires interpretation of a delicate sort, the rule itself is clearly and concisely stated in the words of the First Amendment. Applying that rule to the facts of these cases, we affirm the judgment in No. 142. In No. 119, the judgment is reversed and the cause remanded to the Maryland Court of Appeals for further proceedings consistent with this opinion.

It is so ordered.

CIVIL RIGHTS ACT OF 1964

Public Law 88-352
Title IV—Desegregation of Public Education

Definitions

Sec. 401. As used in this title—

(a) "Commissioner" means the Commissioner of Education.

(b) "Desegregation" means the assignment of students to public schools and within such schools without regard to their race, color, religion, or national origin, but "desegregation" shall not mean the assignment of students to public schools in order to overcome racial imbalance.

(c) "Public school" means any elementary or secondary educational institution, of higher education or any technical or vocational school above the secondary school level, provided that such public school or public college is operated by a State, subdivision of a State, or governmental agency within a State, or operated wholly or predominantly from or through the use of governmental funds or property, or funds or property derived from a governmental source.

(d) "School board" means any agency or agencies which administer a system of one or more public schools and any other agency which is responsible for the assignment of students to or within such system.

Survey and Report of Educational Opportunities

Sec. 402. The Commissioner shall conduct a survey and make a report to the President and the Congress, within two years of the enactment of this title, concerning the lack of availability of equal educational opportunities for individuals by reason of race, color, religion, or national origin in public educational institutions at all levels in the United States, its territories and possessions, and the District of Columbia.

Technical Assistance

Sec. 403. The Commissioner is authorized, upon the application of any school board, State, municipality, school district, or other governmental unit legally responsible for operating a public school or schools, to render technical assistance to such applicant in the preparation, adoption, and implementation of plans for the desegregation of public schools. Such technical assistance may, among other activities, include making available to such agencies information regarding effective methods of coping with special educational problems occasioned by desegregation, and making available to such agencies personnel of the Office of Education or other persons specially equipped to advise and assist them in coping with such problems.

Training Institutes

Sec. 404. The Commissioner is authorized to arrange, through grants or contracts, with institutions of higher education for the operation of short-term or regular session institutes for special training designed to improve the ability of teachers, supervisors, counselors, and other elementary or secondary school personnel to deal effectively with special educational problems occasioned by desegregation. Individuals who attend such an institute on a full-time basis may be paid stipends for the period of their attendance at such institute in amounts specified by the Commissioner in regulations, including allowances for travel to attend such institute.

Grants

Sec. 405. (a) The Commissioner is authorized, upon application of a school board, to make grants to such board to pay, in whole or in part, the cost of—

(1) giving to teachers and other school personnel inservice training in dealing with problems incident to desegregation, and

(2) employing specialists to advise in problems incident to desegregation.

(b) In determining whether to make a grant, and in fixing the amount thereof and the terms and conditions on which it will be made, the Commissioner shall take into consideration the amount available for grants under this section and the other applications which are pending before him; the financial condition of the applicant and the other resources available to it; the nature, extent, and gravity of its problems incident to desegregation; and such other factors as he finds relevant.

Payments

Sec. 406. Payments pursuant to a grant or contract under this title may be made (after necessary adjustments on account of previously made overpayments or underpayments) in advance or by way of reimbursement, and in such installments, as the Commissioner may determine.

Suits by the Attorney General

Sec. 407. (a) Whenever the Attorney General receives a complaint in writing—

(1) signed by a parent or group of parents to the effect that his or their minor children, as members of a class of persons similarly situated, are being deprived by a school board of the equal protection of the laws, or

(2) signed by an individual, or his parent, to the effect that he has been denied admission to or not permitted to continue in attendance at a public college by reason of race, color, religion, or national origin, and the Attorney General believes the complaint is meritorious and certifies that the signer or signers of such complaint are unable, in his judgment, to initiate and maintain appropriate legal proceedings for relief and that the institution of an action will materially further the orderly achievement of desegregation in public education, the Attorney General is authorized, after giving notice of such complaint to the appropriate school board or college authority and after certifying that he is satisfied that such board or authority has had a reasonable time to adjust the conditions alleged in such complaint, to institute for or in the name of the United States a civil action in any appropriate district court of the United States against such parties and for such relief as may be appropriate, and such court shall exercise jurisdiction of proceedings instituted pursuant to this section, provided that nothing herein shall empower any official or court of the United States to issue any order seeking to achieve a racial balance in any school by requiring the transportation of pupils or students from one school to another or one school district to another in order to achieve such racial balance, or otherwise enlarge the existing power of the court to insure compliance with constitutional standards. The Attorney General may implead as defendants such additional parties as are or become necessary to the grant of effective relief hereunder.

(b) The Attorney General may deem a person or persons unable to initiate and maintain appropriate legal proceedings within the meaning of subsection (a) of this section when such person or persons are unable, either directly or through other interested persons or organizations, to bear the expense of the litigation or to obtain effective legal representation; or whenever he is satisfied that the institution of such litigation would jeopardize the personal safety, employment, or economic standing of such person or persons, their families, or their property.

(c) The term "parent" as used in this section includes any person standing in loco parentis. A "complaint" as used in this section is a writing or document within the meaning of section 1001 title 18, United States Code.

Sec. 408. In any action or proceeding under this title the United States shall be liable for costs the same as a private person.

Sec. 409. Nothing in this title shall affect adversely the right of any person to sue for or obtain relief in any court against discrimination in public education.

Sec. 410. Nothing in this title shall prohibit classification and assignment for reasons other than race, color, religion, or national origin.

Chapter 1

[1] John Dewey, *Democracy and Education*, The Macmillan Company, New York, 1916, p. 144.

[2] Ross L. Finney, *A Sociological Philosophy of Education*, The Macmillan Company, New York, 1928.

[3] George S. Counts's book, published in 1929, raised an essential question and challenged educators and sociologists to take another close look at the school's function. Counts's answer seems to have been that the school had better try to change the social order. If the school did not make the effort, what agency or institution would? But this did not end the issue. The point is still debated whether or not the school should try to change the society it serves.

[4] I have dealt at greater length with the educational theories of Plato and Isocrates in *Main Currents in the History of Education*, McGraw-Hill Book Company, New York, 1962, pp. 81–102. See also: J. E. Adamson, *The Theory of Education in Plato's Republic*, Swan Sonnenschein, London, 1903; Richard L. Nettleship, *The Theory of Education in the Republic of Plato*, The University of Chicago Press, Chicago, 1906; and H. I. Marrou, *History of Education in Antiquity*, Sheed & Ward, Inc., New York, 1956.

[5] The clearest formulation of the doctrine of utility was made by Francis Bacon in *The New Atlantis*. This utopian volume was influential in shaping the social and educational views of many prominent American philosophers, chief among whom was John Dewey. Dewey himself acknowledges his debt to Bacon.

[6] Publications of the Institute for Higher Education of Teachers College, Columbia University, have probed and tested the tempers of faculties of liberal arts colleges and professional schools. Highly illuminating data are given in: Paul L. Dressel and Margaret F. Lorimer, *Attitudes of Liberal Arts Faculty Members toward Liberal and Professional Education*; Paul L. Dressel, Lewis B. Mayhew, and Earl J. McGrath, *The Liberal Arts as Viewed by Faculty Members in Professional Schools*; Earl J. McGrath, *Liberal Education in the Pro-*

fessions; Earl J. McGrath and Charles H. Russell, *Are School Teachers Illiberally Educated?* and Earl J. McGrath and Charles H. Russell, *Are Liberal Arts Colleges Becoming Professional Schools?*

[7] The religious-educational question is now in the process of being thoroughly reappraised. The decisions of the United States Supreme Court in the summer of 1963 have led many thoughtful people to reevaluate the entire issue. For the decisions, see Appendix.

[8] This is the title of a book by John L. Childs relative to a subject that has commanded the thought of many sincerely interested persons. Childs's interpretation in *Education and Morals: An Experimentalist Philosophy of Education,* Appleton-Century-Crofts, Inc., New York, 1950, is thoroughly relativistic and, to the Christian humanist, disappointing and unacceptable. No one has any reason to doubt, however, that the author is sincere in holding it and that personally he is an entirely honorable man. This topic has formed the theme of a number of other publications; see especially Robert M. Hutchins, *Morals, Religion and Higher Education,* The University of Chicago Press, Chicago, 1950; R. E. Mason, *Moral Values and Secular Education,* Columbia University Press, New York, 1950; and J. D. Redden and F. A. Ryan, *A Catholic Philosophy of Education,* The Bruce Publishing Company, Milwaukee, 1942, chap. 6.

[9] The possibility of moral education's becoming a specific function of the school's instructional program is the burden of an article by Charles F. Donovan, S.J., "On the Possibility of Moral Education," *Educational Theory,* vol. 12, no. 3, pp. 184–186, July, 1961.

[10] The year-round school is presently a subject of intense debate among many educators. It is by no means certain that we are heading in the direction of the year-round school. For some of the arguments pro and con, see *Theory into Practice,* vol. 1, no. 3, College of Education, The Ohio State University, June, 1962. The entire issue is devoted to this topic.

Chapter 2

[1] For the text of Jefferson's proposal, see Edgar W. Knight and Clifton L. Hall, *Readings in American Educational History,* Appleton-Century-Crofts, Inc., New York, 1951, pp. 299–306.

[2] Quoted in *ibid.,* p. 116.

[3] From *Education in the United States,* 3d rev. ed., by Edgar W. Knight, Copyright, 1951, p. 105. Used by permission of Ginn & Company.

[4] The historical evolution of compulsory attendance excludes both Alaska and Hawaii, for in both of these states compulsory-attendance statutes were enacted during the territorial period.

[5] *Acts and Resolves Passed by the General Court of Massachusetts in the Year 1852,* pp. 170 and 171.

[6] See Appendix.

[7] Quoted in Knight and Hall, *op. cit.,* p. 343.

[8] *Laws of Massachusetts,* Mar. 10, 1827, chap. 143, sec. 7.

[9] Donald Tewksbury, *The Founding of American Colleges and Universities*

before the Civil War, Bureau of Publications, Teachers College, Columbia University, New York, 1932, p. 90.

[10] For the text of the Oregon decision, see Appendix.

[11] For the role of the private college in American higher education, see John S. Brubacher and Willis Rudy, *Higher Education in Transition,* Harper & Row, Publishers, Incorporated, New York, 1958; Richard Hofstadter and C. DeWitt Hardy, *The Development and Scope of Higher Education in the United States,* Columbia University Press, 1952; and Frederick Rudolph, *The American College and University,* Alfred A. Knopf, Inc., New York, 1962.

[12] Religion's place in education forms the theme of Chap. 13. The role of religion in education has been given special emphasis in the following: R. Freeman Butts, *The American Tradition in Religion and Education,* Beacon Press, Boston, 1950; Committee on Religion and Education, *The Relation of Religion to Public Education,* American Council on Education, Washington, 1947; Educational Policies Commission, *Moral and Spiritual Values in the Public Schools,* National Education Association, Washington, 1951; C. L. Hay, *The Blind Spot in American Education,* The Macmillan Company, New York, 1950; Virgil Henry, *The Place of Religion in Public Schools,* Harper & Row, Publishers, Incorporated, New York, 1950; and Vivian T. Thayer, *Religion in Public Education,* The Viking Press, Inc., New York, 1947.

Chapter 3

[1] The school district is treated in some detail on pp. 75–76. For a more elaborate discussion of the American school district, its origin, its evolution, and its present status and structure, see American Association of School Administrators, *School District Organization,* American Association of School Administrators, Washington, 1958. Legal implications relative to school districts are treated in considerable detail by Lee O. Garber and Newton Edwards, *The Law Relating to Creation, Alteration, and Dissolution of School Districts,* The Interstate Printers and Publishers, Danville, Ill., 1962.

[2] Quoted in Edgar W. Knight and Clifton L. Hall, *Readings in American Educational History,* Appleton-Century-Crofts, Inc., New York, 1951, p. 69.

[3] This included the state colleges, as Coulter points out. See E. M. Coulter, *College Life in the Old South,* University of Georgia Press, Athens, 1951.

[4] John Fairfield Sly, *Town Government in Massachusetts (1620–1930).* Harvard University Press, Cambridge, Mass., 1930, pp. 75 and 76.

[5] Section 16, the school section, is still preserved in its original form in many Western states. It has been more common, however, for the states to dispose of this land and use the proceeds from its sale for school purposes. For a more extensive treatment of the impact of the Northwest Ordinances on education, see Hollis P. Allen, *The Federal Government and Education,* McGraw-Hill Book Company, New York, 1950, and Howard C. Taylor, *The Educational Significance of the Early Federal Land Grant Ordinances,* Bureau of Publications, Teachers College, Columbia University, New York, 1922.

[6] For studies of county educational organization, see National Education Association, Department of Rural Education, *The County Superintendent of*

Schools in the United States, 1950 Yearbook, Washington, and Truman M. Pierce, *Leadership in County School Districts and the Administration of Public Education,* George Peabody College for Teachers, Nashville, Tenn., 1954.

[7] The total number of school units is decreasing steadily because of consolidation and redistricting. This reduction has affected the school district from the point of view of numbers, but proportionately its weight is greater than ever before. See *Digest of Educational Statistics,* U.S. Department of Health, Education, and Welfare, Office of Education, 1963, p. 92.

[8] From *Early New England Schools,* by Walter Herbert Small, Copyright 1914, p. 73. Used by permission of Ginn & Company.

[9] *A. H. Andrews Co. v. Delight Special School Dist.,* 95 Ark. 26, 128, S.W. 361.

[10] Compared with the litanies of duties and responsibilities for boards of education given in books on school administration, these responsibilities are somewhat general. However, our interest is not in the board of education as such but in its relationship to education at the local level.

Chapter 4

[1] Quoted in Clement T. Malan, *Indiana School Law and Supreme Court Decisions,* Teachers College Press, Terre Haute, Ind., 1931, p. 451.

[2] *Louisville v. Commonwealth,* 134 Ky. 488, 211 S.W. 411.

[3] *Leeper v. Tennessee,* 103 Tenn. 500 S.W. 962. 48 L.R.A. 167.

[4] *Fogg v. Board of Education,* 76 N.H. 296, 82 Alt. 173, 37 L.R.A. (N.S.) 1110 Ann. Cas. 1912C 758.

[5] *Indiana v. Haworth,* 122 Ind. 462, 23 N.E. 946, 7 L.R.A. 240.

[6] *Nebraska Dist. of Evangelical Lutheran Synod v. McKelvie,* 104 Neb. 93, 175 N.W. 531, 7 A.L.R. 1688.

[7] *Iowa v. Bartels,* 191 Iowa 1060, 181 N.W. 508.

[8] *Meyer v. Nebraska,* 262 U.S. 390. For the text of the Nebraska decision, see Appendix.

[9] See pp. 48–50.

[10] *Pierce v. Society of Sisters,* and *Pierce v. Hill Military Academy,* 268 U.S. 510. For the text of the Oregon decision, see Appendix.

[11] Thomas Bouquillon, *Education: To Whom Does It Belong? with a Rejoinder to Critics,* 2d ed., John A. Murphy Publishing Company, New York, 1892, p. 11. For more recent discussions of this topic, although unfortunately deprived of the context of controversy, see Neil G. McCluskey, S.J., *Catholic Viewpoint on Education,* Hanover House, Doubleday & Company, Inc., Garden City, N.Y., 1959; and Jerome G. Kirwin, *Catholic Viewpoint on Church and State,* Hanover House, Doubleday & Company, Inc., Garden City, N.Y., 1960.

[12] Pius XI, *The Christian Education of Youth,* 1929.

[13] The development, financing, and problems of junior colleges particularly form extensive testimony to the educational variety among states. On this point, see Leland L. Medsker, *The Junior College: Progress and Prospect,* McGraw-Hill Book Company, New York, 1960, pp. 208–286.

Chapter 5

[1] *Brown v. Board of Educ.*, 347 U.S. 483. For the text of the decision, see Appendix.

[2] Literature on the Northwest Ordinance and its effects on education across the nation is not great. Supplementing the grant of the sixteenth section, section twenty-nine was reserved for the advancement of religion, and two entire townships were set aside to help finance and maintain a university. Ordinance of 1787, art. III.

[3] *Ibid.*

[4] *Stat. L.*, 37th Cong., p. 503. Approved July 2, 1862.

[5] Henry S. Brunner, *Land-grant Colleges and Universities,* U.S. Office of Education Bulletin 1962, no. 13, 1962, p. 4.

[6] *Stat. L.*, 39th Cong., p. 434. Approved Mar. 2, 1867.

Chapter 6

[1] *Digest of Educational Statistics*, U.S. Department of Health, Education, and Welfare, Bulletin 1964, no. 18, 1964, pp. 14–15.

[2] See Edward J. Power, *Main Currents in the History of Education,* McGraw-Hill Book Company, New York, 1962, chap. 1.

[3] See Thomas Woody, *Life and Education in Early Societies,* The Macmillan Company, New York, 1949, pp. 55–58.

[4] See pp. 63–71.

[5] See p. 32.

[6] See pp. 173–176.

[7] Quoted in Clifton Johnson, *Old-time Schools and School-books,* The Macmillan Company, New York, 1904, pp. 116 and 117. By permission.

[8] See pp. 176–178.

[9] See pp. 28–29.

[10] See pp. 274–277.

[11] See pp. 278–279.

[12] Quoted in Raymond B. Culver, *Horace Mann and Religion in the Massachusetts Public Schools,* Yale University Press, New Haven, Conn., 1929, p. 36.

[13] For the origin and early history of common school funds, which in many cases led to permanent school funds, see F. W. Blackmar, *History of Federal and State Aid to Higher Education in the United States,* U.S. Bureau of Education Circular of Information 1, 1890, p. 46; and F. H. Swift, *A History of Public Permanent Common School Funds in the United States, 1795–1905,* Holt, Rinehart and Winston, Inc., New York, 1911.

[14] On this point, see pp. 71–73 and 75–76.

[15] *Laws of Massachusetts,* Mar. 10, 1827, chap. 143, sec. 7.

[16] For the evolution of the American teacher and the influence of Carter and Mann on the newly formed normal schools, see pp. 274–278.

[17] See pp. 50–51.

[18] See pp. 367–371.

[19] Quoted in J. A. Burns and Bernard J. Kohlbrenner, *A History of Catholic Education in the United States*, Benziger Bros. Inc., New York, 1937, p. 137.

[20] *Ibid.*, pp. 143 and 144.

[21] For a general evaluation of the work of the Committee of Ten, see pp. 184–186. For the report itself, see Appendix.

[22] The work of this committee is described in the "Report of the Committee on College Entrance Requirements," Proc. NEA, 1899, pp. 632–817, Washington.

[23] A rather dramatic outcome of these approaches has been FLES (Foreign Language in the Elementary School), a program of language instruction that stresses the natural method of learning a language. These programs have been remarkably successful despite obvious difficulties in obtaining teachers qualified to employ a conversational technique. The work of teachers has been cleverly supplemented by carefully designed and effectively presented audio-visual aids.

Chapter 7

[1] Quintilian, *Institutes of Oratory*, Henry G. Bohn, London, 1856, vol. II, p. 25.

[2] Cicero, *The Orator*, G. Bell & Sons, Ltd., London, 1881, vol. I, p. 6.

[3] For this essay, see John Harden Best (ed.), *Classics in Education*, no. 14, *Benjamin Franklin on Education*, Bureau of Publications, Teachers College, Columbia University, 1962, pp. 34–38.

[4] Quoted in Henry Barnard, *Am. J. Educ.*, vol. 27, pp. 441–442, 1878.

[5] Yet Franklin did leave money to the cities of Boston and Philadelphia to be invested by them to maintain a fund upon which medical school scholars might draw. These scholarships are still intact.

[6] See pp. 28–29.

[7] See pp. 64–71.

[8] For the text of the decision, see Appendix.

[9] See pp. 215–216.

[10] In addition to the five members who were presidents of colleges, there were one college professor, two headmasters of private secondary schools, one principal of a public high school, and the United States Commissioner of Education. Charles W. Eliot was the committee's chairman. William T. Harris was the United States Commissioner of Education. Nicholas Murray Butler, then president of Columbia University, was not a member of the Committee of Ten.

[11] See *The Report of the Committee of Ten on Secondary School Studies*, U.S. Bureau of Education, 1893, pp. 51–53.

[12] See *Report of the Committee on College Entrance Requirements*, in Proc. Addresses NEA, 1899, pp. 655–658, Chicago.

[13] See Appendix.

[14] The Eight Year Study published plans and conclusions under the general title *Adventures in American Education*, Harper & Row, Publishers, Incorporated. The study was presented in several volumes: W. M. Aikin, *The Story of the Eight Year Study*; S. P. McCutchen, H. Giles, and A. N. Zechiel, *Exploring the Curriculum*; E. R. Smith and R. W. Tyler, *Appraising and*

Recording Student Progress; Dean Chamberlain, Enid Chamberlain, N. E. Drought, and W. E. Scott, *Did They Succeed in College?* and *Thirty Schools Tell Their Story.*

[15] Educational Policies Commission, *Education for All American Youth,* National Education Association, Washington, 1944, p. 216.

Chapter 8

[1] Second Report, 1957.

[2] These estimates vary considerably because of the variety of selections made of base years from which to predict future college attendance. If the year 1945 is taken rather than, say, 1932, the estimates for the future will vary greatly. Bernard Berelson, *Graduate Education in the United States,* McGraw-Hill Book Company, New York, 1960, handles these estimates and the issues fundamental to them in a conservative manner seeing relatively little indication of crisis thinking with regard to either faculty or enrollment. However, Oliver C. Carmichael in his study of *Graduate Education; a Critique and a Program,* Harper & Row, Publishers, Incorporated, New York, 1961, does not agree that Berelson's premises are valid and sees plenty of reason for alarm.

[3] There are a number of valuable accounts of medieval universities. The definitive work in English is by Hastings Rashdall in F. M. Powicke and A. B. Emden (eds.), *Universities of Europe during the Middle Ages,* Oxford University Press, London, 1936, 3 vols.

[4] The rise of the modern university is discussed by Frederick Paulsen in *German Universities and University Study,* Charles Scribner's Sons, New York, 1906.

[5] Quoted in Perry Miller, *The New England Mind,* The Macmillan Company, New York, 1939, p. 75. By permission.

[6] Edward J. Power, *A History of Catholic Higher Education in the United States,* The Bruce Publishing Company, Milwaukee, 1958, p. 57.

[7] For professional teacher education, see pp. 281–285.

[8] See pp. 111–114.

[9] Donald G. Tewksbury, *The Founding of American Colleges and Universities before the Civil War,* Bureau of Publications, Teachers College, Columbia University, New York, 1932, pp. 167 and 168.

[10] *Digest of Educational Statistics,* Bulletin 1964, no. 18, 1964, p. 74.

[11] See George Paul Schmidt, "Colleges in Ferment," *Am. Historical Rev.,* vol. LIX, pp. 19–42, October, 1953.

[12] *The Report of the President of the University of Chicago, July, 1898–July, 1899,* The University of Chicago Press, 1900, pp. xx–xxi.

Chapter 9

[1] This was Robert M. Hutchins in *The Higher Learning in America,* Yale University Press, New Haven, Conn., 1937, pp. 1–5.

[2] See W. M. Smail, *Quintilian on Education,* Oxford University Press, Lon-

don, 1938. For a summary of Quintilian's principal educational positions, see Edward J. Power, *Main Currents in the History of Education*, McGraw-Hill Book Company, New York, 1962, pp. 147–149.

[3] *Ibid.*, pp. 285–289, 336–346, 300–302, 359, 360, 377–388, 476, 404–408, 476–478.

[4] For a general discussion of the meaning of learning, see Tad W. Guzie, S.J., *The Analogy of Learning: An Essay toward a Thomistic Psychology of Learning*, Sheed & Ward, Inc., New York, 1960.

[5] For a further distinction between self-education and self-teaching, see Mortimer Adler in National Society for the Study of Education, *Philosophies of Education*, Chicago, 1942, Forty-first Yearbook, part I, pp. 213–214.

[6] Connectionism is explained in most books on educational psychology and psychology of learning. For what would seem to be an authentic presentation of its meaning, see Edward L. Thorndike, "The Psychology of Learning," *Educational Psychology*, Teachers College, Columbia University, New York, 1913, vol. II.

[7] Gestalt and topological field theories are treated by K. Koffka, *Principles of Gestalt Psychology*, Harcourt, Brace & World, Inc., New York, 1935; K. Lewin, *A Dynamic Theory of Personality*, McGraw-Hill Book Company, New York, 1935; and K. Lewin, *Principles of Topological Psychology*, McGraw-Hill Book Company, New York, 1936.

[8] Fear of psychoanalysis is now somewhat allayed in the popular mind. Its emphases, which do not directly include learning theory, are treated along with several theories of learning in Louis P. Thorpe and A. M. Schmuller, *Contemporary Theories of Learning*, The Ronald Press Company, New York, 1954.

[9] It is extremely unlikely that any section of a chapter devoted to motivation could be entirely satisfactory: the subject is simply too broad to admit of summary treatment. The reader is directed, therefore, to other more highly specialized books. For example, D. C. McClelland (ed.), *Studies in Motivation*, Appleton-Century-Crofts, Inc., New York, 1955, or C. L. Stacey and M. F. De Martino, *Understanding Human Motivation*, Howard Allen, Inc., Cleveland, 1958.

[10] For an elaboration of process transfer, see C. H. Judd et al., *Education as Cultivation of the Higher Mental Processes*, The Macmillan Company, New York, 1936.

[11] This issue was sharpened considerably, but not settled, in the Eight Year Study. See W. M. Aikin, *The Story of the Eight Year Study*, Harper & Row, Publishers, Incorporated, New York, 1942.

[12] For these classical positions, see E. L. Thorndike, *Educational Psychology: Briefer Course*, Teachers College, Columbia University, New York, 1914, pp. 276 ff., and C. H. Judd et al., *op. cit.*, pp. 200 ff.

[13] Herbart's steps were set forth in his *The Science of Education* (tr. by H. M. Felkin and E. Felkin), Routledge & Kegan Paul, Ltd., London, 1924, and Morrison in his *The Practice of Teaching in the Secondary School*, The University of Chicago Press, Chicago, 1926.

[14] For other delineations of the guidance function, see Percival W. Hutson, *The Guidance Function in Education*, Appleton-Century-Crofts, Inc., New

York, 1958, pp. 76–110, and Donald G. Mortensen and Allen M. Schmuller, *Guidance in Today's Schools,* John Wiley & Sons, Inc., 1959, pp. 3–42.

Chapter 10

[1] For an illuminating and discriminating analysis of the teacher's contribution to the quality of the educational process and the school, see Pierre D. Lambert, "The Teacher and the System," *Peabody J. Educ.,* vol. 40, pp. 94–98, September, 1962.

[2] See Edgar W. Knight and Clifton L. Hall, *Readings in American Educational History,* Appleton-Century-Crofts, Inc., New York, 1951, p. 28.

[3] Relatively little is known of the dame school in America and the literature pertaining to it is not impressive. For some of the details of its mission, see Walter Small, *Early New England Schools,* Ginn and Company, Boston, 1914, pp. 162 ff.

[4] Knight and Hall, *op. cit.,* p. 29.

[5] *Ibid.*

[6] *Ibid.,* p. 31.

[7] Quoted in Willard S. Elsbree, *The American Teacher,* American Book Company, New York, 1939, p. 42.

[8] *Ibid.*

[9] D. D. Runes (ed.), *The Selected Writings of Benjamin Rush,* Philosophical Library, Inc., New York, 1947, p. 114.

[10] *Ibid.*

[11] James G. Carter, *Essays on Popular Education,* quoted in Knight and Hall, *op. cit.,* p. 404.

[12] Henry Barnard, *National Education in Europe: Being an Account of the Organization, Administration, Instruction, and Statistics of Public Schools and Different Grades in the Principal States,* 2d ed., published for the author by Case, Tiffany, & Co., Hartford, Conn., 1854, p. 33.

[13] Henry Barnard was the first United States Commissioner of Education. As commissioner he continued in the *Annual Reports* and elsewhere to encourage the professional upgrading of teachers. See especially Barnard's encouragement of professional upgrading in any early issue of the *American Journal of Education.*

[14] From the *Common School Journal,* Feb. 1, 1839. Quoted in Knight and Hall, *op. cit.,* p. 415.

[15] See pp. 351–352.

[16] See Charles A. Harper, *A Century of Public Teacher Education: The Story of the State Teachers Colleges as They Evolved from the Normal Schools,* American Association of Colleges for Teacher Education, Washington, 1939, pp. 35 and 36.

Chapter 11

[1] I have treated most of these theorists in *Main Currents in the History of Education,* McGraw-Hill Book Company, New York, 1962. In addition, Robert

Ulich's *History of Educational Thought,* American Book Company, New York, 1950, and Percival R. Cole, *History of Educational Thought,* Oxford University Press, London, 1931, may be consulted.

[2] V. T. Thayer in *The Role of the School in American Society,* Dodd, Mead & Company, Inc., New York, 1960, is concerned with the meaning of education and its relationship to society. In connection with this general discussion, one should consult Philip H. Phoenix, *Education and the Common Good: A Moral Philosophy of the Curriculum,* Harper & Row, Publishers, Incorporated, New York, 1961.

[3] On these points the student is advised to read Herbert Johnston, *A Philosophy of Education,* McGraw-Hill Book Company, New York, 1963, and Robert Ulich, *Philosophy of Education,* American Book Company, New York, 1961, pp. 3–140.

[4] Alfred North Whitehead illuminates the entire issue of educational goals and their interpretation in *The Aims of Education and Other Essays,* The Macmillan Company, New York, 1929. This is a perceptive treatment that no student of education should miss reading.

[5] Acceptance of educational philosophy as a directive force is only one interpretation of its role; it may be accepted also as a liberal discipline. Both positions are discussed by Harry Broudy, *Building a Philosophy of Education,* 2d ed., Prentice-Hall, Inc., Englewood Cliffs, N.J., 1961, pp. 3–21, and Philip H. Phoenix, *Philosophy of Education,* Holt, Rinehart and Winston, Inc., New York, 1960, pp. 3–19.

[6] Many authors have written on totalitarianism in education. For good, clear, and relatively brief treatments, see George Z. F. Bereday, William W. Brickman, and Gerald H. Read (eds.), *The Changing Soviet School,* Houghton Mifflin Company, Boston, 1960; George F. Counts, *The Challenge of Soviet Education,* McGraw-Hill Book Company, New York, 1957; and Arthur H. Moehlman and Joseph S. Roucek, *Comparative Education,* Holt, Rinehart and Winston, Inc., New York, 1952.

[7] Theodore Brameld deals with indoctrination and what he cleverly refers to as "defensible partiality" in *Education for the Emerging Age: Newer Ends and Stronger Means,* Harper & Row, Publishers, Incorporated, New York, 1961, pp. 153 and 154. Regardless of the position one takes on such questions, it must be admitted that Brameld's discussion is interesting and penetrating. The literature on indoctrination in education is extensive but not especially impressive.

[8] See Appendix.

[9] William F. Cunningham, *The Pivotal Problems of Education,* The Macmillan Company, New York, 1940, pp. 158–228.

[10] The great exponent of liberal learning, John Henry Newman, in *The Idea of a University,* Doubleday & Company, Inc., Garden City, N.Y., 1959, pp. 144–147, raises the question of merit in connection with liberal studies and concludes that superior merit is not guaranteed by liberal learning. Even to raise the question of merit is to miss the real point of liberal learning.

Chapter 12

[1] We raise the issue of liberal education here only to show that disagreements are possible even with educational doctrines that have been in vogue for thousands of years. Without making any claim for definitiveness of treatment, we have devoted Chap. 15 to liberal and general education, but for more pointed references to the animosities surrounding liberal learning, see Vincent E. Smith, *The School Examined: Its Aim and Content,* The Bruce Publishing Company, Milwaukee, 1960.

[2] For the decisions on prayer and Bible reading, see Appendix. For a more extensive treatment of Bible reading and prayer as plans to return religion to public education, see pp. 380–382. See also Robert F. Drinan, *Religion, the Courts, and Public Policy,* McGraw-Hill Book Company, New York, 1963.

[3] Francis Bacon asserted the primacy of utility and induction. In his famous *Novum Organum* he tried to lead a revolution in human knowledge and redirect education from the routes it had traveled for so long. He argued that education in a world that valued progress could not afford to be restricted by the boundaries of Aristotelian deductive thinking or a theory of learning which prized ornamentation at the expense of useful knowledge. Knowledge, Bacon was convinced, is power. See J. Donald Butler, *Four Philosophies: And Their Practice in Education and Religion,* rev. ed., Harper & Row, Publishers, Incorporated, New York, 1957, pp. 422–427.

[4] William F. Cunningham, *The Pivotal Problems of Education,* The Macmillan Company, New York, 1940, p. 16. By permission.

[5] Harry Broudy, *Building a Philosophy of Education,* Prentice-Hall, Inc., Englewood Cliffs, N.J., 2d ed., 1961, pp. 18 and 19.

[6] See John Dewey, *Experience and Nature,* The Open Court Publishing Company, La Salle, Ill., 1925; Sidney Hook, *The Metaphysics of Pragmatism,* The Open Court Publishing Company, La Salle, Ill., 1927; and John L. Childs, *Education and the Philosophy of Experimentalism,* Appleton-Century-Crofts, Inc., New York, 1931.

[7] The place of the thesis or principle of independence in realist educational theory is made clear by Frederick S. Breed in the National Society for the Study of Education, *Philosophies of Education,* Chicago, 1942, Forty-first Yearbook, part I, pp. 92–94; and John Wild in the National Society for the Study of Education, *Modern Philosophies and Education,* Chicago, 1955, Fifty-fourth Yearbook, part I, p. 17.

[8] George Santayana, in *The Genteel Tradition at Bay,* Charles Scribner's Sons, New York, 1931, pp. 63 and 64, wrote: "Why is naturalism supposed to be favourable to the lower sides of human nature? Are not the higher sides just as natural?"

[9] National Society for the Study of Education, *Philosophies of Education,* Chicago, 1942, Forty-first Yearbook, part I, pp. 253 and 254.

[10] The substantial union of the spiritual and the material constitutes one substance, man. This is a composite.

[11] The evidence for this claim is found mainly in the thirty schools experiment. The conclusions of the study, while questionable if applied with exag-

gerated enthusiasm, suggest that students with varied and unrestricted backgrounds are more successful because of their refined self-reliance. But the point to be made is not that one extreme position is superior to the other—prescription versus freedom—but that students must be restricted enough to encourage the building of discipline and freed to capitalize on their resources of intelligence and motivation. For the report of the thirty schools experiment, see *Thirty Schools Tell Their Story,* Harper & Row, Publishers, Inc., New York, 1942.

[12] John Wild assigns the school these four functions in his chapter on "Education and Human Society: A Realist View," in National Society for the Study of Education, *Modern Philosophies and Education,* Chicago, 1955, Fifty-fourth Yearbook, part I, pp. 28–31.

[13] National Society for the Study of Education, *Philosophies of Education,* Chicago, 1942, Forty-first Yearbook, part I, pp. 77 and 78.

Chapter 13

[1] See pp. 51–52.

[2] The popular Protestant version of the Bible is known as the King James version, undertaken in 1604 to counteract the influence of an English Bible published in Geneva by Calvinist Christians. Fifty-four scholars were commissioned to work on the new version; they represented a variety of points of view, all the way from High Churchmen to uncommitted scripturalists. The rules laid down were that the Bishops' Bible, an earlier English Bible, was to be used as a basis and that departures be made only when demanded by the text. No notes were included except for explanations of Greek and Hebrew words. The finished product was ready in 1611. It has an unequaled quality for clear, idiomatic English.

[3] For both of these decisions, see Appendix.

[4] For the various positions that may be taken on this point, see Edgar W. Knight, *Education in the United States,* 3d rev. ed., Ginn and Company, Boston, 1951, p. 85; Samuel Eliot Morison, *The Puritan Pronaos,* New York University Press, New York, 1936, pp. 15 and 16; Charles Beard and Mary Beard, *The Rise of American Civilization,* The Macmillan Company, New York, vol. I, p. 52; and Merle Curti, *The Social Ideals of American Educators,* Charles Scribner's Sons, New York, 1935, pp. 4 and 5.

[5] Newton Edwards and Herman G. Richey, *The School in the American Social Order,* Houghton Mifflin Company, Boston, 1947, p. 38.

[6] Vernon Louis Parrington, *Main Currents in American Thought,* vol. I, *The Colonial Mind, 1620–1800,* Harcourt, Brace & World, Inc., New York, 1927, p. 21.

[7] See R. Freeman Butts, *The American Tradition in Religion and Education,* Beacon Press, Boston, 1950, pp. 39–110. For an even more uncompromising position, see Paul Blanchard, *Religion and the School: The Great Controversy,* Beacon Press, Boston, 1963.

[8] Albert Ellery Bergh (ed.), *The Writings of Thomas Jefferson.* The Thomas Jefferson Memorial Association, Washington, 1907, vol. II, p. 301, 20 vols.

⁹ See pp. 28–29.

¹⁰ See pp. 215–216.

¹¹ See Alice Felt Tyler, *Freedom's Ferment*, The University of Minnesota Press, Minneapolis, 1927.

¹² Committee on Religion and Education, *The Relation of Religion to Public Education: The Basic Principles*, American Council on Education, Washington, 1947.

¹³ Educational Policies Commission, *Moral and Spiritual Values in Public Schools*, National Education Association, Washington, 1951.

¹⁴ All constitutional authorities agree that some parts of the Bill of Rights do apply to state actions. The link between the Bill of Rights and the states is the Fourteenth Amendment provision that no state may "deprive any person of life, liberty or property without due process of law." For a Bill of Rights provision to be clearly applicable to state actions, "life, liberty or property" must somehow be involved. Neither the school prayer nor the Bible reading cases were involved with life or property. Was liberty involved? The Court, in effect, said it did not have to be, that any required religious exercise in a public school is unconstitutional whether or not there is any infringement of liberty. A suit against "an establishment of religion," by the state, the Court wrote, does not require any proof that "particular religious freedoms are infringed." This doctrine, say some constitutional authorities, is unsound, for the only way a state can violate the Establishment Clause is by depriving a person of liberty; religious exercises cannot be unconstitutional unless there is an element of compulsion. This question of religious exercises, in the opinion of many, is by no means a settled one.

¹⁵ See J. A. Burns and Bernard J. Kohlbrenner, *A History of Catholic Education in the United States*, Benziger Bros. Inc., New York, 1937, pp. 156–165.

¹⁶ For the opinion of the Court in *Zorach v. Clauson*, see Appendix.

¹⁷ For the Court's decision in *McCollum v. Board of Educ.*, see Appendix.

¹⁸ *Cochran v. Board of Educ.*, 281 U.S. 370.

¹⁹ *Everson v. Board of Educ.*, 330 U.S. 1. See Appendix.

²⁰ *Ibid.*

²¹ It should be noted that the "wall of separation" metaphor used by the Court is not in the wording of the First Amendment or elsewhere in the Constitution of the United States but is from a remark made by Thomas Jefferson sometime after the Bill of Rights was adopted. See James M. O'Neill, *Religion and Education under the Constitution*, Harper & Row, Publishers, Incorporated, New York, 1949.

Chapter 14

¹ See pp. 52–55.

² No more dramatic portrait of American secondary education can be drawn than by going directly to the *Reports of the United States Commissioner of Education* covering this period. Together with the more recent *Biennial Survey of Education in the United States* these Reports offer the most comprehensive statistical summary of education available to us.

³ Traditionally the junior high school has been the place where the growing pains of adolescence can be handled in a specially designed program. For an up-to-date view, see James B. Conant, *Education in the Junior High School Years,* Education Testing Service, Princeton, N.J., 1960.

⁴ Herbert A. Carroll, *Genius in the Making,* McGraw-Hill Book Company, New York, 1940, p. 6.

⁵ No systematic view or theory of education entertains a position opposing greater democratization of school opportunities. Obstacles to opportunity and the development of individual talent are always deplored. See, for example, Ernest E. Bayles, *Democratic Educational Theory,* Harper & Row, Publishers, Incorporated, New York, 1960; and Christian O. Weber, *Basic Philosophies of Education,* Holt, Rinehart and Winston, Inc., New York, 1960.

⁶ In this connection the reader might wish to consult E. P. Torrance (ed.), *Talent and Education,* The University of Minnesota Press, Minneapolis, 1960; or Harry J. Baker, *Introduction to Exceptional Children,* 3d ed., The Macmillan Company, New York, 1959.

⁷ A number of interesting and telling points are made by Stanley J. Idzerda, "Honors Programs," *J. Higher Educ.,* vol. 33, pp. 417–423, November, 1962.

⁸ Paul Woodring, *A Fourth of a Nation,* McGraw-Hill Book Company, New York, 1957, pp. 143-158.

Chapter 15

¹ See Herbert Spencer, *Education, Intellectual, Moral, and Physical,* Appleton-Century-Crofts, Inc., New York, 1914, pp. 2–4.

² The literature on Plato's educational views is large and imposing. One hesitates in recommending any secondary source concerning the position he took on the essential meaning of education. Perhaps the best thing for the student to do is to sample Plato's writing for himself. In this connection, see *The Laws* (tr. by R. G. Bury), Harvard University Press, Cambridge, Mass., 1932, book I, vol. I, p. 65.

³ Despite an earlier promise to do so, Aristotle never produced a work on education. There are educational attitudes expressed throughout his works, but the most complete view may be found in *The Politics* (tr. by H. Rackham), Harvard University Press, Cambridge, Mass., 1932, book VIII, p. 637.

⁴ Thomas Henry Huxley, *Science and Education,* Appleton-Century-Crofts, Inc., New York, 1894, p. 86.

⁵ For a review of the doctrine of mental discipline as it worked its way down through history, see Walter B. Kolesnik, *Mental Discipline in Modern Education,* The University of Wisconsin Press, Madison, 1958.

⁶ See John Henry Newman, *The Idea of a University,* discourse 5, any edition.

⁷ See pp. 351–352.

⁸ Jacques Maritain, in National Society for the Study of Education, *Modern Philosophies and Education,* Chicago, 1955, Fifty-fourth Yearbook, part I, p. 77.

⁹ See Spencer, *op. cit.,* and Thorstein Veblen, *The Higher Learning in America,* B. W. Huebsch, Publishers, New York, 1918.

[10] Again, going to the original source is recommended. See John Henry Newman, *The Idea of a University,* any edition.

[11] National Society for the Study of Education, *Modern Philosophies and Education,* Chicago, 1955, Fifty-fourth Yearbook, part I, p. 152.

[12] National Society for the Study of Education, *General Education,* Chicago, 1952, Fifty-first Yearbook, part I, p. vii.

[13] Harvard Committee on the Objectives of Education in a Free Society, *General Education in a Free Society,* Harvard University Press, Cambridge, Mass., 1945, pp. 51, 52, and 93.

[14] For different approaches to elementary school objectives and curricula, see pp. 160–163.

[15] The role of the Committee of Ten in popularizing secondary education is discussed on pp. 184–186.

[16] John Dewey, *Democracy and Education,* The Macmillan Company, New York, 1916, 144 pp. By permission.

INDEX